HENRY VI

TO MY MOTHER

Frontispiece: A portrait of Henry VI, the earliest copy, first recorded in 1542, of an original probably dating from the 1450s.

HENRY VI

Bertram Wolffe

Reader in Medieval History
University of Exeter

METHUEN

First published 1981
by Eyre Methuen Ltd

First published in this paperback edition 1983
by Methuen London Ltd
11 New Fetter Lane, London EC4P 4EE

© *1981 Bertram Wolffe*

Made and printed in Great Britain by
Richard Clay (The Chaucer Press) Ltd
Bungay, Suffolk

ISBN 0 413 52240 7

CONTENTS

CONTENTS

Part V · CIVIL WAR

Part VI · APOTHEOSIS

ILLUSTRATIONS

PLATES

MAPS

GENEALOGIES

Acknowledgements and thanks for permission to reproduce photographs are due to the National Portrait Gallery for plate 1a; to the Dean and Chapter of Westminster for plate 1b; to the British Library for plates 1c, 3a, 3b, 4, 5a, 5b, 6a, 6b, 8a, 10a, 10b, 12b, 15a, 15b, 20a, 20b and 23a; to the Dean and Chapter of Winchester for plate 2a; to the Bodleian Library, Oxford, for plates 2b and 24; to the Bibliothèque Nationale for plates 5c, 13a and 13b; to the Courtauld Institute of Art and the Provost and Fellows of Eton College for plate 7a; to the Royal Commission on Historical Monuments for plates 8b and 23c; to King's College, Cambridge, for plates 10c and 16a; to the National Monuments Record for plate 11b; to the Courtauld Institute of Art for plate 11c; to the Musée du Louvre for plate 12a; to the Victoria and Albert Museum for plate 13c; to the Musée des Beaux Arts de Dijon for plate 14a; to Photographie Giraudon for plate 14b; to the Public Record Office for plates 16b and 17; to the Dean and Chapter of Exeter Cathedral for plate 18; to the British Museum for plate 20c; to Aerofilms Ltd for plates 21 and 22; and to the Dean and Canons of Windsor for plate 23b. The frontispiece is reproduced by gracious permission of Her Majesty the Queen. Plate 7b is from H. C. Maxwell Lyte's *History of Eton College* by permission of Macmillan, London and Basingstoke. Plate 11a is from S. B. Chrimes's *Lancastrians, Yorkists and Henry VII* (Macmillan). Plates 19a and 19b are from J. H. Ramsay's *Lancaster and York* (Oxford University Press, 1892).

The maps and genealogies were re-drawn from the author's roughs by Neil Hyslop.

ACKNOWLEDGEMENTS

I am deeply indebted to all those scholars who, since the war, have revitalized the previously moribund English fifteenth century and whose works I cite in my footnotes and bibliography. My thanks are due to Professor David Douglas, the General Editor of the series, to Professor Stanley Chrimes who encouraged me to write this book and to Professor Alec Myers for his helpful comments after kindly reading the whole of the first draft. I also wish to thank Mrs Elizabeth Burney Parker, Dr Robin Jeffs and Dr Roger Virgoe for allowing me to read and quote from their unpublished theses, Dr and Mrs Patrick Strong for their hospitality and help with the archives of Eton College, Dr S. Bhanji for discussing Henry's mental illness with me in the light of modern medical knowledge, Mr Brian Spencer of the British Library for placing his knowledge of pilgrim badges at my disposal and Miss Ann Mansbridge of Eyre Methuen for her assistance with the illustrations. Writing a biography of such an insubstantial and unsuccessful king as Henry VI has been a long and sometimes dispiriting task which would never have been completed without the constant help, advice and encouragement of my wife, who has also largely compiled the index.

I am indebted to Miss Irene Bell, Mr A. M. Cockerill, Dr R. J. Hetherington and Mr T. B. Pugh for pointing out errors in the original text. While the hardback edition was in the press, Dr and Mrs Strong published the copy of Henry V's will referred to on pp. 28–9 in *E.H.R.*, xcvi (1981), 89–102, with comments which show that Henry VI himself received a copy of the will in 1444.

ABBREVIATIONS

B.I.H.R.	*Bulletin of the Institute of Historical Research*
B.J.R.L.	*Bulletin of the John Rylands Library*
B.L.	British Library
C.C.R.	*Calendar of Close Rolls*
C.P.R.	*Calendar of Patent Rolls*
E.E.T.S.	Early English Text Society
E.H.R.	*English Historical Review*
H.B.C.	*Handbook of British Chronology*
H.M.S.O.	Her Majesty's Stationery Office
P.P.C.	*Proceedings and Ordinances of the Privy Council*
P.R.O.	Public Record Office
R.P.	*Rotuli Parliamentorum*
R.S.	Rolls Series
S.R.	*Statutes of the Realm*
T.R.H.S.	*Transactions of the Royal Historical Society*
V.C.H.	*Victoria County Histories*

PART I

THE MYTH OF THE ROYAL SAINT

Chapter 1

THE MYTH OF THE ROYAL SAINT

Of all the adult English kings from Richard II to Henry VII who cross
the stage in Shakespeare's historical plays, Henry VI alone has yet to
receive a comprehensive modern biography. Indeed, since the mid-
sixteenth century he has hardly been noticed at all by students of the
past and remains today the most shadowy figure of all England's post-
Conquest kings. Most Englishmen and women take their history of the
fifteenth century, in the first instance, from Shakespeare, and Henry's
lifespan from 1421 to 1471 covered half of it, yet even though Shakespeare devoted three plays, *Henry VI* Parts 1, 2 and 3, to him by name,
Henry himself was peripheral to all of them. If he is remembered at
all from Shakespeare it is probably only for the poetry of his soliloquy
on his mole-hill at the battle of Towton, wishing he had been born
a shepherd, not a king. Other English kings of Henry's day and age
have never ceased to interest successive generations as kings; no such
interest has ever been shown in Henry. Such memories of him as do
persist today centre on Eton schoolboys and Christmas carols from
King's College, Cambridge. As king, he is traditionally seen as the
innocent victim of the men and forces which caused the Wars of the
Roses and made his reign, in Hazlitt's phrase, a perfect beargarden.

In the present century the advent of the five-hundredth anniversaries
of his birth and death have generated brief revivals of interest in the
long-neglected Henry VI; in the possibility that he was a saint, whose
blameless, praiseworthy life as well as the miracles worked in his name
after his death, require his canonization. This development focuses
attention on one of the greatest obstacles in the path of a modern
biographer who would penetrate right back to his lifetime in order
to present an authentic picture of the living king. In contrast to the
neglect of later times, the first fifty years after his death saw Henry
VI revered as a royal saint in popular esteem who rivalled St Thomas
Becket in the fame of his cures: the last great posthumous miracle-
worker in England before the Reformation. This early-Tudor, posthumous cult was responsible for the production of almost all the record
of Henry's character and personality which is known today. Modern
advocates of his canonization would gladly accept the succinct character-
study of Henry provided by the Italian humanist Polydore Vergil
who wrote as the official court historiographer of the first Tudor king,

Henry VII. Polydore was hired by Henry VII to set his employer in history as the lawful, godsent ruler and conveniently recorded for his master how the holy man Henry VI, in the year of his death, had actually prophesied that he, Henry of Richmond, his half-brother's son, would in the end inherit his kingdom. When Polydore wrote, Henry VII was petitioning three successive popes, in vain, to canonize Henry VI, so that he could appear as the lawful heir of his sainted uncle.

> King Henry was a man of mild and plain-dealing disposition, who pre-ferred peace before wars, quietness before troubles, honesty before utility, and leisure before business; and to be short, there was not in this world a more pure, honest, and more holy creature. There was in him honest shamefacedness, modesty, innocency and perfect patience, taking all human chances, miseries, and all afflictions in this life in so good part as though he had justly by some offence deserved the same. He ruled his own affec-tions, that he might more easily rule his own subjects; he gaped not after riches, not thirsted for honour and worldly estimation, but was careful only for his soul's health; such things as tended to the salvation thereof he only esteemed for good; and that very wisely; such again as procured the loss thereof he only accounted evil.[1]

Polydore Vergil did not have entirely to invent this picture of Henry and his blameless life. In general those who write about medieval kings have to make do without the help of any intimate, personal memorials of their subject, but Henry VI at first sight appears to be the exception to this rule. When Polydore began work on his English History for Henry VII there already existed a 'Life' of that king's uncle, 'holy King Henry', which appears to constitute a rare, intimate record. It was rescued from centuries of oblivion in 1919 by M. R. James, Provost of Eton College, who published it as a tract on the personality of Henry VI, allegedly written by his spiritual director or confessor, John Blacman. It thus appears to provide all the evidence needed for an intimate life of Henry VI. But is this tract what it seems to be? Can it be accepted as reliable first-hand evidence of the living Henry?

Henry of Windsor, as he was known after his deposition in 1461, was done to death in the Tower during the night of 22–23 May 1471 after ten years of wanderings and imprisonment. He was hastily buried a few miles up-river in the Lady Chapel of Chertsey abbey. Towards the end of the decade the appearance of pilgrims at the grave with thank-offerings indicated that he had become an invocatory miracle-worker. Twenty years later hundreds of attested cases of cures, of calamities averted and misfortunes relieved by his intervention demon-

---

[1] *Polydore Vergil's English History*, ed. Sir Henry Ellis (Camden Society, 1844), 70–1.

strate that by the turn of the century he did indeed rival St
Thomas of Canterbury in public estimation as the most popular saint
in the south-east of England. Richard III felt compelled to remove
the body to Windsor; Henry VII encouraged the cult of his uncle for
obvious political reasons and pressed successive popes hard for his
canonization. Official inquiries were set in motion and the canons of
Windsor duly supplied the commissioners with sworn evidence of
hundreds of posthumous miracles.

But the attainment of sanctity also depended on evidence of fitting
achievements by the postulant during his life on earth. The difficulties
here were great; somehow they had to be met. The result, the
required companion to the record of posthumous miracles, appears to
have been this 'Blacman' tract, or to give it its full title, a 'Compilation
of the Meekness and Good Life of King Henry VI'. It is now known
only from two rare copies of Robert Coplande's printed version, which
was published in 1510[2] and probably written at the behest of Henry
VII himself.[3] It is a collection of a series of apocryphal anecdotes, with
deductions made from them by the collector.[4] Its nature was surely
foreshadowed in a *Historia Regum Angliae* written by a sycophantic priest,
John Rous, between the birth of Prince Arthur in 1486 and Rous's
death in 1491, and dedicated with a fulsome panegyric to Henry VII.
This states that Henry VI had been twice entombed and that many
thought his body should now be entombed elsewhere a third time, a
clear reference to his nephew Henry VII's desire to found his dynasty
on the basis of an official translation of the relics of a new royal saint
to a new chapel, built to house the remains of his sainted uncle and,
ultimately, his own. Rous's description of Henry VI, followed by an
account of his foundations and benefactions, is thus summed up: 'a most
holy man, shamefully expelled from his kingdom, but little given to
the world and worldly affairs which he always committed to his
council'.[5] The legend of holy and blameless Henry had begun.

John Blacman was fellow and precentor of Eton College, 1445–52,
subsequently of King's Hall, Cambridge and later a monk at the Witham
Charterhouse, Somerset, but how long he lived is not known. There
is no evidence to support the contention that he died in 1485 before

[2] According to the eighteenth-century antiquarian Thomas Hearne, who reprinted
150 copies of it.
[3] According to the seventeenth-century Archbishop Sancroft, who annotated his own
copy to that effect.
[4] *Henry the Sixth a reprint of John Blacman's Memoir*, ed. M. R. James (Cambridge,
1919).
[5] B.L., Cotton MS Vespatian A xii, printed by Thomas Hearne in 1716 with a
second edition in 1745.

the advent of the first Tudor king.[6] In any case the title of the printed version on which the attribution of the work is solely based reads *Collectarium ... ex collectione Magistri Joannis Blakman* and the possibility that this merely signified that it was originally found among Blacman's books and manuscript collections at some unknown date cannot be overlooked. It is presented mainly as the recollections of one of Henry's chaplains and other intimates of the king. But the only ones mentioned by name are from his later life after his deposition, the companions of his wanderings in the mid-'sixties, Doctors Manning and Bedon, and Sir Richard Tunstall. Blacman's own name in fact never appeared among the dozens of clerks described as royal chaplains during Henry's lifetime, so it must be very doubtful whether he was the unnamed author who speaks in the first person in this collection. Internal evidence places the composition of the tract in the middle or later years of Henry VII's reign. Henry VI is referred to as rightly included in the register of saints. A long series of miracles worked at his tomb is mentioned. While this cult of a murdered, anointed, popularly sanctified king certainly began at Chertsey in the latter years of Edward IV's reign, the recorded miracles, with one or two exceptions, all date after his translation to Windsor by Richard III on 12 August 1484 and the establishment of a 'long series' required the subsequent passage of quite a few more years. There can be no question of its having been written before the advent of the Tudors because there is a reference to Henry being twice crowned rightful heir of his realm. This would have been treasonable at any time before the battle of Bosworth Field which gave his Tudor nephew the throne. There is also a clear reference to the downfall of the House of York. Those who put him to death are referred to as no longer possessing his inheritance.

The problem before the unknown compiler of this early-Tudor hagiographic collection was that he could not present Henry, like St Louis, as a candidate for sainthood by reason of his kingship. The aim of this collection was therefore to present, as nearly as possible, a Christ-like figure whose kingdom was not of this world, who is alleged to have performed during his lifetime a miracle of loaves, if not of fishes, for his hungry troops on campaign; who 'patiently endured hunger, thirst, mockings, derisions, abuse, and many other hardships', including wounding in the side with a dagger; who foretold his own Christ-like end but was not believed, and who 'finally suffered

---

[6] Dr A. B. Emden in his *Biographical Register of the University of Oxford* (Oxford 1957–9), gives January 1485 as the date of Blacman's death, but he kindly informed me that he based this solely on Sir Wacey Sterry's statement in *Etoniana* 56 (June 1934). Sterry was in error here and appears to have conflated John Blacman with a William Blackden and a John Bonor in transcribing details of probate and obit from the Eton College Audit Rolls and Register.

violent death of the body that others might, as was then the expectation, peaceably possess the kingdom'. In fact there is no evidence that he had ever suffered physical injury prior to his murder, except for an arrow wound in the neck at the first battle of St Albans, or of any ill-treatment during his captivity. This appears to have been comfortable and considerate, with those who wished to do so having free access to his person.

The testimonies of witnesses cited to produce this picture of innocent, holy Henry may be acceptable to the eye of faith, but almost without exception they are incapable of proof, or disproof. Among the alleged intimations of sanctity appear his shocked reaction to the sight of men taking the waters naked at Bath. All one can say from his lifetime is that he had been in Bath more than once. Likewise his alleged grave displeasure at the sight of dancing girls with bared bosoms may or may not be authentic. According to a contemporary, Thomas Gascoigne, who also deplored it, this was no uncommon sight, apparently a fashion in dress from about 1429. Maybe his hat did sometimes fall from his head unnoticed when he was on horseback and his servants retrieved it, especially after 1453 when he lost his wits. The tract solemnly parades such trivialities as evidence of his otherworldliness. The story that he only removed his hat from his head in passing a church when he divined that the sacrament was reserved within, like the miracle of the loaves, reveals the essential nature and purpose of this hagiographic collection. Alas, some of its stories, even if accepted as authentic, are capable of quite different interpretations just as convincing as those put upon them by the pious collector. His assertion that Henry spied on his courtiers through secret windows in order to control the comings and goings of doubtful women has been taken by one modern writer as evidence that he was in fact interested in observing their dalliances in secret![7]

One specific incident cited in the Blacman tract can be shown to be a manifest invention, though based on certain ascertainable facts. Both Eton and King's Colleges benefited by £1,000 from the death in 1447 of King Henry's great-uncle Cardinal Beaufort. The tract states, in proof of Henry's complete lack of avarice, and his laudable liberality, that when Beaufort's executors approached him with a gift of £2,000-worth of gold for his own use, to relieve the burden and necessities of the realm, to their amazement he utterly declined to take it because of his uncle's great generosity to him in his lifetime. They did, however, prevail upon him to accept it on behalf of his two foundations. In fact Beaufort's will had stipulated that Henry should pay exactly this sum

[7] John W. McKenna, 'Piety and Propaganda: the cult of Henry VI', in *Chaucer and Middle English Studies in honour of Rossell Hope Robbins*, ed. Beryl Rowlands (London 1974), 78.

from what he owed his uncle at his death to the two colleges to secure the cardinal a special collect said there daily, and a yearly obit, both at Eton and King's.[8]

One other incident in the Blacman collection has been made the basis for the assertion that Henry had a distaste for public affairs. He is alleged to have complained heavily to Sir Richard Tunstall, his household chamberlain, when they were together in his chamber at Eltham, busy with his holy books, and were interrupted by a certain mighty duke. The story seems to have been awkwardly contrived to use testimony from Tunstall who still flourished at the court of Henry VII, for why, in a royal household stuffed with chaplains, should it be a layman, the household chamberlain, who was helping him with his 'holy' books?[9] Polydore Vergil appears to have been glossing this passage when he alleged that Henry preferred leisure to business. In any case his father Henry V, who can hardly be said to have neglected affairs of state, is equally recorded as refusing to allow them to intrude upon his devotions. The compiler of the Blacman tract himself well knew that for a king to neglect the duties of his kingly office could not be considered a mark of sanctity and his ensuing remarks, that Henry spent all his days, apart from high feasts and Sundays, conscientiously treating of the business of the realm with his council, or reading, were designed to meet this objection. These remarks should therefore be given equal prominence if the tract is to be cited as evidence at all, but of course they simply do not fit the overall picture given of the innocent, retiring, monkish king.

There is no doubt that Henry's failures as a king, which have to be discussed at length in this book, left Eton College and King's College, Cambridge as almost the sole record of his achievements. But how far do these support the view of him set out in the Blacman tract? Not all his contemporaries by any means were impressed by his colleges. His faithful Commons in parliament in 1451, mindful of their pockets in supporting their king's ambition thus to lay up for himself treasure in heaven, told him they considered Eton and King's Colleges to be 'over chargefull and noyus'. In his foundation and development of Eton College, his first love, two of his aims became obsessions. His secretary's letters to Rome show that he was inexorably determined, in spite of all costs, delays and obstacles, to secure for his new college of secular priests an accumulated power to grant indulgences greater

[8] *Henry the Sixth*, 10; *Royal Wills*, ed. J. Nichols (London 1780), 338–9; H. C. Maxwell Lyte, *A History of Eton College* (4th ed., London 1911), 29.

[9] As the modern editor M. R. James is careful to point out (*Henry the Sixth*, 48), this incident is told as related by Tunstall, not, as usually claimed, by the author himself, Henry's claimed 'confessor'. He merely adds that he remembered a similar incident at Windsor.

than was possessed by any other church in his dominions and equal to the greatest in Rome. Secondly, his new minster there was to exceed all other churches and cathedrals of England in sheer size. As and when he discovered the dimensions of various existing cathedrals, plans had to be revised, even at the cost of much destruction of building work already undertaken. His twenty-five scholars, like the equal number of paupers, were originally only a normal, minor appendage to the foundation at Eton, after the standard practice of the time, but when he became acquainted with William Wykeham's unique achievement, Winchester College and its twin foundation New College, Oxford, his soaring ambition here also dictated that both Eton and King's College should have an equal number of seventy scholars each. The intentions and aspirations of the founder of Eton and King's thus provide no evidence of the saintly spirituality which the Blacman tract subsequently found in Henry. Pretentious in his piety as judged by the scale of his foundations, he was nevertheless as conventional and practical minded in it as those most pious but successful of kings, his father Henry V and his nephew Henry VII.

There is equally no contemporary evidence as the Blacman tract suggests, that Henry was uniquely addicted to prayer and private meditation. The unusual fact that as a boy of twelve he had lived with the monks of St Edmundsbury for several months did not, as Cardinal Gasquet would have us believe, indicate an early propensity for the monastic life. On that occasion Henry and his whole court were thrust upon the abbot without notice to enjoy free hospitality from Christmas 1433 to Easter 1434 when his council, who had to provide for his expenses, found themselves totally unable to do so in the severe financial crisis of the autumn of 1433. It is true that altar closets were built for him off the chapels at Sheen and Havering and an oratory constructed for him over the hall porch at Sheen (this latter possibly providing the germ of the idea that he watched the comings and goings of the court to keep out women of easy virtue). However, there is no instance to compare with the devotion of his father, who is recorded as spending the whole night in prayer on the eve of his accession. The only comparable incident cited for our Henry is the testimony of an aged witness to Henry VII's council that he once knelt in prayer for a whole hour with his chamberlain, Lord Cromwell, and his court standing patiently by, before borrowing Cromwell's staff of office to indicate the place for his tomb. This strains credibility, as Lord Cromwell was dead by the time it is alleged to have taken place. On the other hand his love of the ceremony of public worship is firmly attested by the record of his royal chapel and by the accounts of his frequent appearances in the chapel of Winchester College.

Much has been made of the Blacman tract's description of Henry's habit of dressing like a townsman and a farmer in plain dark clothing and blunt-ended footwear, not being content merely to mortify the flesh with the customary hair shirt. The most that can be said in support of this view is that it could well have been his disguise during his wanderings in the north of England in the early 'sixties. General sartorial inferences of this nature are not borne out by contemporary descriptions. There is a fine painting of Henry, one of nine portraits of contemporary rulers, in the diary of the German knight Jörg von Ehingen, who received a decoration, probably the Lancastrian livery collar of esses, from his own hands, some time in 1458 or 1459.[10] It could be taken to bear out the Blacman description only to the very slightest extent in that the shoes, although pointed, are not extravagantly so when compared with some of the other eight kings and princes represented there. Henry is one of three who are portrayed unarmed and one of three not wearing tight hose. But he is represented in a purple hat with a streamer of the same colour, a light blue cloak with crimson collar and white linen showing at the neck and a crimson girdle with gold buckle and pendant. The only unusual feature is that the hands are particularly delicate. The face is an individual one, showing the same protruding lower lip, broad forehead and wide-spaced eyes as the Windsor portrait.[11] Again the costume of the Windsor portrait is certainly not that of a townsman or farmer.

This dubious Blacman picture of a meanly clad king has sometimes been taken as confirmed by another largely apocryphal story of Henry giving away his best robe to St Albans abbey and of the embarrassed servant who had perforce to ask for its return because it was the only decent one he had. The original facts on which this story is based, as related in Abbot Wheathampstead's register, tell a different story. It was customary, when the king visited a church in state, for the ceremonial robe he used on that occasion to be presented to the authorities to be made into vestments. Another instance of this practice is found in the Coventry Leet Book where it is recorded that when Henry visited the church of St Michael there in state on Michaelmas Day 1451 he subsequently sent them his robe of gold 'tussu' furred

[10] The portrait on the jacket of this book is a colour photograph of the original in the Würtembergische Landesbibliothek, Stuttgart, Cod.hist.4⁰,141, printed as *The Diary of Jörg von Ehingen*, ed. Malcolm Letts (O.U.P., 1929), which contains a black and white photograph at p. 50. Jakob von Hefner-Alteneck's *Trachten des christlichen Mittelalters* (Mannheim 1840), II, plate 81 is a colour drawing. The other portraits are of Ladislas of Hungary, Charles VII of France, Henry IV of Castile, Alfonso V of Portugal, James III of Cyprus, René of Anjou, John II of Navarre and Aragon and James II (of the red face) of Scotland.

[11] Roy Strong, *Tudor and Jacobean Portraits* (H.M.S.O., 1969), I, 147. This is the earliest of the Tudor portraits, considered, on costume and portrait formula evolved by Roger van der Weyden, to be a copy of an *ad vivum* likeness of about 1450.

with marten sable.[12] He spent the whole of the Easter festival at St Albans in 1459 and wore the very special, unique robe which was kept solely for his use at the Easter festivities each year and for no other occasion. This was the robe which was nevertheless formally and correctly presented to the abbey on his departure, but his household treasurer immediately redeemed it for fifty marks to be paid at the exchequer and for sufficient costly gold cloth called 'crimesyne thisswe' to make a whole set of vestments and altar cloths worthy of the proto-martyr's altar. This had to be fetched from the great wardrobe in London.[13] The redemption may be compared to the custom in his chapel, where the gold talent equivalent to five nobles by weight, which he offered daily, was daily redeemed by his clerk of the jewels for the payment of seven pence sterling to the dean;[14] or to his offering at the high altar every Good Friday of the gold and silver rings which he wore when he touched for the king's evil. These, together with some of the most precious jewels of the chapel, were then redeemed by his jewel clerk for one hundred marks. In short, this presentation of his best robe was no more than any king would have been expected to do on such an occasion, and its redemption was routine practice.

The concomitant impression of a shabby, indigent and dull, because exceptionally devout, court, generally associated with Henry VI on the basis of the Blacman tract, again is not supported by any contemporary evidence. It is true that one chronicler wrote in the late 'fifties that 'he maintained no household', but it had not always been so. Circum-stances then were quite exceptional. This stricture came after twenty years of intermittent complaint in parliament and elsewhere about the size and expense of a royal establishment which the dean of the chapel royal had stated in 1449 numbered twelve hundred persons, but which had probably been virtually disbanded in 1454 during Henry's first attack of mental illness.[15] A magnificent French embassy of 1445, for which Henry provided a small fleet of ships to bring them across the Channel and three hundred horses to transport them from Dover to the capital, was much impressed by his rich attire, by the ceremony surrounding his person and by the splendour of its reception. A modern discovery in Portuguese archives has revealed that a Portuguese nobleman at Henry's court in 1449 so admired the dignified order and ceremonial of the royal household chapel that he persuaded the dean, William Say, to set down all the details in a book for presentation to his own king, in the hope that he might imitate it. The ceremonies

---

[12] *Coventry Leet Book, or mayor's register 1420–1455*, ed. M. D. Harris (E.E.T.S., 1907–13), 264.

[13] *Registrum Abbatiae Johannis Whetamstede*, etc., I (R.S., 1872), 323–5.

[14] *Liber Regis Capelle*, 61, 63 (see below, p. 12, n. 16).

[15] See below p. 283.

there described are in every sense impressive. The introduction of Burgundian court fashions are sometimes supposed to have transformed a shabby royal household which Henry kept into a court fit for kings under his successor Edward IV. But the discovery of this book, Henry's *Liber Regis Capelle*,[16] must make this doubtful. The elaborate ceremony of his chapel was an integral part of court life and may be taken to indicate a well ordered and dignified royal court in general. It reveals, for example, in its detailed description of the solemn crown-wearing processions, that state crown wearings were now held not merely at the traditional Christmas, Easter and Whitsun festivals but also at Epiphany, All Saints and the two feasts of the Confessor. Similarly, Henry's detailed ordinances for the daily regulation of the whole household, promulgated in 1445, were the first of the century. How far they were observed may be doubtful, but it must at least be stated that the much praised provisions of the 1478 household ordinances of his supplanter Edward IV were in fact largely based on these precedents set in Henry's reign.

It is inconceivable that certain unpalatable basic facts of Henry's rule can have been completely forgotten by the date when the Blacman tract was compiled and indeed traces of them can still be discerned there through the hagiographic mist. It was the fact that policies, actions and attitudes of his had brought great trouble and harm to his subjects which dictated the portrayal of one who was not personally responsible, though such a claim was foreign to the very nature of fifteenth-century kingship. Again the undoubted fact of his recurrent mental incapacity from 1453, never mentioned in the tract, could likewise only be covered by the portrayal of a holy innocent. A series of parliamentary acts of resumption had been necessary to try to undo the damage which his exercise of his powers of patronage had done to the substance of the monarchy; this could only be portrayed as selfless generosity. Setting aside the attribution to him in the tract of supernatural powers of divination, the portrayal which remains there of his strict morality, chastity and scrupulous observance of the requirements of his religion as king, while setting him apart from some of his predecessors on the English throne, could have been applied equally well to others such as his successful father or his nephew Henry VII himself, who probably commissioned this compilation. But for these kings subsequent political circumstances never made desirable the achievement of their canonization.

There is thus no evidence dating from Henry's lifetime to support this posthumous early-Tudor hagiographic picture of Henry as a saintly, blameless, ascetic royal pauper. Yet the only two modern studies

[16] *Liber Regis Capelle, a Manuscript in the Biblioteca Publica, Evora*, ed. Walter Ullmann (Henry Bradshaw Society, 1961).

of him, both published near the five-hundredth anniversary of his birth, are squarely based on an acceptance of the Blacman tract. Mrs Christie in her *Henry VI* accepted it as reliable chronicle material. Cardinal Gasquet in his *Religious Life* went further. He claimed that it presented the only authentic picture of the living king, recovered by early-Tudor England after wilful denigration of Henry by the usurping Yorkists. Thus notions that Henry had been a weak-minded and useless ruler were fabrications of his supplanters and his rule had in fact been just and upright. It is therefore most important to try to recover what Henry's contemporaries did actually say, write and think about him during his lifetime. Such material is extremely scarce, if only because few people ventured to express the unvarnished truth about their king in the king-centred society of fifteenth-century England. In Henry's case we cannot even have the record of an independent life before he became king, as was the case with his two Lancastrian predecessors, his father Henry V and his grandfather Henry IV. Henry VI was unique among English kings in being reared as a king from the cradle. The only child of the illustrious Henry V was not only born in the purple but was hedged about with the divinity of kingship before he was twelve months old.

Nevertheless, there is some evidence of the kind we need. The earliest surviving testimony to his character and abilities dates from 1432, on the approach of his eleventh birthday. It was recorded in a report to the royal council from his tutor Richard Beauchamp, earl of Warwick, made because he required extra powers from them in order to control the boy. Henry, he said, was already showing exceptional precocity, impatience with restrictions and an awareness of the regality which was in him. As a comment on royalty this may not be entirely reliable, but twelve months later Burgundian ambassadors, who had no reason to lie, reported back to their master, Philip duke of Burgundy, that the king was a handsome, robust child who would converse with them in French at his ease. In November 1434, when he was still scarcely thirteen years old, his council had occasion to remonstrate with him over his eagerness to seize the reins of power. There is no other useful comment on the youthful, untried Henry, except that his physical stamina, his ability to endure long and arduous ceremonies with cheerfulness and without fatigue, had already become apparent at his two coronations in London and Paris in 1429–30, with all the journeyings, pageants, thanksgivings, feastings and solemn entries into his cities which they had entailed. When his council began to hand over real powers to him from 1435 they can thus have had no reason to suppose that he would not turn out to be a replica of his formidable father.

That this was what the age required, indeed demanded of him, can hardly be doubted. It can be read between the lines of his 'Mirror for Princes', a manual on king-craft which was presented to him, probably in the late 1440s, after he had been ruling personally for some ten years or so. This is the until recently unknown *Tractatus de regime principum ad regem Henricum sextem.*[17] As its modern editor says, the author, a king's *orator* and *religiosus*, was presenting a Christian mirror for a prince to Henry, concerned with his attainment of ultimate, personal salvation amid all the snares and temptations peculiar to a great and powerful king. At the same time his concern with temporal achievements and the great deal of advice given on secular matters more than justifies its secular title. It shows what the age expected of Henry and is therefore infinitely more valuable than the Blacman tract as a yardstick against which to measure his policies and actions. The only evidence which this author could cite to show Henry as the effective defender of his realm, which he had to be, was the repulse of the duke of Burgundy from Calais and the Scots from Berwick, both of which had happened in 1436, at the end of his minority, hardly achievements personal to him. But the tract cannot have been submitted to the young king at that early date, near the start of his majority, because he was not married until 1445 and 'nostra dulcissima regina', whose marriage, in the author's opinion, brought the blessings of peace to the two kingdoms of England and France in fulfilment of the prophecy of St Bridget, cannot have been his mother, Catherine of Valois, who died in 1437. At no time in her seventeen years as queen and queen dowager of England could such a happy state be considered attained. Rather does this reference, together with another reference to Henry's 'preclarissima regina' point to composition after the truce of Tours in 1444 and after his marriage in 1445, when the author could still praise the success of Henry's peace efforts to date ('pacis tempora tranquillastis ... prestantissime ac metuendissime Rex et princeps gracie celestis spiramine tot remedia pacis elaborastis'). While unable to contemplate that Henry would himself break the truce he had made with the French, the author assured him that should his enemy do so his cause for waging effective war, however long, would be a just one.

This beautiful manuscript, originally prefaced by the king's portrait and bound up with a collection of matutinals and prayers to the Virgin, St Bridget and St John of Bridlington, the most recent English saint, to whom Henry acknowledged a special devotion, was probably the king's own presentation copy. Intended to be Henry's own personal political mirror, it is unambiguous and emphatic on the most controversial issues of this period: to its author, Henry's claim to the French throne was a just one, in pursuit of which, as a proven peacemaker,

[17] B.L., Cotton MS Cleopatra A xiii, printed by Jean-Philippe Genet in *Four English Political Tracts of the Later Middle Ages* (Camden Society, 1977).

he had nevertheless to be prepared to fight bravely in person on the battlefield, with an effective army, should his peacemaking efforts ultimately fail. In this respect within a few years the author, a member of a religious order, but no pacifist, must have been gravely disappointed in his king. In the weightiest problems of governance Henry was here instructed to take the advice of wise and discreet councillors. He was especially advised to guard himself against a partisan dispensation of his patronage. This should never be bestowed in the presence of a few, the unknown author advised, badly needed advice which was patently ignored. The king in his unique position of dignity and responsibility had to ensure that just law was effectively administered. This was his responsibility and in this respect too it cannot be claimed that Henry ever excelled. The author of the *De regimine* was however still able to congratulate his patron on the state of his realm because his reign had so far been undisturbed by horrible rebellions such as had so often marred the reigns of his predecessors. By 1450 this would no longer have been possible. This tract then gave sound advice and indicated how Henry's conduct of affairs was likely to be judged and criticized. It shows that even a member of a religious order expected that his king should fight his people's just battles on the battlefield in person, that he should preside over a government which had no cliques or favourites and that he should actively concern himself to ensure that good justice prevailed in his kingdom. By the very nature of this tract the effective performance of these kingly duties was shown to be necessary even for Henry's personal salvation. This is in stark contrast to the alleged attributes praised in the Blacman tract.

Between 1444 and 1453 Henry presided over the liquidation of our first overseas empire and by his policies provoked the first significant revolt among his English subjects for three-quarters of a century. From this time also dates the work of his first tentative biographer. John Capgrave, an Augustinian friar from King's Lynn, had laboured to produce a collection of the lives of many illustrious Henries for his king's edification and naturally felt bound to include Henry's own life to date at the end. This appears to have been an embarrassing task, particularly since he brought the work to fruition at the unfortunate point in time when not only Paris but also London had rejected Henry. This can only have been during Jack Cade's Kentish rebellion of 1450,[18] when Henry fled from London, since the work was definitely written before the birth of Prince Edward in 1453 and could not therefore apply to his later absences from the capital. Apparently there was little positive Capgrave could say in appreciation of his king,

[18] *Liber de Illustribus Henricis*, ed. F. C. Hingeston (R.S., 1858), also in translation as *The Book of the Illustrious Henries* (London 1858). Capgrave expresses the hope that London will spew out her foulness and welcome Henry back.

except that he had founded colleges, was an example to his subjects in his adoration of the holy cross and had married a wife. Otherwise his life of Henry himself perforce consisted of hopes and the introduction of further edifying exemplars whose names were not Henry. On one score alone he could not restrain his criticism. England's enemies, he lamented, were saying with justifiable scorn, 'Put a sheep on your English noble in place of a ship': the current failure to keep the seas was a disgrace.[19] Living on the Norfolk coast he well knew the dangers from French, Breton and Norman pirates who could land, plunder and depart with impunity. Clearly he expected his king to do something about these misfortunes. But Capgrave did feel it his duty to contradict those of Henry's own subjects who were then proclaiming 'Woe to thee O land when thy king is a child'. He had first heard this said at the time of the boy's Westminster coronation in 1429, and in 1450, when Henry was some twenty-eight years old, men were now saying that the prophecy was being fulfilled. This was not the only reference in these years to the old saw from *Ecclesiastes*, and the natural inference to make is that men were indeed now saying that their adult king was childishly inadequate. Furthermore, Capgrave only lamely attempted to refute them here on a point of theology: the best he could do was to claim that the scripture was meant to refer to corrupt morals, not to the age of a ruler, and so had no relevance to Henry!

In the French wars the years between 1444 and 1450 were years of truce, leading to English military disasters in Normandy and Gascony, the like of which had not been seen since the reign of King John. At home the years from 1450 to 1453 were years of rebellion and armed risings. The period from 1444 to 1453 alone can provide the crucial test of what his subjects thought about Henry in his prime, because the first onset of his mental illness in the summer of 1453 must have coloured all later opinions. We must of course remember the sacred nature of the crowned and anointed king. He was the personification of the unity of the realm and of all due order in society, the linchpin holding it together from dissolution and anarchy. There were dreadful penalties, easily incurred, for any derogation of kingship, because to attack the king was to promote the dissolution of society, a heinous sin as well as a crime. Except in the direst extremities the politically discontented and those who sought to apportion blame for disasters generally accused the king's ministers and alleged favourites in the name of the public weal, not the king himself. The king could do no wrong. Nevertheless, significant comments on King Henry VI were recorded in these years and they cannot be discounted simply because they were the opinions of unimportant, genuinely 'obscure men'. For example, Thomas

[19] An early quotation from the *Libel of English Policy*: see *The Libelle of Englyshe Polycye: A Poem on the Use of Sea-Power, 1436*, ed. G. Warner (Oxford 1926), 3, 61.

Carver, bailiff of the abbot of Reading, in 1444 rashly glossed a court sermon preached before Henry on the text 'Woe to thee O land when thy king is a child'; he suffered most, but not quite all, of the gruesome penalties of treason for it. Obviously, whatever the preacher himself had said before the king, it was not to the effect that the adult king himself was mentally still a child, and Carver did not actually say this either. What he did say was that Henry was a less than perfect king because he was not leading his armies in the field to recover and maintain the rights of his subjects as he should be doing.[20] Other careless talkers now expressed, in part, the guarded, critical, collective views later found in the manifestos of the Cade rebels of 1450.[21] For example, a London draper said in October 1446 that the marquis of Suffolk and Bishop Aiscough so dominated the king 'that his rule is nought' and even blamed them and his other lords for the lack of an heir, since they kept him from having 'his sport' with the queen. But he added, Henry had a child's face, he was not steadfast of wit as previous kings had been and, proof of it, he had lost all his progenitors had gained.[22] In 1447 the yeoman keeper of Gloucester castle, who presumably owed his position to Henry's uncle, Humphrey duke of Gloucester who had died under arrest at the opening of the Bury parliament of 1447, baldly declared that Henry had killed his uncle and he would rather Duke Humphrey had killed the king and queen since the duke would have made the better king. Six months later the keeper of Guildford gaol, on the testimony of the same approver, wished the king hanged and the queen drowned and added that nothing had gone right since this queen, Margaret of Anjou, had come to England in 1445.[23] An alien resident at Ely, a Dutchman, who was alleged to have christened his two fighting cocks Henry of England and Philip of Burgundy and applauded the victory of the latter, incautiously cursed the king for a tax on aliens, prophesied his early death and also said a sheep would be a better emblem than a ship on his noble. He further added that Henry looked more like a child than a man.[24] Men as far apart as Cley in Norfolk and Brightling in Sussex in 1449 and 1450 expressed opinions that Henry was a natural fool and no fit person to govern the kingdom.[25] Men of Wales, Shropshire, Kent and elsewhere, sub-

[20] See below pp. 128–9.
[21] Chiefly discovered by Professor Robin Storey and Dr Roger Virgoe to whose works I am indebted in the first instance for most of the following references.
[22] P.R.O., K.B.9/260/85 (indictment of 11 January 1447).
[23] P.R.O., K.B.9/256/12, allegedly in June and November 1447 respectively (indictments of 23 November 1447).
[24] P.R.O., K.B.9/262/1 (indictment of 21 November 1449), allegedly in October 1449.
[25] P.R.O., K.B.9/262/78; 122/28 (printed by R. F. Hunnisett, 'Treason by Words', *Sussex Notes and Queries*, XIV [Lewes 1954–7], 116–20).

sequent to Henry's humiliation of the duke of York at Dartford in 1452, were indicted for conspiring to levy war against Henry at Baynard's Castle, at Ludlow and in Kent, and for slaying his valet of the chamber, Richard Fazakerley. They were accused of purposing to replace a king who, they said, was neither fit nor able to rule the kingdom, nor ought to rule it. His replacement was to be chosen by authority of a parliament of the whole community of the realm, with the help of their friends and of 'another who was entitled to the crown of England'.

Undoubtedly the fact that Henry occupied the throne by virtue of the usurpation of his grandfather Henry IV in 1399 was remembered throughout his reign,[26] but here in 1452 he was to be deposed, not for a deficient title, but for his unsuitability and inefficiency. In this case the principal accused were gentry, a former Member of Parliament for Warwickshire, Robert Ardern esquire, and John Sharpe, gentleman, of London.[27] Again, after the news of the disaster of the battle of Castillon in 1453 by which English Gascony was finally lost, and, coincidentally, on 1 and 3 August 1453, just about the time when Henry really did go out of his mind at Clarendon, two men in Southwark, having possessed themselves of one of his velvet cloaks, were allegedly engaged in the black art of destroying him. Their treasonable words were 'would God that the captain of Kent had reigned and then we should have had a merry realm, for the king is but a sheep and hath lost all that his father won and would God he had died soon after he was born'. For Jack Cade's head on London Bridge they proposed to substitute the heads of those who were then considered his chief advisers: the chancellor and archbishop of Canterbury and the dukes of Somerset and Buckingham.[28] Thus some of Henry's more articulate, obscure, but careless subjects had such low opinions of their king in his prime as to claim he was simpleminded or dim-witted on the evidence of the failure of his policies. Conspicuously to these ordinary subjects he was not the kind of king his father had been. That was what they wanted and expected.

From late July or early August 1453, for nearly eighteen months, Henry did suffer from totally prostrating mental illness. Then a relapse in the autumn of 1455 was followed by some measure of recovery in the following spring, which was probably never subsequently complete. The fact of his total incapacity was, as far as possible, concealed for eight months, but the death of the chancellor and the consequent in-

[26] Cf. an instance of this in 1440 cited by Hunnisett *op. cit.*, 118, where a Chichester man was indicted for saying the king was no king nor should be and that should be known in a short time.

[27] P.R.O., K.B.9/270/34.

[28] P.R.O., K.B.9/273/103.

ability to use the great seal of England finally forced its complete revelation. Descriptions of him from 1454 must therefore have been affected by the knowledge of this mental collapse. There is a subsequent first-hand description of Henry recorded by Abbot Wheathampstead of St Albans, when he entered in his register details of an act to resume all Henry's lavish grants which was passed in the parliament of 1455–6, and a description of how he had obtained his abbey's exemption from it by expending much time and money up to November 1457. The abbot, who had met the king on a number of occasions, was by nature a verbose and often tediously obscure writer. He began with a lengthy dissertation on the necessity of conciliating the great, rather than of uttering anything which might offend them. Illustrations from ancient times follow and then an example from his own day. A certain lawyer John Holton had been drawn, hanged and quartered merely for writing something derogatory of the king's person. The cautious abbot said he did not know what this was. All he knew of Henry's actions was that, when dealing with petitions, he was indeed a generous king because he did not ask what a man deserved but gave what it was fitting for a king to give! King Henry VI himself was *simplex et probus*. This would normally be translated by a good latinist as 'honest and upright' and Abbot Wheathampstead has thus been cited as strictly contemporary evidence in this instance for accepting the laudatory Blacman memoir of Henry as the true picture.[29] But a few years later, immediately after recording the usurpation of Edward IV in 1461, the abbot gave a further description of Henry, this time in verse, which is seldom cited:

> his mother's stupid offspring, not his father's, a son greatly degenerated from the father, who did not cultivate the art of war ... a mild-spoken, pious king, but half-witted in affairs of state.[30]

In these circumstances one must wonder whether the earlier description of the king as *simplex*, with all the circumlocution surrounding it, was not really a daring *double entendre*.

Another contemporary, the rhyming chronicler John Hardyng, made no comment at all on Henry's personality or abilities in the first version of his chronicle which he dedicated to Henry, his queen and his infant son, in the vain hope, as it turned out, of obtaining a royal

---

[29] *Registrum*, I, 247–68.
[30] *Ibid.*, 415: 'Matris non patris, fuit ortus filius excors:
  Martem non coluit, nimis a patre degeneravit....
  Hic fuit in verbis Rex mitis, Rex pietatis,
  Attamen in factis nimiae vir simplicitatis.'
(The juxtaposition of *excors* and *simplicitatis* in this context makes the intended meaning of *simplicitas* unmistakable here.)

grant of the manor of Geddington in Northamptonshire. But a second version, which he dedicated to Richard duke of York between 1458 and his death in 1460, does describe the king. In a reference to Henry's boyhood tutor, Richard Beauchamp, he projected dim wits and indeed a lack of sound moral judgement right back to his minority:

> Therle Richard, in mykell worthyhead,
> Enfourmed hym, but of his symplehead
> He could litle within his brest conceyve,
> The good from eivill he could uneth perceyve.[31]

Towards the end of his reign the three rebellious magnates – York, Salisbury and Warwick – in their manifesto of 1460 were still observing the fundamental social conventions of the age about the person of the king, so they officially declared that the man they wished to control, but not yet to depose, was 'hymself as noble, as vertuous, as ryghtwys, and blyssed of dysposicione as any prince erthely'. But the chronicler who recorded their manifesto for posterity had himself starkly recorded under the previous year: 'the kyng was simple and lad by covetous counseylle ... the quene with such as were of her affynyte rewled the reaume as her lyked. . . .'[32] Likewise a chronicler of the fenland abbey of Crowland, who had opportunity to observe Henry at close hand, when he stayed there during Lent 1460, wrote of him at this time that in consequence of an illness which had been increasing upon him for many years he had fallen into a weak state of mind and for long remained in a state of imbecility, holding the government of the realm in name only.[33]

With an apparently successful deposition in 1461 came at last completely open contempt from those who had brought it about. The earl of Warwick's brother George Nevill, bishop of Exeter, writing to the papal legate Coppini to announce the decisive Yorkist victory at Towton on Palm Sunday 1461, now referred to Henry as 'this puppet king'.[34] A similar opinion was now expressed by Pope Pius II (1458–64). In his memoirs the pope described Henry as 'more timorous than a woman, utterly devoid of wit or spirit, who left everything in his wife's hand', and he put into Warwick's mouth, when in conversation with his legate at Calais in 1460, the description of Henry as 'a dolt and a fool who is ruled instead of ruling. The royal power is in the hands

---

[31] *The Chronicle of John Hardyng together with the Continuation of Richard Grafton* (ed. Henry Ellis, 1812), 394. The earlier version (B.L. Lansdowne 204) was partially printed by C. L. Kingsford in *E.H.R.*, XXVII (1912), 462–82, 740–53.

[32] *An English Chronicle*, ed. J. S. Davies (Camden Society, 1856), 79, 88–9.

[33] In *Ingulph's Chronicle of the Abbey of Croyland with the Continuations*, ed. and trans. H. T. Riley (Bohn, London, 1854), 420, 424.

[34] *Calendar of State Papers Milan* (H.M.S.O., 1910), I, 61–2.

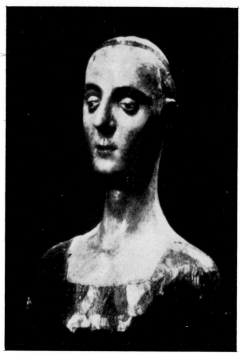

1(a). (*Above left*) Henry V.

1(b). (*Above right*) Queen Catherine of Valois. Funeral effigy in Westminster Abbey.

1(c). (*Left*) The birth of Henry VI from 'The Pageant of the Birth, Life and Death of Richard Beauchamp, earl of Warwick', *c.* 1485–90 (B.L. Cotton. MS Julius E iv, Art. 6, f. 25).

2(a). Cardinal Beaufort. Recumbent effigy on his tomb in his chantry chapel, Winchester Cathedral (late seventeenth century).

2(b). Humphrey duke of Gloucester.

of his wife and those who defile the king's chamber.'[35] It should also be noted that the pope's memoirs alone provide any explanation why in October 1460 Henry agreed to an ill-fated compromise which disinherited his heir Prince Edward of his succession to the kingdom of England in favour of Richard duke of York and his heirs, who then became Protector for the third time. The pope wrote: 'by the wisdom of the Legate the dispute was settled'.[36] In papal eyes this was the best solution for Henry's evident personal deficiencies.

Thus, although at first sight the biographer of King Henry VI is presented with a near-contemporary, ready-made 'Life' of his subject, the early-Tudor Blacman tract, the historical circumstances of its production suggest that it should be discounted in any portrait of the living king. No testimony prior to his death in 1471 supports this hagiographic view of him. The opinions of his contemporaries in fact show that the king in life was adversely judged by criteria quite different from those proposed for his canonization in the early sixteenth century. Henry's biographer in fact is confronted with the normal problems of the biographer of any medieval king. There is no personal memorial and precious little intimate detail on which to base it. He must be brought to life through his actions, through what was done in his name and the consequences thereof.

[35] Constance Head, *Archivum Historiae Pontificae*, VIII (1970), 145, 152, citing the *Commentaries of Pius II on the Memorable Events of his Times*, trans. Florence Alden Gragg and ed. Leona C. Gabel (Smith College Studies in History, vols XXII, XXV, XXX, XXXV, XLIII, Northampton, Mass., 1937–57, reprinted New York, 1959), III, 268, 269–70, IX, 578.

[36] Cited by Miss Head, *op. cit.*, 161, quoting *Commentaries*, III, 271.

Part II

THE MINORITY

Chapter 2

AN INFANT KING

A fifteenth-century English king both reigned and ruled. For his subjects, great and small, his was the supreme authority on earth. He had to be seen by his people, be accessible to his people and, in the ultimate event, personally decide their disputes and determine their requests for favour. He was their personal champion in peace and war. On the personality of the king depended the tone and quality of the life of the nation.

Undoubtedly the king of England had at his disposal to assist him in his task an apparatus of government which was impressive by any fifteenth-century standards. At its head was a council of his choice to advise and to execute his decisions. A representative parliament to tax and legislate had existed for more than a century and a half by 1422. Two great self-sufficient offices, the chancery under the chancellor or keeper of the great seal, and the exchequer under the treasurer of England, directed the administrative and financial systems. In addition the king had the services of his extensive royal household, the offices of his lesser seals, the privy and signet seals, his law courts and judges, his network of administrative and legal officers in the shires, sheriffs, escheators, coroners, customs officials, justices of the peace. Without all these he could not rule and in that sense his powers were limited. Yet all enduring peace, good law, justice and order within the kingdom, its prosperity and its defence against its external enemies, depended on his personal direction of affairs and on his subjects' conviction that the king was personally directing everything in their best interests, that he knew what was going on and that he cared about it. The exacting office of a successful fifteenth-century English king demanded real mental ability and shrewdness in camp and in council, a tough physique, a commanding presence and a royal integrity which could inspire loyal, efficient service.

In the year 1422 the kingdom of England could look back over nine years of glorious rule by King Henry V, a paragon of medieval kingship, who had successfully recreated the martial, imperial ethos of his greatest predecessors on the English throne, Henry II, Edward I and Edward III. In his short reign he had quickly taken a firm grip on his English kingdom, marshalled all its resources for war, defeated the

French at Agincourt and recovered Normandy for the English crown. He had married the French king's daughter and established himself as regent and heir to a second kingdom. Had he lived two months longer he would have been crowned king of France on the death of his father-in-law, the mad Charles VI.

It has been suggested that unrest and uncertainties in his English kingdom led Henry V to re-assert Edward III's claim to the French crown, that his purpose was to provide an outlet in foreign conquest for energies which might otherwise feed the divisions still confronting his usurping dynasty at home. The ease with which he dealt with a plot to assassinate him in 1415 makes this doubtful. On that occasion the very man who was cast for the position of king, Edmund Mortimer, earl of March, divulged the conspirators' activities to Henry in advance. Neither does such a notion fit Henry V's character, with his burning ambition and his belief in the rightness of his cause. In any case, whatever doubts may have remained about the stability of the new Lancastrian dynasty at his accession in 1413, he had certainly given it the stamp of successful kingship and permanency by 1422. The major significance of the French adventure for his successor lay in the fact that Henry V, in claiming the French crown and then dying, undefeated and unspotted by failure, with the necessary conquest of the French kingdom half achieved, left behind him a glorious legend, but a task impossible to fulfil.

Henry's French adventure had been assisted from the start by the internal divisions of French politics, the struggle for power at the French court of the mad king Charles VI, between the great princes of the royal blood, Orleans and Burgundy. His further stroke of good luck came at a moment in the final stages of his conquest of Normandy, when these two rival parties were about to reunite in face of the invader. Duke John the Fearless of Burgundy was assassinated on the bridge at Montereau on 26 August 1419 while in conference with the dauphin Charles, a belated revenge for an earlier murder of Louis duke of Orleans at Burgundy's instigation in 1407. The personal responsibility of the young dauphin for the murder remains a matter for conjecture, but in consequence the new young duke of Burgundy, Philip the Good, bound himself in solemn alliance with the invader Henry V, acknowledging him as rightful king of France. His ally Queen Isabeau repudiated her son the dauphin as illegitimate. It was thus the renewal and extension of this internecine feud in the French royal house which enabled Henry V to enlarge his conquest and authority beyond Normandy to cover half France, to marry Catherine of France and to die regent and heir to Charles VI, leaving his infant son to inherit two kingdoms. But the unresolved problem was the continued existence of a second kingdom of France, dauphinist-Orleanist, or Armagnac France,[1] south of the Loire, which acknowledged the dauphin as Charles VII, by the grace of God, King of France, on the death of Charles VI, in defiance of the allegations of his illegitimacy. This problem of the English claim to the French throne, dependent for its realization on the continued alliance of Burgundy and the further conquest of half the vast kingdom of France, was the *damnosa hereditas* of Henry V to his infant son Henry of Windsor.

With so much dependent on the aims and personality of the king it was only to be expected that the accession of a nine-month-old baby to the English throne should be taken to portend not only the end of his father's grandly designed dual monarchy but also the inevitable collapse of government, law and order and a decline into corruption and chaos at home. One might expect the oft-quoted saying on minorities would be true in its entirety: 'Woe to thee O land when thy king is a child and thy princes eat in the morning.' In fact this infant's princes, his royal uncles and their peers, the Lancastrian lords spiritual and temporal assembled in council or parliament, confounded the preacher. In some respects a period of marking time inevitably followed the nine years of continuous action under Henry V, for only an adult king could initiate new policies. But government did not collapse at Henry V's sudden and unexpected death. Those who found themselves saddled with the responsibility of carrying it on, his brothers, uncles and councillors, strove, not without success, for some fifteen years to continue what they believed had been his policies and to hand on an unimpaired and expanded inheritance to his son. Contests for power and precedence potentially harmful to the cohesion of the body politic inevitably arose in the absence of the strong, effective kingship which alone could permanently limit and control them, but crises were surmounted. The long minority of Henry VI revealed the inherent political maturity of fifteenth-century England. Such was the prestige of English kingship and the fundamental loyalty and ability of the Lancastrian royal family that it was to prove easier for the kingdom to flourish under a minor than under a weak and ineffective adult king who failed to harness its powerful energies, or misdirected them.

Henry of Windsor, only child of King Henry V and Queen Catherine of Valois, was born in Windsor castle on St Nicholas day, 6 December 1421, an event well prepared for and joyfully welcomed. It was assisted by the presence of that precious relic, Our Lord's foreskin, known as the silver jewel, renowned for its help to women in labour, specially

---

[1] In 1410 the young Charles of Orleans married the daughter of Bernard VII, count of Armagnac, and the Orleanist party soon became known as Armagnac.

brought over in good time from France.[2] All the bells of London were rung that day and the mayor commanded Te Deums to be sung in the churches.[3] In France Henry V and the English army besieging Meaux received the news joyfully.[4] The tale that he had wished to avoid a birth at Windsor as a bad omen, foreshadowing the shortness of his own successful reign and the length of his son's days and misfortunes, only began as a piece of Tudor hindsight.[5] Before the child was nine months old the death of his father at Bois de Vincennes in the small hours of 31 August made him king of England. By the death of his French grandfather Charles VI on 21 October 1422 he became the first and last king of the two realms, proclaimed king of France over his grandfather's open grave.[6]

Henry V had probably known, or at the least must have had grounds for hope, that his queen was pregnant when he left England for the last time. The unusually generous gift of the manor of Old Shoreham for life, made at Canterbury when he was organizing his departure, to Elizabeth Ryman, one of the queen's ladies, whom he later commanded to take care of the child from its birth, suggests that this was so. An act of parliament in 1406 had entailed the kingdom of England on the heirs of his body like any other piece of landed estate, so that by the law of the land a child of either sex would have succeeded to the throne in the event of his early death, in preference to his adult brothers.[7] Since he thoroughly revised his will at Dover on 10 June 1421, before sailing to France for the campaign which proved to be his last, it is surprising that he did not see fit to address his mind to the problems which an infant succession would create. Indeed historians have hitherto always assumed that he did so. This 1421 will, which was placed in the care of William Alnwick, keeper of the privy seal, was lost some time before 1445 when the council tried in vain to find it, and its contents thus remained unknown until 1978 when reorganization of the archives at Eton College led to the fascinating rediscovery of a copy of it, along with later codicils added to it, the contents of which have also hitherto been uncertain. This Eton College document now reveals that it was not until Henry V was mortally ill from dysentry and knew he was near to death that he formulated his wishes

[2] Belonging to the abbey of Coulombs, diocese of Chartres, sent to the Sainte Chapelle afterwards and later to the abbey of St Magloire. A. Tuetey, *Journal d'un bourgeois de Paris 1405-1449* (Société de l'Histoire de Paris, 1881), 376, n.2.

[3] B.L., Add. MS 34764, quoted by C. L. Kingsford, *English Historical Literature in the Fifteenth Century*, 169.

[4] *Vita et Gesta Henrici V*, ed. Thomas Hearne (Oxford 1727), 321-2.

[5] *Hall's Chronicle*, ed. Henry Ellis (London 1809), 108.

[6] On 11 November in fulfilment of the treaty of Troyes, 1420.

[7] *S.R.*, II, 151.

for the care of his English inheritance and his infant son, in one of
two codicils drawn up on 26 August 1422 at the castle of Bois de
Vincennes. He intended that Humphrey duke of Gloucester, his
youngest brother, then in his early thirties and guardian, warden or
keeper of England during his absence, should be the child's principal
guardian and protector. His Beaufort uncle Thomas duke of Exeter
was to have the governance of the child's person, with the choice of
appointment of all his personal servants. Thomas Beaufort was the
youngest of the three illegitimate sons of Henry V's grandfather John
of Gaunt by his mistress Catherine Swynford, who had subsequently
been legitimized by King Richard II. Henry IV had specifically
excluded them from the succession to the throne. The eldest of these
three sons, John Beaufort, earl of Somerset, had died in 1410; the
middle one, Henry Beaufort, now bishop of Winchester, was given no
part to play in these arrangements except as an executor of the will.
Henry V nominated two Garter knights, his household steward Sir
Walter Hungerford and his chamberlain Henry, Lord Fitzhugh, to
assist the duke of Exeter in the child's household and laid down that
one or the other of them was to be always with him.[8]

Neither the will of 10 June 1421 nor the written codicils of 26 August
1422 contained any directions for the pressing problems of the government of the French dominions or for the future conduct of the war. But
testimony was later made to the council of the minority by Hungerford and three other survivors of the death-bed scene[9] confirming the
role which Henry V intended his other brother, John duke of Bedford,

[8] Eton College archives contain the only known copy of this 1421 will and the ten
codicils of 26 August 1422, a document to which no reference has hitherto appeared
in print. It reveals the 1421 will to be a revision and extension of the original will
of 24 July 1415 (*Foedera*, IX, 289–93), to which Henry had already added a long
codicil of directions to his feoffees dated 21 July 1417 (J. Nichols, *Royal Wills*, 236–43,
there wrongly described as a second will). Another codicil dated 9 June 1421, the
day before the 1421 will was sealed, written 'in haste with mine own hand, thus
interlined and blotted as it is', the existence, but not the contents, of which is known
from *R.P.*, IV, 299, was especially addressed to the feoffees of his fee simple lands
and so did not concern the government of his heir or the kingdom. There is no
reference to this codicil in the Eton document.

The Latin codicil on the child's guardianship reads in the passage crucial for
Duke Humphrey – 'habeat tutelam et defensionem principales' – exactly as he later
affirmed it did. *Tutela*, a term of Roman civil law, signified the control of the heir's
estate during his minority, though not necessarily the personal care of the child: see
J. S. Roskell, 'The Office and Dignity of Protector of England', *E.H.R.*, LXVIII
(1953), and references given there.

[9] *P.P.C.*, III, 247–8 (25 February 1427): William Alnwick, Doctor of Civil Law,
papal notary and Henry V's secretary and confessor who had probably drawn up
the codicils, by then bishop of Norwich; Humphrey earl of Stafford and Sir Lewis
Robessart, Henry V's standard bearer, by then Lord Bourchier.

who was a year older than Humphrey, to play in this respect.[10] This revealed that the dying king had orally instructed Bedford to 'draw him down into Normandy and keep that country as well as the remnant of his conquest on the best wise that God would give him grace, with the revenues and profits thereof and do therewith as he would with his own'. To Bedford's questioning he had replied that his authority there was to last until his son came of age. Henry V's dying wishes thus became Bedford's prime, sacred duty towards his nephew, even though as the eldest brother he might have expected to become regent in England during the minority. Gloucester had been the one who had initially left England with the king on campaign in June 1421 while Bedford remained behind to govern England. Their roles had been reversed only in April 1422 when Bedford brought out reinforcements and Humphrey returned home to take his place there. Thus circumstances of the moment to a large extent dictated the respective roles which the child's two uncles were to play in the management of his affairs. Henry V seems to have held them both in equal high esteem.

There were English precedents for such a disposal of the governance of the realm and of the heir, by will, during a minority,[11] but the will of Henry V did not prevail for long. According to Duke Humphrey the lords spiritual and temporal back in England, either in great council or parliament, at first agreed to the terms of the codicil and prayed him to undertake the high office which Henry V had assigned to him, but before long objections were raised to the implications of the term of civil law, *tutela* which the writer of the codicil had used. The lords could not accept that the younger brother should be given the power of regent in England which this term would imply. Theirs proved to be the final decision as regards the rule of the kingdom of England, fortified with the assent of the Commons assembled in parliament. Duke Humphrey only received the title of protector and defender and principal councillor of the king which deliberately avoided all imputations of supreme authority of governance which tutor, lieutenant, governor or regent would have carried. In vain he justifiably claimed that this did not give him his due under his brother's will and aptly cited the case of William Marshall, made *Rector Regis et Regni Angliae* for Henry III, even though he 'was not so nigh to the king as my

---

[10] Henry V's other brother, Thomas duke of Clarence, second son of Henry IV and heir presumptive at the time of the 1415 will, had been killed at the battle of Beaugé in 1421.

[11] By Henry III in 1253 and by Edward I in 1272 before he left on crusade before his accession and anticipating his own and his father's deaths. See J. S. Roskell, *op. cit.*, 2, 7.

lord is to our liege lord'.[12] He did not claim to *Rector Regis*, but only of the kingdom, for clearly the will had directed otherwise as regards custody of the child's person. Probably the most important single factor which led to this provision of the dead king's will being set aside was that Bedford, the elder uncle, who found himself regent not only for Normandy and English France but also for Valois France after his nephew's French accession when the duke of Burgundy declined to act there, refused to see his younger brother accepted as regent in England, even though he could not possibly act there himself as well. He made this known publicly in a letter to the mayor and corporation of London, firmly reserving his own claims as next in line to the crown and declaring his belief that his dead brother had in no way intended to prejudice his rights in this matter.[13] Thus the disappointed Gloucester received a summons to the first parliament of the new reign as duke of Gloucester only and a mere commission to open it on his nephew's behalf. His full title, warranted by 'the king by the advice and assent of the lords spiritual and temporal in parliament and the assent of the Commons' on 5 December 1422, was 'Protector and Defender of the kingdom of England and the English church and principal councillor of the lord King', and that only when Bedford was out of the country.[14]

The infant's youngest uncle soon made clear his natural resentment that Henry V's plans for him should be thus set aside. Politics of the minority in England became dominated by rivalry in government between Humphrey and his Beaufort uncle, Henry bishop of Winchester. This suggests that the powerful Beaufort was probably the most influential promoter of the conciliar rule in England which followed and which deprived Humphrey of the power Henry V had intended him to have. No obvious precedent existed for coping with the problems of the accession of an infant in his cradle. Richard II had been nearly ten-and-a-half at his accession in 1377. There had then been no admission that a minority existed at all and the royal authority had been exercised in his name for a few years by a series of councils, nominated by the lords spiritual and temporal meeting in great council or parliament. Edward III was over fourteen at his accession in 1327. He had merely been given a council of lords to advise him. But the accession of the previous youngest of English royal minors, and therefore the most likely precedent to be followed, Henry III in 1216, had been marked by the formal appointment of William Marshall as regent of the king and king-

[12] S. B. Chrimes, 'The Pretensions of the Duke of Gloucester in 1422', *E.H.R.*, XLV (1930), where he prints Gloucester's representations to the lords in the first parliament of the reign (P.R.O., C.49/53/12).

[13] *London and the Kingdom*, ed. R. R. Sharpe (London 1895), III, 367–8, from City of London Letter Book I, fol. 43.

[14] *R.P.*, IV, 174–5.

dom. Duke Humphrey knew this well enough and made the most of it, but to no avail.

The details of the collective conciliar supremacy which governed England from 1422 were in fact only recorded for posterity some five years later as the final outcome of Duke Humphrey's persistent attempts to overturn it, at a point when he did succeed in bringing Henry Beaufort's own secular career as chancellor and principal councillor to an abrupt end, but still failed to further his own. At that point the collective council, first with Bedford's temporary presence and backing, and later by itself in his absence, proved strong enough to uphold as permanent the arrangements made for the government of England within a few weeks of Henry V's death. On 28 January 1427 Beaufort's successor as chancellor, John Kemp, archbishop of York, declared in the Star Chamber on behalf of all his conciliar colleagues, in the presence of the duke of Bedford, that the royal authority, so long as the infant king could not exercise it in person, could not be vested in any other individual. It could only be exercised collectively in the lords spiritual and temporal assembled in parliament or great council, or by the continual council when neither of these two bodies was assembled. It was their responsibility to preserve it intact until it could be handed over to an adult king. Should providence decree that, in the event, that king should not turn out to be the infant Henry then, even so, whosoever it should be (Bedford or Gloucester being envisaged as the only alternative possibilities) would only blame them if meantime they had made it possible for any individual to usurp the royal rights in any way. This view the chancellor declared was based on advice and exhortations they had received from Bedford since his return to England in 1425. The fact that he there and then took a voluntary oath on the gospels to uphold this conciliar supremacy and solidarity confirms that this was indeed so.

According to the conciliar record Duke Humphrey, who was not present, similarly bound himself the next day when visited at his inn by a council deputation. But not before he had observed: 'let my brother govern as his lust whiles he is in this land for after his going over into France I will govern as me seemeth good', and that he would answer for his actions to no man but the king himself when he came of age.[15] In final pursuit of thwarted ambition he chose publicly to challenge the position at the opening of the next parliament, but even without Bedford and Beaufort the lords spiritual and temporal assembled in parliament proved strong enough to maintain this conciliar supremacy.[16]

Thus from September 1422 government by a council had replaced

[15] *P.P.C.*, III, 231–42.
[16] See below pp. 44–5.

government by a king in England, with prospects of unprecedented endurance before it. From the beginning all acts of state were performed by this council which at first consisted of all those lords spiritual and temporal who happened to be within reach of Westminster when the news of Henry V's death first reached them, about 10 September;[17] then by a council of seventeen, nominated by the lords spiritual and temporal at the request of the Commons in the first parliament of the reign, which met at Westminster on 9 November 1422. Their names were announced to the Commons and five articles for the conduct of council meetings submitted for their approval. The Commons added a sixth which was accepted. Of the seventeen nominated councillors, excluding the three great officers (the chancellor, the treasurer and the keeper of the privy seal), a minimum of four would constitute a quorum, but Bedford or Gloucester must be present before any matter which in normal times would have been dealt with by the king and council together could be determined. The council collectively would appoint to all royal offices and benefices except to a limited range of parkerships, foresterships and prebends allowed to the Protector, chancellor and treasurer; a collective and secret conciliar control of the royal revenues would be absolute, and personal responsibility for their actions would be recorded by the clerk of the council who every day would write the names of those council members present when anything was enacted.[18] This process of recording names and responsibility and drawing up articles of conduct, further to strengthen their collective responsibility, was renewed in the 1423-4 parliament.[19] Long afterwards, when the grown king lost his wits and succumbed to debilitating illness, this remarkable precedent of orderly and effective conciliar rule was recalled and resurrected.

These decisions were of considerable personal significance for the royal infant in whose name this conciliar rule was instituted. No regent had been appointed; the person and the office of the king had been declared inseparable and there could be no substitute for him. Thus even while still in his cradle the most solemn acts of state had to be performed in his presence; he had to be made available to his loyal subjects; the quarrels of the great had to be resolved before him. At the hour of vespers on 28 September 1422 the great seal of gold was ceremoniously surrendered in his bedchamber at Windsor by his father's chancellor, the bishop of Durham, and handed by Duke Humphrey to the keeper of the rolls of chancery for temporary safe-keeping. At

[17] *R.P.*, IV, 194. Parliament summoned 29 September, the new king's peace proclaimed 1 October.

[18] *R.P.*, IV, 175-6.

[19] *Ibid.*, IV, 201. The council nominated in the 1423-4 parliament consisted of twenty-three members including the three officers.

two-and-a-half years old Henry was considered able to transfer the
great seal with his own hands.[20] Even before he was two he was on
the move for reasons of state. In the winter of 1423, in spite of the
season, his presence was required at the second parliament of the
reign and on Saturday 13 November 1423 he left Windsor in his
mother's care to fulfil the desire of the Commons, in the words of their
Speaker, to see 'your high and royal person to sit and occupy your
own rightful seat and place in your parliament to whom our recourse
of right must be to have every wrong reformed'. The fact that this
unaccustomed journey was remembered in detail for posterity was
probably due to the scare occasioned by the sudden illness which it
brought on. After the first night at Staines, when carried out to his
mother's conveyance to resume his journey, he 'shrieked and cried and
sprang and would not be carried further'. Mercifully a quiet day at
Staines restored him and the next morning he was 'glad and merry
cheered'. His day of rest at Staines was a Sunday and this was taken
by the chronicler, writing twenty years after, to demonstrate the child's
God-given piety. This interpretation is of interest in showing that by
1443 Henry's scrupulous regard for Sundays and Feast Days had been
remarked. During his personal rule the court never moved on Sundays.
However, his leisurely progress after the alarms at Staines suggest a
more childish reason for the delay. After a further prudent night's
stay at Kingston, and Tuesday spent at Kennington, he rode in state
through the city on the Wednesday in his mother's arms 'with a glad
semblance and merry cheer'. On Thursday 18 November he was
brought to the parliament to be seen and to hear the Speaker's loyal
address, returning to Westminster and then via Waltham to Hertford
castle for Christmas.[21]

This first enforced public appearance at such a tender age was most
likely connected with a treason scare of that year because this parliament went on to enact a new form of treason; attempted escape from
prison by a person under suspicion of treason should be taken as proof
of guilt. There was such a person in custody with the fatal name of
Mortimer, one Sir John, imprisoned in the Tower by Henry V, who
duly attempted to escape and was drawn and hanged on 26 February
1424. At this most critical time for the Lancastrian House no hint of
the rival Mortimer claim to the throne,[22] however faint, could be

[20] *P.P.C.*, VI, 343–7. The second occasion was the appointment of his uncle
Henry Beaufort as chancellor at Hertford castle on 16 July 1424.

[21] MS Harley 565 in *A Chronicle of London*, ed. N. H. Nicholas (London 1827), 111–12,
for the journey; MS Cotton Julius B I for the Speaker's oration in *Chronicles of London*,
ed. C. L. Kingsford (Oxford 1905), 280–1.

[22] By right of descent from Philippa, countess of March, daughter and sole heir
of Lionel duke of Clarence, third son of Edward III, the Lancastrian kings being
descended from John of Gaunt, Edward III's fourth son.

ignored. The informer employed for the trial, a servant of the lieutenant of the Tower, alleged that the accused intended to kill both Gloucester and Beaufort, 'play with his [Beaufort's] money' and make a king of the earl of March, even though March was 'but a dawe' (a fool).[23] Edmund Mortimer, earl of March and Ulster, whose father, Roger, according to later Yorkist tradition, had actually been recognized as King Richard II's heir presumptive, had inevitably been the focus of intrigue since the Lancastrian usurpation of 1399 to which Henry owed his throne. In 1423 March had been nominated as the first lieutenant in Ireland of the new reign. He had initially been allowed to appoint a deputy, but in 1424 he was ordered to his post in person.[24] It may be that, not for the first time, he was the innocent victim of the intrigues of others. But the only recorded explanation for the council's sudden change of mind is that Duke Humphrey was alarmed by the size of the retinue which March brought to the parliament and by the lavish hospitality he dispensed during it from his lodgings at the bishop of Salisbury's inn. Packed off to Ireland out of harm's way he conveniently died of the plague within six months.[25] His lands and claims then devolved on his sister's son, Richard 'Plantagenet', the young duke of York. The keeping of the land during York's minority was bestowed on Duke Humphrey.[26]

The story of the government of the realm during Henry VI's minority and how the collective council and the royal uncles faithfully maintained his rights against the attainment of his majority can be told in some detail. By contrast, information about the domestic life of the royal infant is extremely scanty and can only be gleaned incidentally from financial records. His mother Queen Catherine left him at Windsor in Elizabeth Ryman's care at six months old, to rejoin her husband in France, taking with her a military escort drawn from that part of the royal household which Henry V had left behind him.[27] At his death this became the royal household of the new reign. Sir Robert Babthorp continued in office as steward, but the absence of the treasurer of the household, who also acted as paymaster of the army in France, meant that he had to be temporarily duplicated at home by a commission of the 'clerks of the expenses of the household'[28] for the financial reorganization of the new reign. The first parliament made provision

[23] R.P., IV, 202; Chronicles of London, ed. Kingsford 282–3, 341–2, the only account of this obscure incident.

[24] For March as lieutenant of Ireland, see A. J. Otway-Ruthven, A History of Medieval Ireland (London 1968), 362–3.

[25] Giles's Chronicle, 6.

[26] P.P.C., III, 169. York may have taken the Angevin name 'Plantagenet' about 1448: Gregory's Chronicle, 189.

[27] C.P.R., 1415–22, 443; Chronicles of London ed. Kingsford, 74.

[28] R. L. Storey, 'English Officers of State, 1399–1485', B.I.H.R., XXXI (1958), 87–92.

for household expenses at 10,000 marks a year, but the council considered that a child's household could manage on 3,000 marks for the
moment and the other 7,000 marks was appropriated for pressing
military needs until July 1424.[29] The infant's mainly female entourage
were reappointed under the authority of the new reign. Apart from
Elizabeth Ryman he had a principal nurse, Joan Asteley, paid £20
a year, who had her salary doubled in January 1424, a day nurse,
Matilda Fosbroke, at half that rate, subsequently raised to £20, Agnes
Jakeman, his chamberwoman, and Margaret Brotherman, his laund-
ress, both at £5, with a later doubling of wages. Another personal
attendant, Margaret Brekenam, was not mentioned in the records until
she persuaded the council in 1427 to double her salary of £5 because
it was insufficient to maintain her honestly in her station. There was
a sixth lady, Rose Chetewynd, also at £10, who was commended for
her good service about his person in his tender age in 1429.[30] The
queen returned to England with her husband's corpse about the
beginning of November 1422 and joined her infant son at Windsor
after the funeral on 7 November in Westminster Abbey. She remained
in charge of him until he was seven years old.

On 23 April 1424 the council decided that he should have a governess.
Lady Alice Butler was appointed to train him in courtesy, discipline
and other things necessary for a royal person. She had licence to
administer reasonable chastisement from time to time as the case might
require and a salary of £40 a year during pleasure. Her selection
appears to have been justified, because at Leicester two years later her
remuneration was increased by 40 marks and given to her for life. She
was finally rewarded with an extra 10 marks a year immediately after
Henry officially came of age.[31] He was not educated in solitude. In
1425 the council ordered all heirs of the crown's tenants-in-chief, of
the rank of baron or above, who were in royal wardship during
minority, to be brought up at court, with at least one master provided
for each of them at the royal expense.[32] If Sir John Fortescue's recollections are to be trusted, when he was schooling Henry's son some
forty years later, these noble young orphans were particularly fortunate
to be reared in this 'supreme academy for the nobles of the realm and
a school of vigour, polity and manners by which the realm is honoured
and will flourish'.[33] But Henry's younger companions in the household

---

[29] *C.P.R., 1415–22*, 227, 234.

[30] *Ibid.*, 84, 455, 525, 531.

[31] *P.P.C.*, III, 143; *C.P.R., 1422–29*, 323.

[32] *P.P.C.*, III, 170.

[33] Sir John Fortescue, *De Laudibus Legum Anglie*, ed. and trans. S. B. Chrimes
(Cambridge 1942), 111, 193. This tract is generally accepted as written for Henry
VI's son Prince Edward in exile in France between 1468 and 1471.

were not all to be orphans and infants. The seventeen-year-old duke of York was removed from the care of Henry's Beaufort great-aunt, the widowed Countess of Westmoreland, in April 1428 to reside continuously in the household, and at least three other noble youths who were knighted by Henry at Leicester in 1426 were resident in the court, they and their attendants wearing the king's livery. They were Thomas, Lord Roos, some five years older than the king; James Butler, son and heir of the earl of Ormond, who was no more than eight years old in 1428; and the nineteen-year-old John de Vere, earl of Oxford, who in February 1428 lost his gold collar of the royal livery worth 20 marks when Henry personally removed it from his neck to honour with it a Polish knight then visiting the court.[34] They were to prove three of his most loyal, life-long servants. Dame Butler, who had at least one lady, Griselda Belknap, wearing a silver gilt collar of the king's livery, in her service, had status comparable to a chief officer of the household, authorizing expenditure in the chamber as one of those who 'bore rule about the king's person', together with the household chamberlain Lord Bourchier.[35]

It is possible to gather a few personal details of the lifestyle of the infant Henry from two accounts kept by John Merston, his chamber treasurer.[36] From the expenses paid for one can reconstruct his regular pattern of movement with his attending female entourage, movement not just of essentials but even of the king's portable organs. He lived mainly at Windsor, Eltham and Hertford but he also stayed at the royal hunting lodge at Woodstock, at Kennington and at the Lancastrian castle of Kenilworth. Christmas and New Year expenditure gives some impression of the entertainment available for him. Throughout Christmas at Eltham in 1426 he was entertained by Jack Travaill's London players and also by four boys, protégés of the duke of Exeter,[37] performing interludes. The next year the John Travaill players were again at Eltham, this time with another company, called the Jews of Abingdon. The time for present giving was New Year's Day and the royal child received gifts from his mother, uncles and others. For example, in 1428 Sir John Erpingham presented him with

---

[34] *P.P.C.*, III, 282, 292–3; *Foedera*, X, 387–8.

[35] *P.P.C.*, III, 284–6, *C.P.R.*, *1436–41*, 285; *Foedera*, X. 387–8.

[36] P.R.O., E.404/42/306; E.404/44/334; *Foedera*, X, 387–8.

[37] This is one of the very few references to any contact between the child and his youngest Beaufort great-uncle who was supposed to have taken personal charge of him under his father's will. Exeter can have spent very little time with the boy as he returned to campaign in France in February 1423 and died on 31 December 1426. Likewise the two coadjutors who were never to be away from the infant Henry at the same time can have had little influence on his upbringing. Hungerford was given special dispensation by the council to accompany Exeter to France and Lord Fitzhugh died in January 1424.

coral beads and a gold brooch which had once belonged to King Edward. Henry also made gifts. In 1428, on the advice of Dame Alice, he gave his mother the gold ring set with a ruby which had been his gift from his uncle Bedford in 1426. Purchases made for Henry's personal use in 1426 show that even a five-year-old king was expected to dress impressively. These included a gold chain with pendants of unicorn and serpentine and a gold collar of esses and broomscods, supplied by the London goldsmith John Patyng. The accounts also show that Henry made a Maundy distribution at this early age, bestowing two shillings and nine pence each to thirty-three poor men.

It is impossible to determine when the young Henry first became aware of the animosity and rivalry between his uncle Humphrey and his great-uncle Henry Beaufort which became the principal domestic issue of his minority. Later generations, viewing this first development of domestic faction in the reign in the light of the civil war which dominated its final years, have sometimes discerned two unbroken threads of aim and interest in two parties running right through the minority and through the ensuing period of Henry's personal rule, linking and identifying Humphrey duke of Gloucester with Richard duke of York and the later Yorkist cause, and the Beaufort cardinal with the later interests of his two Beaufort nephews, successive dukes of Somerset, who ultimately became the preferred men of Henry's choice in the execution of policies opposed by Humphrey duke of Gloucester and by Richard duke of York. In this view a developing conflict of policies between parties, the alternatives of war and peace, and an ultimate dynastic conflict of York and Lancaster arose from, or, rather, were grafted on to this initial personal rivalry for power between these two great Lancastrian princes of the blood royal, Gloucester and Beaufort. This simple, comprehensive explanation of forty years of English political history has powerful attractions, but detailed study of the politics of the successive stages of the reign will expose the contradictions undoubtedly inherent in it and suggest essential modifications.

The beginning of the reign saw Duke Humphrey repeatedly thwarted. Cheated, as he believed, of his right to exercise supreme power in England, he was for a time prepared to transfer his ambitions to the continent. The opportunity arose because of the presence in voluntary exile in England of the heiress Jacqueline, countess of Hainault, Holland and Zeeland, a protégée and pensioner of Henry V, whom he had also made godmother to the infant prince. Originally Henry V had sought to marry her to John duke of Bedford, a fine opportunity to extend English influence into the Low Countries, but her overlord the duke of Burgundy, who had similar ambitions, had contrived to marry her to the duke of Brabant, her first cousin and his vassal, whose duchy bisected her territories, with Hainault to the south and Holland and Zeeland to the north. The validity of this marriage remained in doubt for several years until Pope Martin V finally declared it binding on 9 January 1428, but meantime this satisfactory political and strategic arrangement for Burgundy turned out to be a marital disaster for the high-spirited, independent-minded Jacqueline. In England she found a kindred spirit and champion in Duke Humphrey, fell in love with him and married him under a papal dispensation, obtained from the discredited anti-pope Benedict XIII. In October 1424 Gloucester, now styling himself count of Hainault, Holland and Zeeland, left with his wife and an English army to conquer her inheritance. His uncle Bishop Beaufort, made chancellor in July 1424, consequently took his place as principal councillor in England. In February 1425 Beaufort was given an extra salary, indicating that Humphrey's early return to England was not anticipated.[38] Humphrey's conquest of Hainault was suddenly cut short when, early in March, Philip duke of Burgundy issued a challenge to fight him in single combat, rather than slaughter their subjects in public war. It was to make arrangements for this contest, which he eagerly accepted, to be held on St George's Day, 23 April 1425, that Humphrey suddenly and unexpectedly returned to England. Needless to say his brother the duke of Bedford and Burgundy's ally took urgent steps to prevent such a foolish act of bravado in pursuit of a quarrel which was endangering the unity of their joint war effort in France. The pope forbad it and the English parliament, at Bedford's direction, declined to finance it.[39]

The parliament which opened at Westminster on 30 April 1425 had been intended as a demonstration of the harmony and success of the new reign. Henry was again brought to the capital in state for the occasion. Taken from his mother's carriage at St Paul's by Gloucester and his great-uncle Exeter, set upon his feet at the West door, he walked into the choir where he was 'borne up and offered'. Afterwards, 'set upon a courser', he rode through Cheapside and London to Kennington. On the appointed day he was seated on the throne in the Painted Chamber at Westminster to hear his Beaufort great-uncle and chancellor preach on the text 'Glory, honour and peace to every well-doer',[40] giving thanks for his peaceful accession to both kingdoms, for the God-given victory over the French which Bedford had won at Verneuil on 27 August 1424, and for his subsequent

[38] *P.P.C.*, III, 165: 2,000 marks *p.a.*

[39] For the full story of the Hainault, Holland and Zeeland succession dispute and its outcome see Richard Vaughan, *Philip the Good* (London 1970), 31–49.

[40] *Romans*, II, 10.

further conquests in France.[41] The serenity of Beaufort's opening
sermon was in fact illusory. He later claimed that a number of
reliable persons before, during and after the parliament warned him
that Westminster was unsafe for him since Gloucester intended him
actual bodily harm. Beaufort became unpopular in the capital because,
as chancellor and principal councillor in Gloucester's absence, he was
considered personally responsible for certain legislation passed in this
1425 parliament. It granted the first levy of tonnage and poundage
of the reign on native merchants, but only on condition that restrictions
were put on the movements and activities of alien merchants, a condition which the council over which Beaufort presided did not then
enforce. It also made attendance at the annual general chapters and
assemblies of masons a felony, on the grounds that they were defeating
the statute of labourers which it further ordered to be strictly enforced.
For these, or other reasons, a crowd on the wharf near the Crane
Inn in the Vintry threatened to throw the bishop into the river 'to
have taught him to swim with wings', and he was slandered and
threatened in placards which also threatened alien merchants. Beaufort
claimed that Gloucester, after his unexpected return, encouraged the
unrest in the city and the defiance of parliament's enactments.

The most specific bone of contention between them was that the
duke found himself prevented from lodging in the Tower, on Beaufort's
orders. He could thus accuse him of usurping the authority of the whole
council, of attacking the rights of the Protector and Defender of England
and insulting the honour of the City of London to boot. Beaufort had
indeed instructed the governor of the Tower, Sir Richard Wydeville,
to keep Gloucester out and officiously justified this action on the grounds
that in anticipation of possible disturbances in the city, and because
prisoners accused of treason, felony and lollardy were confined therein,
the council had commissioned Wydeville to mount a special guard
there[42] and to admit no one 'stronger than himself'.

It was at the end of October that their differences culminated in
an armed confrontation, ostensibly in a contest to secure custody of
the king. The bishop, from his inn in Southwark, had at his command
many men from the shires, Lancashire and Cheshire being specially
mentioned, and possibly some of the king's household, then at Eltham.
The duke, as Protector of England, summoned to his aid the mayor
and three hundred armed men from the city, together with the appren-
tices of the Inns of Court. The confrontation took place, inevitably,
on London Bridge, but fortunately neither party could cross either
bridge or river. The archbishop of Canterbury and the king's cousin

<hr />

[41] *Chronicles of London*, ed. Kingsford, 285.
[42] *P.P.C.*, III, 167 (26 February 1425).

Prince Peter of Portugal,[43] then in London, came between them and due to their persistent, energetic mediation they were both persuaded to disperse their forces. But the repercussions of such an irresponsible display by the young king's two most powerful princes of the blood in England could hardly fail to have serious consequences. On 5 November Gloucester celebrated a somewhat vainglorious triumph over his uncle Beaufort, parading Henry through the streets of London together with Prince Peter, many lords and the mayor and aldermen in state and subsequently returning him to Eltham. The bishop for his part on All Hallows Eve, in desperate haste and in fear of his life, so he alleged, penned a letter from Southwark to Bedford in France imploring him to come home post haste to prevent a pitched battle and to restrain his unscrupulous brother.

The four-year-old boy may well have been completely unaware of the significance of his ceremonial ride with his uncle Gloucester through London on 5 November 1425. At Leicester in the following May he can scarcely have failed to comprehend something of this acrimonious family feud. Beaufort retired to Merton, to await Bedford's arrival. It was early January 1426 before they entered London together, escorted by the mayor and city dignitaries to separate lodgings in Westminster palace and abbey. A city *en fête* to receive him, and exceptionally lavish presents, do not appear to have won Bedford over to approval of their role in the affair. For all their generosity to him they 'had but little thanks'. London was considered no suitable venue for the urgent reconciliation which Bedford had to bring about between his uncle and his brother. A council meeting fixed for St Albans could not obtain Gloucester's presence. Go-betweens, a powerful committee of arbitration, failed to bring him to Northampton and finally only the most solemn command brought him to a full parliament before the little king himself at Leicester.[44]

Here, on his throne in the great hall of Leicester castle on Monday 18 February 1426, in an atmosphere of crisis, with both Gloucester and Beaufort given strict instructions to limit and control their retinues, and all men forbidden to carry arms, Henry heard his great-uncle Beaufort once again open parliament with a sermon on the text: 'Children listen to your father. Do what I tell you if you wish to be safe.'[45] As recorded on the roll, this was no more than an introduction to the outline of a legislative programme, but it can hardly have been interpreted by his hearers otherwise than as a personal plea for their

[43] Son of Philippa, daughter of John of Gaunt by her marriage to King John I of Portugal.

[44] *P.P.C.*, III, 183–4. According to one chronicler, other weapons being forbidden, men carried clubs, hence 'The Parliament of Bats' (Gregory's Chronicle, 160).

[45] *Ecclesiastes*, III, 2.

support. The king was then removed from the scene and his uncle Bedford was formally appointed his commissioner. The commons in the assembly well appreciated the dangers. They took an unusually long time to present their Speaker and when they did so on 28 February they formally expressed their disquiet at dissensions among the lords, who were all constrained to take a special oath to allay their fears. In the king's absence a commission of ten lords spiritual and temporal then completed the terms of an arbitration. Having failed to bring the recalcitrant pair together in a great council, either at St Albans or Northampton, Bedford now at last had the satisfaction of presenting them both before his nephew in full parliament on 12 March. Here the child heard the archbishop of Canterbury recite a lengthy denial on oath from his great-uncle that he had ever attempted to deprive his grandfather King Henry IV of the governance of the realm or that he had ever plotted to assassinate his father King Henry V. Such was the alleged ancient history which Gloucester raked up in his efforts to get his uncle convicted of treasonable activities against the crown. If the roll is to be believed, no mention was now made of the recent charge of attempting to seize the king's person at Eltham in October, or of depriving Gloucester of his rightful pre-eminence in the land. But the whole arbitration did turn out to be conducted with Gloucester appearing as accuser and Beaufort as defendant. Through Bedford, Henry was then made to declare his acceptance of his great-uncle's declaration of innocence. Gloucester also, with feigned good grace, solemnly affirmed that he would take Beaufort at his word and believe that malicious persons unnamed had misled his uncle about his own intentions: 'Beal Uncle, sithen ye so declare you such a man as ye say, I am ryght glad that hit is so, and for suche I tak yowe.' As instructed they then shook hands.

By his disingenuous use of conciliar authority to humiliate Gloucester during his own brief months as head of the council, Beaufort had in fact put a stop to his own political career. Duke Humphrey had already tried to impose his dismissal from the chancellorship upon Bedford as a prerequisite for any reconciliation,[46] and he was now relieved of it. On 16 March in the abbey of St Mary de Pratis Henry himself handed the great seal of silver to John Kemp, bishop of London and elect of York.[47] Also removed from office at the same time was Beaufort's colleague, the treasurer, John Stafford, bishop of Bath and Wells, who was replaced by Sir Walter Hungerford. With the

[46] P.P.C., III, 185-6.

[47] The earliest and fuller narrative account of the events of 1425-6 is in *Chronicles of London*, ed. Kingsford, 76-94. See also *A London Chronicle*, ed. Nicholas, 114; *R.P.*, IV, 295-9; *P.P.C.*, III, 181-9; *ibid.*, VI, 347-9; Gregory's Chronicle, 158-61; *An English Chronicle*, ed. J. S. Davies, 53-4; Giles's Chronicle, 7-9.

complicity of Treasurer Stafford, Beaufort had been gaining a stranglehold on the chief sources of government finance. He held priority assignments on the major part of the customs and subsidies paid at the ports, the country's only regular national tax, and he had also taken the crown jewels in pawn at his own gross undervaluation.[48] Supreme political influence, coupled with the status of chief creditor of the state, might have made him invincible, but for the unexpected return of Gloucester from Hainault and the resultant open quarrel between them which necessitated the appeal to the superior authority of Bedford. During his brief spell as chief councillor Beaufort had contrived to avoid the redemption of the jewels due at Christmas 1424 and Easter 1425 and had put the national finances even further into his debt. It is true that no accusations on the score of these financial manipulations were made against him at this time, when it was supposed that he would disappear from English politics for good, but they were not overlooked. Duke Humphrey kept them in reserve for future use.[49] On 14 May 1426 at Leicester the council, headed by Bedford and Gloucester, granted their uncle, euphemistically described as the king's 'humble chaplain', formal leave to go on a long-delayed pilgrimage. Once outside England, in St Mary's church at Calais on Lady Day 1427, Bedford gave his blessing to his alternative papal ambitions by placing on his head the Cardinal's Hat which the pope bestowed on him nearly ten years earlier, but which Henry V in his lifetime and, subsequently, the opposition of Archbishop Chichele, had hitherto prevented him from receiving.

Collapse of conciliar rule under the stress of this quarrel between these two overmighty princes of the royal blood had thus been averted by Bedford's intervention. His personal prestige and authority as the first adult representative of the kingship, heir presumptive and victor of Verneuil, acting through the institutions of council and parliament, had thus happily proved sufficient to restore unity in the body politic and in the person of the young king. Summoned to adjudicate and assume supreme control by one party when their quarrel got out of hand, he had in effect temporarily taken upon himself the powers of regency in England which had been denied to his younger brother. His solution was to remove his uncle from the scene, free to pursue his alternative ambitions in the church, and to leave his brother to the council, whose authority he had thus reinforced and could do so again if required. While lacking the drive and magnetism of Henry V he, at least, had inherited the vital qualities of kingship. His reestablishment of the authority of the crown was publicly demonstrated

---

[48] K. B. McFarlane, 'At the deathbed of Cardinal Beaufort', in *Studies in Medieval History Presented to F. M. Powicke*, ed. R. W. Hunt and others (Oxford 1948), 405–28.
[49] McFarlane, *op. cit.*, 416–20.

on Whit Sunday 1426 in the closing session of the Leicester parliament, when he prematurely knighted Henry and he, in his turn, was made to dub some thirty-eight new knights, led by the fourteen-year-old Richard duke of York.[50] New accords on council conduct, backed by Bedford and agreed by Gloucester, were settled at Reading in November. These now amounted to no less than twenty-nine articles.[51] A final tripartite family bond and mutual pact, sealed between the king's two uncles and his mother, to defend and further his interests, left Bedford free to return to France.[52]

Duke Humphrey had thus experienced a vicarious triumph over his uncle, but not to the increase of his own authority. His fundamental loyalty to his nephew need not be doubted, but he still hankered after the position in the governance of the realm which Henry V's will had intended for him. What had appeared to be the public trial of his uncle at Leicester had probably generated views in some quarters that his powers as Protector and Defender of the kingdom and principal councillor of the king were in fact greater than had hitherto been allowed for. At any event in the autumn of 1427, soon after the beginning of a new parliament, with both Bedford and Beaufort out of the country, he again publicly raised the issue on the grounds that differing opinions were being expressed thereon and that he was entitled to a new and public declaration and definition. To emphasize his grievance he openly declared that he would go on strike and absent himself from the parliament, thus making the conclusion of its business impossible, until his position had been clarified. Abstention produced no response, and when on 3 March 1428 he reappeared and demanded a reply, the lords spiritual and temporal had a careful answer ready. Through the mouth of the archbishop of Canterbury they reminded him how in the first parliament of the reign his claims to the governance of the kingdom had been rejected and his present title devised to 'ease and appease' him and to keep peace and tranquility. His attendance at parliament, they declared, was as duke of Gloucester only; in it his powers were no greater than they would be when the king attained his majority. They 'marvelled with all their hearts' that he should not be content with the so recent declaration of his authority and power to which he, along with his brother Bedford, had subscribed, especially since the king had now so far grown in person, wit and understanding since those powers had originally been granted to him, and would take upon himself the exercise of his full royal authority within a few years.

---

[50] *Chronicles of London*, ed. Kingsford, 94–5, 130–1 (38 names), *Foedera*, X, 356 (34 writs sent out).

[51] *P.P.C.*, III, 213–21, dated 24 November (another copy in *R.P.*, V, 407).

[52] Printed in *Correspondence of Thomas Bekynton* (R.S., 1872), i, 138–45, presumably Gloucester's copy since Beckington was his secretary.

The two archbishops, nine bishops, four abbots, the duke of Norfolk, the earls of Huntingdon, Stafford and Salisbury and eight other lords, then set their hand to a formal document requiring him to be content with this affirmation and to obey the king's writ summoning him to the parliament.[53] Thus, in spite of the absence of Bedford and Beaufort, Duke Humphrey proved unable to shake off the superior control of the collective council over the government of the kingdom. Influence over Henry himself was not yet a factor in the governance of the realm.

Henry was still in the overall care of his mother in the spring of 1428, but new arrangements were about to be made to take account of his natural development. The view that he was ever removed from his mother's care because of her association with Owen Tudor, although an act of parliament was passed in 1427 or 1428 prohibiting marriage with the queen dowager without royal licence, has no foundation.[54] Easter 1428 they spent together at Hertford where French players and dancers are recorded as performing before them and on Easter Sunday Abbot John Wheathampstead of St Albans officiated at the castle. On the Friday of Easter week the court moved to the abbey, staying there for nine days until St Alphege's Day (19 April).[55] Fundamental changes in Henry's lifestyle were pending as he approached the age of seven. He was about to be provided with an all-male entourage and a male governor.

Already on 8 May 1428 Richard Beauchamp, earl of Warwick was referred to as the king's 'master' when four knights of the body and four esquires of the body were summoned to take up duties about Henry's person at 100 marks and 50 marks salary a year respectively, each knight to have board and lodgings for himself and for two personal esquires in attendance. At the same time Wallingford and Hertford castles were appointed as the king's summer residences and Windsor and Berkhamsted for the winter.[56] Henry had already been given his own doctor from Easter 1427.[57] The appointment of Warwick

---

[53] R.P., IV, 326–7.

[54] Act found by Dr Griffiths in the archives of the borough of Leicester. See Law Quarterly Review, XCIII (1977), 248–58.

[55] Annales S. Albani, I, 21; P.P.C., III, 294 (payment for French players and dancers coram rege).

[56] P.P.C., III, 294–5; C.P.R., 1422–9, 531. Knights: William Philip, Ralph Rochefort, Walter Beauchamp, William Porter. Esquires: John St Loo, John Chetewynde, Thomas Boulde and William Fitzharry.

[57] Master John Somerset, doctor in medicine at £40 a year, with the furred and lined livery accustomed for royal physicians (ibid., 460), possibly the 'bastard of Somerset' who received a legacy in Cardinal Beaufort's will, son of his brother John earl of Somerset or of John duke of Somerset his nephew: K. B. McFarlane, 'At the deathbed of Cardinal Beaufort', in Studies in Medieval History Presented to F. M. Powicke, 425, n.4

as his governor or tutor, now that Henry had reached the appropriate age, was quite a natural choice. Warwick owed everything to the House of Lancaster. As son and heir of the appellant earl of 1387, who had been condemned to forfeiture and life imprisonment by Richard II in 1397, he had succeeded to the restored earldom at the age of nineteen, in 1401, entirely as a result of the triumph of Henry's grandfather. He was a prominent soldier, a diplomat at the Council of Constance and a king's councillor from 1410, a patron of the poet John Lydgate,[58] and regarded as outstanding for his fluent French. The recital of his numerous qualifications by the council in his patent of appointment on 1 June 1428 – loyalty, knowledge, wisdom, good breeding, prudence and discretion – matched the almost universal praise of contemporary chroniclers. They disprove the other image of the rigid martinet, which seems to have been based solely on his presence at the trial and execution of Joan of Arc four years later. It is true that some evidence survives of a range of miniature swords and a suit of armour 'to learn the king to play, in his tender age ... that the Earl of Warwick made for the king',[59] but this was part of Henry's essential training. Skill and bravery on the battlefield were universally recognized as vital attributes for a fifteenth-century king, even by the most pacific writers of the age.[60] No king could hope to do without them.

Warwick's terms of reference were to train the boy in the moral virtues, literacy, languages, discipline and courtesy and other accomplishments which were meet for such a great prince, only the last two of these five requirements having been specified in Dame Alice's brief of four years earlier. He was to hold before him mirrors and examples of times past; of virtuous kings who had come to good ends and their opposites who had come to bad, with corresponding results for their subjects. He had the assistance of at least one professional tutor, John Somerset, Henry's physician who, in addition to his medical qualifications, had previously been master of a grammar school and was later rewarded for instructing Henry as well as for preserving his health. Warwick's was now to be the principal charge both for Henry's education and for his safety until he reached years of discretion, with power

---

[58] In the autumn of 1426 he commissioned one of the most banal of Lydgate's poems, 'On the English Title to the Crown of France', printed by Thomas Wright in *Political Poems and Songs relating to English History* (R.S., 1861), II, 131–40, from MS Harley 7333, fol. 31.

[59] Cited by R. Pauli, *Geschichte von England*, V, 263 (Gotha 1858), from the Tower records.

[60] 'Tractatus de Regimine Principum ad Regem Henricum Sextum', in *Four English Political Tracts of the Later Middle Ages*, ed. J.-P. Genet (Camden 4th Ser. 18, Royal Historical Society, 1977), 78.

to control access to his charge, subject only to an over-riding responsibility to obtain the confirmation of the royal uncles for any exclusion
he deemed necessary, and subject to the access normally enjoyed by
the great officers of the household and others, duly appointed and
admitted by the steward, according to the old and accustomed rule
of the royal household. For any emergency of pestilence or other danger
he was to have power to move his charge whenever and wherever he
deemed best. At his discretion he could also chastize Henry for mis-
behaviour, refusal to learn, or other disobedience.[61] The rule of women
and the royal infancy were at an end.

[61] *P.P.C.*, III, 296–300 (French and English); *Foedera*, X, 399 (Latin from the Patent
Roll). I am indebted to Dr Nicholas Orme for the references to Somerset as grammar
master and tutor (see *C.P.R., 1429–1436*, 241; Emden, *Biographical Register ... Oxford*,
III, 1727).

Chapter 3

CORONATIONS

There was no English precedent to determine when a king who had succeeded to the throne in his cradle should be crowned. All previous royal minors, even the youngest – Henry III at the age of nine – had so far been considered old enough on accession to undergo the arduous ceremonies of recognition, oath-taking, anointing, crowning and homage, with all the processions, masses and feastings which constituted the medieval coronation. Indeed Henry III had had to undergo them twice, but it was not his extreme youth which had rendered the efficacy of the first time doubtful, only its partly improvised nature, held perforce at Gloucester where the bishop of Winchester, in the absence of the archbishop and St Edward's regalia, had crowned him with a simple circlet of gold.[1] In 1377 the rigours of the full Westminster ceremony at the age of ten had so exhausted Richard II that he had to be carried to his banquet in Westminster Hall.[2]

On St Leonard's Day, Sunday 6 November 1429, Henry of Windsor, scarcely eight years old, was taken in procession to his abbey ceremony in the arms of his tutor the earl of Warwick, but he walked out un-aided at the end to his coronation banquet between the bishops of Durham and Bath, with Warwick bearing his train, having cheerfully survived the full gruelling ceremony. It all began with ceremonial washing and creation of thirty-two knights of the Bath the previous evening; then the morning procession from the Tower to show himself to his people, followed by a solemn seating on the King's Bench in Westminster Hall, a full abbey ceremony, and, finally, the customary gargantuan banquet with the dramatic appearance of the Dymmock champion to defend his right.[3] The day was fine, the crowds huge, several people were crushed to death and a number of cut-purses were imprisoned and had their ears cut off.[4] Observers noted especially the

---

[1] W. Stubbs, *Constitutional History*, II, 18, 31–2.

[2] Walsingham, *Historia Anglicana* (R.S., 1863), 337.

[3] *P.P.C.*, III, 6–7, council orders to supply Philip Dymmock, Esquire, with the accustomed trappings, war-horse and armour for his appearance, dated 4 November 1429. Gregory's Chronicle, 164–70, for the most detailed account, cf. 'On the Coronation of Henry VI. A balade made of the same kynge', printed by T. Wright, *Political Poems*, II, 46–8, from B.L. MS Lansdowne 285 fol. 5.

[4] 'Register of John Amundesham', in *Annales Sancti Albani* (R.S.), I, 43–4.

boy's sad and wise demeanour as he surveyed the assembly from the coronation platform, his repeated long prostrations before the altar and the number of times he was 'stripped of his gear' and reclothed. St Edward's crown proved 'over heavy for him for he was of tender age'. The oath-taking seems to have gone unremarked, although the elaborate symbolism of all the regalia was noted, with the precise significance of each of the separate swords used specified for the first time.[5] The most solemn moment was the anointing by the archbishop of Canterbury, Henry Chichele: 'fyrste hys breste and hys ij tetys, and the myddys of hys backe, and hys hedde, all a-crosse hys ij schydlerys, hys ij elbowys, his pamys of his hondys; and thenne they layde a certayne softe thynge as cotton to all the placys a-noyntyde; and on hys hedde they putt on a whyte coyffe of sylke'. Left *in situ* for eight days, when the bishops washed the oil away 'with whyte wyne i-warmyd leuke warme', this especially solemn consecration must have made an even more lasting impression on the boy himself than on the careful chronicler, although in his grandfather's case the same ritual appears to have been chiefly remembered because it produced an abundant growth of lice on the anointed royal head.[6]

Henry VI was in fact, like his grandfather, anointed from the golden eagle and ampulla, the receptacle of the holy Becket oil, 'with which kings were accustomed to be consecrated'.[7] The legend of the eagle containing a stone flask of oil, presented by the Virgin to the exiled Becket for the anointing of future English kings, first appeared in English history during the reign of Edward II. Fifteenth-century versions state that the vessel had disappeared before the crowning of Richard II, only to be rediscovered in time for the coronation of the usurping Henry IV. The political overtones added to the legend for the first Lancastrian crowning of 1399 are obvious, but its origins had lain in the desire to put the Westminster coronations of our fourteenth-century kings on a par with those of the Most Christian Kings of France. They alone hitherto, having the sacred oil of Clovis for their Rheims coronations, 'did not have to buy their oil at the apothecary's but had it brought direct from Heaven'.[8]

---

[5] In details of the procession (modern transcript) in B. M. Harg. 497, fols 29, 30, partly printed by L. G. Wickham Legg in *English Coronation Records* (Westminster 1901), xxv.

[6] *Chronicon Adae de Usk*, ed. and trans. W. Thompson (London 1904), 298.

[7] *P.P.C.*, III, 7–8, order from the council to the treasurer and chamberlains of the exchequer to deliver the vessels to John Merston, keeper of the jewels for the king's use, dated the day of the coronation, 6 November 1429.

[8] P. E. Schramm, *Der König von Frankreich* (Tubingen 1940), 150. On the legend of the oil reputed to have been brought from heaven during the baptism of Clovis see also F. Oppenheimer, *The Legend of the Sainte Ampoulle* (London 1954). On the Becket legend see most recently T. A. Sandquist, 'The Holy Oil of St Thomas of

1429 saw further significant developments in this respect. Here, in Henry VI's coronation, we have the first clear statement that the ancient English custom of anointing with two comparatively ordinary oils, the oil of the catechumens and chrism, both provided by the abbey sacrist, was abandoned. Henry was anointed solely with the miraculous Becket oil from the golden eagle ampulla. This was solemnly borne in procession with cross and candles from the palace to the high altar by a bishop in full pontificals, 'and at its arrival the king to be crowned must reverently rise from his seat'. The new rubric appears in the up-to-date version of the coronation *ordo* recorded in a book of ceremonies compiled by the dean of the royal chapel, William Say, for presentation to the king of Portugal in the spring of 1449. Along with two other preliminary ceremonies new to the English *ordo*, it was undoubtedly copied from current French practice and designed to emphasize the highest theocratic nature of Henry's kingship. The coronation *ordo* for 1429 had in fact been specifically modified in these respects to conform with the official French *ordo*, as written by command of Charles V in a volume in the royal library of the Louvre, which fell into Bedford's hands in 1423. Thus in 1429 the English coronation service no longer actually began with the more popular or constitutional ceremony of recognition and acceptance, the traditional commencement of the English ceremony. This had significantly been completely omitted from the French coronation since the later thirteenth century.[9]

Henry's Westminster coronation ceremonies were redesigned as befitted the enhanced sanctity and regality of the first king of two realms. The introduction of two extra preliminary ceremonies emphasizing the regality of the king, even before the recognition, together with the procession of the Becket oil from the palace to the abbey, on the pattern of the Rheims practice with the sacred Clovis oil from abbey

Canterbury', in *Essays in Medieval History presented to Bertie Wilkinson*, (ed. T. A. Sandquist and M. R. Powicke, Toronto 1969), 330–44, who nevertheless claims that there is no definite proof that the Becket oil was used for the coronations of Henry V and Henry VI, in spite of its mention in a mid-fifteenth-century account of Henry V's coronation, *Vita et Gesta Henrici Quinti Anglorum Regis*, ed. T. Hearne, 21, and in Henry VI's *Liber Regie Capelle* (see footnote 9).

[9] Charles V's coronation *ordo* is B.L. Cotton Tiberius B. viii, published as *The Coronation Book of Charles V of France*, ed. E. S. Dewick, XVL (Henry Bradshaw Society, London 1898). The evidence for its influence on the English coronation *ordo* is demonstrated in the *Liber Regie Capelle*, ed. Walter Ullman (Henry Bradshaw Society 1961), 26–42, 77, 80, 90. The two other innovations in the French mode were prayers already recognizing the king's full regality, said over the king by the bishop of Durham (matching the role of the bishop of Laon in the Rheims coronations), before he was raised from his seat in Westminster Hall and by the bishop of Bath on his reception at the door of the abbey.

to cathedral, were meant to assimilate English practice to that appropriate for the Most Christian King of France, when Henry entered into his continental heritage. The young Henry's approaching arrival in France had in fact been the very reason for fixing the date for the Westminster coronation. The same theme was continued in the concluding ceremonies of the banquet, eloquently expressed by the elaborate 'subtleties', or set-piece pastry confections, which accompanied each mammoth course. In the first the young king, in armour, was supported by St Edward and St Louis, similarly clad:

> Loo here ben ij kyngys ryght profytabylle and ryght good,
> Holy Synt Edwarde and Synt Lowys.
> Also the branche borne of hyr blode.

The final presentation showed the Virgin, with the Christ Child on her lap, offering to the kneeling Henry, who was supported by St George and St Denis, not one crown but two:

> Borne by dyscent and tytylle of ryght
> Justely to reygne in Ingelonde and yn Fraunce.[10]

As the council had written to the citizens of Ghent on 18 October 1429, it had in fact been arranged that Henry should receive the holy anointing and take the crown of England in the accustomed place at Westminster on 6 November 1429, not for any English reasons of state, but specifically to facilitate and hasten his arrival in France, to take possession of his French kingdom.[11] Thus the Westminster coronation was but the first half of a double ceremony for the hallowing of a king of two realms, who was as much the heir of St Louis as of St Edward, of St Denis as well as St George. Although the splendid Westminster ceremonies bore no obvious signs of hasty preparations, the style and date had in fact been determined by the exigencies of the political and military situation in Henry's second kingdom. This was the reason why, as the crowds on the route to the abbey murmured, it was done much too early.[12]

When Henry first set foot in France on St George's Day 1430, to take seisin of his inheritance there, ten years had passed since the treaty of Troyes. This had provided for the grandiose dual monarchy which was to be the outcome and justification of his father's renewal of the age-old war with the Valois kings. Since Henry's accession, the regent, John duke of Bedford, brother and uncle of kings, had maintained his

---

[10] Gregory's Chronicle, 169–70, for full details and menu.

[11] P.P.C., III, 5–6, and ibid., IV, 10–11, to the inhabitants of Paris, Rouen and other towns of France where it is again stated that this was the reason for the Westminster anointing and crowning.

[12] John Capgrave, De illustribus Henricis, ed. F. C. Hingeston (R.S., 1858), 129–30.

nephew's 'right' there as the sacred duty imposed upon him by the dying Henry V. From the beginning of his regency he had striven hard, by proclamation and pictorial propaganda, to prevent the struggle in France being regarded in its true, natural light as a contest for supremacy between two kings. Severe penalties were laid down for anyone within Henry's obedience who referred to the enemy as 'the French', rather than 'the Armagnacs', or gave a royal title to him 'who calls himself the Dauphin'. The official view of the rightful nature of Henry's title as king of France was expressed in a French poem of 1423. This was written at Bedford's command by Master Lawrence Calot, one of the leading Anglo-Burgundian notaries and a royal secretary, to accompany a pictorial representation of Henry's descent in the eighth degree from St Louis IX, both through his father and his mother.

This pictorial genealogy and the poem both represent the fact of the new dual monarchy, first realized in the person of Henry VI. The strength of Henry's claim to the French throne on the English side is emphasized. Through his father, he is shown as a direct descendant of Philip IV, whereas on his mother's side he is shown as descended from a nephew of Philip IV. The portrayal of fleur-de-lys as well as leopards as background to the medallion of Edward III and his successors suggests that these kings of England were also rightful kings of France. According to the picture, Henry's grandfather Charles VI of France had no son, and the existence of other descendants of St Louis, the Houses of Orleans and Bourbon, was similarly ignored. The poem and genealogy was hung together in Notre Dame[13] and probably in other churches throughout the English obedience. They show that Henry's French claim was presented to the public as founded on an established right of inheritance and it is therefore quite incorrect to assume that the claim to the French throne, based on direct descent, had been abandoned after Henry V was nominated 'heres Francie' in the treaty of Troyes. The French poem was translated into English by John Lydgate, on the earl of Warwick's instructions, in the autumn of 1426, while he was acting as Bedford's lieutenant.[14] A splendid copy of the picture is preserved in a book of romances presented to Margaret of Anjou by John Talbot, earl of Shrewsbury, in 1444.[15] This enables us still to contemplate this genealogy as its original designer urged the reader of this poem to do. In the words of Lydgate's translation:

[13] A canon of Rheims who in 1425 dared to deface the picture was punished partly by having to pay for fresh copies of it.

[14] Details in B. H. Rowe, 'King Henry VI's claim to France in picture and poem', *The Library*, 4th ser., XIII (1933), 77–88, from which this information is taken.

[15] B.L. MS Royal 15 E vi fol. 3a.

3(a). John duke of Bedford kneeling before St George from the Bedford Book of Hours, commissioned by him as a wedding present to Anne of Burgundy in 1423, who presented it to Henry VI at Rouen on Christmas Eve 1430 (B.L. Add. MS 18850, f. 256v).

3(b). Autograph entry of John Somerset, Henry's physician and grammar master, recording the occasion on the duke's orders 'near the image of my said duke of Bedford' B.L. Add. MS 18850 f. 256r).

4. Genealogical chart of the claim of Henry VI to the thrones of England and France (B.L. Royal MS 15 E VI, f. 3a).

Verily liche as ye may se,
The peedegre doth hit specifie,

...

This figure makith clere domonstracione

...

That this Henry

...

is justly borne ...
For to be kyng of Englond and of Fraunce.

The other most effective means of impressing the fact of the dual
monarchy on the minds of his subjects was to strike an entirely new
coinage. During previous English occupations of France, including
Henry V's, the pattern of the Valois coinage had invariably been
followed in English-held territories. In the new circumstances of Henry
VI's succession, the Anglo-Gallic issue were completely redesigned, as
early as November 1422. The pattern followed for these was a coinage
which had been designed to mark the union of Flanders and Burgundy
in the House of Burgundy in 1387, now copied to celebrate the creation
of the dual monarchy of England and France in Henry's person.
It consisted of silver *blancs* and *demi-blancs* and gold *salutes* and *angelots*.
Common to all of them were twin shields of arms of England and
France, with the firm traditional positions of the Virgin and Angel
reversed on the *salutes* so that the Angel of the Annunciation, on the
viewers' right, behind the arms of England, announced to the Virgin
(France), on the left, the coming of a saviour who was, of course, the
infant Henry VI.[16]

Bedford's vision of Henry's inheritance was given substance by his
great victory at the battlefield of Verneuil in 1424. From that point
English France consisted of most of the Ile de France, including Paris,
and of Normandy and Gascony. In addition their Burgundian ally
controlled Picardy and Champagne. The early acquisition of Maine
and Anjou then also seemed imminent, and on 10 August 1425
Bedford took the capital of Maine, Le Mans. Yet another milestone
seemed to have been passed when in 1427 Duke John of Brittany
decided to renounce his allegiance to the Dauphin Charles. English
troops had penetrated to his capital, Rennes, and had roundly defeated
Charles's Breton constable, Arthur of Richmond, on the Breton

---

[16] J. W. McKenna, 'Henry VI of England and the Dual Monarchy: Aspects of
Royal Political Propaganda', *Journal of the Warburg and Courtauld Institutes*, XXXVIII
(1965), 145–51, with plates of the coinage. As Dr McKenna points out, the designer
could not reverse the relative positions of the two shields as an alternative, since the
arms of France, the country for which the coins were struck, necessarily took
precedence on the *heraldic* right, that is the left to the viewer.

marches. The struggle for power between the Constable and Charles's favourite, La Trémoïlle, paralysed the French war effort. Temporary set-backs apart, Bedford, by 1427, seemed poised to execute a great final plan of conquest, to capture Angers and the whole of Anjou and Maine, to go on through Poitou and Saintonge and so link up with English Gascony.

Thus, two years before the young Henry was summoned to France, as Bedford himself later told his boy nephew, 'all things there prospered' for him in his quarrel with his enemies.[17] The events which led to the premature, personal appearance of the nine-year-old king on French soil in fact stretched back no further than the sudden check administered to English fortunes before the walls of Orleans in the spring of 1429. The decision to besiege Angers, taken in the *Grand Conseil* in Paris, probably in May 1428, had been abandoned meantime.[18] The alternative siege of Orleans, 'taken in hand God knoweth by what advice',[19] according to Bedford, on 12 October 1428, came to unexpected grief. The ablest English general, the earl of Salisbury, prime mover in the change of plan, was mortally wounded on the fourth day of the siege and died on 3 November. It had involved attacking the patrimony of Charles duke of Orleans, an English captive since the battle of Agincourt, and this was contrary to the rule of chivalry.[20] It had alienated the principal ally of the English, Philip duke of Burgundy, who was thereby prevented from occupying Orleans in the role of trustee, as proposed by Charles's bastard brother.[21] Consequently he removed his 1,500 soldiers from the combined army. Bedford himself, for reasons not fully explained, never approached nearer than Chartres.

It was in a letter which the continual council in England received shortly before 15 April 1429, complaining of numerous desertions from Salisbury's army, voicing his misgivings about the outcome of the siege and asking for further reinforcements, that Bedford declared the opinion of the *Grand Conseil* that the young king should be speedily crowned in France. Even though the reason he gave for proposing this step was simply the need to take the homage and cement the allegiance of his French subjects, it was probably rumours of plans for the coronation of the Dauphin Charles at Rheims which then prompted Bedford

[17] *P.P.C.*, IV, 223.
[18] B. J. H. Rowe, 'The Estates of Normandy under the duke of Bedford', *E.H.R.*, XLVI (1931), 564–5; *Wars of the English in France during the reign of Henry VI, Letters and Papers*, ed. J. Stevenson (R.S., London 1861–4), II, pt. i, 76ff.
[19] *P.P.C.*, IV, 223.
[20] *Ibid.*, III, 332–3. G. Du Frêne de Beaucort, *Histoire de Charles VII* (Paris 1881–91), I, 31, cites an agreement of 16 and 17 July 1428 between Bedford and Suffolk and Dunois, for his brother, not to attack Charles of Orleans's possessions during his captivity.
[21] Usually known as Dunois. Created count of Dunois 1439.

to press the English council at home to make urgent arrangements for the solemn crowning of his boy nephew there. The jolt which his letter gave to the council in England shows that the fixing of any date for the English coronation for the young king had not then been considered at all.

The death of the English commander at Orleans in November and the lack of a resolute successor, followed by the first appearance of Joan of Arc there on 29 April 1429, sapped the purpose and drive of the English expeditionary force which had been sent out by the English council to be the instrument of final conquest. William de la Pole, the earl of Suffolk, the new commander appointed by Bedford, raised the siege early in May, dispersed his forces under several commanders and was himself defeated and captured at Jargeau on 12 June, while Scales, Talbot and Fastolf suffered a crushing humiliation on the field of Patay on the 18th. The crowning and anointing of Charles VII with the sacred oil of Clovis at Rheims, which Bedford probably feared, became a reality on 18 July. The siege of Paris itself was imminent.

Henry VI's arrival in his second kingdom thus certainly did not happen in a due course of well ordered events. It was part of Bedford's plans to reverse the sudden decline of the English fortunes in France from the spring of 1429. Five years later Bedford described a rapid sequence of events slipping out of his control: he instanced the loss of Rheims, Troyes, Châlons, Laon, Sens, Provins, Senlis, Lagny, Creil, Beauvais and the substance of the counties of Brie, Beauvoisin and part of Picardy, all of which were declaring allegiance to the newly crowned Charles VII and spurning English offers of men and supplies. There were mundane, practical reasons for this sudden, unexpected collapse of the English armies, but Bedford, in retrospect, was clear that it was fundamentally due to the advent of the Maid, Joan of Arc. 'The great stroke' upon Henry's people, he told the young king, was 'caused in great part as I trow of lack of sad belief and unlawful doubt that they had in a disciple and limb of the fiend called the Pucelle that used false enchantment and sorcery'.[22] Only the timely arrival of Henry's great-uncle Cardinal Beaufort with some 3,000 men, diverted to France from a second crusade against the Hussites, at the urgent plea of the council in England, and in defiance of Pope Martin V, saved the fall of Paris.[23]

Beaufort's unexpected re-entry into his nephew's affairs had been made possible by this sudden reversal of English fortunes in France. His enforced exile from England had been sweetened by permission to accept the cardinalate, but in the eyes of the papacy that was to

[22] *P.P.C.*, IV, 223.
[23] Bedford and Beaufort entered Paris on 25 July. Ethel C. Williams, *My Lord of Bedford 1389–1435* (London 1963), 176.

be no unconditional elevation. He was to become a real soldier of
Christ. The colour of his cardinal's robes, Pope Martin informed him,
was to remind him that he must be willing to shed his blood for the
church. Freed of all his English commitments, except for the mere
matter of his Winchester bishopric, he had to shoulder the burden of
a papal legate militant in Germany, Bohemia and Hungary, charged
to exterminate the Hussite heresy.[24] Initially he met with failure there,
defeated on the battlefield of Tachau with a small personal army,
recruited in English France, and a huge, but incoherent mass of German
troops. This compelled him to return uninvited to England, equipped
with a papal licence to preach a crusade and to raise an effective,
professional English army for a second attempt.

The reappearance of his uncle in England, with his authority enhanced as cardinal and papal legate, was naturally most unwelcome
to Duke Humphrey, who now chose to attack him by attempting to
deprive him of the basic source of his riches, the lucrative bishopric
of Winchester, which he still held *in commendam* with his cardinalate.
The young king was made to declare with his own mouth at Westminster on 17 April 1429 his great-uncle's suspension from exercising
the bishop's office of chaplain to the Order of the Garter within his
diocese at Windsor, on St George's Day in the following week.[25] No
financial help for a renewed crusade came either from the clergy in
convocation, or the royal council, who more than halved the permitted
size of the forces he sought to raise.[26] But these still amounted to 250
spears and 2,000 archers, considerably more than the council had themselves been able to muster in response to Bedford's urgent appeal for
reinforcements for the flagging siege of Orleans.[27] On the very day the
council gave permission for the raising of Beaufort's new crusading
force, Talbot, Scales and Fastolf met their disaster at Patay.

Greatly to his credit at this moment of national crisis, patriotism now
overcame the cardinal's papal loyalties. A collusive compact with the
council, sealed at Rochester on 1 July 1429, ensured that Bedford, not
the pope, would have his own services and those of his crusaders. To
save his public face and reconcile his conduct with his higher duty,
a messenger was sent at once to Bedford, ordering him to requisition
Beaufort's army on its passage through France.[28] Thus it was only at
the price of his career in papal service that Beaufort averted the loss
of Paris. The exiled cardinal had therefore undoubtedly earned himself

[24] *Papal Letters*, vii, 25, 30–2.
[25] *P.P.C.*, III, 323.
[26] *Ibid.*, 330, 334 (18 June 1429).
[27] *Ibid.* 322–3, 326; 100 spears and 700 archers against 200 spears and 1,200 archers
requested.
[28] *Ibid.*, 339–44.

a role in his nephew's dual coronation,[29] as well as reinstatement to his seat in the council.[30] Other services quickly consolidated his return to royal favour: his personal loans for the king's affairs in little more than a year before January 1430 amounted to nearly £24,000 and he surrendered, out of pawn, the finest of his spoils from the crown jewels, the Rich Collar of gold, at less than he gave for it,[31] to grace the king's person on his French expedition.

The royal council was now perforce divided into two parts. Most prominent in the section to accompany Henry to France were the earl marshal, the duke of Norfolk, and the earls of Huntingdon and Warwick who, together with the earl of Stafford, also provided the largest contingent of troops. But the principal councillor going abroad with the king was Henry Beaufort himself, who agreed to act 'at the great and busy prayer and instance' of Gloucester and the rest of the council, to be paid at the rate of £1,000 a quarter.[32] Gloucester may have been glad to get him out of the country again, but Beaufort improved the occasion by expatiating on the dangers of dissensions among the king's councillors and captains, stipulating that he would immediately return to England if any such disagreements made his task difficult.[33] The duke of Bedford received real, immediate demotion as a result of Henry's advent in France. Although being allowed to retain Alençon, Anjou and Maine at the king's pleasure, he automatically lost his regency from the day on which the king landed.

There can be no doubt that the collective council, as assembled in England on the eve of Henry's departure, considered itself about to take over the whole direction of affairs in France when Henry was transferred there. Questions raised and answered for the benefit of their departing members under Beaufort's presidency, and recorded in their proceedings, ranged over all the likely problems to be encountered and provide a unique insight into the thinking of Henry's leading advisers on the highest matters of policy in the spring of 1430. Each separate part of the council in England and France was to be sovereign in its decisions, subject to overall consultation in matters touching both.[34] What forces should be raised to accompany Henry? Should they all go out at once or by stages? My lord of Gloucester nor anyone else dared put a limit to what was necessary for the king's safety, but they all knew that everything the kingdom of England could do had been

[29] Subordinate to the archbishop of Canterbury and bishop of London in the Westminster coronation: Gregory's Chronicle, 167.
[30] R.P., IV, 338.
[31] K. B. McFarlane, *Cambridge Medieval History*, VIII, 394.
[32] P.P.C., IV, 34.
[33] Ibid., 35–6.
[34] Ibid., 37.

put in hand and a departure date fixed. Should he be taken direct to Rheims for his coronation or to Paris, where a coronation would be a great confirmation of obedience in his subjects? Bedford, the cardinal, and others of his blood present there, must decide in the circumstances of the moment, but if Rheims was attempted Louviers and Rheims itself must be taken first, and all the country behind his advance secured.

How should possible fighting allies be treated, for example, the dukes of Burgundy and Savoy? How would the finance for 600 spears (and presumably the requisite number of supporting archery) in France be managed? Who would pay the officers of the *Parlement,* the *chambre des comptes* and others of the realm of France? Their costs must be kept to the minimum and would have to be raised locally. How long would the king be absent? Six months? Financial necessity might compel his return after that period as support beyond it could not come from England; it would be up to the council there to raise it locally if necessary. He would need to leave a lieutenant behind him in France when he returned. Who should this be? Bedford, of course, if he would undertake it. If the pope's envoy, the Cardinal de Ste Croix, came to treat of peace, what then? The king's tender age at present made the conclusion of a peace impossible, but a good and reasonable truce would be acceptable, unless a means could be found to victory by further war. Continuous war could not possibly be maintained, so how could the conquest be pursued? By granting to individuals who had the resources to undertake it all the lands they might conquer, subject to the king's over-riding authority to acquire them subsequently by exchange. The English obedience was known to be stuffed with walled towns and castles, both royal and private, with their garrisons all living off the land. How could the burden on the inhabitants be alleviated and the danger of some of them falling into enemy hands by averted? They must be surveyed by the council there and all but the most essential ones slighted.[35]

Such was the English council's appraisal of the hazards facing Henry's coronation expedition to France. In the event Rheims proved inaccessible and Paris itself had to be preserved for the coronation at all costs. By the time Henry VI landed, as a result of the military reverses of 1429, except for isolated garrisons north, east and south of Paris,[36] the English occupation had been withdrawn to the duchy of Normandy and part of the Vexin, the adjacent English-held areas of Maine and Anjou and some of the county of Perche. At this hour of crisis it was vital to establish Henry V's heir on French soil and

[35] *Ibid.,* 91–7.
[36] Notably Creil, Pontoise, Meaux, Montereau and Montargis.

to strengthen his rights by the symbolism of coronation. In the difficult military conditions prevailing, an expedition on as grand a scale as his father's first Agincourt campaign was essential. Loans and parliamentary grants of tonnage and poundage, wool subsidies and direct taxation from his loyal English subjects on this his first and only military venture produced some £120,000, by far the highest grants and receipts since 1418.[37] Professor M. R. Powicke has demonstrated how the whole political community was thoroughly involved in person, as well as purse. Sixteen peers, including seven dukes and earls, thirteen other great captains and twenty lesser ones are known to have contracted for 1,352 men-at-arms and 5,593 archers. Of the twenty lesser captains fifteen were parliamentary knights. For comparison the great muster of 1415 had produced 2,262 men-at-arms and 6,275 archers and the armies of the conquest between 1417 and 1421 by the same reckoning 1,771 men-at-arms and 5,031 archers.[38]

In spite of all this strength, achieving the coronation was a long-drawn-out affair. Three months were spent assembling in Calais, followed by a whole year at Rouen. During this time Joan of Arc was captured by John of Luxembourg at Compiègne in May 1430. Beaufort could again claim personal credit here for he had won over John of Luxembourg to fight on the English side during a rapid embassy to Burgundy in anticipation of the coronation expedition.[39] The witch and sorceress of France, in English and Norman records, was now tried by the church[40] and burnt at the stake under the authority of the English council. Finally the great *chevauchée* from Rouen to Paris was at last undertaken in November. Seventeen separate, successful 'journeys'[41] alone made the safe conducting of the king as far as Paris possible, in which several notable places, including Château-Gaillard and Louviers, were captured, though Melun was lost.

From the day when Henry landed at Calais 'for the safety, defence and good governance and rule of our kingdom of France and the recovery of our rights there', until his re-embarcation early in February 1432, Bedford's title and powers as regent lapsed, the government being taken into the hands of those members of the English council who accompanied the king, reinforced by his *Grand Conseil* in France. At

[37] Anthony B. Steel, *The Receipt of the Exchequer, 1377–1485* (Cambridge 1954), 172–5, and his graphs in Appendix E.

[38] M. R. Powicke, 'Lancastrian Captains', in *Essays in Medieval History presented to Bertie Wilkinson*, ed. T. A. Sandquist and M. R. Powicke (Toronto 1969), 371–82.

[39] *P.P.C.*, IV, 44.

[40] Among the 54 assessors were Norman abbots and 10 theologians from the University of Paris. Ethel C. Williams, *My Lord of Bedford*, 199.

[41] B.L., Cotton Julius B i printed in *A Chronicle of London*, ed. Sir N. H. Nicolas (London 1827), 170–1.

its head Cardinal Beaufort was specially named as abiding personally with the king and representing his interests. Everything was done under this authority, including the burning of Joan of Arc at Rouen on 30 May 1431. Bedford thus had to accept that his regency was an appointment and not a birthright. Confined to his military tasks as commander-in-chief, he himself had been able to return to the near-starving capital from Rouen, bearing supplies by river, in January, but it was not judged safe to bring on the young king until after the capture of Louviers in October.

With an entourage of several thousands, Henry began his solemn entry into Paris for his coronation round about midday on Sunday 2 December 1431, the first day of Advent and four days before his tenth birthday. After spending two nights at St Denis he was met half-way by an escort of burghers, in crimson satin gowns and hoods led by the Provost Simon Morhier. At the entrance to the city he was greeted by the goddess Fame with the nine male worthies and the rarer nine female worthies, all conquerors and warrior women, as the prelude to one of the finest successions of pageants and tableaux fully recorded in the fifteenth century. Having received the various dignitaries of the city in their robes of office, the commandant of the watch, the provost of the merchants, the president and members of the *Parlement*, the *chambre des comptes*, masters of requests, royal secretaries, etc., he proceeded amid shouts of 'Noel!' under an azure canopy worked with golden fleur-de-lys, carried by four aldermen 'as was done for Our Lord at Corpus Christi', through streets festooned with rich hangings. The cardinal of Winchester, four bishops, twenty-five heralds and twenty-five trumpeters went before him. At the outer gate of St Denis was a huge shield of the city arms bearing a silver ship under sail, with a crew of twelve representing bishop, university and city. They presented him with three hearts, opening to release showers of birds and flowers, to signify that the three estates of the realm were opening their hearts with joy at his presence. At the Ponceau St Denis, in a wood within a richly-mounted pavillion, male and female savages fought a mock battle, while below was a fountain of hippocras, with three mermaids swimming in it. These mermaids held the boy's attention for a long time, while the fountain flowed continuously for all who would and could drink of it. In front of La Trinité and stretching to the inner gate of St Denis were *tableaux vivants* of the nativity of the Virgin, her marriage, the Adoration of the Magi, the Massacre of the Innocents, the Flight into Egypt and a good man sowing his corn, who acted his part particularly well. Above the inner gate itself were enacted scenes from the life of St Denis, including the beheading of the glorious martyr, all of which particularly held the attention of his English entourage. Here the drapers took over the canopy from the aldermen, to be succeeded in due course by the grocers, the money changers, the goldsmiths, the furriers, the butchers and, finally, sergeants-at-arms, who delivered it to the prior of St Catherine's, their own foundation, as of right.

In front of their respective churches were assembled the clergy with holy water and relics, most notably the arm of St George which Henry reverently kissed. Before the church of the Innocents a forest had been created in the street where a stag was hunted by horsemen and hounds right to the feet of the king's horse. He graciously spared its life. Outside the Châtelet he was confronted with a representation of himself, a boy of his own age and build, seated on a high platform, beneath a canopy, with two crowns suspended above and the arms of England and France worked on a satin tapestry behind. To the right were represented lords of the royal house of France: Burgundy (the most notable absentee), Anjou, Berry, Nevers, etc., presenting him with a shield of the arms of France and on the left the duke of Bedford, the earls of Warwick and Salisbury and other great English lords, all in their own correct tabards of arms, presenting the arms of England. Also on the right, on a separate lower platform, appeared a pageant of the clergy, the Provost and the citizens of Paris. Finally, before he entered the Palais, the butchers of Paris presented him with a live stag, caparisoned with the arms of his two kingdoms, which was conveyed to the Hôtel des Tournelles where he was to dine. At the Palais the clergy of the Sainte Chapelle and members of the university greeted him and after viewing and kissing the relics he proceeded to his dinner where Anne duchess of Bedford and the ladies were waiting to receive him. After dinner he resumed his progress, doffing his hat to his grandmother Queen Isabeau, waiting at the window of the Hôtel de St Pol with her ladies. The following day he removed to the castle of Vincennes to await his coronation. It is surprising that, unlike the accounts of the rather less arduous progress awaiting him on his return to London, no one here remarked on the boy's obviously quite remarkable stamina.

Early on Sunday 16 December, on foot from the Palais, attended by a numerous company of ecclesiastics, nobility and townsfolk 'all singing very tunefully', he processed to Notre Dame for his coronation. Here a huge platform, approached by steps wide enough for a procession of ten abreast, painted azure and starred with fleur-de-lys, led through the nave, under the crucifix, into the choir. The 'Bourgeois of Paris' records simply that the coronation ceremonies were more in the English than the French mode and that a large silver-gilt pot containing the wine at the offertory was afterwards seized by the king's officers and only returned to the canons as their perquisite as a result of a long and costly law suit. The alleged Englishness of the ceremony is at first sight surprising, since the English coronation *ordo* had already been revised on the basis of Charles V's French *ordo*. It may have been partly a question of personnel, since the cardinal of Winchester himself not only did the crowning this time, but also insisted on singing the mass, to the great displeasure of the bishop of Paris. But the part of the ceremony which would undoubtedly appear foreign to a Parisian spectator was the recognition, with its great shouts from the four corners of the cathedral, which had not been seen at a French coronation for more than 150 years.

Afterwards, at the Palais, was held the traditional coronation banquet in the great hall at a great marble table, with the king served in state by all the appropriate officers. Monstrelet describes four of the elaborate 'subtleties': a figure of Our Lady with an infant king crowned by her side, a fleur-de-lys surmounted with a crown of gold and supported by two angels, a lady and a peacock and a lady and a swan. The anonymous 'Bourgeois of Paris', again derogatory, says the food, like the organization, was shocking; the English were again in charge and most of it had been cooked the previous Thursday. Away from the high table chaos reigned with the *Parlement*, the university, the provost of the merchants and the aldermen all unable to find seats, unless they sat amid the ravenous common herd who had waited since early morning to guzzle and steal. Only the thieves had a heyday, stealing hoods and cutting off purses. The bread and circuses were mean and despicable, ending with one single, small tournament. Paris, unaccustomed to coronations, had yet done more to honour this boy king than ever it had done for any other, yet these events brought little profit to the traders and craftsmen who had a right to expect them. Moreover, the king left the impoverished city on St Stephen's Day to endure a bitter winter of inflated prices, scarcity of fuel and provisions, without even doing the final things which were confidently expected of him: releasing prisoners and abolishing evil taxes.[42]

The memories retained by the young Henry of this climax to what was to be his one and only visit to his French kingdom remain a matter for some conjecture. It is hardly surprising however that he subsequently regarded himself as the rightful king of France. One precious

[42] The sources for Henry's solemn entry into Paris and his coronation there are: (1) the City of London Letter Book 'K' printed in calendar by R. R. Sharpe (London 1911) and in full by Jules Delpit, *Collection générale des documents français qui se trouvent en Angleterre* (Paris 1847), 239–44, who considered this account to have been compiled by the official master of ceremonies; (2) *The Brut*, 458–61 (probably derived from 1); (3) *The Journal d'un Bourgeois de Paris* (ed. A. Tuetey, Paris 1881), 274–9, well and conveniently translated by Janet Shirley as *A Parisian Journal 1405–1449* (Oxford 1968), 268–73, from which quotations are taken; (4) Enguerrand de Monstrelet, *Chronique*, ed. L. Douët-d'Arcq (Société de l'histoire de France, Paris 1857–62), V, 1–7, in Johnes's translation vol. I, 596–7.

and practical memento of his French coronation was his beautiful, illuminated, personal psalter, executed for him in Paris, probably as a gift from his mother, since her name-saint is conspicuous in one of the miniatures portraying the child king and elsewhere in the volume.[43] Another splendid memento of his visit, which he might have been expected equally to treasure and to have ensured its transport back to London, was left behind forgotten. On Christmas Eve 1430 Anne duchess of Bedford, with her husband's consent, presented him with the illuminated Bedford Book of Hours in the Paris Use, which the duke had given her as his wedding present. John Somerset, Henry's personal physician, recorded the presentation on a blank page.[44] But Henry left it to fall into the hands of his adversary of France when he took Rouen in 1449 and to be treasured by the French royal family until it returned to English hands in the eighteenth century.[45]

Henry landed at Dover on 9 February 1432, reached Eltham about St Valentine's Day[46] and made a solemn entry into London on 21 February, through festive streets displaying pageants appropriate to a now twice-crowned king entering into his estate, or, as London was privileged to call itself, his 'chamber'.[47] The city dignitaries rode out to meet him at Blackheath: the mayor in red velvet, the sheriffs and aldermen in furred scarlet cloaks, the crafts in white livery, embroidered with their own devices and alien merchants in their national costumes. After a loyal address the mayor conducted him into the city. At the entry to the bridge, raised on a pillar between antelopes bearing the arms of England and France, the now traditional giant, a sturdy champion, declared confusion to his enemies. At the centre of the bridge three empresses, Nature, Grace and Fortune, presented him with gifts: strength and comeliness, knowledge and understanding, pros-

[43] B.L. Cotton, Domitian, A. xvii.

[44] B.L. Add. MS 18850. Somerset's latin autograph note of the occasion with his sign manual is on fol. 256 r. 'prope imagine dicti domini mei ducis Bedfordie' which is fol. 256, v, as, he states, Bedford subsequently asked him to record it. He describes himself as 'Regis ad personam tuitor ad sanitatem vite pro consuasione consulens tunc presens et predicta cognoscens'.

[45] Ethel C. Williams, *My Lord of Bedford*, 249–50.

[46] *Chronicle of London* (ed. Nicolas), 119; Gregory's Chronicle, 173.

[47] *Chronicle of London* (ed. Kingsford), 97–116, which is John Lydgate's verses 'On the coming of the King out of France to London', written to the order of the City. Another description is in Gregory's Chronicle, 173–5. His state entry took place 'towards the end of windy February', on a Thursday when the Calends of March had begun. His first recorded act after his return seems to have been to preside over the surrender of the Great Seal by John Kemp on the afternoon of 25 February (*P.P.C.*, VI, 349). The writ cited by Kingsford and Ramsay (*Foedera*, X, 500) as evidence that he 'signed' at Westminster on 16 February is in fact only a routine privy seal writ of that date authenticated as 'teste rege'.

perity and riches, while their fourteen attendant maidens welcomed him in song. In Cornhill there was first a tabernacle of wisdom, with the seven sciences in attendance: Priscian for grammar, Aristotle for logic, Cicero for rhetoric, Boethius for music, Pythogoras for arithmetic, Euclid for geometry and Albunisar for astronomy. On the castellated conduit called the Tun, in the middle of Cornhill, was a child king enthroned, with Mercy, Truth and Clemency to govern him and attended by two judges and eight sergeants-at-law. At the Great Conduit, at the junction of Poultry and Cheapside, specially appropriate in view of the name of the mayor, John Wells, three virgins, Mercy, Grace and Pity, drew up wines of temperance, good governance and consolation from a well amid a bower of fruit trees, and Enoch and Elias blessed the king. At Chepe Cross was a royal castle of jasper, with the inevitable branching genealogical tree demonstrating, yet again, his descent from St Edward and St Louis and matched this time by a tree of Jesse demonstrating the descent of Jesus from King David. Finally, at the Little Conduit, at the west end of Cheapside, stood a representation of the Trinity, with a great multitude of angels.

There followed a solemn service of thanksgiving at St Paul's and then a further procession escorted by the mayor and citizens to Westminster abbey, where the chapter met him with the relics and the sceptre of St Edward. Long and heavy as this was, the young king still had the strength to bear it on his shoulder into the minster. After the singing of a Te Deum he was finally escorted to Westminster palace where, on the Saturday, a deputation of mayor, sheriffs and aldermen waited upon him with a present of a golden casket containing £1,000 in gold.

The tremendous English national effort which culminated in Henry VI's coronation in Paris brought little tangible gain to anyone. Nevertheless, Henry had safely entered into possession of his French patrimony as a crowned and anointed king. It is true that no subsequent resumption of military advance ever took place, and this coronation *chevauchée* was 'the swan song of Lancastrian military glory'.[48] However, apart from the subsequent loss of the French capital itself, a tenuous and illusory possession, which had been vital only for this one event, little more was lost. The English-held territories, as stabilized in 1431, now remained essentially intact until English plans of military advance were finally abandoned, and all hopes were transferred to peace negotiations at Tours in 1444.

[48] M.R. Powicke, *op. cit.*, 378.

Chapter 4

ROYAL ADOLESCENCE

Fifteenth-century kings were expected to grow up fast. After the ceremony and pageantry of the coronation years there would be only six more, 1432–7, before Henry was invested with the full responsibilities of kingship. These were years of indecision and inaction by those who still governed in his name, even of helpless waiting for the young king's assumption of power. The boy himself looked forward eagerly to that inevitable event and just before his thirteenth birthday in November 1434 his councillors had to warn him that he was not yet competent to assume control. It was the unlooked-for death of his uncle Bedford in 1435, still only in his mid-forties, which hastened the end of the minority, for in the last two years of his life, initially at the request of the Commons in parliament, Bedford was called upon to assume supreme direction of his nephew's English as well as French affairs. The vacuum created by his death was thus complete and neither Gloucester nor Beaufort was ever regarded as an acceptable replacement. It was the immediate need to replace Bedford in his military post as Captain of Calais which provided the very first planned personal involvement in Henry's affairs, leading through increasing participation to his full assumption of power in December 1437. There was no reason to expect that at sixteen years of age the son of Henry V would not be equal to the task.

The coronation, even of an eight-year-old king, could be no empty ceremony; apart from his own appreciation of his enhanced status, it entailed specific changes in the conduct of his affairs. With the existence of a crowned and anointed king the protectorate was at an end and Gloucester and Bedford were henceforth styled principal councillors only.[1] But Henry's absence from England for his French coronation meant that a deputy was required. On 23 December 1429 Duke Humphrey was nominated king's lieutenant in the kingdom of England at a salary of 2,000 marks until Henry's departure for France[2] and 4,000 marks *per annum* thereafter. As king's lieutenant in England from April 1430 to February 1432 Duke Humphrey had in fact acquired greater power than he had ever had as Protector. His new importance as the royal deputy was further enhanced by his prompt and personal

[1] *R.P.*, IV, 337 (15 November 1429).
[2] *P.P.C.*, IV, 12.

suppression of a Lollard conspiracy which was discovered in May 1431. Centred on Abingdon, its handbills had been found, and arrests made, over an area as widespread as Coventry, Salisbury and London. The seditious writings were in substance a revival of the 1410 parliamentary petition for the confiscation of the temporalities of the church and, as such, directed only against the ecclesiastical establishment. Humphrey's duties as king's lieutenant certainly included the defence of the church, but the Lollard leader, William Perkins or Mandeville, called himself Jack Sharp of Wigmoreland, the Mortimer heartlands, just as Jack Cade was later to call himself Mortimer in 1450, and such a potentially political and anti-Lancastrian association must have seemed genuinely dangerous when kings and lords were absent abroad in strength.[3] Apart from receiving specific reimbursement for his expenses in crushing the rising,[4] as his terms of appointment merited, Gloucester had been voted a fifty per cent increase in salary and a continuing fee of 5,000 marks *per annum*, even after the king's return. This had been proposed in the council and carried by John, Lord Scrope of Masham,[5] supported by a newcomer to the council, William de la Pole, earl of Suffolk,[6] and others, in spite of the opposition of Hungerford and Chancellor Kemp who maintained he should expect to revert to his former 2,000 marks on the king's return. Gloucester intended to retain not only his higher salary but also his increased powers when the king returned to England.

Henry had been given his own signet seal and a secretary, William Hayton,[7] with at least one clerk, William Crosby, to write for it, before he left for France. The signet in English history had hitherto been essentially an instrument of personal rule, but this could hardly have been expected of an eight-year-old boy and provision was made for both halves of the council to oversee any grants he might make with it.[8] There is no evidence that he did make any grants,[9] but the new signet office was certainly active. When Duke Humphrey, as

[3] *Ibid.*, IV, 89, 99, 107, and chronicle references in Stubbs, III, 115, and Ramsay, I, 437.

[4] *P.P.C.*, IV, 91.

[5] *Ibid.*, 104, 105–6 (18 November 1431).

[6] First admitted and sworn to the council on 30 November 1430 with the approval of all existing members except the chancellor and treasurer, then absent. The treasurer subsequently agreed (*ibid.*, 108).

[7] A. J. Otway-Ruthven, *The King's Secretary and the Signet Office in the XV Century* (Cambridge 1939), 13–14, 33–4.

[8] *P.P.C.*, IV, 38.

[9] The petition printed in *P.P.C.*, IV, 67, minuted 'R.H. we have granted this bille' and dated there 13 September 1430 (9 Henry VI) is in fact 9 Henry V, 1421. The original is in B.L. Cotton Vespasian F. iii fol. 5, 'Royal and Noble Autographs', No. 6.

Warden of the Cinque Ports, received his instructions to prepare for Henry's re-entry into his English kingdom, the instrument was a letter under the signet, written in Abbeville on 18 January 1432.[10] At a council meeting on 1 March 1432 Hayton was peremptorily dismissed. Henry's signet was sealed up under the duke of Gloucester's signet and given into the custody of the exchequer. The same council minute recorded the dismissal of four other principal officers of the royal household, which shows that the coronations and the French expedition had caused Duke Humphrey to fear a palace revolution centred on the possibility of Henry's first personal exercise of authority. The dismissed household chamberlain, Ralph, Lord Cromwell, was replaced by Sir William Philip, the steward, Lord Tiptoft, by Sir Robert Babthorpe, Master Robert Gilbert, dean of the chapel, by Master Robert Praty and the almoner, John de la Bere, by Master Robert Felton. The new appointees were ordered to appear before Gloucester himself to receive their charges without delay.[11] Four days earlier the treasurer, Sir Walter Hungerford, had been replaced by John, Lord Scrope of Masham.[12] Archbishop Kemp had retired from the chancellorship on 25 February and been replaced by John Stafford, bishop of Bath and Wells.[13] Lord Cromwell, at least, made a spirited protest against his dismissal, producing testimonies from Bedford and others who had been with Henry in France. He received no satisfaction beyond a declaration that Gloucester and the other lords of the council present on 1 March had been pleased so to decide.[14]

A new attack had already been launched on Gloucester's most powerful opponent, Cardinal Beaufort, while he was still absent with the king in France, with a view to preventing his return. In the council on 6 November 1431 Gloucester produced historical evidence that acceptance of a cardinalate by an English bishop had always meant resignation of his see and he extracted from the bishop of Worcester confirmation of his suspicions that Beaufort had in fact already purchased a papal dispensation to exempt his city and diocese from the jurisdiction of Canterbury. If Gloucester could get his way, Beaufort was now to be required to pay back all the revenues of Winchester, the richest of English sees and the fundamental source of his wealth, which he had received since 1426.[15] On 28 November the duke

[10] P.R.O., C.81/1367/1.

[11] P.P.C., IV, 110.

[12] Ibid., 102 (26 February 1432). C.P.R., 1429–1436, 187.

[13] Ill on 30 November 1430 (P.P.C., IV, 108); unable to open parliament on 12 January 1431 (R.P., IV, 367).

[14] Ibid., IV, 392.

[15] P.P.C., IV, 100–1.

succeeded in getting writs of praemunire and attachment prepared, with the joint objectives of crippling his uncle financially and preventing his return to English politics, but in view of Beaufort's royal blood and his recent great services to the king he found that he could only get the consent of the council to holding the writs in suspension until Beaufort could return to England to be heard.[16] In thus trying to manipulate the law to remove this greatest potential obstacle to his dominance of the young king, Gloucester was here his own worst enemy, because rumours of impending treason charges brought the cardinal back post-haste when, it seems, he had otherwise been bent on following up renewed possibilities of service in the papal cause and his own, which might well have kept him permanently out of England.

Subsequent events did not follow the earlier pattern of Beaufort's 1426 humiliation. The new chancellor's oration to parliament on 12 May 1432 on the text 'Fear God, honour the king', appropriate to the dignity of the now twice-crowned king there present, was followed next day by an oration from Gloucester, still, as he stressed, the king's nearest male relative and chief councillor in Bedford's absence. He declared that he was backed by a council which was of one mind in advising the king now and for the future, until he should come to years of puberty and discretion. This statement was communicated to the Commons when they presented their Speaker,[17] but if it was intended as a challenge to overawe Beaufort it failed. Not only did the cardinal successfully demand public acceptance of his loyalty and innocence from Henry himself, but this was recorded under the great seal and Gloucester and all the other lords had to give their approval. Moreover, Beaufort also obtained a statutory guarantee, originating in the Commons House, both as cardinal and bishop of Winchester, that he would be subjected to no further harassment under provisors or praemunire. On 6 February 1432 Gloucester had had 6,000 marks' worth of his uncle's jewels and plate seized in the customs at Sandwich. These were now ordered to be restored to him and it can have been small consolation to the duke that their restoration was now made conditional on Beaufort's making further substantial loans in the king's services.[18] It is noteworthy that Bedford's services as mediator between his brother and uncle, as in 1425–6, were not required this time. In view of the young king's enhanced status he may well have been no mere figurehead in this accommodation which was reached in his presence and declared for him among his lords in parliament in June 1432. The issue was certainly not to Gloucester's liking, as he made

[16] *Ibid.*, 104–5.
[17] *R.P.*, IV, 389.
[18] *Ibid.*, 390–2, *P.P.C.*, IV, 162–3.

clear when he raked up this 1432 bone of contention in his better known personal attack on his uncle eight years later.[19]

It is no surprise to find the earl of Warwick stating in late November 1432, on the approach of Henry's eleventh birthday, that the boy had grown 'in stature of his person' in the four and a half years of his tutorship and 'in conceit and knowledge of his high and royal authority', and thanking God for it. But the occasion of these remarks was not mere praise. It was his tutor's acknowledged inability any longer to administer correction and to control him which had forced him to appeal to the council for added powers. He consequently requested a clear, formal demonstration to Henry that his uncle Gloucester and all the council were still firmly behind him in his task. They were to explain to the king himself the need for new measures to support Warwick in doing his duty and also to move him not to bear any grudge against his tutor on that account. Warwick asked for and was given power to order his movements more strictly than before, to regulate all access to him, to remove unsuitable persons from his service and to be always present himself, or by deputy, at royal audiences. All this was necessary, he said, because unnamed persons in his absence had already stirred the boy from his learning and had told him things he ought not to hear. Subject to exceptions being made for princes of the blood, persons of the highest estate and the great officers of the household, all the new powers asked for were now granted to Warwick, but the principal councillor himself and the rest of the council were to be consulted before any changes were made among the knights and esquires of the body.[20]

1433 saw Henry's council faced with insoluble problems which were to dog the footsteps of the young king and his advisers for the next twenty years. They could not conceive of any means of defending and consolidating the French inheritance which did not involve further aggressive conquest, yet it was impossible to raise finance from either kingdom adequate for this. A negotiated peace was not a viable alternative because the two rival French coronations at Rheims and Paris had created a fundamental block to peace by negotiation. As Berry herald put it, each party demanded, rightly or wrongly, to have the kingdom of France and each wished to be called the king of France. Since 1422 Bedford had striven militarily and diplomatically to assert his nephew's claims to the uttermost. There was no going back on these. While it is possible that Henry V himself might have envisaged ultimate peace terms of his own which would have admitted of compromise over the title to the French crown, Bedford and the other

[19] Stevenson, *Wars*, II, 442.
[20] *P.P.C.*, IV, 132–7 (council minutes, 29 November 1432).

councillors of the minority never could do so. Moves for peace earlier than March 1431 were not contemplated at all. Only then were steps taken to remove the specific ban on negotiations with 'Charles the Dauphin' without the assent of the three estates of both realms, which the treaty of Troyes had imposed. Even then it was papal intervention alone which compelled the formal consideration of peace, simply on Christian and moral grounds, although the grievous burden of the war was cited as a subsidiary reason for finally getting this ban removed in parliament.[21] In fact peace negotiations thus only began when rival coronations were about to make peace by agreement impossible. Two years of negotiations under papal auspices revealed that even a meeting of principals or plenipotentiaries from both sides was unattainable. In April and May 1433 Bedford and Gloucester went to Calais for a whole month, and the dukes of Orleans and Bourbon, with other French prisoners, were moved to Dover for six weeks to be at hand to assist negotiations, but the promised French emissaries failed to appear.

The papal initiative had also brought another danger nearer, the alternative of a separate peace between Burgundy and Charles VII. Burgundy's absence from Henry's Paris coronation had been conspicuous. He was in fact already negotiating what ultimately turned out to be a separate peace, a course which the papacy pressed upon him as a duty should the English prove recalcitrant. Philip of Burgundy, for his part, feared that there were also secret Anglo-French negotiations in hand to his detriment, involving Henry's marriage to one of Charles VII's daughters. Consequently he sent an embassy to London under Hugh de Lannoy, designed to find out if there was any truth in such rumours. Lannoy was received in personal audience by Henry at his Guildford hunting lodge on 26 June 1433. According to his report the king, a fine looking, sturdy child, asked very pleasantly in French after the duke and conversed with the embassy for a while before summoning his lords who knelt around him while Burgundy's letters were read. They remarked on the presence among his entourage of another 'very gracious and clever child', Gilles, younger son of the duke of Brittany,[22] with whom they also spoke, evidence that Henry still had the allegiance of one other important ally, the duke of Brittany. Their audience, and subsequent consultations with the English lords, convinced them that Burgundy's fears were quite unfounded. It was also through this embassy, as a result of their chance encounter at Calais on their return journey with one Jean de Saveuse, who had had

---

[21] R.P., IV, 371, wrongly printed in P.P.C., IV, 279–80 under the date 8 July 1434.
[22] £20 to be paid to Gilles being about the person of the king 28 August 1432. P.P.C., IV, 128. Agreement on his return to Brittany in spite of the very great and singular pleasure the king had in his company P.P.C., IV, 278 (Gravesend 6 July 1434).

direct access to Charles VII, that Philip of Burgundy was informed that, on Charles VII's part, any peace with Henry VI depended absolutely on his willingness to relinquish his claim to the French crown. Lannoy's sealed despatch from Henry, when opened, revealed that Henry and his councillors had no intention at all of abandoning his crown and sovereignty of France.[23] So Burgundy was now fully informed of the uncompromising stand of both Henry and Charles. It was also at this time that the first secret direct Orleans-Burgundian contacts were established. This was brought about by the accident that the earl of Suffolk had a Burgundian barber from Lille with access to his French prisoner, Charles of Orleans. This was to lead eventually to the release of the duke of Orleans and to an Orleans-Burgundian alliance.

The complete failure of the Calais negotiations was followed by urgent representations by the people of Normandy to Bedford for provision of effective defence. This was why he returned to England in 1433 to obtain it.[24] Here, from 18 June 1433, he automatically took over the role of principal councillor.[25] He had also been stung into action by rumours, which he claimed had been put about in England, that his carelessness and negligence were responsible for the declining fortunes of Henry's French inheritance. Parliament had been summoned and, as soon as its opening formalities were completed, he rose on 13 July to demand that his attackers should identify themselves. A brief consultation of those about the king resulted in a formal declaration by the chancellor on behalf of Henry, his uncle Gloucester, and all the lords present, that no such allegations were known to them. Henry then personally thanked him profusely for his services and expressed his joy at having him once more in his presence. From this moment Bedford dominated the assembly. Ralph, Lord Cromwell, who now replaced Duke Humphrey's nominee Lord Scrope as treasurer, must be considered his choice[26] and, possibly also, the earl of Suffolk who replaced Robert Babthorpe, Gloucester's man, as steward of the household.[27] On 3 November Bedford led the Lords at the request of the Commons in taking an oath not to harbour or maintain criminals and later he administered a similar oath to all members of the Commons House, calling each member by name.[28]

[23] Stevenson, *Wars*, II, part I, 218–62.
[24] *P.P.C.*, IV, 257; *R.P.*, IV, 420.
[25] *P.P.C.*, IV, 218.
[26] *Ibid.*, 175 (11 August), although Scrope was ill and confined to his chamber on 15 December (*R.P.*, IV, 422).
[27] This could have been as early as 20 April, but Suffolk was first referred to as steward on 14 August 1433 (R. L. Storey, 'English officers of State', *B.I.H.R.*, XXXI [1958], 89).
[28] *R.P.*, IV, 'Domum ipsirum Communium'.

Bedford had returned to England for only the second time in ten years specifically to obtain adequate funds and support for his continuing role as regent in France. But it soon became clear that he was wanted in England. At the end of November the Speaker of the Commons appeared before the king and the lords to deliver a panegyric on Bedford for securing and consolidating the king's French possessions, which they said could now more easily spare him, for his noble example in upholding the law, personally bringing criminals to justice, truly paying for his victuals and wisely advising the king. The purpose was to make him remain in England at the head of the government and, after consultation with Gloucester, the cardinal, the two archbishops and certain other lords unnamed, Henry ordered the chancellor to ask all the assembled lords whether they supported the Commons' request. With their support he secured Bedford's agreement.[29] The next day in the Star Chamber the duke raised the question of his salary, recalling that he, or his brother, had in the past been paid as much as 8,000 marks *per annum* (£5,333 13s 4d). At this none of the other councillors ventured to speak. He then proposed, in view of the king's great necessity, to take only £1,500 a year, with another £500 for each journey to or from France.[30] On 18 December he laid before parliament his conditions for assuming his own new responsibilities, but only 'as far as it may goodly be with the weal of his [the king's] lands and lordships beyond the sea', thus not abdicating what he still considered to be his primary charge, as laid upon him by his brother Henry V, but taking on additional responsibilities in England until the king could exercise the governance of the realm in his own person. Parliament now, in fact, gave him a new controlling interest over Henry's government without any specific new title to formalize it: a new personal nomination of the continual council, a guarantee that none of the great officers of state, including those of the duchy of Lancaster, would be replaced without his approval, no parliament called without his assent and presence, and no bishop appointed without his assent.[31] On 28 November Duke Humphrey *faute de mieux* also had to accept a mere £1,000 *per annum* for attendance at the council,[32] and when the new councillors were nominated in Henry's presence on 21 December the cardinal, the two archbishops and the bishops of Ely and Lincoln all agreed to give their services free in term time.[33] The

---

[29] *Ibid.*, 423 (24 November).

[30] *Ibid.*, 424–5.

[31] *Ibid.*, 423–4.

[32] *P.P.C.*, IV, 185–6.

[33] *R.P.*, IV, 446, the other members being the bishops of Rochester and Bath (the chancellor), the earls of Huntingdon, Warwick, Stafford, Suffolk and Northumberland, Ralph Lord Cromwell (the treasurer) and John Lord Tiptoft.

Commons finally granted one tenth and fifteenth, the standard form of direct taxation, to be levied in two instalments in 1434 and 1435 but, for the first time, with a deduction of £4,000 from the total sum because of poverty, distress and inability to bear the previous level of taxation prevalent throughout the country.[34]

Cromwell's appointment as treasurer had demonstrated that this was no time to expect massive financial assistance for the prosecution of the war in France. There was a financial crisis of the gravest magnitude in the aftermath of the enormously expensive coronation sortie of 1430-2. It was customary throughout the fifteenth century for the treasurer to 'declare the state of the realm' in general terms to parliament, but 1433 revealed for the first time that such general statements could be based on very detailed, comprehensive surveys of expenditure and revenue prepared by the treasurer's staff in the exchequer. When Cromwell took over the treasurership on 11 August 1433, parliament had already been informed that even the normal expenses of government could not be covered to the sum of £35,000 or more. When parliament was suddenly prorogued on 13 August because of plague in London he had to be given emergency powers to restrain all assignments already made prior to 20 July, in order to secure an essential £2,000 for Henry's personal expenses and the expenses of his household, until the reassembly of parliament on the quindene of Michaelmas. After reassembly (13 October), Cromwell was ready with further evidence of the seriousness of the financial situation. He now claimed that the earlier statement, alarming as it had been, had had little effect on the parliament. It seems that Cromwell feared that he would be blamed for the crippling lack of funds. Consequently on 18 October he laid before the Lords books and records of exchequer revenues and financial commitments. They had to undertake first to examine these, and then to instruct him how to provide for all the expenses of government, with a clear order of priorities for the limited resources available. A digest of these exchequer documents was also handed in to the Lords, sectionalized under the names of the various exchequer staff who had prepared it. This was subsequently read out to the Commons and sewn on to the roll of the parliament. Thus there survives for this year a survey of the resources and financial commitments of English government, unique in its detail and comprehensiveness, made only some three years before Henry assumed personal direction of affairs.[35] The gross annual revenues of the crown amounted to £54,000, of which £31,000 came from indirect taxation, that is, from import and export duties, the customs, tonnage and poundage and wool subsidies levied at the ports. These provided £27,000 net,

[34] *Ibid.*, 425-6.
[35] *Ibid.*, 420-1, 432-9.

which was the major part of the current disposable income, because the remaining £23,000 of the gross sum, which alone might be called the permanent revenues of the crown, bore long-term charges, consisting mainly of fees and annuities, amounting to £14,000. Foreseeable expenses for the coming year amounted to £57,000 and there were debts outstanding of £165,000. At the end of his budget Cromwell clearly stated that there was no provision made for the defence of Henry's French possessions. Neither was there any money even for the immediate expenses of the king himself and his household.

These were the circumstances which caused the young king to spend the next four months in a monastery. It was the custom on the Feast of All Saints each year to decide where the king should spend Christmas. In the midst of this financial crisis, with no provision made for household expenses beyond the quindene of Michaelmas, and no parliamentary grants yet offered, the council now took the novel, emergency decision to send Henry and his household for a protracted stay, at no cost, from Christmas 1433 to St George's Day 1434, to the monastery of Bury St Edmunds. Doubtless this was a financial decision. The abbot William Curteys, then at his manor of Elmswell some ten miles to the east of the town, received this unprecedented council order with astonishment. Nevertheless, mindful of the especial honour and obligation of entertaining this twice-crowned king of two realms, so he said, he immediately engaged eighty workmen for a month to put his dilapidated palace into order and prudently arranged to share both the honours and the expenses with the prior and convent. Even before the king's arrival he had to feed an advance party of one hundred officials of various grades. A magnificent reception was required for the king himself, so at the abbot's direction five hundred of his towns-men in red livery, led by their aldermen and burgesses in scarlet, rode out on Christmas Eve to meet the king and his mile-long train on Newmarket heath. Entering the precincts of the monastery by the south gate, Henry was assisted from his horse by his tutor Warwick, to be greeted by his confessor, William Alnwick, who was also the bishop of Norwich, and the abbot, in full pontificals, together with all the monks in the abbey's best copes. Censed and sprinkled with holy water, he reverently kissed the cross which the abbot presented to him and processed to the high altar to the singing of the antiphon for the service of St Edmund: 'Ave rex gentis Anglorum'. After praying at the saint's shrine and thanking the abbot for his reception, the king and his nobles moved on to occupy his palace throughout the Christmas festivities, in all of which he participated in regal state until Epiphany. The abbot was careful to present suitable precious gifts not only to the king but also to his nobles according to rank. Probably among the Near Year gifts which Henry now received was the splendid dedicatory manuscript of John Lydgate's Life of St Edmund which shows him kneeling in prayer before St Edmund's shrine.[36]

From 6 to 23 January Henry moved to the prior's lodging, considered especially pleasant because of its proximity to the water and enclosed vineyard and, being easily accessible to the open country, allowing him to make frequent excursions hunting both fox and hare. Then it was the turn of the abbot's manor house at Elmswell to accommodate him and his court, completely in the country, where the sports of fishing and fowling could most easily be provided and provisions were especially plentiful. For Lent, 25 February to 11 April that year, he returned to the prior's lodgings and then back to the abbot's palace for the Easter festivities, until the time set for his departure for Windsor. When this approached, the duke of Gloucester and the various dignitaries of the court were solemnly admitted into the fraternity of the monastery and Henry himself, at his own request, in spite of his youth, was also solemnly enrolled in the fraternity by the abbot in a special ceremony in the chapter house. At the moment of departure, Gloucester prostrated himself before the king and requested him to express his final thanks to the abbot for his lavish presents and indefatigable hospitality. This the boy did, taking him by the hand, commending himself and his people to God and St Edmund and thanking the abbot joyfully and profusely.

The circumstances and details of this prolonged monastic visit of 1433–4, as minutely described in the abbot's register,[37] if considered independently of posthumous assertions about Henry's character, are hardly material for the view that he was, from birth, and by nature, more monk than monarch. It was in fact a state visit on a grand scale, very expensive for the abbot and community and, though possibly also made to seem desirable as part of the boy's education, was occasioned by immediate financial necessity, not planned to accommodate his youthful wishes.

Cromwell's budget had contained a memorandum 'To provide for the kingdom of France' and highlighted the fact that there was no current provision at all from English revenues for the defence of Henry's French possessions. Normandy and Maine were indeed normally expected to finance themselves. Only when special new expeditionary forces were sent out, such as Salisbury's in 1428, the coronation expedition of 1431 or on the appointment of a new lieutenant there, did the English exchequer contribute to the cost of waging war and then only for the first six months after landing. With Bedford con-

[36] B.L. MS Harley 2278, the original book presented to the king: dedication on fol. 119v.
[37] First printed in *Archaeolgia*, XV, 65–71 and in Dugdale's *Monasticon* (ed. Caley and Ellis, 1821), III, 99.

strained to remain in England to rule the country, and the king and court in a monastery, the problems of the French possessions, which had actually brought him back across the Channel in June 1433, were apparently ignored until April 1434. But the very purpose of Bedford's visit had been to secure some permanent provision from England, and rumours of the raising of a great French army of attack, with repeated appeals for help from Normandy, persisted. A few days after the court's departure from Bury, a great council assembled in the parliament chamber at Westminster on 26 April 1434, specifically summoned to deal with this problem. It was first confronted with ambitious plans put forward not by Bedford but by Duke Humphrey. Impatient at his elder brother's unaccustomed presence and pre-eminence in England, he now proposed to usurp his vacant place in France.

Bedford took this as a new personal attack upon his regency there and demanded the right to make a studied reply, which Gloucester then counter-challenged as a slight on his honour. Such an open and tedious quarrel, with both of them meticulously preparing their written cases, could only be settled in the king's presence, as had been the previous quarrels between two of his three nearest princes of the blood in 1426 and 1432. It is natural to assume that Henry was advised here by the cardinal, for once not a party to the dispute, even though the record does not say so. The solution, 'by advice of the council', was to silence both of them, to have them both surrender their written evidences into Henry's own hands for destruction, for him to declare that the honour of neither of his most loyal uncles had been besmirched, and to forbid any further argument.

This scene in the great chamber of the bishop of Durham's London palace on 8 May 1434,[38] in the presence of the cardinal, the two archbishops and sixty-five other members of the great council, can hardly have strengthened the case for the continuance of conciliar government in the mind of the thirteen-year-old king. Moreover, the great council as a body considered that its honour and competence had also been put in doubt. Rumours were soon current that the two dukes had made offers, and submitted plans, which would solve the insoluble problems of France at no public cost and to the relief of many years' taxation, which the council had irresponsibly laid aside. Gloucester, at least, had openly appealed to public opinion in support of his plan, which was apparently sufficiently detailed to be roughly costed: some £50,000, which the council declared was an utterly impossible sum to think of, when commissioners sent out into the counties to raise loans could not get any money, even on the security of the crown jewels. They therefore petitioned Henry that Gloucester should be formally challenged to request the summoning of a parliament

[38] *P.P.C.*, IV, 210–13.

and put his wholly admirable but financially impossible plan to it, in order to clear them of the imputations of negligence.[39] After the king's enforced reconciliation of the two royal dukes no more was heard of Gloucester's plan.

The council minutes for 14 and 15 June 1434 do, however, show that Bedford, on the other hand, did subsequently submit his plans in writing to Henry, embedded in a long justification of his whole regency since the death of Henry V, and these, in substance, were finally adopted. They involved the appropriation to war expenses of the only permanent item of royal revenue not covered by Cromwell's budget, the major portion of the personal patrimony of the royal house, the part of the duchy of Lancaster which Henry V had enfeoffed for the fulfilment of his will. Some £5,000 gross and £2,500 net of duchy revenues had been included in Cromwell's budget, though carefully excluded from his totals since he had no control over them. A further £4,000 per annum was being enjoyed by Queen Catherine. It was the remainder, currently producing about £6,000 per annum, still under control of the cardinal and Henry V's other surviving feoffees, which Bedford now asked should be henceforth set aside to finance 200 lances and 600 bowmen for duty in France.[40] He proposed to double this force by drawing upon the Calais garrison from which, if he were given the supreme command of it, he confidently predicted he could extract a mobile field force without weakening its defences.[41] Finally he undertook to devote his own personal income from Normandy for two years from Michaelmas 1434 to the same cause. Had he lived, it is possible that these arrangements, which were approved in outline by the council,[42] might have provided the basis for the permanent English field force which was so conspicuously lacking in France. But the trustees of the duchy imposed the condition that they should be provided with alternative income. While in fact, under pressure, they loaned some £114,000 towards the conduct of the war between the death of Henry V and their dissolution in 1441, all this had to be, and was, repaid.[43] In the end, when Henry was given personal control, the duchy revenues went not to financing the war but to building Eton College.

Bedford was eager to return to France, while at the same time maintaining his new pre-eminence in the English government and henceforth he proposed to travel to and fro as and when required.[44]

[39] Ibid., 213–16.
[40] Ibid., 226–7.
[41] Ibid., 228–9.
[42] Ibid., 229–32.
[43] Figures in R. Somerville, History of the Duchy of Lancaster, I (London 1953), 206, 208, with details of lands 339–40.
[44] P.P.C., IV, 227.

On 20 June 1434 in the Star Chamber he also extracted an oath from eleven members of the council, led by the cardinal, but not including Gloucester, that they would continue to observe the articles of the previous 18 December after his departure.[45] In fact his return could only be managed by courtesy of his uncle, who now furnished a loan of 10,000 marks for the defence and safeguard of Henry's realm of France and another 3,000 marks to provide Bedford's escort of 100 lances and 300 bowmen when the council found they could not raise even that sum by any other means. The whole sum was secured for repayment on the tenth and fifteenth granted in 1433 and due for payment in 1434 and 1435. Moreover, Beaufort laid down further stringent conditions: a full account and payment of what was still owing for his expenses in attendance on Henry in France from 1430 to 1432; a declaration from the king's own mouth that £6,000 which he had advanced to secure the return of his jewels in 1432 would be repaid on good assignment; the repayment of a further 5,000 marks from the tenth and fifteenth which he had loaned for war expenses while he, Bedford and Gloucester, had been together at Calais, and the surrender to him, in pledge, of 7,000 marks' worth of crown jewels, plus personal guarantees from his fellow councillors for another 3,000 marks. Finally he requested and was given leave to go abroad at will, taking such valuables as he wished with him.[46] Thus more than one-third of the 1433 lay taxation, demonstrably the only possible ultimate source of war finance, was mortgaged to Beaufort in advance of payment.

Bedford returned for the last time to face the problems of Normandy early in July 1434.[47] One other project was sanctioned before he left, destined for a very long time ahead to produce no results, but which was ultimately to have the most profound consequences for his nephew. With approval not only of the cardinal and Bedford but also of Duke Humphrey, who otherwise seems to have played no part whatsoever in Bedford's final arrangements for the government of England and France to the end of the minority, the earl of Suffolk's prisoner, Charles duke of Orleans,[48] was to be allowed to attempt peace negotiations with his fellow princes of the blood in France. Orleans had already been bound on oath, in secrecy, to accept Henry as the only king of France.[49] Under the strictest safeguards for his safe custody by land and sea and of collective conciliar responsibility for all his movements and negotiations (no one person being able to give any orders whatsoever in these respects), Suffolk was now instructed to convey to him

[45] Ibid., 243–4, referring to R.P., IV, 423–4 (see above p. 72).
[46] P.P.C., IV, 232–9, 244–5, 247–54.
[47] He was still at Gravesend on 6 July (ibid., 278).
[48] Delivered into Suffolk's custody on 21 July 1432 (ibid., 124).
[49] Agreement of 15 August 1433 (Foedera, X, 566–63).

the council's permission to meet and negotiate with other French princes of the blood at Calais, with their English counterparts, Bedford, Gloucester and Beaufort, standing by.[50]

Bedford was still only in his mid-forties when he died the following year. It is idle to speculate on what might have happened had he lived as long as his brother Gloucester, who was only a year his junior, but one cannot see him consenting to the surrender of his patrimony of Maine and Anjou. From the moment Henry V died, he had loyally tried to carry out his will in France, having successes both as a soldier and a diplomat. He made clear, however, that he was not going to allow his younger brother, Humphrey, to assume a power in England superior to his own. He may have been actuated by personal ambition in this, but he probably also showed sound judgement in view of some of Humphrey's hasty and ill-considered acts. Faced with the impossibility of ruling himself in both England and France he threw the whole weight of his personal authority behind the council, maintaining its power against Gloucester and Beaufort, and also accepting that his own power should be restricted by the council's articles. In this he showed considerable statesmanship. The council was probably the only way the country could be ruled efficiently through the minority and the king's power kept undiminished for his ultimate assumption of power. For the thirteen years that he was the principal power in his nephew's two kingdoms, he showed the qualities of kingship while never usurping his nephew's position. He controlled the ambitions of others and had the respect of council and parliament. After his death there was no successor to his unique position, no one who could restrain the ambitious about the young king and no one who could guide the developing king towards the highest attributes of kingship.

Henry, left in the control of Warwick and Suffolk, his new steward of the household,[51] spent the late summer of 1434 at Kenilworth.[52] Approaching the age of thirteen he was already eager to participate in affairs of state. Childish meddling this may have been, but it now caused its own crisis of confidence for the council in England. Throughout the minority the main instrument of conciliar government, the privy seal, had been static at Westminster, like the government to whose acts it gave expression. From 10–14 November 1434 writs under the privy seal were suddenly changed to dating at Cirencester[53] and the explana-

---

[50] At Gravesend on 1 July (*P.P.C.*, IV, 259–61).

[51] Powers granted to these two and the officers about the king 'for evident causes and necessity' to move him as the case may require, Gravesend 1 July (*ibid.*, 261).

[52] John Benet's Chronicle, ed. G. L. & M. A. Harriss in *Camden Miscellany*, XXIV, 184.

[53] P.R.O., C.81/699/2977–2983; *C.P.R., 1429–1436*, 450.

tion is found in a council minute of 12 November.[54] 'Motions and stirrings' had been made to Henry which had caused him 'to depart and choose, namely in matters of great weight and difficulty', suggesting to his alarmed council that he was intending to 'change the rule and governance that afore this in his tender age hath by his great council in parliament and else been advised and appointed for the good and surety of his noble person and of this land'. Consequently the whole council arrived post-haste to confront him at Cirencester, armed with a lengthy protestation which the chancellor read out to the boy word for word. The tone was remarkably deferential and the fundamental implication obvious: if he wished to end the conciliar rule of his minority there was nothing they could do to stop it. Nevertheless, while stressing his 'great understanding and feeling as ever they saw or knew in any prince or other person of his age' and their belief that he was likely to reach a stage of maturity adequate to assume the responsibilities of kingship 'as soon as any is possible by nature', they made it crystal clear that, in their collective wisdom, anyone who put him in conceit or opinion that such a stage had yet been reached was guilty of action prejudicial and perilous to him and to his people. Twenty-one other councillors, headed by the cardinal, heard the chancellor, the bishop of Bath and Wells, read out this protestation, which Henry, according to the record, willingly accepted. He gladly undertook for the future not to agree or assent to any such 'motion or stirring' again, until he had consulted the great or continual council. The specific nature of the offending initiative is shrouded in mystery, but Gloucester's name alone is conspicuous in its absence from the protesting council thus assembled in Henry's presence. Had he been responsible for Henry's throwing off conciliar restraint? In spite of Warwick's increased powers over the previous three years, Henry had clearly outwitted his immediate official entourage, because both Warwick and Suffolk, the two chief councillors about the king's person, were present and subscribed to the protestation.

Henry's inevitable involvement in affairs of state, other than in a 'dignified' capacity, was in fact not far distant. He appears to have been kept in the West until Easter 1435 and then to have spent that whole summer hunting in Rockingham forest, staying at Higham Ferrers castle until Michaelmas 1435.[55] It was Bedford's death in September which began his participation in affairs of state. A council warrant of 1 October 1435 recorded his presence, his first, at a meeting of the continuous council, held at Kennington, which included Gloucester, the cardinal, Warwick and Huntingdon. It met urgently to appoint a new Captain of Calais, Richard Wydeville, in place of

[54] *P.P.C.*, IV, 287–9.
[55] Benet's Chronicle, 184.

the deceased Bedford.[56] This exactly accords with views of the council expressed to the Norman estates round about his fourteenth birthday, two months later, that they had decided he should henceforth be party to and constantly attend to affairs of state.[57] As further evidence of his participation there is a privy seal writ, dated for the first time in the reign at a royal palace other than Westminster, on 10 April 1436, which may have been his very first official act of state: the presentation of his 'beloved chaplain', Doctor William Aiscough, to the parish church of Ditton in the diocese of Ely during the vacancy of the bishopric.[58] From 21 July 1436 the privy seal once more became mobile, with writs sealed at Canterbury, where Henry is known to have been, attending the departure of his uncle Gloucester on an expedition to Calais to make war on his defaulting ally the duke of Burgundy.[59] While still at Canterbury on 28 July he personally granted an important part of Bedford's lands in England, the manor of Canford and town of Poole in Dorset to Cardinal Beaufort, 'our great-uncle for his great services' for life, rendering nothing for them, and he simply signed the warrant 'Henry' at the bottom.[60] On 5 August, at Merton priory, he granted prebends to his clerk and chaplain Thomas Lisieux and to Duke Humphrey's dean of the chapel Richard Wyot, again signing the instrument with his own hand, 'Henry', at the top left of the document, the normal position for the royal sign manual.[61] From early October 1436 his itinerary can henceforth be followed from the dating clauses of instruments of government. His signet seal, released from the custody of his uncle Gloucester, reappeared in use at Eltham palace on 8 January 1437.[62] Also from August 1436 members of the council ceased to sign measures passed in the council, which had been the normal method of authentication of acts of state during the minority. That minority was now coming to an end.

Henry's initiation into affairs of state thus came just too late for him to exercise any influence over the crucial course of events in France which began in the spring of 1434, leading to the tripartite Congress of Arras, formally opened early in August 1435, and to a separate peace, concluded in September 1435, between Charles VII and the principal English ally, Philip of Burgundy. French-Burgundian negotia-

[56] P.R.O., C.81/1545/55 at Eltham.
[57] See below p. 88.
[58] P.R.O., C.81/702/3262.
[59] P.R.O., C.81/703/3365–3377; E.404/52/385; *London Calendar of Letter Books Letter Book*, K, 206.
[60] P.R.O., E.28/57, dated 28 July, 14 Henry VI.
[61] *P.P.C.*, IV, 345 from B.L. Cotton Vespasian F. iii fol. 7b; P.R.O., C.81/703/3378, 3379 (the privy seal writs).
[62] P.R.O., P.S.O. 1/5/230.

tions began at Chambéry in February 1434, as a continuation of interminable family efforts to heal the Armagnac-Burgundian rift of 1419 in which the French king's mother-in-law, Queen Yolande of Aragon,[63] had laboured ever since Charles's succession. This specific occasion was Burgundy's presence in Chambéry for the marriage of his cousin Louis count of Geneva.[64] It was at a further family gathering at Nevers in January 1435 that what turned out to be the final terms of the Congress of Arras were agreed between Burgundy on the one hand and Charles VII's ambassadors on the other. Offers made on behalf of Charles VII for public atonement and reparation for his share in the death of Burgundy's father, Duke John the Fearless, in 1419, were accepted, and it was decided that if the English could not be brought to terms, Burgundy was to get all the lands pertaining to the French crown on both banks of the Somme, the county of Ponthieu, the towns of Montreuil, Doullens, Saint-Riquier and all other places on the side of Artois and Flanders. This was to be subject to homage, but performance of homage was to be delayed for face-saving during Philip's life-time. The sovereignty would pass to Burgundy in perpetuity unless Charles VII redeemed these lands for the sum of 400,000 écus d'or. Various possible Valois-Burgundian marriages were also discussed. A journée was fixed for Arras on 1 July 1435 and if Henry VI's government of the minority refused to entertain plans for peace and rejected reasonable offers, then Burgundy, saving his honour, would sign a separate agreement with Charles VII. This was asking the impossible from the English negotiators so the subsequent peace negotiations at Arras were doomed to failure. The English council could have no authority to agree to any settlement. They had to maintain the king's 'right', including the claim to the French throne, to the full. All they could hope for from the negotiations were temporary expedients to postpone a final settlement until Henry came of age and could decide for himself.

Burgundy's defection aroused the bitter anger of public opinion in England and greatly moved the young Henry. When the duke's emissaries were sent to London in late September 1435, to attempt to explain and justify their master's treachery, they went in fear of their lives. Their letters, when opened before the king, were found to be addressed to Henry, for the first time, as mere king of England and not as Philip's sovereign lord. The significance of this was not lost on the boy and caused his eyes to fill with tears which ran down his

[63] Daughter of John I of Aragon, m.1400 Louis II of Anjou, king of Sicily, who died 1417. Their daughter, Marie of Anjou, betrothed from 1413 to Charles of Ponthieu who became King Charles VII.

[64] Eldest son of Amadeus VIII duke of Savoy, who had married Philip's aunt, Mary of Burgundy.

cheeks. He said he feared for the whole future of his dominions in France because of this Burgundian reconciliation with his adversary.[65] Even twenty years later the thought of his 'good uncle' of Burgundy's treachery still rankled.[66] The duke of Alençon's emissary, who had two conversations with him in London early in 1456, reported that he then declared that Burgundy was the one man in the world on whom he would most wish to make war and that he would indeed yet do it if only he lived long enough, 'because he abandoned me in my boyhood, despite all his oaths to me, when I had never done him any wrong'.[67] This incident provides some insight into the character of Henry. For once his feelings were revealed. It is natural to assume that his coronation and anointing as King of France would have made a lasting impression on the nine-year-old boy, and now the emotional reaction of the adolescent shows how deep was his conviction of his own right to France. The fact that twenty years later he had still not forgotten Burgundy's betrayal confirms his sense of injury and also reveals a perhaps unexpected, unchristian and unforgiving nature. On the more practical level he showed that he was well enough informed to under-stand the significance and danger of Burgundy's *volte face*. His presence at Canterbury the following year, to speed his uncle Gloucester at the outset of his campaign against Burgundy, shows his support for that warlike policy and his wish twenty years later to make war on Burgundy shows him as no pacifist, even though he had by then proved to be no practical soldier.

[65] Monstrelet, chap. cxci, col. V, 192, and Marie-Rose Thielemans, *Bourgogne et L'Angleterre: relations politiques et économiques entre les Pays-Bas bourguignons et l'Angleterre, 1435–67* (Brussels 1966), 65–7.

[66] Philip the Good's first wife (died 8 July 1422) was Michelle of France, daughter of Charles VI and sister of Henry VI's mother. 'Bel oncle' was the mode of address he used for Burgundy as for Beaufort and Gloucester and for Charles VII after he ceased to be 'our adversary of France' from 1444 (Stevenson, *Wars*, II, part i, 250, 262).

[67] 'Parce qu'il m'a abandonné dans ma jeunesse, combien qu'il m'ait fait le serment, et sans que oncques lui eusse meffait': quoted by Beaucourt, vi, 137, from the deposition of Edmond Gallet, MS fr. 18441, f. 112v.

Part III

MAJORITY RULE

Chapter 5

THE ATTAINMENT OF POWER

From 13 November 1437 the full powers of personal kingship in England were formally and fully restored and vested in Henry of Windsor, albeit he was still scarcely sixteen years old. This has been disputed by some historians, who believe that the council of the minority were determined to cling to power as long as they possibly could. The official records of the event and subsequent detailed workings of government show that this was not so. By November 1437 Henry had already undergone a two-year period of initiation into the conduct of affairs of state, begun soon after the death of his uncle Bedford in the autumn of 1435. Traditionally a major part of the duties of personal kingship consisted in granting or refusing requests submitted in the form of petitions: for grants of land, money, offices, benefices, annuities, pensions or pardons of crime. But a surprising further variety of state matters could be couched in the form of a petition, all things which in a period of active, adult kingship only the king's personal grant could make effective. Petitions, equally from the highest in the land or the humblest, could only reach the king via those who had access to his person, the normal channels being either through his council or through his household chamberlain.[1] He could signify his will by writing his sign manual on the document, or by the mere act of handing it to the head of one of his writing departments, his chancellor, the keeper of his privy seal, or his secretary who kept his signet seal. Alternatively he could hand it to the household chamberlain. In the case of the latter, who was most constantly with the king, but did not control his own writing office, this officer would himself sign the document for authentication before it was passed on to the appropriate writing department. Such was the traditional machinery, but the unique situation of supreme power being gradually transferred from a council to a king from 1435 led to the development of a further method for Henry. A privy seal clerk, who was already serving as clerk to the council, was now employed additionally to maintain contact between council and king, and he began to endorse or subscribe the petitions with a

[1] For a detailed examination of fifteenth-century machinery of government in full working order during one earlier year of personal rule, September 1404 to September 1405 see A. L. Brown, 'The Authorization of Letters under the Great Seal', *B.I.H.R.*, xxxvii (1964), 125–55.

note of the date, place and people present at the time when Henry signified his will in the matter.

It is clear, at least from July 1436, when Henry, merely by signing his name 'Henry' at the bottom of a petition, personally granted certain valuable lands which had been Bedford's to his Beaufort great-uncle for life, that the process of granting royal graces was re-established.[2] On 23 November 1436 he alienated the islands of Jersey and Guernsey, also former possessions of Bedford, to his uncle Gloucester and his heirs male by minuting Gloucester's petition 'R.H. nous avouns graunte'.[3] In another grant to Gloucester, made on 19 December 1436 at Eltham palace, the clerk in attendance recorded that Henry simply handed the document to the keeper of the privy seal, 'present Ralph Botiller, knight and others'.[4] Another early, solitary example of authentication was the application of a wooden stamp signature 'Henry'. But Henry wrote an autograph initial 'R' before and 'nous avouns graunte' after it.[5] The existence of a wooden stamp signature would have meant that persons other than the king might have applied it to documents and its use was not repeated. Between 7 November 1436 and the end of that month Henry signed at least twenty-seven petitions, so there can be no doubt that well before his fifteenth birthday he had been given the wide range of powers of kingship which can be described as royal graces. Some instruction in their exercise was definitely provided by the council because on 21 November 1436 their minutes included a memo to advise him to give office only to such persons as the office were 'convenient to', that is, in the conventions of that time, not to high estate a small office, nor to low estate a great one.[6]

His English council had informed the Estates of Normandy that from his fourteenth birthday (6 December 1435) Henry had at last begun to hear and attend constantly to his affairs. In May 1436 his tutor the earl of Warwick was discharged from his duties about the king's person, but no successor was appointed, another indication that his initiation into the processes of government was in progress.[7] Since there is no record of his making grants before July 1436 this initiation must, in the first instance, have consisted of the communication to him of the contents of state papers and his attendance at meetings of the continual council and the intermittent great councils which still

    [2] P.R.O., E.28/57 dated 28 July, 14 Henry VI.

    [3] P.R.O., E.28/58/66; *P.P.C.*, V, 5.

    [4] P.R.O., E.28/58/75.

    [5] P.R.O., E.28/58 dated 27 October 15 Henry VI, petition from Master Richard Praty dean of the Chapel Royal for presentation to the parish church of Prescot, exhibited in Pedestal 14 in the P.R.O. Museum.

    [6] *P.P.C.*, V, 3.

    [7] *C.P.R., 1429–1436*, 589, dated 19 May.

governed the country. This was of course now in addition to those 'dignified' appearances at parliaments which had been his lot from birth. Consequently some meetings of the continual council were now held, with Henry's presence noted, in royal palaces, as distinct from its official home, the Star Chamber. One such meeting was recorded as early as October 1435 when they met at Kennington palace to appoint a successor to Bedford in the key military post of Captain of Calais.[8]

The detailed workings of government are actually preserved for these years in a unique, if intermittent, record extending from 21 November 1436 to 22 July 1446. The ravages of time alone could be responsible for the haphazard degree of survival, but the need for this new record probably only arose because of the new factor of the young king's involvement in the processes of government. The council of the minority had had its proceedings written up *ex post facto* by its privy seal clerk, Richard Caudray, who had kept the record from 1421 until the summer of 1435, selecting for preservation those items considered most important, but in November 1435 another clerk of the privy seal office, Henry Benet, began a new, rough but instant record of its proceedings.[9] It reveals that, prior to the complete transference of power, some matters before the council had already been considered by the king. In a minor matter, for example, one William Peres, a converted Moslem, had petitioned for sustenance. On 2 May 1437 the clerk, Henry Benet, noted that the treasurer reported to the council that the king wished the suppliant to have 2d per day, which was then done.[10] Again, on a rather more important matter, shortly before 8 June 1437 a problem arose in the council regarding Henry's ex-tutor, the earl of Warwick, who was then reluctantly about to take up the lieutenancy in France which Richard duke of York had insisted on relinquishing. Among the conditions which he had laid down for acceptance was one which he absolutely insisted on having, and he said he would not go without it. This was a firm undertaking that Henry would personally accept an enfeoffment of the lordship of Abergavenny from him for two years and one week, and subsequently grant it back to him, the surest means he could think of to establish and preserve his rights therein during his absence. When this came before the council the archbishop of York said he knew that Henry had in fact already agreed to this on Whitmonday 20 May while he was at Merton Priory, but other council members were not satisfied that he had. Therefore the keeper of the privy seal was sent to the

[8] See above p. 80–1.
[9] These records are discussed by A. L. Brown in *The Early History of the Clerkship of the Council* (University of Glasgow, 1969).
[10] *P.P.C.*, V, 22–3.

king who was then at Copped Hall near Waltham Abbey, where he had audience on 7 June. He had been instructed to ascertain Henry's wishes on this matter as well as on a pardon for Lord Willoughby and on other things which the clerk did not specify. Presented with a schedule of the items concerned and asked if he had already given his assent the king replied that 'he was not advised that he had', but if his council approved then he agreed. When the privy seal reported back to the council in the Star Chamber next day they affirmed that they were still in agreement and that the schedule should now pass by warrant under the privy seal in its present form, which was done.[11] Thus new channels of communication for purposes of government had had to be established between the king and the council. The great officers themselves might now have to attend the king on government business and the whole council might meet in his presence away from Westminster.[12]

There were now instances recorded of his personal wishes being expressed and met. Soon after the death of his mother (2 or 3 January 1437) he summoned his step-father to his presence. Owen Tudor was Queen Catherine's clandestine second husband, by whom she had had four or more children. He was ultimately brought to Henry, not without difficulty, through the agency of the duke of Gloucester, though their conversation is unfortunately not recorded. On another occasion a deadlock in the council had to be settled by his personal intervention. Weak, faulty and subject to changes and reversals as his decisions proved to be, from the autumn of 1437 Henry had to take the final decisions if disagreement arose in the council. On 24 October 1437 agreement could not be reached as to whether the captive duke of Orleans should be allowed to go to Cherbourg on a peace mission to meet his fellow lords of the Valois blood only if he paid the considerable expenses involved himself. Gloucester, Beaufort and Archbishop Kemp, in agreement for once, stood out against the rest in maintaining that the king should not pay the expenses, since in negotiations with his adversary of France one concession on his part would only lead to another being demanded. The duke of Orleans was therefore brought to Henry at Sheen the following Monday, to commune with him about the prospects of peace. Henry's final decision was to pay his expenses out of a lay tenth and fifteenth.[13]

On All Saints Day 1437 Henry presided in state over his court at

[11] Ibid., 29–30, 40–1.
[12] For example on 13 and 17 October 1437 at Kennington palace on the second occasion in the king's chamber (P.R.O., C.81/1545/60, 63). On 21 October he attended a meeting of the great council in the parliament chamber at Westminster (P.R.O., E.28/58/9).
[13] P.P.C., V, 67–8, 86.

Merton Priory wearing his crown, when it was recorded that he changed the name of Anjou herald to Lancaster herald and created a new pursuivant called Collar. The presence of the earls of Warwick and Stafford was noted in the chamberlain's warrant as witnesses. The occasion was only recorded at all because it involved a financial transaction, paying for two silver bells presented to the heralds.[14] But this formal crown-wearing may have marked his assumption of full ruling powers, because within a few days the council's arrangements for the transference of power to the king were formally ratified by the appointment and commissioning of a new council. Someone had found a detailed definition of the functions of a royal council, made for Henry's grandfather in 1406, which was now made to serve again in the different circumstances of 1437. This document of 1406 had described the council as existing to lighten the king's burden in the governance of his realm; to conserve his rights; to oversee the collection and just augmentation of his revenues; to preserve the laws, customs and statutes; to see that right and justice was done to rich and poor alike. Written precedents were scarce, and even this one was not entirely apposite to the needs of 1437, because Henry's grandfather in 1406 had then been stricken with illness and had consequently been *increasing* the power of his council. Some historians have therefore supposed that the same was happening in 1437. But while the 1437 document was in large part an English translation of the French document of 1406, there were essential differences between them. In 1437, publication of the names of the new council members in parliament was not an issue, as it had been in 1406, because the council was now losing, not gaining, power. There was now no order that the king's instruments endorsed by the chamberlain, or his letters under the signet, or his other warrants directed to the chancellor, treasurer or keeper of the privy seal, should be submitted to the council before they passed, as in 1406. There was now no provision that these officers should not act without conciliar approval. Moreover, additions made to the 1406 document now ensured reservation to the king of all matters of royal grace and included new provisions for limiting the council's powers. In all matters of great weight and charge they were to debate, but not to reach a conclusion without the king's advice. In other matters, which were within their competence to conclude, they must no longer do so if there was significant variance of opinion, for example half against half or two-thirds against one-third, and the king must be informed of the differing opinions so that he himself might conclude the matter. In short the new council, appointed at the attainment of Henry's majority in 1437, was to have no authority to act in matters of royal grace and

14 *Ibid.*, 63.

its initiative was to be confined to minor matters over which it could reach near unanimity. Their role would henceforth be entirely determined by what the king chose to refer to them and by what they did in advising him in his presence.[15]

Fifteen members of the old council were reappointed[16] and four new ones added.[17] They were placed under contract to the king and their terms of appointment registered in indentures, exchanged with him. Hereafter the council kept its own set terms in the Star Chamber, fixing their length itself.[18] But it now also met in the royal palaces when summoned by the king. In composition this new council was a conservative body, nicely balanced as regards princes of the blood, spiritual lords, lay lords and royal officers, but its functions had now been reduced to those traditionally performed by English royal councils: advising the king and executing his decisions. There are no grounds whatsoever for believing that the council of the minority was greedy to maintain itself in power, and determined in this document to preserve its supreme authority intact, while conceding only a semblance of power to the young king. All the evidence points the other way.

Until 1437 there was nothing to suggest that Henry was unlikely to develop into an able and thoroughly satisfactory king; in fact quite the reverse. The record of his childhood and adolescence, even allowing for natural partiality in describing a king, suggests physical strength, normal but not excessive piety and the natural ambition of a young monarch to become king, in fact as well as name, just as soon, if not sooner, than his advisers approved. There could therefore be no reason at all for the council needing to maintain their power once the king came of age. They had shown great restraint in governing during the minority so that Henry should come to power with undiminished royal authority. They had achieved their end and in 1437 it was time for the normal processes of royal government to be resumed.

[15] *Ibid.*, 71–2; VI, 312–15 (12–13 November 1437).

[16] The duke of Gloucester, Cardinal Beaufort, Henry Chichele archbishop of Canterbury, John Kemp archbishop of York, William Alnwick bishop of Lincoln, John earl of Huntingdon, Humphrey earl of Stafford, Henry earl of Northumberland, William earl of Suffolk, Walter Lord Hungerford, John Lord Tiptoft, John Stafford bishop of Bath and Wells, the chancellor, Ralph Lord Cromwell, the treasurer, William Lyndwood, the keeper of the privy seal and William Philip, knight, the chamberlain.

[17] Thomas Rodbury, bishop of St David's, Richard earl of Salisbury, John Stourton, knight, and Robert Rolleston, the keeper of the great wardrobe.

[18] *P.P.C.*, V, 73.

Chapter 6

THE ROYAL ENTOURAGE

The governance of England from 1422 to 1437 had been vested in the council and was static, conducted from one centre, the Star Chamber in Westminster Palace. Even a few council meetings held in Cardinal Beaufort's lodgings had been sufficient to draw protests from Duke Humphrey, as evidence of his uncle's unlawful usurpation of power. But from 1437 the centre of government became the household of a peripatetic king, moving from palace to palace with royal officers, clerks and seals in attendance as required.[1] Henry's main residences proved to be Windsor castle or the principal lodge in the park there, Sheen (now Richmond) and Eltham. Kennington[2] and Westminster were less popular but much used. Transfers of the court by land between these palaces were frequent, but communication by river made them all easily accessible to one another for the king, four of them being directly on the river. A royal barge was permanently stationed at Lambeth, adjacent to Kennington palace, for passage over to Westminster and elsewhere and there was a royal ferry boat at Sheen manor in the charge of the keeper of the king's ferry.[3] After the death of Duke Humphrey in 1447, when his manor of Greenwich was given to Queen Margaret, this became a further royal residence with river access. Both Sheen and Eltham were twice extensively rebuilt, extended and refurbished in the 1430s and 1440s to meet the needs of the burgeoning, peripatetic royal household.

With no dowager queen left alive after 1437, no royal offspring to provide for, no brothers and only one uncle, and with both the duchies of Lancaster and Cornwall in hand, Henry had a wider choice of

---

[1] John Stafford as chancellor was frequently present with the king in his household. While still bishop of Bath and Wells he occasionally sealed documents with the great seal at his manor of Dogmersfield, as well as at Westminster, when he was not in the household; after he became archbishop of Canterbury, sometimes at Canterbury. The keeper of the privy seal, the seal and his clerks were even more frequently in the royal household; the secretary, the signet seal and its clerks were always there, although their movements from palace to palace did not always coincide to the exact day with the king's movements as recorded in the household accounts. The treasurer's movements cannot be so precisely ascertained, although he too was often present at court from 1437.

[2] A duchy of Cornwall manor.

[3] P.R.O., P.S.O. 1/17.

habitable royal residences than any king of England before him. Other castles and houses kept in repair for royal occupation included three hunting lodges in the vast area of the great park of Windsor (Easthampstead, Henley-on-the-Heath and Guildford). A wider circle included Havering-atte-Bower, normally a queen's residence, Berkhamsted castle,[4] Hertford castle,[5] which was surveyed for renovation and extension by Lord Bardolf, Henry's household chamberlain, soon after Queen Joan's death in 1437, King's Langley, also previously occupied by Queen Joan, Copped Hall near Waltham, Pleshey[6] and Odiham. Clarendon and Woodstock were at a greater distance. In the Midlands the duchy of Lancaster castles of Leicester and Kenilworth, the latter with its lodge of Pleasance in the Marsh, Goodrest Lodge four miles to the south, and Fulbrook Lodge three miles south of Warwick, which had belonged to his uncle Bedford, also accommodated Henry. Nottingham and Pontefract castles were put into a good state of repair and Pontefract partly rebuilt at this time, although Nottingham saw him only once and Pontefract twice before 1450. Bishops' palaces, abbeys and priories, a few houses of the nobility and often tented camps, briefly provided the court with additional accommodation on his progresses. Between 1437 and 1453 these, rather than Westminster, were the places from which government was conducted.

With the exception of the years 1442 and 1443, royal progresses were made every year between 1437 and 1453 outside the inner circuit of royal residences between Windsor and Greenwich. The shortest period in any one year was twenty-seven days in 1441, which yet took Henry to Canterbury, Winchester and Cambridge. Between his return to Eltham on 13 January 1442, from a pilgrimage to Canterbury, and 23 March 1444, when he left Sheen for Woodstock, he did not move away from the Thames-side palaces. It has been suggested that this comparatively static period marked an early illness, but there is no evidence of this, and during that time he still moved about freely between his Thames-side residences, also using the hunting lodges in Windsor great park for short periods. This prolonged stay in the environs of London was more likely due to pressure of work or inclination. For the remaining eleven years between 1437 and 1450, his progresses beyond his normal residences averaged about 90 days a year, the longest period being 120 days in 1448. In 1451 a new policy developed; the 253 days he spent away in the two years 1451 and 1452 were mainly occupied in judicial progresses with his judges.

The king's mobile household consisted of the personnel of his court, his entourage, and those who provided for their everyday needs. The

---

[4] Duchy of Cornwall manor.
[5] Duchy of Lancaster manor.
[6] Duchy of Lancaster manor.

whole body moved from one royal palace to another, each of which kept only a minimum staff of keepers, parkers, bedders and gardeners in permanent residence. In 1445 very precise and elaborate regulations were promulgated in parliament to order the numbers, conduct and discipline of this entourage which was then rapidly increasing in size, to define their duties and the duties of those who fed and clothed them, to regulate the purchase and consumption of provisions and to control entrance and exit from the precincts. Set over all were the 'sovereigns' of the household, the great officers ruling all its various departments. 'Above stairs' were the chapel, hall, wardrobe, counting house and chamber. The chamber was the king's own living quarters, itself a considerable suite of rooms with its own hall, where the elite personnel about the king dined and the king's secretary sat with his clerks of the signet, performing their writing duties. 'Below stairs' were the stables, the mews, the kitchen, pantry and all other domestic offices. By 1449 there were normally twelve hundred souls within this household verge or precincts, under the exempt episcopal and archidiaconal jurisdiction of the dean of the royal chapel. Henry's entourage was headed by the king's confessor, always a bishop, the chamberlain of England, who was only occasionally in the king's presence when the office was held by Gloucester, but almost continuously so when he was succeeded by Suffolk, the seneschal or keeper of the household, the keeper of the great wardrobe, the household chamberlain, the king's carvers, who were two or three knights of the chamber, the master of the horse, the controller and the cofferer, the dean of the chapel, the royal almoner and a host of select esquires and yeomen of the body in the chamber, and yeomen of the hall.

Ordered magnificence was expected of a medieval king's household. When the Commons in parliament were petitioning Henry VII in 1485 to order an act of resumption, the proceeds from it were to go first to meet the regular expenses of his household which they considered amounted to some £14,000 *per annum*, and they referred back to the household of his uncle, King Henry VI, as a precedent for an 'Honourable Household ... kept and borne Worshipfully and Honourably, as it accordeth to the Honour of your Estate and your said Realm, by the which your Adversaries and Enemies shall fall into the dread wherin heretofore they have been'.[7] But a royal household could easily become a burden on the realm, and a centre of faction, both in affairs of state and in the local government of the shires, because of the privileged positions in the realm which its personnel could so easily acquire. Such indeed rapidly became this 'worshipful and great household' of Henry VI, which Sir John Fortescue, looking back some

[7] *R.P.*, VI, 336.

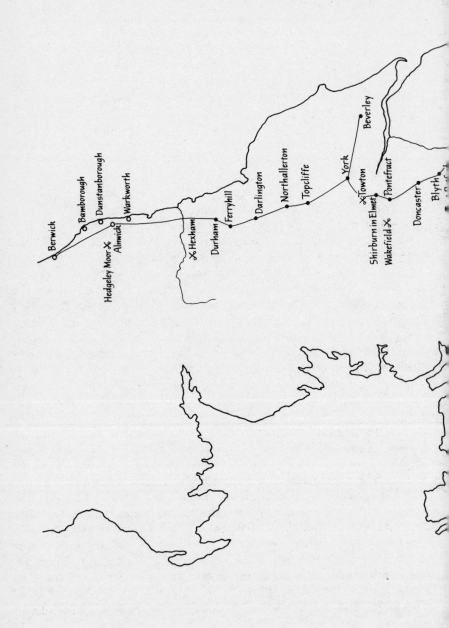

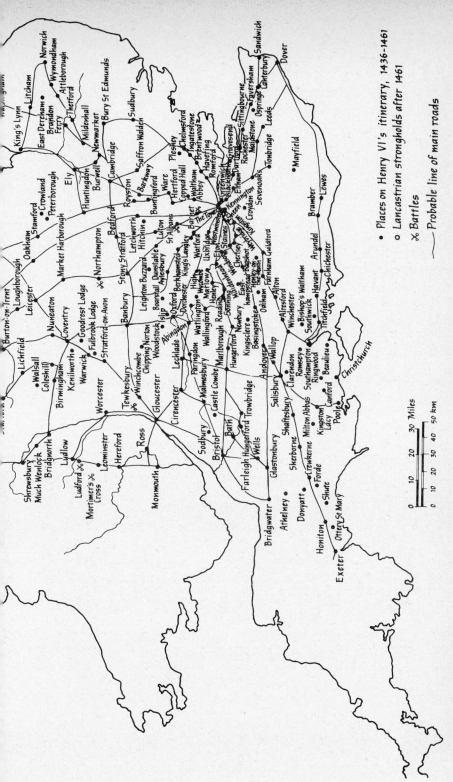

Legend:
- Places on Henry VI's itinerary, 1436–1461
- o Lancastrian strongholds after 1461
- ✗ Battles
- — Probable line of main roads

1 England and Wales

twenty-five years later, thought Henry should forbear to re-establish for the first year of his Readeption in 1470 to prevent a repetition of the way his affairs had been conducted in the pre-Yorkist period.[8] Its personnel required very careful selection and control and strict rules for their conduct had to be established. Whether the royal household functioned as a blessing rather than as a burden on the realm depended essentially on the ability of the king to control and direct its activities.

An establishment drawn up for Henry's household in 1445 made provision for a total of 53 knights and esquires of the hall and chamber and 36 chamber valets or yeomen. But an extra provision in this 1445 ordinance allowed for a surplus of king's esquires and officers beyond the appointed number, who were only to come to court at the five principal feasts of the year, at parliaments, great councils, levees for receiving strangers and on other occasions when specially summoned by the steward and the 'sovereigns'.[9] The treasurers' and controllers' accounts in fact reveal that in the following year numbers far in excess of these – 254 knights and esquires and 223 yeomen – were wearing the king's livery. By 1451 these figures had risen to 301 knights and esquires and 228 yeomen. The earliest figures after Henry attained his majority are for 1439: 128 knights and esquires and 172 yeomen. The equivalent figures for the first year of his father's reign had been 75 knights and esquires and 181 yeomen. Thus the number of Henry's household retainers, above stairs, of rank of esquire and higher, more than doubled during fifteen years of personal rule and, together with the yeomen of the household, reached a grand total of a little short of 550 by 1451. The comparable totals of chaplains and clerks of the chapel, which stood at 26 in 1413, and 28 in 1439, had risen to 37 by 1448–9, as against an establishment of 20 in the ordinances of 1445 and 1454.

Henry's mobile household establishment thus became the largest single institution in the realm, at least twice the size, above stairs, of a parliament in session. Its influence and tentacles stretched throughout the kingdom, since most of those household men who wore his livery were also domiciled somewhere in the shires and held local offices there, and elsewhere, in person, or by deputy. According to Sir John Fortescue, the king had more than a thousand offices at his disposal, without including those in the duchy of Cornwall, the principality of Wales and the earldom of Chester.[10] The majority of these now went to household men and their nominees. It has been calculated that 63 household men held the key office of sheriff on one or more occasions between 1437 and 1461. In 1448 alone fourteen of

[8] *Fortescue on the Governance of England*, ed. Charles Plummer (Oxford 1885), 352–3.
[9] Printed by A. R. Myers, *The Household of Edward IV* (Manchester 1959), 66.
[10] *Governance*, 151.

the thirty-six counties of England had household men as sheriffs.[11] Administratively the sheriff and his undersheriff were the king's local men-of-all-work, serving writs, empanelling juries, collecting debts, holding elections to parliament, etc., and raising the fencible men of the county for the king's service. Increasing numbers of household men now appear among the Justices of the Peace. In 1437, 327 persons served on the commissions of the peace in the English shires. By 1449 this number had risen to 440.[12] Whereas in 1437 members of the household, 27 in all, made up only one-twelfth of the total, by 1449 this figure had risen to 76, so that one in six of the J.P.s in the shires were now receiving the royal livery.

Within an overall total of 51 peers of the realm and rather more than 2,100 armigerous gentry in England in 1436,[13] the upper strata of society who considered themselves able to sit on commissions of peace or in parliament, this rapidly expanding household of Henry's majority thus grew to be the greatest political affinity, or faction, in the kingdom. It is generally supposed that it had been the landed wealth and retainer power of John of Gaunt, duke of Lancaster and king of Castile, the most over-mighty subject in English history, which had enabled his son, Henry of Bolingbroke, Henry VI's grandfather, to seize the throne of England in 1399 and found the Lancastrian dynasty. At the height of his power, John of Gaunt had retained seven bannerets and 195 knights and esquires.[14] But this was less than two-thirds of the size which his great-grandson's establishment had reached by 1451. By comparison, in 1448 the best documented affinity of any fifteenth-century magnate, the affinity of Henry VI's most wealthy subject Humphrey Stafford, duke of Buckingham, who had lands in twenty-two counties, consisted of ten knights and twenty-six esquires.[15]

It has further been suggested that the Lancastrian party built up by John of Gaunt was carefully enhanced and maintained by his son and grandson, Henry IV and Henry V, as an invincible political connection, but that it disintegrated in the nerveless hands of Henry

[11] Robin Jeffs, 'The Later Medieval Sheriff and the Royal Household, 1437-1547' (unpublished Oxford D. Phil. thesis, 1960), 55-7.

[12] i.e. 327 persons on the commissions at 13 November 1437 named 628 times; 440 persons on the commissions at 31 December 1449 named 740 times.

[13] This figure represents those who were assessed at £20 per annum or above in the income tax returns of 1436 and a statute of 1439-40 laid down that Justices of the Peace must hold a landed income of not less than £20 per annum. Comparable income and status was required for election to parliament.

[14] K. B. McFarlane, 'Bastard Feudalism', B.I.H.R., XX (1943-5), 165.

[15] Carole Rawcliffe, The Staffords, earl of Stafford and dukes of Buckingham 1394-1512 (Cambridge 1978), 72-5.

VI.[16] In fact it was the size and expense of Henry VI's very substantial affinity and the privileged positions which its members abused, which caused growing resentment, jealousy and division among his subjects and lowered royal power and authority to the level of faction. It is true that the revenues of the duchy of Lancaster no longer formed the basis for it. But this was not due to a personal change of design on Henry's part or to weakness or neglect. In his use of the duchy Henry VI in fact followed a pattern mainly determined by his father. In 1419 rather less than £13,500 of duchy revenues had been at Henry V's disposal, above the unavoidable sums spent on internal administration, in fees, wages, etc. A little more than £5,000 *per annum* had certainly then been spent on annuities, which allegedly still secured a duchy of Lancaster affinity. But Henry V had tied up £6,000 *per annum* of these revenues for the performance of his will, an arrangement which lasted until 1443, and he endowed his queen with another £4,000 *per annum*. Humphrey duke of Gloucester took over £2,500 *per annum* as Protector and principal councillor of the realm. The budget which Treasurer Cromwell presented to parliament in 1433 revealed that less than £2,500 *per annum* was then at the crown's disposal. This sum was clearly increased substantially with the death of Queen Catherine in 1437 and from 1439 to 1458, under various arrangements made in parliament, the net revenues of the duchy were actually paid towards the expenses of the king's household. Nevertheless from 1445 these were again diminished because his new queen, Margaret of Anjou, began to absorb some £4,000 *per annum* and Henry, following his father's precedent and regarding the duchy essentially as his personal estate, chose to set aside another like sum to build and endow his colleges at Eton and Cambridge.

Henry's affinity was in fact built up on the basis of the crown lands and permanent revenues of the crown, which came into his hands in unusual profusion. With no heir to the throne, the lands of the duchy of Cornwall, the principality of Wales and the earldom of Chester were at his disposal from the beginning. The deaths of his three uncles, Clarence (1421), Bedford (1435) and Gloucester (1447), without legitimate issue, together with both the queens dowager, Joan and Catherine, in 1437, left him in a most unusual position, with absolutely no royal family to provide for, except his own queen from 1445. The revenues of this profusion of crown lands thus made available went not to the national exchequer but mainly to his household affinity who enjoyed their resources in the main in addition to their normal fees and wages of office. Between 1437 and 1450 Henry made at least 192 choice grants of royal lands and properties for terms of years, lives,

[16] T. B. Pugh, 'The magnates, knights and gentry', in *Fifteenth-century England*, ed. S. B. Chrimes and others (Manchester 1972), 107-8.

5(a). Henry VI as a child in the arms of his tutor, Richard Beauchamp, earl of Warwick, from the 'Rous Roll', an illustrated history of the earls of Warwick by their family historian, John Rous (B.L. Add. MS 48976, f. 957).

5(b). The coronation of Henry VI as king of England from 'The Pageant of the Birth, Life and Death of Richard Beauchamp, earl of Warwick' (B.L. Cotton. MS Julius E iv, f. 23v).

5(c). The coronation of Henry VI as king of France from Jehan de Waurin's 'Recueil des Chroniques de Grand Bretagne'.

6(a). Henry VI aged nine supported by St Catherine with the Virgin and Child and Angels from the king's personal psalter (B.L. Cotton. MS Domitian A XVII, f. 75r).

6(b). Henry VI aged twelve kneeling before St Edmund's shrine, from the dedicatory manuscript of John Lydgate's 'Life of St Edmund', probably presented to Henry on New Year's Day 1434 at Bury St Edmunds Abbey (B.L. Harley MS 2278, f. 4v).

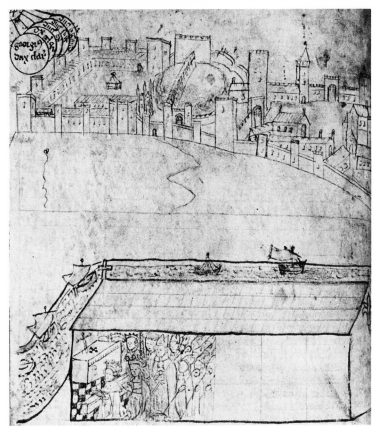

7(a). Henry VI, presenting relics, with Queen Margaret in the unfinished Eton College chapel, with Windsor castle in the background. From John Blacman's copy of the 'Polychronicon'.

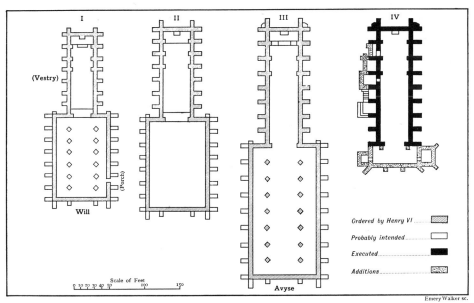

7(b). Successive changes in the plans for Eton College chapel.

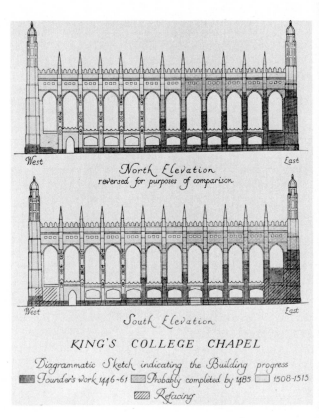

8(a). Drawing, *c.* 1448, of a tower intended for King's College, Cambridge (B.L. Cotton. MS Augustus I, i.3).

or in fee, over and above grants of offices, to 169 persons. These grantees included 9 great lords, some of whom were household members, 74 others wearing his livery, who were more or less permanent residents in the household, another 15 who can only be described as 'country' members and 22 with positions in the royal service who had easy access to the household.[17] These extraordinary material grants of royal favour were topped up with a uniquely lavish distribution of honours.[18] All this came under very heavy criticism in parliament and elsewhere from 1449, as unprecedented dilapidation of the financial resources of the monarchy and the creation of privileged factions within the administrative and judicial system.

Henry's rule from 1437 to 1450 was thus undoubtedly centred on his household. With government directed from a peripatetic household, members of the council which operated from one static centre at Westminster were now at a distinct disadvantage unless they also happened to be household officers, because they were dependent upon the king's personal summons before they could meet in his presence. Many years later in 1470, after Henry had lost his throne and briefly recovered it, the exiled Sir John Fortescue, who had been his Chief Justice of the King's Bench from 1442, warned Henry, through the medium of his pupil Prince Edward, how dangerous it was to allow himself to be counselled by men of his chamber, or of his household generally, men not qualified and with no right to advise him.[19] He was writing from his own experience in Henry's council during the 1440s. This was also the sound, unheeded advice given to him by the author of his 'Mirror of Princes'. For a king to be thus ruled by 'private Counselloures', Fortescue wrote, was the surest means to civil strife.[20] This was also the contemporary charge levied against Henry's so-called favourites in the crisis of 1450 because they, according to their detractors, had constituted the government of the country during the king's majority rule. The degree of privilege and private profit they had gained from the king's service was then taken to fix upon them responsibility for abuses of the law and corruption of government at home, as well as for the policies followed in France which led to the loss of Normandy, to Henry's financial bankruptcy and to grave damage to the material interests and pride of the crown and his subjects.

The main evidence of how the kingdom of England was governed, and through whom it was done at this time, comes from documents published by Sir Harris Nicolas under the title *Proceedings and Ordinances*

[17] For details see B. P. Wolffe, *The Royal Demesne in English History* (London 1971), 248–89.

[18] See below, pp. 215–6.

[19] *Governance*, 350.

[20] *Ibid.*, 348.

of the Privy Council in England.[21] This collection lumps together, quite indiscriminately under this one misleading classification, all the records of three quite distinct kinds of governmental meetings: the council in Star Chamber, the council meeting with the king in his various palaces and the king signifying his will in the presence of a few advisers and servants who were not necessarily councillors at all. In the latter case an attendance of at least two was normally recorded, but there were cases where Adam Moleyns, who was both clerk of the council and the privy seal clerk attendant on the king from May 1438, was alone in the king's presence when he granted petitions and issued warrants. By careful attention to the nature of each of the separate documents which are all thus indiscriminately classified by Nicolas as council proceedings, and by reading the endorsements on the hundreds of similar unprinted documents for the period of Henry's personal rule still existing in the Public Record Office, it is possible to show who actually were the regular companions of Henry's working days and who exercised power under or over him.

Henry thus made appointments, grants, etc., in the presence of a certain entourage which was only partly identical with the membership of his council. Such records as survive indicate that matters of general policy were still discussed, often indecisively, in his council, either when it was summoned to his presence, or without him, in the Star Chamber. But on all these matters final decisions, wise or unwise, were now his alone. An intermittent written dialogue between king and council can be studied with ease up to 22 July 1446 when the record of it fails, and throughout that period the pattern remained the same. For example, on 18 November 1437 a long council debate on the question whether to restore the forfeited franchises of the city of Norwich and whether to prohibit the export of wool and cloth was concluded: 'this to be had to the king'. The clerk's jottings were necessary to enable him to rehearse the conciliar discussion to Henry for his approval or otherwise. Equally necessary was his record of what was done when he was in the king's presence and not with the council; he reported back, for example, that on 13 May 1438, in the king's secret chamber at Kennington, with Gloucester, the chancellor, Suffolk and the Privy Seal present, Henry granted three bills and had rehearsed to him what had been discussed in the council the day before.[22] One of the most detailed accounts of decisions taken in a matter of the greatest weight, the launching of a large-scale expeditionary force against France in 1442 and 1443, shows how the council was merely the executant of the decisions taken over its commander, its size, its destination, places of assembly, date of departure, etc. Every matter was referred to the

[21] Record Commission, 6 vols (London 1834–7).
[22] *P.P.C.*, V, 98.

king for final decision after full and, it must be said, inconclusive discussions in council, some of them in his presence. The most vital decision, the selection of commander, was certainly taken by Henry himself and another equally vital one, its destination, by Henry and the commander together.[23]

When the record fails in July 1446, the council were still executing the king's decisions. He had recently personally decided to meet his uncle Charles VII of France and the lords spiritual and temporal in parliament, not to be saddled with the responsibility for it, had put on record that it was his personal decision.[24] The council were now perforce settling the location, between Mantes and Melun; they were executing his orders to move Eleanor Cobham, the disgraced and divorced wife of the heir presumptive, Duke Humphrey, to stricter and remoter confinement in the Isle of Man; determining wages for various ambassadors according to precedent; conveying to the duke of York a temporizing answer from Henry as to his future as lieutenant in Normandy; and, finally, deputing the treasurer to ascertain the king's final wishes on the numbers of his escort, the place of assembly and the date of departure for his visit to France.[25] Typically of Henry, that meeting never actually took place.

Most of the mere executive work of government was still undoubtedly carried out through the council, sitting without the king. The historian of the king's council thought that it was only from 1446, when the council minutes fail, that the most vital processes of government were withdrawn into the innermost recesses of the household[26] and a simultaneous decline in the volume of documents, issuing under the privy seal, by authority of king and council, may seem to bear this out.[27] But routine meetings of the council never ceased and surviving isolated summonses to council meetings indicate that matters were still discussed there, after 1446 as before. Moreover, the numbers of instruments minuted with presences around the king by a privy seal clerk, on occasions other than council meetings, also show a simultaneous decline. On the other hand, comparable direct warrants under the sign manual, subscribed by the signet clerks Robert Osbern, John Blakeney and Robert Repynghale, who were not accustomed to note presences, continued much as before 1446, if anything increasing in

[23] *Ibid.*, 218, 223–4, 225–8, 229, 232, 233, 234–7, 251–64, 267, 279, 280–1, 284–90, 292–4.

[24] *R.P.*, V, 102–3.

[25] *P.P.C.*, VI, 50–4.

[26] J. F. Baldwin, *The King's Council in England during the Middle Ages* (Oxford 1913), 191.

[27] P.R.O., E.28, files 75–8 *passim*.

number.[28] The conclusion must be therefore that the ravages of time
are responsible for the imbalance in the record, that 1446 was no
turning-point, and that the practice since 1437, which had established
that some members of Henry's household were the more important
and favoured of his advisers, prevailed throughout the period of his
personal rule, not just after 1446.

If we described as the king's ministers those persons whose names
appear as the most frequent witnesses to his acts of state, both inside
and outside council meetings and ignore for this purpose those present
ex officio, equally at council meetings or in the household, as chancellor,
treasurer, keeper of the privy seal, secretary, or household chamberlain,
then already from 1437 the most important was the earl, later marquis
and duke, of Suffolk, steward of the household, who was to succeed
Humphrey duke of Gloucester as Great Chamberlain of England in
1447. Most assiduous in attendance with him were William Aiscough,
Henry's confessor, bishop of Salisbury from 1438 and a councillor from
1441; England's first viscount, John, Lord Beaumont, who married the
daughter of Lord Bardolf, the household chamberlain, received
Bedford's former viscounty of Beaumont in France, became a councillor
from 1443 and Constable of England from 1445; Master Adam
Moleyns, privy seal clerk in attendance and clerk of the council from
May 1438, a councillor in his own right and keeper of the privy seal
from early 1444, dean of Salisbury and bishop of Chichester from 1445;
James Fiennes, esquire and knight of the body from 1438 to 1447 when
he became household chamberlain, and then treasurer of England in
1449, a peer of the realm as Lord Say and Sele and a councillor from
1447; John Sutton, Lord Dudley, a councillor from 1443, and, from
about 1445, Reginald Boulers, abbot of Gloucester, made bishop of
Hereford in 1450, and also a councillor from 1445. These seven, who
were most constantly in the king's presence when he carried out the
duties of kingship, can be considered as the ministers of his personal rule.
It is a striking fact that four of them actually lost their lives in 1450 for
their alleged responsibilities, and Beaumont alone among them escaped
attack in the political proscriptions and lampoons of that year.

There were twelve others whose names appear frequently as witnesses
to the king's acts of state. These were ten knights and esquires of
Henry's household,[29] mainly gentlemen of his chamber, together with
the privy seal clerk Thomas Kent, also clerk of the council from 1443,
and the signet clerk, John Blakeney. Among these the two Beauchamps,
both king's carvers, entered the peerage, John as Lord Beauchamp of

---

[28] P.R.O., C.81, files 1437–54 *passim*.

[29] John Hampton, John Noreys, Thomas Scargill, Master John Somerset, Edmund
Hungerford, John and William Beauchamp, John Saintlo, John Pennycook, John
Trevelyan.

Powicke in 1447, and William as Lord St Amand in 1449. None of
these twelve prominent members of Henry's entourage, in spite of their
obvious influence, ever received appointment to the council. Of the
eleven still alive in 1450 only three of them escaped proscription and
denigration in the crisis which then destroyed Suffolk, Fiennes, Moleyns
and Aiscough.[30]

---

[30] The two Beauchamps and Thomas Scargill. John Saintlo died in 1448. A list of
twenty-nine people whose banishment from court was urged in a parliamentary
petition of 1451 is printed in *R.P.*, V, 216, and a largely identical list of thirty-two
persons allegedly indicted at Rochester in August 1450 by C. L. Kingsford, *Eng. Hist.
Lit.*, 364–5 from B.L., Cotton Roll, ii, 23. For contemporary political lampoons see
Political Poems and Songs, ed. Thomas Wright (R.S., 1861), ii, 222, 232, 234.

Chapter 7

PATRONAGE, FACTION AND INJUSTICE IN ENGLAND, 1437–1450

The royal entourage had great opportunities to exert influence on the king in their own and their adherents' interests. The surviving evidence of Henry's personal acts, done in this entourage which surrounded him from 1437, displays an open-handedness in the dispensation of patronage which might, at first, have been seen as largely inevitable in a good-natured boy of sixteen, set in the supreme seat of power after an upbringing uniquely sheltered and elevated right from birth. But it must soon have begun to disturb those great officers about him who were themselves bound by the responsibility of office to see certain principles followed. They certainly strove diplomatically to correct his weaknesses. As his lack of sound political sense became obvious, access to his person carried particularly heavy responsibilities. These were not fulfilled by all his entourage, or by all those whose rank alone was sufficient to give them the privileges of access when they wished to exercise it. Two very early instances are recorded of apparently mind-less grants from which his council, sitting in the Star Chamber at Westminster, clearly hoped he would learn. On 11 February 1438 the council clerk, Henry Benet, noted that he was charged to speak to the king about the way pardons should be granted. He had given one to a collector of customs by which the crown had lost 2,000 marks. The next day he again made a note to draw Henry's attention to a grant he had made of the office of constable and steward of Chirk castle, whereby he had lost another 1,000 marks.[1] On 25 May he sold the lordship and castle outright to his great-uncle, the cardinal, who had no cause to acquire land for himself, but never missed a chance of using his ecclesiastical wealth to endow his Beaufort nephews. This sale was particularly unwise, especially as Henry's father, by contrast, in 1418, had bought Chirk for the crown for cash. Henry's Lord Chief Justice, Sir John Fortescue, was later to cite this sale as the most glaring instance of wanton alienation of crown lands he could think of.[2]

Three years later Henry's lack of judgement and appreciation of the consequence of his actions gave cause for alarm. In the autumn of 1440 the council had been dealing with breaches of the peace by Thomas Courtenay, thirteenth earl of Devon, and by the king's knight and

[1] *P.P.C.*, V, 88, 89.
[2] *C.P.R., 1416–1422*, 172; *1436–1441*, 276, 311; *The Governance of England*, 134.

steward of the duchy of Cornwall manors in Cornwall, Sir William Bonville of Shute. The earl had had to be forbidden to use his office of Justice of the Peace against Bonville and ordered, in October 1440, to make personal complaint to Henry if he had any grievance against Bonville.[3] Bonville had appeared in person before the council and been bound over to keep the peace; Devon had been excused personal appearance there because of illness, but had been visited by the king's household knight and councillor, Sir John Stourton, to take appropriate assurances from him.[4] On 21 November 1441 Sir Philip Chetwynd was to be before the council about an assault made upon him and some Bristol merchants at Hungerford on their way to London by an un-identified armed band, who were thought to be the earl's men who had mistaken them for Bonville's supporters.[5] It is quite impossible to believe that Henry was not made aware of the feud. Yet in the spring of 1441 he had granted the stewardship of the duchy of Cornwall, which Bonville had exercised in Cornwall since 1437, to his antagonist Devon. Within a week of the earl's patent being sealed, the serious conse-quences of what he had done were brought home to him. At Sheen on 14 May 1441, in the presence of Suffolk, Treasurer Cromwell, Beaumont, the household chamberlain and Moleyns, he had to com-mand the chancellor to send an immediate order to the earl, under the great seal, not to meddle with the office until a council meeting could be convened to ordain what should be done, in view of the 'great trouble in the said county to great distress of our true subjects and disturbing of our peace' likely to ensue from the consequent reopening of their quarrel.[6] Much council time was subsequently taken up that year composing the differences of Devon and Bonville. In the end they appeared separately before Henry in his chamber and bound them-selves each to surrender their patent of office, to accept arbitration and to allow the stewardship to be held by 'an indifferent man' meantime. Bonville was constrained to accept the seneschalry of Gascony in the following year, but attempts to get Devon away to Normandy to rescue besieged Avranches, citing the example of how his father had re-sponded to Henry V's personal appeal when Cherbourg was threat-ened, met with no success.[7] Thus the king had exacerbated rather than checked, controlled or solved the differences of his unruly subjects.

The picture thus gained of Henry of Windsor's vacillation and un-certain judgement in his exercise of the powers of kingship is not what one would have expected from the son of Henry V, especially after

[3] P.R.O., E.28/64/30.
[4] P.R.O., E.28/65/19.
[5] *P.P.C.*, V, 159–61, 166.
[6] P.R.O., E.28/68/22; *C.P.R., 1436–1441*, 532.
[7] *P.P.C.*, V, 173–5, 203, 240.

the apparent promise of his minority. He was well enough served by his councillors, but nothing of importance was done or could be done without his approval and assent, and it is clear that his own personal wishes and decisions could brook no delay or circumvention. For example, Cardinal Beaufort died at Wolvesey on 11 April 1447 and that very same day Henry sent a signet letter from Windsor, ordering the prior and chapter at Winchester to elect William Wainfleet as his great-uncle's successor. This must have crossed a request for free election, sealed in the chapter house of St Swithun's on 12 April and carried by a delegation to Windsor, because another peremptory order followed from Windsor on 13 April ordering Wainfleet's immediate election on Saturday 15 April, without waiting for back-dated letters under the great seal which would follow. The chancellor sealed letters patent committing the temporalities to Wainfleet at Canterbury which he back-dated to 11 April 'per ipsum regem et de data predicta auctoritate parliamenti', although no parliament was sitting, and in spite of the statute of 18 Henry VI forbidding this practice. The licence to elect under the great seal duly followed, dated at Canterbury 15 April. Writs went out from Westminster *per ipsum regem*, under the normal process, on 4 June, to the escheators, ordering the delivery of the temporalities. The papal letters of approval, stated in these writs to have been already received, must have been assumed, unless they had indeed been obtained meantime with most unusual promptitude.[8]

Henry also considered that he was perfectly free to change his mind if he wished to do so. In 1448, on the death of Robert Gilbert, bishop of London, he recommended Thomas Kemp, his chaplain and the archbishop's nephew, for the vacant see. The papal letters of approval were duly sent. Some time before 19 May 1449 he wrote asking for the translation of Marmaduke Lumley, bishop of Carlisle and treasurer of England since 1446, to the see of London. Lumley was about to relinquish the treasurership to Lord Say and Sele, the king's chamberlain, and it may have been belatedly desired to take advantage of the London vacancy to keep him close at hand. Suffolk also wrote to the pope, recommending Lumley, in support of the change of plan.[9] But Pope Nicholas V refused to undo what he had already done, rejecting the joint efforts of king and minister when they claimed that Henry's original letter had been surreptitious and that his proctor in Rome, William Gray, had been responsible for it. In a salutary homily to Henry, the pope defended the honour of Gray, sent Henry back a copy of his original letter to show how genuine it had been and called to

---

[8] Richard Chandler, *The Life of William Waynflete* (London 1811), 299–305, 314–18, citing Pat.25 Henry VI pt. 2 m.29, 30, 36 and *Foedera*, XI, 172.

[9] This may indicate arrogance in the Great Chamberlain of England but can hardly prove that Suffolk had compelled Henry to change his mind as has been suggested.

mind some essential attributes of kingship: gravity in taking advice, constancy when he had accepted it. Such changes of mind or readiness to believe slander were deplorable in a king.[10]

An effective king had to be able to stand up to the unscrupulous pressure under which he made his grants and appointments. Henry's failures in this respect can be further well illustrated by similar incidents involving the later squire of the body, Thomas Daniel. The same day in 1441 when his mistake over the duchy appointment was made clear to him, it also emerged that the chamberlain of Chester, John Trout-beck, had had to be ordered to return letters under the royal signet of arms and the duchy of Lancaster eagle signet, granting Daniel the manor of Frodsham rent free for life. Henry, it was now said, had been misinformed that this manor was only worth £20 *per annum*. The chamberlain had been instructed from Westminster to hold the grant in abeyance meantime, since Lord Cromwell, the treasurer, who was present at Sheen on 14 May, had realized that it was worth very much more and Daniel was therefore very properly restricted to a £20 *per annum* grant from it.[11] A few years later the same avaricious Daniel secured from the pliant king a reversion of John Troutbeck's own office of chamberlain of Chester held for life, immediately after his death or earlier, to have 'quiet entry ... if so be that the aforesaid John Troutbeck have offended or offend in any other wise than he should do in his said office'. John Trevelyan, yeoman of the crown, was his agent in the matter and carried the bill bearing Henry's assent to Moleyns, newly made keeper of the privy seal, with a verbal message 'that he should speed the bill in all haste'.[12] Troutbeck had himself received the office from his father, to hold by himself or by sufficient deputy, on 16 June 1439, and might reasonably have expected to pass it on to his own son in due course. Daniel's grant was dated 13 February 1445 and it is no surprise to find that on 29 March following, at Windsor, Troutbeck himself secured from Henry an exemplification of his letters patent of 1439, declaring his exemplary service in the office and safeguarding himself against any removal by virtue of other letters patent for the office obtained subsequently to that date. This Henry, impartially or indifferently, handed personally to Moleyns, also with a special order to expedite it: 'et tradita mihi cum speciali iussu ad expediendum'.[13] Such ambivalent actions can hardly have created confidence in his kingship.

The role of household squires and yeomen such as Daniel and

---

[10] *Correspondence of Bekynton*, I, 155–9.
[11] *P.P.C.*, V, 144–5.
[12] P.R.O., E.28/68/17.
[13] P.R.O., E.28/75/44.

Trevelyan in Henry's appointments is further revealed in a covering letter written by John Hampton to Moleyns, as keeper of the privy seal, from Staines on 5 May 1445 to accompany a petition from Thomas Burghill for the office of collector and receiver of the king's rents and dues at Calais, for which Hampton had just obtained Henry's assent under his sign manual. The king's secretary Richard Andrew was not at court, so he had been unable to get an immediate signet warrant to send to Moleyns, but he feared that Master John Langton, the treasurer of Calais, although he had promised 'afore time that my said well beloved should have had it', was at the same time suing for a man of his own to have the office. 'Wherefore I beseech your good lordship as ever I shall desire that be unto your pleasure ye will speed my said well beloved afore any other in this matter. And almighty Jesus preserve your good estate. Written at Staines the V day of May in haste. Hampton by mine own hand.'[14] While making sure that the chancellor received a warrant that he would execute without question, speed was of the essence because parliament in 1439, in order to close one abuse in the undignified scramble for grants which Henry's majority had unloosed, had determined that the chancellor should henceforth not issue any letters patent bearing a date earlier than that of the delivery of the warrant into chancery.[15]

The ability of various household men to obtain all manner of grants great and small from Henry clearly soon became well known to suitors, informers, etc., who would share the proceeds of their grants with them in return for their promotion of them. For example, on 8 April 1445 Hampton obtained the royal assent by sign manual to a petition of his own and Thomas Hampton's granting them all the king's rights in ten pokes of wool which had been discovered at Titchfield by two local informers 'in a barn of William Uvedale set upon the sea bank under straw in manner suspect there and hid for to be carried unto parts of beyond sea not customed nor coketted'.[16] They commonly promoted bills for one another. A petition for John Say, yeoman of the crown, to have the office of keeper of the privy palace at Westminster and granted under the sign manual on 3 March 1445, is again endorsed as promoted by John Trevelyan, yeoman of the crown, 'to my lord privy seal in the king's behalf, praying and commanding him upon the said bill to do make letters under the privy seal unto my lord chancellor, etc.'[17]

The greatest could suffer from Henry's unlimited and haphazard

[14] P.R.O., E.28/75/60, 61.
[15] Statute 18 Henry VI c.l.
[16] P.R.O., E.28/75/51.
[17] P.R.O., E.28/75/5.

granting of favours. Humphrey duke of Gloucester had to petition on
10 March 1445 that he might in future be allowed to see all warrants
under the privy seal before they were issued, if they concerned the
royal forests and parks. Henry had committed to him the rule and
governance of these, but so many warrants had been directed and
executed there to the great damage of trees, underwood, vert and game,
that he was left with responsibility, but no control.[18] Richard duke
of York, absent as Henry's lieutenant in France and Normandy, wrote
on 9 March 1445 to complain that in his absence Sir John Paunce-
foot's feoffees had disinherited him of his manor and lordship of
Crickhowell, by granting the king a reversion of it and that Henry
had ratified and approved the arrangement. He now petitioned for
leave to sue for his title in the high court of parliament, which was
granted.[19] On the other hand there was one family whom absence from
court or service abroad did not damage. Edmund Beaufort, marquis of
Dorset on 4 October 1444 was given thirteen manors in Somerset and
Dorset for himself and his heirs male which Henry V had decreed should
be perpetually joined to the duchy of Cornwall. At the same time Henry
similarly granted him the valuable earldom of Richmond lands, the
manors of Bassingbourn and Babraham in Cambridgeshire, the whole
grant being worth over £400 *per annum*. Possibly the cardinal was
watching over his nephew's interests at court. He had himself already
acquired Chirk and Chirklands, the manors of Henstridge, Charlton
Camville, Canford and Poole, in Somerset and Dorset, through Henry's
alienations, to bequeath to his Beaufort nephew.[20]

A full survey of the bounty lavished on members of Henry's household, over and above the normal fees and wages of their offices,
between 1437 and 1450, would entail consideration of grants to eight
members of the nobility, fourteen king's knights and forty-five king's
esquires, not to mention gentlemen ushers of the chamber, king's
sergeants, clerks, etc. However, its extent and variety can be suggested
by what three of them at different levels in the household hierarchy
received: the earl of Suffolk, established as head of the household from
1433, James Fiennes, who rose from esquire of the body in 1438 to
be household chamberlain, treasurer of England and Lord Say and
Sele by 1449, and John Hampton who became an esquire of the body
in 1438 and remained so to the end of the reign.

William de la Pole, earl of Suffolk, the household steward, surpassed
all his predecessors and competitors in the acquisition of major offices,

---

[18] P.R.O., E.28/75/13.
[19] P.R.O., E.28/75/17.
[20] *R.P.*, II, 141; V, 446; *C.P.R., 1441–1446*; Wolffe, *The Royal Demesne*, 102,
281.

with all the powers and patronage they each entailed, as well as vast acres of crown lands which Henry granted to him for life, or to him and his heirs in perpetuity. By 1446 he was steward of the Chiltern Hundreds, constable of Wallingford castle, steward of the honours of Wallingford and St Valery, chief justice of Chester, Flint and North Wales, chief steward of the North Parts of the duchy of Lancaster and steward and surveyor of all mines in England and Wales. In 1447 he acquired the Chamberlainship of England, and the wardenship of the New Forest. In 1448 he became Captain of Calais. His share of the crown lands included the manors of Woodstock, Handborough, Wootton and Stonesfield, with the hundred of Wootton in Oxfordshire, the manor of Swaffham in Norfolk, and East Worldham, Nutley, Benesworth and part of Woolmer forest in Hampshire. All these grants were for life, rent free; the Welsh castles and lordships of Pembroke, Cilgerran, Emlyn Is-Cych and Dyffryn Breuan he received in perpetuity. Raised to marquis in 1444 and duke in 1448, he secured the additional earldom of Pembroke, along with the Welsh lands, on the death of Humphrey duke of Gloucester in 1447. The wardships he acquired were the greatest in the land, including the heiresses of Warwick and Somerset.[21]

An equally impressive though lesser patrimony fell into the lap of his household colleague James Fiennes of Knole, by Sevenoaks in Kent. As an esquire of the body his grants at first, understandably, came in smaller parcels than Suffolk's. In 1437 he was given £40 a year from the manor of Headington and Bullingdon hundred, Oxfordshire and the alien priory manor of Monkecourt in Kent, with exemption from clerical taxation for it. In 1440 he added the manor of Capel to his Kentish possessions, followed by the manor of Huntingfield with land in Chelsfield in 1441. When Henry wanted Monkecourt for King's College, Cambridge, Fiennes exchanged it with him for the manor of Witley in Surrey. In 1444 he was given the manors of Solihull and Sheldon in Warwickshire. His offices included spells as sheriff of Kent, Surrey and Sussex, the chamberlainship of the exchequer, constableship of Rochester castle, bailiff of Otford and Uckfield Stonham and of Loxfield hundred in Kent and Surrey, while the temporalities of the archbishopric of Canterbury were in Henry's hands, and steward of the duke of Warwick's lands in Kent and Sussex during minority. From 1447 he was the king's household chamberlain, constable of Dover castle and Warden of the Cinque Ports. To all these were added pensions at the exchequer, on the issues of the county of Kent, and on the customs in the port of London, and a string of royal forfeitures and wardships. He also received apartments in Westminster

---

[21] Mainly listed by K. B. McFarlane in the *Cambridge Medieval History*, VIII, 403.

palace, the Tower, Eltham and Sheen. Only after ten years in the household did he become a member of the council, in 1447.[22]

John Hampton of Stourton, Staffordshire, was already an established usher of the chamber in 1437, enjoying the additional offices of constable of Chester and water bailiff of Plymouth, master of the ordnance, life sheriff of Merioneth and steward of Morfe and Shirlet. Promoted to squire of the body in 1438, he had acquired additional pensions amounting to £122 a year out of the revenues of Coventry, Worcester, Bridgnorth and London by 1440. Henry also gave him £9 a year of the issues of the forest of Kinver and £7 3s 4d of the issues of the manor of Rowley Regis, Staffordshire; £8 a year, with Bewes Hampton, of the issues of Wrockwardine, Shropshire, the offices of master of the horse, constable of Colchester castle and captaincy of Hammes castle in the marches of Picardy. He was also master of the queen's horses from 1445. He specialized in picking up wardships, forfeitures and reversions. In 1439 he had the keeping of the manor of Aston Botterell, Shropshire and marriage of the heir, the reversion of the keeping of Kempton park and lodge, and two tuns of Gascon wine a year for life. 1444 and 1445 were good years when he acquired an additional £4 3s 8d pension which fell in, payable from the issues of Bridgnorth, a ship, the *Katherine*, forfeited for exporting uncustomed wool, various consignments of wool discovered being exported uncustomed, and a surety of £40 forfeited by the citizens of Coventry for breaking the peace. In 1446 he picked up the keeping of an idiot, in 1447 forfeitures incurred by a Genoese merchant and by the citizens of Cambridge, and the reversion of the manor of Newport and Birchhanger in Sussex.[23]

It is hard to believe that in the 1440s Henry weighed the consequences of granting any petition which reached him, or refused it, and this must have been the situation which the council in the Star Chamber, at some date which cannot be precisely determined, tried to remedy in a discreet and diplomatic memorandum. He duly approved it with his sign manual. It is now pasted, without date, in the Cotton collection printed by Nicolas, immediately after a document dated 4 March 1444.[24] It amounted to a plan to constitute an advisory body of receivers and triers for royal petitions, something like those

[22] *C.P.R.*, *1436–1441*, 77, 248, 382, 402, 414, 423, 428, 470, 485, 493, 511, 529; *1441–1446*, 76, 133, 140, 160, 161, 169, 187, 279, 296, 355, 401, 445; *1446–1452*, 1, 45, 63, 87.

[23] *Ibid.*, *1436–1441*, 221, 237, 239–40, 285, 300, 349, 404, 431, 432, 454; *1441–1446*, 2–3, 35, 226, 229, 258, 318, 344, 356, 452; *1446–1452*, 33, 34, 46, 106, 107, 214, 256, 300, 332.

[24] *P.P.C.*, VI, 316–20; S. B. Chrimes and A. L. Brown, *Select Documents of English Constitutional History* (London 1961), 277–9; B.L. Cotton Cleopatra F v 112b.

long since automatically appointed at the beginning of every parliament
to process petitions received in parliament. It was proposed that henceforth the sponsor of any petition to the king, whether a member of
the council or any other with access to the king's person, should have
to subscribe his name to it. Then certain persons, nominated by Henry,
would first receive them all. If they were matters affecting justice and
the common law they would then be sent to the council, if matters
of grace, taken to Henry. But first a clear summary of the contents of
each would be written on the back for his easy comprehension, so that
he might the better decide whether to grant or refuse it, in whole or
part, or to remit it to the council for their advice. What he granted,
where and when, and in whose presence, especially noting which lords,
if any, were there at the time, should then be subscribed on it. The
king would then sign it immediately and command his chamberlain
either to sign it also or to take it to the secretary. To prevent the
dangerous practice of granting the same thing to two persons in the
future, everything which the king granted should be minuted: 'provided
always that the king hath not granted the things asked to any other
person afor this time'.

There was in future to be only one channel by which these petitions,
once they had been made into warrants by the king's approval, should
reach the chancellor for execution under the great seal: first to the signet
office, then to the privy seal office, then to the chancellor. The
diplomatic but revealing reason given for this was that 'such things
as passeth the hands of many persons shall the more readily and
sadly pass and any hurt that should else more grow to the king or
to prejudice of any other person the more to be eschewed'. It was
recommended that the signet office, Henry's most intimate writing
office, should henceforth keep all originals and copies of their consequent warrants to the privy seal, clearly something not previously
done. In this connection it must be mentioned that on 16 October 1444
Henry duly assigned the highest chamber in the tower next to the
Lancaster Tower in Windsor castle to his secretary and the signet office
clerks as their first permanent, static base for storing their records.[25]

The crux of this document was the role envisaged for the keeper
of the privy seal: he would scrutinize the grants before allowing them
to pass and, at his discretion, refer them to the council, who would
refer them back to the king if they thought this advisable. The
deferential tone of the memorandum submitted 'only by way of
advertisement ... for they in no wise think nor have will to do ... any
thing but that the king's good grace do at all times as it shall please
him and use his power and will as it pertaineth to his royal estate',

---

[25] P.R.O., C.81/1435/1789; Sir Henry Maxwell Lyte, *Historical Notes on the use of the
Great Seal* (H.M.S.O., 1926), 122.

shows how powerless the council really were in this situation. Indeed, such explicit conciliar supervision of royal acts was incompatible with the exercise of real kingship. To sweeten the pill, the document concluded with a special new oath of loyalty and impartiality, to be taken by the new 'receivers and triers', and other recommendations to ensure the integrity and impartiality of royal councillors.

Since the document bears the royal sign manual, Henry must actually have approved it. But a privy seal writ was soon issued from his lodge in Windsor park, on 7 November 1444, for letters patent under the great seal to be made reaffirming the validity of all direct warrants to the chancellor made since the tenth year of his reign (1431–2) until that date, whether under his sign manual, his signets, or endorsed by his chamberlain or the clerk of the council. He thus appears soon to have changed his mind, although it is possible that this privy seal writ was merely to ensure that the new measure of conciliar control he was now accepting should not affect the validity of his past acts.[26] The real test of the effectiveness of the council's laudable plans to supervise the ineffective king ought to be whether or not the records of the privy seal and signet reveal any consequent changes. The answer is that the files of direct warrants under the sign manual and signets covering 1444[27] are the smallest of any before the period of Henry's madness, while the corresponding files of council and privy seal warrants to the chancellor do seem to provide some evidence of restriction to conciliar supervision.[28] But the files for these and subsequent years in both series also demonstrate that these changes, if made, were but partly and temporarily applied, and direct warrants under the sign manual subscribed by the three signet clerks Robert Osbern, John Blakeney and Robert Repynghale, which should have been eliminated by the proposed council reform, substantially increased in volume again from 1445 until the autumn of 1453.

The favoured circle who had access to Henry's person between 1437 and 1450 and received grants of lands, offices and privileges stretching throughout the land, were not only the channels of royal authority at the centre, but also in the localities. Some of the most favoured, like James Fiennes, Lord Say and Sele, in Kent and Sussex, received their bounty in lands, offices and privileges mainly, but never entirely, in one territorial area. For example, John Viscount Beaumont received his grants mainly in Lincolnshire, Ralph Lord Cromwell in Derbyshire, Nottinghamshire, Lincolnshire and Yorkshire, John Lord Beauchamp of Powicke in Gloucestershire and the Marches of Wales, John Lord Stourton and Sir Edmund Hungerford in Wiltshire, Sir Thomas Stanley

[26] C.P.R., 1441–1446, 312–13; Chrimes & Brown, op. cit., 279–80.
[27] P.R.O., C.81/1434, 1435.
[28] Files E.28/72, 73 as also noted by Baldwin, op. cit., 189.

in North Wales, Cheshire and Lancashire. This also applied to some of the lesser fry. The squire of the body, John Trevelyan, received most of his extensive rewards in his home county of Cornwall. Others, however, who were equally favoured, such as Ralph Butler Lord Sudeley, William Beauchamp Lord St Amand and John Somerset, the king's physician, received as many, if not more, grants scattered haphazardly throughout the kingdom. The conclusion must be that it was the local interest, preference and early knowledge of what became available, on the part of the recipients, which produced these territorial groupings and not any conscious policy on Henry's part. In theory Henry's ability to dispose of so much valuable patronage in lands, offices and privileges throughout the kingdom, and the concentration of them in the hands of members of his household, should have given him an invincible royal affinity, with roots in every shire of England. In fact it only served to generate the same jealousies and resentments in the localities as in government at the centre. From the later 1440s evidence begins to accumulate of the royal power and influence being regarded as support for territorial factions. In 1449 the Commons in parliament complained that the king's duty to keep the peace, dispense justice and maintain the law of the land was no longer being fulfilled as it had been, and consequently 'murders, manslaughters, rapes, robberies, riots, affrays and other inconveniences greater than before, now late have grown within this your realm'.[29] These were the words of the preamble to a petition for the punishment of the king's squire, William Tailboys, of South Kyme in Lincolnshire, who had set upon Lord Cromwell with an armed band at the entrance to the Star Chamber, a glaring instance of a local feud being carried into the very precincts of the palace of Westminster. Tailboys enjoyed the protection of Suffolk and Viscount Beaumont, and had been allegedly saved from the execution of judicial writs against him by Suffolk's intervention.[30] According to contemporary complaints it was the king's favour, operating through members of Henry's household in their localities and through their privileged agents and servants, which was now bringing the machinery of royal justice into growing disrepute.

One of the two fundamental duties of a medieval king was to judge his people. The other was to fight their battles.[31] Henry VI did neither. The two duties were not mutually exclusive or incompatible, since the previous reign had been outstanding in both respects. In spite of Henry V's almost continuous absence on the conquest of France, while he was abroad his mere shadow, it was said, maintained a healthy

[29] *R.P.*, V, 200.
[30] R. L. Storey, *The End of the House of Lancaster*, 53.
[31] 1 Samuel VIII, 20, cited in *De Laudibus Legem Anglie* of Sir John Fortescue (ed. S. B. Chrimes), 2.

respect for law and order in England. He was a tireless correspondent, issuing orders and directives in English, in his own hand, to his servants back home; his tremendous energy enabled him to poke his finger into all manner of his subjects' concerns. He was never the tool of any faction. Evidence survives of his personally punishing a prominent Oxford esquire, Reginald Malyns, in July 1419, for bribing a jury with money, food and drink. Dangerous quarrels between three powerful baronial families were peacefully settled in his council between 1415 and 1420.[32] Likewise the duke of Bedford, during Henry VI's minority, in 1433, was praised for upholding the law and for bringing criminals to justice. Some rulers did it, some did not; how it was done is difficult to determine, but undoubtedly mere charisma, as well as energetic, strategic personal intervention was important. Between 1437 and 1450 throughout the shires of England the personal influence of the king in the field of justice, law and order was at best a negative one. In so far as he allowed the royal power to be associated with faction, it was positively harmful.

Lawlessness and disorder are almost impossible to quantify for any epoch, but specialized studies of almost any specific, limited period of English history in the later middle ages, from the later thirteenth to the early sixteenth centuries, tend to come up with evidence of outstanding lawlessness.[33] The pattern of later-medieval law and order, and the undoubted elements of endemic disorder in it, was probably set at the end of the thirteenth century with the collapse of law enforcement from the centre by the general eyres, due to the impossible burdens then placed upon them and to their local unpopularity. The multiplication of more specialized, real property assizes never filled the gap and the ensuing enforced delegation of royal authority to the local gentry, first as keepers of the peace and, later, as justices of the peace, with statutory powers to imprison and punish, ensured, in the long run, that the commission of the peace would become more an instrument of local politics than an effective grass-roots agency of the common law and royal authority in England. Likewise the later-medieval sheriff, the king's only server of writs and empaneller of juries, was emasculated as an effective, impartial agent of central government by a diminishing financial role, by his being deprived of control of the crown lands within the area of his shrievalty and by parliament's insistence on his annual appointment and prohibition of reappointment within three years. Even in the 1330s, one of the few periods intensively studied in this respect, English society was already looking back to a mythical golden age of effective law enforcement and had allegedly 'largely ceased to

[32] K. B. McFarlane, *The Nobility of Later Medieval England*, 118–19.
[33] See John Bellamy, *Crime and Public Order in England in the Later Middle Ages* (London 1973), 3–10.

place its trust in royal justice', seeking security in 'local bands and private associations'.[34]

Another consideration which partially explains an endemic lawlessness in later-medieval England, not peculiar to the personal rule of Henry VI, was that, by contrast with modern society, public opinion was not naturally inclined to respect and obey the law. The author of the only detailed, large-scale study of the workings of an English court of law during this period has demonstrated that the fifteenth-century land-hungry gentry and their superiors, as well as the prosperous mercantile classes, demanded from the law courts not abstract or perfect justice but assistance in furthering their own private objectives.[35] The correspondence and complaints of the Paston, Plumpton and Cely families, stretching backwards and forwards beyond this reign, like the petitions and depositions which form the judicial records themselves, must always be evaluated in the light of their one-sided self-interest. An action at law was a skilled and unscrupulous contest to outwit your opponent by any possible means to hand. No prudent man, however skilled in that exercise, relied on the letter of the law alone to protect or further his interests. The particular advice given to the next-generation John Paston in 1461 can be taken as generally followed: 'Make you so strong in lordship and in law that ye reck not much whether the [law] be good or bad.'[36]

In the maintenance of law and order in the localities, the authority of the local lords was undoubtedly of vital importance. The commissions of the peace for the thirty-six counties of England in the mid-fifteenth century were always headed by those temporal lords who had estates within the county and by the bishop of the diocese, where similarly appropriate. The power of the nobility, where they lived and exercised it, could be the most important element making for peace and quiet. In a famous 'king's speech', prepared for the opening of parliament in 1483, the royal chancellor, Bishop Russell, declared that 'the politic rule of every region, well ordained, standeth in the nobles'.[37] This maxim was equally applicable to the reign of Henry VI, because the parts of his kingdom where public order was most disturbed were not those where the great lords were constantly resident, but, for example, South Wales and the Marches, where the lords were absentee landlords and where the conduct of affairs was left to their local officials,

---

[34] Alan Harding, *The Law Courts of Medieval England* (London 1973), chapter 3, and especially p. 91 with quotations and the detailed references there given.

[35] Margaret Hastings, *The Court of Common Pleas in Fifteenth Century England* (Ithaca, New York, 1947), especially chapter XV, 'Delays and hindrances to Justice'.

[36] *Ibid.*, 226–7, 259–60.

[37] *Grants of the Reign of King Edward the Fifth*, ed. J. G. Nichols (Camden Soc., 1854), xliii.

mainly selected from the Welsh squirearchy. Likewise disturbances and local discontents which were revealed in 1450 in Kent, Sussex, East Anglia and Wiltshire also had this element in common. They arose where the lords of the area were absent because constantly employed at the centre in the king's service: in Kent and Sussex the treasurer, Lord Say, and the chancellor, the archbishop of Canterbury; in East Anglia, the duke of Suffolk, and in Wiltshire, where the courtier Bishop Aiscough, Lord Stourton and Sir Edmund Hungerford held sway. The brutal murder of Henry's confessor, the bishop of Salisbury, by his tenants at Edington began the disturbances there. He was making for the safety of Sherborne castle on 29 June 1450 on what was probably only his first or second visit to his diocese during his twelve-year episcopate. The complaints of abuse and corruption of the processes of the law which appeared in 1450 were mainly against the lesser gentry, lawyers and officials who were operating under the 'good lordship' of the absentee great.[38] Grievances against the king's ministers were most keenly felt in localities where they delegated their local responsibilities to concentrate on their position in the king's entourage.

In such circumstances the influence of a good or bad resident territorial magnate undoubtedly had a great effect on the general state of law and order. A failure of belief in the king at the top as the ultimate, impartial and effective agent of justice, whether through his local agents or through his council, or approached personally, could lead to total collapse. The dangers inherent in these conditions which existed in England from the fourteenth to the sixteenth centuries are well illustrated by the conduct of justices of the peace in Bedfordshire in 1436, the type of quarrel between local magnates of more or less equal importance, competing for authority in one locality during Henry's personal rule, which has been seen as the kind of situation which finally escalated into civil war. It was a quarrel between powerful commissioners of the peace who tried to use the commission against one another. Two members of the commission of the peace for Bedford-shire, naming another with them without his knowledge, had obtained a special legal commission and attempted, under its authority, to hold sessions outside the village church at Silsoe. The village belonged to Lord Grey of Ruthyn, another of the J.P.s for Bedfordshire. He duly appeared there when he learnt of this, suitably accompanied by his retainers as befitted his station, to protect his tenants' interests. He was supported by yet another J.P., John Enderby, also with an armed following, who proposed they should hold rival sessions and maintained that the special commission had been fraudulently obtained with the intention of injuring Grey's tenants. It was further alleged by one of Grey's party that the other local magnate, Lord Fanhope, was behind

[38] See below pp. 124–5, 234–5.

it all and Fanhope himself, yet another of the Bedford justices, also duly turned up to view the situation. Finding himself outnumbered there by the combined Grey-Enderby party, he sent back to his nearby manor of Ampthill for his armour and for more men. Under these conditions no party could hold sessions and the attempt was abandoned.[39] This particular precarious balance in local politics in Bedfordshire was still unchanged two years later, as revealed by a second incident which has become known as 'the Bedford riots'. Four of the same local gentry, still justices of the peace under the 1437 commission, attempted to hold sessions by themselves in the lawful place, the shire hall at Bedford. Again this was by authority of a limited special commission which they had obtained and again they were allegedly interrupted by Lord Fanhope, also still a justice of the peace, who proceeded to set up a rival court at the opposite end of the hall and to summon some, but not all, of the other justices present, to join him there. In this case each side reported the other to the king and council, under the provisions of Statute 13 Henry IV chapter 7, for causing a riot; first the four justices of the peace who had obtained the special commission of oyer and terminer and then Fanhope and his supporters in retaliation. Large numbers of men, forty-five on one side and one hundred on the other, were named and counter-named as being involved, and much larger unnamed bodies alleged to have been in support.

A long and inconclusive examination of the principals on both sides by the royal council followed. It emerged that neither side was entirely blameless, that a report against Fanhope, by those who had obtained the special commission of oyer and terminer in the first place, had probably been a fabrication and their original commission obtained for dishonest purposes. Both sides obtained Henry's pardon as a result of this Star Chamber inquiry and in a Great Council meeting on 23 February 1439 Henry granted Fanhope's request for an exemplification of the proceedings to be made under the great seal.[40] Thus Lords Fanhope and Grey were repeatedly able to take the law into their own hands with impunity, only checked by the ability of others to do the same. Commissions of the peace were discredited and fraudulent powers obtained from Henry's council, but it all ended with pardons all round and without punishments. The comparable Courtenay-Bonville dispute of 1441, already described, similarly ended inconclusively, and, as it turned out, was left to simmer before breaking out with renewed violence some ten years later.

A similar quarrel, but between lesser, gentry families, the Staffords of Grafton and the Harcourts of Stanton Harcourt, occurred when an

---

[39] *C.P.R., 1436–1441*, 87; *P.P.C.*, V, 35–8, 57–9.
[40] *Select Cases before the King's Council*, ed. I. S. Leadam and J. F. Baldwin (Selden Soc., 1918), 104–7; *C.P.R., 1436–1441*, 246, 282, 578.

old land dispute led to an affray and slaying in Coventry in May 1448. This was exacerbated by Sir Robert Harcourt's ability, through his court connections, to get the king to stay proceedings begun against him for the murder of Richard Stafford. Richard's father, Sir Humphrey Stafford, unable to get his son's murder 'by the course of your law duly punished', was ultimately provoked into taking the law into his own hands. On 1 May 1450, with a force of some 200 Warwickshire tenants and supporters, he attempted to storm and burn out his enemies in their manor-house and church at Stanton Harcourt. The surviving parties to this dispute obtained pardons, without any punishment, later that year.[41]

Sir James Ramsay was the first to compile a catalogue of incidents of the domestic disorder in England in the 1440s, which he did not hesitate to describe as anarchic, and he first laid the blame squarely on the 'simple' king for these 'premonitory symptoms of civil war'.[42] In fact this is a mistaken explanation of the origins and causes of the civil wars or Wars of the Roses, which followed in the 1450s. The later outbreak of armed conflict on a national scale did certainly develop from a feud and rivalry between two of Henry's greatest subjects, Richard duke of York and Edmund Beaufort, duke of Somerset, to which other families attached themselves, but this Yorkist-Beaufort enmity arose not out of English domestic history, but out of the conduct of the war in France. It grew out of the changing dispositions, vacillations and suspicions engendered by Henry's policies there, not in England. It was a rivalry exacerbated during the years while Henry's marriage remained childless, by fears on York's part, after the death of Humphrey duke of Gloucester in 1447 made him heir presumptive, that he would be disinherited by allegations of treason, in favour of the Beauforts, in succession to the throne. Following the decline in Henry's mental powers, the later, direct dynastic issue between York and Lancaster was grafted on to this original contest. However, it is certainly true that the same unhappy ability in Henry to generate and feed unrest and insecurity was evident in his actions at home, for almost all of Ramsay's incidents of domestic disorder in the 1440s, since supplemented and developed by Professor Storey, contain the same disturbing element: the royal power in Henry's hands appeared to be used and was alleged to be used, as an instrument of faction. Thus a dangerous new factor added to the already general tendency of disrespect for and manipulation of the law: the feeling that royal power was partisan and was being used as such in the administration of justice.

From the evidence of the Paston Letters it appears that in Norfolk

[41] *Paston Letters*, I, 73–5; Storey, *op. cit.*, 57–8.
[42] *Lancaster and York*, II, 49–53.

the 'princypall rewle and governaunce throwh all this schir', which the duke who bore its name claimed in 1452[43] was his by right, under the king, had, during the 1440s, been usurped by king's household men. Generally alleged to operate under the impregnable protection of the duke of Suffolk, the most prominent and hated perverters of the law, according to the Pastons, were Sir Thomas Tuddenham, John Heydon, John Ulveston and Thomas Daniel. Tuddenham, of Oxburgh, Norfolk, keeper of the king's wardrobe from 1446, repeatedly M.P. for Norfolk and sometime sheriff, held the chief stewardship of the North Parts of the duchy of Lancaster jointly with Suffolk and was himself steward of the duchy in Norfolk, Suffolk and Cambridgeshire, jointly with Heydon, from 1443.[44] He also 'occupied and governed' Suffolk's honour of Richmond manor of Swaffham as steward and farmer.[45] His associate, John Heydon of Baconsthorpe, Norfolk, sometime recorder of Norwich, J.P. and M.P. for Norfolk, engineered Lord Moleyns's sack and seizure of their manor of Gresham, according to the Pastons, while Sir John Fastolf complained in 1450 that Heydon had wronged him over the past thirteen years with continual distraints. While 'the world was alwey set after his rule', he said, legal action against Heydon had been pointless.[46] John Ulveston of Debenham, Suffolk, employed by Henry as receiver of Eton College, a lawyer, M.P. for Yarmouth, J.P. in Suffolk, king's escheator in Norfolk and Suffolk, was also the keeper of the writs and rolls of the Court of Common Pleas so had special facilities for the misuse of legal instruments. Thomas Daniel, referred to by Margaret Paston as 'my lord Daniel',[47] squire of the body, king's remembrancer in the exchequer, was established at Roydon by Castle Rising, Norfolk, from 1447. He first entered the county by the king's grant of Castle Rising according to Lord Scales, who complained about his interference with one of his tenants in 1450.[48] Another protected lawbreaker and manipulator was Charles Nowell, Daniel's bailiff of Bradeston, against whose misdeeds ten gentlemen of Norfolk jointly petitioned. He was the man who, with an armed band, set upon Paston and his men at the door of Norwich cathedral.[49]

According to Judge Yelverton only the fall of Suffolk and the discomfiture of the king's household men in 1450 made possible the appointment of an impartial sheriff and undersheriff for Norfolk and

---

[43] *Paston Letters*, I, 230.
[44] R. Somerville, *History of the Duchy of Lancaster*, I, 420, 594.
[45] *Paston Letters*, I, 203.
[46] *Ibid.*, I, 81–2, 116.
[47] *Ibid.*, I, 70.
[48] *Ibid.*, I, 117.
[49] *Ibid.*, I, 231–4.

Suffolk, as a start to getting proper remedies at law.[50] Tenants of
Swaffham in 1451, with some exaggeration, complained of sixteen years
of Tuddenham's misrule there,[51] while twenty-four separate charges
were prepared against Tuddenham and Heydon ready for a new and
impartial commission of oyer and terminer, which it was hoped the
duke of Norfolk would head in 1451. A separate list of twenty-two of
their victims was compiled, headed by Yelverton, Fastolf and Paston.[52]
The activities of which these men were accused, by virtue of their many
offices, included forcing juries to perjure themselves, issuing forged
returns and inquisitions, retaining against the law, making unjust
presentments and imprisonments, exacting obligations of money by
threats and menaces, falsely outlawing men, manipulating the customs
due on wool exports and overawing lawcourts. Tuddenham and
Heydon mustered 400 knights, esquires and yeomen successfully to
influence a commission of oyer and terminer meeting at Walsingham,
after their ally Judge Prisot had removed it there from Norwich.[53] Fastolf
claimed to have lost the manor of Dedham, Essex, through the false
representations and testimonies of these men, acting as the duke of
Suffolk's council.[54] In 1448 he had lost his Norfolk manor of Titchwell,
which he had bought dearly for £400 in 1431, to Sir Edward Hull
and Thomas Wake, not by an unimpeachable judicial verdict, but
through Heydon's intervention in the legal process and Hull's superior
influence as Henry's knight of the body and member of the tight circle
of royal intimates.[55] Over Lord Moleyns's burning and sacking of
Gresham the sheriff declared that it was the king's wish that he empanel
a jury to acquit him, and he dared not disregard it, even though
Paston said such a writ could be bought for a noble.[56]

   In all these incidents right was probably never entirely on one side,
but the common theme running through them all was that in the 1440s
the royal powers of justice in the localities could be manipulated with
impunity by those who enjoyed Henry's access and favour. The second
set of impeachment charges laid against the duke of Suffolk in 1450,
produced when his impeachment on higher matters of state appeared
to be failing, made the same allegations. These concerned his 'insatiable
covertise' in engrossing the king's lands, revenues and offices to himself, which gave him the powers complained of, and made general
references to the damage done to the efficiency of the king's courts by

[50] *Ibid.*, I, 165.
[51] *Ibid.*, I, 203.
[52] *Paston Letters*, I, 188–93.
[53] *Ibid.*, I, 210–12.
[54] *Ibid.*, I, 359.
[55] P. S. Lewis, 'Sir John Fastolf's Lawsuit over Titchwell 1448–55', *The Historical Journal*, I (1958), 1–20.
[56] *Paston Letters*, I, 207–8, 213–16.

his procuring excessive liberties, privileges and franchises for suitors, preventing the execution of writs, securing a pardon for Tailboys, and influencing the selection of sheriffs. Thus 'they that would not be of his affinite in their contreys were oversette, every matere true or fals that he favoured was furthered and spedde, and true maters of such persones as had not his favour were hyndred and put abakke', whereby justice miscarried, true men were hanged, thieves saved, and men lost their lands.[57] Royal power had become the tool of faction. The misuse of royal power was commonly alleged even in cases where legal rights were duly upheld. In serious riots at Norwich in 1445, over jurisdiction disputed between the city and the cathedral priory, Henry's council probably dispensed good law, if bad politics, by upholding the rights of the ecclesiastical authorities, suspending the city's liberties and fining them heavily. But in 1450 the citizens of Norwich laid their consequent misfortunes at the door of Suffolk and his councillors who, they claimed, were responsible for the crown's partiality against them.[58]

Undoubtedly assertions made in city records and the Paston Letters cannot always be taken at their face value, but the complaints of the Cade rebels in 1450, about conditions in Kent and Sussex during the 1440s, also bear remarkable similarities to the Norfolk scene. Here James Fiennes, Lord Say and Sele, Henry's household chamberlain and treasurer of England, was principally blamed, together with his local associates, 'the great extortioners Slegge, Crowmer, Isle and Robert Est'.[59] As a result of the privileged, illegal activities of these men, the rebels claimed, gentlemen of Kent could have no security in goods or lands. Fiennes and William Isle represented Kent together in parliament in 1441–2, and Fiennes and Crowmer in 1446–7, when Slegge was member for Dover.[60] Slegge was certainly closely associated with Fiennes in land dealings.[61] William Crowmer, Fiennes's son-in-law, son of a mayor of London and himself a king's squire, was sheriff of Kent in 1444–5 and 1448–50, William Isle in 1446–7 and Stephen Slegge in 1448–9.[62] They served on various commissions together, including the commissions of the peace. Robert Est, a lawyer and keeper of Maidstone gaol, was escheator in Kent in 1447 and had been coroner in 1445.[63] As collectors of taxes, justices of the peace and oyer and terminer, sheriffs, escheators, coroners, constable of Dover castle, with its special jurisdiction, and Warden of the Cinque Ports,

---

[57] R.P., V, 177; Historical Manuscripts Commission, Third Report, Appendix, 280.
[58] Storey, op. cit., 217–25.
[59] John Stow's Annales, 390.
[60] Returns of Names and Members of Parliament, I, 336.
[61] C.C.R., 1447–1454, 54, 56, 58.
[62] P.R.O., List and Indexes, IX, 68.
[63] C.C.R., 1441–1447, 321; C.F.R., XVIII, 83.

they undoubtedly administered the south-east during the 'forties. The complaints of 1450 were an indictment of their power to distort the operation of justice. Men were summoned to courts without due notice and lost their cases by default, collectors serving writs of the exchequer extorted much more than they were authorized to collect, the offices of sheriff and undersheriff were bought and sold, influence at court secured them the lands and goods of innocent men, who were afterwards falsely condemned to forfeiture. The court of Dover extended its jurisdiction illegally over the whole county, while the barons of the Cinque Ports abused their exemptions from taxation at the cost of the rest of the county. These 'great rulers of the shire' themselves chose the knights of the shire for parliament who chose the dishonest collectors of taxes.

Again, there was doubtless some exaggeration in these charges, but an examination, published by Dr Roger Virgoe, of local presentments before commissioners of oyer and terminer, sitting from August to October 1450 at Rochester, Maidstone, Canterbury and Dartford confirms that conditions in Kent during the 'forties presented a sorry condemnation of royal government and justice as administered by Say and his associates.[64] Over three-quarters of the ninety presentments before these commissioners concerned events from 1445 and consisted of charges of corruption and extortion by the sheriffs and their undersheriffs, bailiffs, gaol keepers and stewards, men who were principally the king's officers or those of the archbishop of Canterbury, or Lord Say and Sele. Stephen Slegge of Wouldham and Robert Est of Maidstone were the two most frequently presented, for corrupt land deals, false outlawries, unlawful seizures of goods, forcible expulsions and extortions of fines by virtue of their offices.

Nine times between 1438 and 1448 Henry perambulated through the area of Kent from which Jack Cade's rebellion drew its supporters in 1450. Each year, from 1446 to 1449 inclusive, he was in Norfolk and Suffolk where, according to the Paston Letters, and the records of the city of Norwich, members of the duke of Suffolk's affinity corrupted and perverted the administration of royal justice to their own mercenary ends. But there is no record that during these years he ever took his judges with him on commissions of oyer and terminer, as became his constant practice from 1451 to 1453, or that he ever personally heard any complaints or did justice himself.

Indeed King Henry VI would certainly not have made a good Lord Chief Justice, the office which the chronicler John Hardyng later urged him to take personally into his own hands as a remedy for the general lawlessness of the late 1440s. Apart from mere weakness and inaction he had other undesirable personal traits, vindictiveness and a degree

[64] *Documents illustrative of Medieval Kentish Society*, ed. F. R. H. Du Boulay, 220–43.

of credulity which jars with the popular, pious and enlightened image of the founder of Eton and King's. These appeared in his over-reactions in certain judicial processes during the 1440s, which were set in motion by allegations of treason against his person. Two of these concerned the greatest in the land, the third, one of his ordinary subjects. Humphrey duke of Gloucester had returned in triumph from his Calais expedition in 1436 where he had put the traitorous duke of Burgundy to ignominious rout. He and his second duchess, the unfortunate Jacqueline of Hainault's lady-in-waiting, Eleanor Cobham, then stood high in royal favour[65] and Duke Humphrey's views prevailed with the young king in the closing stages of the Gravelines peace conference of 1439.[66] This harmony between the king and his uncle and heir presumptive was not destined to last for long. In 1440 Gloucester presumed to oppose his release of the duke of Orleans from captivity and the role proposed for Orleans in future peace negotiations with France. The duke put his adamant opposition to these royal policies on record by exemplification under the great seal, as an outspoken arraignment of the two cardinals Beaufort and Kemp, whom he professed to hold responsible. But Henry replied personally to him in a detailed, reasoned argument, claiming these decisions as his very own. His uncle had thus become a serious political nuisance and the Gloucesters the objects of the king's displeasure. Consequently, when the duchess behaved foolishly and recklessly and laid herself open to a possible charge of treason, she received no mercy from Henry and in 1441 London witnessed the astonishing exemplary punishment of this first lady of the land, charged with imagining Henry's death, seeking by means of witchcraft and sorcery to accomplish it, and thus to bring her husband, and herself, to the throne. To have submitted Duchess Eleanor to the fearful death reserved for heretics and traitors, and duly suffered by two of her accomplices, would, of course, have been unthinkable. Nevertheless, several days of humiliating public penance, walking through the principal streets of the capital in a fashion normally reserved for common prostitutes, were imposed upon her, followed by perpetual imprisonment in five successive royal strongholds under strict guard of officers deputed from the royal household.[67]

The scandal had broken about a month after the date allegedly

---

[65] Giles's Chronicle, 30, *Excerpta Historica*, 148.

[66] See below p. 148.

[67] This trial is fully discussed and all sources of evidence reviewed by R. A. Griffiths, 'The trial of Eleanor Cobham: an episode in the fall of Duke Humphrey of Gloucester', *B.J.R.L.*, LI (1968–9), 381–99. Dr Griffiths has also disproved the hitherto accepted belief that she finally died in prison on the Isle of Man in 1457: 'Richard duke of York and the royal household in Wales, 1449–50', *The Welsh History Review*, VIII (1976), 14–25.

predicted for the king's death had safely passed, at the end of June 1441, with the arrest of her accomplices in the black arts, the fashionable astrologer and necromancer and member of Humphrey's household, Master Roger Bolingbroke; the rector of St Stephen's Walbrook, a canon of the king's own palace chapel of St Stephen's Westminster, Master Thomas Southwell; Eleanor's secretary and chaplain who was also secretary to the duke, John Home; and the 'witch of Eye', or Ebury, by Westminster, Margery Jourdemain. Bolingbroke had allegedly presided over ceremonies designed to foretell the date of the young king's death for the foolish gratification of the wife of the heir presumptive, and a resulting prediction of an early demise had spread among the London populace, Bolingbroke himself informing an esquire of the household and sergeant of the king's tents, John Solers. Margery Jourdemain, a well-known sorceress, had also been consulted by Eleanor to provide potions to make her pregnant by the duke and provide him with a legitimate heir.

Such charges of treasonable witchcraft against royal ladies in England were not in themselves an entirely new thing. Henry IV's Queen, Joan of Navarre, had been so charged some twenty years before, but, in contrast to Eleanor's fate, Joan's rank had prevented her from being brought to trial, and an honourable, if not luxurious, brief imprisonment had been followed by her return to court, where she had been quite prominent during Henry VI's infancy.[68] Henry now showed no such leniency to Eleanor. Gloucester's inability to protect his wife and the ruin of his influence over his nephew were now made manifest. Her examinations before an ecclesiastical tribunal, consisting of the two cardinals, the archbishop of Canterbury and three bishops, were completed by 25 July. They secured admission of certain of the charges. After extensive inquiries by a joint civic and conciliar committee into the alleged plot against the king's life and the trials and deaths of her accomplices, who turned evidence against her, she performed her public penance in mid-November, was solemnly divorced from her husband and finally proceeded to her lifelong incarceration which Henry announced on 19 January 1442. Moved from Leeds castle, where Queen Joan had served her brief imprisonment, to Chester, in the charge of Sir Thomas Stanley, controller of the household and Lord of the Isle of Man, and kept under the strictest guards, her subsequent peregrinations were prompted by Henry's periodic fears that attempts might be made to free her. In 1443 he was roused to anger by a Greenwich woman who reviled him to his face for his treatment of the duchess. She was pressed to death for the offence, and Eleanor was moved to Kenilworth under the charge of Lord Sudeley, the house-

[68] See A. R. Myers, 'The Captivity of a Royal Witch', *B.J.R.L.*, XXIV (1940), 263–84; XXVI (1941–2), 82–100.

hold chamberlain and constable of the castle there. Shipped off in 1446
to the distant Isle of Man, fears of a possible French or Scottish raid
there brought her back to Beaumaris in 1449, where she ended her
days in 1452 in the care of Sir William Beauchamp, the king's carver
and constable of the castle. Charges were made against members of
Duke Humphrey's household in 1447, not only that they intended to
make the duke king, but that it was planned to rescue Eleanor and
make her queen. Her presence at Beaumaris, when Richard duke of
York landed there in early September 1450, on his unbidden return
from Ireland, may well have been a factor in prompting the decision
to send household men to oppose him. Feared as a possible source of
future discontent, even as a threat to Henry's throne, the hapless
Eleanor was also a martyr to the rights of women. Her final sentence
for treason had been decreed by Henry without any trial by a duly
constituted, secular court of law. This caused much apprehension, on
a wider if less exalted issue, so much so that the next parliament in
1442, in a petition introduced into the Commons House, appealed to
Magna Carta on behalf of such defenceless women in general and
ensured that in future, but not retrospectively, peeresses in their own
right, or as wives of their husbands, were guaranteed the same trial
by their peerage, for charges of felony and treason, as was enjoyed by
their husbands.[69]

Another over-reaction to an alleged personal attack occurred in 1444
when careless talk brought a charge of treason upon the head of the
abbot of Reading's bailiff, Thomas Carver. He had ventured to contrast the unmartial Henry unfavourably with the valiant French
dauphin, then leading his father's armies in Gascony; all they had in
common, he said, was their age.[70] The Truce of Tours was then in
the making. Six years or more had passed since the king had attained
his official majority, and continued English losses in Gascony and
central France had culminated in the failure of a major expedition in
1443, led not by the king but by the duke of Somerset. Throughout
the shires, down at least to the level of such lesser gentry where few
can have been without neighbours or friends who had served in France,
there was much disappointment and bitterness. Now at this small verbal
sign of discontent, a massive judicial exercise was mounted to secure
an exemplary sentence and to strike terror into eastern Berkshire, an
area prominent in the king's habitual perambulations. It was a 'sledge-
hammer to crack a nut'.[71] Carver's words resulted in successive special
commissions of inquiry, leading in turn to two separate trials, the first

[69] *R.P.*, V, 56.
[70] See below p. 161.
[71] For this and what follows see C. A. F. Meekings, 'Thomas Kerver's Case', *E.H.R.*,
XC (1975), 331–45.

in King's Bench, which rightly failed to secure a conviction on such unsubstantial grounds, the second under an oyer and terminer commission, with sharpened charges, which finally produced the required result: conviction for imagining Henry's death and for seeking to accomplish it by the incitement of others! The special commissions were carefully staffed by household men,[72] three of the juries of inquisition employed had as their foreman William Staverton, a yeoman of the chamber. The victim was not only removed from the Tower in July to confinement in Wallingford castle, under the charge of its constable, Suffolk, the household steward, but immediately returned there after being cut down from the gallows, under escort of John Say, a trusted yeoman of the chamber. His exemplary punishment across twenty miles of Berkshire, the last three of these dragged either on a hurdle or at a horse's tail, was abruptly terminated only at the very moment of death by an eagle signet writ, signed by Henry in his lodge in the park at Windsor on 4 August 1444. This extraordinary writ ordered the pardon to be kept secret so that the punishment could shine forth as a deterrent 'even to those nearest to the king in blood'.

The most sinister event of all in the 1440s was the public degradation and death of the man who was indeed the nearest in blood to the king, the duke of Gloucester himself, at Bury St Edmunds in February 1447.[73] One chronicler described it as treason against the victim, rather than against the king.[74] According to another source Henry had previously forbidden his uncle his presence from about 1445 or 1446, and had fortified himself with armed guards against him.[75] This might be regarded simply as a projection back in time of the actual situation early in 1447, except that Abbot Wheathampstead, when describing later persistent attempts to clear the duke's name, which Henry persistently refused to accept, also asserted that the king

---

[72] The first by the lawyer William Tresham, king's servant retained at £20 a year, later chancellor of the duchy of Lancaster, several times Speaker of the Commons, Sir Thomas Stanley, controller of the household, John Noreys of Bray, Berks., squire of the body and Thomas Browne, king's squire, lawyer, later under-treasurer of England; the second by the two Chief Justices, the earl of Suffolk, king's household steward, Sir Thomas Stanley and John Noreys again and Richard Restwold of Sonning, Berks., king's squire and justice of the peace.

[73] Sources for the death of Gloucester, of which there is no good modern account, are: J. A. Giles's Chronicle, 33–4, Gregory's Chronicle, 187–8, The Brut, ed. F. T. Brie (E.E.T.S.), 512–13, Benet's Chronicle, 192–3, J. S. Davies's Chronicle, 62–3 and John Fox's memoranda there printed, 116–18, Chronicle of London, ed. Kingsford, 157–8, J. Gairdner's Three Fifteenth-Century Chronicles ('A Short English Chronicle'), 65, Bale's Chronicle, in Six Town Chronicles, ed. Flenley 121–2 and Rawlinson B 355, ibid., 104. Also Foedera, XI, 178 and E.H.R. XXIX (1914), 513 (Hatfield MS 281, ed. C. L. Kingsford), H. Ellis, Letters 2nd series, I, 108.

[74] 'A Short English Chronicle' in Three Fifteenth-Century Chronicles (ed. Gairdner), 65.

[75] Giles's Chronicle.

himself became convinced that his uncle and heir presumptive was himself secretly and assiduously labouring to encompass his death and to usurp the throne.[76] Henry first conceived these suspicions through a bishop who revealed to him something he had heard in the confessional.[77]

On 25 September 1446 summonses to a council meeting for 11 October were sent out from the royal court, then at Marlow, to twelve councillors. It was to assemble to discuss business for a new parliament, although the last one was but five months dispersed, and especially to plan Henry's intended 'personal convention with our uncle of France'. Gloucester and York were notable omissions from the list of summonses.[78] When Henry was returning to Windsor, late in January 1447, from a progress which had taken him as far as Southampton, he wrote from Alresford to the chancellor about the coming parliament. Its venue had already been fixed for Cambridge and then changed to Winchester because of a pestilence there. But now all those concerned were to be speedily informed that 'we now be fully deliberated and advised that our said parliament shall be holden at our town of St Edmunds Bury'.[79] Three years later it was already believed that the principal intended business of this parliament, the destruction of Gloucester, had been finally fixed on by Henry to take place at Bury on the advice of Suffolk, in country where he was most powerful.[80] Henry had decided upon his uncle's destruction. One chronicler, who accurately lists the places of Henry's nights' lodgings at Cambridge, Newmarket and Royston on the way, noted the unusually large guard which now surrounded him day and night, for fear of his uncle. Duke Humphrey was in fact coming innocently to the parliament as bidden, intending, it was said, to plead with his nephew on behalf of the incarcerated Eleanor.[81]

The parliament which assembled there in Henry's presence in the abbey refectory on Friday 10 February first heard the chancellor preach

---

[76] *Registrum*, I (R.S., 1872), 179.

[77] Lines in a poem entitled 'On the mutability of worldly changes' printed by C. L. Kingsford in *English Historical Literature*, 395–7.

[78] P.R.O., E.28/77/3: writs to Cardinal Kemp, the bishops of Norwich, Bath, Rochester and Lincoln, the dukes of Exeter and Buckingham, Lords Cromwell and Hungerford, Sir John Stourton, the marquises of Dorset and Suffolk.

[79] P.R.O., C.81/1370/41.

[80] The earliest allegation that he had been murdered was in the manifesto of the Cade rebels in June 1450: he had died as a result of the accusation of one false traitor whereas Suffolk, impeached by the Commons representing 24,000 of the king's good subjects, might not be put to death by lawful means as he should have been (*Three Fifteenth-Century Chronicles*, 95, 97): cf. the petition for the attainder of the dead Suffolk submitted in the parliament which assembled on 6 November 1450 (*R.P.*, V, 226).

[81] 'Brief Notes' (MS Lambeth 448) in *Three Fifteenth-Century Chronicles*, 149–50.

a pertinent sermon on the theme of good and bad councillors to the text: 'To the counsellors of peace is joy.'[82] No business ultimately appeared on its roll concerning the Gloucesters, except an act to debar the duchess, 'for her great misgovernance', from receiving any dower or jointure from the dead Humphrey's lands.[83] The suspicion must be strong that these lands were previously bespoke, judging by the indecent haste with which they began to be granted to the queen, the king's foundations and members of the royal household on 23 February, the very day of the duke's death.[84] The chroniclers also noted the unusual guard of armed men kept about the town 'secretly commanded to watch for safety of the king's person', and lords riding thither 'with great power as they should have ridden to war'. Gloucester arrived on Saturday 18 February, with a household retinue of some eighty men, no great size for his rank, as he had been ordered to do. He was met by Sir John Stourton and Sir Thomas Stanley, the treasurer and controller of the royal household, and ordered straight to his lodgings, without being given access to the king. After dinner, at Henry's command, he was placed under arrest there by the Constable of England, Viscount Beaumont, the duke of Buckingham, the marquis of Dorset, the earl of Salisbury and Lord Sudeley, and put in the charge of Thomas Calbrose, sergeant-at-arms, and two yeomen of the chamber, Bartholomew Halley and Thomas Pulford. Later that day a progressive arrest of some fifty members of his entourage began, which continued until Shrove Tuesday 21 February. They were despatched to widely scattered places, some to the Tower, some to Winchester, some to Nottingham, some to Northampton. On 23 February the duke died, and his body, which exhibited no signs of violence, was exposed for viewing by the whole parliament next day. The earliest accounts make no mention of foul play. It was said, and it was most likely true, that he died of sheer depression and despair at being prevented from appearing there to identify his accusers and to answer the charges of treason preferred against him. Again, no record of these charges remains, though it is alleged that Henry especially feared him because Humphrey would have done his utmost to prevent Henry's surrender of Maine and Anjou, at that time so crucial to the furtherance of his peace policy.

It is understandable that such an arrest should have prostrated the prince who is remembered as the good Duke Humphrey. Even though he was given this title by posterity principally as the opponent of the

[82] *R.P.*, V, 128 (Proverbs, XL, 20).

[83] *R.P.*, V, 135.

[84] Ramsay, *Lancaster and York*, II, 75, 77, citing *Foedera*, XL, 155 and *R.P.*, V, 132, 133, the earliest being a grant of Baynard's Castle to King's College, Cambridge that day.

unsuccessful policies of Henry and his agents, this appellation does suggest qualities hoped for and revered in a prince of the blood, which were so conspicuously lacking in his nephew the king. He had the adventurous spirit and courage of his Lancastrian forbears and, had he not been overshadowed and constrained by Bedford and Beaufort, he might have matured into a respected elder statesman. His fundamental loyalty to his nephew cannot be doubted and now that it is known that Humphrey really was designated regent of England by Henry V in his will one has more sympathy for and understanding of his resentment and frustration at his failure to be accepted in that position. As the only surviving prince of the Lancastrian blood royal after 1435 he alone was sufficiently powerful and courageous openly to oppose the haphazard, ignominious peace policies of Henry and his queen from 1445. It was for this, not treason, that he was unworthily attacked at Bury St Edmunds. In view of the way his duchess Eleanor was being punished for her foolishness it is not surprising that he should have despaired at his arrest. It was a mortal blow that his years of loyalty and service were rewarded by such a despicable attack on his honour.

Of the members of Gloucester's household, his bastard son Arthur, Sir Roger Chamberlain, Richard Middleton esquire, Thomas Herbert esquire, Richard Neadham, a London mercer in Gloucester's service, and four others unnamed, were finally indicted before the marquis of Suffolk and others at Dartford on 8 July 1447, charged with conspiring at Greenwich, and assembling there on 11 February, in strength, to march to Bury, to kill the king and to make Gloucester and Eleanor king and queen, maintaining that they had the support of a great part of the people of England. Sentenced for high treason on 12 July and taken to the Marshalsea, the King's Bench prison in Southwark, they were drawn from St George's Fields on 14 July, over London Bridge to Tyburn, tied to hurdles and clad in velvet doublets, the bastard Arthur with a gold cross held between his manacles, all loudly protesting their innocence of treason. This was an unpleasant and unpopular sight for the London populace and disturbing for a French peace delegation, who also witnessed it. Hanged, cut down alive, stripped for quartering and beheading, and the knife put to their throats, they were spared by the last minute appearance of Suffolk bearing Henry's pardon, granted not on the merits of the case but in honour of the pope's Eton indulgences at the approaching Feast of the Assumption. In it was included the same warning, as in Thomas Carver's case, to those even nearest in blood to the king, not to presume on Henry's mercy for any comparable behaviour.

Such was the nature of the domestic history of England in the 1440s, with the crown reduced to the level of faction in the hands of an ineffective king who often appeared unable to comprehend the likely consequences of his actions. Henry was a dangerous compound of forcefulness and weakness, unable to establish a firm, purposeful grip on the government of the realm, but willing and able to destroy his uncle and heir presumptive who opposed his misguided policies, on spurious charges of planning to usurp the throne. Some modern historians have discerned in the uncontrolled feuding of the 1440s the seed-bed of the civil wars which sprang up in the following decade. However, near-contemporary narrative accounts of these years which are fairly plentiful, while full of the misfortunes of the Gloucesters, make no mention of the unregulated disputes of the nobility and gentry which are alleged to have escalated into civil war.[85] The greatest single interest for all of them was the conduct of the war in France and the fate of Henry's other kingdom; the truce, the king's marriage, the intermittent peace negotiations and controversies over English-held Anjou and Maine, leading to military defeats and national disaster. It therefore comes as no surprise to discover that the earliest attempt to deduce cause and effect for the troubles of the next decade from the depressing events of the 1440s looked not to conditions within the kingdom of England but to the affairs of Henry's French kingdom. This is an exposition in the continuation of the Brut chronicle to 1461, written up in its final form between 1464 and 1470,[86] which Caxton selected for his 1480 edition of the chronicles of England. Adopted by Shakespeare through the medium of the Tudor chroniclers, Hall and Hollinshed, it thus provided the inspiration for the crucial final scene of his *Henry VI* Part 1 and the opening scene of *Henry VI* Part 2 which together set the stage for Shakespeare's ensuing immortal version of the Wars of the Roses. This unknown continuator of the Brut deduced that Henry never prospered from 1445; fortune then turned against him in Normandy, France, Gascony and England, because he broke a marriage contract already concluded with the sister of the powerful and wealthy count of Armagnac in favour of a marriage with Margaret, the daughter of the impoverished duke of Anjou, surrendering to the French the English-held counties of Anjou and Maine, which opened the door for the conquest of Normandy. All this was done for no *quid pro quo* whatsoever, except his dowerless bride. Moreover, Henry squandered a whole fifteenth and tenth simply on the cost of bringing this penniless queen over to England. Great princes ought to keep

[85] This includes the Brut continuation, Giles's Chronicle, John Benet's Chronicle, Bale's Chronicle and Rawlinson B 355 ed. R. Flenley in *Six Town Chronicles*, Gregory's Chronicle, *Chronicles of London*, ed. C. L. Kingsford, *A Chronicle of London*, ed. N. H. Nicolas, a Short English Chronicle and the Brief Latin Chronicle, both in *Three Fifteenth-Century Chronicles*, ed. James Gairdner and *An English Chronicle*, ed. J. S. Davies.
[86] C. L. Kingsford, *English Historical Literature*, 119.

their promises and by their policies augment and conserve the resources of the realm, not deplete them. Consequent troubles within the kingdom of England itself began to show from the moment when the noble duke of Gloucester was destroyed at Bury St Edmunds in 1447, because he would have prevented the delivery of Anjou and Maine to the French king. The commons of the realm began to murmur and finally rebelled against such folly and injustice, the loss of Normandy and Gascony ensued, the lords of the realm were split over the issue, the king was deposed and his queen and her son forced to flee to Scotland and then to France, to take refuge back in the family lands from which she had first emerged in 1445 to trouble England.[87] This ancient, reasoned exposition of the downfall of the House of Lancaster, which looked for and found cause and effect in the conduct of war and diplomacy rather than in domestic feudings and disorders, serious as these may have been, in spite of its obvious crudities and inaccuracies, first showed real insight into the relationship between Henry's personal rule from 1437 to 1450 and the events of the next decade.

After a brief look at Henry as the founder of Eton and King's Colleges it therefore remains to examine his conduct of war and diplomacy in order to give that full picture of his personal rule to 1450 without which no sound understanding of the events of the 1450s can possibly be attained.

[87] *The Brut*, 511–13.

Chapter 8

THE FOUNDER OF ETON AND KING'S

The story of the two royal institutions of Eton College and King's College, Cambridge, is obviously very germane to a biography of Henry VI. The terms of their foundation, and their history during the period while their founder exercised personal control over them, can tell us much about the nature and purposes of the man who chose to devote a major part of the resources of the English crown to their creation. They belong to the early stages of his personal rule and the earliest documents of Eton College reveal that, far from shrinking from affairs of state as he is represented in the tradition of early-Tudor hagiography, the young king regarded his assumption of the government of the realm in both his kingdoms in 1437 as cause for celebration and the expression of gratitude to his creator. That was why he founded Eton. It was his wish and intention to mark the attainment of his majority rule with a distinctive, commemorative act which would make a unique contribution to the record of monasteries and great churches built by his forbears,[1] as a gift to God, that He might direct all his future actions as king.[2] This was how he rationalized his foundation of Eton College in letters patent of 1440, and again in 1446, when he had to relieve the parishioners of Eton of the heavy burdens which he had unwittingly imposed upon them by appropriating their church and making it collegiate to further his great symbolic design.

Execution of this intention to mark his attainment of power in this fashion was somewhat slow in appearing; his first specific step was to purchase the advowson of the parish church of Eton and two houses to the north of the churchyard in August 1440,[3] followed by a declaration of intent to found a college of priests there on 12 September.[4]

---

[1] Preamble of letters patent for the foundation of Eton College dated at Sheen 11 October 1440. *Correspondence of Thomas Bekynton*, ed. G. Williams (R.S., 1872), II, 279–85.

[2] Eton College Charter of 17 July 1446 printed by M. R. James in *Etoniana*, April 1920, 387.

[3] R. Willis and J. W. Clark, *The Architectural History of the University of Cambridge ... and Eton* (C.U.P., 1886), I, 313–14, citing Eton College muniments.

[4] *Correspondence of Bekynton*, II, 287–90.

The same day he enfeoffed twelve feoffees with all the possessions of alien priories in England, Wales and the Marches of Wales, with reversion of all grants hitherto made from them, in order to provide the initial means to endow his new college.[5] Three of these same feoffees, together with the canonist William Lyndwood, keeper of the privy seal, were also nominated by William Alnwick, bishop of Lincoln, within whose diocese Eton lay, as his commissaries to convert the parochial church into a collegiate one, to receive the rector's resignation and to install a provost in his place.[6] Thomas Beckington, Henry's secretary, was involved in the plan in four different capacities: as archdeacon of Buckingham, surrendering his archidiaconal jurisdiction over the church and parish to the new provost, as Henry's feoffee, as his bishop's commissary and as Henry's secretary, conducting negotiations with his agents in Rome to secure the unprecedented papal privileges which the young king required for his new foundation. Perhaps it was he, rather than Archbishop Chichele, who first sowed the seed in the king's mind.

This first Eton foundation of 11 October 1440 was to consist of a provost, 10 priests, 4 clerks, 6 choristers, 25 poor scholars to learn grammar under a schoolmaster, who was also to be bound to teach any others who would come to him from anywhere in England free of charge, and 25 paupers and enfeebled men, whose purpose was to pray for Henry, for the souls of his parents, his forbears and all faithful departed, and for his own soul in due course. The college was licensed to acquire the considerable income of 1,000 marks ($£666$ 13s 4d) *per annum*.[7] He declared that he had selected this old parish church to raise it from poverty to distinction because it was so near to his birthplace and already dedicated to the incomparable festival of the Assumption of the Blessed Virgin, whom he especially delighted to honour.[8]

At about the same time, on 14 September 1440, royal commissioners

---

[5] P.R.O., E.28/65/4: Henry Chichele, archbishop of Canterbury, John Stafford the chancellor and bishop of Bath, John Lowe, bishop of St Asaph, William Aiscough, the king's confessor and bishop of Salisbury, Suffolk, John Somerset, Thomas Beckington, the king's secretary, Richard Andrew, first Warden of All Souls and destined to be Beckington's successor in office, Adam Moleyns, the two household squires John Hampton and James Fiennes and the lawyer and Speaker of the House of Commons, William Tresham (their appointment on 12 September being indicated in this petition for letters patent under the great seal without charge, granted under the sign manual and signet in the presence of Suffolk and Moleyns and minuted by Beckington).

[6] *Correspondence of Bekynton*, II, 274–8: Aiscough, Beckington and Andrew.

[7] *Ibid.*, 279–85.

[8] *Etoniana*, April 1920, 387.

acquired for Henry land at Cambridge[9] to found a college of a rector and twelve scholars, or more or less according to the resources available, on the site subsequently known as the Old Court of King's College, to be licensed to acquire land and advowsons worth £200 *per annum*. This house was to be called the Royal College of Saint Nicholas, his birthday saint, to be devoted to the extirpation of the heresy then current in England, to the augmentation of the priesthood and the adornment of holy mother church. It was quite unconnected with Eton, except that both were to be endowed with alien priory lands, and it was not singled out, as in the case of Eton, to be the memorial of his assumption of the governance of the realm. Both these foundations had more in common with earlier fifteenth-century collegiate churches and university colleges than with those undoubted models for their subsequent refoundation, William Wykeham's grand twin pioneering educational institutions of 1382, Winchester School and New College, Oxford.[10] Building materials were being prepared for the Cambridge college from 14 February 1441 and Henry himself laid the foundation there on Passion Sunday, 2 April 1441. The source of this information also states that he had then already performed a similar ceremony for the new minster intended to replace the parish church at Eton, but there is no evidence of building operations there, either repairs, alterations or new construction, until 3 July 1441.[11]

Henry's initial plan for his Eton foundation thus did not envisage its development principally as an educational institution. His original prime concern was to obtain for the appropriated church from the pope the maximum possible spiritual privileges and immunities. To this end a second envoy, Richard Chester, was sent out to join his permanent proctor in Rome, Andrew Hulse, in October 1440, followed within a few months by a third, Richard Caunton. Between them they secured papal confirmation of the foundation and the same indulgences for a visit to Eton on the feast of the Assumption as for a visit to

[9] J. Saltmarsh, 'King's College', in *V.C.H. Cambridge*, III (1959), 376, citing King's College muniments; *Arch. Hist.*, I, 317–18. The Commissioners were John Fray, Chief Baron of the Exchequer, Master John Somerset, here described as of the exchequer and John Langton, Chancellor of the University. There is a plan of the Old Court in *Arch. Hist.*, I, 322. The refoundation charter of 1443 (J. Heywood and T. Wright, *The Ancient Laws of the Fifteenth Century for King's College Cambridge and ... Eton College*, [London 1850], 1–13), recites the foundation charter of 12 February 1441 (*C.P.R. 1436–41*, 521–3).

[10] E. F. Jacob, *Archbishop Henry Chichele* (London 1967), 87–90; Nicholas Orme, *English Schools in the Middle Ages* (London 1973), 198; *V.C.H. Northamptonshire*, II, 170–7 (Fotheringay, 1411), 177–9 (Higham Ferrers, 1422).

[11] *Arch. Hist.*, I, 317, 321–3 quoting verses in King's College muniments. John Capgrave, *Liber de Illustribus Henricis*, ed. F. C. Hingeston (R.S., 1858), 133 is the other authority for Henry's performance of the Eton ceremony, but he gives no date.

St Peter ad Vincula in Rome on the first day of August. A fourth
envoy, Vincent Clement, succeeded in getting these extended in 1442
for Henry's lifetime, to cover plenary remission of sins, and powers for
the provost to hear confessions and give full absolution to the personnel
of the college. But Henry was still not satisfied. The hapless Clement
was constantly in fear that failure might blight his career by losing
him the royal favour, as he laboured mightily for a further twelve
months from May 1443 to obtain in perpetuity for Eton the power
to grant these indulgences. Secretary Beckington urged upon him that
the stream of instructions he sent to him were in great part framed
and dictated by Henry himself. Henry daily asked him when would
he have news of Master Vincent; when would his letters arrive? The
clause in perpetuity, costing at least one thousand ducats, was finally
obtained in a bull dated 11 May 1444.[12] Such was Henry's delight
as 15 August, the feast of the Assumption, approached that year, that
he felt moved to perform a specific act of gratitude for it. He spared
the life of Thomas Carver, gentleman, of Reading, who on 3 August
was condemned to a traitor's death for derogatory remarks made about
Henry's kingship.[13] It was the receipt of yet another papal bull in
1447, extending seven years' and seven lents' indulgences for a visit
to the Eton shrines to cover further feast days, which occasioned his
ultimate release. Gratitude for this final bull of 1447 also caused Henry
to spare the lives of members of Duke Humphrey's household who had
been charged with conspiring to depose him.[14] These indulgences were
expected to spread the fame of the new foundation far and wide. In
1445, in anticipation of a great concourse of pilgrims, the college hired
thirty beds for confessors and other servants, while an addition which
Henry later made to the statutes required all fellows of the college to
take an oath that if they were subsequently raised to the episcopate
they would always return to Eton every year to assist at the feast of
the Assumption of the Blessed Virgin.[15]

Henry later referred to the establishment of his two remodelled, and
interdependent, royal colleges in their final forms as 'the primer
notable work purposed by me after that I ... took unto myself the

[12] *Correspondence of Bekynton*, I, lxxxi–lxxxviii and letters and bulls cited there.
[13] P.R.O., C.81/1370/13 dated 4 August 1444 under the sign manual.
[14] P.R.O., C.81/1370/52 dated 25 August 1447 under the sign manual addressed
to the chancellor for the constable of the castle, replacing a recent similar writ to the
Lord Chief Justice Fortescue who had sentenced him but who had replied that he
had no power to order Carver's release. H. C. Maxwell Lyte, *History of Eton College*
(London, 4th edn 1911), 24, citing Patent Roll 25 Hen. VI pt. 2 m.18 and m.12,
the second entry being printed in *Foedera*. The bull is printed in *Correspondence of Bekynton*,
II, 309–11, misdated 1446.
[15] Maxwell Lyte, *op. cit.*, 25; *Anc. Laws*, 619–20.

rule of my said Realms'.[16] Yet the development of these two institutions had from the beginning mirrored frequent changes of purpose and ambition. There is in fact no evidence of such a dual determination in the initial foundations of 1440–1. The seeds of a plan to transform them both in pattern, and to link them into imitations of the twin Wykehamist foundations, were probably sown when he paid his first of many visits to the Winchester College from 5 to 7 August 1441.[17] As late as 3 February 1441 he had granted some lands of the Ogbourne alien priory in frankalmoign to support five scholars at Oxford, provided they had been nurtured in grammar at Eton.[18] Indeed, one historian of Eton College has asserted that the statutes of the initial foundation, which William Wainfleet swore to keep at his installation as provost of Eton on 21 December 1443, provided for scholars at Oxford, not Cambridge.[19] This would indeed have been a more logical development as the King's Hall at Cambridge, as endowed by Edward II, already existed to provide education for the children of the royal household chapel. The details of these earliest Eton statutes cannot now be known, since they are no longer extant,[20] but it is clear that on 10 July 1443 the statutes for the first foundation of King's College, which were still being compiled by William Alnwick, bishop of Lincoln, William Aiscough, bishop of Salisbury and William Lyndwood, the canonist and keeper of the privy seal, John Somerset and John Langton, were not completed when Henry relieved them of their duties and took the task into his own hands. This date is important as the first firm evidence of the radical change of plan,[21] an intention confirmed by the conclusion of a quadripartite pact of perpetual alliance for mutual support in lawsuits between Winchester College, New College, Eton and King's on 1 July 1444.[22] The acquisition of a new site for King's,

[16] Henry's 'will' or intention of 1448 in *Arch. Hist.*, I, 353, from Eton College records Vol. 39/75.

[17] Subsequently in 1444, 1445, 1446, 1447, 1449 (twice), 1451, 1452 (see Itinerary).

[18] *C.P.R., 1441–1446*, 46.

[19] A. F. Leach, 'Eton College' in *V.C.H. Buckinghamshire*, II, 153, with no reference given, but he was discussing the incident described rather differently by Maxwell Lyte, *op. cit.*, 18, on the authority of Eton College muniments Drawer 46 no. 1, now E.C.R. 54/10. An early reference to Wainfleet, the former headmaster of Winchester, as Provost is in P.R.O., E.28/71 dated 30 September 1442.

[20] They are not the much annotated and altered copy, mentioned in Heywood and Wright *op. cit.*, xxxiii–xxxiv, as disappearing from the library of St John's College, Cambridge in the early eighteenth century, which has recently been rediscovered and donated to Eton College by St John's. These date from July 1446, if not earlier, but are of the second foundation.

[21] Saltmarsh, *op. cit.*, 377, quoting the second foundation charter of King's College printed in *Anc. Laws*, I.

[22] Printed by M. E. C. Walcott, *William of Wykeham and his Colleges* (1852), 141–3, cited by Saltmarsh, *loc. cit.*

six or seven times the size of the original and to the south of it, was begun on 26 August 1443,[23] causing a clearance of buildings and closing of thoroughfares in the heart of Cambridge the like of which had not been seen since William the Conqueror cleared the site for his castle there.[24] The earliest specific statement that King's was now to be a foundation of 70 fellows and scholars, not 12, with an establishment of 10 secular priests, 6 clerks and 16 choristers for the chapel, dates from 1445.[25] At Eton the acquisition of small properties adjacent to the original church and churchyard site had proceeded piecemeal, but likewise a major addition of over eleven acres was made on 9 August 1443,[26] though the date of the enlarged Eton foundation of 70 scholars, with the addition of an usher to assist the schoolmaster, 10 extra priests, 6 more clerks, 10 more boy choristers and a reduction from 25 almsmen to 13 weak, old, single men, or disabled young paupers,[27] is not exactly known.

Henry's personal assumption of responsibility for new statutes for King's College hardly produced quick results and when these did ultimately emerge they turned out to be almost entirely *verbatim* copies of the Wykehamist statutes of 1382. These statutes gave the rector his new title of provost and changed the name of the college to the Royal College of the Blessed Mary and Saint Nicholas, specifically because of the new affiliation to Eton.[28] They were delivered to King's in 1447 by a commission consisting of the marquis of Suffolk, Bishop Alnwick, Bishop Lyhert of Norwich, Beckington, now bishop of Bath and Wells, Richard Andrew, his successor as Henry's secretary, and possibly Aiscough. The first and only rector and first provost since the 1443 foundation, William Millington, found some of them so objectionable that he refused to swear obedience to them and was forced to resign.[29] The mention of prayers for Wainfleet as bishop of Winchester in the comparable Eton statutes indicates that they also cannot be earlier than 1447. The most notable differences between the new Eton statutes and the Winchester statutes from which they were copied arose from the contrast between a mere college chapel at Winchester and the vast collegiate church of the royal foundation envisaged at Eton; also in the greater emphasis at Eton on the priestly vocation of the

---

[23] *Arch. Hist.*, I, 337, Saltmarsh, *op. cit.*, 377, 386.

[24] *Ibid.*, 386.

[25] *Ibid.*, citing *Papal Letters 1431–1447*, 479.

[26] *Arch. Hist.*, 315–16.

[27] *Anc. Laws.*, 478, 540, 541, 601.

[28] *Ibid.*, 6–7.

[29] *Correspondence of Bekynton*, II, 159, 164, 171, where Suffolk is described as Great Chamberlain of England, an office he only received after the death of Duke Humphrey in 1447; Saltmarsh, *op. cit.*, 378.

70 scholars, together with a rigid insistence that they should not be villein born or illegitimate, have visible bodily defects or any incurable disease, and that immediate expulsion should fall on any who were subsequently discovered to have got in under false pretences on any of these points. The intended grandiose scale of Eton is further indicated by a proposed addition to the somewhat earlier 'St John's College' version of these statutes,[30] one apparently never adopted, that an annual Maundy distribution there should be made to one thousand paupers!

Henry had intended personally to lay the foundation stone of his first chapel at King's College, Cambridge, next to the Old Court, on 29 September 1444, but because of pestilence in Cambridge he finally sent Suffolk to do it instead.[31] After his change of plan much of the original building design was abandoned, in anticipation that the college would soon occupy its grander new home, though owing to the misfortunes which befell their founder from 1461 this original chapel survived until 1536 and the Old Court buildings, in the event, provided the major part of the college's living accommodation until well into the eighteenth century.[32] On St James's Day, 25 July 1446, Henry did lay the first stone of his second chapel, the beginning of the existing splendid King's College building,[33] which was to form the northern side of a magnificent new quadrangle of unprecedented size, with a smaller court of domestic offices and a great cloistered cemetery between the college and the river, with a lofty four-storied bell and muniment tower in the centre of its western side. The details of the plan were all minutely specified in Henry's 'will' of 1448, to be financed by annual payments of £1,000 from the duchy of Lancaster revenues, but from 1455 funds began to dry up and by 1461 only the eastern range of the great quadrangle had been started and raised several feet above ground for most of its length, with more substantial parts of two turrets standing at its northern end. The roofless shell of the great chapel then stood sixty or seventy feet high at the east end, sloping down to seven or eight feet westwards, with only two side chapels completed.[34] Within these buildings the full complement of fellows and scholars was reached in 1451 and the income of the college exceeded £1,000 a year by the

---

[30] See above p. 139 n. 20.

[31] Saltmarsh, 378 note 32, where he provides a cogent explanation of why the reference in the register of Abbot Curteys of Bury St Edmunds to the event refers to this date and to the *first* chapel.

[32] Saltmarsh, 388.

[33] Verses from King's College Muniments Box M.9. f. 16a cited by Saltmarsh, 378, and printed by Willis and Clark, *Arch. Hist.*, I, 465; *R.P.*, V, 164 a.

[34] Saltmarsh, 389, deduced from the evidence of the kind of stone used only during Henry's reign, detailed by Willis & Clark, *Arch. Hist.*, I, 486–9.

time of Henry's deposition, when it possessed lands in twenty-one
counties by royal grant.[35]

More frequent, drastic changes of plan dogged the construction of
the Eton college minster, which remained throughout the very heart
of all Henry's interests and ambitions for his foundations. The original
draft from his 'will' or intention of 12 March 1448 contained a
specific comparison of his then intended measurements for the Eton
minster choir with the chapel of New College (called Winchester
College), Oxford, expressing Henry's satisfaction in its superiority over
the Wykehamist design. But this 'will', for all its solemnity, tone of
finality and no less than five separate impressive royal seals,[36] was soon
altered. Had it been carried out it would have involved the complete
demolition of the northern and eastern sides of the domestic cloister
buildings which had already been constructed.[37] Not that this in itself
would have been any obstacle to Henry's burgeoning ambitions. Within
the next nine months he decided further to enlarge the minster, but
this in such a way as to involve the demolition of all the seven years'
continuous work already done on that building, since he now required
both the choir and nave to be lengthened by fifteen feet each and
widened by three feet, with the aisles widened by one foot. This wanton
sacrifice was indeed carried out, but only after Henry had yet again
changed his mind, to a plan on an even grander scale. In January
1449 he sent the Eton clerk of works, Roger Keys, with three servants,
on a nine-day tour to measure the choirs and naves of Salisbury
and Winchester cathedrals. The result was a third and final design,[38]
with the Eton minster choir increased by a further twenty-two feet in
length and a further five feet in width, and the nave by a staggering
further thirty-nine feet and five feet respectively. The present building
at Eton is the choir only of this ultimate, vast design, with a small
ante-chapel added later, *in lieu* of a nave, by Wainfleet at his own
expense to accommodate the parishioners as a stop gap completion
when royal funds ran out. Had the whole ever been completed, across
the Eton High Street, it would have been comparable to any of the
medieval cathedrals, with a nave as long as Lincoln's, and would have
been exceeded in width only by York Minster, the whole being thirty
feet longer than the comparable design for King's College chapel as
it now stands.[39]

[35] Saltmarsh, 379.

[36] The duchy of Lancaster great seal (72mm) and signet of the eagle, the great seal
of England, the signet of arms and a unique seal (80mm) appointed for the use of
Henry's feoffees of those duchy lands now appropriated to the two foundations.

[37] Maxwell Lyte, *op. cit.*, 45.

[38] Eton College Records, Vol. 39/81, 'the kynges owne avyse', printed in *Arch. Hist.*,
I, 366–7.

[39] Maxwell Lyte, *op. cit.*, 48–9.

This final design required the demolition of the first choir, which was already being roofed, and its stalls constructed, from Michaelmas 1448. Only the foundations below ground were retained and a new start was made outside them. This was apparently done 'for dread of hurting and impairing of the said grounds', especially to be feared in view of an initial 'enhancing' or artificially raising of the site by some three feet as a precaution against floods.[40] This final rebuilding was begun in 1449[41] and understandable doubts about the foundations for the huge new structure provide a perfect explanation why Henry now sent a yeoman of the chamber to Wykeham's college at Winchester, which lay on a similar, potentially unstable river-side site, to obtain a sample of soil dug from its foundation, together with an account of what was found in the course of the necessary excavations. He had already had the Winchester buildings surveyed once before by a royal mason in July 1443, at the time of his previous major changes of plan.[42] This incident thus gives no support to the other more romantic explanation, hazarded by Leach and chiming in with the early-Tudor hagiographic portraits of Henry, that he was here seeking to transfer the spirit of Winchester to Eton by a symbolic mixing of the soils!

Thus Henry's achievements in brick and stone at Eton, by the time of his deposition, considerable as they were, would obviously have been very much greater still but for his frequent changes of plan and his destruction of a full seven year's work on his first new church in 1448, to make way for the huge replacement of which only the choir was ever to be built. The east window of this choir was ready to receive its iron-work in 1458-9, but the west end seems to have been still unfinished when Wainfleet resumed building at his own expense in 1469, and the roof had only just been completed in 1475.[43] Demolition of the old parish church in the cemetery to the south of the present chapel, itself repeatedly altered, enlarged and embellished to meet the needs of the new foundation during its protracted wait for its new church, could only be begun after 1476 when Wainfleet had added his small nave or ante-chapel for the use of the parishioners to Henry's choir.[44] £15,000–£16,000 had been spent on building, demolition and rebuilding by 1461.[45] Over one and a half million

[40] Diagram of this enhancing of different levels for the various buildings in Willis & Clark, *Arch. Hist.*, I, 364.

[41] *Ibid.*, 401–2.

[42] Winchester College Muniments 22123 (bursar's account roll for 1448–9) and information from Mr Peter Gwyn, archivist of the College, to whom I am indebted for the references and full transcript of the entry first printed by T. F. Kirby, *Annals of Winchester College* (London and Winchester 1892), 193.

[43] *Arch. Hist.*, I, 409, 428–9.

[44] Maxwell Lyte, *Eton College*, 74–5, *Arch. Hist.*, I, 388, 393–5.

[45] *Ibid.*, 405

bricks were delivered to the site between 1442 and 1444, with as many
as 140 pressed building workers employed at the peak time of 1442,
rising again to 118 in 1448, but from 1453 there was a considerable
accumulation of unused materials on the site and building operations
declined dramatically.[46]

It seems that the full complement of 70 poor scholars and 16
choristers was already reached by 1447 and when 15 scholar vacancies
were filled in 1453 a waiting list of a further 65 was compiled.[47] The
more modest domestic building in the college, all in brick, must clearly
have progressed much more rapidly by these dates than the stone
church building and did not suffer anything like the same delays and
set-backs occasioned by demolitions to make way for Henry's ever increasing, more ambitious plans. The north and east sides of the existing
cloister building (called the quadrant in the 'will') were built between
1443 and 1448 and the whole quadrant finished by 1459–60. The
ancient red brick range containing 'Lower School', with the dormitory
called 'Long Chamber' above, on the north side of School Yard, is
most probably the building where Beckington held his banquet in 1443,
after his consecration as bishop of Bath and Wells within the rising
walls of the first chapel. The 'almshouse', to house the poor men and
college servants, and the granary were finished in 1447; the hall, in
its present position on the southern side of the cloisters, was built between 1443 and 1450, but only after it had been converted to a new
design begun in 1447. A new kitchen was begun in 1449 and was being
floored in 1451.[48]

As is well known, evil days descended upon Eton, as upon King's,
in the founder's lifetime with Henry's deposition in 1461. This was not
a possibility which he had anticipated could occur before his death.
His final Eton statute was designed to provide against any drying up
of funds after his demise. This confirms in which portion of his twin
foundations his very heart and ambitions really lay. For when he
defined his absolute, irreducible minimum for the survival of the Eton
establishment, he considered the provision for scholars not worthy of
mention. The fact that he could contemplate that, in extremities, the
school would completely disappear, shows that he should not be considered primarily as an enlighted promoter of education. His final

---

[46] For details of the work force see Douglas Knoop and G. P. Jones, 'The Building
of Eton College 1442–1460', *Transactions of the Quatuor Coronati Lodge*, XLVI (1933),
70–114.

[47] Maxwell Lyte, *Eton College*, 20, 59.

[48] *Arch. Hist.*, I, 395, 430, 433, 439, 440, but contrast Leach in *V.C.H. Bucks.*, II,
155, where he states that there are doubts whether the present Long Chamber and
headmaster's and usher's chambers and the old Lower School beneath it were in the
school yard before the sixteenth century.

Eton statute provided for four chaplains, four clerks, of whom one should be skilled in playing the organ, and eight choristers. In this ultimate injunction, laid on the provost and fellows under the penalties of perjury, he required 400 marks *per annum*, or at the very least 300 marks, to be applied, before all other charges whatsoever, to the completion of the minster.[49] No such provision at the expense of all else was ever written into the King's College statutes.[50] From the windows of his birthplace, Henry's eyes were undoubtedly fixed on the most highly privileged, vast, projected minster, rising so slowly under his vacillating direction from the fields of Eton.[51] In spite of what was said in the early sixteenth century, when Henry VII was labouring for his canonization, one cannot doubt that if his own wishes had been fulfilled neither Chertsey nor Windsor nor Westminster, who squabbled over them, would have received his mortal remains. He would surely have been buried by choice in his most glorious and most privileged minster of the Assumption of Our Lady at Eton. The foundation of Eton and King's thus throws considerable light on the character and interests of the king. That he should choose this means to symbolize his assumption of power, rather than some martial exploit, sets the tone of his personal rule. His constant changes of plan, regardless of expense, show his impractical nature and lack of steadfast purpose. His ambition to surpass all other foundations in privileges and grandeur reveals the ostentatious nature of his piety. His slavish modelling of Eton and King's on Winchester and New College reveals no originality of concept, nor does his addition of scholars as a less important appendage suggest any Renaissance interest in learning. Nevertheless, Henry's foundations at Eton and King's were the only great achievements of his reign, so although his prime interest in them was not as centres of scholarship, it is just that these foundations, with their splendid buildings, should perpetuate his memory.

[49] *Anc. Laws*, 621-3.

[50] *Ibid.*, 167-9.

[51] On 12 July 1455, no doubt appreciating his own incapacity, though ostensibly because of pressing affairs of state, he resigned his hitherto personal oversight of the statutes of his two foundations to William Wainfleet and John Chedworth, bishop of Lincoln, for the rest of his life: *Anc. Laws*, 623-4, wrongly dated 1445.

Chapter 9

WAR AND PEACE: THE PROBLEMS OF NORMANDY AND GASCONY, 1437–1443

When Henry entered fully and without opposition into his peaceful and secure English inheritance in 1437 the problems facing his French inheritance were many, and its future uncertain. His uncle Bedford and the councils of the minority had perforce kept all alternatives for future action there open to him: war or peace, resolute defence of English Normandy, Calais and Gascony, or sustained military effort to complete the conquest; insistence on his title to the French throne and arms, or their relinquishment in return for some *quid pro quo*, perhaps the English-held lands in France in complete sovereignty, or even in homage to his uncle Charles VII. Undoubtedly Henry's own attitude to the problems of the English occupation and claims in France would henceforth be of paramount importance. Sad to say, the lack of consistent purpose, random changes of plan and undue susceptibility to influence by persons with wills stronger than his own, already revealed in his kingly acts at home and in the history of the royal foundations, were equally apparent in the affairs of his second kingdom. An account of these years shows that contradictory policies were pursued at the same time. Peace negotiations were continued, while preparations were made for war, Normandy and Gascony were considered separately, and yet were expected to act complementarily. The overall picture has to be built up gradually because it is crucial to an understanding of Henry and his reign. In foreign policy there is more evidence of Henry's personal involvement than in England and more positive indication of his thinking. His failures here were to have fundamental repercussions on his rule in England.

Moves for a new, comprehensive peace conference first arose at Gravelines in 1438, where attempts were being made to re-establish normal Anglo-Burgundian commercial relations. The duke of Burgundy initiated them, prompted by a deepening realization of how little he had gained, and how much he stood to lose, from his unilateral agreement with Charles VII at Arras in 1435. His chief agent was his third duchess, Isabel of Portugal, the grand-daughter of John of Gaunt, who, unlike her husband, proved acceptable to the English because of her Lancastrian blood. The English, of course, did not know that along with Burgundy's chancellor Nicholas Rolin and other influential Burgundian councillors she was already Charles VII's pensioner. He had successfully bribed her in 1435 at the Arras congress to act in the French interest.[1] Her English feelers for peace moves were made through her uncle Cardinal Henry Beaufort. Together these two succeeded in assembling a tripartite conference at Gravelines in June 1439 to which Henry gladly undertook to send a powerful delegation.[2] Its leader, Archbishop Kemp, received their official instructions from his own hands at Kennington on 21 May 1439. These were noteworthy chiefly for their rigid maintenance of his claim to the French throne and arms and for the almost complete absence of possible concessions, except for an expressed willingness to ransom the duke of Orleans for 100,000 marks.[3] But four days later Henry gave different, secret directions to his Beaufort great-uncle, making him his plenipotentiary with complete discretion to negotiate and conclude a binding agreement within the terms of his word-of-mouth instructions. Beaufort alone was told 'all the king's mind and intent as regards the crown'.[4] It may be that these secret instructions of 25 May 1439 were the very first step towards implementing the policy of peace by concession and compromise, leading to the truce and marriage of 1444–5 which came so disastrously to grief in 1450.

The conference warily assembled near Gravelines in an elaborate, isolated, temporary town of wooden and canvas pavillions, erected on the next best thing to neutral territory, an open site in the Calais march by the Gravelines road, at the Anglo-Burgundian frontier. Negotiations alternated with lavish displays of mutual hospitality, dominated by the duchess and the cardinal. Together with the duke of Orleans, who had been brought as far as Calais on parole by the English to assist in the attainment of peace, they were accepted as mediators between the French and English delegations.[5] The full extent of Beaufort's reserve powers was never disclosed, though they were real enough, because he was able on his own authority to purge the English instructions of some features which were most obnoxious to the French, for example, changing the insulting form of address for their king, 'Charles of Valois', to 'our adversary of France'. On 18 July, in a bid to break complete deadlock, the cardinal and the duchess took the actual negotiations into their own hands. According to what emerged in a final draft, and from what Beaufort subsequently told Henry's

[1] Richard Vaughan, *Philip the Good* (London 1970), 100–1, and references there to the work of Dr Thielemans.

[2] M. R. Thielemans, *Bourgogne et Angleterre*, 111–63; C. T. Allmand, 'The Anglo-French Negotiations of 1439', *B.I.H.R.*, XL (1967), 1–33; Richard Vaughan, *op. cit.*, 107–9.

[3] *P.P.C.*, V, 345–62.

[4] *Foedera*, X, 732–3, from French Roll 17 Hen. VI. m.6; *P.P.C.*, V, 361.

[5] Documents relating to the conference, mainly from the French side, are printed by C. T. Allmand in *Camden Miscellany XXIV* (Royal Historical Society, 1972), 79–149.

secretary Beckington, who was present throughout and subsequently wrote an account of the proceedings,[6] they agreed orally to the following proposals: a truce for thirty, twenty or fifteen years, on the basis of the territorial *status quo* in Normandy with its appurtenances and appendances, Calais and its marches, and Gascony, during which time Henry would cease to use the title of King of France. He might resume it at any time and renew the war, after giving a year's notice of his intentions. Permanent peace could be made at any point within the period of truce if Henry decided to make renunciation of the crown and to do homage for the lands he held. Charles VII should make no demand for homage from Henry meantime and the duke of Orleans should be released without ransom.

The task of agreeing and formulating these original oral proposals in writing proved formidable enough. The official English embassy understandably shied away from a first draft which, among other unacceptable points, left the precise extent of the lands to be held by Henry in homage to the decision of the French king and demanded prior renunciation of all the English conquests and of the claim to the French throne. For a long time Beaufort and the duchess simply could not agree in writing what they had orally understood, or misunderstood, from each other, even though the duchess was reduced to tears in the attempt (or tried to use tears as a weapon, Beckington was not sure which). On 29 July both sides finally agreed to an adjournment until 11 September, for the reference back to King Henry and to Charles VII of a final draft produced by the duchess with the assistance of the captive duke of Orleans. In spite of his plenipotentiary powers and secret instructions, this was not a package for which Beaufort was willing to accept full responsibility. Henry's assent had therefore to be publicly and formally given. Kemp was sent back to England to try it out on the young king.

According to Humphrey duke of Gloucester, the archbishop of York laboured mightily at Windsor to gain Henry's acceptance.[7] But this time Gloucester and the other lords of Henry's council, with the cardinal absent, persuaded him to send back a resounding disavowal, dated from Langley on 30 August, of any intention whatsoever to put his French title in abeyance. The cardinal's proposed terms in fact bore a remarkable likeness to the ones previously put forward on behalf of Charles VII by that Burgundian embassy to London in late September 1435 which had then been so furiously rejected.[8] Three main proposi-

---

[6] Printed in *P.P.C.*, V, 334–407.   [7] Stevenson, *Wars*, II, 446.

[8] Thielemans, *op. cit.*, 66, though the earlier offer had been better in that reasonable ransom was to be paid for Orleans and the impossibility of demanding homage from Henry VI in person after his crowning recognized. His heir was to do the homage and have the title of duke of Normandy.

9. Coinage of Henry VI. The two upper panels show (obverse and reverse, *left to right*) a gold noble, silver groat, half groat and penny from London and York; in the centre is a groat from the Calais mint which struck coins of the same type, weight, etc., as the English money. The two lower panels show an Anglo-Gallic gold salute from St Lô, a gold angelot from Paris, a silver grand blanc from Rouen and a billon denier tournois from Auxerre.

10(a). Obverse and reverse of the great silver seal of Henry VI (diameter 114 mm).

10(b). Henry VI's great seal for French affairs (obverse) (diameter 98 mm).

10(c). Five seals appended to the King's College, Cambridge, version of the king's 'will'. (*Left to right*) duchy of Lancaster great seàl (72 mm); signet of the eagle; great seal of England; signet of arms; a unique seal (80 mm) appointed for the use of Henry's feoffees of those duchy lands appropriated to his two foundations.

tions were now specifically selected for rejection as 'right unreasonable': temporary renunciation of the French title, release of the duke of Orleans without ransom, and restitution of dispossessed lay and ecclesiastical properties during the truce. A cogently argued, detailed and outspoken memorandum of advice, by that part of the council still in England, was appended to the answer to supply reasons for the rejection. Acceptance would 'show too great a simpleness and lack of foresight in him that accepteth it', because of the irreparable loss involved for Henry in damaged prestige, firmness and credibility of purpose and shaken legal title.[9] But the basic fear expressed in this council memorandum was of an insidious French reconquest of Normandy under cover of a truce. It is nevertheless significant that in one important respect Henry's answer differed from the conciliar advice appended to it, because he still agreed to release the duke of Orleans for a fixed period in return for hostages and financial pledges, but specifically and only in order that he might work towards the achievement of a peace and would return to captivity by a definite date if he failed.[10]

The young king thus appears to have changed his mind under different pressures. In the event this final English decision, mixing general intransigence with some concession over Orleans, was of little significance because the French king, although he subsequently denied it, did not think fit even to send his ambassadors back to the conference with any answer at all.[11] Henry, for his part, speedily agreed to efforts being made for a new convention to be held in March or April 1440[12] and then, under further pressure and after further bitter argument in the council, finally agreed unilaterally to the release of the duke of Orleans, specifically to further the cause of peace. Charles VII for his part did summon a meeting of the Estates General to Orleans for 25 September 1439 to advise on the Gravelines proposals, and then adjourned it to Bourges for February 1440 because the dauphin would not attend. This reassembly was prevented by the revolt of the French nobility and the dauphin known as the *Praguerie*. There are two quite contrary versions as to whether the assembly at Orleans reached a

[9] *P.P.C.*, V, 388–95.
[10] *Ibid.*, 391.
[11] According to what Beaufort told the English embassy, Charles VII had informed Orleans and the duchess meantime that he could not agree to the mode of peace proposed by them without the advice and assent of his lords of the blood and his council which the dauphin could not attend before 25 September in Paris, therefore he required postponement of any further meeting; *P.P.C.*, V, 396.
[12] Stevenson, *Wars*, II, 446.

decision[13] over peace negotiations, but the remonstrances which the
princes, including the released Orleans, later addressed to Charles from
Nevers in 1442 accused him of evasion and procrastination over the
Gravelines proposals.[14] This elicited the reply that he had only engaged
in those negotiations to secure the release of the duke of Orleans and
that for nothing in the world would he ever abandon to the English
any territory unless it was to be held in the sovereignty and jurisdiction of his crown. For a perpetual record of the matter he had ordered
this reply to be registered in his *chambre des comptes*.[15]

It appears, therefore, that short of a complete English military
victory, now a remote possibility, a final peace could only ever be
obtained on the basis of Henry's renunciation of his claim to the French
crown and arms, and a willingness to hold whatever he did hold in
France on the same terms as Charles VII's other vassals. This solution
would have been gladly accepted by the inhabitants of Normandy. The
duchy of Normandy by 1439 was neither a mere unwilling English
colony nor a limb severed from the Valois kingdom of France. The
uncertainty about the outcome of interminable, elaborate, ineffective
peace negotiations was more disturbing to the duchy than the military
reverses which the English cause undoubtedly suffered, on balance, between 1435 and 1441. In truth only two of these reverses adversely
affected Normandy, and even they did not endanger the English
occupation as a whole, that is, the loss of Dieppe in 1435, with its
valuable port and its herring trade, and the French recapture of
Louviers in 1440, which brought an isolated French garrison within
fifty miles of the capital, to the south of Rouen. Otherwise the
permanent English losses of this period were well outside the duchy,
being isolated fortresses then still remaining to the south, east and
north of Paris, notably Montereau (1437), Montargis (1438), Meaux
(in 1439 while the Gravelines conference was in session), Creil and
Pontoise (1441). These merely confirmed the verdict of the 1429–30
campaign that the Ile de France was lost for ever. What worried the
particularist sentiments of the people of the duchy was not English
oppression but the inadequacies and possible impermanence of the
English occupation as indicated by the repeated negotiations for peace.

---

[13]Jacques Garillot, *Les Etats généraux de 1439* (Nancy 1947), 17, quoting the conflicting evidence: Berry herald, 404, and a royal letter to the inhabitants of Lunel
printed in Beaucourt, *Charles VII*, iii, 528–9. The chronicle of Berry herald is printed
by Denys Godefroy in *Histoire de Charles VII Roy de France par Jean Chartier, Souschantier
de S. Denys, Jaques le Bouvier, dit Berry, Roy d'Armes, Mattieu de Coucy et autres autheurs
du temps* (Paris 1661), 369–480.
[14]*Chronique de Mathieu D'Escouchy*, ed. G. du Fresne de Beaucourt (Paris 1864), iii
(Pièces justificatives), 58, 61, 62.
[15]Monstrelet, vi, 27–49.

At Arras the Norman towns would have been quite happy with terms which left Normandy to the English crown, as it had been held by the Plantagenets.[16] From 1435 withdrawal to the frontiers of the duchy, seemingly made inevitable by the general pattern of the military reverses, and the necessary concentration of all government and administration at Rouen, led to a growing desire there to consolidate what was still held, to hold on to Normandy and Maine and nothing more.[17] This was the ambition of the Anglo-Norman establishment, including the old warrior servants of Bedford like Sir Thomas Scales the seneschal, Sir Andrew Ogard and Sir William Oldhall, who were to figure so prominently in York's council and entourage when he became Henry's lieutenant there; also the public servants which the new university of Caen, Bedford's foundation, began to produce, and Henry's Norman councillors like the ex-abbot of Mont St Michel, the abbot of Fécamp, and Zano di Castiglione, bishop of Bayeux, friend of Gloucester and York. But during these years the alternative, coherent policy to peace, consolidation and strengthening of what was still held, as expressed notably by York's 'energetic but frustrated efforts to retain the duchy as a Lancastrian domain', received little appreciation or purposeful support from Henry and the English council at home, because it would have closed the door to the pursuit of other possible courses: the abiding dream of further conquest and the ultimate realization of a completely Lancastrian kingdom of France.

In June 1441 Henry's council in Normandy wrote the young king an emotional and exaggerated letter imploring effective decisions and assistance in the grievous sickness of that body politic, the duchy of Normandy, which, they said, God had committed to his change. The hearts of his subjects, they said, were cast down, enfeebled, frozen and withdrawn from his love by their fears for the future. They alleged he had abandoned his charge 'as a ship tossed about on the sea by many winds, without captain, without steersman, without rudder, without sail, tossed, staggering and driving among the stormy waves, filled with the storms of sharp fortune and all adversity, far from the haven of safety and human help'. Specifically they complained that they had been buoyed up with false and contradictory hopes; his letters to them had long since announced the imminent arrival of the duke of Gloucester as his lieutenant. He did not come. The arrival of the Duke of York had now been repeatedly promised to them and to various towns in the duchy, at various dates. They now equally had no hope of this. They had last written at the fall of Creil: they now

[16] Joycelyne C. Dickinson, *The Congress of Arras, 1435* (Oxford 1955), 151-4.
[17] For the rest of this paragraph see E. M. Burney, 'The English Rule in Normandy, 1435-1450' (unpublished Oxford B.Litt. thesis, 1958, in the Bodleian Library), 147-54.

wrote urgently to inform him of the impending siege of Pontoise. Lord
Talbot was raising all the troops he could to do his best there, but
it was a great misfortune for Henry that such an able and loyal
servant could not be given the means to act effectively.[18] Similar
sentiments, in flowery Latin rather than Norman French, had been
expressed somewhat earlier by Gloucester's friend in Bayeux, Zano di
Castiglione, who appealed ominously to history. The name of King
John, who lost the duchy of Normandy for the English, was still held
in execration there, he said. What was needed was another Henry V
and vital English self-interest by itself ought to secure the sending of
adequate military aid for its defence, because the only alternative to
effective defence of the duchy would ultimately be a repeat of the 1066
Norman invasion of England.[19]

Finally John Smert Garter King of Arms also expressed the apparent,
genuine widespread feelings of apprehension and neglect when he wrote
urgently to the chancellor in England from Cherbourg in 1441. A
chance encounter with a poursuivant of the duke of Alençon, who was
on his way to the chancellor of Normandy at Rouen, as Garter made
his way downstream to Harfleur, had alerted him to impending
betrayals of various English-held strongholds to the enemy, one of
which, Argentan, had just been saved by this timely information. The
duke of York had meantime at last taken up his post as lieutenant.
Garter, sent by him on embassy to the duke of Brittany, now had great
hopes of York and of the king's goodwill towards Normandy. He had
just taken leave of York and wished him well, the very day he marched
out of Rouen towards Pontoise. He had himself given York other unspecified secret information he had acquired about the 'injustice which
reigned in the king's jurisdiction and of the vices and sin which were
among the people of our nation', and he pinned his hopes on York
being able to overcome these and to re-establish justice on a triumphant
return from Pontoise.[20]

The facts about the supreme direction of affairs in Normandy since
the end of Henry's minority had certainly not been encouraging. The
young king showed no intention of appearing a second time in person
in his French domains as the leader of his people. Consequently there
had now to be a viceroy and there were few who could undertake such
a post. The king's honour and the pride of Normandy demanded he
should be a powerful prince of the blood royal. The last conciliar
appointment had been Richard duke of York, Humphrey of Glouces-

---

[18] Stevenson, *Wars*, II, 603–7.
[19] *Correspondence of Bekynton*, I, 289–95, undated, though placed by the editor under
1435.
[20] Stevenson, *Wars*, I, 192–3, 21 July 1441, wrongly dated 1447 (Beaucourt, iii, 23,
quoting the original).

ter's former ward, the prince of the blood royal nearest to Henry apart from the Beauforts and the Holand earl of Huntingdon. York had been commissioned on 1 May 1436, while still not twenty-five years old, but already an experienced soldier, and with Talbot's assistance in 1436 and 1437 had effectively consolidated the English position in upper Normandy and Picardy. According to later generations, apparently on lost contemporary Norman authority, he had also established good order and justice.[21] His commission had not been designed to extend beyond the attainment of Henry's majority[22] and he himself was consequently pressing to return by April 1437. The young king seems already to have been reluctant to employ York in any capacity. His name was conspicuous by its absence from the new council appointed by Henry in November 1437 to mark his own assumption of power.

York's first successor in Normandy, appointed by Henry, was a political compromise, the king's tutor, Richard earl of Warwick, an unwilling and elderly stop-gap of fifty-seven, who most inconveniently died in harness on 30 April 1439. The office was then put into commission with both Beaufort brothers, the cardinal's nephews, prominent members of it, until the king, as he now said, could either appear there in person, or make up his mind whom to appoint as his deputy. He was a long time in deciding. First Humphrey of Gloucester was made 'general gouverneur' *in absentia* and the elder Beaufort earl of Somerset, already on the spot but a soldier rusty from seventeen years of captivity in French hands, was appointed 'lieutenant et gouverneur général sur le fait de guerre', a title which he ambiguously retained even after York's ultimate reappointment. Finally, with obvious reluctance, York was at last acknowledged to be the only possible satisfactory, long-term candidate and reappointed on a five-year term from 2 July 1440 until Michaelmas 1445. He made conditions, insisting on Henry's formal conferment upon him of all the powers which his uncle Bedford had had. A whole further twelve months was needed to organize his return. By the time he landed at Harfleur in June 1441, with a large army and an English council of his own choosing,[23] Somerset was back in England and the floundering Norman ship of state once more had a reasonably competent captain and steersman after four years of stop-gaps and political compromises which had followed Henry's personal assumption of power.

York had been advised in drawing up his conditions by his own council, which included Sir John Fastolf, Sir William Oldhall and Sir William ap Thomas, all able and experienced in Norman affairs, and

[21] E. M. Burney, *op. cit.*, 127, quoting Hall's chronicle, 181, citing an unidentified Norman chronicle.

[22] *P.P.C.*, V, 7: 'almost expired', 7 April 1437.

[23] *Ibid.*, 142–3; Stevenson, *Wars*, II 585–6.

he had required this council to be augmented by the addition of at least one bishop (he specified Norwich, Salisbury or Lincoln), one lord (Viscount Beaumont, Lord Hungerford or Lord Fanhope) and a knight (Sir Ralph Butler, Sir John Stourton or Sir John Popham). He was thus clearly demanding the secondment to him of a representative selection of those about Henry who were known to enjoy his confidence. He also requested the services of a further notable number of knights, esquires, yeomen and others from Henry's own household. The era of Bedford's administration was now to be revived. His powers were to be those of Bedford, or of those which Gloucester 'had or should have had now late'. He was to be able to call upon the assistance of the duke of Brittany, to have £20,000 *per annum* from England, on firm surety and assignments, which were not to be diverted or employed to other purposes (a significant requirement),[24] so that he should have no cause to leave the king's service there (as had ominously just happened to the earl of Huntingdon in the comparable post in Gascony) and sufficient extra for 'great war or laying great sieges'. For the expenses of his household he was to have 30,000 francs *per annum* (12,000 less than Bedford, 6,000 more than Warwick). Also, from the king, were to come sixteen pieces of artillery with twenty-six gunners and all other necessary arms and ammunition. He was to have the right to return to England if the appointments were not fully kept (as they were not), after due notification to the king and council. He also specified power to appoint to all military posts in Normandy, over-riding with his own nominees any existing life or term of years grants unless they were being adequately performed in person or by deputy.

Avoiding the traditional wasteful and profitless siege warfare condemned by Fastolf, he marked his advent in Normandy by a brilliant Seine and Oise campaign, conducted in conjunction with Talbot and centred on Pontoise, in the course of which the French king and the dauphin, harried to and fro over the rivers, were ignominiously chased almost to the gates of Paris. The pursuers found the royal bed still warm at Poissy. But inexorable logistics dictated an autumn return to Rouen for the triumphant but exhausted and near-starving army.[25] Charles VII took Pontoise by assault on 19 September 1441 and the 1442 campaigning season was notable only for Talbot's capture of Conches and siege of Dieppe.

For 1441–2 York's £20,000 was paid promptly, largely by diverting assignments intended for Henry's own household, but after that he had to wait until February 1444 for anything more from England, when

---

[24] He was still owed at least 1,150 marks from his last lieutenancy (Stevenson, *Wars*, II, lxxi–lxxii) and Warwick for his long-standing service in France was some £10,000 out of pocket in 1438 (*ibid.*, lxix–lx).

[25] See A. H. Burne, *The Agincourt War* (London 1956), 293–302, for this campaign.

he received a further £10,300.[26] It was not that all sources of financial support from England suddenly failed. Other expensive and contradictory projects had meantime secured the attention of Henry's weak and vacillating resolve. York had at last been given a long-term, well-endowed appointment 'for the defence and conservation of the duchy of Normandy and realm of France'. But the year 1443 saw Henry, with the administrative assistance of his English council, marshalling the resources of the English kingdom for a contradictory, grandiose plan in which York would play no part, a revived plan of complete conquest, of the thwarted, expansionist ambitions of 1428, with the elder Somerset now cast in the role then played by the earl of Salisbury. But this was no long-term, carefully thought out master-plan to determine the future of Henry's French kingdom. An opportunity to employ this force in this manner was hastily contrived out of the near-desperate needs of Henry's other duchy, Gascony, and at the expense of resources already promised to Normandy. As it turned out, it provided no benefit whatsoever, either to the duchy of Normandy or to the southern duchy whose cries for help had first occasioned the raising of its great army.

The appointment of John Holand earl of Huntingdon as lieutenant general of English Gascony for nine years, in the midst of the preparations for the peace conference of Gravelines, had been the first such military appointment since Thomas earl of Dorset's in 1413.[27] It was occasioned by aggressive French expeditions against the duchy in 1438, planned by Charles VII, which had advanced on Gascony from the Agenais, Armagnac and Béarn, under the Castilian *routier* Roderigo de Villandrando, Poton de Saintrailles, Alexander bastard of Bourbon and Charles II sire d'Albret. The ravaging of the whole of the Médoc and its occupation as far as Soulac at the mouth of the Gironde culminated in the capture of the Saint-Seurin suburb of Bordeaux, which lost 800 men in an unsuccessful sortie against them. This French tide ultimately spent itself and fell back, due to lack of sufficient artillery, provisions and the hostility of the countryside, but savage war had been carried into the heart of English-held areas which had been free of it for many years before. The solitary key fortress-town of Tartas in the Landes, to the far south on a tributary of the Adour (some forty-five miles north-east of Bayonne), held by Charles II, sire d'Albret, now became a symbol for deciding the loyalties of all the feudal lords of the Midi.[28]

[26] Jacob, *The Fifteenth Century* (Oxford 1961), 467–8.
[27] Stevenson, *Wars*, II, 549–50, 551–2, 27 March 1439; M. G. A. Vale, *English Gascony 1399–1453* (O.U.P., 1970), 246, quoting P.R.O., Gascon Rolls C.61/129 m.21 and m.16. Acting by 11 August 1439, C.61/129 m.7. Returned to England by 21 December 1440, C.61/130 m.10.   [28] Beaucourt, *op. cit.*, III, 14–6.

At the end of August 1440 the earl of Huntingdon and the seneschal of Gascony, Thomas Rampston, began a long siege of Tartas and ultimately obtained terms for a conditional surrender of the city from Albret.[29] On 21 January 1441 Rampston signed a local treaty which would give joint possession of Tartas to Albret and the English, with the assent of the viscount of Lomagne, eldest son and heir of Jean IV, count of Armagnac, mutual exchange of hostages and a truce of twenty years between Albret and the English. But all this was made conditional on the issue of a trial of strength, a journée, to be held between English and French forces at Tartas on a stipulated day. This day was finally postponed, at the request of the English captains on the spot, to St John's Day (24 June) 1442.[30] The stronger army, English or French, which appeared in the field before Tartas on that date, would thus secure the allegiance of the lords of the Midi. Before February 1442 Charles VII sent most solemn and binding letters to Albret, promising, in view of his composition to hand over Tartas to the English on 24 June, that he would be there with the greatest force he could muster on that day.[31]

Gloucester had publicly indicted Henry's wavering policy towards Gascony in June 1440 as part of his condemnation of the release of Orleans, complaining that Huntingdon's indentures were not being kept and that he most probably would have to abandon his charge. He also warned about the danger inherent for English Gascony in alliances then pending between Orleans and the houses of Armagnac, Foix and Albret.[32] Huntingdon was in fact recalled some time before 21 December 1440, why is not known,[33] and the affairs of Gascony left without supreme direction. Nearly twelve months later nothing had yet been done towards facing up to the pending trial of strength at Tartas on 24 June 1442. Ambassadors from the three estates of Gascony, pressing for provision to be made before the appointed day, were then promised by the chancellor, John Stafford, bishop of Bath and Wells, that the council would put their case to Henry.[34] Nothing further happened. No decisive confrontation in the field, as planned by Huntingdon, was forthcoming. Charles VII, by contrast, kept his word to Albret and appeared before Tartas in strength on the appointed day. Thus he gained the allegiance of the feudal lords of the Midi, as well

[29] Ibid., 233; A. Vallet de Viriville, Histoire de Charles VII (Paris 1862–5), II, 437.
[30] Beaucourt, op. cit., III, 233.
[31] Chronique de Mathieu d'Escouchy, III (Preuves), 45.
[32] Foedera, X, 765–6.
[33] Vale, op. cit., 115–16, quoting C.61/130 m.10.
[34] P.P.C., V, 161, 21 November 1441, but they thought it should be held by an Englishman.

as possession of Tartas, because the English made no appearance there to oppose him.

Amid all these problems of his French inheritance, the defence of Normandy and Gascony, the assertion of his right to the French crown with the consequent commitment to aggressive war, and the impossible pursuit of peace terms acceptable to two sides with irreconcilable claims, it was the attainment of peace by negotiation which proved to be Henry's over-riding interest. Hence the release of Orleans on 5 November 1440.[35] Henry thought this would open a line of direct, fruitful contact between himself and Charles VII, his uncle of France, which would ultimately lead to peace.

Charles duke of Orleans, premier prince of the Valois blood royal, and a prisoner in England since his capture at Agincourt in 1415, was released by Henry, after twenty-five years of captivity, specifically to bring about realistic peace terms through the special personal influence which, it was believed, only he could exert over Charles VII. Henry reached this decision after considering written submissions weighing the advantages and disadvantages likely to ensue, which were provided for him by the council at his request. His uncle Gloucester was adamantly opposed to the release and said so with the utmost publicity. A striking act of open government then followed, made necessary by his uncle's attitude when he demanded, and was granted, an exemplification under the great seal of his arguments against the release.[36] Through the council the king himself now issued his own counter-manifesto of justification.[37] Gloucester had pursued a vendetta against the two cardinals, Beaufort and Kemp, for their role in the abortive peace conference of Gravelines and stigmatized the release of Orleans as their doing.[38] When the mass began after Orleans had solemnly sworn on the high altar in Westminster Abbey to observe the conditions imposed upon him as a peacemaker, Gloucester ostentatiously marched out and took to his barge.[39]

Gloucester's accusation has led to Beaufort's part in Henry's peace policy being exaggerated. The details of the negotiations at Gravelines show that Beaufort was only the executant of Henry's policy and any decisions had to be referred back to him. Beaufort and Kemp were

[35] The date on which he left London with an English escort which returned home on 2 April 1442 (Stevenson, *Wars*, II, 460–2).

[36] *Foedera*, X, 764–7, dated at Kennington 2 June and enrolled on the patent roll 18 Henry VI pt. 3 m.17, a whole membrane to itself.

[37] B.L. MS Cotton Vitellius A xvi fol. 102 printed by Kingsford, *Chronicles of London*, states that the articles of the release were presented to the parliament which met on 14 January 1440.

[38] Stevenson, *Wars*, II, 440–51.

[39] *Paston Letters*, I, 40.

the first of a long line of ministers who were saddled with the responsibility for policy which was actually the king's. On this occasion the king cleared his ministers of such responsibility, openly and unequivocally stating in his counter-proclamation[40] that the release of Orleans was *his* own personal doing, made not of 'simpleness or self-will', but of 'his own advice and courage', stirred by God and reason, in the best interest of himself and his people. Some of the reasons behind it were necessarily his secrets, he said, but he could state publicly that it was done specifically because, in his considered opinion, it would lead to the attainment of peace. The history of one hundred years of conflict, and the present position in France, he declared, both showed that a complete English conquest of the might of France was impossible. Even Edward III had been content with less than this, and Henry's father, just before his death, was about to treat for peace, as those then about him and still living had told him. Henry believed (mistakenly) that his adversary was really disposed and inclined towards peace and (again mistakenly) that Charles VII had himself made the release of Orleans a *sine qua non* of any treaty. It was thought that those about his adversary who opposed a treaty were the very ones who opposed the release of Orleans, since they feared for their influence at the French court should he return (here again Henry was wrong in his diagnosis). A subsidiary reason given was that it was contrary to the law of arms to keep a man in perpetual prison when he was prepared to offer reasonable finance, and a bad example for a king to set. Orleans had never had access to English state secrets and it was unlikely that a man who had been kept out of affairs of state and the conduct of the war for a quarter of a century would be much of an asset to his adversary (this turned out to be true only so long as Orleans and Charles VII remained at loggerheads). Finally both Charles VII and the dauphin would be solemnly bound as parties to any agreement. Orleans's task was specifically to resolve the contention between the two kings over the right and title to the *Regnum Francie*. No hostages were to be taken, but he was bound to return to captivity if he had failed after twelve months. Success would bring cancellation of his ransom and Pope Eugenius IV, through the agency of the apostolic court and chamber, would mediate over any breach of the terms.[41]

All this was wishful thinking. Three years later Orleans was still at liberty and nothing had been achieved, not because, as Gloucester had feared, the able Orleans had at once proved a god-send to a dim-witted French king and dauphin, but because Charles VII had declined to receive him and had not taken him into his confidence, let alone been

[40] Stevenson, *Wars*, II, 451–60.
[41] Indenture for release, *Foedera*, X, 776–82 (Orleans's half), 782–86 (Henry's half), Westminster 2 July 1440.

influenced by him. The French king, when approving his release, had bound himself only to accept a 'fitting and reasonable peace',[42] which to him meant no concession over sovereignty in any part of the *Regnum Francie* and, equally, no concession at all over the title to the French crown and arms.

The duke of Orleans, thus released by Henry specifically to bring about realistic peace terms, was in fact rebuffed by Charles VII. The French king flatly refused to receive him in state when he proposed to present himself at court. He had first made a triumphal progress through Northern France, with nothing short of regal honours, fresh from a lavish reception by Burgundy. He had declared his adhesion to the treaty of Arras, had been installed as a knight of the Burgundian Golden Fleece and had married Burgundy's niece Mary of Cleves.[43] Rebuffed by Charles VII, Orleans withdrew in frustration to his own estates. He became involved in a new *Praguerie* of the French princes of the blood, designed to impose their will on Charles VII, their lawful sovereign. Henry's reliance on the good offices of Orleans for the achievement of peace thus enmeshed his interests with those of the rebellious princes and immeasurably complicated both the diplomatic and the military position. Among the diplomatic consequences were proposals for Henry's marriage to a daughter of Jean IV, count of Armagnac, one of the leaders of this rebellious league of French princes. He was led to offer the hand of one of his daughters to the young Henry VI at the instigation of the princes of France in order to add the support of the English king to their coalition against Charles VII.

In 1442 the count of Armagnac sent his chancellor Jean de Batute, archdeacon of Saint-Antonin at Rodez, to London to broach this subject of marriage between Henry VI and one of his three daughters, at the king's selection. He acted, the count specifically stated, at the request of the dukes of Brittany, Orleans and Alençon. The overtures were favourably received by the young king, and he even at first authorized the opening of negotiations on the basis of a firm choice of one of the maidens. He sent ambassadors, his secretary Thomas Beckington and his household knight Sir Robert Roos, to accompany the archdeacon on his return to his master. But Henry soon had regrets, not about marrying at all, but about thus closing his options of choice among three maidens in advance. He sent hot-foot after his ambassadors to Plymouth with messages signed 'of our owne hand, the which as ye wot well we be not much accustomed for to do in other cases'. The ambassadors, duly checked, sent the messenger, the king's esquire, Nicholas Huse, back to Windsor post-haste for new credentials and received in reply their final instructions. They were to obtain portraits

---

[42] Charles VII's confirmation, *ibid.*, 798–800, St Omer, 6 August 1440.
[43] Beaucourt, *op. cit.*, IV, 159–64.

of all three daughters 'in their kirtles simple and their visages, like as
ye see their stature and their beauty and colour of skin and their
countenances, with all manner of features'. They were to base themselves
on Bordeaux or Bayonne, while a portrait painter did this work and
an envoy was to be sent back to the king with the likenesses so that
he could signify his final choice.

Henry thus appears to have shown a quite normal interest in the
fair sex, but his intimate negotiations, alas, were not to be allowed
to proceed smoothly. Charles VII, accompanied by the dauphin and
most of the nobility of south-west France, including the count of
Armagnac's own heir, the viscount of Lomagne, set out from Toulouse
on 11 June 1442 at the head of a considerable force en route for the
Tartas journée and to reconquer English Gascony. The marriage
embassy had in fact learnt something of these intentions from Sir
Edward Hull even before they embarked for Gascony, as early as 15
June. They had met him by chance at Enmore in Somerset, on his
way to court. Hull had been sent by the terrified community of Bordeaux
to solicit Henry's immediate aid. Before they themselves landed at
Bordeaux on 16 July, Tartas had actually fallen, Thomas Rampston,
seneschal of Gascony, had been captured, the road to Bayonne was
cut, Dax was under siege and communications with Armagnac already
uncertain. To the north of the mouth of the Gironde Royan had
capitulated. With Saintonge and the Landes lost, Entre deux Mers and
Médoc were in immediate danger. So much for the activities of Orleans
the peace-maker.

A more immediate task for Henry's ambassadors than pursuing his
courtship thus turned out to be controlling the mounting tide of panic
in Bordeaux. A public reading and display of Henry's signet letters
declaring that massive aid would quickly follow had some effect. The
Armagnac archdeacon himself hurried on to rejoin his master at
Lectoure, but Roos was forced to accept the post of regent *ad interim*
at Bordeaux and communication with the count of Armagnac soon
became very slow and difficult. No local portrait painter could be found;
further progress to a meeting came to turn on the production of safe
conducts from Charles VII, unlikely in the extreme, in spite of the
facile optimism or, more likely, cautious procrastination of the count,
since it was clear that Charles was now well aware of the conspiracy
to bind Armagnac into alliance against him and was determined to
isolate the count from his new-found friends.

It was not until late October 1442 that Sir Edward Hull arrived back
in Bordeaux from England with a portrait painter, one Hans, who was
sent forward to Armagnac on 3 November with appropriate messages
concealed inside a pastoral staff in case of capture by the French. By
22 November Hans was reported diligently at work and had finished

one likeness in four or five days. But no further progress with the portraits was ever reported: a letter of 3 January 1443 arrived in Bordeaux on 14 January stating that the cold winter was preventing Master Hans's colours from mixing. By then Beckington had left to return home empty-handed. He put to sea on 17 January. Unlucky in the weather and driven into a Breton port, he only presented himself to Henry at Maidenhead on 20 February and found there his fellow ambassador Roos, who had left Bordeaux several days later than himself.[44] This was the last heard of Henry's courtship of the daughters of Armagnac. The French king alone determined the issue. Later that year Charles VII sent the dauphin in his role of governor of Languedoc at the head of an army to execute judgement on Jean IV of Armagnac for two other offences: continuing to style himself count by the grace of God, for which title he had solicited the support of the Paris *Parlement*, and for refusing to surrender lands belonging to Charles's deceased tenant-in-chief Marguerite countess of Comminges. Henry VI's would-be father-in-law, together with his family, were imprisoned and his patrimony taken into the French king's hands.[45]

In the midst of his exasperating, long-distance negotiations with Jean IV of Armagnac, perforce conducted from Bordeaux, Sir Robert Roos had threatened on 24 August 1442 that the prevaricating count would himself be the first target of a new English army, coming to the aid of the Gascons in their resistance to Charles VII's aggression. Indeed, by 21 September 1442, Henry had decided that the pleas for help from Bordeaux would be answered by a force commanded by John Beaufort, earl of Somerset.[46] But progress here was slow. In November measures were taken to provide for an advance party under Sir William Bonville, who was made seneschal of Gascony on 1 December, and he finally sailed from Plymouth with 600 men some time before 2 March 1443.[47] Meantime, although the main force was being raised, the onset of the severe winter, and Charles VII's withdrawal from Gascony, relieved the immediate pressure. In this breathing space a new debate was raised: the relative needs of Normandy and Gascony.

In Normandy York was occupied clearing the potential dangers of French garrisons in the English rear, but Granville had fallen by treachery to the French commander of Mont St Michel in November

[44] *Correspondence of Bekynton*, II, 177–248, from MS Ashmole 789 fol. 174, also printed in trans. by Sir Nicholas Harris Nicolas in 1828 as *A Journal by one of the suite of Thomas Beckington*; Beaucourt, *op. cit.*, III, 240–52.

[45] *Ibid.*, III, 30–1, 252–5. See also for a recent investigation of the Armagnac affair Samuel E. Dicks, 'Henry VI and the Daughters of Armagnac: a Problem in Medieval Diplomacy', *Emporia State Research Studies*, XV (Kansas 1967), 5–12.

[46] *Correspondence of Bekynton*, II, 201, 216–17.

[47] Vale, *op. cit.*, 124, quoting *C.P.R., 1441–1446*, 154 and E.403/747.

and Talbot was locked in a protracted siege of Dieppe. Intelligence from the Council of Basle and elsewhere suggested that Charles VII had now turned his attention to Normandy[48] and that he was even preparing an assault on Rouen. He had kept Whitsun at Poitiers in company with King René of Anjou and the duke of Orleans, who was by now reconciled to him, and he had made the dauphin Louis governor-general for the lands between the Seine and Somme. On 14 August 1443 Louis duly appeared before Dieppe with a substantial force.[49]

From this background of competing claims of Gascony and Normandy emerged the ultimate English plan, not of aid to existing hard-pressed areas but of new aggression and conquest in areas between Gascony and Normandy. Put in charge of John Beaufort, newly created duke of Somerset,[50] as commander-in-chief, this was bound to rouse the resentment of York and also of Somerset's own younger brother the earl of Dorset. In April 1443 Henry informed York 'it is seemed full behoveful and necessary that the manner and conduct of the war be changed', and that he had appointed Somerset to 'use most cruel and mortal war that he can and may, in the king's right to fight his adversary and get the victory of him'.[51] Here the king again gave unmistakable evidence of that ambivalence in decision which was ultimately to cost him all his French possessions and much else besides.

On 6 February 1443, in Henry's secret chamber at Westminster, Henry required the assembled council to debate in his presence the alternative merits of possible action, either in Gascony or Normandy. The various advices tendered led nowhere. The treasurer, Cromwell, on financial grounds, appeared to favour sticking to the original Gascon plan because he considered previous outlays on Normandy had not produced value for money; the two cardinals wanted to know exactly what forces could be raised, but on the vital question of priority Kemp could only offer prayer, and Beaufort a suggestion that the lords temporal and spiritual be consulted.

The issue had in fact already been pre-empted by the king's designation of Somerset as his chosen commander-in-chief for the original Gascon expedition,[52] because Henry allowed Somerset's own personal wishes ultimately to prevail in deciding where this force should be used. But Somerset was a sick man, too sick even to attend at Westminster, so Adam Moleyns was deputed to attend on him personally to ascertain

---

[48] *P.P.C.*, V, 261.
[49] Berry herald, 423.
[50] *P.P.C.*, V, 253, 30 March 1443.
[51] *Ibid.*, 260 (5 April 1443).
[52] The men of Bordeaux were informed of this in a letter dated from Windsor 21 September 1442.

what his wishes were.[53] It was in fact nearly a month before the possibility of two separate expeditions being mounted, one for Normandy and one for Gascony, was finally scotched by Treasurer Cromwell simply on financial grounds. He especially urgently pressed for a decision by the king, the council and the commander-in-chief on where the one expedition should go. He wished to get on with the job of indenting for the wages.[54] The army meantime was still being raised ostensibly, to relieve Bordeaux and Bayonne, the original intention.[55] Everything now had to hang on the duke of Somerset's recovery. Not until 9 March did Moleyns, supported by Sir John Stourton, manage his personal visit.[56] Ships were ordered to the Camber to be ready to sail on St George's Day[57] but it was 30 March 1443 before Somerset was even well enough to appear at Eltham to discuss with the king various written advices and demands he had meantime submitted to him as the conditions on which he offered his services. It now emerged that he intended to use the great army for an assault on those parts of Anjou and Maine not under English control. The ultimate English plan was thus not to give aid to existing hard-pressed forces but to launch new aggressive conquest in the area between Gascony and Normandy. Whatever the appearances still kept up, the relief of Gascony had now become a secondary consideration.

Somerset's wish to carve out a patrimony for himself in Anjou and Maine, or Alençon, or in all three counties, cannot be doubted. He requested Henry to grant him the county of Alençon to himself and his heirs. He also wanted Anjou and Maine. But his younger brother Edmund earl of Dorset[58] already held Maine by Henry's grant, although Henry's French council was objecting to the grant being made under the French seal. Pending the settlement of his brother's rights, Somerset was given the governorship of Anjou and Maine for seven years.[59] If the younger Beaufort was not actually count of Maine in 1443 he had exercised power and authority there for a number of years. At the end of a campaign which he had waged there in 1438, he had made a tripartite agreement with the French duke of Alençon and count of Maine to put the possessions of these two princes under the protection of *appatis*. In this agreement he had been styled captain

[53] *P.P.C.*, 223–4, 225–7.
[54] *Ibid.*, 229, 2 March.
[55] *Ibid.*, 234.
[56] *Ibid.*, 234–5.
[57] *Ibid.*, 241.
[58] Raised to marquis of Dorset, 24 June 1443.
[59] P.R.O., Chancery Miscellanea, C.47/26/28 (Articles for the earl of Somerset with the king's answers, dated under the privy seal at Eltham, 30 March 1443); *P.P.C.*, V, 251–6, 263.

general and governor of the king in the regions of Anjou and Maine, etc.[60]

Thus, as a result of the elder Beaufort's ambitions and Henry's weak accommodation of them, there was now a new source of conflict over Bedford's former Angevin patrimony between the two Beaufort brothers themselves. But the intentions of the new commander-in-chief also raised another, much more serious, conflict of interests: between him and Richard duke of York, the king's already established lieutenant-general and governor of the realm of France and Normandy. Somerset's powers were to be declared in two separate commissions under separate seals, one for France under Henry's French seal and one for Gascony under the English seal, but a declaration that his powers would in no way be detrimental to York could hardly disguise the contradictions, implied criticisms and mark of no confidence in York which the mere fact of this new, ill-defined Beaufort appointment implied. On 30 March Henry blithely 'granted' Somerset, who was himself very anxious over this point, that he would have York's good will towards him.[61]

The elder Somerset from the start proved to be an exacting and un-generous recipient of Henry's favour. All his demands were conceded by Henry: provision for his widow, for a possible unborn child, the title of duke, with precedence over the duke of Norfolk because of his nearness in blood and the magnitude of the service he was about to perform and, finally, a promise of a considerable landed endowment in England. The king gave him the lands of the earldom of Kendal, last held by the duke of Bedford. This was Somerset's own choice of land and the young king gave it to him personally, after the council had refused to advise for or against it. Two months later Somerset made an appearance in the council chamber simply to accuse the treasurer, Cromwell, of delaying the implementation of this grant and Henry duly ordered the council to take collective responsibility for its fulfilment.[62]

On 5 April Garter was briefed to go out to Normandy and put York in the picture. He was to represent Somerset's advent into a part of Normandy as a defence and shield for York because he would meet and fight Charles VII wherever he might be in the areas not yet in Henry's obedience and, by his offensive there, would finally be able to pass over the Loire in triumph, to link up with English Gascony. All the defences of Normandy must be on maximum alert and York must, in addition, give all possible help and comfort to Somerset. While

[60] Treaty of Harcourt, 20 December 1438, in J. Du Mont, *Corps universel diplomatique du droit des gens* (8 vols, Amsterdam and The Hague, 1726–31), t. III, pte. I, 60, and also in Frédéric Leonard, *Recueil des Traitez* (Paris 1693), t. I, 457; cf. *P.P.C.*, V, 15. For *appatis* see below p. 180.

[61] P.R.O., C.47/26/28.

[62] *P.P.C.*, IV, 281.

the king would do all in his power to send York reinforcements, he trusted he would understand that the vast expense of mounting Somerset's expedition had made it quite impossible to deliver the £20,000 now due to him. Garter was to impart these high matters on the future conduct of the war to York as a prime secret, to be divulged to no one else. Such was the full extent of Somerset's specious instructions, as far as the knowledge of them could be trusted by word of mouth, even to the king's personal deputy and representative in France.[63] Further than that, as the malicious bishop of Lisieux after-wards put it, Somerset declared that he would burn his own shirt if it discovered his military intentions. Whether or not he himself ever discovered them was still a secret at the end of the campaign.[64]

St George's Day came and went without the departure of the great army. So did the months of May and June. On 6 July Cromwell resigned from the treasurership with the enterprise still unlaunched, on the plea that a day longer under the strains of office in those circumstances would irretrievably ruin his health.[65] Some three days later Somerset sued for a third delay in his musters, though requiring continued payment meantime. The council now estimated that every day he had tarried in England since he had undertaken to muster on 17 June cost the king £500 and even Henry's patience with his pampered and pernickety commander now at last gave out. He sharply contrasted this unprecedented selfishness, ingratitude and rapacity with the practice of his uncle Gloucester who in similar circumstances in 1436 had himself borne the costs of transporting his army to France when he failed to fulfil his contract by the lack of a mere two men in his musters. Somerset was now roundly told that his parasitic forces were a greater burden on the shires than four complete subsidies would have been, and a comfort only to the king's enemies.[66]

Early in August 1443[67] Somerset at last landed at Cherbourg with a force of some 8,000 men, a heavy artillery train, siege and bridging stores, etc. Purveyance of horses, carts and men and local taxation, levied for his transportation without any authority from York, proved necessary to enable him to pass safely through Normandy because no provision had been made at home for his transport beyond the port.[68]

[63] *Ibid.*, 259–63.

[64] T. Basin, *Histoire des règnes de Charles VII et de Louis XI*, ed. J. Quicherat (Paris 1855), I, 149–52.

[65] *P.P.C.*, V, 299–300.

[66] *Ibid.*, 303–4, 409–14.

[67] Ramsay, *op. cit.*, II, 55, quoting Issues, Easter 21 Henry VI m.14 (sailed by 15 August).

[68] Burney, *op. cit.*, 206–9, quoting *P.P.C.*, V, 257, and Arch. Nat. K.68/19, accounts of his debts to the crown as granted to Margaret of Anjou in 1446.

The greater part of the English forces already on the frontiers of Normandy made their way towards him, expecting to be engaged in battle, and swelled his numbers to some 10,000 combatants.[69] Ironically, to the north, on 14 August, the dauphin forced the raising of Talbot's nine-month siege of Dieppe, dramatically highlighting the effects of the abandonment of the needs of Normandy which this great new enterprise inevitably signified.[70]

The scanty information about it which York had been allowed had quickly caused him to despatch a powerful embassy led by Talbot, Sir Andrew Ogard, John Stanlow and the French secretary, Master John Rinel, to impress on Henry his alarms and fears of the consequences. But Henry had no personal inclination to listen or to reply. That unpleasant task was deputed to a council meeting of 21 June 1443 which was then otherwise busy approving the cost of a novel bridge of barrels intended for Somerset's river crossings. York received only a letter appealing to his cousinage and good personal relations with Somerset and repeating Somerset's personal assurances that absolutely no 'disworship' was intended towards him.[71]

John Beaufort, duke of Somerset, the eldest surviving son of the senior of John of Gaunt's three illegitimate sons by Catherine Swynford, was a man of straw. Captured by the French while in his early teens at Beaugé in 1421, in the army of his step-father the duke of Clarence, he had spent seventeen years in French captivity. The need to find 16,000 marks from his own resources to pay for his ransom, after his release in 1438, probably lay behind the extraordinarily demanding 'articles of his desires' with which he conditioned his appointment to lead the original relief force to Gascony, and which had now burgeoned under his soaring ambition into this grandiose expeditionary force of 1443. In his few brief years of freedom he had certainly served with some credit in the armies of Normandy and had, for a few months, been acting governor of Normandy before York's second appointment in 1440. But his only qualification for receiving the mantle of Henry V, as deputy for his unmartial son, was his nearness in the half-blood to his royal cousin. His obvious ill-health, an adult lifetime of captivity and a lack of substance of his own to maintain his high estate combined to make him singularly unqualified to hold this supremely demanding office for the re-opening of the conquest of France which had now been conferred upon him.

The facts of his 1443 campaign are not in dispute. Proceeding down

---

[69] Berry herald, 424. Stevenson, *Wars*, II, 347–9.

[70] Berry herald, 423.

[71] *P.P.C.*, V, 288–9 (presence: the Chancellor, the bishop of St Davids, Adam Moleyns, the duke of Somerset himself, the earls of Stafford, Northumberland and Suffolk).

the marches of Brittany and Alençon he besieged and took the stronghold of La Guerche by assault or composition. According to the contemporary heralds' accounts this belonged to the French duke of
Alençon,[72] a peer of France and, at that time, Charles VII's
commander-in-chief in the area. Somerset believed it did.[73] He then
stayed for some two months before Alençon's other stronghold of
Pouancé, and ravaged the country between Angers, Craon and
Château Gontier from that base, but quite failed to find any major
French force to fight. His army was next reported successfully
besieging Beaumont-sur-Sarthe and, finally, after its surrender, the
English commander moved not south to cross the Loire with his bridge
of boats but northwards to reinforce the frontier garrisons of Normandy.
From here he took final, ignominious refuge with York in Rouen, from
where he returned, sick and discredited, to England. He died the
following May, 1444, allegedly by his own hand, from chagrin at his
disgrace and failure, but certainly from no sudden unexpected illness
as one chronicler has it, for bad health had dogged him from before the
onset of his campaign.

Further charges of his crass stupidity on the campaign, taken to bear
out Thomas Basin's picture of the elder Beaufort as a vain, presump-
tuous, secretive and purposeless commander appear to have been unjustified. The most serious of these charges was that he had deliberately
attacked the territory of Henry's ally and vassal, the young duke of
Brittany, Francis I, then in perfect peace and harmony with Henry,
thus seriously undermining one vital prop of Henry's French inheritance. The duke certainly sent an outraged complaint to the English
court through his brother Gilles, Henry's youthful friend and companion, that this new lieutenant and captain general of Henry's realm
of France, quite unprovoked, had sacked his town of La Guerche and
ransomed it for 20,000 saluts. Ironically it had been Somerset himself,
when earlier briefly in office as Henry's lieutenant general and governor
for war in his realms of France and Normandy, who, on 11 July 1440,
had concluded the final treaty of peace and friendship between the
duke's father, the old Duke John of Brittany, and Henry VI.[74] From
Sheen on 17 December 1443 Henry sent on a copy of the complaint
to Somerset and ordered him to make full restitution if the facts were
as he had stated.[75] But the history of La Guerche in the campaign
of the frontierless Breton March suggests that Somerset was correct in

---

[72] Monstrelet, *Chronique*, vi, 66–7; Waurin, *Recueil des chroniques*, ed. W. & E. L. C. P.
Hardy (R.S., 1884), iv (1431–47), 375–6.
[73] Berry herald, 424.
[74] Pierre Hyacinthe Morice, *Mémoires pour servir de preuves à l'histoire de Bretagne*
(Paris 1742–6), ii, cols 1329–31, 1342–3; *Foedera*, X, 788; Stevenson, *Wars*, II, 304–5.
[75] *P.P.C.*, VI, 11–13, 17–18, 22–3.

regarding this as a hostile garrison. The old duke of Brittany, who had captured it from the duke of Alençon in 1432, along with Pouancé, had subsequently restored both strongholds to Alençon under conditions of obedience,[76] but Somerset's younger brother Dorset had deemed it prudent to take it on his very similar 1438 campaign south from the Cotentin, without any international complications.[77] It was certainly garrisoned for Charles VII in 1440.[78] Somerset's fault was that he allowed immediate military considerations to prevail, without considering possible diplomatic consequences, when the vital allegiance of Brittany was in the balance and Duke Francis was urgently considering on which side his best interests lay.

The best of the French chroniclers says mildly that the English much blamed Somerset for thus exploiting and wasting their grand army to no purpose. He had indeed dissipated the strength of a fine and costly force; he had effected no relief to Gascony; he had completely failed to bring a French field force to battle and he had achieved nothing, at great cost, in his other declared role as a shield and defence of Normandy. Such was Henry VI's one and only effort to make 'cruel and mortal war'. The supreme fault surely lay not in the personal shortcomings, however apparent, of the hapless Lancastrian prince of the half-blood who was allowed to formulate and execute his own plan of campaign without consideration of its overall consequences, but in Henry's vacillating direction of the affairs of his French inheritance. If a scheme of this nature for further conquest was to be attempted – a renewal of his illustrious father's campaigns – then it was Henry's prime duty, not Somerset's, to lead it in person in the field. Most seriously of all for the future, the elevation of the elder Beaufort brother at the expense and neglect of Richard duke of York sowed the seeds of a deadly enmity between him and the House of Beaufort which was to lead ultimately to civil war.

[76] Morice, *Preuves*, II, cols 1238–50.

[77] Kingsford, *Chronicles of London*, 145. Since it is here mentioned in close proximity to the taking of Saint Aignan-sur-Roe this is unlikely to have been La Guierche, some fourteen kilometres north of Le Mans as identified by Beaucourt, *op. cit.*, III, 16, quoting Berry's reference to it, 400.

[78] See map in Philippe Contamine, *Guerre, état et société au fin du Moyen Age* (Paris 1972), 264.

Chapter 10

MARRIAGE AND TRUCE, 1443-1445

Somerset's grandiose campaign, launched so belatedly in August 1443, had been planned because of the apparently total failure of peace through negotiation on which Henry had pinned his hopes in 1440, when he had released his prisoner, the premier Valois prince of the blood royal, Charles duke of Orleans. After 1439 Charles VII took no part in peace negotiations which continued between England and Burgundy only and led finally to a separate perpetual truce between them, signed by the duchess Isabel and Richard duke of York at Dijon on 23 April 1443.[1] The French king's antipathy towards Henry's former ally, the duke of Burgundy, and his desire to injure his interests persisted.[2] He firmly vetoed a marriage arranged by treaty on 4 February 1443 between Margaret of Anjou, the daughter of his queen's brother, René duke of Anjou, and Charles count of Nevers, Burgundy's nephew, even though papal dispensation had already been obtained for it.[3] This intervention to prevent Margaret of Anjou's marriage into the House of Burgundy may have been prompted only by a desire to prevent an alliance of Angevin and Burgundian interests, but within a very few months she was designated for the role of Henry's consort and queen of England.

A new peace initiative had originated from the French side towards direct Anglo-French negotiations by September 1442. In that month Henry appointed a peace embassy which, he stated, he did as a result of recent letters received both from Charles VII and from Charles duke of Orleans.[4] They had been reconciled at Limoges in May 1442 and Orleans became the king's pensioner, a check to the coalition of confederate princes from which it never recovered.[5] Detailed plans for these new peace negotiations with Henry were most probably formulated at a meeting in Poitiers at Whitsun 1443 when Charles VII dined with the dauphin, Charles of Orleans, the brothers René and Charles count of Maine, and the papal nuncio, the bishop of Brescia, who was under recent explicit orders to work for an Anglo-

[1] Beaucourt, *op. cit.*, III, 262.
[2] Richard Vaughan, *op. cit.*, 113-18.
[3] Beaucourt, *op. cit.*, III, 260.
[4] *Foedera*, XI, 13.
[5] Beaucourt, *op. cit.*, III, 260, 265.

French peace.[6] Henry had at first appointed an embassy under Richard duke of York, made up from the Anglo-Norman establishment, as a result of the new French initiative, and debated with his council what instructions they should be given.[7] The duke of Brittany promptly offered his services as a mediator, but when negotiations did begin, they were actually to be conducted on the English side by a completely new team from England. The leader of it, William de la Pole, earl of Suffolk, Orleans's former custodian, was the man asked for by Charles VII himself.

More than once in later years Charles maintained that in 1443 he had been poised to throw the English out of Normandy and had had no need to re-open peace negotiations,[8] but it is very doubtful whether he was so confident militarily at that stage, especially as the peace initiative then came from him. The offer of an Angevin bride for Henry, linked to the conclusion of a short truce, was in fact a cleverly calculated act of policy on Charles's part. Thomas Basin was surely wrong on several counts when he stated that the resultant English embassy to Tours in 1444 laboured for an alliance with one of Charles's numerous daughters, and then only accepted Margaret as second best.[9] In the first place, even if Charles had been amenable to accepting his nephew Henry as his son-in-law, there was no choice available among his own offspring. Of his twelve children, born to his queen Marie of Anjou by 1444, eight were girls. Three boys and two girls were already dead. The eldest daughter, Radegonde, a sickly girl of eighteen, was long since betrothed to Sigismund duke of Austria and died in 1445. Catherine, already married to Burgundy's heir, died in 1446. Yolande, nine years old, had been betrothed to Amadeus prince of Piedmont since infancy and was being brought up at the court of Savoy. There remained one of two twins born in 1438, destined to survive only to the age of eight; Madeleine, only born on 1 December 1443, and finally Jeanne, the third daughter and fifth child, still unmarried and not betrothed, the one and only marriageable daughter of them all, born about 1430 and roughly of an age with Margaret of Anjou (born 23 or 25 March 1429).[10]

There is no evidence that either side, French or English, at this

---

[6] *Ibid.*, 265.

[7] *P.P.C.*, V, 210–3. It was decided to press for a truce in default of a peace, both Cardinal Beaufort and Gloucester agreeing. The next day, with Gloucester absent, it was advised to accept a short truce if a long one could not be got (7 & 8 October 1442).

[8] Stevenson, *Wars*, I, 119, 243–4 (in July 1445 and again on the eve of the final declaration of war in 1449).

[9] T. Basin, *op. cit.*, I, 154–6.

[10] A. Lecoy de la Marche, *Le Roi René*, 2 vols (Paris 1875), I, 231.

time proposed a marriage between Henry and his first cousin Jeanne, or that the English ever made an issue of the obvious disparagement to Henry in Charles's offer of the French queen's dowerless niece, Margaret of Anjou. Mere consanguinity, especially in view of the madness of their grandfather, the poor health and survival rate of her brothers and sisters and possibly the unjustifiably poor reputation of the capabilities of Charles VII himself in England, may have made a marriage with Jeanne appear not worth having. But this is unlikely, because Richard duke of York soon afterwards was ambitious enough to seek Jeanne as a bride for his heir Edward of Rouen, through the good offices of Suffolk and Margaret of Anjou. Charles VII then offered only the infant Madeleine for a second English marriage, useless to York, who wanted a bride of an age to produce an heir. It is hardly surprising that Charles VII was not willing to offer Jeanne to Henry, considering the trouble which had come to his house from the previous two English marriages of French princesses close in line of succession.[11] His antipathy towards an English marriage some ten years before at Arras can hardly have been forgotten. But the basic fact was that only Margaret of Anjou was on offer because he saw the possibility of an Angevin marriage as a potent means of furthering his interests against England.

From the English point of view Margaret was at least healthy breeding stock; the House of Anjou was demonstrably fecund. Also the queen's brother René duke of Anjou was titular king of Jerusalem and Sicily, as well as duke of Bar and Lorraine by right of his wife, and count of Provence, which could be taken to lessen the degree of disparagement. There were two surviving daughters of Anjou, but the elder was already betrothed to Ferry of Lorraine, son of Antoine de Vaudemont, a political alliance destined to strengthen René's hold over his wife's patrimony of Lorraine. Margaret's father René, like Charles VII, was now prepared to sacrifice his second daughter towards a profitable accommodation with the nephew of England.[12] The Angevins themselves had the prospect of doing very well out of this match, in return for their compliance in their king's act of high policy: no less than the peaceful recovery, with the help of their sovereign, of the English-held county of Maine, the most recent and strongly held English conquest and strategically, the key to Normandy, as well as English abandonment of their efforts against Anjou. Maine was the patrimony of the French king's companion and favourite, René's younger brother, Charles of Maine. Charles VII made the

[11] Isabella to Edward II and Catherine to Henry V. Jeanne was betrothed in 1446 to Jean count of Claremont, heir to the duke of Bourbon, as a matter of internal politics.

[12] Charles VII's only other niece, Jeanne, daughter of his sister Isabella and of Charles of Orleans, had long since been married to the count of Alençon.

Anjou marriage essential to the conclusion of even a short truce. But Henry and his council had already decided in October 1442 that a short truce would not be acceptable, in default of that final peace settlement which had been made impossible by the impasse over the title to the *Regnum Francie* and the question of sovereignty over the English-held lands. The *quid pro quo* of such substantial concessions by Henry and the English was never specified, beyond the understanding that his Valois uncle would be made amenable to a peace settlement thereby. In this vital matter Henry, who had never known his father, but had been reared by his Valois mother, began to show himself more of a Valois than a Plantagenet or Lancastrian.

Charles VII's purposes in peace negotiation with his nephew of England are revealed by the terms of the powers of attorney by which René of Anjou made Charles's ambassadors to London in October 1445 his own plenipotentiaries, superior to his personal representatives: the marriage was executed by the good pleasure and will of Charles under the hope that for the affinity and love between Henry and René which should reasonably ensue from it, the differences outstanding in the achievement of final peace between Charles and Henry could be more swiftly settled. Furthermore, by the above means, 'the county of Maine or what our dear son holds of it, will be made over to us as we have requested'. In return for this, René had permission from Charles VII to make an alliance for life and a twenty-year truce with his new son-in-law.[13] The unilateral surrender of English Maine from son-in-law to father-in-law was thus boldly requested at an early stage by the Angevins and, by 17 October 1445 at the latest, they had formally made Charles VII their agent in this. The French were later to maintain that Adam Moleyns, second-in-charge of the Tours embassy and treaty, had instructions from Henry to implement this surrender when he was again in France, even as early as September 1445. It was also later asserted more than once that Henry gave an oral undertaking to surrender it by 1 October 1445 to the great French embassy to London in July that year.[14] This surrender of Maine was to become the most bitter charge laid against the duke of Suffolk when final disaster in Normandy overwhelmed Henry's government. Suffolk always strenuously protested his innocence and certainly no promises appear to have been given at Tours in May 1444. Nevertheless, Charles VII and the Angevins un-

---

[13] 'Procuration donnée a Guillaume Cousinot et à Jean Harvart pour négocier la paix avec leroi d'Angleterre', printed by A. Lecoy de la Marche, *op. cit.*, II, 'Pièces justificatives,' 258–9, dated at the castle of Angers, 17 October 1445.

[14] Beaucourt, *op. cit.*, IV, 284–5, citing MS français 18442, f. 173; *Chronique de Mathieu D'Escouchy* (ed. Beaucourt), III, 194.

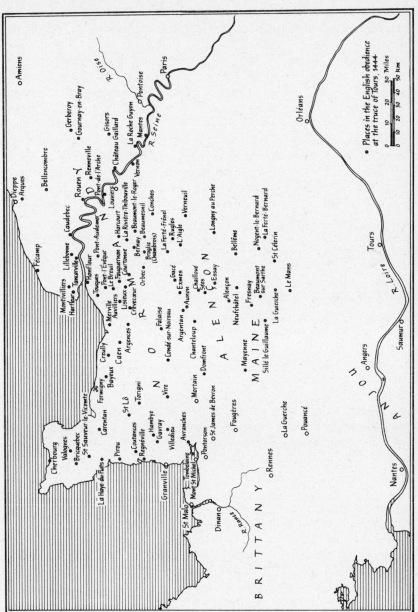

2 English Normandy and Maine

Amiens

Dieppe
Arques

Bellencombre

Fécamp
Montivilliers
Harfleur
Tancarville
Lillebonne
Caudebec

Gerberoy
Gournay-en-Bray

Rouen
Renneville
Pont-de-l'Arche
Gisors
Château Gaillard
La Roche Guyon
Mantes
Vernon
Paris

Honfleur
Pont-l'Évêque
Touques
Le Breuil
Pont-Audemer
Louviers
Harcourt
Beaumont-le-Roger
Pontoise
R. Seine
R. Oise

Merville
Auvillers
Lisieux
Fauguernon
Courtonne
La Rivière-Thibouville
Beaumesnil
Comches
Verneuil

St James de Beuvron
Pirou
Coutances
Regnéville
Hambye
Gavray
Villedieu
Avranches
Tombelaine
Mont St Michel
Granville
St Malo
Dinan
R. Rance

Briquebec
St Sauveur-le-Vicomte
La Haye du Puits
Carentan
Formigny
Bayeux
St Lô
Torigni
Vire
Mortain
Domfront
Chanteloup
Condé-sur-Noireau
Falaise
Argentan
Aunou
Exmes
Gacé
Orbec
Brionne
Broglie
(Chambrais)
Bernay
La Ferté-Frénel
L'Aigle
Rugles
Longny au Perche
Bellême
Nogent-le-Bernard
La Ferté-Bernard
St Céterin
Beaumont
sur-Sarthe
Fresnay
Le Mans
La Guerche
Alençon
Sées
Séez
St Essay
Neufchâtel
Silié le Guillaume
Mayenne

Crévecœur
Creully
Caen
Argences

Valognes
Cherbourg

Fougères
Rennes
La Guerche
Pouancé
St Denis

Orléans

Tours
R. Loire
Saumur
Angers
Nantes

BRITTANY

MAINE
ALENÇON
N O R M A N D Y
ANJOU

● Places in the English obedience
at the truce of Tours, 1444

0 10 20 30 Miles
0 10 20 30 40 50 Km

doubtedly had it very much in mind from the beginning of these new negotiations.

The earl of Suffolk, steward and head of the king's household, was understandably nervous at being singled out by his king's adversary to lead this new Tours peace mission. He prudently made his doubts public before the king, Gloucester, and most of the other lords of the council in Henry's privy chamber at Westminster on 1 February 1444.[15] He pointedly recalled the opprobrium which had fallen on the heads of earlier peace negotiators, much mightier than himself, saying also that there was already talk in London of his unsuitability for the task because of his former captivity in France, his close association with Orleans as his keeper during his captivity in England, and the French indication that he would be *persona grata* to them. Henry nevertheless ordered the chancellor formally to declare that it was his own high commandment, and the desire of all the lords present, that Suffolk should undertake the task and he would not have him discharged of it. No protest by Gloucester is recorded on this occasion. Suffolk then requested that if the embassy had to consist of men of 'easy degree' like himself, and be few in number, his few chosen colleagues should be shrewd and able. This was granted: he was in fact to be accompanied by a household team, Master Adam Moleyns, doctor of laws, dean of Salisbury, made keeper of the privy seal on 11 February, Robert Roos the king's carver, Master Richard Andrew, doctor of laws, the king's secretary, and John Wenlock, the king's squire. From Rouen they were to be joined by the chancellor of Normandy, Thomas Hoo, a former retainer of Suffolk's. The purpose of Henry's new embassy, succinctly stated, was 'to satisfy our mind's whole and singular desire for a good peace and the marriage of our person'.[16] It is thus inconceivable that the Angevin marriage was not fixed and personally accepted by Henry himself before the embassy left. As the result of previous overtures for his marriage had shown, no one else could select his bride. A joint delegation from Aragon and Navarre, offering a choice of Spanish princesses in 1430, had been plainly told that the lords of the blood royal and the council could not undertake the grave responsibility of choosing a wife for Henry. Other possibilities, of a Habsburg marriage raised when the Garter was sent to Albert of Austria on the eve of his election to the empire in 1438, and Portuguese proposals in the early 1440s, had all come to nothing for the same reasons.[17] He had also clearly shown, in ad-

---

[15] *P.P.C.*, VI, 32–5, wrongly dated there 1445.

[16] *Foedera*, XI, 53 and 59–67, for the diplomatic history of the truce, and Bodleian Library MS Digby, 196, fols 155v, 156r, a Latin narration of the English embassy.

[17] See John Ferguson, *English Diplomacy, 1422–1461* (O.U.P., 1972), 48, 51, 53–4, 223–5.

vance of the embassy for the Armagnac match, that his own personal wishes and decision would be paramount in selecting his consort. Marriages of kings, like treaties with foreign princes, were matters for kings alone.

Suffolk's departure was imminent on 14 February 1444.[18] Charles VII arranged to have him met from Calais, but he announced his landing at Harfleur round about 15 March to Orleans and Pierre de Brézé, intending to proceed via Rouen to Le Mans. Charles VII had installed himself in the castle of Montils-les-Tours and summoned there all the princes of the blood, including Burgundy, who alone did not come. Arrangements for the conference to be held at Vendôme, protected by local truces, fell through because Charles succumbed to a serious illness[19] and the English embassy, with its French escort headed by Orleans and his bastard brother, consequently went on to Blois and finally down river to Tours on 26 April.

Here, on the sixth day of the conference, at his first meeting with Charles VII, Suffolk presented a letter under Henry's signet and sign manual of greeting and hope for a successful outcome of negotiations with his 'dear uncle of France'. Now, for the first time, Charles was no longer styled his adversary. The negotiations were interspersed with appropriate festivities: the marriage of Charles of Anjou to Isabella of Luxembourg; an archery contest between the king's Scots guard and English archers and, on 1 May, the dauphine at the head of three hundred gallants riding out to bring in the May. Some formal negotiations were certainly held for the conclusion of a perpetual peace, but they came to nothing. The French offered Gascony, Quercy, Périgord, Calais and Guînes, to be held in homage to Charles VII. The English wanted the lands which they had claimed before their claim to the French throne had been advanced, that is Gascony and Normandy in full sovereignty, for which, most significantly, Henry was now prepared to abandon his claim to the French throne. This vital English change of position and bargaining counter, so cavalierly revealed at Tours to no purpose, is known from the later negotiations conducted in London with the great French embassy of July 1445, when Suffolk and the new archbishop of Rheims, Jacques Jouvenel des Ursins, summarized these preliminary parleyings of Tours. The French clearly had not been prepared to make any concessions at all at Tours and had not allowed for any progress whatsoever to a final peace treaty there.[20]

The French were, however, very ready to make progress with the marriage negotiations. The marriage treaty with King René was con-

[18] *Correspondence of Bekynton*, I, 175.
[19] Stevenson, *Wars*, I, 67–76.
[20] *Ibid.*, 131–3, 157.

cluded on 22 May 1444.[21] Margaret renounced all claims to any of
her father's possessions, a renunciation which Henry was to confirm
after consummation of the marriage. Her dower was to consist merely
of her mother's empty claims to the kingdom of Majorca and 20,000
francs. René undertook to send an embassy to England to fix the date
of the marriage and the place where she should be handed over to
Henry. On 24 May in the church of St Martin, in the presence of
her aunt and mother, the queens of France and Sicily, and all the
princes of the French blood royal, Charles VII in person, doffing his
hat, handed the young princess to the papal legate for betrothal to
Suffolk, who was standing proxy for his king, while the people shouted
'Noel'. Festivities at the abbey of Saint-Julien then continued into the
small hours. The whole congress terminated with the signing of a mere
twenty-one-month truce on 28 May. This was the second, attainable
purpose for which Charles had designated a suitable commission on
20 May consisting of Charles duke of Orleans, Louis count of
Vendôme, Suffolk's French equivalent as Grand Master of the royal
household, Pierre de Brézé, lord of Varenne and Bertrand de Beauvau
lord of Précigny and a servant of René of Anjou. They did have
powers to negotiate truces particular or general with a view to arriving
at a permanent peace, but the ultimate formal goal of a final peace
settlement in fact remained as remote as ever.

Charles VII had good reasons to be very satisfied with this outcome.
The concessions had all been one-sided. He had acquired the prospect
of an attractive and able personal agent as the consort of his nephew
of England[22] and he had a truce of limited duration, the extension
of which would be the subject of further bargaining. On this point
Henry had fundamentally shifted his position since Gravelines in 1439,
when the basic English fear had been that Charles VII would use
a short truce for an insidious conquest of Normandy. Thirdly, Charles
now knew that Henry's title to the French throne was negotiable. But,
fourthly, and in fact in the long run the most significant of his
triumphs over his English nephew at Tours, both the English and the
French versions of the truce terms, which were mutually ratified in
Paris and Rouen to run from sunrise on 1 July 1444 to sunrise on 1
April 1446, included the duke of Brittany, not among the allies and
subjects of the king of England, but in due order among the allies
and subjects of Charles VII, after the dauphin, Orleans and Burgundy
and before Bourbon, Alençon and Charles of Anjou, count of Maine.[23]

[21] Beaucourt, *op. cit.*, III, 276–7, quoting from an early-sixteenth-century copy in
the B.N. of the lost original, MS Latin 10151.

[22] Thomas Basin says 'filiam specie et formam praestantem, quae tunc "maturo
viro foret et plenis nubilis annis"'.

[23] René of Anjou appeared as king of Sicily and Jerusalem, after the king of
Castile and before the king of Scotland.

It is hard to realize that Henry VI and his negotiators at that time attached no special significance to this formal acknowledgement of the loss of the vital Breton alliance.

   ` John V duke of Brittany, of the House of Montfort, who died in 1442, had repeatedly been caught in the vice of the English and French claims to the French throne and had attempted to keep his duchy free from the ravages of war by accommodating whichever side was the stronger at the moment. Charles VII always had the possibility of bringing pressure to bear upon him through the family of Clisson-Penthiève, representatives of a rival Blois claim to the duchy, as well as through his power to confiscate certain lands which the duke held of the French crown outside the bounds of the duchy. Thus he had rendered homage to Charles VII in 1425, although he had been a firm supporter of the treaty of Troyes. Successful English attacks on Brittany, and the absence of aid from Charles VII, had brought him back into an English alliance in 1427, with a declaration of perpetual homage to the infant Henry VI and a reaffirmation of his adherence to the treaty of Troyes. In a most solemn declaration of homage to Henry he then undertook to perform it in person when Henry should come to France, as his predecessors had been accustomed to do to the kings of France. He furthermore insisted on subscription to this declaration of homage by the Breton estates, his chancellor, bishops, lords, cathedral chapters, a number of towns and his near relatives, including the later Duke Francis himself, then count of Montfort, his eldest son and successor. There is no record of this homage ever being personally rendered while Henry was in France. Subsequent successes of French arms forced the duke into yet another treaty of amity with Charles VII in 1431, but, together with the Dauphin Louis, King René of Anjou, the dukes of Bourbon and Alençon and the count of Armagnac, he was involved in the *Praguerie* of 1440. Finally the duke signed a new treaty of peace with Henry on 11 July 1440[24] which, among other more important general matters, mentioned St Malo as being given to his younger son Gilles, Henry's 'dear cousin', to be kept to ensure free intercourse between the two principals, a port from which all ships of the adversary Charles VII, and even Breton ships hostile to Henry VI, should be excluded. At the time of his death the duke was attempting to mediate between the two sides.

   The young Henry had become personally attached to the House of Montfort. An important aspect of John V's relations with England had been his decision to send his youngest and favourite son Gilles, then eight years old, to be brought up with the young Henry VI

---

[24] *Foedera*, X, 385; Morice, *Preuves*, II, cols 1200-2, 1204-5, 1329-42 (11 July and 18 October 1440).

under the tutorship of Richard Beauchamp, earl of Warwick. They were cousins through their mothers Jeanne and Catherine, daughters of Charles VI of France, and no more than two years separated them in age. Lavishly provided for by his father, the young Gilles also received a maintenance allowance of 250 marks from the English exchequer. The two boys became greatly attached to one another and it was with much reluctance that the English council agreed to Gilles's return to his father in August 1434, heaping praises upon him for the pleasure and satisfaction which the young king had found in his company.[25] Gilles's special captaincy of St Malo was a memorial to his own, and his father's, particularly close English affiliations.

Such was the background to the reappearance of Gilles at Henry VI's court in June 1443[26] at the head of a Breton embassy. The vasion of his territory, on which Henry gave him immediate satisfaction who had only recently succeeded his father on 28 August 1442, had sent his younger brother to ask for the restoration of the earldom of Richmond, which had been held by the Montfort family for two centuries from 1136, and again during the reign of Richard II. Gilles was authorized personally to enter Henry's service and to offer Duke Francis's own services as mediator in the renewed peace negotiations with the king of France. Henry's ready acceptance of the personal allegiance and service of Gilles of Brittany in the autumn of 1443 was to have far-reaching, long-term consequences, at least as significant as his grasping at the Angevin marriage, and his decision to make a unilateral surrender of the county of Maine to his new father-in-law. Its special importance arose from Henry's careless acceptance of the loss of the allegiance of Duke Francis at Tours in May 1444 and the consequent separate English and French allegiances of the two Montfort brothers.

Gilles's service to Henry VI, proffered and accepted in 1443, was to be open-ended, at the king's discretion, in peace and war. His brother the duke also asked to be included by Henry, on honourable terms, in any peace treaty he made with Charles VII. But in October or November 1443 Gilles was reporting that Charles VII had requested the presence of his brother the duke in his entourage, along with his princes of the blood, to meet Henry VI's ambassadors, Suffolk and the others, a request he said the duke would not answer until Henry had declared his wishes in the matter. At this time the duke also made his complaint against the elder Somerset's alleged invasion of his territory, on which Henry gave him immediate satisfaction and at the same time confirmed the fact of the approaching peace

[25] *Foedera*, IX, 48; *P.P.C.*, IV, 128, 151, 181.
[26] Morice, *Preuves*, II, col. 1371.

conference. With regard to the duke's claim to the earldom of Richmond an evasive reply was made. It was said that diligent search of the records revealed only its continuous history in the hands of the House of Lancaster ever since its conferment on John of Gaunt in 1342. This was untrue. The Montforts had held it for much of Richard II's reign and, perhaps more to the point in 1443, Henry had alienated most of the lands of the earldom to Richard Nevill, earl of Salisbury. Gilles formally entered Henry's service with an annual pension of 1,000 marks on 12 December 1443, with the king taking great interest in it and personally settling the details: a gift of two service books from the effects of the cardinal of Luxembourg for his chapel, a cup of gold worth 100 marks with £100 in it and advance payment of his first quarter's pension.[27] On 28 August Charles VII, fully appreciating the danger that Gilles's embassy might result in a new strengthened alliance between Henry and Duke Francis, had already confiscated Gilles's French lands of Chantocé and Ingrandes on the Loire which he had inherited from his father, for treason with the English.[28]

It has been claimed that Somerset's idiotic blunder over La Guerche threw Duke Francis into the arms of Charles VII at Tours, or alternatively that Somerset, in spite of being immediately disowned by Henry, had in fact only been following his instructions to demonstrate the English power to the young duke of Brittany when he was wavering in his allegiance.[29] But contemporary evidence states that La Guerche, like Pouancé, was held for the duke of Alençon, Charles VII's commander-in-chief in the area, and suggests that its capture was the result merely of a local military decision taken on the spot. The fact was that Henry VI and those who had his ear, in their eagerness to come to terms with Charles VII, utterly failed to realize until too late the great potential importance of the Breton allegiance. It was Charles VII, not Henry, who managed to ensure that Duke Francis appeared at Tours as his ally, if not yet as his vassal. Henry was left only with the troublesome allegiance of his brother Gilles. Shortly after the Tours negotiations Gilles abducted and married an eight-year-old Breton heiress, Françoise de Dinan, and, with her patrimony of Châteaubriant, La Hardouinaie, Montrafilant and Le Guildo, became at a stroke one of the greatest landowners in Brittany. Established in the fine stronghold of Le Guildo on the Arguenon estuary to the west of Dinard, he remained a firm adherent of the English interest and entitled to Henry's support, a potential menace to his brother's new French allegiance and thus also to Charles VII's in-

[27] *P.P.C.*, VI, 3–23, Stevenson, *Wars*, I, 439, 440–1.
[28] Morice, *Preuves*, II, col. 1362.
[29] See above pp. 167–8.

tended reassertion of Valois sovereignty over Brittany.[30]

An English embassy to collect Henry's bride left England on 13 November 1444 and the marriage ceremony was performed at Nancy by Charles VII's councillor, Louis d'Haraucourt, bishop of Toul, early in March 1445. Suffolk, now raised to the marquisate, once more stood proxy for his king. The mounting of such a major expedition could hardly have been done in shorter time. The services of some 70 ships were required to transport the substantial household of Suffolk and his lady, together with Beatrice Lady Talbot and a suite of 5 barons and baronesses, 17 knights, 65 esquires and 215 yeomen, the escort deemed appropriate for the new queen. It cost the English exchequer, over six months, £5,573 17s 5d, that is £434 5d more than had been made available for John Brecknock, the receiver general of the duchy of Cornwall, and John Everdon, clerk of accounts in Henry's household, who were deputed to manage the finances.[31]

No further negotiations were conducted by Suffolk on this his second assignment beyond completing the necessary financial arrangements for the truce. These were an agreement about division of *appatis* or 'protection' moneys, which the coming of the truce would entail, the means of support which the garrison troops of both sides levied in time of war from the various local communities within their range of influence. From the date of the truce all these would be taken under control of higher authority by both sides within their designated areas of jurisdiction. It had emerged that the French would lose thereby, since at the date of the truce *appatis* levied by the French in the disputed frontier regions considerably exceeded those levied there by the English. To compensate for the discrepancy, Suffolk at Nancy agreed to pay Charles VII 4,500 *livres tournois* and a further 1,078 *livres tournois* each quarter to the garrison of Bellême, sums which were subsequently charged on the revenues of Normandy until the renewal of the war.[32] It was by later agreeing to forgo these Norman contributions that Charles VII could claim to have provided compensation for those dispossesed in Le Mans, at ten years' purchase, when Henry finally handed it over.[33] Apart from one other agreement made by Suffolk on his return journey at Rouen on 3 April 1445 regarding

---

[30] A. Bourdeaut, 'Gilles de Bretagne entre la France et l'Angleterre', *Mémoires de la société d'histoire et d'archéologie de Bretagne*, I (1920), 68.

[31] Stevenson, *Wars*, I, 443–60. Commissioners to solicit loans for the expenses of conducting her to England and her coronation. *P.P.C.*, VI, 322–5.

[32] Beaucourt, *op. cit.*, IV, 18, 144, citing contemporary references to this agreement; C. de Beaurepaire, *Les Etats de Normandie sous la Domination Anglaise* (Evreux 1859), 86.

[33] *Foedera*, XI, 203–4. For *appatis* in general see A. Lecoy de la Marche, *op. cit.*, I, 521–2; Stevenson *Wars*, II, 550; Philippe Contamine, *op. cit.*, 248–50.

11(a). Richard duke of York: statue formerly on the Welsh bridge, Shrewsbury, now on the old Market House.

11(b). Tomb effigy of John Beaufort, duke of Somerset, in Wimborne Minster, Dorset.

11(c). Richard Nevill, earl of Salisbury; Edmund Beaufort, duke of Somerset; and Richard Nevill, earl of Warwick, the 'Kingmaker', from the south side of the tomb of Richard Beauchamp, earl of Warwick, in St Mary's, Warwick.

12(a). King Charles VII
of France by
Jehan Fouquet
(Louvre, Paris).

12(b). Charles duke of Orleans in
the Tower of London (B.L.
Royal MS 16 F II, f. 173).

compensation for violations of the truce and the payment of income due to churches and individuals who had lands and rents under control of the other side,[34] there is no evidence whatsoever of any further negotiations. The contemporary charge of Thomas Gascoigne, who tells the story three times over, that Suffolk at Nancy was compelled to promise to hand over Maine without conditions, or return to England empty-handed without Henry's bride, is entirely without foundation.[35] Suffolk's report to parliament on 2 June 1445 did state that he had had conversations with French ambassadors arranging for an embassy to England to discuss peace terms with Henry, but he had not presumed to discuss any details of a settlement. He also claimed that a truce meant no loss of vigilance in the English lands and that he had advised the duke of York to strengthen and provision the frontier towns of Normandy and Maine as 'a great means to the better conclusion of peace'.[36] The ending of York's lieutenancy in September 1445 meant that this was never done.

The undoubted delay of some two to three months after Suffolk's arrival in Nancy, the capital of Lorraine, was in fact clearly explained by the military activities of Charles VII, who had taken immediate and full advantage of the new freedom of action presented by the truce of Tours to concentrate his resources and energies on problems in the eastern confines of his kingdom where Henry VI's new father-in-law was also closely involved as duke of Lorraine and Bar by right of his wife. The 'Bourgeois of Paris' regarded this as an irresponsible abandonment of the kingdom by Charles and the dauphin to make a war in Lorraine and Germany, leaving the English free to strengthen and provision their castles,[37] but in fact they had taken the English troops under Mathew Gough with them! The problems and dangers of English soldiery unemployed because of the truce were for the moment shelved by allowing English men-at-arms led by Mathew Gough to enlist under the dauphin to fight in Germany. After five months subduing the country between Strasbourg and Basle, the dauphin was recalled to the court at Nancy from where his father and René of Anjou were conducting a siege of Metz, a city tenacious of its independence of the duke of Lorraine and of Valois France. Only on 28 February 1445 was a treaty of peace signed with the stubborn city and Charles, at last, free to welcome Suffolk and attend to the marriage of Margaret.[38]

[34] Beaucourt, *op. cit.*, IV, 144.
[35] *Loci Libro Veritatis*, ed. J. E. Thorold Rogers (Oxford 1881), 190, 204, 219, elaborated by Ramsay, *Lancaster and York*, II, 62–3.
[36] *R.P.*, V, 118–20.
[37] *Journal* (ed. Tuetey), 375.
[38] Berry herald, 425, 426, Beaucourt, *op. cit.*, IV, 57, Stevenson, *Wars*, I, 119.

After eight days of festivities she was conducted two leagues from Nancy by Charles VII himself, where she bade him a tearful farewell, escorted by her father as far as Bar-le-Duc and then by her brother and her cousin the duke of Alençon to Paris, where the canons of Notre-Dame accorded her the honours of a queen regnant, by order of Charles VII. Received by the duke of York at Pontoise, she proceeded by river to Rouen and then again down river to Harfleur, where she embarked on the *Cock John* of Cherbourg, landing at Porchester on 9 April. For the next seven days she lay sick at Southampton 'of the labour and indisposition of the sea by occasion of which the pocks be broken out upon her'. Henry, impatiently awaiting her at Southwick, consequently had to arrange for deputies to hold the Garter feast of Saint George at Windsor on his behalf.[39] They were finally married by his confessor, William Aiscough, bishop of Salisbury, in the Premonstratensian abbey of Titchfield on Thursday 22 April, the vigil of St George. She made her state entry into London from Blackheath on 28 May, and was crowned in Westminster Abbey on Sunday 30 May.[40]

Margaret of Anjou came dowerless to England but, in the words of St Bridget, the hope was 'Fiat pax per matrimonium'.[41] John Stafford, archbishop of Canterbury and chancellor, took for his text at the opening of parliament on 25 February 1445 'Righteousness and peace have kissed each other'.[42] Marriage and truce had been made by Henry in trust to that prime end, although he also believed, according to the instructions given to his commissioners soliciting loans to pay for it, that the whole kingdom would have cause to thank God for the provision of this queen 'of a high and noble birth, greatly endowed with gifts of grace and nature'.[43] Peace and Plenty was also the message of the pageant which greeted her on London Bridge and Henry's biographer Capgrave reiterated the theme: everyone considered these nuptials pleasing to the church and state 'pro eo quod pax et abundantia frugum cum ipsis adventarent'. Against this a more realistic commentator added the succinct marginal comment: 'compilator adulavit'.[44]

The new queen, although she was only fifteen at the time of her

---

[39] *P.P.C.*, VI, xvi.

[40] Ramsay, *Lancaster and York*, II, 64, chronicle references there given and Benet's Chronicle, 190–1, Davies's Chronicle, 61–2, Bale (ed. Flenley), 119–20, Stow, *Annales*, 384–5, Gregory's Chronicle, 185–6 (Stow and Gregory for processions and pageants).

[41] Stevenson, *Wars*, I, 139.

[42] *R.P.*, V, 66.

[43] *P.P.C.*, VI, 323.

[44] Johannis Capgrave, *Liber de Illustribus Henricis*, ed. F. C. Hingeston (R. S., 1858), 135.

marriage, was soon to be a powerful influence in her new country. Charles VII had hoped that the marriage would bring him a pleasing advocate at the court of his nephew and he must have been very well satisfied with his protégée. It is not surprising that she soon established herself in the heart of Henry VI, who had little family to absorb his affections. He had already shown himself very easily influenced by those closest to him and Margaret obviously sustained his resolve to continue with his unpopular and disastrous French policy. Her association with this policy led to her marriage being regarded as the beginning of Henry's failures. The English always showed a dislike of foreign queens who meddled in politics. The last one to have done so before Margaret was Isabella, queen of Edward II, and the next, another French princess, Henrietta Maria, Charles I's queen. One should not pursue a comparison too far, but it cannot be entirely coincidence that those three queens each saw civil war in England and the violent death of her husband.

Back in Nancy Charles VII had taken a muster of all the French troops who had been summoned to Germany and before Metz. The best of them, 1,500 lances and 4,500 archers, were formed into companies under fifteen captains and lodged in different areas of the kingdom to provide for their support, with each man-at-arms drawing quarterly pay of 30 francs a month. A special *taille des gens d'armes* was instituted to pay their wages; the rest were sent home with pardons. Thus in the conditions of peace brought about by the truce of Tours the permanent French army, vainly foreshadowed in the great Ordinance of 1439,[45] could now be founded. By contrast, in spite of Suffolk's assurances to parliament, the English garrisons were allowed to fall into a state of demoralization and penury and no field force was maintained. The widely different treatment of their armies is a practical expression of the fundamentally different approach of Charles and Henry to the truce. To Charles it was merely a short truce of which he intended to take full diplomatic and military advantage, whereas Henry believed it was the first stage towards a permanent peace and began to act as though that peace was already achieved. His failure to maintain his forces on a war footing, like his unilateral diplomatic concessions, further weakened his future negotiating position and handed the initiative to his adversary.

[45] Berry herald, 427; Beaucourt, *op. cit.*, III, 402–16.

Chapter 11

SURRENDER AND DEFEAT, 1445–1450

At Tours the English conditions for a final peace were possession of Normandy and Gascony in complete sovereignty in return for the abandonment of the title to the French throne. These were spurned by Charles VII[1] who had other ideas; as he himself declared,[2] he personally employed himself with all his heart to further the Angevin marriage by which Henry was absorbed into the Valois family. This was to be the means by which peace would be achieved and it should be followed by a short truce to allow time for the achievement. Consequently, as the members of the French embassy which came to England in July 1445 were instructed to make clear, they came as the king's own kinsmen and most intimate councillors and from now on all diplomatic exchanges between the two kings were to be conducted in a close family context, with Charles affirming that in cordial love and affection his nephew Henry was next in his heart to the dauphin,[3] and Henry reciprocating that his uncle Charles was the person in the world whom he loved best, after his wife.[4] These were no mere pious formalities. Behind the official, diplomatic exchanges, which were themselves couched in such intimate terms, there also began a further direct, personal correspondence between Henry and Margaret and their uncle Charles, written from England by the French secretaries Jean Rinel, Gervase le Vulre and Michael de Paris.[5] Several examples of these from the French archives chart the vital, decisive influence of these personal exchanges at the highest level. On 17 December 1445, at Sheen, Margaret acknowledged a personal communication from her uncle, brought by the master of requests of his household, Guillaume Cousinot, and his carver Jean Harvart. She sent oral messages by them in return, but also affirmed in writing her intention to do what he had asked, to work on Henry for the delivery to Charles of the county of Maine.[6] On 20 May 1446, at Windsor,

[1] Stevenson, *Wars*, I, 151–2.
[2] *Ibid.*, 118.
[3] *Ibid.*, 109.
[4] *Ibid.*, 116.
[5] Over two dozen examples of this correspondence are recorded in print, most of them by Beaucourt in his edition of the *Chronique de Mathieu D'Escouchy*, vol. III (*Preuves*).
[6] Stevenson, *Wars*, I, 164–7, signed Marguerite (MS fr. 4054, f. 37).

Michael de Paris wrote on her behalf in answer to other requests from Charles, affirming that she would also make every effort to be present in person at Henry's projected face-to-face meeting with his uncle.[7] The most vital communication of all was a personal letter under the signet and sign manual, which Henry himself sent to Charles from Windsor on 22 December 1445, firmly undertaking, on the word of a king, all excuses and hindrances laid aside, to accede to his request for the complete surrender of Le Mans and the county of Maine, as his most dear and well-beloved companion the queen had repeatedly requested him to do. His only reason for this was that his uncle of France had informed him that this would be one of the best and aptest means of arriving at a final peace![8]

The proceedings of the first and greatest French embassy of July 1445, arising from the truce of Tours, were recorded in full detail by more than one of its members.[9] There had been nothing like it since 1415. It was led by Charles VII's close kinsman Louis prince of Bourbon, count of Vendôme and Chartres, sovereign master of the household, Jacques Jouvenel des Ursins, archbishop of Rheims, president of the *chambre des comptes*, and Bertrand de Beauvau, lord of Précigny, king's chamberlain and councillor. These three were the principal negotiators. Other members were the count of Laval, introduced as the French king's cousin and Henry's cousin german, Guillaume Cousinot, master of requests, and Etienne Chevalier, king's secretary. In addition there were supporting embassies from the king of Castile, René of Anjou and John duke of Alençon. The ambassadors of the duke of Burgundy failed to arrive in time because of difficulties over a safe-conduct. Over 300 horses were needed to move them all to London. They were shepherded in batches across the Channel from Calais by Garter and reached London in easy stages, with suitable escorts, via Canterbury, Rochester and Maidstone, for an impressive civic welcome to the city on Wednesday 14 July. They met Henry at Westminster three times. On the Thursday he received them, richly clad and in impressive formal state. Later in this audience he moved about among them, doffing his cap to them, conversing in French and even patting them on the back, striving hard to generate an atmosphere of the utmost friendliness. He reproved his chancellor in English for a polished latin oration which was not friendly enough for his liking. Suffolk was the councillor most familiar to the Frenchmen and his words were later repeatedly recalled to show his extreme good will towards their master. Gloucester, by contrast, was something of a bugbear, and they professed to have seen Henry openly express his

[7] *Ibid.*, 183–6, signed Marguerite (MS fr. 4054, f. 33).
[8] *Ibid.*, II, pt. ii, 639–42.
[9] *Ibid.*, 87–159.

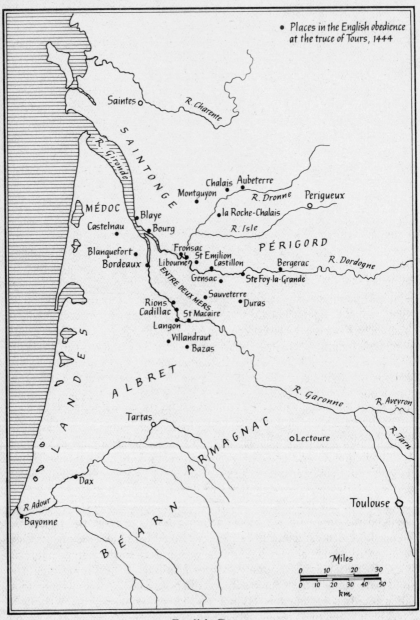

Places in the English obedience at the truce of Tours, 1444

Saintes

R. Charente

SAINTONGE

R. Gironde

Chalais   Aubeterre

Montguyon

R. Dronne   Perigueux

MÉDOC   Blaye

la Roche-Chalais

Castelnau   Bourg

R. Isle

PÉRIGORD

Blanquefort   Fronsac

St Emilion

Bordeaux   Libourne   Castillon   Bergerac   R. Dordogne

Gensac   Ste Foy-la-Grande

ENTRE DEUX MERS

Sauveterre

Rions   Duras

Cadillac   St Macaire

Langon

Villandraut

Bazas

ALBRET

R. Garonne   R. Aveyron

Tartas   R. Tarn

Lectoure

ARMAGNAC

Dax

BÉARN

R. Adour   Toulouse

Bayonne

Miles
0   10   20   30

0   10   20   30   40   50
km

3   English Gascony

pleasure at seeing his uncle's discomfiture at the turn of events.

On the 16th, Friday, they assembled in the king's great chamber, prior to being received in his privy chamber. Here Suffolk, in the eyes of the French, both before and during the audience, dominated the scene. This audience was designed to generate further intimacy and confidence between the two sides and to dispel any fears that the French might have about disunity in Henry's councils. Suffolk, they reported, specifically denied rumours that Gloucester had tried to prevent a successful outcome of the Tours conference, but affirmed that even if he had wished to do so he had no power. Again, when he gave them audience, Henry talked familiarly to the ambassadors and finally deputed the cardinal of York, Suffolk and Ralph Butler, the treasurer, to conduct negotiations with them. The king then retired to Windsor for the weekend and more permanent lodgings were provided for the ambassadors, who were given a sight-seeing tour of the city on the Sunday.

On Monday morning at 8 a.m. serious negotiations began in the new refectory at Blackfriars. Suffolk and the archbishop in turn recapitulated the position as it had been left at Tours where, it now appeared, Charles VII's maximum offer had been Guienne,[10] Quercy, Périgord, Calais and Guînes with full homage, that is, what the French said the English had claimed before they claimed the crown as well. Cardinal Kemp said that historically what they claimed before the crown included Poitou and Normandy, but Suffolk cut short the ensuing wrangle over history with a plea for thorough frankness, before suggesting dinner. A further meeting next day made no progress, but the following day's parley extracted the addition of Limousin. Suffolk's reputed *rapport*, which he claimed to have established with Charles VII at Tours, had clearly made Henry's deputies certain that the French still had something up their sleeves. They had, but it was only Saintonge, and at the end of the day on Wednesday 21 July they finally convinced the thoroughly disillusioned English negotiators that they had reached the very limit of their instructions. They had been expected to offer more than ever before, but they had offered less; the cardinal now admitted that no more could be done by them; Henry, at Windsor, would have to be consulted. This turned out to be the cue for which the Frenchmen were waiting. Précigny exclaimed: 'Would to God that they [the two kings] would meet, and would see each other', to which all chorused 'Amen'. Suffolk left for Windsor after dinner to brief Henry.

On Friday 30 July Henry received both delegations in audience at Fulham Palace. The upshot of this final meeting was that Henry now

---

[10] i.e. Gascony, which the French normally called Guienne and the English indifferently Gascony or Aquitaine. The French defined this as the three seneschalries of Bordeaux, Landes and Bazadais.

gave a firm undertaking to meet his uncle Charles VII in France, in spite of all the formidable problems involved in such a journey. The Frenchmen then suggested a six-month prolongation of the truce to All Saints Day 1446, to allow for it. A request from the English delegates for a longer extension revealed that the Frenchmen had had instructions all the time covering precisely what they had now suggested, but now absolutely no more latitude whatsoever. They could only suggest taking back English envoys to make this request for a longer truce to Charles himself. If that was all, the French still had had a most pleasant and successful embassy but there was more: Précigny, who had first suggested the personal meeting, subsequently revealed that Henry also gave him an oral undertaking that he would surrender Maine before 1 October 1445.[11]

It fell to the lot of Adam Moleyns, former clerk of the council, now keeper of the privy seal, and about to be made bishop of Chichester, to return with the ambassadors to France to secure the further prolongation of the truce. The French subsequently alleged that on this visit to France in the autumn of 1445 he was charged to implement the surrender of Maine.[12] At all events, the further prolongation of the truce, which he requested, was made the official occasion for an immediate new French embassy, led by Guillaume Cousinot, master of requests of the household, and Jean Harvart the king's carver. With them went King René's personal representatives Auvergnas Chaperon and Charles de Castillon. René gave separate powers of attorney to each pair at Angers on 17 October,[13] but only to Charles's representatives did he give power to negotiate over the surrender of Maine in return for an alliance for life between the Angevins and Henry and a twenty-year truce between them. Chaperon's and Castillon's instructions were somewhat cryptically minuted by Pierre de Brézé, seneschal of Poitou, Charles's chamberlain and principal and intimate adviser,[14] as being subordinate to the other, only to be used to avoid a breakdown of negotiations over the delivery of Maine. The House of Anjou would thus be allowed to recover Maine only through the licence and agency of the French king, their sovereign lord. This was undoubtedly the real purpose of the new mission. On

---

[11] B.N. MS fr. 18442, f. 173, subsequent instructions to the French negotiators; Beaucourt, *op. cit.*, IV, 285 n. The allegation that the undertaking to surrender Maine was first made 'de bouche' by Henry is repeated in B.N. MS fr. 4054, f. 71, printed in Eschoucy (ed. Beaucourt), III (*Preuves*), 194 (letters from French ambassadors to their English opposite numbers, 1448).

[12] B.N. MS fr. 18442, f. 173.

[13] Lecoy de la Marche, *op. cit.*, II, 258–60 (see above p. 172); Arch. Nat. P. 1334[18] no. 106.

[14] Beaucourt, *op. cit.*, IV, 208, no. 8.

12 November Henry appointed Suffolk, Moleyns, John Viscount Beaumont and his chamberlain and treasurer, Sudeley, to treat with them. York, who still considered himself Henry's lieutenant of France, was now back in England, but he was given no part in these negotiations. The official agreements which emerged were for a second prolongation of the truce to 1 April 1447 and an undertaking that Henry would go to France to meet his uncle before 1 November 1446.[15] The real product of this second French embassy was the secret undertaking given by Henry, in the letter under the signet and sign manual to his uncle Charles on 22 December, that he would surrender Maine by 30 April 1446.[16] So secret was this pledge that Henry sent a quite separate letter under the sign manual on the same day to the French king which made no mention of Maine. This acknowledged his personal communications via Moleyns, Cousinot and Harvart, and assured him that delay over their proposed personal meeting and the concomitant extension of the truce were necessary only because of his current great preoccupation with the affairs of parliament.[17] Thus it is probable that in 1444 and 1445 Suffolk was aware of the French soundings for the surrender of Maine and certain that Moleyns was involved in them prior to his elevation to the episcopate.[18] But none of Henry's negotiators could or did give the vital, explicit commitment to surrender, which lay hidden behind the public documents. This was the undertaking Henry gave personally and secretly in the letter written by his French secretary to his uncle on 22 December 1445. From that moment Charles VII quite legitimately took this unilateral concession in the cause of peace to be legally binding and cleverly made its implementation the condition for any further extension of the truce.

1446 should thus have been a year of great events. On 2 January Garter, also charged with unspecified verbal messages, bore Henry's greetings to his uncle, written by Michael de Paris and signed by the king, reaffirming his intention to cross to France.[19] The practical details of implementing the truce were not proving difficult. Between the end of March and early May a quite successful convention was held at Evreux and Louviers to settle arguments about disputed revenues and alleged excesses and violations by both sides.[20] But who would implement the surrender of Maine? It could hardly be done without

[15] *Foedera*, XI, 106-7, 108-14.
[16] See above p. 185.
[17] Escouchy (ed. Beaucourt), III (*Preuves*), 151-3. Parliament was dissolved on 9 April 1446.
[18] He received the temporalities on 3 December 1445.
[19] Stevenson, *Wars*, II, pt. i, 368-71.
[20] *Ibid.*, I, 178-82.

the cooperation of the king's lieutenant in France and the government in Rouen; also of Edmund Beaufort, marquis of Dorset and
count of Maine,[21] and of the garrisons there who claimed to hold it
in his name. The duke of York had gone home to attend parliament
and defend his reputation in the autumn of 1445.[22] Although his term
of office had expired at Michaelmas 1445, for many months he daily
expected orders to return, though this was obviously now bound up
with the king's projected journey. Parliament was told on 9 April that
the king, of his own mind and by divine inspiration, not by the
promptings of his council, had determined to go to France to meet
his uncle in September 1446 and duly revoked the clause of the treaty
of Troyes forbidding negotiations with the 'dauphin Charles' without
the consent of the Estates.[23] 30 April, the date for the projected surrender of Maine, passed unnoticed, at least as far as the official records
went. Mathew Gough bore personal messages from Henry to Charles
on 2 July.[24] York, still in England, was promised wages for 200 spears
and the bows on 20 July, three months in hand at the lower English rates and then month by month at the higher French rates, in
anticipation of his return, presumably as Henry's right-hand man.
The council proceeded to solicit loans and to arrest shipping for the
king's expedition on the same day.[25]

The idea was for a personal convention of the two kings on the
river between Meulan and Mantes.[26] The Estates of Normandy
granted 130,000 *livres tournois*. In preparation for the meeting Charles
VII had Jean Jouvenal des Ursins, bishop of Laon, draw him up a
schedule of transcribed documents relative to his rights in the English
occupied lands, to the claims of the kings of England to the French
crown and to the validity of the treaty of Troyes.[27] But doubts had
been voiced on the English side; the meeting might have to be postponed until the following March.[28] Moleyns and John Sutton, Lord
Dudley, appointed to go on embassy[29] originally to arrange the day
and place, in fact went to request a postponement, a most unwelcome
suggestion to Charles, so he said, and in his eyes a great detriment

---

[21] First unequivocally styled count of Maine on 23 September 1447 (below p. 194n),
but see above pp. 163-4 for evidence of a grant and authority exercised there before
1443.
[22] Before 21 September: *ibid.*, 163.
[23] *R.P.*, V, 102-3.
[24] Escouchy (ed. Beaucourt), III (*Preuves*), 156-7.
[25] *P.P.C.*, VI, 46-9, 52-3.
[26] *Ibid.*, 53, 54.
[27] *Foedera*, IX, 138-9.
[28] *P.P.C.*, VI, 51.
[29] *Foedera*, XI, 138-9.

and injury to the cause of peace. So important did he consider it that he flatly refused to agree, thus putting his nephew Henry in default of yet another promise. He insisted on sending yet another embassy to England to bargain about it. Cousinot and Havart, appointed for this purpose on this their second embassy, did not arrive in London until December when the original final date for the meeting (1 November), like the original date for the surrender of Maine (30 April), was now past. Effusions of good will from Charles VII did not conceal the hard fact that he now made fulfilment of the promise to surrender Maine a *sine qua non* of fixing a new date for the personal meeting. Cousinot and Harvart, he maintained, could be given formal seisin of Maine and they could give a secret, conditional undertaking to prorogue the personal meeting of the two kings in advance if necessary, but to no one except to Henry and Suffolk.[30] Nothing at all was achieved on either of these two points and by the following February (1447) Moleyns and Dudley, with the French secretary Michael de Paris, were back again in the French court at Tours, accompanied by Mathew Gough, by which date the expiration of the truce itself had once more become imminent (1 April 1447). On 22 February 1447, at the second treaty of Tours, they secured a further breathing space to 1 January 1448, during which time the two kings should come together at a place and time still to be fixed.[31]

What had gone wrong? It is easy to imagine the many misgivings which Henry VI's councillors had over his dual, personal decisions for the cause of peace to 'employ a great part of his heritage which he had had in France [Maine], and *de propriae personae commercio* [this personal meeting with Charles VII]'.[32] This latter would be a costly and hazardous affair. The finance and logistics of mounting another expedition, at least on the scale of the coronation *chevauchée*, or of Somerset's more recent 1443 expedition, probably simply could not have been managed successfully in the time available before the original date of 1 November 1446, less than twelve months ahead. It has been suggested that postponement began because of the high politics involved in the decision as to who should accompany him in the highest position of authority. The recalled York? Apparently as late as 20 July 1446 he received positive reassurance on this score. The ailing Gloucester? Who among the princes of the blood could best be trusted to implement the king's policies to which he had committed his agents, in the Angevin marriage and the truce of Tours? In

[30] Beaucourt, *op. cit.*, IV, 289, citing B.N. MS Clairambault, 307, pp. 570–61; *Foedera*, XI, 152–3, 14 December 1446.
[31] Beaucourt, *op. cit.*, IV, 290; *Foedera*, XI, 153–5.
[32] Stevenson, *Wars*, I, 147, his final words, through Cardinal Kemp to the embassy of July 1445.

the event it was another royal deputy, Edmund Beaufort, now earl of Somerset,[33] who finally received the appointment of king's lieutenant in December 1446,[34] but he was not to set foot in Normandy until March 1448! Pliancy in the furtherance of Henry's wishes, rather than military or administrative ability, was now the most desirable qualification for this office. However, Somerset in his own right as a prince of the blood and a hitherto successful soldier, the victor of Harfleur in 1440, of the relief of Calais in 1442 and Bedford's successor in the campaigns in Maine and Anjou, would appear to have had the military competence for the office.

The dangers inherent in personal interviews between kings and princes in the fifteenth century, and their conspicuous, inevitable lack of success for one side or the other, have been graphically preserved for us by Philippe de Commynes.[35] Yet the fervour with which both sides had greeted the original suggestion at the deadlocked meeting of the great embassy showed that personal decisions by the two kings alone could determine the issue. It could be that, having reacted on impulse to Précigny's original stage-managed suggestion, Henry's advisers later more prudently feared that he would be as clay in the hands of his wily uncle. The sad and simple explanation is that the English had allowed themselves to become hooked on a series of truces of limited duration, each extension of which Charles VII now made dependent on one condition after another. Ultimately, quite other issues, involving the allegiance of Brittany, fatally endangered the truce. It was a diplomatic game in which the French had early gained the upper hand and never subsequently lost it.

After the second treaty of Tours, 22 February 1447, Moleyns and his companions returned to London to announce the coming of a second large-scale, high-powered French embassy to London, this time headed by Dunois, Beauvau, Cousinot, Havart and Jean Jouguet, notary and secretary of the king of France. No diplomatic stone was left unturned by Charles VII to secure a peace satisfactory to himself thereby. He even wrote in advance to the city of London on 2 May 1447, soliciting its good offices for the success of his embassy.[36] On 1 July Henry designated the duke of Buckingham, Suffolk, Moleyns,

---

[33] By the death of his brother John, 27 May 1444.

[34] His commission delivered 24 December 1446: Burney, *op. cit.*, 145.

[35] Philippe de Commynes, *Memoirs*, ed. & trans. Michael Jones (Harmondsworth 1972), 141-5; two great princes of equal power should meet each other only when they were both very young and had thoughts only for their pleasures.

[36] Jules Delpit, *Collection générale des documents français*, i, 263; *Calendar of Letter Books of the City of London*, Letter Book K, ed. R. R. Sharpe (London 1911), 320.

John, Lord Scrope and John, Lord Dudley to negotiate with them.[37] On 27 July 1447 a new treaty was signed, extending the date for the personal meeting to 1 May 1448. It appears from the next subsequent extension of the truce recorded that the truce itself was likewise extended at the same time, exactly to the same date and not beyond that date.[38]

These concessions were only bought on 27 July 1447 by the most solemn undertaking in the form of letters patent, exemplifying Henry's personal promise of 22 December 1445 to surrender Maine, written by the clerk of the council Thomas Kent and handed over to the French ambassadors in the presence of the earl of Somerset, who personally stood to lose most by the loss of Maine, 'and many others of our blood and of our council', 'after great and ripe deliberation'.[39] A final date, and Charles VII at least meant it to be so, was fixed for the surrender of Maine: 1 November 1447. Was the matter now out in the open at last? There had been rumours; Suffolk had already been blamed. As recently as 25 May 1447, as a result of his petition to Henry, he had been granted the opportunity to make a solemn declaration in the king's chamber, in the royal presence before eight spiritual and lay peers, including York 'and others our servants, familiars and domestics', that he had never been a party to any proposals for the surrender of Maine. The king wished to silence the malicious rumours stirring about this.[40] Now, only two months later, Henry was formally binding members of his council and entourage to the execution of that same execrated policy which had in truth been his own for the last two years. Charles VII, in his instructions to his ambassadors, had made it an absolute condition binding on his negotiators that they must now have the firmest possible undertaking to deliver Maine before making any other treaty.[41] This was the crunch over Maine and administrative action followed swiftly the next day to secure its implementation. By signet letter, which he signed in the presence of Suffolk on 28 July 1447, Henry ordered the English captains Mathew Gough and Fulk Eyton to receive Maine from the hands of Edmund Beaufort, earl of Somerset, not in his capacity as his lieutenant of Normandy and France, but as count of Maine by Henry's grant, and styled the marquis and earl of Dorset because this had been his title when he had received this former patrimony of his

[37] *Foedera*, XI, 175–6.
[38] *Ibid.*, 193–6.
[39] Stevenson, *Wars*, II, pt. ii, 693, 694. According to the French (see below p. 195) these were the duke of Buckingham, the duke of Suffolk, Adam Moleyns, lords Scrope and Dudley and Thomas Kent.
[40] *Foedera*, XI, 172–4.
[41] *Ibid.*, 184.

uncle Bedford. Somerset and his lieutenants in Maine and Anjou were commanded to provide soldiers if necessary, at the request of Gough and Eyton, to effect the surrender.[42] The same day (28 July) a personal letter, written by Rinel and signed by Henry, went off to Charles VII, informing him what had been done about the surrender of Maine and announcing a further embassy, led by the bishop of Norwich, the king's councillor, going to Lyons on the affairs of the church, which would visit him on the way.[43] It was this embassy, consisting of Walter, bishop of Norwich, Robert Botyll, prior of St John, John, Lord Dudley, Vincent Clement, president of the chamber of accounts at Rouen, and Thomas Kent, clerk of the council, which confirmed the 27 July agreement at Bourges on 15 October 1447 and secured, by way of reward for Henry, a further extension of the truce from 1 May 1448 to 1 January 1449.[44] Charles VII wrote to Henry on 17 October with the news of it, Garter delivered the letter and was sent back with a reply on 11 December 1447. In this Henry joyously confirmed the extended truce and informed Charles that he was now sending the earl of Somerset to Normandy to deal with any past or future infractions of the truce.[45]

By this date, of course, Henry's royal gift of all he held, or rather of all Somerset held by his previous gift, in Anjou and Maine should have been handed over to Charles VII's emissaries. But serious difficulties began when Gough and Eyton presented themselves at Le Mans before their comrades-in-arms, Somerset's lieutenants Osborne Mundeford, captain of Le Mans and Beaumont-sur-Sarthe, and Sir Richard Frogenhall, captain of Mayenne. Nothing more than a polite charade ensued in which Mundeford declined to make the delivery because the king's agents did not have specific orders signed and sealed from the middleman, Somerset, and he had no letters of discharge either from Henry or from Somerset. Gough and Eyton retired to await further instructions.[46] It was a full month before they could be ordered by Henry from Eltham to try again, now armed with letters patent for Mundeford's and Frogenhall's discharge and sufficient acquittances.[47] On 28 October, when he realized that 1 November 1447 must pass without his promise being fulfilled, Henry sent peremptory orders to Somerset to secure the obedience of his officers, in an

[42] Stevenson, *Wars*, II, pt. ii, 692–702, 704. Somerset is there styled count of Maine, captain general and governor of the counties of Anjou and Maine on 23 September 1447.

[43] Printed by J. Quicherat in his edition of T. Basin's *Histoire des règnes de Charles VII et de Louis XI*, IV, 286–9, from the original B.N. MS Du Puy vol. 760 f. 161.

[44] *Foedera*, XI, 189–91 (confirmation), 193–4 and *C.C.R. 1447–54*, 37–8.

[45] Escouchy (ed. Beaucourt), III (*Preuves*), 172–5.

[46] Stevenson, *Wars*, II, pt. ii, 704–10.

[47] *Ibid.*, 702–3.

angry letter accusing him of besmirching his honour and incurring his bitter displeasure.[48]

Cousinot and Harvart had duly appeared as Charles VII's plenipotentiaries at the council house at Le Mans on 31 October 1447, to arrange the final delivery. They were received by Mundeford, now supported by Sir Nicholas Molineux, master of the chamber of accounts at Rouen, and Thomas Dirhill, viscount of Alençon in the English obedience. They had meantime contrived further delaying tactics. They presented themselves as formally nominated in a notarial instrument, attested under Henry's French seal at Rouen on 9 September, to negotiate terms of compensation for all those about to be dispossessed of lands and property in Maine, before any surrender could be discussed.[49] Protracted negotiations on 1 November made no progress. The exasperated French presented notarially attested copies of all the relevant, authentic documents, which were subjected to minute scrutiny. They were then queried because of two alterations in them and because the notaries concerned were unknown to the English. The Englishmen knew that Henry was to receive a licence from Charles VII for the Angevins to make alliances with him for their lives, and truces to cover Anjou and Maine for twenty years. These must be delivered first, they now said. The French replied that they were being kept for safety along with the other original documents in Sablé. The Englishmen could be taken there and allowed to examine all the original documents. As for the compensation, Somerset had already received what had been requested on the occasion of the treaty of 27 July 1447 in London, as the duke of Buckingham, Suffolk, Adam Moleyns, lords Scrope and Dudley and the secretary Master Thomas Kent could testify. They said that the whole question of universal peace could turn on the surrender of Maine. Every sovereign prince could and ought, in a treaty of peace, to dispose of his subjects' goods and chattels without their consent or will, as both canon and civil law affirmed. Those who opposed him in this incurred capital penalties.[50] All this was to no avail. Finally a deputation of English knights and esquires, led by John de Montague, bastard of Salisbury, and Sir John Fastolf's proctor, John Daubenay, interrupted the proceedings, demanding compensation on their own behalf and on behalf of many others. The Frenchmen retired under protest, with nothing achieved, and the Englishmen withdrew to the chapter house of the cathedral to draw up a notarial instrument of the proceedings, sealed and attested by the bishop and chapter, priests and notaries and by some forty knights, esquires and others.[51]

[48] *Ibid.*, 692–6.   [50] *Ibid.*, 650–87.
[49] *Ibid.*, 646–50.   [51] *Ibid.*, 687–92.

It is difficult not to accept the charge of 'subterfuges and pretences and simulations' levied by the French against Gough and Eyton. The situation was farcical where those who were designated by Henry to provide his envoys with soldiers to enforce the surrender were the very officers who were called upon to make it. On 30 December 1447 Gough actually reached agreement with Charles VII's commissioners, Dunois, Brézé and Beauvau, on the objections raised by Mundeford and Frogenhall, and formally bound himself to make the surrender by 15 January 1448. But his colleague Eyton, who was conveniently not then present, refused to ratify it, demanding further delay until Candlemas (2 February). On 14 January Charles VII even accepted this further extension.[52] At the end of December Charles VII had sent out heralds to proclaim the latest extension of the truce, made on 15 October 1447,[53] to 1 January 1449, and in fact he was still concerned to play the issue of Le Mans in a low key because he was secretly planning alternative action, the first mobilization of his new army. He had no desire as yet to see any resumption of hostilities and he had no intention of being deemed the truce-breaker. At this stage, apparently still in some hopes of a peaceful surrender, he decided to appeal to the only other possible authority, Henry VI's council in Rouen, to ask them to discipline Gough, Eyton, Mundeford and the rest and to declare them outside the operation of the truce. Since the expiration of York's lieutenant-governorship, English France and Normandy had been nominally ruled by a commission, prominent on which were Sir Thomas Hoo, chancellor of France and Normandy, and Sir Robert Roos, both agents and signatories of the original truce of Tours. Somerset, although appointed to succeed York in December 1446, had still not set foot in Normandy. Meantime, by 20 January 1448, Hoo knew that the French mobilization was in progress and wrote with the utmost alarm and urgency to Brézé, as the author and very originator of the truce, he said, and with whom he claimed to be on intimate terms, desperately imploring him to halt it. In spite of Gough and Eyton, he declared, Le Mans would be peacefully given up.[54] The upshot of a conference at Rouen at the end of January was a further and final extension of the delivery date to 8 February 1448 at the cost of formally outlawing Gough, Eyton, Mundeford and their fellows should they not comply.[55]

A military investment of Le Mans began on 10 February 1448 after

[52] *Ibid.*, 710–3.

[53] R. Planchenault, 'La délivrance du Mans en 1448', *Revue Historique et Archéologique du Maine*, LXXIX (1923), 188, 198; Escouchy (ed. Beaucourt), III (*Preuves*), 176.

[54] Stevenson, *Wars*, 198.

[55] Escouchy (ed. Beaucourt), III (*Preuves*), 182–3; Stevenson, *Wars*, I, 365–6.

a smooth mobilization closely supervised by Charles himself.[56] This was the first test of the new permanent army as organized at Nancy in 1445. By 10 February he had assembled at Le Mans from 6,000 to 7,000 troops, with a large artillery train and siege engines. The English garrison, reinforced from Normandy, allegedly by the notorious freebooters of Lord Camoys, numbered some 2,500.[57] When Brézé approached the suburbs on 13 February, backed by the massive French force, his progress was resisted, but contact was ultimately established with Gough, Eyton and Mundeford and local truces established for parleys. Gough and Eyton continued in negotiations and produced a new trump card which the French naturally found most strange and exasperating: they alleged that they had just received fresh instructions direct from Henry himself, under his privy seal, ordering them to make no surrender pending the arrival of fresh ambassadors from England. The Frenchmen were very sceptical, but ultimately agreed to further truces until noon on 19 February, to enable reference to be made back to Charles VII. But they were finally forced to flee in disorder when Mundeford sallied out of the castle intent on capturing them, with a force of six or seven hundred armed men, calling for combat.

Charles VII, at Lavardin, now sent his cup-bearer Raordin Regnault, off to England with two long, up-to-the-minute, detailed accounts of these abortive negotiations, omitting nothing except the vital fact of his investing army in position around Le Mans.[58] But Henry had indeed already appointed new plenipotentiaries, Adam Moleyns, Reginald Boulers, abbot of Gloucester, and Sir Robert Roos, on 30 January, to treat with Charles's commissaries.[59] Gough and Eyton on 13 February were thus telling the truth and had been speedily and accurately informed. Later, on Sunday 18 February, Hoo wrote again in mounting alarm to Brézé to inform him that Moleyns and his fellows had landed at Honfleur the previous Thursday and were hastening to Lavardin. He knew that Garter had already been sent to Lavardin to Charles VII with news of this embassy and could therefore see no justification for the provoking and dangerous siege while negotiations and the truce continued.[60] On 22 February Garter,

---

[56] Planchenault, *op. cit.*, 196–202, gives specific details from records at Angers how heralds and messengers were sent out to summon the captains of the army to appear by various routes with their contingents from all corners of France and provision made for artillery, stores, billetting, musters, etc. for the siege of Le Mans. *op. cit.*, 196–202.

[57] Berry herald, 430.

[58] His own is printed from B.N. MS Baluze 9037–7 by Stevenson, *Wars*, I, 361–8, wrongly dated 1445. The other, from Pierre Brézé and the rest of the French commissioners, is printed in Escouchy (ed. Beaucourt), III (*Preuves*), 181–92.

[59] *Foedera*, XI, 196–7.   [60] Stevenson, *Wars*, I, 202–6.

clearly a model herald, hastening on his return from Lavardin to meet Moleyns and Roos at Alençon with Charles VII's letters of safe conduct, declined the escort offered him by Brézé, who was travelling via Le Mans, because this would be an embarrassing sight to both of them. He was given Touraine herald to conduct him by an alternative route, but he too felt bound to complain that Moleyns and Roos, who he considered as close to his king and as devoted to peace as any man, were not being received with the honour due to them.[61]

Crisis on the spot was now matched by belatedly expressed alarm in England. By 31 January the council there had had their own disturbing reports of Charles VII's military preparations against Maine and considered that Edmund Beaufort should take up his duties as king's lieutenant in Normandy, France and Gascony at once and on a war footing. He received £2,275 as immediate payment for the first quarter's wages of 1,000 archers, part of his £20,000 *per annum* and 1,000 marks was paid out for his shipping on 5 March. Next day accurate news of the 'mighty siege' and 'sharp war' at Le Mans secured him a further advance of £2,500 for a further force of 200 spears and 2,000 bows.[62]

Henry's promise to surrender Maine, a unilateral gesture in return for nothing more than his Valois uncle's unspecified goodwill towards a peace settlement, had thus divided and confused his own councillors at home and demoralized his administration and garrisons in France. Charles VII had been able to use to the full the opportunities provided by the truce for the organization and development of his military forces. Moreover, he had now conducted a successful trial mobilization, with palpable justification, to ensure possession of what had become his legal right, which only Henry's rebellious subjects were withholding from him.

Moleyns and Roos appear to have reached Lavardin by 6 March,[63] and a treaty was signed on the 11th, followed by separate conventions regarding the truce and the surrenders on 15 March. Compensation, at ten years purchase, was now agreed for the dispossessed, to be paid by cancelling the annual sums from the revenues of Normandy due to Charles as agreed by Suffolk at Nancy in 1445. The English would thus pay the compensation themselves! All English-held Maine, except Fresnay, was to be surrendered and consequently the truce could be extended to 1 April 1450.[64]

[61] Escouchy (ed. Beaucourt), III (*Preuves*), 197–8.
[62] Stevenson, *Wars*, I, 479–83.
[63] Escouchy (ed. Beaucourt), III (*Preuves*), 180.
[64] *Foedera*, XI, 199–203 (French version), 203–4 (compensation terms), 206–10 (English version); Stevenson, *Wars*, I, 207–8, and II, pt. ii, 717–18 for conventions of 15 March.

The siege of Le Mans by Charles VII's new army was indeed a reality. Three heavy skirmishes took place and the walls, gates and some buildings of the town were heavily damaged.[65] It was Charles VII's successful investment of the city which made ultimate surrender inevitable. This came at 10 p.m. on 15 March 1448, when Osbert Mundeford, styled bailiff of Maine, read out aloud on the bridge at the entrance to the castle a notarial instrument on behalf of Mathew Gough and Fulk Eyton. Its points were (1) that the 'peaceful' surrender was now made for the benefit of René of Anjou and Charles of Maine only; (2) for the achievement of a good, firm and secure peace only; (3) that the sovereignty was expressly reserved to Henry and his heirs; (4) that if anything was attempted against the above, then the gift was revoked and Henry re-entered into full possession.[66] On the 16th the defenders marched out in company with Moleyns and Roos, equipped with six months' provisions.[67] On 12 June 1448 Gough and Eyton received Henry's discharge and commendation as good and faithful executors of their charge to deliver Maine![68] In fact it was now abundantly clear that the valuable bargaining counter of Henry's marriage and much more besides had been thrown away at Tours in May 1444. Three years of wrangling under cover of a precarious truce and the ultimate threat of Charles VII's *force majeure* had at last accomplished a surrender which seriously undermined the English position in France and had no point other than the empty fulfilment of Henry's irresponsible personal promise, made 'on the word of a king' to his new-found, dearly beloved Uncle Charles.

The treaty of Lavardin of 11 March 1448, which in theory implemented the final surrender of Maine, differed from the truce of Tours in one very significant respect. The English version, which the French ratified, includes the duke of Brittany among the 'colligate confoederate, amici, auxiliantes, fautores et adhaerantes' of Henry VI, listed after the king of Portugal and before the duke of York. The French version, which the English ratified, includes him among Charles VII's 'seigneurs les ducs'. Thus in the spring of 1448 Henry and his negotiators were now aware of the vital importance of the duke of Brittany's allegiance, which they had cavalierly ignored at Tours and the two sides consequently had to leave this issue undecided in order to be able to formalize the final surrender of Maine. The disputed allegiance of Brittany now replaced possession of Maine as the principal danger to the continuation of the truce. This was on two counts. In the first place no provision was made to accommodate

---

[65] Escouchy (ed. Beaucourt), I, 128–31.
[66] Drawn up and attested by the public notary Jean Brandelli: *Foedera*, XI, 204–6.
[67] Planchenault, *op. cit.*, 195.
[68] *Foedera*, XI, 215–6.

the dispossessed from Le Mans, and the other English garrisons in Maine, elsewhere. They found themselves new homes in the dismantled fortress of St James de Bevron, in the marches between Brittany and English Normandy and built two new fortresses in Mortain, allegedly arousing the alarm of the duke of Brittany and inviting the opportunist claim of Charles VII that these moves constituted serious infringements of the truce in a frontier area. Secondly, Henry had himself become concerned and involved in the quarrel between his friend and ally Gilles of Brittany, who had stoutly maintained his English allegiance, and his brother, the duke, who was supported by Charles VII.

Gilles's problems stemmed in the first instance from discontent with his appanage, which consisted of certain rents on the ducal demesne, but land situated only outside the duchy and subject to homage to René count of Anjou and to Charles VII. He had contemptuously renounced these before four public notaries at Le Guildo on 23 December 1445 as derogatory to his dignity. Gilles first drew Henry, his acknowledged overlord, into his dispute with his brother the duke through his close contacts with the English authorities in Normandy, Mathew Gough, Chancellor Hoo and Sir Robert Roos. Requests to Hoo and Roos for advice about the payment of his English pension and how he should behave when Henry made his intended journey into France were passed on to Henry himself. Advised to contact Henry direct, he sent an envoy to England whose instructions, dated at Biron on 5 July 1445, were intercepted by his brother the duke. They were taken to constitute treason with the English because in them he allegedly offered to lay his grievance over his appanage before Henry's council in France or England and to accept him as his principal lord. He also offered Henry his further services subject to the truce, undertook to place his castles in Brittany at Henry's disposal and requested that Henry's subjects in France be called upon to give him aid if he required it. His friend Mathew Gough went on a mission of reconciliation to the duke to explain all this away as harmless early in October 1445, and Gilles and his brother the duke were formally reconciled by their uncle Arthur de Richemont, constable of France, at Rieux on 19 October. But the price Gilles had to pay was the surrender of St Malo and Moncontour and an undertaking to break off his English contacts. A letter under Henry's sign manual and signet, written by Gervais le Vulre at Westminster on 25 October 1445 reveals that out of affection for Gilles and their nearness of blood (their mothers were sisters, daughters of Charles VI of France), Henry had personally interceded with the duke to give Gilles an honourable Breton endowment. In this letter Henry also expressed his disbelief that the duke could disapprove of Gilles's Anglo-Norman contacts and had informed him that he had instructed Chancellor Hoo and others in his service there to do all in their power to serve Gilles. When Gilles at Le Guildo on 23 December 1445 solemnly renounced his French appanage and continued his English contacts he was duly encouraged, especially by Mathew Gough, with strong assurances of Henry's great affection and with hopes that he might receive the earldom of Richmond and other English favours.

On 16 March 1446 the duke, by contrast, decided to cement his links with the Valois by performing homage to Charles VII at Chinon. This he did standing for Brittany and kneeling in liege homage only for his French lands, just as previous dukes had done. The allegiance of Brittany was always to Charles VII, if not to Henry VI, a vital factor in the Anglo-French struggle. Charles never overlooked it. As he himself said, it was 'a matter of the highest importance which touches the king nearer than almost any other which can arise in this realm'. Although the form of Duke Francis's homage was displeasing to the French chancellor and others of Charles's entourage, Charles himself was not too particular. He took it graciously and willingly and improved the occasion by absolving the duke from the odium of his father's English adherence and his own homage which he had done to Henry while himself under age.[69]

Late in April 1446 Gilles began to fear for his personal safety in Brittany. He requested the English captain of Avranches to send him an English bodyguard of twenty-five men to his castle of Le Guildo. Hoo and Roos gave their approval, provided the guards were not taken from the garrison strength. But in June 1446 he successfully defied emissaries from his brother, sent to summon him to answer further charges of planning a military coup with the English, and ignored advice from the English captains to leave Le Guildo and come to Normandy with his family and followers. He was consequently arrested by a trick on 26 June. A French force, sent by Charles VII under Admiral Coëtivi, was admitted to his castle at Le Guildo in the mistaken belief that they were a friendly mission from his uncle of France. The Frenchmen conveyed him to the duke; the duke put him on trial before the Estates of Brittany and the process dragged on until July 1447 with no conclusive issue. Gilles was then confined by the duke in various strongholds: Châteaubriant, Moncontour, Touffon and, finally, La Hardouinaie where he was murdered on the night of 24 April 1450.[70]

It seems that Gilles genuinely regarded himself as Henry's man and

[69] P. Jeulin, 'L'hommage de la Bretagne', *Annales de Bretagne*, XLI (1934), 446-8; Morice, *Preuves*, II, cols 1399-1400. Stevenson, *Wars*, I, 263 (July 1449).

[70] See A. Bourdeaut, *op. cit.*, and Morice, *Preuves*, II, for a comprehensive collection of the relevant correspondence and treaties.

protected by the terms of the truce of Tours. Whatever his differences with his brother the duke, he was totally unprepared for a French attack upon him in breach of the truce. The *Boke of Noblesse*, originally written in the early 1450s to promote and justify an English reconquest, confirms that the 'grete adversarie of Fraunce Charles the vii[the]' was currently regarded in England as the first truce-breaker by this arrest of Gilles, for which the subsequent English attack on Fougères was a legitimate retaliation.[71] When Henry VI himself was ultimately convinced, in August 1448, that their Valois uncle Charles VII, not Duke Francis, had been responsible for his arrest, he too regarded this as a breach of the truce. Some of Gilles's servants fled to England where they were warmly received by Henry. As early as 1446 one of Gilles's valets was busy at court trying to get a military expedition launched into Brittany to rescue his master. Lodged with Suffolk, he was wearing the SS collar of the Lancastrian royal livery. Montauban, the principal stronghold of Gilles's gaoler Arthur de Montauban, was the first objective suggested for such an expedition. Similar plans were also made among the English captains in Normandy. To this end Mathew Gough sought the services of Francois de Surienne's famous *échelleur*, Thomassin Duquesne.[72]

Thus for more than one reason the allegiance of Brittany belatedly became of prime importance to Henry VI, as it always had been to Charles VII, and Henry's negotiators began a tussle to compel the duke's representatives to accept English injunctions. From 1447 English versions of the Anglo-French negotiations extending the truces no longer specified the French allies among whom the duke of Brittany had originally been included at Tours.[73] At the conclusion of the treaty of Lavardin on 11 March 1448, prior to the surrender of Le Mans on the 15th, Moleyns and Roos, sent out by Henry as plenipotentiaries direct from London, were under strict instructions not to treat on the question whether the duke of Brittany was a subject of Charles VII. They were instructed categorically to affirm that he was not so. Therefore the English version included him among Henry's vassals. The duke of Somerset, as Henry's lieutenant of France and Normandy, pointedly referred Charles VII to these facts at the ultimate conference held at Port St Ouen from 15 to 20 June 1449 in proof of his stance that he himself had no power to accept that Brittany was included in the truce as Charles's vassal. On this score the French king repeatedly accused Somerset of prevarication and deceit. But Somerset correctly pointed out that Henry's own personal

[71] *Book of Noblesse*, ed. J. G. Nichols (Roxburghe Club, London 1860), 3, 5, and see below p. 266.

[72] Stevenson, *op. cit.*, I, 281 (deposition of de Surienne).

[73] *Foedera*, XI, 164, 193.

emissaries, sent post-haste to negotiate the final surrender of Le Mans, had been strictly forbidden to do this and he did not have that power either. The French notaries at Port St Ouen in 1449 duly recorded Somerset's version of the Lavardin proceedings and there is no record that any French protest had been made at Moleyns's and Roos's stand on that earlier occasion. The historian of Brittany pertinently remarks that it is very strange that neither the French nor the Breton negotiators at any time accused the English of falsifying that crucial treaty of Lavardin by which the surrender of Le Mans was secured.[74] Clearly, they had to accept it, in order to get the surrender agreed to there. The graphic story of a false, inaccurate version of the treaty giving Henry the allegiance of Brittany, foisted upon the French by the cunning English in a ditch, by candlelight, outside the gates of Le Mans, goes back no further than 1464, when Louis XI was marshalling evidence to use against Edward IV who had renewed the English claims to the French inheritance and to the Breton allegiance.[75]

Moleyns and Roos were ordered to remain in France in the spring of 1448 to treat for a final peace settlement, after their success in securing the ultimate surrender of Maine without a gross violation of the truce or, indeed, a general outbreak of war. To them were added Reginald Boulers, abbot of Gloucester, Osborne Mundeford and Somerset himself, who was now, at last, actually present as Henry's lieutenant in France and Normandy. This group were now Henry's commissioners to treat for the permanent peace which should have been attainable now that the alleged primary obstacle to that end, inability to surrender Maine, had finally been removed.[76] In June Somerset sent Mundeford to join Moleyns and Roos, still with Charles VII, but excused himself, because of his recent arrival and personal inexperience in the matter.[77] Alas, the re-occupation of St James de Bevron and Mortain by the dispossessed and disinherited garrisons of Maine had meantime reduced the level of the peace negotiations to a fresh wrangle about these alleged new infringements of the truce.

In negotiations at Louviers on 24 August 1448 Moleyns, the principal English negotiator, endeavoured to justify the English diplomatic stance. He maintained that St James de Bevron and the other fortresses in question had previously been in English hands. Their re-

---

[74] Charles Taillandier, *Histoire ecclésiastique et civile de Bretagne* (Paris 1756), 21.

[75] *Pretentions des Anglais à la couronne de France*, ed. Robert Anstruther (Roxburghe Club, vol. 64, 1847), 88-117, dated by A. Bossuat, *Perrinet Gressart et François de Surienne, agents de L'Angleterre* (Paris 1936), 331-2, to 1464.

[76] French Rolls 36 Hen. VI, m.6, 6 April 1448 (*Deputy Keeper's Report*, XLVIII, Appendix).

[77] Escouchy (ed. Beaucourt), III, 210, 14 June 1448.

occupation could not have infringed the truce with Charles VII because they lay in the marches towards Brittany, whose duke owed allegiance to Henry VI. There could thus be no question of a frontier there between English and French territory. With the French contention that international law forbad the occupation of marches during a truce Moleyns agreed, but countered that Henry had the right to take what action he deemed fit because his vassal Francis duke of Brittany had failed to do justice to his subjects as he was bound to do. This was a clear reference to Gilles's predicament. But the presence of Michel de Parthenay, constable of Rennes, declaring that his master the duke was in fact the subject of Charles VII and repudiating the English allegiance, proved an insurmountable obstacle to progress here and Moleyns adjourned the conference on the lame excuse that Somerset, the king's new lieutenant in Normandy and France, must be consulted.[78] In fact he sent Garter back to England with a request for specific guidance in this impasse. Henry and his council duly considered the problem and produced a revealingly futile memorandum on 30 October 1448. This instructed the ambassadors to make the maximum use of the old patents of oaths of allegiance, given by the previous duke of Brittany and by all the notable people of the duchy, including the present duke, and Henry declared he would take his stand on these and in no way allow them to be impugned. If the Breton ambassadors still could not be moved, then the English ambassadors were to allow discussion to continue under due legal protest but prevaricate as much as possible by securing long prorogations for further references back to the two principals Henry and Charles. In this way a rupture must be prevented.[79] These were the barren delaying tactics pursued. Consequently what turned out to be the final meeting of the English and French ambassadors for peace at Vaudreuil on 15 November 1448 made no progress.[80]

Meantime Moleyns and Roos had been negotiating equally inconclusively for the release of Gilles of Brittany, soliciting directly to the duke while seeking the assistance of Charles VII to this end. They did not know that on 21 July 1448 Charles himself laid down the most stringent conditions, which he required the duke to see observed, before Gilles could be released. Gilles must do direct, personal homage to him; firm undertakings must be given by Henry VI and papal sanctions be obtained to back these up. Finally, he stipulated that on no account must the release appear to be made at the behest of the English.[81] On 20 August 1448 Henry himself sent yet another of his

[78] Morice, *Preuves*, II, cols 1430–7.
[79] *P.P.C.*, V. 62–4.
[80] Morice, *Preuves*, II, cols 1439–41.
[81] *Ibid.*, cols 1412–15.

personal letters to Charles, via Garter, because the duke of Brittany had now directly informed his ambassadors that the arrest and detention of Gilles had been made on the advice and initiative of Charles VII and that he could only release him with Charles's consent. The pathetic declaration of his nephew Henry's great love for Gilles, above all normal sentiments between cousins, his complete trust in his uncle Charles's good intentions, and references to the long and fearsome hardships which his friend and cousin, Charles's Breton nephew, was known to have endured, alike failed to move the French king. He took no steps to secure Gilles's release or to restore his sequestered property.[82]

The new, obstinate English stand over the Breton allegiance and the re-establishment of English forces in the Breton marches acquired sharper point and purpose when, in the small hours of 23 or 24 March 1449, an Aragonese captain in English service, François de Surienne, knight of the Garter in the stall of John Holand duke of Exeter, English military commander and king's councillor, seized the important Breton town and fortress of Fougères by surprise assault. Punitive military effort had now been added to the diplomatic exertions designed to ensure the safety and secure the release of Gilles of Brittany. It does not seem to have been thought that Gilles was detained in Fougères; the object was to secure the border fortress as a valuable bargaining pledge. Any fears that Charles VII would represent this as a flagrant breach of the truce, absolving him from its observation, and declare open war to drive the English from Normandy, appear to have been cavalierly discounted in England. According to de Surienne's subsequent letters of 15 March 1450, the first such moves to secure the release of Gilles of Brittany by force had come from Mathew Gough and others in Normandy, when they had asked to borrow his escalade-master and some of his soldiers. Then Jean le Roussellet, his marshal at Verneuil, who had been on a mission to England, brought back the suggestion, made by the duke of Suffolk, that de Surienne himself should capture Fougères and hold it, subject to Suffolk's guidance. De Surienne in reply sent another messenger to England, one Raoul de Vatonne, asking for a secure base on the borders of Brittany from which to mount the operation. It was Suffolk who arranged for him to receive Condé-sur-Noireau (Calvados) from Sir John Fastolf for this purpose.

The decisive stage in his acceptance of this task was a personal visit he made to England, apparently some time in 1447, during which Suffolk personally encouraged him in the enterprise and told him he had settled it all with Henry. From this point the capture of Fougères was a secret, fall-back policy to secure the release of Gilles

[82] *Ibid.*, 1429–30, received at Mehun-sur-Loire 24 September.

if diplomacy failed. Somerset, at his house at Blackfriars, newly appointed governor of Normandy but then still in England, also assured de Surienne, newly made knight of the Garter for his intended services, that these contingency plans had the king's approval and declared that such an enterprise would be entirely worthy of a Garter knight. Later, when present and in command in Normandy, Somerset, through intermediaries, expressed fears that the enterprise might be prematurely discovered and fail, and therefore pressed for its speedy execution, personally intervening to secure the making of special assault tools, the manufacture of which was illegal (long pincers for cutting gate fastenings, etc.). After the capture he sent Mortain herald to congratulate de Surienne and to make sure he held it firmly, supplying him with bows, arrows and gunpowder when requested.

De Surienne, once in possession, confidently rejected terms offered by the duke of Brittany for surrender of the place and sent his own pursuivant, Bon Désir, direct to Suffolk in England for his further instructions. He duly received letters back from both Henry and Suffolk ordering him to hold the place firmly until further notice. Moreover, Somerset also wrote to the same effect, under his own signet and sign manual, also promising reinforcements. Since his assault force had been largely drawn piecemeal from garrisons of many different captains in Normandy, and these could not stay with him beyond Michaelmas 1449, de Surienne sent one Guillim de Lille to England to Suffolk with details of his needs. De Lille returned and assured him that Henry had been informed and had appointed Sir Robert Vere to reinforce him, pending the crossing over of a great army. Vere indeed got as far as Caen, but no further, and the duke of Brittany, on learning of his approach, laid siege to Fougères. De Surienne considered he needed at least 1,000 fighting men to hold it and he had only 400. Yet, in spite of being out-gunned and undermanned, he ignored repeated requests of his followers to make terms, even though a number of them fraternized with the enemy and gave away his secrets. He succeeded in holding Fougères for five weeks until, finally, his garrison would no longer obey his orders and he had to surrender. He could see no future for himself except to retire with his family to Aragon, and sent back his Garter to Henry by the herald Longueville, in disgust at his betrayal. He might have had 50,000 gold crowns cash down and other inducements for an earlier surrender to the duke of Brittany and he indignantly repudiated any suggestions of dishonourable conduct and aspersions that he had acted on his own initiative in undertaking the capture. He had acted on explicit orders from England. Such was his own justification for his actions.[83] The depositions subsequently taken

[83] De Surienne's own story is in Stevenson, *Wars*, I, 278–98.

by the French at Rouen from October to December 1449 before Guillaume Jouvenel des Ursins, chancellor of France, specifically to prove the responsibility of the English government for the assault on Fougères, even allowing for the desire of the witnesses to please their French conquerors, only serve to confirm that the prudent, self-interested de Surienne was not the kind of rash captain who would do such a thing on his own initiative. He was convinced that his orders came from Henry in England and there is no room for doubt that they had done so.[84]

Somerset had arrived in Rouen in March 1448 to fulfil three roles: commander-in-chief and head of the English government in Normandy, posts kept vacant by the king's vacillation since Michaelmas 1445, and, by far the most important job in Henry's eyes, to act as conservator of the truce. His insistence on addressing Charles VII only as 'the uncle in France', which Charles found derogatory to his honour and contrary to the practice of Somerset's predecessor York,[85] was no new, pointless discourtesy: Henry's claim to the French crown was now no longer negotiable and was perforce re-asserted because the allegiance of Brittany could only be claimed in his capacity as king of France. The English envoys to maintain the truce admitted this at their final meeting with Charles at Roches Tranchelion on 31 July 1449.[86] Time and again, both through his envoys, meeting with Somerset's envoys, and in his letters directly to Henry, Charles asserted that Somerset, as Henry's plenipotentiary over the truce, yet refused to do justice over St James de Bevron, Mortain and Fougères. Persistently and unvaryingly Somerset claimed that he had not been given such powers. In English eyes affairs on the borders of Brittany and Normandy were no concern of Charles VII. The adamant stand by both Henry and Charles that the allegiance of Brittany was not negotiable must exonerate the loyal and unfortunate Somerset from the French charges of duplicity. He had in fact no power to accept the incidents of St James de Bevron and Mortain as breaches of the truce, or power to order or compel de Surienne to surrender Fougères to the duke of Brittany, as the French insisted it should be surrendered. This point was emphasized by a direct appeal which de Surienne made to Henry over Somerset's head.[87] Complete absence of any mention of the allegiance of Brittany in the direct cor-

---

[84] Printed by J. Quicherat in his edition of Thomas Basin's *Histoire*, IV, 290–347.

[85] Stevenson, *op. cit.*, I, 82, 214, 216–17, 241–2; Escouchy (ed. Beaucourt), III, 243–4.

[86] Proceedings at Rouches Tranchelion (Indre-et-Loire) printed *ibid.*, 243–51 and partly by Stevenson, *Wars*, I, 243–64 (mis-dated).

[87] *Narrative of the Expulsion of the English from Normandy 1449–50*, ed. J. Stevenson (R.S., 1863), 408.

respondence between the two kings, Charles and Henry, obscures this vital point. Instruction given to Harvart, Charles's personal envoy, sent to Henry in June 1449, specifically ordered him not to discuss it.[88] Thus the conferences of 20 June 1449 at Port St Ouen, from 25 June to 4 July at Louviers and the abbey of Bonport[89] and, finally, at Roches Tranchelion on 31 July 1449, all failed on the basic question of the allegiance of Brittany. The truce thus ultimately foundered. At Tours, in their eagerness to secure the Angevin marriage and the truce, the English had neglected the Breton allegiance. From 1447 they attempted to resurrect it. Henry refused to abandon his childhood friend, Gilles of Brittany, his liegeman and subject, whose detention by Charles VII he ultimately regarded as the first breach of the truce, and he made his release a *sine qua non* for the surrender of Fougères. The allegiance of Brittany was of greater importance to Charles VII even than the possession of Maine had been. In the ultimate event, at the final meeting of 31 July 1449, held by Charles VII to justify the resumption of hostilities, the chancellor of France was made to declare that the restoration of Fougères was a lesser thing than the issue of Breton homage.[90] It was defence of his vassal's rights which provided Charles VII with his justification for reopening the war.

For a full month after de Surienne's daring feat of arms, this contingent English plan to secure Gilles's release if negotiation failed actually seemed assured of success. Charles's ambassadors, Cousinot and Pierre de Fontenil, were with Somerset in Rouen from 7–22 April 1449 and, although the capture of Fougères had been common knowledge even before their departure on 7 April, they made no mention of it in their negotiations. It seems that Charles VII, even at that late stage, was still not quite sure of his vassal duke. The terrified Duke Francis had fled from Rennes to Vannes on the first news of the English attack.[91] At first he actually proposed to surrender Gilles. He sent the pursuivant Malo to Somerset at Rouen[92] and Michel de Parthenay to Fougères where, according to the English ambassadors at Roches Tranchelion, confirmed as true by de Surienne's letter to Henry, and by the depositions recorded at the French inquiry, he not only offered to release his brother, but also to pay de Surienne handsomely into the bargain to surrender the fortress.[93] But, in fact, a train of events had begun on 10 April which

[88] Escouchy (ed. Beaucourt), III (*Preuves*), 225 (instruction given 3 June 1449).

[89] For Port St Ouen, Louviers and Bonport see *Narratives*, 379–514, previously printed by Morice, *Preuves*, II, cols 1454–1508.

[90] Escouchy (ed. Beaucourt), III (*Preuves*), 256 cf. Stevenson, *Wars*, I, 263.

[91] Bourdeaut, *op. cit.*, 108.

[92] Bossuat, *op. cit.*, 325, quoting B.M. Add. MS 11509, fol. 24v.

[93] Escouchy (ed. Beaucourt), III (*Preuves*), 250; Stevenson, *Wars*, I, 296; deposition of Jacquemin de Molineaux in T. Basin's *Histoire*, ed. J. Quicherat, IV, 326.

led swiftly to the complete expulsion of the English forces from the whole of Normandy, branded with the full guilt of breaking the truce. That day Charles knew for certain that the duke was appealing to him for assistance as his vassal.[94] This at last put right on Charles's side. He was now entitled to claim that the English had broken the truce by their acts at St James de Bevron, Mortain and Fougères. An offensive and defensive alliance between Charles and Francis to drive the English from Normandy was drafted at Rennes on 17 June and confirmed on 27 June.[95] Charles gave power to Dunois, as his lieutenant general, to treat for the surrender of places in Normandy on 17 July[96] and through his chancellor, after consultations with his council and the lords of his blood, he declared himself absolved from the truce of Tours to Somerset's ambassadors at Roches Tranchelion on 31 July 1449.

The military recovery of Normandy by French and Breton forces, for which the investment of Le Mans had been a valuable dress rehearsal, now proceeded with astonishing speed. No acknowledgement of the desperately dangerous weakness of Normandy, demoralized by five years of precariously maintained truce and the forcible amputation of Maine, appears to have been made by Henry before May 1449.[97] On 27 May provision was made for 100 men-at-arms and 1,200 archers to muster at Portsmouth on 11 June.[98] On 20 and 22 December Henry was reduced to pledging his jewels and plate for the renewed war, which he had never believed would happen.[99] De Surienne was forced to make a composition for Fougères on 1 November and by 1450 only Honfleur, Caen, Bayeux, Cherbourg, Fresnay, Domfront, Saint-Sauveur, Vire, Falaise and a few other small places were left of English Normandy. The battle of Formigny of 15 April 1450 administered the *coup de grâce*; the fall of Cherbourg on 12 August completed a reconquest which had taken little over a year. All the English high hopes placed on the Angevin marriage and truce at Tours in May 1444 had come to nothing. Charles VII, as the inscription on his portrait proclaimed, was 'Le Trèsvictorieux Roi de France'. In his own good time, in one year and six days, he had

[94] Morice, *Preuves*, II, col. 1485.

[95] *Ibid.*, cols 1451-4, 1508-10.

[96] *Ordonnances des roys de France de la troisième race*, 22 vols (Paris 1723-1846), XIV, 59-61.

[97] Bossuat, *op. cit.*, 333. Citing Talbot's urgent appeal for reinforcements on 11 April to which Henry took a month to reply. Letter to Talbot and the Rouen council of 12 May (P.R.O., E. 28/78) and *ibid.*, 13 May 1449, his letter to Jean Salvin, bailli of Rouen.

[98] Bossuat, *op. cit.*, 333-4, citing E.101/71/4 no. 923, 27 May 1449, and E.403/775, 29 July 1449.

[99] Stevenson, *Wars*, I, 503-8.

conquered Henry's duchy of Normandy, six whole days' marches long and four broad, six bishoprics, one noble archbishopric and a hundred towns and castles, not counting those destroyed by the war.[100] Henry by contrast, as the contemptuous jingle now ran among his own subjects, was no king at all; 'The king's son, lost all his father won'.

Undoubtedly Henry himself bore the ultimate responsibility for the loss of Normandy, brought about by his marriage and truce policy of 1444 and the means by which it was implemented and continued up to the summer of 1449. As a result of it Charles VII was able completely to transform his position from a general stalemate in 1443 to a point where he was poised for reconquest, with every appearance of right on his side, a splendid war machine to hand and a firm treaty guaranteeing every assistance from the duke of Brittany. Nevertheless, under Henry, the loyal but supine duke of Somerset, who had accepted from him the supreme appointment of lieutenant and commander-in-chief in France and Normandy in December 1446, could be held immediately responsible for the military disasters. York had returned to England, in September 1445, taking with him his personal retinue, for which he was subsequently criticized by Henry's entourage, and was never allowed to return. After his withdrawal there was no English field force in Normandy and no commander-in-chief at all until Somerset was finally allowed to take up his hitherto sinecure appointment in March 1448. Even then he was content to accept Henry's interpretation of his appointment as being primarily to maintain, at all cost, a truce which was still, quite unrealistically, expected to lead to a final peace. His loyal prevarications over Fougères finally gave Charles VII the excuse he needed to resume hostilities which the English had neither forseen nor provided for. Consequently numerous but isolated and neglected English garrisons, each one only capable of a few weeks' resistance, fell in rapid succession before the French and Breton armies which were launched against them in July 1449. These armies were some 30,000 strong and serviced with effective siege artillery. For comparison, even under Bedford the total English forces had never exceeded 15,000. With the exception of limited forces, perhaps totalling 1,500, which he sent out from Caen, Bayeux and Vire to the assistance of Kyriell's small relieving army of 2,500 in April 1450, Somerset's strategy, if so it could be called, was merely for each garrison to sit tight and wait to be invested.[101] He did nothing to check the escalating collapse of the English positions and in the situation which had been allowed to develop by the summer of 1449 there was probably nothing else he could have done.

The personal participation of the commander-in-chief in operations

[100] Berry herald, 456.
[101] A. H. Burne, *The Agincourt War*, 310–12.

was thus confined to making the two most important and humiliating surrenders of the campaign. On 29 October 1446, after he had lost the allegiance of his capital city Rouen and had retreated into the citadel there, he made a degrading composition with Charles VII to secure the release of himself, his duchess and their children, and the English garrison. This involved the surrender of all the English strongholds still held in the Pays de Caux: Arques, Caudebec, Montivilliers, Lillebonne, Tancarville and Honfleur; a ransom of 50,000 crowns and the delivery into French hands of John Talbot, earl of Shrewsbury, Normandy's only remaining successful English general, together with four other hostages. The refusal of the commander of Honfleur to obey his orders left Talbot in captivity until 21 July 1450, when the garrison of Falaise successfully made his release a condition of their capitulation. In Caen, the second city of Normandy and Somerset's final place of refuge with his family, he surrendered the stronghold to the Count of Dunois on 1 July 1450, handing over eighteen hostages to be held until he and his family, and the 4,000-strong English garrison, had departed directly from France by Oistreham, the port of Caen. Somerset, in his disgrace, made by sea first for Calais, not England, presumably fearful of the nature of his reception. Henry, however, persisted in maintaining him in favour and two months later appointed him to a further supreme military command as Constable of England. A year later he received the other highest military office, the captaincy of Calais. The abject surrenders Somerset made to the French and his part in the surrender of Maine were to be the principal grounds on which Richard duke of York, whom he had supplanted in France, blamed him for the disasters of the reign and later rose in armed strength to compel Henry to consent to his destruction as a menace to the safety of the realm.

The first victims of the loss of Maine, Anjou and Normandy were the thousands of English combatants, their families and dependants, including Norman-born wives and sympathizers, who were allowed to depart to England with only their lives and personal possessions when there remained nowhere else for them to go; refugees from the four final, simultaneous sieges of Caen, Falaise, Domfront and Cherbourg in July and early August 1450. According to Berry herald they numbered some 4,000 from Caen and a further 2,300 combatants with their dependants from Falaise, Domfront and Cherbourg.[102] Abandoned by Henry's government, destitute and permanently embittered, they could do little immediately to help themselves other than petition and beg at the impoverished royal household for relief and

[102] Berry herald, 452–6.

sustenance.[103] Their past and present commanders and captains, who had other resources in England to fall back on, had, of course, lost most in lands, rents and offices. Somerset's own lost princely patrimony of Harcourt, Mortain and Maine was nearly equalled by York's apanage, the counties and lordships of Evreux, Beaumont-le-Rogier, Orbec, Conches and Bretheuil.[104] Some, like Sir John Fastolf, whose lands in Normandy and Maine had once produced a clear £675 *per annum*, while still losing heavily in the débâcle, had managed to salvage something by prudent sales in advance.[105] Even in the final years absentee landlords like York and his henchmen Scales, Oldhall and Ogard, who had left their own officials behind them, were still being remitted substantial sums to England.[106] But Somerset alone, prime target for the accumulated resentment of the dispossessed Anglo-Norman establishment, was alleged to have received compensation for losses from Henry, for his own and what had been intended for others, for the surrendering garrisons of Maine.[107] The rest, great and small, were hardly likely to be content with memories of past benefits enjoyed during thirty years of English occupation and could be expected to make common cause against those whom they held responsible for their current misfortunes.

[103] P.R.O., E.28/80/83, August 1450: £50 paid to Lord Scales to feed soldiers daily troubling the king's household.

[104] Burney, *op. cit.*, 248.

[105] K. B. McFarlane, 'The Investment of Sir John Fastolf's Profits of War', *T.R.H.S.*, 5th Series (1957).

[106] Burney, *op. cit.*, 257, citing P.R.O., C.47/25/9/18–21 to show £600 paid to York, £200 to Scales, 2,000 gold saluts to Oldhall and 1,500 silver saluts to Ogard from the profits of their Norman estates in 1448.

[107] Included in York's accusations made against Somerset in 1452, printed by Gairdner in *Paston Letters, Introduction*, cxxiii.

13(a). René of Anjou: a miniature painted by himself in his Book of Hours.

13(b). Margaret of Anjou, René's daughter, painted by him in his Book of Hours.

13(c). Queen Margaret of Anjou. A medal struck in 1463 by Pietro de Milan.

14(a). Philip the Good, duke of Burgundy.

14(b). Isabel of Portugal, duchess of Burgundy (Louvre, Paris).

Part IV

THE AFTERMATH OF DEFEAT

Chapter 12

PARLIAMENTARY OPPOSITION AND POPULAR RISINGS, 1449–1450

During the first half-century of its existence, to 1449, the Lancastrian dynasty had had remarkably little trouble from its parliaments. With the exception of an awkward initial five or six years, the frequent assemblies which it called, thirty-seven in all, had served it well, cooperating obediently in royal policies. Fifteenth-century parliaments were still intermittent bodies, summoned and dissolved entirely at the king's will to give effect and authority to royal policies throughout the shires of England. They were his cash-producing, legislating and publicity agencies. Nevertheless, parliament, when assembled, was a well-established institution with recognized powers, privileges and procedures. During Henry's long minority, those members summoned by individual writs, the 'Upper House', peers of parliament, or lords spiritual and temporal, who assembled about the throne in the parliament chamber proper, in theory a body of some thirty-five lay and forty-eight spiritual peers, enjoyed a peak period of political power. Whenever parliament was sitting they took over from the council as the ultimate authority in the land. After Henry had attained his majority, the lay peerage had been expanded and their formal dignities had been enhanced and graded to a unique degree. In 1441 additions to the basic grade of peer began to be made by charter and patent with a solemnity hitherto reserved, with two solitary exceptions, for earls. By 1449 ten new peers of the realm had been so created.[1] In addition another eight swelled the ranks of the peerage by being summoned to the parliaments of 1445, 1447 or February 1449 for the first time by personal writs.[2] In the same period there were six creations to dukedoms, two creations to a new dignity of marquis, set between

---

[1] Sudeley (Butler) 1441, Millbrook (Cornwall) 1442, Lisle (Talbot) 1444, Saye and Sele (Fiennes) 1447, Beauchamp of Powicke 1447, Hoo 1448, Rivers (Wydeville) 1448, Stourton 1448, Rougemont-Grey (Grey) 1449, Egremont (Percy) 1449. There had only been two previous such creations of baronies by patent: Beauchamp of Kidderminster in 1387 and Fanhope (Cornwall) in 1432. Sir John Cornwall married into the royal family (Henry IV's sister). The 1442 Millbrook patent was probably a confirmation after Henry came of age of the 1432 patent.

[2] Edward Brook, Lord Cobham, Robert Hungerford, Lord Moleyns, 1445; Edward Grey, Lord Ferrers of Groby, Henry Percy, Lord Poynings, 1447; William Beauchamp, Lord St Amand, William Bonville, Lord Bonville, William Bourchier, Lord Fitzwarren, Henry Bromflete, Lord de Vescy, February 1449.

dukes and earls, five creations to earldoms and two to another new dignity of viscount, an importation from France.[3]

This marked enhancing of the dignity of the lay peers of the realm and the increase in their numbers during Henry's personal rule emphasizes the growing importance of the peerage in fifteenth-century English society. It did not, however, reflect an increase in the political importance of the 'Upper House' itself. Indeed, with the re-establishment of personal rule, the powers of the lords spiritual and temporal assembled in parliament had declined, like those of the council. Also, recent study of attendance of the lords, both spiritual and temporal, at parliaments, has revealed a wide discrepancy between numbers of peers summoned to parliament and the consistently low numbers attending. In 1435, for example, only twenty-four lords appeared out of the eighty summoned. Attendances at great councils, called to discuss affairs of state, normally exceeded the attendance of peers at sessions of parliament.[4] The more important section of a mid-fifteenth-century parliament in session was undoubtedly the representative, elected members, the Commons, or 'Lower House'.

At the beginning of Henry's majority rule the Commons in parliament were made up of 74 'knights of the shire', so-called, although most of them were esquires in status, two from each of the 37 English counties,[5] and 190 burgess members, two each from 93 cities and

---

[3] Dukes: Somerset (John Beaufort) 1443, Exeter (John Holand) 1444, Buckingham (Humphrey Stafford) 1444, Warwick (Henry Beauchamp) 1445, Somerset (Edmund Beaufort) 1448, Suffolk (William de la Pole) 1448. Marquises: Dorset (Edmund Beaufort) 1443, Suffolk (William de la Pole) 1444. The short-lived title of Marquis of Dublin (1385-6), conferred by Richard II on Robert de Vere in the Irish peerage, may be taken as a solitary precedent here. Earls: Dorset (Edmund Beaufort) 1441, Shrewsbury (John Talbot) 1442, Wiltshire (James Butler) 1449, Worcester (John Tiptoft) 1449, Warwick (Richard-Nevill, recognized by right of his wife) 1449. In addition Kendal went to John Beaufort in 1443 by creation and Pembroke to William de la Pole, marquis of Suffolk in 1447. Viscounts: Beaumont (John, Lord Beaumont, count of Boulogne) 1440, Bourchier (Henry, Lord Bourchier, count of Eu) 1445. These 17 creations and elevations thus involved only 12 individuals.

[4] J. S. Roskell, 'The Problem of the Attendance of the Lords in Medieval Parliaments', *B.I.H.R.*, XXIX (1956), 153-204, from which the following figures are extracted:

Date of Assembly	1435	1439	1449	1449-50	1453-4	1459
Parliaments						
Total Peers summoned	80			92	105	97
Maximum attendance of peers at one session	24			46[i]	27	66[ii]
Great Councils						
Total attendance at one session of Great Councils	30	38	33		28	

i) Special meeting in king's chamber at his command to hear his sentence on Suffolk.
ii) Special session to take an oath of allegiance to King Henry and Prince Edward.

[5] The palatine counties of Cheshire and Durham not sending members.

boroughs, and four from London. The increasing status and importance of the Commons is evident from the establishment of the first statutory code of parliamentary electoral law between 1406 and 1445. From 1406 sheriffs were bound to make returns of shire 'knights', freely elected in the shire courts or assemblies, by indenture bearing the seals of all the electors, under penalty of £100 if the Justices of Assize found any irregularity (1410), and all electors and elected in shires and towns were to be residents (1413). The right to vote had now become a valued piece of property which was restricted in the shires, from 1429, to those freeholders having land worth at least 40/- *per annum*. Finally, in 1445 the same system of indentured returns was to be applied by the sheriff to city and borough elections and 'knights' of the shire were to be selected only from notable esquires, gentlemen by birth, able to take up knighthood, if not already dubbed knights, and not from those of yeomen status or below.[6] How far these conditions of free election, residence and status were observed is a measure of the influence which could be exerted over elections by the king and his officers or by individual lords.

At first sight it might appear that considerable royal patronage was exercised in elections. The number of household servants who were also members of parliament varied considerably from rather more than a fifth to below a twelfth of the identifiable membership of the Commons.[7] From 1442 it was made easier for household members to obtain seats by the creation of new parliamentary boroughs. By 1453 twelve had been created, providing twenty-four new seats, many of which

[6] *S.R.*, II, 156, 162, 170, 243, 340.

[7] Totals from J. C. Wedgwood and Anne D. Holt, *History of Parliament 1439–1509 Biographies* (H.M.S.O., 1936), and Household accounts, mainly P.R.O., E.101/410/6:

Date of Parliament	1439	1442	1445	1447	1449 (1)	1449–1450	1450–1451	1453	1455	1459	1460
Possible total membership of the Lower House	264	268	268	272	276	278	280	288	288	250	288
Number of names known	108	268	122	272	274	272	268	278	204	167	164
Number of members of household elected	24	31	25	53	49	35	30	61	26	34	14
Number of these elected for boroughs	4	12	7	24	22	19	15	25	17	13	8
Number of holders of crown lands present	10	15	8	21	27	12	7	18	15	11	

were occupied by men in the lower ranks of the household. Some of five small boroughs newly created in Wiltshire were also controlled by those magnates who could be expected to be loyal to Henry's government. With the exception of Plymouth, all these new boroughs returned members of the household to parliament on one or more occasions between 1442 and 1460.[8] Studies of borough representation during this reign have now revealed that outside patronage of any kind was still not the deciding factor in the majority of borough elections. Rather more than half of the borough representation was still by resident burgesses, as laid down by the 1413 statute.[9] For the rest a mixture of candidates, outside gentry, lawyers and royal servants, put in by noble or ecclesiastical patrons or owners, was blurring the difference in status between knights of the shire and burgesses of the boroughs. The household element in the boroughs remained fairly constant, but it was never more than twenty-five members, at most an eighth of the overall borough membership.

On the whole knights of the shire predominated in the household contingent and fluctuations in its share of the county representation were much more pronounced than in the borough membership. There is no evidence that the shire seats were subject to any permanent or consistent form of patronage. In addition to the king, a few of the greatest nobility could exert some influence over the choice of knights of the shire. The best known instance of this, of the dukes of York and Norfolk deciding together who should represent Norfolk in the 1450–1 parliament, resulted only in their securing one of the two members between them. It is true that in the 1455 parliament, after York's victory at the first battle of St Albans, they again acted in concert and, on that occasion, secured both seats, but considerable local resentment was expressed that the gentlemen of the shire should as a result have to suffer as their representative John Howard, Norfolk's kinsman and ultimate successor in the dukedom, who was a 'strange man' (i.e. unknown in the locality) with no livelihood or standing in the shire.[10] This was stigmatized as an 'evil precedent'. Deference to great lords was a factor in deciding some shire elections, but on the whole 'knights' were freely elected and represented the local county community, possibly in some form of rotation where separately identifiable local interests were in

[8] From 1442: Plymouth and Downton; from 1447 Windsor and Wooton Bassett; from 1449 Westbury, Haytesbury and Hindon; from 1453 Gatton, Bramber, Coventry, Poole and Steyning. Some of these had occasionally returned members in the previous century.

[9] Similar conclusions reached both by J. S. Roskell, *The Commons in the Parliament of 1422* (Manchester U.P., 1954), 133, and Roger Virgoe, 'The Parliament of 1449–50' (unpublished London Ph.D. thesis, 1964), 136.

[10] *Paston Letters*, I, 150, 157, 160, 161, 337, 340, 341.

conflict. The knights of the shire assembled in parliament were consequently neither credulous nor easily led, either by the king or great lords. Some of them were men of substance, equal to if not surpassing members of the baronage in landed wealth, with wide experience of rule in the shires, and with a certain long-standing continuity of membership in the Commons. Community of aim, outlook and interest was needed to bind them to the support of a government, or of great lords.[11] The number of household servants in the Commons reflected not so much any consistent attempt at patronage, but the standing of the government at the time of the elections. It was a barometer of the decline and recovery of royal influence. In 1447 there were 29 household knights of the shire; this dropped to 15 in 1450 and rose again to 36 in 1453. The size of the household or government element in the Commons thus provides an indication of the political standing of Henry's government in successive parliaments. On all counts this plumbed the depths in 1449.

In 1449 and 1450 England was in the grip of political, military and economic disasters which constituted a damning indictment of Henry's personal rule since 1437. However, incompetent and unreliable as the king had proved to be, direct criticism of him was muted and almost non-existent, for the king could do no wrong. No prudent person would criticize the king himself, unless he was able and willing to take his criticism to its logical conclusion and challenge his possession of the throne. That possibility had already found expression by 1450, but as yet there was no determined or convincing alternative candidate for the kingship. A real change of government was therefore out of the question. Nevertheless, in 1450 the Commons assembled in parliament, backed up by popular rebellion, did achieve the next best thing. They exacted retribution from Henry's advisers and the executants of his policies for the evils of misgovernment and current disasters.

The parliament called for 6 November 1449 assembled and deliberated in an atmosphere of mounting crisis. In France, after the renewal of hostilities in May 1449, Henry suffered humiliating military disasters leading to total defeat in war such as no king of England had experienced since the reign of John. It was a picture of unmitigated gloom, not only on land, where the defeat and dissolution of his armed forces terminated in the complete expulsion of the English from Normandy, but also by sea. With no adequate naval force, without the French seaboard, and deprived of the Breton alliance, Henry was unable to keep the narrow seas open for trade. He could not stop a damaging series of French raids on English coastal towns in the

[11] See the masterly article by K. B. McFarlane, 'Parliament and "Bastard Feudalism"', *T.R.H.S.*, XXVI (1944), 53–79, based on the records of the graduated income taxes of 1411 and 1435 and discussion of the disputed elections of the 1450s.

south and east. He not only could not prevent piracy but actually licensed some himself. Most notorious here was an attack by Robert Winnington on the Bay salt fleet of Hanseatic, Flemish and Dutch ships in May 1449, made under protection of Henry's letters of marque. In the opinion of the Prussian agent in London, in June 1450, the Kentish rebels rose primarily to demand the restoration of the lost Hanseatic trade and the punishment of pirates who were supported by Henry's entourage, some of whom had shares in their enterprises.[12] Sea-borne trade with Normandy, Poitou and Gascony collapsed. From 1447 Philip duke of Burgundy chose to impose one of his periodic protectionist embargoes on the entry of English cloth to the Low Countries for the benefit of his cloth-making towns in Flanders, Brabant, Holland and Zeeland. Over all the ports of England between 1448 and 1449 exports of cloth fell by 32 per cent and miscellaneous exports by 35 per cent, while imports of wine dropped by 50 per cent in 1450. In 1449–50 exports from Sandwich, the hub of Kentish trade, fell from 182 sacks of wool to 25, and woollen cloths from 2,078 to 237. Wine imports dropped from 1,042 to 271 tuns.[13] These were the circumstances in which the centre of affairs moved from royal court and council to parliament where the chief agent of Henry's policies, the duke of Suffolk, was impeached, and all those associated with Henry's government and household came under attack. In June 1450 the south-eastern shires rose in rebellion to support the actions of parliament. It was the Commons in parliament, not the Lords, who now destroyed the king's chief executive, and the major cause of his downfall as revealed by the articles of impeachment was the loss of Normandy. Apportioning blame for this disaster was to become a major issue in domestic politics for the rest of the reign.

The first mention at a high level that the loss of Normandy was even a possibility came in a quarrel between the dispossessed lieutenant, Richard duke of York, and Henry's chief diplomatic agent, the keeper of the privy seal and bishop of Chichester, Adam Moleyns. This must have taken place not later than 6 July 1449,[14] when York was at last constrained to take up his uncongenial new post in Ireland, to which he had been appointed in 1447, to get him out of the way. York petitioned the king to clear his name against Moleyns's alleged slander that it was his past misconduct as lieutenant in Normandy which was responsible for impending disaster there. A frightened but casuistic Moleyns claimed in reply that he would never be such a fool as to criticize a prince as powerful and beyond reproach as the duke of

[12] Studies in English Trade in the Fifteenth Century, ed. Eileen Power and M. M. Postan (London 1933), 128–9.
[13] Ibid., 330–60 (figures for individual ports), 402 (consolidated table).
[14] J. Otway-Ruthven, A History of Medieval Ireland (London 1968), 379.

York, that Normandy was still not lost if it was effectively reinforced, and that he was anyway known in the council as a consistent advocate of the vigorous policy of defence,[15] of which York had been the prime exponent. One of the better chroniclers asserts that it was during and immediately after the Winchester session of 16 June to 16 July 1449 that common report first began to single out Suffolk, not York, as to blame for everything: for defeats at the hands of the Scots in the previous autumn, for the current losses to the French and for the king's impoverishment, as revealed by a desperate request for assistance from Somerset, York's supplanter as lieutenant in Normandy, which Henry could not meet and which he ordered to be read out in the full parliament. The same source noted the truculence of the Commons in this assembly and their refusal to make any effective grant of supply unless Henry agreed to resume all the grants he had made from his livelihood. Henry's adamant refusal caused its dissolution on 16 July.[16]

As the first parliament of 1449 had refused to provide finance for the urgent needs of the defence of Normandy, another parliament was called almost immediately, for 6 November. When it assembled, all criticism concentrated on Suffolk's head. Before it met, Rouen, the capital of Normandy, was lost and the new lieutenant, Somerset, had made his first humiliating surrender to the French. The brave but minor captain Sir Thomas Kyriell had been commissioned to raise a relieving force, but this turned out to be pathetically small; too little and too late as always with this king, says one latin chronicle. In any case, it could not leave until the following March. On 9 January some of its discontented, unpaid soldiery, waiting to embark at Portsmouth, murdered the keeper of the privy seal, Adam Moleyns, and he, it seems, *in extremis*, made specific allegations against his colleague Suffolk of responsibility for the surrender of Maine, of which the troops were accusing him.

Consequently on 22 January 1450 Suffolk, using the defence which had served him well in 1447[17] when he had been accused of engineering the surrender of Maine, petitioned the king, detailing the long, loyal and costly service of himself and his family to his House, and alleging himself the victim of widespread, malicious, baseless slander, 'almost in every Commons mouth', originating from the confession of the dying Privy Seal, that he was guilty of some unspecified treason with the French. He asked that his desire to answer any man's general or specific charges be entered on the parliament roll. Such aggressive

---

[15] 'Articles of the duke of York against the bishop of Chichester' (B.L. MS Harley 543, fols 161r.–163r., in the hand of John Stow).

[16] *R.P.*, V, 147–8; Bale's Chronicle in *Six Town Chronicles* (ed. Flenley), 125; cf. John Benet's Chronicle, 195.

[17] See above, 193.

defence, backed up by Henry, had worked well in 1447. This time it did not. Four days later, he ventured to address the Commons in person in his defence, but they immediately reacted with a deputation to the chancellor requesting his commitment to ward, since, they said, he had now, by his own actions, personally admitted the strength of the rumours against him.[18]

There is one solitary, anonymous chronicle account which alleges that Lord Cromwell put the Commons up to this attack, a royal councillor prepared to ruin a fellow councillor for mere personal reasons.[19] Suffolk had exercised his 'good lordship' on behalf of the king's squire William Tailboys of South Kyme in Lincolnshire, a near neighbour to Cromwell at Tattershall, and at odds with one John Dymoke, who in turn had invoked the 'good lordship' of Cromwell. In 1448 Dymoke secured a powerful commission of *oyer et terminer* headed by the earl of Salisbury and Cromwell, which was preparing to do justice on Tailboys when it was superseded, at his petition, by one with more restricted power, composed of three judges and only one lay member. Tailboys had thus successfully petitioned the council against that first commission and the clerk of the council had minuted his petition that certain persons 'be assigned and no other'. Tailboys, also an enemy of the Pastons, operating under the protection of Suffolk, is normally portrayed as the very personification of the evils of 'good lordship'.[20] In these years he was actually attendant on the king's person. He had a spell in the Marshalsea in consequence of his dispute with Dymoke, but Suffolk presided, with Viscount Beaumont, over negotiations which ultimately led to Henry's pardoning him, on 8 November 1448, after Dymoke had been given some degree of satisfaction. In a further dispute Cromwell's castle at Tattershall was used as a prison to hold one of Tailboys's men whom, his master alleged, in an appeal to Viscount Beaumont for help, Cromwell was determined to hang as a common thief. Finally, on 28 November 1449 Cromwell was jostled, with, it seems, murderous intent, by Tailboys, at the very entrance to the council chamber in Westminster palace. Consequently he was again put in prison, this time in the Tower, for brawling in the palace precincts.

It is true that when the original indictment of Suffolk was rejected, further charges laid against him included a reference to his connection with Tailboys, alleging that he had intervened to pervert the course

---

[18] *R.P.*, V, 176ff.

[19] 'William Worcester', 'Annales', printed in *Wars of the English in France*, ed. Stevenson, *Wars*, II, pt. ii, 766.

[20] It is hard to find any contemporary who had a good word to say for him, although they did exist; the chronicler of the abbey of Crowland remembered him with gratitude for his vigorous defence of the abbey's rights against Thomas Lord Dacre in 1447.

of justice in his favour, but there is no need or justification for thus reducing Suffolk's impeachment primarily to this low, sordid plane of a personal vendetta.[21] To do so is to ignore the high issues of national policy and responsibility most prominent in the indictment, which the pettiness and patent absurdity of some of the lesser charges in the impeachment cannot conceal. Moreover, it is hardly likely that Henry, who in spite of his other shortcomings was consistently loyal to those who served him loyally, would have taken Cromwell into his closest personal service as his household chamberlain after the death of his principal agent and loyal minister Suffolk if he had been the prime mover in it.[22] All other sources, of which Davies's English chronicle is typical, stress the initial initiative of the Commons themselves here over matters of high policy: 'All the people of this land and especially the Commons, cried against the said duke of Suffolk and said he was a traitor and at instance and petition of the said Commons of the parliament holden at Westminster he was arrested and put in the Tower.'[23] This impeachment, the first since Suffolk's grandfather Michael de la Pole, minister of Richard II, had been brought low in 1386, was in reality an indictment of the whole of Henry's regime. It was the first stage of a threefold attack on the inefficiency of his royal government, the second being the acts of resumption and the third the rising of the Cade rebels in support of the activities of the Commons.

Suffolk had risen to eminence without any great achievement to his credit. In 1428 he became commander of the English forces before Orleans on the death of Salisbury and was responsible for raising that siege; later he lost the battle at Jargeau where he was captured. On his release he became a member of the council and in 1433 the steward of the household. From that moment he was constantly in the king's presence and employed about the king's business, acting as proxy for his master, whether laying a foundation stone at King's or marrying Margaret of Anjou; sitting in judgement on a minor traitor or leading a major embassy. We have the evidence from both Henry and Suffolk that the policy towards France was Henry's and that Suffolk was only the faithful executant. On the question of overseas affairs he was therefore unjustly accused. On the other hand, as the minister closest to the king, he must have had extensive influence. He used that position to his own financial advantage, but we have no evidence of him using

[21] *C.P.R.*, *1446–1452*, 187–8, 189, 210–2; P.R.O., E.28/77/53 (3 June 1448); *Paston Letters*, I, 96–8; The Crowland Continuator in *Ingulph's Chronicle of the Abbey of Croyland*, ed. & trans. H. T. Riley (London 1854), 405. See also R. L. Storey, 'Lincolnshire in the Wars of the Roses', *Nottingham Medieval Studies*, XIV (1970), 77–8.

[22] King's household chamberlain by 18 May 1451 (*C.P.R.*, *1446–1452*, 452).

[23] Davies's Chronicle, 68–9.

it to influence the king wisely in matters of high policy. For his sins of omission in this respect he merited the attack made on him.

On Tuesday 27 January the chancellor informed the king and lords, in the council chamber of parliament, of the Commons' request for impeachment. The lords took the measured advice of the judges, which was that no specific charges had been brought against Suffolk, and they unanimously advised against his arrest. They would not willingly provide one of their order as a scapegoat for the collapse of policies which were royal policies. But the very next day the Speaker of the Commons, in his own House, before a deputation of the chancellor and lords whose presence they had requested, made the most specific and alarmist accusations to press home their charge: the king was in danger, Charles of France was making ready to invade England. Suffolk had planned this and had fortified and provisioned his castle of Wallingford to serve as a place of refuge and succour for the invaders. This in itself should now be sufficient suspicion of treason to compel proceedings, they said, although they had further accusations to prepare. On the basis of these wild, baseless allegations Suffolk was sent to the Tower.

On 7 February the further charges were ready. Again, in their own House, through their Speaker William Tresham and before another delegation of the chancellor and a notable number of lords, they formally accused and impeached William de la Pole, duke of Suffolk, of high treason. Tresham handed the bill of accusation to the chancellor and the lords with the request that it should be enacted and proceedings taken against the duke according to the law and custom of the kingdom of England. The charges could hardly have been more specific. They said that on 20 July 1447, in the parish of St Sepulchre in the ward of Farringdon Within, he had conspired with the French embassy to facilitate a French invasion, to kill the king and make his own son John king by virtue of his marriage to his ward, the Lady Margaret Beaufort, daughter of the elder Beaufort duke of Somerset who died in 1444, pretending her to be next in line of succession to the throne in default of Henry's issue. Since his arrest that marriage had now in fact been solemnized. For bribes and promises, they said, he had earlier, while the first of the king's councillors, contrived the release of the duke of Orleans on 20 January 1439, clean contrary to the will of Henry V, to the end that the king's great adversary might conquer Henry's realm of France, duchies of Normandy and Gascony and counties of Anjou and Maine. This was now finally about to be accomplished as a result of Suffolk's unauthorized promise to surrender Anjou and Maine to the Angevins, made at Tours in 1444, and his revealing the king's innermost diplomatic and military secrets to his adversaries in 1447. He alone was responsible for the failure of all the great embassies and had on one occasion in the Star Chamber actually boasted of his honoured place in the councils of the French king. He had been responsible also for the duke of Brittany's inclusion among the subjects and allies of Henry's adversary at Tours in 1444, so that he too became an enemy, thereby causing the imprisonment of Henry's loyal sworn man Gilles of Brittany and putting him in peril of his life. Apart from his alleged attempt on the throne, all these original charges against Suffolk were thus concerned with foreign affairs and the conduct of the war. He was in fact impeached for the loss of Maine, Anjou and Normandy. Many of the things alleged had indeed happened, though not by Suffolk's fault or instigation. There is a remarkable parallel here with the dilemma confronting King Charles II two centuries later, when he fought to prevent the impeachment of a loyal servant, the earl of Danby, arraigned on similar capital charges of collusion with the French, when he had in fact merely been carrying out his master's own pro-French policies.

On 12 February 1450 the bill of impeachment was read before the Lords, who decided to send it to the judges for advice. But Henry would not have this done. Consequently, like Danby in 1679, Suffolk remained in the Tower. On 7 March the lords then present in parliament declared by a majority that he ought to be brought to his answer. The Commons meantime had not been idle and on 9 March they requested yet another lords' deputation to receive eighteen further charges: a truly formidable hotchpotch of half truths and untruths, repetitive in their general purport, but with even further spurious circumstantial details added. Suffolk was now charged with sole responsibility for the failure of the Armagnac marriage, and the consequent loss of the allegiance of the great lords of the Midi, since he was alleged to have given Charles VII advance notice of those plans. He was also charged with responsibility for persuading Henry to bind himself to a personal meeting with his great adversary in France, a plan of great potential danger for the king's safety and of impossible financial cost. This he had achieved, they said, by causing the French ambassadors to be admitted to Henry's presence for a secret discussion, without the assent or knowledge of other lords of the council. He was also charged with the responsibility of sending English soldiers to fight for the dauphin against Henry's German allies after the truce of Tours. They claimed he had alienated Henry's patrimony in Gascony, most notably to his nephew by marriage, Jean de Foix, viscount of Castillon, whom he had also made earl of Kendal, and that he had secured £1,300 worth of English revenues for Margaret of Anjou's aunt, the queen of France. Now, for the first time, allegations of his malign and corrupt influence on government at home were brought in. For sixteen years, it was said, he had also bled the king white, causing Henry to squander his inheritance on him and his friends; he had wasted the king's treasure, the £60,000 left by Lord Sudeley in the treasury when he resigned the treasurership (1446); he had also misemployed subsidies, purloined obligations, procured offices for unworthy persons, interfered with the normal course of justice and nominated sheriffs.

On 9 March Henry had him brought out of the Tower to Westminster to the parliament chamber, ostensibly to receive copies of these charges against him. Under the friendly guard of three household esquires he was then lodged for safety in the jewel house tower of the palace and given time to prepare an answer. Three days later he was brought back to the parliament chamber and on his knees before the king and lords utterly denied the original treasonable charges. On two points he was able to make statements which are at least, in part, verifiable from the records: other councillors knew as much as he did about the intended delivery of Maine (some others certainly had from late July 1447); the dead Moleyns, not he, had been the actual deliverer of Maine, which was also true. On a third point he did not deny his claim, made in Star Chamber, to knowledge of Charles VII's privy counsels, but he had made it, he said, to demonstrate the strength of his declared belief in the sincerity of the French king's desire for peace (i.e. he had been mistaken in this, but not disloyal). For the rest, significantly, he declared himself willing to prove his innocence 'in what wise the king will rule him to'. He made no claim for trial by his peers. He put his fate entirely in Henry's own hands.

Suffolk also now put in a written reply to the second lot of charges. This lost 'book', which must have contained a detailed justificatory *curriculum vitae*, produced in its turn a detailed *riposte*, possibly again prepared on behalf of the Commons, but showing a new personal tone of malice and scurrility which suggests it was an individual product.[24] In its imperfect surviving state it begins with charges of his adultery with a nun, giving her name and identifying their illegitimate daughter. Taking its cue from the nature of Suffolk's 'book', it then proceeded to belittle all his long record of military and diplomatic service. A number of otherwise unknown facts emerge from it. If it can be believed, then the English garrisons before the original truce of 1444 amounted to some 14,000 men; by the date of the first extension of it they were down to 8,000. Suffolk had actually admitted that his plenipotentiary powers, at Tours and in Lorraine, had been ample to cover the surrender of Anjou and Maine, but had absolutely denied that he ever consented even to discuss it, in spite of pressing attempts of the French to get him to do so. This final replication is also notable for its itemized demonstration of his 'insatiable covetise' at the king's

[24] *Historical Manuscripts Commission, Third Report* (London 1872) (muniments of the family of Neville of Holt), 279–80.

expense, to a figure of some 5,000 marks *per annum* in lands and offices, acquired by more than thirty patents, quite apart from his exploitation of 'the best revenues of all this land', the customs and subsidies, in the one specific instance cited amounting to a gain of another 5,000 marks through his wool factor, Simon Pygot of Lynn.

Thus Suffolk was the scapegoat for Henry's loss of his French lands. He also personified the abuse and prostitution of royal power in the localities to private ends which had become the hallmark of Henry's personal rule. There can be no doubt that he had acquired the substance fitting for a great duke entirely through royal service. His enhanced status and very great rewards had even so not made him able to bear unscathed the responsibilities he had shouldered for his king. He had expressed premonitions of personal disaster in 1443 before he undertook the peace negotiations and, fundamentally, he must have known that only royal blood in his veins, if even that, could save a loyal servant of a king who was incompetently pursuing such unpopular policies. Perhaps the most significant sentence in this long, final, vitriolic attack was this: if he persisted in denying responsibility for what happened, then 'let him tell the said defaults or misdeeds and lay them upon them that are guilty and tell what it is that passeth his power to amend'. This, of course, was utterly impossible, except by directly attacking the king himself, and Henry's loyalty to him was all he had left to depend on.

The next day Henry requested the lords through the mouth of the Lord Chief Justice to say what action they would advise. They deferred their answer until the following Monday, to give themselves time to consider, but what their answer would have been was never stated. Instead, on Tuesday 17 March, the king took the initiative. He summoned all his lords 'then being in town', forty-five of them including the chancellor, to his innermost chamber, identified in the record by its gavel window overlooking a cloister in Westminster palace. Here the duke of Suffolk was sent for and, kneeling, was asked, yet again, what answer he made to the Commons' charges. Again he denied them utterly, adding finally and pointedly that it was impossible that such great things could be brought about by him alone. Again he did not claim his right to trial by his peers, but submitted himself wholly to the king's will. The chancellor then read out Henry's prepared decision. On the first eight capital charges he declared him neither cleared nor convicted; on the second bill of lesser charges, for 'misprisions not criminal', he pronounced him banished from all his realms for five years from 1 May, on the prior understanding that he would not show or allow any malice of any kind against any person of whatever rank, for what had been done to him. This was done entirely on Henry's own will, not by way of legal judgement, nor by advice of the lords who thereupon, through the constable, Viscount Beaumont, requested that it should be so enacted on the parliament roll, to preserve intact their rights and their successors' rights to trial by their peerage in like cases in the future.[25] 'William Worcester' alleges that, while Suffolk was still in the custody of the household at Westminster, the frustrated Commons laboured to have him attainted of treason by bill,[26] to force Henry's hand. Such a bill in fact was presented, and rejected, in the next parliament, even though Suffolk was then dead.[27]

In the passions roused by Henry's refusal to allow the legal condemnation and destruction of this loyal servant whose innocence he alone could have proved, criticism of the king himself only found expression anonymously, or in the mouths of his humblest subjects. Henry released Suffolk from the palace under cover of darkness on the day he pronounced his sentence and he fled from the city, barely escaping from some 2,000 angry citizens, who managed only to seize one of his packhorses and rob some of his attendants.[28] From this time probably dates the most extreme of the political lampoons, such as the 'Warning to King Henry', which warned about the probable consequences of a pardon for Suffolk. This placard demanded his condemnation as essential justice, and as the price of any parliamentary grant. The king was now advised to look to his own position if he stood by traitors.[29] A London vintner's servant, who was executed for planning a rising on 21 March, was alleged to have proclaimed that for letting Suffolk escape justice Henry would lose his crown.[30]

Suffolk was the scapegoat for Henry's own failures. The well-known letter of advice which the duke wrote to his son on the day he sailed into exile, whatever it may disclose of the writer's character, is chiefly notable for the expressions of utter loyalty to Henry, and for the insistence that the same complete devotion should be shown to him by his heir.[31] Suffolk then believed he was going into temporary exile in the territory of the duke of Burgundy. His actual fate on 2 May, beheaded on the gunwale of a small boat in Dover Roads by sailors from the ship *Nicholas of the Tower*, in open defiance of royal safe conduct and authority, was seen by its perpetrators as an act of justice upon both king and minister. Recent research has now made this quite clear. The many pardons issued to Kentish rebels in 1451 contained

[25] *R.P.*, V, 182–3.
[26] 'Annales', 766.
[27] *R.P.*, V, 226.
[28] 'A London Chronicle', ed. C. L. Kingsford in *E.H.R.*, XXIX (1914), 515, 'Annales', 767.
[29] *Political Poems and Songs*, ed. Thomas Wright, II. (R.S., 1861), 229–32.
[30] Cited by Roger Virgoe, 'The Death of William de la Pole, duke of Suffolk', *B.J.R.L.*, XLVII (1965), 491.
[31] *Paston Letters*, I, 121.

a proviso of exclusion for offences committed at sea to the king's dishonour and when, finally, in June that year, two shipmen were brought
to trial for Suffolk's murder, they were also indicted for accusing the
king himself of misgovernment and of harbouring traitors about his
person. They were alleged to have declared, when they were shown
the royal safe conduct on which the duke relied, that they recognized
no such king; that the crown of the realm was the community of the
realm and that they would now make another person from outside
the kingdom king in his place.[32] This in some measure echoes the final
lines of the 'Warning to King Henry':

> O rex, si rex es, rege te, vel eris sine re rex;
> Nomen habes sine re, nisi te recte regas.[33]

The Commons' impeachment of Suffolk was only one half of a two-
pronged parliamentary attack on the agents of Henry's personal rule.
The other plan was to enforce legislation to recover all the material
benefits which Suffolk and his household colleagues had gained from
their privileged positions in the royal service. To this end a bill was
promoted to resume into the king's hands all lands, offices, pensions
and gifts made by Henry, or earlier in his name, since his accession.
The only precedent for such an attempt to compel a king to annul
royal acts went back to 1404, when parliament had similarly tried
to make his grandfather Henry IV undo the costly arrangements by
which he had rewarded the supporters of his usurpation. In that similar
situation Henry IV's resistance had been determined, clever and
successful. In the spring of 1450 his much less able grandson had first
to admit a partial defeat, which became total in the following parliament of 1450–1.

The first two sessions of the parliament which impeached Suffolk,
in the turbulent capital at Blackfriars and at Westminster between
6 November 1449 and 30 March 1450, had otherwise been singularly
unproductive. Officially summoned to handle arduous affairs of the
kingdom which could not be dealt with in any other way, which was
circumlocution for the paramount need for substantial grants of
taxation, the Commons stubbornly refused to grant anything at all.
Apart from listening to the desperate appeal from Somerset for assistance for Normandy, they were treated to an exposition of the 'state
of the realm', in other words a financial summary of the king's resources,
debts and obligations for the next twelve months, best calculated to
impress his needs upon them.[34] As with the previous assembly, the

---

[32] Roger Virgoe, *op. cit.*, 489–502.
[33] Wright, *Political Poems*, 231.
[34] Mentioned with some details in the preambles to the two acts of resumption
of 1450 and 1451.

appalling financial situation thus revealed led them to demand not simply redress of grievances but retribution before supply. After Palm Sunday, 29 March 1450, at the approach of Easter, the weary king, 'for intimate reasons' unspecified, took the first of what was to be many similar decisions to withdraw from London and retreat to the security and more favourable atmosphere of the Lancastrian Midlands, there to hold the next session of parliament at Leicester. John Paston received a letter from the parliament at Leicester, dated 6 May, informing him of Suffolk's death, that Calais was threatened with attack, and that the king at Leicester had accepted a resumption 'in some but not in all'.[35] This resumption, coupled with the destruction of Suffolk, was the Commons' panacea for all the nation's grievances, for the loss of the French lands, the years of crippling taxation to no successful purpose, the evils of a royal household which lived off the land without paying for what it took, and for the scandal of royal servants who corrupted the administrative and judicial systems of the kingdom and contrived to enrich themselves while the king went bankrupt.

The determination of this parliament to make Henry rescind his grants had been common knowledge inside and outside the assembly since its inception. The Kentish rebels rose in arms while it was still sitting at Leicester, claiming that those about the king were preventing its acceptance. This belief was not very wide of the mark, because it was only after Suffolk had been removed from the political scene, Normandy irretrievably lost, and Calais threatened, that any degree of resumption was accepted. When it was, no attempt was made to modify the original bill's sweeping provisions, which suggests that the final decision to accept it was a sudden one, typical of Henry. Instead it was accepted wholesale, but with a clause reserving the king's right to make exceptions appended to it. In this way it was hoped to get away with a gesture and only limited concessions.

Fifteen modifying clauses and 186 separate clauses of exemption, the result of petitions, were subsequently added to the act. All these petitions were personally signed and authorized by Henry himself. Some of these were in fact harmless and necessary in order to avoid an utter and complete annulment of all acts of state made over the previous twenty-eight years. But the crucial exemptions were those made for the household men, which at first sight appear to be the least controversial, because in a number of cases they specifically stated that certain grants they had obtained would be surrendered. When their original petitions for exemption are consulted it becomes clear that some kind of conference or committee had in the first instance agreed in advance what they should keep and what they should be prepared to lose. As enrolled on the parliament roll their surrenders totalled some £700

[35] *Paston Letters*, I, 126–7.

per annum, but figures on a separate list of 101 household men raise this total to about £1,800 *per annum* and further reveal that they were actually retaining specific items of royal revenues totalling £3,750 *per annum*.[36] Beyond this figure the greatest of the survivors, Cromwell, Say, Sudeley, Beauchamp and others, had blanket exemptions covering all their grants in the widest possible terms. Six months' discussion of the measure had left plenty of time for individuals and corporate bodies to prepare for the possible event. Exemption certificates were reaching the exchequer by 13 August 1450 although it did not receive a copy of the act itself until 15 October 1450. Administrative action on the act was slow and ineffective. No writs went out to the shires ordering inquisitions into holders of crown lands and revenues until the spring of 1451.

Nevertheless, the formal annulment by act of parliament of grants, antedated to take effect from 6 November 1449, the opening day of the parliament, was sufficient to create much uncertainty in the land market. Something of a scramble for new leases ensued. Some unfortunates who were absent, even the greatest, such as York in Ireland, Somerset in Normandy and of course the family of the dead Suffolk, lost heavily. In some cases Suffolk's former colleagues benefited. Lord Beauchamp secured a twelve-year lease of his county and lordship of Pembroke. His Oxfordshire lands (Woodstock, Handborough, Wootton and Stonesfield) were taken over by Lord Sudeley. Some had post-dated patents ready in case grants covered by the act should be resumed. Some household men lost rent-free grants or grants at nominal rates to colleagues who, with foreknowledge, stepped in smartly to secure them for themselves on less favourable but still remunerative terms.[37] Such was the half-hearted, dilatory and deceptive act which, nevertheless, still constituted a parliamentary triumph. Along with it were passed a detailed reservation of specific items of the king's endowed revenues for the expenses of his household and a graduated tax on incomes from land and offices. A further grant of the normal tenths and fifteenths, even in halves, such as had been reluctantly granted in 1447, was still out of the question, and Henry, in his extreme poverty, had to be content with this still novel, limited, income tax which in fact produced no more than £5,000 to repay loans over the next three years.[38]

After 7 June news of the Kentish rising made the king's return to London from Leicester imperative. In the ensuing confusion, the parliament was not so much dissolved as faded away. The Kentish rebels

---

[36] P.R.O., E.163/8/14.

[37] For a more detailed discussion of this act and its consequences see Wolffe, *The Royal Demesne*, 124–30.

[38] *R.P.*, V, 172–4; P.R.O., E.359/29.

actually thought the king brought it back to London with him. They regarded themselves not as rebels, but as petitioners, seeking to back up the demands of parliament and they sent it a copy of their articles of complaint to Westminster. This rising, or petitioning, by the men of Kent, East Sussex, Surrey and Middlesex, known as Jack Cade's rebellion, seems to have been initially organized in the Ashford area, in the religious gatherings on Whitsunday, 24 May 1450.[39] The final spark to action there was the threat made to the whole county by the sheriff of Kent and Sussex in retaliation for the death of Suffolk. The duke's headless body had been found on Dover sands and, according to the first article of the rebels' complaint, William Crowmer, sheriff of Kent and Sussex, son-in-law of the treasurer, Lord Say, had taken custody of it and threatened that the king would now turn the whole county of Kent into a deer forest, in punishment. Such a threat was enough to coalesce all the grievances in this most politically conscious, responsive and best-informed area of England, lying as it did between the capital and disintegrating English Normandy, its coastal areas fully exposed to French raids, its trade and well-being most immediately susceptible to the severe economic crisis of 1449–50. Beginning in Ashford, a march on London rapidly gathered contingents by the way until they reached Blackheath, the obvious, final place of assembly outside London, on 11 and 12 June. Here they established a strong encampment, efficiently staked about to prevent its being over-run by cavalry. When the news reached Henry in Leicester he appointed two Kentish lords, the duke of Buckingham, of Penshurst, and Lord Rivers, of the Mote, by Maidstone, to head the vanguard of a battle force to accompany him back to London.[40] Here he established himself at St John's Hospital in Clerkenwell on Saturday 13 June. Nothing was done on Sunday, but on the Monday morning he sent out heralds to Blackheath to order the encamped host in his name to withdraw. These heralds returned with the message that those assembled on Blackheath declared they were not rebels, but petitioners, gathered for his right and his people's rights. They would not withdraw without redress of their grievances.

Their captain, at least from this 15 June, when a spokesman was required to address the king's envoys, was a man who styled himself John Mortimer and John Amendall and claimed to be a cousin of the duke of York.[41] In truth, according to the proclamations issued for his apprehension on 10 July, he was John Cade, a sanctuary man

[39] Helen M. Lyle, *The Rebellion of Jack Cade 1450* (Historical Association, 1950), 9.

[40] Commissions of array to go against the rebels were issued to Beaumont, Lovell, Scales, Rivers, Dudley, Buckingham, Oxford, Devon and Arundel from Leicester on 6 June and Newport Pagnel on 10 June (*C.P.R., 1446–1452*, 385).

[41] Giles's Chronicle, 39; *The Brut*, 517.

and outlaw, an Irishman and ex-soldier, who had taken service with the French.[42] In contrast to their spokesman, those of his host who are identifiable were impeccably respectable, including as they did eighteen esquires, with several former sheriffs among them. Cade's carver or sword-bearer was Robert Poynings of Maidstone, M.P. for Sussex in the next parliament, grandson of Lord Grey of Ruthyn and son-in-law of Judge Paston. Seventy-four of the rebels styled themselves gentlemen; there were the mayor of Queenborough and the bailiff of Sandwich among them; over 500 styled themselves yeomen and there were very many tradesmen and craftsmen present: farriers, saddlers, brewers, vintners, innkeepers, fullers, weavers, tailors, masons, tilers, coopers and butchers, sailors and many husbandmen. Inevitably there were many without any designation, but the most striking aspect of all is the way their 3,000 or more ultimate pardons[43] were grouped together in their hundreds of origin, under constables. Fifty-three constables from thirty-one of the sixty-eight hundreds of Kent headed their named contingents, sometimes followed by the note 'and all others of the said hundred'. In addition there were constables and their contingents from fourteen Sussex hundreds, three from Surrey, one from Middlesex and four from Surrey towns.

It looks as though this was in fact a levy of the fencible men, mainly of Kent and East Sussex, raised for this mass petitioning of the king and parliament, and, they claimed, to defend the king and realm against the traitors about his person. This suspicion is strengthened almost to certainty by the fact that in their midst were at least five commissioners of array for Kent, who had been appointed with eight others on 14 April 1450, in the face of threatened French invasion, to array and muster all fencible men of the county, and to set up beacons.[44] The two principal commissioners now numbered among the Kentish host were Sir John Cheyne of Eastchurch in Sheppey, justice of the peace, king's sergeant-at-arms, M.P. for Kent in the previous parliament, and William Haute of Bishopsbourne, brother-in-law of Lord Rivers, justice of the peace and shire knight in the next parliament. The three other rebel commissioners of array were William Manston, John Fogge of Great Chart near Ashford, Haute's son-in-law, and William Hextal of Peckham, an associate of the Stafford duke of Buckingham, M.P. for Bletchingley, a Stafford borough, in the previous

[42] The principal documents for the Kentish rising are in John Stow's *Annales* (1631 ed.), 388–92; *Three Fifteenth-Century Chronicles* (ed. Gairdner), 94–9; *Historical Manuscripts Commission Eighth Report Part I* (1881), 266 (b)–269 (a) from the muniments of Magdalen College, Oxford, cf. G. Kriehn; *The English Rising of 1450* (Strasbourg 1892), and Helen M. Lyle, *op. cit.*

[43] *C.P.R., 1446–1452*, 338–74 (3,327 names, with some duplication).

[44] *Ibid.*, 383.

parliament, and for Kent in 1453–4. With the exception of the sparsely populated areas of the Isle of Thanet and Romney Marshes, all areas of Kent supplied contingents of fencible men to Blackheath: the areas bordering the main highway all the way from Dover, through Ashford, Canterbury, Sittingbourne, Maidstone and Wrotham to Southwark; the Weald and the whole of the Thames estuary from Deptford to beyond the Isle of Sheppey.

Placards of the rebels' complaints and grievances, one of which was secured for his master by Sir John Fastolf's servant Payn, from the Blackheath camp,[45] were condensed by the captain, or by his secretary Henry Wilkhouse, public notary and procurator of the bishop of Rochester,[46] into five requests for presentation to the king. Henry should resume his lost demesnes in order to re-establish his power and dignity: he should banish from his presence and punish according to the law 'all the false progeny of the duke of Suffolk', and replace them by the lords of his blood, York, Exeter, Buckingham and Norfolk, York being specifically referred to as exiled from his presence; those who had encompassed the death of Gloucester should be punished, together with those who had lost the overseas possessions: 'and our true lords, knights and esquires, and many a good yeoman lost and sold ere they went, the which is great pity to hear'. They wanted the removal of abuses of the law immediately affecting them: extortions of green wax,[47] judgements of King's Bench, the insufferable purveyance for Henry's household and the statute of labourers. They demanded relief from the corrupt practices of certain named influential local individuals: Stephen Slegg, William Crowmer, William Isle and Robert Est.[48] The misdeeds of such royal servants and servants of the 'great rulers of the shire' were linked with abuses perpetrated by members of Henry's household government on the national plane. This was chiefly because the courtier Lord Say, treasurer of England, chamberlain of the household, Warden of the Cinque Ports, constable of Dover castle, chief recipient of Henry's bounty in Kent and Sussex, and a great ruler of the shire from his seat of Knole castle near Sevenoaks, personified both. Specific local complaints included interference with the free election of the knights of the shire, corruption in the choice of tax collectors and in levying taxes, extortion by the sheriffs and under-sheriffs, false charges of treason, laid so that those who had the king's ear could get the lands of those accused, tax concessions made to the barons of the Cinque Ports, which then had to be made up out of the

[45] *Paston Letters*, I, 131–5.
[46] Identified by Dr Roger Virgoe (see below p. 239n).
[47] Green wax was used to seal the exchequer writs issued to sheriffs for collection of fines incurred in the law courts.
[48] See above, pp. 124–5.

county quota, feigned indictments for alleged hunting offences, illegal exactions of castle ward dues throughout the shire, enforced by the court of Dover castle, and the remoteness of the justices of the peace sessions from much of the county, five days' journey being necessary to get to them from the west of Kent.

Rebellions normally lift the lid on the state of the realm and reveal its inside workings. This Kentish rising was no exception. The opinion of Sir John Fortescue on the root cause of rebellion, a rare event among the common people of England, is apposite here: 'when they lack good they will arise, saying that they lack justice'.[49] The picture revealed is one of endemic, corrupt local government and justice, its failings exacerbated by sudden, severe economic depression caused by political events. The great lords of Kent, both lay and ecclesiastical, were constantly absent on royal service and the localities ruled by their agents. The community of the shire looked to parliament, now moved off to the remote Midlands, for redress of all the multifarious grievances summed up in the phrase 'lack of governance'. They were determined to assist the Commons in parliament in their efforts to obtain reform and redress.

The 'Lower House' in parliament had made a scapegoat of the king's chief executive for the accumulating failures of past policies. The king's opposition to his impeachment and the only slight success of their resumption bill suggested that Henry was not amenable to change. These requests of the men of Kent, the most articulate section of the kingdom, presented from a local viewpoint but basically identical with the Commons' demands, now met the same negative response. Robert Bale's London chronicle, which is noteworthy for its precise chronology[50] of these years, shows that much of the king's considerable army was moved to within sight of the Blackheath camp at Henry's command that same Monday 15 June, after his herald's return. The following morning he at first proposed to move against them himself, but was persuaded to delay while a deputation consisting of the duke of Buckingham and the two archbishops, all three commissioners of the peace for Kent, plus his friend the bishop of Winchester and the constable, Viscount Beaumont, went to reason with them. They returned with the captain's specific requests, having bound themselves to return by a fixed time to deliver the king's answer. But this answer never arrived because Henry simply refused to consider them. Instead, on the Wednesday, the rebel host received intelligence that Henry was indeed taking the field in person against them. Such a respectable assembly would not face the king's banner in the field, which would be manifest

---

[49] *The Governance of England*, 140.
[50] In *Six Town Chronicles of England* (ed. Flenley), 129ff.

treason, so they dispersed under cover of darkness, leaving an empty heath for him to occupy on the Thursday morning.

Further reinforcements for Henry's host, notably from Lancashire and Cheshire, continued to arrive throughout that day and night. He now allowed the vanguard of his army to deploy their forces to hunt down the retreating rebels in the Kentish countryside. Among the leaders of this foray were the earl of Northumberland, lords Rivers, Scales and Grey, Sir Humphrey Stafford of Grafton and William Stafford, both kinsmen of the duke of Buckingham and of the archbishop of Canterbury, Sir Thomas Stanley, the controller of the household and other household men, John Sutton, Lord Dudley, Sir Robert Wingfield and Thomas Daniel, Henry's esquire of the body. On Thursday afternoon he received the shock news that the Staffords had been routed and slain with many of their men, somewhere in wooded country between Bromley and Sevenoaks. On the Friday morning, when Henry ordered the host to stand to arms for further pursuit of the rebels, he was faced with mutiny in his own ranks. A great shout of 'destroy the traitors about the king' went up and a call to finish the captain's work for him.

A weak *volte face* by Henry now followed under this sudden pressure, in marked contrast to his refusal to consider the petitions of his loyal rebels only three days previously. First Lord Say and William Crowmer were arrested and despatched to the Tower.[51] He issued a proclamation against traitors, which was taken to mean further arrests of some not present, including Thomas Daniel, and this quieted the host. But the incipient mutiny had revealed its unreliability and a lame dispersal back through the city now began. Henry himself withdrew to nearby Greenwich, returned up-river to the city on 20 June, and then retired to Westminster. From here, having qualms about the safety of Lord Say, he sent secretly to the Tower for him to join him, but the constable, the young duke of Exeter, declined to sanction his release. Henry had decided to flee out of harm's way, back to his Lancaster estates, and was unmoved by a deputation of the mayor of London and his fellows sent to Westminster to implore him to stay with them to face the reassembling rebels.[52] In marked contrast to his predecessor Richard II, who in his youth had personally confronted his rebellious peasants in almost identical circumstances at Mile End in 1381, Henry had no spirit for a personal encounter. By 26 June, if not before, he was in Berkhamsted castle. It was the council who ordered the Tower to

[51] It was not simply for their own safety, since a commission was issued to the sergeants-at-arms at the Tower to seize all the goods of the 'late treasurer' Lord Say in Kent on 24 June (*C.P.R., 1446–1452*, 390). John, Lord Beauchamp of Powicke was made treasurer in his place from 22 June (*ibid.*, 330).

[52] 'A Short English Chronicle' in *Three Fifteenth-Century Chronicles* (ed. Gairdner), 67.

be victualled against siege on 30 June.[53] By 7 July Henry had withdrawn
to the Midlands and was secure in the castle of Kenilworth with levies
from the four northern counties and from Cheshire and Lancashire
alerted to his call.[54]

The rash sorties of the household men into the hostile Kent countryside between 18 and 20 June had thus destroyed the king's apparent
position of strength at Blackheath and rekindled the dying rebellion.
On Tuesday 23 June the captain re-established his camp at Blackheath
and finally moved to occupy Southwark on Thursday 2 July. A supporting great fellowship now came out of Essex and occupied Mile End
outside Aldgate the same day. There were undoubtedly sympathizers
within the city itself, since at noon that day Cade was able to cross
over London Bridge and cut the drawbridge ropes, so from that Friday
afternoon until the following Sunday evening the men of Kent crossed
into the city and returned to Southwark at will. They pillaged the
house of Alderman Philip Malpas, the chief of Cade's opponents within
the city, and contrived to get hold of Say and Crowmer. Some twenty
persons, including the dead duke of Suffolk and his duchess, the bishop
of Salisbury, Lord Say, William Crowmer, Thomas Daniel, John Say
and other household members, were indicted at the Guildhall before
the Chief Baron of the Exchequer, Peter Ardern, and two other judges,
Nicholas Assheton and Robert Danvers. These commissioners were
members of a powerful commission of oyer and terminer for London
and the suburbs, headed by Lord Scales, keeper of the Tower, the
mayor, Thomas Chalton, and the Chief Justice, issued by the council
from Westminster on 1 July, both as a concession and as a precaution
against anticipated disorders.[55] The treasurer of England, Lord Say,
was arraigned in person at the Guildhall. When he tried to claim
trial by his peers he was dragged from the court and summarily executed
by Cade's men in Cheapside. Crowmer was executed at Mile End
among the Essex men. On the Sunday a joint force of citizens and
the Tower garrison under Lord Scales attempted to bar the bridge
to the rebels and fought them all night to a standstill, with many
casualties on both sides, including among the slain Mathew Gough,
veteran captain of the French wars, and an alderman, John Sutton.
Finally, on the Monday morning, during a truce, the two archbishops
and the bishop of Winchester crossed over to persuade the captain
and his men to accept a royal pardon, prepared at the instigation

[53] *P.P.C.*, VI, 95.

[54] *Ibid.*, 95–6; P.R.O., C.81/1371/23: orders from Berkhamsted castle on 1 July to
prepare commissions for the earls of Salisbury and Northumberland, Ralph, Lord
Greystock, lords Clifford and Egremont, for the four northern counties and Sir William
Stanley and Sir Thomas Harrington for Cheshire and Lancashire, to array the people
in their best and most defensible array to be ready when Henry sent for them.

[55] *C.P.R.*, *1446–1452*, 388, 433–5; Benet's Chronicle, 200, 'William Worcester', 768.

of Queen Margaret, who was still at Greenwich. This was issued to some 3,000 of them that day and the next, 6 and 7 July. It is the enrolment of these pardons which enables the composition of the rebellion to be ascertained with such accuracy. With the exception of the captain's own pardon, which was in any case granted under his false name, all of them were honoured to the letter.

Over a century ago Bishop Stubbs wrote that Cade's rebellion, more than anything else in the reign, proved Henry's utter incapacity for government.[56] It was a political demonstration of his loyal subjects from four counties, supported by all sections of the community except the lords, although the substantial gentry element in it kept out of the limelight; a localized expression of a deep national sense of humiliation and frustration. The king, when confronted by several thousand of his loyal subjects demanding redress, had declined to consider their petitions and had raised his standard in the field against them. They dared not and would not fight him face to face and dispersed, but he simply threw away his enormous personal advantage as their sovereign. He allowed sections of his army under his hated household men to ravage the countryside in pursuit, and they met with sharp defeat in the process. This led to mutiny in his own forces who then showed sympathy with the rebels, so Henry abandoned his army and his capital and withdrew to his private Lancastrian domains. He had handled rebellion at home as badly as he had previously managed the affairs of his French kingdom in the loss of which lay the basic cause of all his troubles from 1449.

[56] *Constitutional History*, III, 155.

Chapter 13

THE FRUSTRATION OF
RICHARD DUKE OF YORK, 1450-1453

Some two weeks after the rebels dispersed from London with their pardons Henry regarded it as safe to return south and took up the discarded reins of government once more at a great council meeting, summoned to meet him at St Albans on 24 July.[1] He re-entered the capital on the 28th and was honourably received there, in spite of his cowardly desertion of a month before. He offered at St Paul's and would have proceeded to Eton to celebrate the Feast of the Assumption, but was prevented by the multitude of destitute and disorderly soldiers coming from Normandy.[2] Fear of renewed widespread insurrection in Kent and elsewhere now prompted an important concession. Sixteen commissioners of oyer and terminer headed by the two archbishops, Bishop Wainfleet, the duke of Buckingham and Lord Sudeley, were sent into Kent, not as used to be supposed further to supress rebellion, but genuinely to inquire into grievances.[3] There were no government indictments laid before this commission. The ninety or so presentments made before them in August, September and October at Rochester, Maidstone, Canterbury and Dartford all came from the juries of the county. Among these were many laid against the household men, who had made the futile *chevauchées* of 18 to 20 June into Kent, for plundering provisions and horses, stealing cash, plate, jewellery and household goods.[4] Of the rest, over one-third were against the alleged oppressers and extortioners whose misdeeds had been among the grievances of the rebels: sheriffs and their undersheriffs, gaol keepers and stewards in royal service and in the service of Lord Say, the archbishop of Canterbury and other Kentish lords.[5] Among those so indicted was Alexander

[1] Benet's Chronicle, 202.

[2] *Ibid;* soldiers still bothering the household were given 15 days' maintenance on 25 August 1450 (P.R.O., E.28/80/83).

[3] *C.P.R., 1446-1452*, 388, dated 1 August 1450. The rest were all legal men apart from one king's sergeant-at-arms, William Wangford: eight high court judges, Thomas Burgoyne, under-sheriff of London, and William Laken, lawyer, later sergeant-at-law and judge.

[4] The most prominent of these were John Sutton lord Dudley, Thomas Daniel, Sir Thomas Stanley, Richard Wydeville lord Rivers and Sir Robert Wingfield (see note 5 below).

[5] Roger Virgoe, 'Some Ancient Indictments in the King's Bench referring to Kent, 1450-1452'; in *Documents Illustrative of Medieval Kentish Society*, ed. F. R. H. Du Boulay (Records Publication Committee of the Kent Archaeological Society, XVII, Ashford 1964), 214-65.

Iden of Milton, the new sheriff of Kent and Sussex, who had captured and killed the captain of Kent and been rewarded for it. When Henry later recovered sufficient confidence to set up further commissions of oyer and terminer to punish disorder these were directed to ignore offences committed before 8 July, the day after the Cade rebels had received their pardons.

A new dimension was given to the troubles of Henry and his household when news reached them, probably towards the end of August, that the exiled Richard duke of York, without any royal command or permission asked or received, was on his way back from Ireland.[6] His defeated and disgraced successor in Normandy, Edmund duke of Somerset, had already returned among his demoralized troops, passing through London on 1 August. Defeats of such magnitude can hardly have been much recommendation for a new military appointment, but Henry was sure of his loyalty and obedience and it was probably apprehension at the news of York's pending return that caused Henry to make Somerset Constable of England on 11 September. York's name had been used by malcontents since the beginning of the year as a potential reformer who had a prime right to prominence in Henry's councils. A charade had been acted before Henry as he passed through Stony Stratford on his way to the Leicester parliament when a sailor, John Harries, threshed with a flail before the king to show how York would deal with the traitors about him. The foolhardy man suffered a traitor's death in April for his demonstration.[7] But undoubtedly some men also saw York as an alternative king. A man was indicted at Ipswich and hanged and quartered for plotting in January to put York on the throne,[8] one of Moleyns's murderers made similar threats to Henry's face.[9] Jack Cade usurped York's family name of Mortimer and called for his return from exile and Cade's placards showed that his followers felt the need to deny any wish to depose Henry and make York king in his stead. These were false, treasonable intentions, they alleged, which had been fathered on them by the king's entourage. York was quite untainted by any of the disasters of recent years. As heir male and heir general of Edward III he was the sole person who could dispute the Lancastrian title. Later tradition maintained that Roger Mortimer, fourth earl of March, had been proclaimed

[6] At Dublin on 14 August, at Trim on 26 August; J. Otway-Ruthven, *A History of Medieval Ireland* (London 1968), 383.

[7] 'John Piggot's Memoranda', printed by C. L. Kingsford in *English Historical Literature*, 371.

[8] The earliest known reference to York as a challenge to Henry's throne, detailed by Dr Roger Virgoe in his unpublished London Ph.D. thesis 'The Parliament of 1449–1450' (1964), 198–9, from P.R.O., K.B.9/265/12–29.

[9] *Paston Letters, Introduction,* xciv–xcv.

Richard II's heir presumptive in 1385.[10] There may be some doubt whether York, distant relative as he was to Henry himself, was widely regarded as his heir presumptive in 1450, but he was actually proposed as his 'heir apparent' in the parliament of 1451 by the lawyer member for Bristol, Thomas Yonge,[11] who had been York's attorney in England during his absence in Ireland.[12]

York re-entered the kingdom as he had left it, by the haven of Beaumaris on Anglesey. From Beaumaris he passed to his estates in the Welsh marches, to strengthen his following before proceeding in military array to the capital. He communicated by letter and petition with the king and what he wrote was intended to be made public. Men were uncertain of the significance of his return and none more so than Henry himself. Two of the most prominent and unpopular members of the king's household, John, Lord Dudley and Reginald Boulers, fled to York for protection.[13] The Speaker of parliament, William Tresham, wearing Henry's SS collar of livery,[14] set out to meet him and was cut down by followers of Lord Grey of Ruthin on the king's highway. Henry had approved hasty and ineffective arrangements to oppose his return, chiefly by members of his household whose local interest lay in North Wales and the western counties. According to York's complaints they were specifically instructed to imprison him at Conway, kill his chamberlain and right-hand man, Sir William Oldhall, and detain two others of his council, Sir Walter Devereux and Sir Edmund Mulso.[15] Perhaps their loyal zeal had simply outrun their instructions, since the king himself stated, in his first reply to York's letters, that they had been sent to ascertain his intentions

---

[10] York's great-grandparents were Philippa, daughter of Lionel duke of Clarence, second son of Edward III, and Edmund Mortimer, 3rd earl of March. He had inherited the Mortimer lands and title from his uncle Edmund Mortimer, 5th earl of March (d.s.p. 1425). See above, p. 35.

[11] 'William Worcester', in Stevenson, *Wars*, II, pt. ii, 770.

[12] *C.P.R., 1446–1452*, 245.

[13] Benet's Chronicle, 202. The people of Gloucester had risen up against the abbey, proclaiming Boulers a traitor and blaming him for the loss of Normandy: 'Gloucester Annals', in Kingsford, *English Historical Literature*, 355.

[14] *R.P.*, V, 211–3.

[15] Those whom York alleged had opposed his entry on Henry's instruction are all precisely identified by R. A. Griffiths, 'Richard duke of York and the Royal Household in Wales, 1449–50', *The Welsh History Review*, VIII (1976), 14–25: Sir Thomas Stanley, constable of Chester, chamberlain of North Wales, controller of the household, Thomas Norris, sergeant-at-arms there and a household esquire, William Griffiths, esquire of the chamber, Richard Belth, groom of the chamber, and others in North Wales on the orders of William Say, usher of the chamber; Thomas Pulford, usher of the chamber from Chester, William Elton, yeoman of the crown from Worcester, William Broke, yeoman of the crown from Gloucester. Also John Talbot viscount Lisle from Holt castle, apparently the only non-household agent and possibly Lionel Lord Welles and Richard Waller, two other members of the royal household.

and to oppose them only if they were hostile. Henry doubted his loyalty, though there are no grounds for disbelieving York's own stated reasons at this stage for thus returning unbidden in strength. He rightly claimed that his name had been linked with treasonable movements; he further genuinely believed that there were those who were actually labouring to have him indicted for treason. He could not have forgotten the fate of Duke Humphrey who had died under arrest, in a cloud of royal mistrust and disapproval, in 1447. He said he came to clear his own name and to prevent the corrupting of his blood. This suggests that he already had the prospect of a *natural* succession to the still child-less Henry in mind. At any rate, he was determined, amid all the unrest and uncertainty in England in 1450, to assert and keep open his rights.

York's first two communications to Henry indicate that he was returning, in the first instance, in some apprehension, to defend his own good name and his own interests, not to play the reformer, anti-household advocate, or House of Commons man, let alone to topple Henry from his throne. His attainder in 1459 alleged that he finally forced his way into Henry's presence in Westminster palace on 27 September 1450, beating down the resistance of his guards,[16] but their surviving exchanges of correspondence, and the most reliable of the chroniclers, suggest that their personal encounter on that occasion, as one would expect in the royal presence, was at least calm and orderly.[17] By this date Henry had issued a formal, written public declaration that he accepted him as his true subject and well-beloved cousin. Never-theless, York's second interview with the king, before 6 October, reveals that by then he had rapidly donned the reformer's mantle and espoused an anti-household cause which was conveniently personified now not by the duke of Suffolk but by York's erstwhile rival for pre-eminence in Normandy, the Beaufort duke of Somerset. According to Abbot Wheathampstead, the old resentment at his replacement by Somerset as king's lieutenant in Normandy, as he had previously been superseded in authority by his elder brother John Beaufort, followed by his relegation to Ireland, now got the better of him, when he saw his former rival, in spite of his failures and disgrace, once more exalted in the king's favour.[18] York's entourage knew that, when he was with the king on this second occasion, he caused consternation in the royal

[16] *R.P.*, V, 346, 'with great multitude of people harnessed and arrayed in manner of war and there beat down the spears and walls in your chamber'.

[17] Benet's Chronicle, 202. Their exchange of letters most recently and accurately printed from Beverley Corporation Archives with commentary by R. A. Griffiths, 'Duke Richard of York's intentions in 1450 and the origins of the Wars of the Roses', *Journal of Medieval History*, I (1975), 187–210.

[18] *Registrum*, I, 160–1.

household by pressing Henry to do justice to those commonly spoken of as traitors, and desired 'much after the Commons desire'. His chamberlain, Sir William Oldhall, had also been with the king and Henry had actually asked them to look favourably upon his esquire of the body John Pennycook, who was unable to gather his rents in areas dominated by York's lordships, only to be told that 'western men' would not receive royal courtiers favourably, even if ordered to do so under York's own seal.[19] Oldhall also alleged that on their march to the capital near St Albans only his personal intervention had saved the former chancellor of Normandy, Sir Thomas Hoo, from death at the hands of their followers. Once again, dealings between York and his king were publicized on both sides. Henry's formal reply to his requests for reform was to announce his intention to establish a 'sad and sub-stantial council', giving them greater powers than ever he had done before.[20] York would be one member, but only one among equals. The king's philosophical justification on this occasion for taking the advice of many rather than one, in a body where the advice of the greatest and the least should be of equal weight, was later hailed by the authors of York's attainder in 1459 as evidence that the spirit of the wisdom of God in Henry had prompted that clever counter to York's over-weening ambition.

Parliament had been summoned by writs dated 5 September 1450 to meet again at Westminster on 6 November.[21] The causes were to provide for the defence of the realm, for the safekeeping of the sea, for urgent help to the people of Gascony in their defence against the French, and for the pacification and punishment of riotously disposed people disturbing and endangering the kingdom by their gatherings and insurrections.[22] Such unrest was evident in the capital. On 29 October the mayor of London's procession was harassed by disorderly soldiers. On 30 October and 1 November York's arms and the royal arms were set up in various places in the city and suburbs in apposition, by rival parties.[23] York and his wife's nephew, Norfolk, had been exerting their combined influence on the shire elections in Norfolk, Northamptonshire and Oxfordshire with only moderate success,[24] but York's chamberlain Sir William Oldhall was chosen as Speaker. York and Norfolk reappeared in the city in great strength on 23 and 24 November and the tension increased. Retrospectively, this appearance

[19] Paston Letters, I, 150–1.
[20] Griffiths, op. cit., 205–6.
[21] H.B.C., 532.
[22] R.P., V, 210.
[23] Bale's Chronicle, 136.
[24] Paston Letters, Introduction, xcviii; I, 160–2; K. B. McFarlane in Proceedings of the British Academy, L (1965), 89–91.

in such armed strength was treated by Henry as an abortive dress rehearsal for York's later armed Dartford rising; some of his retinue who accompanied him to this parliament from Royston, Stamford and Grantham were subsequently indicted as rebels for it during Henry's judicial progress through the eastern shires in the autumn of 1452.[25] On 30 November a great shout was made in Westminster Hall for justice on traitors, allegedly engineered by Sir William Oldhall. Somerset was assaulted while he sat at dinner at Blackfriars on 1 December.[26] He escaped by river in the barge of his brother-in-law, the earl of Devon, and Henry had him put in the Tower for his own safety. Two days later, in a hollow gesture of unity, Henry rode through the unruly capital with the duke of York and almost all the nobility and gentry who were present at the parliament, apparently in dutiful obedience: an impressive array of military strength 10,000 strong; a noble sight indeed, recorded one chronicler, if it had taken place in France.[27] But the problems which had led to the impeachment of Suffolk and the rebellion were still unresolved. The winter parliament of 1450–1 was essentially a continuation of the interrupted 1450 Leicester session, except that now the Commons had the backing of Richard duke of York, and the mantle of Suffolk had descended on Somerset. The Commons in the new parliament presented their petition of resumption afresh and the list which they drew up of those whom they required to be removed from the king's entourage was now headed by the duke of Somerset.[28]

York himself was appointed to head a commission of oyer and terminer on 14 December to do justice on new rebels, traitors and others in Kent and Sussex,[29] but there is no evidence that he ever acted, or that he had now been admitted to Henry's confidence and favour. He was still under suspicion as the root cause of the continuing disturbances. Somerset was released from the Tower to spend his Christmas at Blackfriars.[30] After Christmas Henry felt the need to make hitherto unprecedented personal efforts in the field of justice, law and order. Now, for the first time, he showed signs of exertion to defend his throne. On 25 January, before he set out on the very first judicial progress he had ever made, he issued instructions cancelling previous orders that certain of his acts should not pass without the advice of the council,[31] indicating that his decision to increase the powers of

[25] P.R.O., K.B.9/7/10; 65a/19, 36, 39.
[26] Bale's Chronicle, 137.
[27] Benet's Chronicle, 203; Gregory's Chronicle, 196.
[28] R.P., V. 216, 217.
[29] C.P.R., 1446–1452, 435.
[30] Benet's Chronicle, 204.
[31] P.R.O., Exch. K. R. Mem. Rolls, E.159/227, Brevia, Hilary m.23.

15(a). John Talbot, earl of Shrewsbury, presents a volume of poems and romances to Queen Margaret (B.L. Royal MS 15 E VI, f. 2b).

15(b). King Henry presides over a Chapter of the Order of the Garter (B.L. Royal MS 15 E VI, f. 439).

16(a). Henry VI with his Lords and Commons in Parliament. Miniatures around the initial
H in King's College Charter of 16 March 1446.

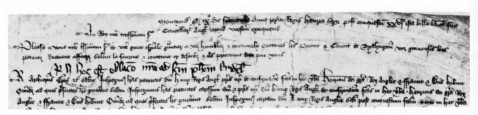

16(b). Henry VI, confirming the Charters of the Prior and Convent of Bridlington,
makes it a personal oblation to St John of Bridlington. He writes: 'RH hec est oblacō
n̄ra ad Scm̄ Johēm Bridel̄', 9 November 1447.

his council, his only concession to York, had been short-lived. On 28 January Henry himself left for an armed, punitive and exemplary judicial progress into Kent with an entourage several thousand strong, headed by the dukes of Somerset and Exeter, four earls, five other peers of the realm and three judges. There followed a 'harvest of heads' throughout the shire which continued until his return to the capital on 23 February. A host of as yet unpunished miscreants waited at Blackheath[32] to beg his mercy and he then 'rode right royally through the city'.[33] In the midst of his Kentish progress he had reaffirmed York's appointment to Ireland for the remaining seven years of the original ten-year term,[34] presumably to get him out of the way. In March and April he appointed new commissions of oyer and terminer which acquitted the household men on the treasonable indictments laid against them in 1450.[35] Little was done meantime in the parliament, which had met from 20 January to 29 March and re-assembled on 5 May, but in the last days of its life at the end of the month or beginning of June[36] he finally answered both a petition for the banishment of thirty members of his entourage and the new resumption petition. He partially accepted the first, but exempted all peers of the realm named in it and declined to remove certain unspecified persons whom, he said, he was accustomed to have about him. Should he have to take the field against enemies within or without the land, he warned, he would summon to his presence whom he pleased.

The second petition for a resumption had been more boldly phrased than the first. For example earlier, generous exceptions made for the king's two foundations were omitted: their endowments were now described as 'over chargefull and noyus'. One new request was that all exchanges of land to which the king had been a party should be reversed. Most significantly, the new petition contained a clause to appoint a committee to supervise all Henry's future grants: the chancellor, the treasurer, the keeper of the privy seal and six lords of the council, who were to sign all instruments they authorized. Acceptance of a grant not so authenticated was to bring forfeiture of all the grantee's freehold possessions. All Henry's grants, and those made in his name since the first day of his reign, were again to be annulled with effect from 6 November 1449, that is, the assembly date of the previous parliament, and the operative date of the earlier, abortive act. This petition for resumption now received a favourable

[32] Benet's Chronicle, 204; C.P.R., 1446–1452, 442; Gregory's Chronicle, 197; John Piggot's Memoranda in Kingsford, English Historical Literature, 372.
[33] Chronicles of London (ed. Kingsford), 162.
[34] C.P.R., 1452–1461, 202 (there referred to as made on 11 February 1451).
[35] Ibid., 443–5; 'William Worcester', in Stevenson, Wars, II, pt. ii, 770.
[36] Benet's Chronicle, 204.

but firm answer. The previous act had been largely invalidated by 186 clauses of exemption. None of these applied to the new act. It is true that Henry reserved his right to make exemptions, but only during the remaining life of the parliament. By the time parliament was dissolved, Henry had added forty-three provisos of exemption, but this time they were almost all couched in general, not personal terms. The patent and fine rolls, receipt rolls and household accounts show that this second resumption, unlike the first, was no half-hearted matter. It was made effective.

The final acceptance of this act destroyed the validity of Henry's grants and leases. Consequently in June and July there was a scramble for new ones. Again, in the last three months of the year, when the returns which sheriffs and escheators had to make under the act were coming in, the number of new leases rose again. At least eighty-five new leases were taken out in 1451. Little if anything had yet been done to implement the earlier act, but the two acts were now operated jointly and as a result at least twenty-four units of permanently alienated lands and properties were recovered and let out again to farm for terms of years at the current rate of extent, several cases of recovered alienated lands were kept in hand, and at least forty-four instances of life grants recovered were changed to leases for terms of years. Many leases for terms of years were shortened after recovery and the farms raised. For the first time within living memory, and possibly for much longer, an element of financial competition now entered into royal leasing. The act stipulated that he who offered most should get the lease unless the previous holder would match his offer.[37]

Henry had at last made a real concession to public opinion as expressed by the Commons in parliament. There appears to have been no political discrimination against new would-be lessees of the resumed lands. In many cases the existing holders, including the household men, got them back on the new and less favourable terms. Jointly held and syndicate leases, taken out by men unknown on the political scene, began to appear, confirming that financial considerations began to operate in the re-leasing. In addition the act annulled a host of annuities, liberties and privileges. The greatest, including both York and Somerset, suffered, as well as many household men. Many grantees quickly got their grants regranted and backdated, but, significantly, many did not. The financial records of government over these years reveal that prior to this resumption cash payments made by farmers of royal lands into the exchequer and assignments made on them were negligible. As a result of these resumptions farms and rents from the resumed lands became, for the time being, sound assignments for the payment of the king's debts, for defending the borders, for repaying

[37] For full details of the effects of the act see B. P. Wolffe, *The Royal Demesne*, 248–89.

loans and current expenses.[38] In May 1450 a sum of £5,661 0s 11d *per annum* had been ordered to be levied from lands and customs revenues for the expenses of the royal household. Twelve selected units of land laid under contribution there could only have contributed £40 at that time. By the summer of 1451 the whole £1,500 charged on these twelve units could be met.[39] Again the receipts which the treasurer of the household acknowledged direct from the exchequer in the 1440s averaged less than £3,000 *per annum*. In the regnal year 1450–1 this figure rose to over £10,500.[40] Thus the parliamentary resumption had restored a considerable measure of control over the endowed revenues of the crown to the exchequer of which the agents of Henry's personal rule since 1437 had hitherto deprived it. The unpaid expenses of the royal household, which had become such a public scandal, could now be made a primary charge on this newly-freed income. So it continued for a time.

The Commons had resubmitted their petition for a resumption because they rightly said their previous one had 'not been effectually had' and asked for 'good and effectual conclusion' to it. At last they had got it. Henry now allowed the arrangements he had made for the use of the crown lands over the previous ten years or so to be almost entirely undone. York, Somerset, the other great lords and the knights and esquires of the household surrendered grants in fee and for life in a manner without precedent. The flow of alienations, life grants and extravagant annuities after 1451 was reduced to a trickle. It is true that the queen benefited hugely, and Henry thereby also found the means adequately to endow his two half-brothers, Edmund and Jasper Tudor, newly created earls of Richmond and Pembroke, with the most important of the resumed lands. The hereditary patrimony of the prince of Wales, duke of Cornwall and earl of Chester was also largely freed of encumbrances for the heir to the throne, when he should appear. But these were all quite legitimate and accepted charges for the crown lands. The actual and potential financial yield of the king's hereditary patrimony should not be exaggerated. Taxation in its different forms provided by far the major part of the revenues of later-medieval English kings. Nevertheless, Henry could hardly have made any other move more calculated to restore and enhance the standing of his government, once the effects were seen.

[38] P.R.O., Exch. of Receipt E.410/814, 820, 821, 824, 827 (Michaelmas 1449–Easter 1452), show the impression made on the receipt rolls.

[39] i.e. on the manors of Bradwell, Hadley, Havering (Essex), Kingsthorpe, Fawsley, Geddington, Brigstock (Northants), Swaffham (Norfolk), Bassingbourne and Badburgham (Cambs.), a large group of manors known as the Gurney lands (Somerset and Dorset), manors in the Isle of Wight, and the lordships of Pembroke and Cilgerran in Wales.

[40] P.R.O., Exch. K.R. Various Accts., E.101/409/9, 11; 410/6.

With parliament dissolved, it was the turn of Surrey, Sussex, Hampshire and Wiltshire, from 22 June to 27 July 1451, to experience a personal, punitive judicial perambulation on which Henry's entourage was almost identical with that of January into Kent, though strengthened judicially by the presence of the Lord Chief Justice.[41] A second royal visitation of Kent on the same lines followed between 30 July and 20 August.[42] The records of the cases heard on all three of these personal visitations reveal the punishment of further lesser risings after the pattern of Cade's, notably one led by Henry Hasildene in Sussex and Kent and another by William Beerbrewer in Wiltshire. It is improbable that Henry presided over them all himself, but on each of these perambulations there is evidence that at Lewes, Salisbury and Canterbury he did personally sit in judgement with his judges.[43]

Thus by mid-summer 1451 Henry's combination of belated concession to public opinion and unusually firm personal action in the shires had restored an appreciable measure of strength to his government at home. Throughout these months Richard duke of York, now identified with would-be reformers and tainted with suspicion of aspiring to the throne, was conspicuous only by his renewed absence from the king's presence and his complete lack of involvement in affairs of state. Henry's personal attitude towards his suspected would-be supplanter was succinctly expressed by one of the better chroniclers: 'When need demands, or necessity compels, we will invoke your aid.'[44] This aid was in fact never sought. Although York was still in London over Christmas 1450,[45] it was probably on the further prorogation of parliament in the New Year that he departed once more into virtual exile at Ludlow. He had offered his services as the king's principal adviser; he had revealed a smouldering, vindictive hostility to Somerset, who had taken Suffolk's place in Henry's service; he was certainly not prepared to run in joint harness with the Beaufort duke. Thus he was once again untouched by the continuing momentum of disaster abroad and from the New Year of 1451 was in a position, from the sidelines once more, to make vociferous and alarming complaints against Henry's government in general and Somerset in particular.

When the surrender of Cherbourg on 12 August 1450 completed the conquest of Normandy, Charles VII apportioned garrisons for its

---

[41] C.P.R., 1446–1452, 477, Benet's Chronicle, 205.

[42] C.P.R., 1446–1452, 477.

[43] P.R.O., P.S.O.1/19/992; E.28/81/60; Virgoe, 'Some Ancient Indictments', 243–55.

[44] Giles's Chronicle, 42.

[45] Benet's Chronicle, 204: 'at Stratford' which, mentioned together with the location of Henry at Westminster and Somerset at the Blackfriars, presumably meant Stratford-at-Bow. This is confirmed by John Piggot's Memoranda in Kingsford, *English Historical Literature*, 372.

defence and turned his full attention to the reduction of English Gascony, sending the surplus of his forces by sea from Normandy to the marches of Guienne. Henry at last made plans to counter this new, singleminded threat to his most ancient French possessions, but their failure to reach maturity was to be as miserable a tale of half-hearted incapacity as any of his previous mishandlings of the affairs of his French kingdom. Richard Wydeville, Lord Rivers, was appointed seneschal of Gascony and commissioned on 30 August 1450 to be ready to sail from Plymouth to Bordeaux with 4,000 men by 21 September. Eighty-six ships great and small, from as far away as Lynn and Calais, were commandeered and gradually assembled in Plymouth and adjacent south-western ports. But it appears that loans were only being raised to pay the soldiers in late February and March 1451 on the security of an as yet unpaid tenth, granted by the clergy of the Canterbury province in November 1449. By early February the still unpaid ships' captains and crews were threatening to disperse and efforts had to be made locally to detain them by force and to summon defaulters before the council. They finally received assignments of over £3,000 on the London customs early in June. The final date of assembly of the force had been repeatedly postponed until 1 March and musters, first attempted for 26 March, were then successively postponed to 30 May. Unpaid mariners and soldiers were disturbing the county of Cornwall in June, when Henry compelled the Genoese merchants to loan him £8,000 by seizing their alum cargoes to that value.[46] How much of this forced loan, if any, went to pay for Rivers's expedition is not known, but Henry was also concurrently pledging and selling jewels and plate for their wages. As late as 8 July 1451 Thomas Gill was appointed the king's special courier to travel with Rivers and return, immediately after landing, with a report on the disposition of the country, but the ill-fated expedition, thus assembling and waiting for nearly twelve months, on which £13,000 was spent to no purpose, never left port. By July Gascony was almost completely lost to the French and fear of a French attack on Calais had now become uppermost in the minds of the king and his advisers.

Charles VII had made a significant start to the conquest of English Gascony in the autumn of 1450, notably with the capture of Bergerac and Bazas and a humiliating decimation of a field force at Blanquefort, only some five miles from Bordeaux. Nothing had been retrieved there when the French opened their spring campaign in May 1451 for a systematic reduction of all strongholds, with several armies operating

[46] *C.P.R., 1446–1452*, 389, 410, 411, 414, 437, 438, 444, 447–50, 462, 476, 478; P.R.O., E.28/81/30, 38; Ramsay, *Lancaster and York*, II, 146; Benet's Chronicle, 205; John Piggot's Memoranda in Kingsford, *English Historical Literature*, 372; *R.P.*, V, 214–15; Bale's Chronicle, 138.

at once, in a fashion reminiscent of the rapid Normandy conquest. The successive capture of Montguyon, of Blaye and Bourg, together dominating the navigation of the Gironde, and of Castillon, was followed by the simultaneous investment of Fronsac, the main English-manned stronghold on the Dordogne, Libourne, Dax and Rions. Ominously these two latter towns in the south were invested by the counts of Armagnac and Foix and the Sire d'Albret, indicating the full involvement of the great lords of the Midi in the French conquest from this point. The whole future of the English duchy, the ancient inheritance of Eleanor of Aquitaine, with the exception of the port of Bayonne in the remote south, which still confidently waited for English aid, was at length made to depend on a formal *journée*, reminiscent of the trial of strength arranged at Tartas in 1442, to be held before Fronsac on the eve of St John the Baptist (24 June). On that day, as at Tartas, the French held the field in strength and no English forces appeared. Fronsac, the key and entry to the English duchy, perforce then surrendered. Bordeaux admitted the enemy forces under Charles VII's lieutenant-general, Dunois, on 30 June. Bayonne was finally entered after siege on 21 August. A few days later the barons of the Bordelais and the three estates of Bordeaux, Dax and Bayonne went to Taillebourg to do homage to the French king.[47] Henry had now lost the whole of the ancient English duchy of Gascony.

There is no evidence to determine exactly when Henry decided against sending the Rivers expedition to Gascony. Even before the fall of Bayonne he had turned his attention to the needs of Calais. Londoners paid a tax for the relief of Calais on 17 July 1451, alleged to be sufficient to provide 1,000 men.[48] Henry was selling a great gold spice plate for the maintenance of the Calais garrison on 22 July and reinforcements were being introduced there from 10 August. Henry again showed his supreme faith in Edmund duke of Somerset by appointing him Captain of Calais on 21 September.[49] By the end of the year Rivers himself arrived in Calais with 60 lances and 530 archers.[50] The irresolute switch from Bordeaux to Calais was reminiscent of the elder Somerset's vacillation between Gascony and Normandy in 1443. In any case the problems of Gascony and Calais were now overshadowed by the urgent need for a considerable armed force at home.

In September 1451 Richard duke of York, now based on his castle

---

[47] Berry Herald, 458–67.
[48] Bale's Chronicle, 138; Benet's Chronicle, 205.
[49] French Roll, 30 Henry VI m. 17, cited in *P.P.C.*, VI, xxxvii.
[50] P.R.O., E.28/81/48; E.28/84/320 (treasurer of Calais' account). The forces sent consisted of men-at-arms on horseback at 12d a day, men-at-arms on foot at 8d a day and archers at 6d a day. The periods paid for varied from 6 to 13 weeks.

of Ludlow in the Welsh marches, supported by Robert Hungerford, Lord Moleyns and Sir William Herbert, intervened, on his own initiative, to settle a dispute in the county of Somerset. This had led to armed confrontation there between the duke of Somerset's brother-in-law, Thomas Courtenay, earl of Devon, supported by Edward Brook, Lord Cobham on one side, and William, Lord Bonville of Chewton and Shute, who was allied with James Butler, earl of Wiltshire on the other. In spite of recent careful investigation of the dispute[51] its origins remain sadly obscure, but it may well have first arisen as a family quarrel between Courtenay and Bonville who were quite closely related,[52] along the lines of their disagreement of ten years previously. York headed the commission of the peace for the county of Somerset. It is unlikely that York's intervention had anything to do with personal enmity towards the Butlers in Ireland at this stage, because he had left Wiltshire's father, the Butler earl of Ormond, as his deputy there is August 1450, when he made his return to England.[53] Devon had marched from Tiverton across the county of Somerset, with a substantial force, to bring Wiltshire to battle at Lackham near Bath, on his way spurning the peacemaking efforts of Bishop Beckington, another Somerset justice of the peace, and of the dean of Wells. He had turned back to besiege Bonville in Taunton castle when he found his first quarry, Wiltshire, had flown from Lackham in dutiful answer to a summons to the king at Coventry. It was during this investment of Taunton that York and his assistants appeared on the scene and intervened between Courtenay and Bonville, a course he could only have taken in an official capacity as the principal member of the commission of the peace for that county. His prestige, and the superior might of his 2,000-strong force, quickly brought the earl and Bonville to terms.[54]

Henry, however, was not prepared to accept that York's intervention had been made disinterestedly in the cause of law and order in the west. This was possibly the last point in the relations between the king and York when a peaceful settlement could have been secured. Since his return from Ireland in August 1450 York had acted entirely consistently as an upholder of good government. He was associated

[51] R. L. Storey, *The End of the House of Lancaster*, 89–92, mainly from K.B.9/267 no. 44.

[52] See J. R. Lander in *B.J.R.L.* (1960), 60. Bonville was the earl's uncle by marriage, and one of his daughters had married Sir Philip Courtenay of Powderham who in the later troubles of 1455 was definitely linked with Bonville against the earl's family at Tiverton.

[53] J. Otway-Ruthven, *A History of Medieval Ireland*, 384–5.

[54] Storey, *loc. cit.*; Benet's Chronicle, 205; 'William Worcester' in Stevenson, *Wars*, II, pt. ii, 770.

with the demand for reform, but when the king at last took action through judicial progresses and the acts of resumption to meet these demands, York returned to his castle of Ludlow. His personal assistance had been spurned but the tenor of his advice followed, so he had no cause for complaint. The following year this intervention in the Courtenay-Bonville dispute could be entirely justified as his duty as the senior member of the justices for that county. York's power could not be ignored by the king. If it was to be contained, his services had to be accepted at their face value. Henry now chose to continue to show his distrust of York thus forcing him into open opposition. Lumping him with the other principals concerned in the dispute, he summoned all of them indiscriminately to answer for a flagrant breach of the peace.[55] On 9 September he set out for the Midlands to hold a countil meeting at Coventry, which was becoming his normal refuge in difficult situations, in the heart of Lancastrian territory. He was powerfully supported by his nobility, notably by York's brother-in-law Richard earl of Salisbury, and by Humphrey Stafford, duke of Buckingham, both of whom were later paid handsomely for contributing to the strong force about his person.[56] This journey was in a sense yet another personal oyer and terminer, this time directly to judge noble peacebreakers and, according to one chronicler, to impose the arbitration of certain lords in his presence upon the variances of York and Somerset, which he proposed to treat as a mere personal matter between them.[57] Wiltshire, Bonville and Moleyns all suffered a month's confinement in Berkhamsted and Wallingford castles for their parts in the disturbances. Cobham was ultimately detained for two years or more.[58] Once again, York's proffered services had been rejected. York and Devon, temporarily thrown together, simply declined to respond to Henry's frequent summonses.

The activities of Sir William Oldhall, York's right-hand man, during this period suggest that support for York was being expressed in word and deed. Oldhall had taken sanctuary in the royal chapel of St Martin-le-Grand in London. From subsequent indictments in Easter Term

[55] Benet's Chronicle, 205, 'iratus rex valde cum illis omnibus'; Giles's Chronicle, 43, though the summons to Coventry is there dated after the Purification, possibly a mistake for the Nativity of the Virgin (8 September). Henry began his journey to Coventry from Windsor on 9 September, reaching Windsor on the return on 12 October.

[56] Recorded in exchequer records (Devon, Issues, 475, 478) because, as Fortescue wrote (Governance, 125), when the king rode out in his own person mightily accompanied no man was bound to serve him in such a case at his own expense. Ramsay, Lancaster and York, II, 152, noted that the second instance of payment in Devon, Issues, was misdated to 1452.

[57] 'William Worcester', in Stevenson, Wars, II, pt. ii, 770, 771.

[58] Benet's Chronicle, 205; R.P., V, 248; P.R.O., K.B.27/774 Rex, 27.

1452 it appeared that he had been made liable for detention by an accusation made by a king's esquire, Walter Burgh, the member for Downton in the last parliament, that he had stolen Somerset's goods at Blackfriars on 1 December 1450. Further charges claimed he was responsible for raising the great shout against traitors in Westminster Hall while the law-courts were in session there, for assembling traitors there himself again on 20 July 1451, and for planning a rebellion in mid-September 1451 to seize the Great Seal and deprive Henry of his crown. Still later indictments alleged that he had instigated an assembly at York's castle of Fotheringhay on 11 November 1451 to encompass Henry's death, and to depose him in favour of York. The earls of Shrewsbury and Wiltshire and Lords Moleyns and Lisle were sent with 400 men to extract him from sanctuary for confinement in Westminster palace on 28 January 1452,[59] presumably for questioning and safer custody, as a suspected rallying point for York's supporters in London, since his indictment for high treason in the Reading parliament of 1453 accused him of helping to prepare his master's armed rising of February 1452. Dean Cowdray of St Martin's, absent when the seizure was made, was nevertheless able to insist on his orderly reinstatement there, which duly took place under the supervision of the duke of Somerset two days later, but a guard of Henry's yeomen of the household was left posted round the sanctuary.[60]

From Ludlow on 9 January 1452 York at length issued an open manifesto of loyalty to his sovereign to counter the king's reported great displeasure. In it he called upon Henry's intimate adviser, whom he had earlier protected from the public wrath, the bishop of Hereford and former abbot of Gloucester, Reginald Boulers, and his own former deputy in Normandy, John Talbot, earl of Shrewsbury, to act as his intermediaries with the king and publicly to witness his oath of loyalty on the sacraments if Henry would not send two or three lords to him at Ludlow for this purpose.[61] Ominously he claimed that Henry's unjustified mistrust of him was entirely due to sinister information fed to him by his 'enemies, adversaries and evil-willers'. By 3 February he had tired of waiting and decided to use force. He sent written appeals to numerous towns for support in an armed demonstration to remove the duke of Somerset from Henry's presence as a danger to the safety of the realm. He referred back to the advice which he had pressed

[59] Benet's Chronicle, 205–6; Bale's Chronicle, 139.
[60] Details in J. S. Roskell's article, 'Sir William Oldhall, Speaker in the Parliament of 1450–1', *Nottingham Medieval Studies*, V (1961), 87–112, from the King's Bench Coram Rege Roll, amplifying older accounts by C. E. Johnston in *E.H.R.*, XXV (1910), 715–22, and A. J. Kempe, *Historical Notes of the Collegiate Church of St. Martin-le-Grand* (London 1825), 140–4; Devon, *Issues*, 476; *R.P.*, V, 452–3.
[61] *Paston Letters, Introduction*, cxi.

upon Henry in October 1450 which the king had ignored, with consequent further disasters. Again he alleged that efforts were being made to have him arraigned for treason, his blood corrupted, and he and his heirs disinherited.[62]

Henry had sent Thomas Kent on a mission to York and it was after his return on 13 February 1452 that preparation against York increased.[63] Copies of York's manifestos seeking support had been sent on to Henry by at least seven loyal towns, including Oxford, Colchester and Canterbury, and on 17 February he sent back orders to them to resist him.[64] These privy seal letters of 17 February refer to earlier proclamations by which Henry had already made it 'openly and universally known throughout this our land' that rebellion was planned under feigned and pretended claims to be acting for the common good and various commissions had either in fact gone out, or were in process of being issued, ordering the raising of loyal forces to stand against those endeavouring to subvert the king's estate and destroy certain of its loyal subjects. Buckingham, Bonville, Sir Philip Courtenay of Powderham and John Dynham of Nutwell had been named to muster and march against them in the south-west, Lord Scales in Norfolk and Suffolk, Lord Audley, Lord Bergavenny, the governor of Leeds castle, the sheriff and many gentry in Kent.[65] The sheriff of Surrey and Sussex raised the men of his shires as instructed and duly brought them to the king at Blackheath.[66] All the nobility had been summoned to Henry's presence to assist him to 'rebuke and chastise' his rebels and Lord Cobham, who had ignored the summons, was sent a second stern warning to present himself 'incontinent upon the sight of these further letters' on 17 February.[67] It is therefore inconceivable that York could have expected a peaceful, compliant reception from Henry who had already declared him a rebel and Somerset loyal. He set out, as his letter to the citizens of Shrewsbury on 3 February clearly indicated, with the firm intention of bending Henry to his will by force of arms.[68]

Leaving London on 16 February, with instructions to close its gates against York,[69] Henry marched north via Barnet, St Albans, Dunstable and Stony Stratford to reach Northampton on 22 February. Intelligence that York had crossed the Thames by Kingston Bridge, after

[62] Ibid., cxii–cxiii; P.P.C., VI, 90–9, misdated to 1450.
[63] Bale's Chronicle, 139.
[64] P.P.C., VI, 90–2.
[65] C.P.R., 1446–1452, 537, 577 (14 and 17 February).
[66] Devon, Issues, 476.
[67] P.P.C., VI, 116; Devon, Issues, 475–6; Bale's Chronicle, 139.
[68] In the words of Giles's Chronicle (p. 43): 'campum auscepit ibidem suae fortunae eventus expectare'.
[69] Davies's Chronicle, 70.

London had duly refused passage to his herald, brought him back
to the capital on 27 February. Crossing over London Bridge to Southwark next day, and to Blackheath and Welling on 1 March, the main
royal force was finally drawn up on the heath where the Cade rebels
had defied the king in June 1450. York was discovered strongly
entrenched a few miles to the east on Dartford heath,[70] with
an impressive artillery train and supported by the earl of Devon to
the south, Lord Cobham north towards the river, and seven ships with
supplies on the Thames. In spite of York's strength, variously and
inflatedly estimated at between 10,000 and 20,000 men,[71] Henry's force
was indubitably the stronger. According to Abbot Wheathamstead
it was three times the size of York's.[72] Henry had had ample warning
on this occasion to prepare for his first military confrontation with
his cousin of York.

On 2 March an embassy of lords, led by the bishops of Winchester
and Ely, the earls of Salisbury and Warwick, Viscount Bourchier and
Lord Sudeley, prevailed upon York to face facts and submit himself
to Henry in his tent at Blackheath. The next day,[73] kneeling before
him, together with Devon and Cobham, he presented lengthy articles
of complaint against Somerset, vainly accusing him on old scores of
making unprincipled financial profit from the surrender of Maine, of
personal responsibility for the attack on Fougères, of the treasonable
surrender of Rouen, of a shameful final composition with the enemy,
made to save his family and his own skin, and, finally, the only
item of recent history, of demoralizing the English garrison at Calais
by intruding himself, the very personification of corruption and defeat,
as their captain there.[74] Henry in his proclamation to the shires had
already indicated his full confidence in those persons under attack.
Any alternative explanation that he had now tricked York into submission with a prior promise to have Somerset tried on these charges
must therefore be rejected.[75]

York was conducted back through the city in the midst of the royal
army, escorted by two bishops, and a few days later made to swear
the most solemn oath of allegiance and loyalty to Henry on the
Evangelists at the high altar of St Paul's, touching the cross and

[70] Benet's Chronicle, 206.

[71] Davies's Chronicle, 70; B.L. Cotton Roll, ii, 23, printed by Gairdner in *Paston
Letters, Introduction*, ccclxxxiv.

[72] Davies's Chronicle, 70, Wheathampstead, *Registrum*, I, 162; *R.P.*, V, 346.

[73] The most precise chronology is that of College of Arms Arundel MS, 19, printed
by Kingsford, *English Historical Literature*, 297–8.

[74] Benet's Chronicle, 207; B.L. Cotton Vespatian C. xiv, f. 40 printed in *Paston Letters,
Introduction*, cxix–cxxiii.

[75] *Chronicle of London* (ed. Kingsford), 163; *Short English Chronicle* (ed. Gairdner), 69;
The Brut, 520.

receiving the sacrament in Henry's presence, with the cathedral filled to capacity. Subsequently he affixed his seal and sign manual to a written version of his oath, recording that, henceforth, he would come at the king's commandment whenever summoned and would never again make any assembly of his people without his command or licence, or attempt anything 'by way of faite' (armed force) against the king or any of his subjects.[76] He was then allowed to depart. Henry moved to Windsor on 22 March and was in his favourite Winchester for the Palm Sunday weekend, returning to Windsor for Maundy Thursday. Here on Good Friday, somewhat belatedly following the example of the pope's general jubilee, indulgences and pardons of 1450,[77] he proclaimed the offer of a general pardon, in honour of the loyal subjects, Christ's crucifixion and the Virgin, to all who had been guilty of disloyalty to himself in great or small matters and would sue to chancery for it. Only the murderers of Moleyns and Aiscough were specifically excluded from his clemency. Some 2,500 people ultimately availed themselves of the privilege, including York, Devon, Sir William Oldhall, Thomas Yonge and a majority of others who had had no connection with the rebellion.[78]

The kingdom was at peace and the loyalty of at least the vast majority of his subjects had apparently been conclusively demonstrated.[79] The king was now ruling his kingdom. Indeed, he could claim that, had it not been for the fractious antics of the duke of York, which had menaced the peace and unity of his realm, he might well by now have been emulating his illustrious father by personally leading an expedition to France. Such had at last been declared to be his intention. Commissioners were appointed from 26 January 1452 to solicit contributions towards the cost of an expedition to France.[80] Their instructions declared that Henry had now resolved that attack was the best form of defence and would in person lead his army to the marches of Calais to seek out his adversary and destroy him, before Charles VII could himself attack England's sole remaining continental possession with a view to invading the kingdom of England itself. The same day

[76] Giles's Chronicle, 43; Short English Chronicle, 69; R.P., V, 346–7.

[77] This pardon, 'the greatest pardon that ever came to England from the Conquest unto this time of my year being mayor of London', was not preached in England until 1451, the year of Gregory's mayoralty (Gregory's Chronicle, 197).

[78] Wheathampstead, Registrum, I, 85–91; Storey, 216; Paston Letters, Introduction, cxxvi–cxxvii, from Pardon Roll c.67/40.

[79] 'That year it was competent well and peaceable as for any rising among ourselves for every man was in charity, but somewhat the hearts of the people hung and sorrowed for that the duke of Gloucester was dead and some said that the duke of York had great wrong, but what wrong there was no man that durst say' (Gregory's Chronicle, 197–8).

[80] C.P.R., 1446–1452, 512–13 (Kent); 513 (Surrey & Sussex, 9 February).

Lords Rivers and Welles and Osborne Mundeford in Calais were commissioned to requisition all ships there and bring them over to Sandwich 'for our crossing into our kingdom of France which, God willing we are disposed and determined to undertake with the greatest possible diligence and expedition'. Orders to arrest all carracks in the port of Southampton until further notice, to provide transport, had already been issued.[81]

There is some evidence that Charles VII was planning an attack on Calais[82] and it might be supposed that the mention of Henry's initiative personally to lead a counter-invasion was merely a desperate ruse to obtain finance to resist him. Nevertheless, as soon as York's rebellion had been mastered, letters went out on 14 March to Lord Clifford to assemble a fleet in the Downs off Sandwich and the Camber, again stressing Henry's intention to 'go over in our own person'. A credence, which Clifford was given to show to all people concerned, reveals that Henry had personally discussed his plans with him and further letters eight days later set out his requirements in detail. Ships available included the *Grâce Dieu* of Calais, the *Anthony*, the *George* and the *Valentine* of Hull and the *Trinity* of Dartmouth. Clifford was to acquire others and victual them all so that he had at least 1,000 sailors, who would be paid 12d a week. The masters of the vessels, who were all to be knights and notable esquires, would receive 10 marks or £10 at his discretion, besides their spoils of war. Clifford's own fee was to be 100 marks and the earl of Shrewsbury would command the fleet once it was assembled.[83] But after this no more was heard of Henry's determination to face his adversary of France on the battlefield. On his past record one must doubt whether he would ever have brought his plans to the point of execution, even in the most favourable circumstances. In fact he had to turn his attention to the disturbing situation in England. In April and May there were further risings, the aftermath of Dartford, in Kent and the Welsh marches involving servants and advisers of Richard duke of York. 1452 was to be notable for Henry not as the year in which he personally invaded France but as the year in which these further risings and continuing doubts about York's intentions moved him to undertake his longest and most ambitious exemplary and punitive judicial progress, covering eleven western shires, from 30 June until 5 September.

Apart from references in one chronicle, details of these further troubles are only known from oyer and terminer proceedings at Dartford in Kent in May and at Ludlow, Bridgnorth and Shrewsbury in August and September. Although the outbreaks were scattered over

[81] P.R.O., E.28/82/5 (19 January 1452).
[82] Beaucourt, *Charles VII*, V, 34, 264, cited by Ramsay, *Lancaster and York*, II, 153.
[83] P.R.O., P.S.O.1/19/982; C.81/1546/54; *C.P.R., 1446-1452*, 537; *P.P.C.*, VI, 119-25.

different parts of the country, they were not isolated incidents. It seems that some of York's followers from Dartford, on the way home, planned further rebellion near their leader's London residence of Baynard's castle on 6 March. Later, in Ludlow, they slew one of Henry's yeomen of the chamber, Richard Fazakerley, sent to arrest various members of York's following, provoking a rising there on 20 April. These men of Wales and Shropshire, at Baynard's castle and back in their own country, made clear their intention to put York on the throne, while not actually naming him. They said that, through a parliament of the whole realm and with the assistance of another 'who was entitled to the crown of England',[84] they would deprive Henry of his crown and royal power because he was 'not able nor of sufficient power to rule the aforesaid kingdom, nor by right ought to have done so'.[85] From 6–8 May there was a further rising in Kent under the captain John Wilkins. This had some connection with the earlier disturbance in Ludlow. Two persons were named in both the Kent and Shropshire indictments, John Sharp, gentleman, of London and Robert Ardern, esquire, former member of parliament for Warwickshire and sheriff of Warwickshire and Leicestershire. Ardern was confined in Kenilworth castle until taken to Ludlow by yeomen of the household to stand trial there in the autumn. The disturbances at Ludlow and the Kentish rising were both notable for their alleged political objectives. Some 300 men rose in the villages north and east of Sevenoaks and between Gravesend and Rochester under John Wilkins from Stratford-on-Avon in Warwickshire, claiming that Cade was still alive, that help was coming from York's son, the earl of March, and from Lord Cobham, and that within a few days, with 5,000 men, they would kill those about the king and depose him. They would take upon themselves the rule of the kingdom and have all the petitions of the last parliament fulfilled. The rising was nipped in the bud with remarkable speed. The earl of Shrewsbury and seven other commissioners of oyer and terminer, including the judges Bingham and Portington, sat in judgement at Dartford from 12 to 16 May. Twenty-eight of the accused were hanged forthwith, and another 'harvest of heads' sent to London.[86] Thirty-eight of the rebels obtained pardons on 17 June.[87] Malicious accusations, even made to Henry in person, caused suspicion of complicity in the rebellion to fall upon his household chamberlain, Ralph, Lord Cromwell, who was said to have been compromised by

[84] P.R.O., K.B.9/103/15; 3270/32; 'per alium qui corone Anglie est hereditabilis'.
[85] 'non habilis nec de potestate gubernare regnum predictum nec illud regnum de recte regere debuisset'.
[86] Indictments printed by Virgoe, op. cit., 256–65; Benet's Chronicle, 207; B.L. Cotton Roll ii, 23, printed in Kingsford, English Historical Literature, 368.
[87] C.P.R., 1446–1452, 553–4.

Wilkins's ultimate confession, while he was being taken from the Tower to his execution at Dartford, after intensive interrogation by the council. The unfortunate chamberlain had to go to extreme lengths in obtaining sworn testimonies and counter-accusations and in character assassination of his accuser, a London priest Robert Colynson, withdrawing from council meetings until Henry finally, but belatedly, declared himself satisfied of his innocence at Eltham on 4 February 1453.[88]

The journey which Henry began from Eltham on 23 June 1452 turned out to be the longest royal progress and judicial perambulation of the reign. It extended west to Exeter, through Somerset and Wiltshire, to cross the Severn at Gloucester, to his father's birth-place at Monmouth, north through the Welsh march to Ludlow and Bridgnorth and thence to Kenilworth and Coventry, returning via Banbury, Woodstock, High Wycombe and Sheen to Eltham on 6 September.[89] His entourage was very substantial, augmented from those fifteen lords and their retinues and the six judges named in a commission of oyer and terminer for Bristol and eleven counties on 6 July. The dukes of Buckingham and Somerset and the earls of Wiltshire and Worcester headed this commission, which included Lord Bonville of Chewton and Shute. Conspicuous by their absence from it were Richard duke of York at Ludlow and the Courtenay earl of Devon at Tiverton.[90]

Henry's progress through Devon was recorded with daily chronological accuracy, from a lost Exeter latin chronicle, by John Hooker, chamberlain of the city, in the mid-sixteenth century. The knights, esquires and nobility of the county from near and far met him 'with his great train of noble gentlemen and others' at the county boundary and conducted him to Forde abbey for the night of Wednesday 14 July. The next day he visited Bonville's place at Shute on the way to Ottery St Mary, and went on to Exeter on Monday 17 July, arriving after dinner. Three hundred or more persons, headed by the mayor, all in the livery of the city, rode out to meet him at Clyst Honiton. At Livery Dole, at the approaches to the city, he was met by the Franciscans and Dominicans. The priors of St Nicholas and St John, with all the city clergy in their copes and vestments, with two crosses born before them, greeted him at the high cross outside the South Gate and 'incensed the king with their frankincense and perfumes'. Henry kissed the cross, received the keys of the city and then proceeded through the South Gate, which was gorgeously adorned with painted scenes. The mayor, bareheaded and carrying the mace before him, led the way up South Street which was hung with silks and tapestries,

[88] *Ibid.*, 93–102 (exemplification made under the great seal at Cromwell's request).
[89] See detailed itinerary below pp. 369–70.
[90] *C.P.R., 1446–1452*, 580–1.

past the Carfax fountain, running with wine for the occasion, into the suitably decorated High Street as far as the Broad Gate to the Close. Here he was received by the bishop, canons and quire, and dismounted to process on foot and offer at the high altar. He was lodged in the bishop's palace for that night and the next. On the Wednesday he left by the East Gate for Honiton and from thence he passed into Somerset, to Donyatt near Ilminster on 20 July. The bishop, the canons and the city fathers shared his expenses in Exeter and the mayor presented him with £50 when he left. Two judges and Lord Bonville also received gifts. The judicial sessions were held in the bishop's hall by the unnamed justices under the direction of the duke of Somerset. Two men who were tried there, and condemned to death for treason, were subsequently pardoned by Henry at the suit of the bishop and canons, who successfully claimed that the king's judges had sat in judgement contrary to the privileges of their sanctuary.[91] Henry's presence on a judicial progress in the heart of Courtenay country was in any case exemplary as well as punitive and a few pardons after conviction were quite germane to his purpose.

It has hitherto been assumed that the climax of this perambulation came later, when Richard duke of York was honoured by his sovereign with a visit to Ludlow castle on 12 and 13 August 1452.[92] In fact the household accounts show that Henry stayed not with York at Ludlow but with the Carmelite Friars.[93] Moreover, judicial sessions were held on 10, 11 and 12 August at Ludlow, before the earl of Wiltshire, and before Judges Portington and Byngham at Bridgenorth. Those principally tried and condemned were York's followers, accused of the rebellions in London, Kent and the Welsh marches in March and April 1452 and now specially assembled there in York's own country for exemplary trial.[94] One strongly Yorkist chronicler later describes, under 1452, what must have been this punitive occasion in grossly exaggerated terms: he states that on Somerset's advice Henry rode to various towns of the duke of York where his tenants had to appear naked before him with nooses round their necks to beg for mercy because they had earlier taken the field with their lord against Somerset. The most atrocious weather imaginable was thrown in for full measure, making the account at first sight appear altogether too improbable: they were made to appear naked before the king to beg for pardon

[91] Exeter City Archives, Hooker Bk 51, fols 309 v-310, 317v. Bk 55 (Freeman's Bk), f. 39; Receiver's Rolls, 30–31 Hen. VI (dorse).

[92] J. Gairdner, *Paston Letters, Introduction*, cxxxii–cxxxiv; Ramsay, *Lancaster and York*, II, 151.

[93] P.R.O., E.101/410/9.

[94] P.R.O., K.B.9/103/2; 103/15; 270/34.

in ice and snow.[95] Nevertheless, the judicial records do confirm that Henry's visit to York's heart-land in August 1452 was no honour, but a demonstration of the strength of the House of Lancaster to the very face of his disloyal, Yorkist would-be heir.

Returning to Eltham on 6 September 1452 Henry spent a month there, at Sheen and at Greenwich with his queen, before setting out about 9 October for a further judicial perambulation through the other principal area of York's influence south of Trent: Hertfordshire and Essex, Cambridgeshire, Huntingdonshire, Northamptonshire and Lincolnshire. This occupied him, his loyal leading magnates, headed by the dukes of Exeter, Norfolk and Somerset, the earls of Oxford, Wiltshire and Worcester, together with Viscounts Beaumont, Bourchier and Lisle, seven barons, the Lord Chief Justice and eight of his fellow justices, until he returned to Eltham from Barking abbey on 11 November.[96] Not all of this company were with him all the time, or involved in the trials. Those who held sessions at York's town of Grantham, while Henry was at Newark, on 24 October, were Lord Moleyns and Judges Prisot, Markham and Danvers. They tried and condemned to a traitor's death, his quarters to be exposed wherever Henry should assign, one John Wynawey, accused of raising rebellion at another of York's towns, Stamford, on 24 February, designed to encompass the death and destruction of the king.[97]

Christmas and the first half of January 1453 were spent with the queen at Greenwich. Here Henry held an investiture for the knighting of his two half-brothers Edmund and Jasper Tudor, creating them earls of Richmond and Pembroke.[98] During this visit to the queen at Greenwich Prince Edward must have been conceived.[99] What was to be Henry's last judicial progress followed from Greenwich on 8 February, through Essex, Norfolk and Suffolk, until he arrived at Reading via Berkhamsted castle for the opening of a new parliament on 6 March. Again the commission of oyer and terminer, issued on 8 January, comprised a similar impressive selection of nobility, the Lord Chief Justice and eight fellow judges.[100] Henry's long-expected appearance at Norwich, foreshadowed in earlier addresses of the duke

[95] MS Bodley, Rawlinson B.355, printed in Six Town Chronicles (ed. R. Flenley), 107.

[96] C.P.R., 1452–1461, 54 (commission of oyer and terminer dated 28 September 1452). For detailed itinerary see below, p. 370.

[97] P.R.O., C.81/1371/31.

[98] Benet's Chronicle, 208; 'William Worcester', in Stevenson, Wars, II, pt. ii, 770; C.C.R., VI, 122.

[99] Born on the translation of Edward the Confessor (13 October) but also, as Giles's Chronicle, 44, puts it, 'ut verisimile est, iuxta conputationem mensium, infra die Natale sancti Edwardi [5 January] erat a matre conceptus'.

[100] C.P.R., 1452–1461, 60.

of Norfolk to the county, in which he had declared himself especially appointed as his personal representative to establish good order and bear rule there meantime, seems to have taken place on 18 February.[101] Henry was now clear about who were his friends and enemies. York was superseded as lieutenant of Ireland from 5 March 1453 by James Butler, earl of Wiltshire. When Somerset was given a life grant of all the principal offices in the royal forests and parks south of Trent, this was declared to be a reward for his good services 'on both sides of the sea'. Devon joined Cobham in prison. Bonville was exalted in the west country as life constable of Exeter castle and conservator of the Exe from source to sea. Sir William Oldhall's freehold lands and property were granted in fee to Somerset and to the newly created earl of Pembroke.[102]

The year 1452 had thus been notable for Henry's re-establishment of order and confidence in his regime throughout the English shires, in the face of York's first serious challenge. It was also the first, and last, year of triumph abroad. Henry's idea of a personal expedition against his beloved uncle Charles, who had once more officially reverted to his original role of 'principal enemy and adversary', had typically failed to materialize, though the idea had not yet been abandoned for ever. It may be that the personal expedition to Calais, planned in the spring, had languished in port for six months or more until the autumn, as had previously happened over Rivers's Gascony force in 1450–1. If so, it was the advent of a secret embassy from Bordeaux, led by the lord of Lesparre in Médoc in early September, offering to return to English obedience if they received sufficient substantial encouragement, which gave it a more practical purpose and converted it back into an expeditionary force to Bordeaux under John Talbot, earl of Shrewsbury, newly made Lieutenant of Aquitaine. Landing in Médoc, Shrewsbury established himself there without difficulty, was duly admitted into Bordeaux on 22 October, and quickly recovered the allegiance of most of the Bordelais, Libourne, St Emilion and Castillon in Perigord. French arms had not been able to erase overnight the ties and loyalties of the three-hundred-year-old English allegiance. In the spring, substantial reinforcements were sent out under Talbot's son, Viscount Lisle, Lords Moleyns and Camoys and the bastard of Somerset. They captured the key fortress of Fronsac and no checks were suffered by this impressive English reconquest until a fresh French army under Charles VII's grand master of the household, Jacques

---

[101] P.R.O., C.81/1371/33; *Paston Letters*, I, 229–30. The only commission of oyer and terminer issued specifically for Norfolk and headed by the duke was dated 4 September 1452 (*C.P.R., 1452–1461*, 54–5).

[102] *Ibid.*, 82–3, 88, 91, 102, 103, 111; Benet's Chronicle, 208; *R.P.*, V, 265–6.

de Chabannes, appeared at Castillon in Perigord early in June.[103]

The expedition to Bordeaux under the veteran Talbot was now regarded as a great revival of national effort in a righteous cause. Cardinal Archbishop Kemp, newly transferred to Canterbury, required prayers and processions to be held throughout his province for the success of this just war against a crafty, deceitful adversary who had ignored the spirit of truces and abstinences from war and had taken unscrupulous advantage of them to build up armies and alliances for ultimate conquest, thereby revealing what his true intentions had been from the outset.[104] This was the light in which his master's disastrous and futile peace policy now appeared, even to one of Henry's oldest and closest advisers. Kemp had been Cardinal Beaufort's partner in the early peace moves opposed by Gloucester and had survived unscathed the reckoning of 1450, continuing to hold, together, the highest secular and ecclesiastical office in the land. The loss of Normandy had opened the eyes even of the peacemakers.

The parliament which met at Reading on 6 March 1453 thus did so in circumstances uniquely favourable for Henry. It was summoned to 'promote the cause of sound and firm government within the realm of England and its external defence'. One solitary chronicler states that the Commons on assembly protested that free elections had not been allowed in the shires,[105] and the composition of the Lower House at first sight may appear to substantiate this, for out of 278 known members, 61 were household men, a figure more than double that for the 1450-1 assembly, nearly double the total in 1449-50 and the highest of the whole reign.[106] However, the temper of this parliament showed a remarkable change from the assemblies of 1449-51. It turned out to be the most cooperative and generous one Henry ever met, so one must conclude that our solitary chronicler was voicing a dissenting and minority complaint. Henry's stock had risen substantially since 1450 and for this reason he now secured a uniquely amenable parliament. The successful reconquest of Gascony probably stood him in greatest stead, though the effective resumption of 1451, the efficient manner in which York's rebellion had been handled, and the wide-ranging royal judicial progresses all contributed.

Indicative of the general mood of the Commons who assembled at Reading on 6 March 1453 were their petitions concerning the events of the past three years. They now called for a formal parliamentary condemnation of Cade, his rebellion and all its aims; of all judicial

[103] Berry herald, 468; C.P.R., 1452-1461, 78, 108; Benet's Chronicle, 209.
[104] D. Wilkins, Concilia, III, 560, proclamation dated at Croydon 1 October 1452 from Kemp's Register, f. 234.
[105] Bale's Chronicle, 139-40.
[106] See above, p. 217.

sentences which had been passed under its pressure by various commissions; of attacks on the king's advisers; of the attempts to remove some of them from his presence; of all rebellions and of all the implied stains upon Henry's honour which had masqueraded as plans for reform. All these unpleasant memories should now be obliterated. Thanks to 'the victorious knighthood of You our Sovereign Lord' the difficulties had been overcome. How easy it was to be a real king with just a little consistent effort! The former Speaker and York's chamberlain, Sir William Oldhall, was made the special scapegoat and exemplary victim, by a parliamentary act of forfeiture, for being *deus ex machina* to Cade, Wilkins and other rebels, especially 'those persons [unnamed] in the field at Dartford'. 'Those persons' were merely declared deprived of all their royal grants. The grants of Oldhall's lands to the duke of Somerset and the Tudor brothers were upheld. It is curious that no mention whatsoever was made of York, Devon or Cobham and that Oldhall should be thus singled out, but the explanation was probably the dangers of the special statutory penalties of *scandalum magnatum* against those who defamed peers of the realm and perhaps a feeling of responsibility especially to punish their own.[107]

The most outstanding expression of this parliament's pro-royal sentiments was its financial generosity which provoked Henry's personal, oral expression of gratitude on 28 March for its 'fidelity, concern and immense good will' towards his person. A fifteenth and tenth, to be paid half on 11 November and half a year later, was by itself not especially remarkable. But he was also now granted tonnage and poundage, the wool subsidies and poll-taxes on aliens, not, as customary, merely for a further few years, but for life, an honour which had only been bestowed once before on a Lancastrian king: on his illustrious father, after his Agincourt victory. Moreover, the rate of subsidy was raised from 40/- to 50/- for natives and from 63/4 to the impossible figure of 100/- for aliens, a level so high that it could not be collected, and had to be remitted in the following year. The convocations of Canterbury and York also granted a tenth.[108]

Finally there was another grant unique in English history, although the possibility seems to have been suggested in 1449.[109] It was financially equivalent to three further tenths and fifteenths and consisted of provision for the raising of 20,000 archers for six months' service, to be provided by all the lords, counties, cities and towns of England and Wales, including contingents from the palatine counties of Chester, Durham

---

[107] *R.P.*, V, 265-6, 329. For *scandalum magnatum* see Stat. 3 Ed. I, c.34; 2 Ric. II, c.5; 12 Ric. II, c.11.

[108] *R.P.*, V, 228-30, 269; Wilkins, *Concilia, III, 563, 564.*

[109] See the seventeenth-century copy of proceedings of a 1449 council or parliament printed by A. R. Myers in *B.J.R.L.*, XXII (1938), 402-4.

and Lancashire.[110] At first sight the terms of this grant appear disingenuous in the extreme and have led to the quite unjustified inference that it was made for home service for Henry's use in anticipation of civil war.[111] On the one hand it was baldly stated to be a once-for-all levy 'for the defence of the kingdom of England', not to be taken as a precedent for the future. On the other it was stipulated that, after the detailed local allocating of responsibility for personnel and finance had been made, then four months' notice should be given by proclamation of the date and place of muster, to be the same for the entire force. This was then to be kept together, whole, entire and undivided, in Henry's service for the full six months. With the necessary accompaniment of men-at-arms from the royal retinues this would have constituted a huge fighting force. For comparison, the total personnel of the army with which Charles VII conquered Gascony was estimated by the French heralds at 20,000 men.[112] Six months was the normal period for which initial financial provision was attempted for any new expeditionary force sent out to Normandy or Gascony from England during this reign, after which the occupied lands were expected to provide the major part of its sustenance. Such a once-for-all force, which could only be mustered at four months' notice, would have been patently useless either to repel an invasion or to master another rising by York. It was not so intended. By the spring of 1453 Henry had received a convincing demonstration of the loyalty of all his nobility, except three, and of their willingness to support him in the field against any who tried to force their will upon him 'by way of faite'. Evidently therefore the declared purpose of this grant 'for the defence of the realm', for its 'external defence', was a euphemism for an expeditionary force with which Henry could reconquer his French kingdom at his pleasure. This was still expected of him, and any indication of its imminence, as always, met with a generous response. The four months' notice specified was just about the reasonable minimum required to find and assemble the necessary ships, ordnance and provisions for such a force which, for once, would now assemble with its vital wages taken care of for six months in advance.

If there could be any doubts about this interpretation they are dispelled by the immediate fate of this extraordinary military grant,

[110] *R.P.*, V, 230–3 (reduced to 13,000 from the English Commons, 3,000 from the lords, 3,000 from Wales and Cheshire and 1,000 being remitted by the king's grace out of gratitude: 'for the great kindness that we have found in our said Commons in this our present parliament') cf. *C.P.R., 1452–1461*, 406–10, November and December 1457 when the allocation was finally made.

[111] Ramsay, *Lancaster and York*, II, 161, repeated in effect by A. Steel, *Receipt of the Exchequer*, 273.

[112] Berry herald, 464.

exactly in keeping with Henry's previously declared intentions and numerous false starts. Before the Easter recess it was postponed for two years in favour of an immediate further grant of another half tenth and fifteenth to finance reinforcements for the successful Talbot in Gascony. Unusually productive loans for this purpose had already been put in hand in January.[113] There was a significant proviso to the postponement: 'unless that his Excellence would take upon him the labour in his most royal person with the said 13,000 archers',[114] an obvious reference to the glorious possibility that Henry, in spite of earlier false starts, might still lead an expeditionary force in person. The Commons now made their emergency grant of extra finance for the Gascony army in exactly the same euphemistic terms as for the original 20,000 archers. It was 'for the purveyance of good for the defence of this land'.[115]

These were the circumstances for which Sir John Fastolf's secretary William Worcester composed his original *Boke of Noblesse*,[116] ready for presentation to Henry on such an occasion, to urge and encourage him to undertake a personal expedition to avenge the great wrongs which he and his subjects had suffered by 'unjust dissimilacions, undre the umbre and coloure of trewis and abstinence of werre late hadde and sacred at the cite of Tairs ... and sethe contynued 'forthe the said trewes from yere to yere, to this land grete charge and cost, till they had conspired and wrought their avauntage, as it approvethe dailie of experience'.[117] Subsequent revisions of his text, for presentation *faute de mieux* to the more valiant Edward IV, fail to conceal the fact that it was originally written to promote an early reconquest of France when the psychological shock of expulsion and the material losses were still fresh in English minds. The purposeful generosity of parliament in this respect suggests that in 1453 Worcester's passionate plea for a revival of the spirit and aims of Henry V did not speak merely for a dwindling, embittered circle of the materially dispossessed. It was not for lack of will on the part of Henry's subjects in general that no further Lancastrian conquest of France was ever launched.

[113] Benet's Chronicle, 208–9; *C.P.R., 1452–1461*, 52; Steel, *op. cit.*, 272.
[114] Henry had generously reduced the size of the grant, see above, p. 265, n. 11.
[115] *R.P.*, V, 233.
[116] K. B. McFarlane, 'William Worcester: A Preliminary Survey', in *Studies Presented to Sir Hilary Jenkinson*, ed. J. Conway Davies (Oxford 1957), 211–2.
[117] *Boke of Noblesse*, 5.

Chapter 14

MADNESS, 1453–1455

The early summer of 1453 thus saw Henry as a stronger and more active king than he had ever been before in all his previous fifteen years of personal rule. Indeed, he seems suddenly to have become an altogether more virile person, even begetting an heir after seven years of fruitless marriage. The reason he gave for proroguing parliament at Reading on 2 July was that he wished to be free to undertake another of his successful judicial perambulations. He had spent twelve months countering the effects of York's rebellion by exemplary punishment of his rank and file supporters in their localities. Quite separate and unrelated disturbances had now arisen in Yorkshire which appeared to require similar treatment.

For fifty years or more the Percy and Nevill families had been rivals for offices and land in the north of England, especially for the two posts of greatest influence there which the crown could offer, the wardenships of the east and west marches towards Scotland. During Henry's personal rule the balance of power there had been significantly tipped in favour of the Nevills. Cecily Nevill, sister of the effective head of the numerous Nevill clan, Richard Nevill, earl of Salisbury, was married to Richard duke of York, but the Nevills, who rose to exercise the predominant power in the north, did so chiefly through their Beaufort connections. They were the junior branch of the numerous Nevill family, children of the second marriage of their father Ralph Nevill of Raby, first earl of Westmorland, to Joan Beaufort, daughter of John of Gaunt[1] and it was basically from possession of Joan Beaufort's lands in Yorkshire and the court influence of their uncle, Cardinal Beaufort, that Richard Nevill, earl of Salisbury became one of the wealthiest peers of the realm, with estates worth some £3,000 per annum.[2] He had acquired the title and estates of the earldom of Salisbury by his marriage to the heiress of the last Montague earl of Salisbury who died at Orleans in 1428. The York marriage of his sister was only one of five noble Nevill alliances and such relationships

[1] The senior branch of the Nevills, Ralph's descendants by his first marriage to Margaret, daughter of Hugh earl of Stafford: Ralph, 2nd earl of Westmorland, John, Lord Nevill etc., played little part in the politics of Henry VI's reign.

[2] Storey, *The End of the House of Lancaster*, 114.

meant little among the frequently inter-related upper echelons of fifteenth-century English society, except insofar as they involved the acquisition and transfer of substantial estates. All the marriages of the male Nevills did so. Richard's brothers William, George and Edward married the baronial heiresses of Fauconberg, Latimer and Aber-gavenny. The only other brother, Robert, was a priest, provided for with the palatine bishopric of Durham from 1438 to 1457. Salisbury's eldest son Richard became the wealthiest of the clan when he acquired the title and estates of the Beauchamp earldom of Warwick by his marriage to Anne, heiress of Henry's tutor Richard Beauchamp, earl of Warwick. By 1453 the Nevill-York marriage had had no political significance. Next after the Stafford duke of Buckingham Richard Nevill, earl of Salisbury, had been the most prominent supporter of Henry in the field against York at Dartford in 1452.

The disturbances in Yorkshire which appeared to require Henry's personal attention in July 1453 were caused by the landless younger sons of the Percy earl of Northumberland and the Nevill earl of Salis-bury, Thomas Percy, Lord Egremont and Sir John Nevill, possibly resulting from rivalries generated in the conduct of the 1448–9 war with Scotland.[3] Repeated summonses before the council to Egremont to answer for breaches of the king's peace and peremptory letters to both of them on 26 June had been ignored.[4] Efforts to get the par-ticularly militant Egremont out of the way by persuading him to raise a force for Gascony on 7 July proved fruitless.[5] The appointment on 16 July of a powerful commission of oyer and terminer for the North Riding, headed by Salisbury, Northumberland and Viscount Beau-mont and including the three judges Ardern, Portington and Danvers, and some household men, thus similar in composition to the commis-sions which had accompanied Henry's previous perambulations to punish York's followers, suggests that his intended destination in the first half of July was the North. But this powerful commission was replaced on 27 July by one with more limited powers (to command appearances before the council only and to imprison those who refused to find security for their appearance), covering the whole four northern counties, but consisting only of Sir William Lucy and the same three judges. This stop-gap arrangement had become necessary because another magnate dispute had suddenly arisen potentially much more serious than the territorially remote squabbles of the younger sons of Percy and Nevill.

On 21 July Henry presided over a council meeting at Sheen to settle pressing differences between Edmund Beaufort, duke of Somerset, and Richard Nevill, earl of Warwick, over the possession of the lordship

[3] *Ibid.*, 124ff.   [5] P.R.O., E.28/83/21.
[4] *P.P.C.*, VI, 140–2; P.R.O., E.28/83/19A.

of Glamorgan and Morgannok in South Wales. The conflict here had arisen because Henry had recently granted to Somerset the keeping of these lands, which had been held by Warwick since 1450. As a result Warwick was maintaining the two principal strongholds there, the castles and towns of Cardiff and Cowbridge, against Somerset by force of arms. The two of them were related by their marriages to half-sisters, daughters of the Beauchamp earl of Warwick.[6] They had already been involved in rival family claims on the Beauchamp inheritance, but this dispute in South Wales was over Despencer lands and Somerset and his wife had no right by inheritance to these. Half these Despencer lands were held by Warwick's wife Anne, the daughter of Isabel Despencer, Richard Beauchamp's second wife. These lands were not in dispute. The other half were held by George Nevill, the grandson of Isabel Despencer by an earlier marriage.[7] He was a minor, and Warwick had acquired his wardship in 1450, thus placing the whole Despencer inheritance under his control. It was probably assumed to be in the king's hands again under the acts of resumption of 1450–1, and therefore available for granting to Somerset who received on 15 June 1453 the keeping of all the lands of George Nevill still in the king's hands.[8] This attempt by Somerset thus to dispossess Warwick and his wife was as deplorable as the king's continued rash indifference to the probable consequences of his grants. The news that Warwick was holding the lordship against Somerset in a state of war was the alarming matter before Henry and his councillors, Somerset, but not Warwick, being present among them, at Sheen, on Saturday 21 July. The decision of the meeting was to send Warwick a peremptory order to disperse his armed followers and to hand the lordships over to John, Lord Dudley, until Henry, with his council, had decided what should be done. The execution of a note 'item sembable to the duke of Somerset, mutatis mutandis', himself taking part in the deliberations, would hardly be sufficient to make the king's actions appear impartial in Warwick's eyes.[9] There is no evidence that he ever surrendered the lordship to Dudley or to anyone else.

[6] Somerset was married to Eleanor, daughter of Richard Beauchamp, earl of Warwick (d. 1439), by his first wife Elizabeth Berkeley. Warwick was married to Anne, Beauchamp's daughter by his second wife, Isabel Despencer.

[7] Isabel Despencer was previously married to the Beauchamp earl of Worcester. Their daughter Elisabeth (d. 1448) married Edward Nevill, Lord Abergavenny, and her heir was George Nevill.

[8] *C.P.R., 1445–1452*, 111, 162; *ibid., 1452–1461*, 34–5. The grant to Somerset was backdated to the date of the death of Anne Beauchamp (1449), only child of Henry duke of Warwick (d. 1445), Isabel Despencer's son.

[9] P.R.O., E.28/83/41 (draft and final version of letters to Warwick and his countess finalized at Westminster 27 July). The other councillors present were the chancellor and treasurer, the prior of St John, dean of St Severin and Thomas Thorpe.

By 31 July Henry and the court were at the duchy of Lancaster manor of Kingston Lacy in Dorset, near Wimborne Minster,[10] where Henry had stayed for five nights on his 1452 western progress. The most likely explanation is that Henry was making for the scene of trouble himself, following his previous convenient route to the west. Kingston Lacy lies beyond the royal hunting lodge at Clarendon by any route from London and it is possible that the king had journeyed even further west before something caused him to turn back. He was certainly at Clarendon by 5 August and is alleged to have been there about the festival of St Peter's Chains (1 August), which is the date for the onset of his madness there as given by Benet's Chronicle. There is no record of who accompanied him, except that one chronicler says Somerset took him there.[11] The loss of his senses at Clarendon is thus not precisely dateable and the exact cause likewise remains a matter for conjecture. But he was able to receive the kiss of homage from Sir William Stourton at Clarendon on 7 August[12] and the devastating news of the death of Talbot and the annihilation of his army at Castillon must have reached Henry during the first week in August. He had only used the ancient royal hunting lodge of Clarendon twice before, although, like Kingston Lacy, it was kept in repair in the custody of a member of the household. Its present isolation and remoteness, three miles east of Salisbury, buried and forgotten in a large modern game-park, makes it much less accessible now than it was in the fifteenth century, when the highway from Salisbury to Winchester, on the main route from the west country, passed through the ancient park. It is unlikely that he had travelled so far west and beyond Clarendon merely for the hunting there. He may well have joined this route to return to the capital when he received the news of Castillon. The shock of such a disaster, clearly indicating the utter loss of English Gascony and, by implication, his own further failure and the rightness of York's predictions, may well have caused the onset of psychotic illness, most likely depressive stupor, which deprived him of his wits for the next eighteen months.[13]

[10] P.R.O., E.404/69/215.

[11] Gregory's Chronicle, 199.

[12] P.R.O., C.81/1371/41.

[13] The nature of his illness in the light of modern medical knowledge and opinion has already been discussed in print by R. L. Storey, *The End of the House of Lancaster*, 136n., 252n., by John Saltmarsh, *King Henry VI and the Royal Foundations* (Cambridge 1972), 11–12, and by Basil Clarke, *Mental Disorder in Earlier Britain* (Cardiff 1975), 176–206, but evidence relevant to Henry's condition is in effect confined to the report of one single interview with representatives of the peerage on the eve of the Annunciation, Sunday 24 March 1454, at Windsor and the report of his behaviour during recovery on 30 December 1454 at Greenwich (see below, pp. 272–3). I am greatly indebted to Dr S. Bhanji, consultant psychiatrist at the Exe Vale Hospital, Digby, Exeter, and

The few chroniclers who give any dates and details were writing some years later and there are no strictly contemporary reports of his condition at Clarendon, where he remained until before Christmas 1453. Dates given for the onset vary from 7 July to 10 August. Giles's Chronicle, which gives the impossibly early 7 July, is the source for the fact that a sudden shock or fright caused him to fall into this sickness which neither doctors nor medicines could cure and which deprived him of normal senses and intelligence adequate to direct affairs of state until about the feast of the Circumcision (1 January) 1455.[14] There is no evidence of earlier physical ill-health or mental disease in Henry himself, but there most probably was an inherited genetic component to his illness. On his mother's side there had been the notorious mental derangement of his Valois grandfather, King Charles VI of France. His was a manic state of raging madness in a violent, choleric, fast-living person, but comparable with Henry's in the sudden initial onset at the same time of year, while on a journey, and in the recurrence of attacks. In Charles's case it occurred on a military expedition when he was riding, armed, and complaining of the heat, in pursuit of the would-be assassins of his constable, through the forest of Le Mans. The onset in Charles's case was recorded in detail. He was startled by the sudden appearance of a well-meaning stranger, whom he mistook for an assassin, who seized his bridle to warn him of an ambush ahead.[15] At the sound of clashing steel from a dropped lance he flew into a demented rage, allegedly killing four men before he was restrained. There was never any suggestion of violence in Henry's condition but that does not exclude an inherited predisposition, as the actual symptoms displayed in his case would also be influenced by his own environmental background, personality and intelligence.

No apparent specialization among the court physicians and surgeons, who were licenced by the council to treat Henry on 15 March 1454, sheds any further light on the nature of his illness. Neither does the

---

senior lecturer in adult mental illness in the University of Exeter, for his comments on Henry's condition. There is insufficient information for a definite diagnosis. The differential diagnosis includes depressive stupor, schizophrenic stupor and some form of organic brain disease. His apparent good recovery from the first attack, with retention of his intellectual powers, rules out the latter and is similarly against a diagnosis of catatonic schizophrenia.

[14] Giles's Chronicle, 44; Benet's Chronicle, 210; B.L. MS. Royal 13 c.1. 'William Worcester', in Stevenson, Wars, II, pt. ii, 771, also says 'rex Henricus VI subito cecidit in gravem infirmitatem capitis ita quod extractus a mente videbatur'. The Royal MS seems to suggest that the onset was in the middle of the night. Bale's Chronicle (Six Town Chronicles, 140) says that he was already indisposed at Clarendon when he 'suddenly was taken and smitten with a frenzy and his wit and reason withdrawn'. Clearly there is no eye-witness account of the onset of the illness.

[15] A. Coville in Cambridge Medieval History, VII, 372-3.

whole gamut of draughts and confections, ointments, laxatives, head-purges, gargles, baths, poultices and bleedings which they were authorized to administer at their discretion.[16] The first indication that Henry's was not a once-for-all illness dates from 5 June 1455 when Gilbert Kemer, dean of Salisbury, formerly physician to his uncle Humphrey, was summoned from Salisbury to Windsor to attend the king 'as we be occupied and laboured *as ye know well* with sickness and infirmities'.[17] In view of the proximity of Clarendon to Salisbury and the wording of this summons, it may well be that this most eminent dietician had attended him there on the first occasion. The only genuine eye-witness account of his condition in the depth of his first attack is a report rendered to parliament on Lady Day 1454.[18] A deputation from the lords spiritual and temporal had waited on Henry at Windsor the day before. They had arrived in time to watch the king dining and when he had finished his dinner their spokesman, the bishop of Chester, had attempted to carry out their instructions which, in essence, were to get him urgently to nominate a new chancellor and archbishop of Canterbury, vacancies caused by the death of Cardinal Kemp on 22 March. The bishop received absolutely no response in words or movement from Henry and they all then tried their utmost to move him by prayers, exhortations and unspecified actions as each thought fit, ending in a state of hopelessly unproductive, sorrowful embarrassment. The bishop of Winchester then relieved the tension by suggesting dinner for themselves. After they had dined they returned to find him as he had been before. They repeated their earlier charades with such variations as had since occurred to them, but still with no result. Finally they had him led into his bedchamber, between two of his attendants, and there tried a third time to elicit a response. They could get no answer, nor any indication that he might wish to see them at any future time, so, sorrowfully, they came away. The only other description of him at this time, by the garrulous and inventive Abbot Wheathampstead, is probably nothing but a gloss on their report and in any case tells us little more: he had no sense of time or memory, almost no control over his limbs, could not stand upright or walk or indeed move unaided from the place where he was seated.[19] By March 1454 the stupor was thus even deeper than on an earlier occasion when he had at least raised and lowered his eyes to his infant son, who had been brought to him at Windsor, at Christmas 1453 or the New Year 1454.[20] During this first illness, as would be expected, he required constant

[16] *P.P.C.*, VI, 166–7.
[17] *Foedera*, XI, 366.
[18] *R.P.*, V, 241–2.
[19] *Registrum*, I, 163.
[20] *Paston Letters*, I, 263–4.

watching and attention day and night, duties falling on the grooms and pages of his chamber.[21]

Henry's public appearance to receive the kiss of homage from the new archbishop of Canterbury on 22 August 1454, a ceremony only omitted by sanction of parliament in time of pestilence, and to hand him his cross, must be taken as the first indications of returning senses,[22] though, at his final recovery, he had forgotten it. He had substantially recovered by 27 December, when he ordered his almoner to ride to Canterbury and his secretary to Westminster, to make thank offerings at the shrines of St Thomas and the Confessor. On 30 December he learnt his fourteen-month-old son's name for the first time, inquired who were his godfathers (Kemp and Somerset),[23] and expressed himself well pleased. At this point the queen told him that Cardinal Archbishop Kemp was dead, which he did not know. He had in fact suffered a complete amnesia for the period of his illness, not knowing what had been said to him or where he had been. He was now for the moment free of all worries: 'in charity with all the world and so he would all the lords were'. Wainfleet and Robert Botyll, the Prior of St John, two of his intimate councillors, in audience on 7 January 1455 found him completely lucid and fully recovered and wept for joy at it. He could now say matins of Our Lady and evensong and hear Mass with due appreciation.[24] Could he resume the government?

For a while after the onset of his illness the processes of government gradually ran down headless. With one solitary exception, dated 3 October 1453, privy seal writs ceased to be dated at Clarendon from 11 August. Some other warrants, bearing the royal sign manual, but dateable only from their delivery clauses, continued to reach the chancellor at Malling in Kent until 22 October. Minor administrative uncertainty was inevitable, but the council at Westminster could and did continue to give effect to measures already generally decided before Henry's departure. More than twenty cajoling and threatening letters went out to the Percies and Nevills and their supporters, including the two earls, in late July and early August, ordering attendance on Sir William Lucy and his fellow justices and arrangements for the assembly of reinforcements for Shrewsbury in Gascony continued uninterrupted

---

[21] P.R.O., E.28/84/20. This petition for payment of their wages, 22 May 1454, states that this was so.

[22] *P.P.C.*, VI, 211; *R.P.*, V, 31; *Paston Letters*, I, 303. The eye witness William Paston mentioned, but did not specify, the nature of the 'demeaning' between them. He also referred to the bishop of Ely doing his fealty on 6 September, the date of the letter, by which time there was great pestilence in the city which he was about to leave in haste.

[23] Davies's Chronicle, 70.

[24] *Paston Letters*, I, 315-16.

until 14 August in spite of the annihilation of the English army at Castillon on 17 July.[25] But the ultimate source of authority was paralysed; how could the disputes of the great now be settled, or their claims maintained, except by their taking the law into their own hands? Thus bickerings of the Percies and the Nevills now erupted into open armed conflict. At Heworth near York on 24 August, where a force of over 700 Percy retainers and servants, led by the earl of Northumberland's younger sons Thomas Percy, Lord Egremont, and Sir Richard Percy, ambushed a strong party of Nevills which included the earl of Salisbury, his countess Alice, his sons Thomas and John, and Thomas's newly married wife Matilda, niece and joint-heiress of Ralph, Lord Cromwell. The Nevills were returning as a family from the wedding at Tattershall and making for their manor of Sheriff Hutton some twelve miles north of York. The immediate cause of this particular confrontation was the potential damage which this marriage would do to Percy interests. Cromwell, by Henry's grant, had obtained the former Percy manors of Wressle (Yorkshire) and Burwell (Lincolnshire), forfeited in the disposal of Percy estates which had followed their unsuccessful rising against Henry IV. The earl of Northumberland, seeking to reconstitute his grandfather's estates, had made counter claims to these manors, but now by this Cromwell-Nevill marriage they would strengthen the position of his rivals, the increasingly powerful Nevill family. The fighting was inconclusive. So far as is recorded, none of the principals was injured, though substantial slaughter of their followers on both sides was alleged. For the first time in the reign, armed confrontation between the great had ended in open warfare.[26]

Another landed dispute of the great also involved the acquisitive Cromwell, this time with Lord Grey of Ruthyn and the young duke of Exeter, Henry Holand, a dispute which was soon to bind Percy and Holand together in armed pursuit of their aims. Exeter, a notoriously unstable character, was doubly of the blood royal. He was the great-grandson of Richard II's mother Joan from her first marriage to Sir Thomas Holand. She was the daughter of Edmund of Woodstock, earl of Kent, youngest son of Edward I. He was also the grandson of Elizabeth of Lancaster, duchess of Exeter, daughter of John of Gaunt and sister of Henry IV, who had married as her third husband the dashing Lancastrian knight 'Green Cornwaille', later Lord Fanhope. After Fanhope's death Cromwell had purchased the manors of Ampt-

[25] *P.P.C.*, VI, 146–57.

[26] This Percy-Nevill dispute has been exhaustively examined, chiefly from King's Bench indictments of May to August 1454 (K.B.9/148 and K.B.9/149), by R. A. Griffiths, 'Local rivalries and national politics: the Percies, the Nevilles and the duke of Exeter, 1452–55', *Speculum*, XLIII (1968), 589–632.

hill, Millbrook and Grange (Bedfordshire) from his executors, by prior arrangement with Fanhope. In 1452 Exeter had claimed these lands. Lord Grey of Ruthyn, as another grandson of Elizabeth of Lancaster, had claims equally as strong, or as weak, as Exeter's. Grey came to an agreement with Cromwell, but Exeter forcibly dispossessed Cromwell of Ampthill in 1453. On 4 July all three parties had appeared at Westminster, supported by armed forces, to overawe a court sitting by virtue of a writ of novel disseisin, sued out by Cromwell against Exeter. Henry had consequently consigned all three magnates to a brief spell of imprisonment in Windsor, Wallingford and Pevensey castles, before dismissing them back to their respective estates. On 19 January 1454 a newsletter from London reported that Exeter and Thomas Percy, Lord Egremont, had been together at Tuxford, some twenty miles south of Doncaster, to make a sworn confederation in furtherance of their common aims against the Nevills, Cromwell, and any of their supporters.[27]

Official pretence that Henry was still in control, and merely absent for unavoidable reasons, was actually kept up until 23 March 1454, but some steps had to be taken in the council to cope with such un-avoidable, new and mounting problems by those of its members present at Westminster in October 1453. It may have been the failure of a very sparsely attended council meeting, consisting only of the chancellor, the duke of Buckingham and the bishop of Hereford, on 8 October, to get any response to most strongly worded reprimands, appeals and summonses to the two northern earls and the two principals in the Percy-Nevill quarrel, Egremont and Sir John Nevill, which led to the summoning of a great council to take up the reins of government which had fallen from Henry's grasp. Its declared purpose, most notably and understandably in view of the several festering magnate disputes, was 'to set rest and union betwixt the lords of this land'. At the back of their minds they must also have realized that the oldest and most potentially dangerous York-Somerset quarrel would have to be taken into consideration. At first they evaded the issue by simply not summoning York to council meetings. It was another, comparatively small council group of five bishops, led by the bishop of Winchester, with the treasurer, the earl of Worcester, Sudeley, John, Lord Dudley, and the premier baron, the Prior of St John, who on 23 October despatched a special messenger to apologize for this 'oversight' and to urge York to attend.[28] Their move had presumably been made much easier from 13 October, when Queen Margaret gave birth to a son. York now had no right to any exalted treatment as Henry's presumptive successor, or as automatic regent by right of an

[27] Griffiths, *op. cit.*, 606–8; Benet's Chronicle, 210; *Paston Letters*, I, 264.
[28] *P.P.C.*, VI, 160–4.

entitlement to the succession. From 13 October he could be treated as Somerset's equal.

York was in London from 12 November, and immediately showed that he had no intention of letting bygones be bygones and would take full advantage of Henry's illness. York was not just raking up past history out of jealousy and resentment to destroy a rival. He had either to remove Somerset or cooperate with him. As far as he was concerned Somerset's past failures made it impossible to work with him. Through the medium of the duke of Norfolk, he at once reasserted the old charges against Somerset. The loss of Normandy and now Gascony, he claimed, were both due to his cowardly and treasonable acts. Those who thought that Somerset's culpable acts in the royal service, whatever they had been, were less than treasonable, and those who thought that peace and unity among the lords should be achieved at all costs, in the desperate circumstances of the king's incapacity, were brushed aside.[29] On 21 November York required, and was given, a public declaration, under the great seal, from his fellow councillors, among whom Somerset and Beaumont were the only noticeable absentees, that all men were free to attend upon him and serve him. He alleged (and this is incidentally confirmed as true by a letter of 6 October 1454 to John Paston), that Henry, the queen and Somerset had made efforts to ostracize him, by warning men to keep away from him at various times over the previous two years, on pain of the royal displeasure.[30] This is the earliest indication of Queen Margaret's hostility to York, even if we take it only as a reflection of her husband's basic attitude towards him. Somerset, by contrast, was established as her trusted confidant and adviser as well as Henry's. Her receiver-general's accounts at Michaelmas 1453, in recording an annuity payment of 100 marks to Somerset, speak of him as her most dear cousin, of his good counsel and worthy service given and to be given, and of the great affection and kindness he had shown in matters vital to her.[31] From 23 November 1453 York's ascendancy in the great council was evident when Somerset was committed to the Tower and the earl of Devon freed from Wallingford castle to take his place in the council, where his declarations of his innocence of all treasonable allegations made against him were accepted.[32] As was subsequently declared in parliament, York took the charges made against Devon, his earlier accomplice, as charges directed against himself.[33]

---

[29] *Paston Letters*, I, 259–61 (Norfolk's indictment of Somerset); Benet's Chronicle, 210, dates York's entry into the council and Norfolk's indictment both to 12 November.
[30] *C.P.R., 1452–1461*, 143–4; *Paston Letters*, I, 403–6.
[31] A. R. Myers, 'The Household of Queen Margaret of Anjou', *B.J.R.L.*, XL (1957–8), 418.
[32] Benet's Chronicle, 211.   [33] *R.P.*, V, 249.

A newsletter, written by a well-wisher of the duke of Norfolk, which had mentioned the sworn pact between Exeter and Egremont on 19 January, also gave an invaluable insight into the political situation at Westminster after the Christmas and New Year festivals in anticipation of the assembly of parliament due on 11 January 1454.[34] The writer knew of unsuccessful attempts made at court, by the queen and the duke of Buckingham, to rouse Henry from his stupor through his infant son and described the consequent, universal state of uncertainty and apprehension with which the great were preparing for the approaching assembly. The cardinal archbishop and chancellor, considered to be Somerset's principal friend,[35] was surrounding himself with an armed guard. Some of Henry's household men, Tresham, Joseph, Daniel and Trevelyan, had framed a bill to provide a permanent garrison at Windsor for the protection of the insane king and his infant heir. Somerset, from the Tower, had secured all the lodgings to be had in its vicinity for his servants and retainers and had spies placed in all the great households. Buckingham had ordered 2,000 badges for his followers and the other magnates coming were all strongly supported. The most prudent, like Warwick, were bringing a second substantial band quite apart from their escort and, following York's example, transporting their armour and arms separately in carts to avoid any accusation of making a rising. Some eight or nine worthy people had gathered all this intelligence for Norfolk's benefit. He was now warned by his correspondent also to take all these sensible precautions, lest the chancellor should issue writs against him. He was advised to be ready to counter any charges against himself by pointing to the great activity being made on Somerset's behalf, which he could legitimately claim was directed against himself. The Speaker of the parliament, Thomas Thorpe, was busy working against York; Henry's Tudor half-brothers, apparently coming to Westminster in York's company, were likely to be arrested on arrival. But the most interesting items of news concerned the queen's entry into politics as the champion of the Lancastrian interests. She had had prepared a bill under five heads, which included a claim to be nominated regent for her husband, with control over all state appointments and royal patronage, civil and ecclesiastical, and the provision of livelihood sufficient to maintain the king, the prince and herself.

York was expected on 25 January and was certainly present in great council meetings, where high matters of state were being decided, by 9 February, when certain royal powers were delegated to Salisbury and Warwick as keepers of the west march towards Scotland.[36] Three

[34] *Paston Letters*, I, 263–8.
[35] Benet's Chronicle, 211.
[36] P.R.O., C.81/1546/66.

days earlier the council had been made aware that there were two lieutenants of Ireland by Henry's appointment and had instructed the treasurer to retain the emoluments of the office.[37] A few days after Dartford, Henry had given the lieutenancy to York's deputy's courtier son, James Butler, earl of Wiltshire, who had appointed his own deputy, the archbishop of Armagh, in June 1453. But in the changed circumstances of the king's total incapacity York had now secured a new ratification of his original ten-year appointment to run its full term from 1447. Nothing more was now heard of Wiltshire's appointment. At the end of his original term in 1457, York was to receive a new grant for a further ten years.[38] Council members were now subscribing their names to the acts of the council as had not been done since the end of the minority. On 6 February they had also instructed the treasurer to go to Reading where the parliament was due to assemble on 11 February and move it to Westminster for the 14th.

On 13 February 1454 York's pre-eminence in the council was officially established. An assembly of twenty-eight lords in the great council chamber, among whom only Somerset, Northumberland, Wiltshire, Beaumont and Bonville were noticeable absentees, nominated him as king's lieutenant, to open and preside over the parliament.[39] The de facto power in the land was now the whole council and, while parliament was in session, the lords spiritual and temporal. Men still petitioned the king by the advice of his council to grant, etc., but petitions were now endorsed 'by advice of the council' only, and signed by all present.[40] On 15 March York, Wiltshire and Beaumont were all among twenty-two lords signing the creation in parliament of the infant Edward as prince of Wales and earl of Chester, so at this point York specifically recognized the Lancastrian succession. The number of lords absent from this session of parliament was very high (60 out of a possible total of 105). Such reluctance to participate in affairs during Henry's incapacity clearly disturbed the new lieutenant since within a fortnight of its assembly graduated fines for non-attendance were being imposed, making this assembly unique in the middle ages.[41]

[37] P.R.O., E.28/84/1; C.81/1546/65. Parliament had already been prorogued by the chancellor on 12 November to 11 February 1454, acting on a council decision of 6 November.

[38] C.P.R., 1452–1461, 202, 311 (York's ratification dated 1 December 1454 and renewal dated 6 March 1457); 82 (Wiltshire's grant from 6 March 1453 and appointment of deputy 25 June 1453).

[39] P.R.O., C.81/1546/68. York naturally did not sign. E.28/81/1 and C.81/1546/65 show that he was present that day.

[40] P.R.O., C.81/1546/71, livery clause of 12 March with 20 signatures.

[41] J. S. Roskell, 'The Problem of the Attendance of the Lords in Medieval Parliaments', B.I.H.R., XXIX (1956), 189–92; R.P., V, 248.

A similar reluctance to obey summonses to great council meetings, except among regular councillors, was also evident,[42] but threats of penalties here against absentees were apparently quite ineffective.[43] However, there is no sign that council membership was restricted to any clique or party.[44] Only the imprisoned Somerset and the distant Northumberland were continual absentees among the regular councillors. The king's resumption of power was to be duly indicated by a return of the old form of documents from 25 February 1455, with a sign manual superscribed on petitions, and a presence, in place of signatures, written out by the clerk at the bottom.

There was certainly no particular enthusiasm for York's presidency in the Commons of this parliament and understandably so, since one of his first actions was to cause the imprisonment of their Speaker Thomas Thorpe. Wearing a second hat as a Baron of the Exchequer, Thorpe had confiscated some of York's property stored in the bishop of Durham's town house and a Middlesex jury had found for York, imposing a £1,000 penalty. The new lieutenant refused to countenance a Commons' petition for his release on the grounds that parliamentary privilege had been broken, and forced them to elect a new Speaker. Through him, Thomas Charlton, on 19 February, they rejected outright requests for £40,000 for the defence of Calais and wanted to know what had happened to all the earlier grants of the Reading parliament. Moreover, they persistently requested the appointment of a 'sad and wise' council which they claimed Henry had promised them, and were clearly not impressed by what had been done in his name so far.[45]

No official mention had been made of his illness, even yet. How long this formal pretence could have been kept up is questionable, but another act of God now intervened. Chancellor Kemp died on 22 March and from that moment not even a semblance of government could be carried on because the great seals of England were now unusable. They were perforce solemnly secured under the private seals of various lords and lodged in the exchequer. It was now at last imperative that the king's will be ascertained, or that his total incapacity be publicly demonstrated, since the chancery was now as paralysed as he was. Consequently the deputation of lords spiritual and temporal, led by the bishop of Winchester and the earl of Warwick, waited upon him at Windsor, on the eve of the Annunciation, with the duty of reporting back exactly what happened for enrolment on the parliament roll. This was the interview which produced the first and last

[42] P.R.O., E.28/85/1, 73; *P.P.C.*, VI, 216–17.
[43] Roskell, *op. cit.*, 193; *P.P.C.*, VI, 233.
[44] P.R.O., C.81/1546/72. cf. *P.P.C.*, VI, 166–74.
[45] *R.P.*, V, 238–41.

full description of Henry's condition.[46] They had first to inform Henry of the assembly of parliament and the appointment of York to preside over it. If there was any sign that communication had been established, he was then to be told of Kemp's death and the sealing up of the seals, and pressed to nominate a new chancellor and archbishop. Furthermore, he was to be asked either to approve the membership of the acting council or to change it, since the Commons persisted in calling for a 'sad and substantial council'. The completely negative results of this interview, reported on 25 March, may have been anticipated, because, only two days later on 27 March, York was appointed by his peers as Protector and Defender of the kingdom of England and Chief Councillor of the king. 1422 had been taken as the precedent. But what is most noticeable is not so much the speed of the final decision to institute a protectorate, following the ultimate official report on Henry's condition, but the eight-month delay before any decision had been taken at all.

The office of Protector and Defender of the kingdom of England, now conferred on York by his peers on 27 March, was deliberately based on the precedent of the minority, since it resurrected Duke Humphrey's title which had avoided the implications of tutor, lieutenant, governor or regent, all of which implied authority of government. It thus confined his duties to protecting and defending the kingdom from its enemies outward and inward, while making him first among equals in the council. He, for his part, required the fact that he had not sought the position and that the peers of the realm, the ultimate authority in the kingdom, had requested him to take it, to be enrolled on record. They, the lords spiritual and temporal in parliament assembled, required it to be recorded that they were compelled by circumstances to nominate and appoint him. The appointment was in formal terms during the king's pleasure. It envisaged the possibility of a partial recovery, which might make it advisable for York to continue in office, to prevent the king's recovery being retarded by the burdens of kingship. The only finality which could be foreseen at that moment was that if Edward prince of Wales wished to take it upon himself when he reached years of discretion, he should be free to do so. Separate letters patent reserved the prince's rights here. Governmentally the duties of York's additional position as chief of the king's council, *primus inter pares*, were not spelled out in detail as they had been in 1422 but his limited rights, and those of the prince if he took the office upon himself, to royal patronage in offices and benefices were to be the same as Duke Humphrey had had[47] and for the rest, royal patronage was to be exercised by the council.

[46] *Ibid.*, 241–2 and see above, pp. 272–3.
[47] See above, p.33.

His salary was to be 2,000 marks *per annum*, with supplementary payment for necessary, unforeseen expenses. All the statutory rights and royal gifts so far granted to Queen Margaret were specifically reserved to her.[48]

In the remaining days of the parliament it granted no further supply, but was used to give ultimate authority to a number of measures appropriate to current circumstances: the imprisoned Somerset was deprived of the captaincy of Calais and York's appointment in his stead approved; the earl of Salisbury, York's brother-in-law, was appointed as the first lay chancellor of the reign. Together with Shrewsbury, Worcester, Wiltshire and Lord Stourton he was also nominated to keep the seas for three years and tunnage and poundage officially appropriated to pay for this. Fresh financial appropriations on the existing revenues, at a much reduced scale of 10,000 marks, not to be exceeded, were made for the stricken royal household in response, it was said, to repeated remonstrances against the excesses of royal purveyors. Any magnates of the realm who declined to obey royal writs of summons before the council were made liable to forfeiture and loss of their peerages.[49]

This last measure indicated that Richard duke of York would inevitably have to take up the exercise of royal authority over the disputes of his peers at the point where Henry had relinquished it once parliament was dissolved.[50] He was on his way north by 16 May and established in York about the 19th,[51] accompanied on his royal judicial progress by the earl of Warwick, Lords Cromwell, Greystock and Fitzhugh and the judges Richard Bingham, Ralph Pole, John Prisot and John Portington.[52] This impressive armed oyer and terminer was designed for the exemplary punishment of the followers of Exeter, Egremont and Richard Percy. York's own interest, the crown's interests through the royal Protector in punishing flagrant breaches of the king's peace, and the private interests of the Nevills and Lord Cromwell were for the moment conveniently and effectively identical. In addition to the indictment of over 700 Percy supporters, almost entirely Yorkshiremen, for the affray at Heworth on 24 August 1453, and for concomitant disturbances in York and elsewhere, the Protector and his fellow commissioners were also concerned with further more serious armed assemblies, principally at the Percy manors of Topcliffe on 17 October 1453 and Spofforth and York on 21 May 1454.

---

[48] *R.P.*, V, 242–4, including enrolment of concurrent letters patent dated 3 April.
[49] *Foedera*, XI, 344; *R.P.*, V, 244–7, 254–6, 266–7; *P.P.C.*, VI, 199–206, P.R.O., E.28/84/59.
[50] Shortly before Easter (21 April).
[51] Griffiths in *Speculum*, XLIII, 612ff.
[52] P.R.O., K.B.9/149; *Paston Letters*, I, 290.

The duke of Exeter and Lord Egremont, who were alleged to be in alliance with King James of Scotland, were, it seems, aiming to raise the whole north of England in rebellion against the Protector, if not against the helpless king. They assembled, with banners displayed, under Exeter, who was taking regal power upon himself, claiming to be the rightful duke of Lancaster and handing out liveries in the Lancastrian colours 'white and bloody' with the words 'take here the duke of Lancaster's livery'. Consequently another two hundred or more named adherents, some from Cumberland and Lancashire, and from Exeter's Bedfordshire estates, and many more unidentified, were indicted for this rebellion. It has recently been cogently argued from the evidence of these indictments made before York in June 1454, and the current records of the reactions of the council, that the Lancastrian Exeter saw himself as the alternative, rightful Protector to the Plantagenet York. In the absence of any other unquestionably legitimate male descendants of John of Gaunt, apart from his two royal great-grandsons (the prostrate Henry himself and King Alfonso of Portugal), Henry Holand, duke of Exeter, the third great-grandson of John of Gaunt through his younger daughter Elizabeth,[53] saw himself as the rightful, supreme champion of the Lancastrian interest during Henry's incapacity.[54]

No direct confrontation between Exeter with his Percy allies and the Protector in fact ever took place. They and their supporters were condemned as traitors by York and his fellow commissioners. Exeter, who fled south, was taken from Westminster sanctuary by York on 23 July and lodged in Pontefract castle. The fugitive Egremont and Richard Percy were finally captured in an armed affray with Sir Thomas Nevill at Stamford Bridge, near York, early in November. They were first confined in the Nevill castle of Middleham, then handed over to the Protector, tried, condemned, and consigned to Newgate.[55] Thus the Nevills triumphed over the Percies and York defeated his new, would-be Lancastrian rival for pre-eminence in the realm. He was back in the council at Westminster from the north by 8 July and then returned to York, where a further final session was held on 3 August. After this any further action against Northumberland and Percy associates could be safely respited until the next Yorkshire sessions due after Easter 1455.[56]

On 23 July 1454 the council approved a severe reduction in the king's stables. Thirty-one of the king's horses were dispersed among

[53] Alfonso of Portugal being the grandson of Philippa, John of Gaunt's elder daughter.

[54] R. A. Griffiths, op. cit., 612ff., using K.B.9/149, K.B.27/778 Rex m.3d and P.P.C., VI, 189–90, 195–7.

[55] Griffiths, op. cit., 620, 622; Benet's Chronicle, 212; Giles's Chronicle, 45–6.

[56] P.R.O., E.28/85/62.

the nobility and another 15 were given to the king's almoner Henry Sever, leaving the now immobile household with 25 only and a stable staff reduced from 39 to 9.[57] Measures were also pending severely to reduce the whole royal household establishment. On the other hand York was authorized to give the king's livery collar to eighty gentlemen of his own choice.[58] It could be argued that the reduction of the royal stables was intended only as a necessary and temporary measure. The drastic reduction of the household establishment announced on 13 November was, however, intended to be permanent and was justified not on the grounds of Henry's illness but because, it was claimed, Henry had himself been about to make such a reduction on the eve of his collapse. This is most unlikely. A straight comparison with all those receiving fees and wages in 1452 shows reductions of about one-third, but this does not reveal the true nature of the exercise. Below stairs there was in fact no great change in numbers, but the knights, esquires and gentlemen of the household, numbering 301 on the 1452 roll, were now officially reduced to 24, while the yeomen of the crown and chamber were reduced from 72 to 31. A medical staff of eight: two master physicians, John Fauceby and William Hatclyff, three yeomen assistants and a sergeant surgeon, a yeoman and a groom, were retained to attend the sick king. Queen Margaret was allowed to retain a household of 120 persons, which was slightly more than she had in 1452, and an establishment of 39 was now provided for the infant prince.[59] There can be no doubt that Henry, on his recovery, could quickly have restored the position, if such numbers were in fact immediately deprived of his livery. Ordinances on the size of the household and the reality did not necessarily correspond. The ordinance of 1445 had envisaged an establishment of only one-quarter of the then current number of household knights and esquires, but the accounts for 1447 show that the actual total by then stood at five times that number. Household men were the ubiquitous agents of personal influence and rule throughout the shires; there could never be enough of them from that point of view, and their numbers had been steadily increasing throughout the 1440s. The reductions now to be enforced brought their numbers down far below the establishment of 1445, and even lower than Henry V's establishment on which these reforms of 1454 were supposedly based.[60] The reference in this measure to the duty of the great council to effect this drastic reduction and relieve the country of the burden of supporting such a huge household *before* Henry recovered his health, after which they might be held to account

[57] *P.P.C.*, VI, 209–14.
[58] *P.P.C.*, VI, 209–10; P.R.O., E.28/85/58.
[59] *P.P.C.*, VI, 220–33.
[60] See above, p. 98.

for their stewardship if they did not do it, suggests that these household reforms were rushed through because recovery may indeed have been on the way by early November. Somerset's fortunes since his imprisonment in the autumn of 1453 suggest the same. On 18 July York had been able to stall a move in the council to have him released on bail, by asking that the opinions of the judges first be obtained, and declaring that he himself could not agree to his release because the meeting was not so well attended (there were nineteen present) as the one which committed him had been.[61] The record suggests that this 'poorly attended' great council had in fact been summoned to try Somerset. A few days later the duke of Norfolk was ordered to be prepared to present charges against Somerset to another great council on 28 October,[62] but this trial never took place.

By the autumn of 1454 the Protector had thus crushed rebellion and was in effective control of council and royal household. He had not, however, managed to deal decisively with the problem of his chosen enemy Somerset and, most galling for the man who had persistently accused his Beaufort rival of responsibility for the loss of the overseas possessions, had also failed utterly to establish his own authority in Calais and its marches. His own appointment as captain of Calais, giving him complete charge in place of Somerset, was formally exemplified under the great seal on 17 July, but Somerset's lieutenants there, lords Rivers and Welles, still remained in control. Maintaining the Calais garrison was one of the heaviest single items for which the English exchequer was regularly responsible, since local revenues there accounted for under one-third of its peace-time cost and less than one-fifth in wartime.[63] In the 1440s the wages of the garrison were continuously in arrears and captains of Calais normally ended their periods of command severely out of pocket, but Somerset, with Henry's support, and contrary to York's allegations, had been unusually successful in securing appropriations and guarantees from the wool customs and lay subsidies for the current wages of a well-equipped garrison, which he had built up almost to war strength by 1453. Now no money reached Calais from England after July 1453. In February 1454 parliament refused to grant £40,000 requested for the garrison and York only succeeded in making less substantial, alternative arrangements for loans

[61] *P.P.C.*, VI, 206–7; P.R.O., E.28/85/49 (18 July).

[62] *P.P.C.*, VI, 218–19; P.R.O., E.28/85/59 (23 July); *P.P.C.*, VI, 216–17 and P.R.O., E.28/85/73 shows that those who had failed to appear for the 25 June great council had been ordered on 24 July to do so for the new one for 21 October.

[63] J. L. Kirby, 'The Financing of Calais under Henry V', *B.I.H.R.*, XXIII (1950), 166–8 (£11,000–£12,000 in peacetime, £19,000 in war). See G. L. Harriss, 'The Struggle for Calais, An Aspect of the Rivalry between Lancaster and York', *E.H.R.*, LXXV (1960), 30–53 for what follows.

from the Company of the Staple. But early in May, before he could
get his envoy Viscount Bourchier there, bearing 6,000 marks in cash,
the garrison mutinied and seized all the stocks of victuals and wool
in the town belonging to the Company of the Staple, in order to sell
them in lieu of their unpaid wages. The Protector, torn between the
outraged Merchants of the Staple, who alone could supply the cash
guarantees adequate to satisfy the garrison, and mutinous soldiers, who
refused to admit his emissaries, was reduced to legalizing the garrison's
sales of wool in August. But he was still ordering Somerset formally
to surrender his command on 4 November. Political and financial
factors thus combined to impede York's attempt to establish his control
over Calais and when Henry recovered his senses Somerset's captains,
Rivers and Welles, were still in command.

Henry's loss of his faculties had rescued York from a political
oblivion which might otherwise have been permanent. He had been
given the unexpected chance of establishing an ascendancy in the state
and, with a little further time, the outstanding problems of Calais would
no doubt have been resolved in his favour. But Henry was reported
fully restored to health in the first week of January 1455. Although
the end of his Protectorate cannot be precisely dated, the decisions
the king then took quickly dissolved all York's authority. York last
signed a council document on 30 December.[64] The royal sign manual
reappeared on an order for the removal of the duke of Exeter from
Pontefract to Wallingford castle on 3 February 1455.[65] The chancellor,
Richard Nevill, earl of Salisbury, who was also constable of Pontefract
castle, ignored it. Somerset was legally freed from the Tower on 4
February, although he may in fact already have been released on bail
on 26 January, at which point York is alleged to have resigned from
his protectorate. But another month passed before the political situation
was made crystal clear. At Greenwich on 4 March Henry personally
presided over a council meeting and repudiated all the charges of
treason against Somerset, declaring him to be his trusted servant and
loyal subject. He formally took the captaincy of Calais into his own
hands and then returned it to Somerset. He bound York and Somerset,
under bonds of 20,000 marks each, to keep the peace until 20 June,
to allow for an arbitration of several lords over what he once more
insisted on regarding as the purely personal disputes between them.
On 7 March Salisbury was dismissed, or resigned, as chancellor, being
replaced by the archbishop of Canterbury, Thomas Bourchier, a
resumption of the normal high ecclesiastical tradition of the office
which, until Salisbury's appointment during Henry's madness, had
been an unbroken one since 1412. On 13 March the new chancellor,

[64] P.R.O., C.18/1546/84a.
[65] P.R.O., E.28/86/1; *P.P.C.*, VI, 234.

under pain of forfeiture of 10,000 marks for non-compliance, was ordered to release the duke of Exeter from Pontefract, where he was now stated to be imprisoned due to 'sinister information made upon him by certain persons not well disposed'.[66] On 15 March the earl of Worcester was replaced as treasurer by the earl of Wiltshire, who had earlier vainly contended for York's lieutenancy of Ireland. Contemporary comment on how these changes were received is almost entirely lacking, except that Salisbury was reported to have resigned the great seal rather than agree to the release of Exeter.[67] Opinions vary as to when an alliance between York and the Nevills was finally cemented, but it was this alliance which now, within two months, enabled the demoted Protector to rise in successful armed rebellion to assassinate their respective enemies and rivals, Somerset and Northumberland, and to capture the king. Most likely it was these partisan decisions which Henry took immediately after his recovery, most notably the release of the duke of Exeter, which now gave Richard duke of York a substantial party in the state. In the 1440s the activities of Henry's household had associated the king with local factions. Now, in the uncertainties of his resumption of power, he was again associating himself with faction, this time on a national scale. He was thus uniting against himself all the opponents of those he favoured. It was this which now gave Richard duke of York the broader support and following which had been so conspicuously lacking at the time of his Dartford humiliation in 1452.

[66] The chronology of these changes has been elucidated by R. L. Griffiths in *Speculum*, XLIII (1968), 624–5; cf. C. A. J. Armstrong, 'Politics and the Battle of St Albans, 1455', *B.I.H.R.*, XXXIII (1960), 8–9.

[67] Giles's Chronicle, 47.

Part V

CIVIL WAR

Chapter 15

THE FIRST BATTLE OF ST ALBANS
AND ITS CONSEQUENCES

Whatever York, as Protector, had done in his own interests his protectorate had undoubtedly maintained and enhanced the royal power. But his imprisonment of Somerset and attempt to secure the office of Captain of Calais for himself had meant undoing decisions which had been Henry's own. Henry thus quite fittingly marked his resumption of royal power by taking this disputed office into his own hands, releasing Somerset and declaring him innocent of the charges against him. Forthwith restoring him to the Calais command was equally an act of legitimate royal authority, though perhaps an unwise one. The release of the militant duke of Exeter, Percy ally and proven Nevill enemy, was mindless and foolish, for it made clear Henry's personal belief that York, as Protector, had been bent on usurping the royal power in his own interest; that he regarded the rebellious Holand duke as loyal to the Lancastrian throne and acting merely against Plantagenet pretensions. It convinced the Nevills that Henry's restoration to health, if such it was, meant that their achievements in their struggle with the Percys were now all at risk. Acceptance of Salisbury's resignation from the chancellorship, or his actual dismissal to facilitate a return to the high ecclesiastical tradition of the office which Henry himself had hitherto maintained, was equally unwise. 'The steryng or moevyng of the male journey of Seynt Albones'[1] arose directly out of these royal decisions. It has now been thoroughly re-investigated by C. A. J. Armstrong, mainly relying not, as hitherto, on the well-known but partisan Yorkist account in English used by John Stow, but on two other little-known and neutral accounts in French, the 'Dijon Relation' and the 'Fastolf Relation'.[2] The indecisive, ambivalent actions which were characteristic of the king before the onset of his madness were now increasingly obvious and rapidly led to an armed clash and politically motivated assassinations in the main street of St Albans on 22 May 1455. This marked the beginning of the longest period of intermittent civil war in English history which, for want of a better title, and by long-established convention, we call the Wars of the Roses.

[1] *Paston Letters*, I, 345.
[2] 'Politics and the Battle of St Albans', *B.I.H.R.*, XXXIII (1960), 1–72, now the indispensable account of politics in 1455 and 1456.

If Henry did fully recover his wits in the New Year 1455, his political judgement was still as weak as it had been. His restoration of Somerset and Exeter to favour caused York, Salisbury and Warwick to flee the court early in March, resolved to form an alliance and, if necessary, to impose their will on him by force of arms. The king's reaction, to some extent, followed the lines of his moves to meet York's similar threat of 1451–2, but this time it was dilatory and lethargic, in contrast to the timely and successful counter-measures which had led to York's humiliation at Dartford. On 21 April 1455 a great council was summoned to assemble at Leicester for 21 May. According to York and his allies its declared purpose, as stated in the writs of summons to it, was to provide for the threatened safety of the king. This they took to be directed against themselves. Precisely what was intended cannot be ascertained. Imposition of the arbitration between York and Somerset, which Henry had ordered to be prepared by certain lords, was due by 20 June. Behind Somerset were both the king and the queen and the declaration of this award was probably intended to be made the occasion of some exemplary humiliation of York at the hands of the establishment, reminiscent of his public submission and oath-taking at the high altar of St Paul's after his failure to secure the dismissal of Somerset in 1452. Whatever was intended was to be staged in a hand-picked assembly in the queen's castle, town and honour of Leicester in the heart of the Lancastrian homelands. The writs, sent out on 21 April by special messengers to selected individuals in the shires, were designed to produce a nominated assembly of lords, knights and esquires, after the manner of a parliament, but with no burgesses and with no elections.[3] York and his friends must have recalled with apprehension the sinister precedent at Bury St Edmunds in 1447, when Duke Humphrey had been arrested, dutifully obeying a summons to a specially staged parliament. Although some bows and guns were ordered for what the exchequer later called the king's 'parliamentary journey' of May 1455[4] timely, efficient preparations and precautions for it on the pattern of 1447 and 1452 were unaccountably not repeated. It seems that Henry, possibly relying on York's earlier solemn public undertaking never again to attempt anything by way of force, at first considered that no show of military power would be necessary. Urgent messages requiring troops from the city of Coventry were not sent out until 18 May.[5] Similar, last-minute, military summonses to various

[3] The resulting assembly can hardly be considered anti-'Yorkist', but it consisted of men handpicked for their loyalty, stability and substance. Of 45 shire nominees identifiable in a surviving list of those sent privy seal writs of summons for 21 May and dated 21 April, 14 were household members, 35 had sat in previous parliaments, 34 were justices of the peace and 25 had been sheriffs (*P.P.C.*, VI, 339–42).
[4] P.R.O., E.404/70/3/2, 71/pt.1/57.   [5] *Coventry Leet Book*, 247–8.

lords, rather than reluctance of the nobility to support the king, probably explains the late arrival at St Albans, after the battle, of a number of magnate contingents. The need to meet at Leicester was itself an admission of weakness, only partially due to Somerset's unpopularity in London, and to the queen's dominance of Henry, since it repeated Henry's own reaction both to the impeachment of Suffolk and to the Cade rebels in 1450. It foreshadowed the semi-permanent withdrawal of the king and court to areas assumed to have the greatest loyalty in the few remaining years of his dynasty from August 1456.

The decision to hold this punitive assembly had been taken at an earlier, select great council meeting, to which York and the Nevills had not been summoned, held at Westminster in April, round about the date when the writs were sent out for the Leicester assembly. This later drew justifiable protests from them at the 'jelosy had ayenst us'. Preparing their army in the north, they were made exactly aware of the king's intended movements by the writs of summons which they did receive to the proposed Leicester assembly. Accordingly they planned to intercept Henry at St Albans on his way to Leicester. As in February 1452, Henry followed up the writs to the dissident lords with personal emissaries, one of whom was Salisbury's son-in-law, the ex-treasurer of the protectorate, John Tiptoft, earl of Worcester, to persuade them to attend peaceably at Leicester. York detained these envoys until his forces were well on their way towards the king, to preserve secrecy about his movements. Finally, on 19 May, the new chancellor was ordered to prepare letters under the great seal to York, Norfolk, Salisbury and Warwick warning them that they would be treated as traitors and public enemies if they did not disband almost all their followers. York could keep 200 and the others 160 each.

Henry did not leave Westminster for Leicester until 21 May, the appointed day of assembly. He was overtaken at 10 a.m. at Kilburn, some four miles on his way, by a messenger from the chancellor, forwarding a petitionary letter which he had received from York and the Nevills, probably their reply to his threat to treat them as traitors. It had been signed and sealed by them at Royston in Hertfordshire the day before. In it they complained of their omission from the Westminster council of the previous month and the consequent, invidious nature of the proposed Leicester assembly. They demanded on behalf of their followers that the chancellor should publicly excommunicate the traitors about the king and, as head of justice in the land, summon a truly representative council. On these conditions they would lay down their arms. That day they advanced to Ware, only fifteen miles from St Albans, and from there York sent his confessor, William Willeflete, with a second letter, direct to Henry, reaffirming their loyalty, asserting that they were only coming to protect him from his enemies and enclosing a copy of their previous letter to the chancellor. Willeflete reached the royal quarters at Watford, seven miles south of St Albans, at 2 a.m. on Thursday 22 May, and handed his communication to the earl of Devon.

Soon after the king and his company left Watford, en route for St Albans, where he intended to have his dinner that day, they were halted by another messenger who informed them that York and his associates were already close at hand, with forces superior to his own. They had in fact taken up positions in the countryside about St Albans at 7 o'clock that morning. Divided counsels now ensued in the royal company. Prudent advice, presumably Somerset's, to stand and fortify themselves where they were, was rejected. Henry, with his customary waywardness, now summarily removed the duke of Somerset from the office of constable and put the temporizing duke of Buckingham in charge of the whole army. This meant accepting Buckingham's contrary advice to proceed to St Albans as intended. The new constable was confident that York and his associates would not fight, and would be willing to negotiate with him and certain bishops who had been summoned to the royal host, but had not yet arrived. Henry, it appears, had set out with only one senior ecclesiastic in his company, the Percy bishop of Carlisle, hardly likely to be a mediator acceptable to his family's Nevill adversaries. When Henry arrived at St Albans, probably about 9 o'clock, he certainly had with him the more distinguished part of the nobility – two dukes and their heirs, four earls and six barons, together with his normal household establishment – but the ensuing conflict suggests that some of these were lukewarm for a fight. York, with only his thirteen-year-old son, the earl of March, the two Nevill earls, Salisbury and Warwick, Henry, Viscount Bourchier, and his son Humphrey, the later Lord Cromwell, nevertheless had the greater and superior fighting force.

It must be assumed that Henry, in spite of having accepted Buckingham's assurances that negotiations not hostilities would ensue, was nevertheless prepared for a fight when he reached St Albans, since he did not make for his usual quarters in the abbey but took up a position and raised his banner in the centre of the town, at Goslaw in St Peter's Street, the better to direct operations. After a provocative and futile defiance, sent to York by Somerset through the duke of Exeter's pursuivant Lesparre, threatening forfeiture if he and his fellowship did not depart, courteous and elaborate negotiations did indeed follow. They were conducted through Buckingham herald on the one part and Mowbray herald on the other, although Mowbray's master, the duke of Norfolk, was not himself present in the Yorkist host. By that time York and his allies were assembled on the Kay field, situated within crossbow range, to the east of the town. There can be no certainty

17. Creation of Edward, the king's first-born son, as prince of Wales and earl of Chester in Parliament, 15 March 1454, signed by twenty-two lords spiritual and temporal including Richard duke of York.

18. Queen Margaret writes in kingly style under her signet and sign manual to Exeter Cathedral Chapter to reinforce Henry's commands, 7 November 1457.

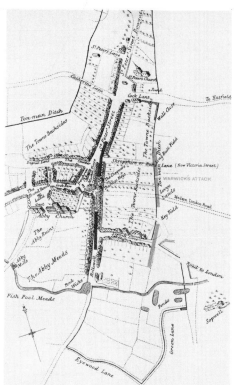

19(a). First battle of St Albans. The two superimposed dark blocks in Hollowell Street and St Peter's Street show the positions of the king's forces. The three lighter blocks to the east show the original position of York's forces who attacked along Sopwell Lane and Butts Lane and across the Town Backsides in the centre, where Warwick first penetrated the king's position between the Cross Keys and the Chequers.

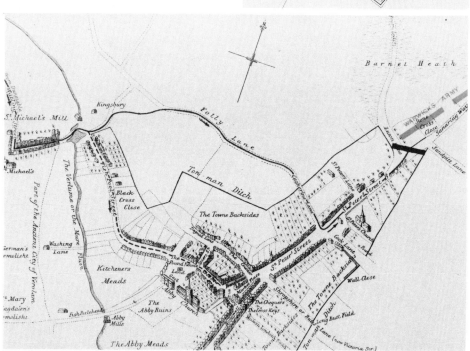

19(b). Second battle of St Albans. The lighter superimposed blocks show Warwick's encampment on Barnet Heath and an outpost of archers in Frenchrow in the town centre. The dotted line represents the first advance of Queen Margaret's troops up Fish Pool Street and Cook Row which was repulsed by the archers. The solid line along Folly Lane and Catherine Lane into St Peter's Street represents their second, successful advance through the town to Bowgate from where they turned Warwick's flank and began the rout of his army.

(a). Henry VI, swan and antelope, from Writhe's Garter Memorial (B.L. Add. MS 37340, f. IV).

(b). Richard duke of York, falcon and fetter-lock, from Fenn's Book of Badges (B.L. Add. MS 40742, f. 5).

(c). Gold and white enamel swan pendant livery badge of Margaret of Anjou, found near the battlefield of St Albans.

that all the messages which York now sent to Henry did reach him; the blatant official exoneration and justification of their treasonable acts, which York and his supporters forced upon the ensuing July parliament, baldly laid the blame for everything on three individuals, Somerset, Thomas Thorpe and William Joseph, who, it was claimed, intercepted and concealed vital communications. But negotiations clearly failed because of stubbornness on both sides. York would not accept Buckingham's fundamental proposal to retire for a night to Barnet or Hatfield and to appoint at least one noble plenipotentiary to talk on his behalf. On the other hand Mowbray herald, who did reach the royal presence, still found that this availed him nothing, because Henry simply referred him back to the duke of Buckingham. In the final resort Buckingham himself could only reply to York's increasingly pressing demands for a reply from Henry's own lips that the king was not disposed to give him any answer. According to the Yorkist 'Stow Relation', York's demands included the delivery to him of 'such as we wol accuse' and Henry sent back the answer that, rather than deliver any lord present with him, he would live or die for their sakes in that quarrel, that day. This is clearly a speech made up by the 'relator', but the king's well-attested silence in effect did mean no more and no less than that.[6]

The first battle of St Albans is remembered as a short, sharp 'affray in a street', St Peter's Street, and the central market place, perhaps of no more than half an hour's duration, once the insurgents had broken through the barriers set up around the unwalled town in three or four different places. The preliminary assault lasted perhaps an hour or so. Scattered fighting and much looting continued possibly for one or two hours after the main engagement. The defeated were despoiled of all their possessions and ransomed like Frenchmen, but for the principals the fight was over when Somerset, who had taken refuge in a house, was deliberately cut down as he tried to make a fighting exit. As soon as possible York secured the king's person and removed him to the safety of the abbey. The slaying of the earl of Northumberland and the aggressive Lord Clifford may have been deliberate Nevill action, but equally may have been accidental. Henry himself, standing almost alone by his overturned banner, by chance received a slight flesh wound in the shoulder or neck. Hardly more than forty were slain, among whom were a high proportion of household men, which tends to disprove the charge of cowardice levied against those around the king. Many of these received wounds on the face, neck, arm and hand, suggesting that, as one contemporary account relates, the king's entourage did not fully arm themselves until the attackers burst in upon them. The general Lancastrian incompetence in the conduct of the

[6] *Paston Letters*, I, 328-9.

fight must be laid on Henry's own shoulders, but perhaps also, some of them were indeed lukewarm about fighting at all, for the earl of Devon and Lord Fauconberg, and a number of other former associates of York, present in the royal company, may not have been enthusiastic in defending Somerset. Only the wounded Buckingham and the earl of Wiltshire among the great, both of whom took refuge in the abbey, were pursued by York. Wiltshire escaped in disguise, but the arrogant York compelled Henry to order Buckingham's surrender, under threat of violation of sanctuary.

Thus York had finally achieved by force of arms in half an hour what in politics had painfully eluded him for the last five years: the elimination of his chief political rival, the head of the legitimized Beaufort house, and control of the king's person. Had Henry himself perished in the fight, with or without Somerset, York's cause, whatever it was, would have been irretrievably lost, for apart from the odium of regicide there would have been only the prospect of a second long minority before him in which Queen Margaret, no more his friend than Henry himself, would almost certainly have played a major role.[7] Moreover, as time was to demonstrate, however great Henry's own limitations as king, none of York's principal associates ever saw him as the alternative.

There is no record of the effect on Henry of the trauma of the battle-field, which at the age of thirty-three was still unknown to him. Standing by his banner, set down and abandoned by its bearer, variously reported to be his carver, Sir Philip Wentworth, his steward, Lord Sudeley, and the treasurer, Wiltshire, with his household men being cut down around him, he must have anticipated for himself the fate shortly to be meted out to Somerset. If shock had indeed caused the original onset of his illness, a further relapse now seemed most probable and he was certainly sick again within the fortnight. Moreover, the physician Gilbert Kemer, summoned from Salisbury to attend him at Windsor on 5 June, was assumed to know the nature of his illness.[8] From the end of the battle until the day in parliament the following February when he personally terminated York's second spell as Protector and Defender of the Realm and principal councillor,[9] Henry was in any case now more or less a puppet in the hands of York and his associates. The day after the battle they escorted him back to London, York riding on his right, Salisbury on his left and Warwick ahead, bearing his sword. Before lodging him in the bishop of London's palace that same evening they paraded him through the streets of the capital,

[7] Cf. Armstrong, *op. cit.*, 42–8.
[8] See above, p. 272.
[9] *R.P.*, V, 321–2 (25 February 1456). York became Protector again on 19 November 1455.

ostentatiously showing him all possible honour and deference, as from completely loyal subjects. On the Sunday, Whitsunday, they staged a crown-wearing in St Paul's where, apparently at his own insistence, Henry received his crown from York's hands.[10] New dispositions of offices were already known in the capital that same day; York had taken the constableship of England and Warwick the captaincy of Calais, though he found himself refused admission by the garrison there, as previously York had been. Their other noble associate, the chancellor's brother, Viscount Bourchier, took the treasurership in place of the fugitive Wiltshire. The three leaders, with the earl of Devon, now 'kept the roialte and sport' for the whole week and a proclamation, made in Henry's name, forbade all talk about the battle.

York had now to try to consolidate their position by means of a parliament. Writs of summons were promptly issued on Whitmonday. Meantime Henry was first moved to Windsor and then to Hertford castle, with the queen and infant prince, until the parliament assembled on 9 July. York at nearby Ware kept a close eye on him, with Salisbury at The Rye, seat of York's councillor Sir Andrew Ogard, and Warwick only a few miles away with Sir William Oldhall, whose forfeiture had just been reversed, at his residence at Hunsdon.[11] They considered it essential that Henry himself should be made to open the parliament and special payments made to three surgeons for their great labour and care to the king's person at this time probably indicate successful efforts to make him presentable for the occasion.[12] That Henry realized his own limitations at this time is clear, because on 12 July he made over to Wainfleet and John Chedworth, bishop of Lincoln, the oversight, correction and reformation of the statutes of his two beloved colleges for the rest of his natural life, a task which he had hitherto personally supervised.[13]

York had been supported at St Albans by only a tiny, though powerful, minority of the peerage. The backing of a substantial concourse of peers in the assembly was almost as vital as that the king should be seen to preside over it. Henry's chief supporter in the battle, the duke of Buckingham, had since been bound over under substantial bonds to support them; even Wiltshire was summoned, though without success. A superficially respectable total for the first session was achieved, but including the unique number of 18 abbots and 2 priors out of a possible total of 27 religious, together with the 2 archbishops

[10] Armstrong, *op. cit.*, 51, 54; Benet's Chronicle, 214.

[11] Armstrong, *op. cit.*, 26, 54; *Paston Letters*, I, 334, 335–6; P.R.O., E.28/86, 6 June 1455.

[12] Issue Roll E.403/801, m.7 dated 16 July, cited by J. R. Lander, 'The Duke of York's Second Protectorate, 1455–1456', *B.J.R.L.*, XLIII (1960), 51, n. 4.

[13] *Ancient Laws*, 623–4, but wrongly dated there to 1445, not 1455.

and 11 bishops. Sixty lords spiritual and temporal took a personal oath of allegiance to Henry on 24 July. Each of the temporal lords, led by York, took him by the hand in turn, but there were only 27 of them out of a possible total of 53. After the end of the second session, on 11 December, 65 out of the total of 100 peers who had been summoned were sent writs of privy seal warning them that their absences had been noted and commanding them under threat of severe and unprecedented penalties to attend at the next session fixed for 14 January.[14] For the Commons also there was no great enthusiasm to be elected.[15] The names of 204 elected members of this parliament are known, compared with 278 for the 1453-4 assembly. It is difficult to say how successful 'Yorkist' electoral management at this election was. There had been 'besy labor made in sondry wises by certain persones' (unnamed) to get their nominees elected in Kent.[16] But whether these efforts had any connection with central politics is impossible to determine. Kent elected Sir Gervase Clifton, who was to lose his head for his support of Queen Margaret at Tewkesbury, and Sir Thomas Kyriell, whom she beheaded for treason in support of the earls at St Albans in 1461. The duchess of Norfolk considered it very necessary that this time knights of the shire for the county should be her husband's 'menyal servants' and his two nominees, John Howard and Sir Roger Chamberlain, were duly returned, albeit with much local resentment about Howard because he was a stranger to the shire.[17] Predictably this parliament did contain very many fewer members of Henry's household, only 26 compared with 61 in the previous 1453-4 assembly.

The parliament duly opened on 9 July with Henry on his throne and York most prominent as the principal trier of petitions for England, Wales, Ireland and Scotland. Its proceedings were given an unusual air of businesslike efficiency by the appointment of five separate committees to see to the rule and financing of the royal household, the financial needs of Calais and Berwick, the keeping of the seas, the retention of bullion within the kingdom and the suppression of disorder in Wales. Two other subjects were also generally to be considered: how to employ the 13,000 archers granted by the previous parliament and how to secure harmony among all the lords of the land.[18] But the primary work of the assembly was to accept and approve a specious

---

[14] See J. S. Roskell in *B.I.H.R.*, XXIX (1956), 193-5.

[15] 'Sum men holde it right straunge to be in this Parlement and me thenketh they be wyse men that soo doo': John Jenny to John Paston, 24 June 1455 (*Paston Letters*, I, 340-1).

[16] *P.P.C.*, VI, 246-7.

[17] *Paston Letters*, I, 337, 340, 341-2.

[18] *R.P.*, V, 279-80.

justification of the treasonable actions of York, Warwick and Salisbury
and all their supporters, in giving the king battle at St Albans. This
was urgently presented on 18 July after Warwick and Cromwell had
publicly quarrelled the previous day over who had been responsible.
Henry's general pardon of Easter 1452 had proved to be ineffective
as protection for the Dartford rebels. Another was now issued, but
an additional 'parliamentary pardon', by legislation, was designed as
the better way of giving the perpetrators of St Albans full legal protection against everybody, including the king. The spurious history of
events recounted in it does not bear examination. It was only made
acceptable, in spite of bitter feeling in many quarters,[19] by the device
of heaping the entire blame on three scapegoats: the dead Somerset,
York's enemy Thomas Thorpe and the insignificant William Joseph
of the royal household.[20] Before the end of the first session, on 31 July,
a petition got up in the Commons to rehabilitate the memory of
Humphrey duke of Gloucester by proclamation, declared him to have
been Henry's true subject, in life and death. Thus York henceforth
identified himself with a growing tradition of the good Duke Humphrey
as patron of loyal opponents of Lancastrian misrule, falsely accused
of treason.[21]

A further act of resumption, presented early in the parliament,[22]
but only accepted in modified form towards the end, after Henry had
terminated York's second protectorate, gives some reliable indication
of the Commons' temper. In its original form it sought yet another
annulment of Henry's grants from the coming Michaelmas 1455. It
was markedly less respectful to the House of Lancaster than earlier
acts, requesting the resumption of all duchy of Lancaster lands put
in feoffment to perform their wills, either by Henry or his father. This,
if accepted, would thus have anticipated Edward IV's disendowment
of Eton and King's Colleges. All reversionary grants of Humphrey
duke of Gloucester's offices, now alleged to have been obtained by
members of the court in anticipation of his early demise, were to be
annulled, together with certain life grants of royal offices in Ireland,
now established as York's own special sphere of influence. The
exemption proposed for Queen Margaret slightingly specified that what
she already had should not be exceeded; no exemption at all was
requested for Henry's Tudor half-brothers. Penalties of the Statute
of Provisors were to be invoked against anyone accepting a grant
contrary to the act after Michaelmas, with a 1,000-mark forfeiture
imposed for every offence. The Commons themselves were to have

[19] Armstrong, op. cit., 61; Paston Letters, I, 346.
[20] R.P., V, 280–2, 283–4; Armstrong, op. cit., 58–62.
[21] R.P., V, 335a; Armstrong, op. cit., 62.
[22] R.P., V, 300–3.

the right to veto any exemptions, which were to be proposed only during the lifetime of the parliament. The survival of many petitions for exemption, but with the decisions of the 'lords spiritual and temporal' rather than the Commons upon them, shows that a further thorough reduction of annuities and pensions still held by household members and others was indeed intended under this act.[23] However, it had not received the royal assent when Henry removed York from his second protectorate in February 1456, on which observers considered its fate depended.

When the prorogued parliament reassembled on 12 November 1455 it found that Henry was not there to open it and that York had been appointed his lieutenant to do so in his name only the day before.[25] Henry had been returned to Hertford castle towards the end of August and reports were about in London at the end of October that he was once more incapacitated.[26] York, Warwick and Salisbury were still spoken of as in control of his movements and probably had intended to bring him back to Westminster formally to preside over the assembly once more. This was not to be. On the second day of the session the Commons began to petition the lords through their Speaker to appoint York Protector again, as previously when Henry had lost his wits. How could their constituents know whom to petition otherwise, they asked, and alarming riots in the West Country between Courtenay and Bonville followers, they maintained, clearly showed the need for a punitive force under royal command. It is not impossible that York put them up to it, but the mere absence of Henry, without any explanation given, is really sufficient in itself to explain the Commons' alarm. They repeated their petition two days later, and as soon as Speaker Burley had left, the lords did elect York as Protector for the second time. But he protested his unworthiness and required time to formulate his conditions. After the weekend Burley was back again, repeating the request and asking for adjournment of the parliament so that York and other lords could leave urgently to settle the disturbed West Country. He had to wait a further two days before York's conditions had been drawn up. These included the nomination of a new council, a guarantee that they should be paid for their attendance, a substantial,

[23] There are some 30 examples of such reductions in P.R.O., S.C.8/28, 105, 117, 124, 138, 141 and C.49/61, 63, 64, 65. The family of the dead Somerset, Henry Holand, duke of Exeter, Lord Cromwell and Sir Thomas Stanley were conspicuous losers under the act. The chief beneficiary, as it turned out, was the infant prince of Wales.

[24] *Paston Letters*, I, 378, 9 February 1456; 'The resumption, men truste, shall forthe, and my Lordes of Yorkes first power of protectorship stande, and elles not' (John Bocking to Sir John Fastolf).

[25] *R.P.*, V, 284.

[26] *Paston Letters*, I, 352.

guaranteed salary, with a down payment of 1,000 marks in advance, for himself and a new guarantee of tenure. He would no longer accept an appointment during royal pleasure. It now had to be until he should be relieved of it by the king in parliament, on the advice of the lords spiritual and temporal. Subject to three extra safeguards over salary and tenure, he accepted the office from 19 November 1455 and his patent clearly stated that the cause was once again the sickness with which it had pleased the Almighty to inflict the king. Involvement in affairs of state would prevent his recovery.

There are thus no grounds for believing that Henry was not once again seriously ill with his original complaint: the terms on which York was again made Protector and Defender of the Realm and the king's principal councillor, as well as the cause stated, were identical, except for his extra conditions, with those of March 1454. Moreover, once again the really long-term possibility that it might be the infant prince of Wales who ultimately relieved York of his office when he reached years of discretion and not Henry, was envisaged and allowed for.[27] One new step was taken. On 22 November the governance of the realm was formally committed to the council and the record of it enrolled on the parliament roll, together with York's patent. Henry's inability to govern was thus confirmed, along with his inability to perform the formal duties of kingship. Yet Henry's transference of governmental powers to the council, for which there was no precedent in 1453-4, does indicate that he was still capable of some action at that stage. Moreover, it did contain one reservation: 'in all such matters as touch the honour, worship and surety of his [Henry's] most noble person they shall let his Highness have knowledge what direction they take in them'.[28] This does suggest that the loss of his faculties this time, though serious enough, was something less than total and that he was himself conscious of his limitations. The councillors, headed by York as principal councillor, began to sign official acts on 19 November, as had been customary during the minority and the first protectorate.[29] Henceforth appointments were no longer made by the succinct royal formula 'during pleasure', but by the cumbersome but significant 'until he be removed by advice of the lords spiritual and temporal of our council for the time being because of reasonable offence in the exercise of the said office proved before the said lords'.[30] The council, not the Protector, was henceforth, in theory, the supreme power in the land. There are some signs during the few remaining years of

[27] R.P., V, 284-9, cf. ibid., 242-4.
[28] Ibid., 289-90.
[29] P.R.O., E.28/87/3.
[30] P.R.O., E.28/87/29A, inserted into a grant of 16 December (cf. C.P.R., 1452-1461, 276).

the reign that Henry did at times exert his will on the conduct of affairs, but the council's delegated powers were never formally rescinded. Although the royal sign manual reappeared on documents from 16 March 1456,[31] signatures of the council members meeting in Star Chamber did continue to appear intermittently until the end of the reign. Perhaps most significantly, there is no contemporary notice at any time of Henry's subsequent full return to health.

There is no record of when Henry was moved from Hertford to Westminster, but he was there at hand in the palace on 25 February 1456.On that day he appeared in the parliament chamber and, following to the letter the terms agreed for York's dismissal, relieved him of his protectorate – in parliament, with the advice and assent of the assembled lords, ordering him no longer to meddle with the office.[32] What caused this exertion is explained in Benet's chronicle. The occasion was the passage of the controversial resumption act being ardently pressed for by York and the Commons. Almost all the lords present were against it and they fetched in Henry as the only superior authority to prevent its passage, at which York resigned his office and left the parliament.[33] Divided opinions in the upper chamber over this punitive resumption act would be consistent with John Bocking's letter of 9 February.[34] In fact, a compromise measure was now given the royal assent.[35] York lost his title, but not immediately his employment. The final act of resumption specifically rejected the proposed penalties of Provisors and forfeiture; Henry reserved his prerogative in all things, with the right to make whatever exemptions he pleased, by advice of the lords during the life of the parliament (143 exemptions followed). Exemption for his own enfeoffments for Eton and King's College and for Queen Margaret were to be complete, except that she was to surrender and be compensated for any lands which should belong to the prince of Wales's inheritance. This was to be preserved intact for him until he reached the age of fourteen. The Tudor half-brothers were also fully exempted. There was to be no question of submitting the exemptions to the Commons. This act of resumption is therefore further evidence that Henry was again briefly active in government at this point. Reductions in the exemption petitions imposed by the 'lords spiritual and temporal' were not rescinded, though some of them were subsequently regranted. Likewise a much reduced provision of grant for his household at £3,943 19s 4¾d, made some time before 1 January 1456 for the twelve months to 30 September 1456, was

[31] P.R.O., C.81/1546/89C.
[32] R.P., V, 321–2.
[33] Benet's Chronicle, 216.
[34] See above, p. 298, n. 24.
[35] R.P., V, 303–20.

not altered, suggesting that the severe establishment reduction of 1454[36] had indeed been carried out.

The political circumstances at the opening of this third, post-Christmas session of this parliament are fortunately described in the Paston Letters, which henceforth provide almost the only insight into politics and government for the rest of the reign. On Monday 9 February 1456 an apprehensive York and Warwick arrived before any other lords with substantial numbers of followers, in martial array. On the previous Saturday the writer (John Bocking to Sir John Fastolf) had heard that York would be discharged from office on arrival and he thought he would have been 'distrussid' (distressed) had he not arrived in force. But Henry, it seems, was in fact disposed to keep him on, again an indication that he realized his own limitations. However, he was now to be only principal councillor, not Protector, called chief councillor and lieutenant. This was what happened and it was not to the queen's liking. Bocking also referred to Queen Margaret as a 'grete and stronge labourid woman, for she spareth noo peyne to sue hire thinges to an intent and conclusion to hir power'.[37]

Henry had been ill in varying degrees since St Albans. There was talk that his wound received there had done permanent damage. During the first two sessions of the parliament, the first of which he had formally presided over, the second of which he could not, York, Warwick and Salisbury had maintained control of him. He had now asserted himself in February 1456, which meant changes, but the history of the remaining five years of the reign suggest that henceforth political life consisted of struggles to manipulate him; that his mental if not his physical health was henceforth precarious and his periods of effectiveness few and far between. Until the middle of August there was no sudden change in the direction of affairs of state. York's loss of the protectorate did not mean dismissal for himself or his principal associates, Salisbury and Warwick. They continued as councillors. In contrast to his treatment of York in the spring of 1455 Henry did not now dismiss Warwick as Captain of Calais. Indeed Warwick, who was still being 'obstinately kept out'[38] of Calais, in spite of apparently satisfactory financial arrangements ultimately agreed with the Staple merchants for payment of the soldiers' wages,[39] only secured admission

---

[36] *Ibid.*, 320. This parliament, in giving formal livery of the duchy of Cornwall, principality of Wales and earldom of Chester to the prince, stipulated that the contributions made from these revenues to the royal household expenses must continue (*ibid.*, 294).

[37] *Paston Letters*, I, 377–8.

[38] *R.P.*, V, 341.

[39] P.R.O., C.81/1546/89a, b (27 and 31 October 1455).

there in April 1456, after commissioners to give satisfaction to the rebellious garrison had been sent in March.[40] In fact he owed his admission to Calais to Henry's recovered ability to act in affairs of state. Henry approved the arrangements on 16 March with the issue of a full pardon under his sign manual to the garrison of Calais, their agents and factors, for all their illegal acts in seizing and selling the Staplers' wool and authorized the treasurer of Calais to issue individual pardons to all concerned.[41]

On 16 May it was rumoured in London that Henry himself would march against the Scots.[42] In fact it was York who was employed, as though he was still Protector, to lead an army north against James II of Scotland who had declared war, broken the truce and brazenly offered York support in asserting a claim to the throne.[43] On 28 June, writing to Charles VII, he had declared his belief that York was the rightful king of England,[44] thus indubitably revealing how widespread such notions were, even if hardly mentioned in England, or entertained by York himself. In face of this threat of foreign invasion a vehement and contemptuous defiance under the great seal was sent to James in Henry's name from Windsor on 26 July and another by York on 24 August when he reached Durham. York's appearance in the North was sufficient to cause James to retire from Northumberland.[45]

In the summer of 1456, therefore, the feeble-minded king, while reasserting his nominal rule, seems at last to have admitted the advisability of employing York in a prominent role in the government of the realm. For a king who was no longer able to govern or lead his armies in the field, this was a most sensible decision, even a generous one, considering York's earlier defiance of his wishes to chose his own advisers, and the hurt he had received at his hands. But round about 17 August all was now changed by the actions of the rash and despotic queen. She either persuaded her husband to remove himself, or carried him off, to her castle of Kenilworth, where the defences were strengthened with cannon and other implements of war against his rival.[46] A considerable battery of twenty-six new field guns (serpentines), a culverin and other armaments were further added in the spring.[47]

[40] P.R.O., E.404/70/3/44 (16 March 1456).

[41] P.R.O., C.81/1546/89c, authenticated by the sign manual only; C.81/1546/89d dated 1 May 1456 repeated with the sign manual and 7 council signatures including Salisbury's.

[42] Paston Letters, I, 388.

[43] Correspondence of Bekynton, II, 139–41; Devon, Issues, 480–1.

[44] Stevenson, Wars, I, 323.

[45] Foedera, XI, 383; Correspondence of Bekynton, II, 142–4; Ramsay, Lancaster and York, II, 195.

[46] Devon, Issues, 481.

[47] Ibid., 482.

Henceforward it is difficult to believe that there was any conscious, identifiable purpose of Henry's own behind his different movements. It is out of the question that he was simply being taken down to sport in the Midlands, away from the unruly Londoners, as Ramsay suggested.[48] For one thing the establishment of the court at Coventry was marked by a complete change in the great offices. The two Bourchier brothers, archbishop and viscount, lost their posts, Bishop Wainfleet of Winchester becoming chancellor and the Talbot marcher earl of Shrewsbury treasurer. Margaret's own chancellor, Laurence Booth, was given the key central administrative office of keeper of the privy seal on 24 September and made bishop of Durham when Salisbury's brother Robert Nevill died in July 1457.[49] Contemporary opinion blamed the queen for these developments. At Oxford Thomas Gascoigne wrote that it was all her doing: she had had Henry removed for safe keeping to her seat 'in Cheshire'.[50] From this point, Gascoigne continues, Queen Margaret conducted the affairs of the kingdom at her will, by right means or wrong, not caring which, as various people said: 'What will be the end of it God knows'. Gascoigne died in March 1458. Queen Margaret was not prepared to see York's employment continued and reacted accordingly. The Paston Letters reveal that she had been in the Midlands all the summer with the infant prince, at Tutbury on 15 May, when another battle on the St Albans pattern was rumoured;[51] at Chester on 7 June, when York had been at Sandal in Yorkshire. Each of them was then said to be watching for a move from the other.[52]

Professor Storey has recently produced another explanation for Henry's withdrawal from the southern part of his kingdom. He sees it as a response to new armed risings, this time in Wales, by York's Welsh tenants, which revived Henry's fears about York's intentions. If York was not personally involved, after Dartford and St Albans it was natural to think that he was. Sir Walter Devereux of Weobly, York's tenant and constable of his castle of Wigmore, had raised and held the city of Hereford in support of York's Dartford expedition and had been indicted of treason there before Somerset and his fellow

---

[48] *Lancaster and York*, II, 198–9.

[49] *H.B.C.*, 85, 92, 93, 221: 24 September (Booth), 5 October (Shrewsbury), 11 October (Wainfleet).

[50] Thomas Gascoigne's theological dictionary (*Loci et Libro Veritatum*, ed. J. E. Thorold Rogers, Oxford 1881), 214, sub 'Regnum Angliae': 'regina traxit ad locum mansionis suae, in comitatu Chestyr'. The editor suggests that for the ecclesiastic Gascoigne the diocese of Coventry and Lichfield, commonly called the bishopric of Chester in the fifteenth century, explains this reference. Henry was at Lichfield 29 August–8 September and entered Coventry with the queen on 14 September.

[51] *Paston Letters*, I, 387.

[52] *Ibid.*, 392–3.

commissioners during Henry's punitive visit in August 1452.[53] He had
been arraigned there a second time, before Lord Audley and William
Yelverton on 20 July 1453, when he pleaded the 1452 pardon which
he had meantime purchased. After the Yorkist victory at St Albans,
a special act of parliament affirmed its validity.[54] But at Easter 1456
he was involved, with his son-in-law Sir William Herbert of Raglan,
the future Yorkist earl of Pembroke, in the intimidation of a coroner
at Bradwardine and of the king's justices at Hereford. Here they
imprisoned the mayor and held the city a second time for several days
over the murder of one Walter Vaughan. They compelled the unfortunate justices there to pronounce death sentences on several
allegedly innocent Hereford men, whom they then proceeded to hang.
On 8 August 1456 they assembled a considerable force at Hereford,
stated to number 2,000 men, and on the 10th marched on Carmarthen
and Aberystwyth castles. These they took by assault, imprisoning
Henry's Tudor half-brother Edmund, whom they found at Carmarthen, and at Aberystwyth they seized Robert ap Rees, the keeper of
the seal of the principality. This they used to appoint themselves as
a royal commission, holding sessions and freeing felons and malefactors.
There was conflict over the control of these two castles. York had
now taken over Somerset's posts of constable there, but had been as yet
unable to expel Somerset's Welsh deputy, Griffith ap Nicholas. A petition
accepted by the 1455 parliament from Griffith ap David ap Thomas,
who had fallen foul of Somerset's deputy and been imprisoned by him,
authorized York to expel him from these castles after the end of
February 1456, but meantime Henry granted them to his half-brother
Jasper earl of Pembroke, before York could take possession.[55] In August
York was in arms in the border country opposing the Scots, dutifully
facing the nation's external enemies in the place of his unmartial and
enfeebled king. These disturbances in Wales may have appeared to
be the acts of his subordinates, committed with his approval, and it
is possible that news of their seizure of the Welsh castles reaching
London did cause the feeble Henry to lose his new-found trust in York
and withdraw for safety to the queen and prince at Kenilworth. He
had certainly never been prone to trust him for long, or to give him
the benefit of the doubt. Whatever the immediate cause of Henry's
withdrawal from the south, whether he fled to the queen's protection,

[53] See R. L. Storey, *The End of the House of Lancaster*, 178–82, 228–30; R. A. Griffiths,
'Gruffyd Ap Nicholas and the Fall of the House of Lancaster', *The Welsh History Review*,
II (1965), 224ff, and H. T. Evans, *Wales and the Wars of the Roses* (Cambridge 1915),
96ff, for the rest of this paragraph.
[54] *R.P.*, V, 342.
[55] *C.P.R., 1452–1461*, 340; P.R.O., S.C.8/115/5703 as cited by Professor Storey, *op.
cit.*, 179.

or she had him carried off there, the result was the same. His retreat to Kenilworth and Coventry proved to be semi-permanent.

August 1456 began a complete change in Henry's pattern of movements. Windsor, Sheen, Eltham and Kennington, Eton, Winchester and Canterbury now saw him no more. The court took up residence in the Midlands. Westminster palace alone, save for the occasional transit stay at Berkhamsted, and at the queen's manor of Greenwich, housed him on his one or two visits south. His itinerary over the next four years cannot be continuously plotted in detail, possibly partly due to a chance absence of household accounts, but also due to the severely diminished level of government business, less even than during his first madness. The government of the realm had been largely abandoned. From mid-August 1456 until Salisbury and Warwick took him into custody at the battle of Northampton on 10 July 1460, even without counting occasions when a monastery provided a convenient night's lodging in transit, he now spent fully one-third of his time in abbeys and priories.[56] There was no precedent for a king thus spending so much time in religious houses, except for the solitary example during the financial crisis of 1433–4 when, as a boy of twelve, the council had put him in the care of the abbot and prior of Bury from Christmas to Easter. The comparative seclusion and time-absorbing ritual of monastic life now became especially attractive and congenial to him and at the same time eased the financial straits of the fugitive royal household, largely cut off from its normal sources of supply. Queen Margaret's castles of Kenilworth, refortified and refurbished with new ordnance, and, to a lesser extent, Leicester, were the royal residences used. Specific contemporary references to his state of health in these years are rare, but in 1457 there was mention of the inordinate amount of sleep he had required since St Albans[57] and the Crowland chronicler, who in 1460 closely observed him in his own abbey, in retreat from the world during Lent, aptly remarked that he had fallen into a weak state of mind after remaining for a time in a state of imbecility and held the government of the realm in name only.[58]

The civic records of Coventry, where the priory now provided his favourite residence of all, preserve accounts of his visits both before and after his initial illness. The contrast is instructive. In 1451 the 'receavinge the king' reveals quite a lively monarch, complimenting the mayor on his speech of welcome: 'Well seyde Sir Meyre, take your hors'; summoning him and his brethren to talk with him in his chamber,

---

[56] Coventry, Leicester, Northampton, St Albans, Reading, Chertsey, Peterborough and Crowland.
[57] Cited by R. L. Storey, op. cit., 184, from P.R.O., K.B.9/287, no. 53.
[58] See above, p. 20.

and treating them to a short discourse on the governance of the city. When he bade them farewell at the city bounds he gave them another homily, which the clerk thought worthy to be recorded verbatim. It was to the effect that although they had not asked it of him, he had decided to make their bailiffs sheriffs in token of the good order prevailing in this best ruled of cities, but if they would continue to enjoy his good lordship they must allow no riots or conventicles in their midst and take no liveries from lords, knights or esquires. By contrast, on the Feast of the Exaltation of the Holy Cross (14 September) 1457 it was Queen Margaret who made the triumphal entry into the city, greeted by adulatory pageants of prophets and patron saints, cardinal virtues and nine conquerors to do her honour. The conquerors were Hector, Alexander, Joshua, David, Judas, Arthur, Charlemagne, Julius Caesar, Geoffrey of Bouillon and, finally, St Margaret herself, represented slaying a great dragon by a miracle. Henry went silent and unnoticed. Were it not for one specific reference to his presence, and hopes for his good health, in Judas's oration, for the tun of wine which the mayor gave him and for the presents given to his household men, by advice of his council, there would be no knowing that he was there at all. Naturally he was still shown all kingly deference, but no more of his speeches were recorded then or on subsequent visits other than notes of his formal expressions of thanks. It was Queen Margaret alone who came from nearby Kenilworth at Corpus Christi, specially to view the famous pageants. Moreover, when a great council held there from February to March 1457 came to an end, the mayor and his fellows discovered to their cost that even the special honours which they had expected to reserve only for the arrival or departure of a king and had never before shown to a queen, had now always to be shown to this queen, on pain of her grave displeasure.[59] The civic records of Coventry do show that Henry could now again take part in processions and services and thus once again perform the dignified duties of kingship. Otherwise his activities were at a very low level. The two ecclesiastical great officers, the chancellor and the keeper of the privy seal, and the courtier treasurers Shrewsbury and Wiltshire, seem to have been kept mainly in attendance on him,[60] but at his best he carried out the duties of government only for brief, intermittent periods. The words of an anonymous English chronicler thus now succinctly expressed the situation: 'the reame of Englonde was out of all gouernaunce . . . for the kyng was simple . . . held ne householde ne meyntened no warres'.[61] So it appeared to this southern chronicler, with an absentee

---

[59] *Coventry Leet Book*, 263–6, 286–92, 297, 298, 299–300, 301.

[60] The note of places where the great seal was affixed to documents in *C.P.R., 1452–1461, passim* shows how closely the chancellor's movements coincided with the king's.

[61] Davies's Chronicle, 79; see above, p. 20.

king, a constant fear of French invasion and nothing being done to recover the lost French lands.

The view of this chronicler is supported by the meagre documentary evidence. Little was done beyond the dispensation of patronage,[62] and the devising of financial shifts for the maintenance of the court. The council in Star Chamber at Westminster continued a few routine activities, while some instruments of Henry's government from Coventry were now issued by advice of 'the lords of his household and council'.[63] That the withdrawal to the Midlands was envisaged as semi-permanent is confirmed by the special administrative arrangements made for household finance. William Grimsby, treasurer of the chamber and keeper of the jewels with the king, and also under-treasurer of the exchequer at Westminster, had a deputy, Richard Davy, clerk of the jewels, who was authorized to act for him at Westminster during his absences with the court. These two were given powers at their discretion to earmark sums of money and assignments at the exchequer for household use, to be recorded on the exchequer receipt rolls as 'for the king in his chamber by the hand of William Grimsby', who was to render account to no one except Henry in person.[64] From 12 March 1456 followed three years and eight months without a parliament, a period unique in the reign.[65] This was possible because no parliament was now required to secure the fundamental source of English government finance, the customs and subsidies, because the 1453 parliament had at last granted them to Henry for life. A major part of these had been set aside for the maintenance of Calais, but from December 1458 £1,000 each quarter were secured in loans for four years from the mayor and society of the Calais Staple for household expenses, in return for licences to export wool and woolfells free of customs duties, and a monopoly of export through the Calais Staple of all wools and woolfells exported to the Low Countries.[66] Otherwise the household, apart from monastic and civic charity, and loans from its own wealthier members,[67] now came to depend on a new monopoly of the so-called hereditary revenues of the crown. Grimsby was able

[62] The files of Warrants for the Great Seal 1456–1458 (P.R.O., C.81/1465, 6, 7, 8) consist of 194 pieces almost entirely authenticated solely by Henry's sign manual.
[63] P.R.O., C.81/1466/12 (1 August 1457).
[64] P.R.O., E.404/71/1/58 (Coventry 12 March 1457).
[65] 12 March 1456–20 November 1459.
[66] C.P.R., 1452–1461, 500–1.
[67] References (P.R.O., E.404/71/2/11–85) given by Storey, op. cit., 182, reveal the earl of Shrewsbury paying out of his own pocket on nine occasions over £300 for various envoys and messengers, for armaments, to buy a ship for the passage of soldiers to Calais and for Henry's wedding present to the duke of Buckingham's daughter (cf. 71/1/98; 71/2/37), the chamberlain Sir Thomas Stanley and the squire of the body John Hampton making similar payments.

to pre-empt all possible sources of revenue from the sheriffs in the shires, however small.[68] Some sheriffs, many of whom were also members of the household,[69] were made directly responsible for paying household wages. The sheriff of Somerset and Dorset, for example, henceforth had to pay for the whole upkeep of the royal pack of hounds.[70] All manner of fines imposed by the exchequer for non-return of writs, etc., or by the law courts for gaol escapes, etc., were similarly pre-empted. A fine on the earl of Devon for his transgressions 'vi et armis' against Nicholas Radford was among these, though a subsequent entry of this as a 'mutuum per duas tallias' from the chamber to the exchequer indicates that it was not collected.[71] When such dues proved difficult to levy, as in the case of the issues of the temporalities of the vacant bishopric of Durham, special commissioners might be appointed, though in this case officials of the bishopric resisted attempts to levy the money and payment had to wait until Margaret's chancellor and keeper of the privy seal, Laurence Booth, was himself put into the vacant bishopric.[72] Efforts were also made fully to exploit the crown's feudal dues for the benefit of the household. Fines for licences to enter into inheritance were paid directly into the chamber, or jewel house, at Coventry.[73] Writs and proclamations were issued to distrain all men holding lands worth £40 *per annum* or more to become knights at Pentecost 1457, and fines totalling £1,089 from those who failed to comply had been levied for the household by May 1460.[74] Grimsby was also made responsible for the purveyance of victuals for the household[75] and Davy removed Henry's jewels from the exchequer of receipt to Coventry on 7 December 1456.[76]

The English chronicle records that the royal debts increased daily as creditors could get no payment and that heavy impositions on the people lost Henry their hearts, because they could see no end-product from them, other than the queen and courtiers lining their own pockets. He instanced 'taxes, tallages and fifteenths',[77] but there was no new

---

[68] P.R.O., E.401/863 under 15 November 1458: items of between £10 and £40 from 21 sheriffs totalling £506 13s 4d.

[69] There were only 7 out of 34 counties which did not have a member of the household as sheriff at some time between 1456 and 1460 (see Robin Jeffs, *op. cit.*, 341–3).

[70] P.R.O., E.28/88/31 2 November 1458.

[71] P.R.O., E.401/863 under December 1458.

[72] P.R.O., C.81/1467/1; *C.P.R., 1452–1461*, 360–8; Devon, *Issues*, 483 (£710 8s 10½d ultimately paid by Booth. He was given £226 13s 4d for collecting it.)

[73] *C.P.R., 1452–1461*, 355 (Coventry, 1 March 1457, 100 marks from Somerset's heir).

[74] P.R.O., C.81/1546/92; E.28/88/26; *C.P.R., 1452–1461*, 295–8, 432; *Foedera*, XI, 389. I am indebted to Dr Robin Jeffs for the total taken from P.R.O., E.370/2/22 (roll of fines).

[75] P.R.O., E.404/71/4/25.

[76] P.R.O., E.404/71/1/40.

[77] Davies's Chronicle, 79.

21(a). Harlech castle.

21(b). Bamborough castle.

22(a). Dunstanborough castle.

22(b). Alnwick castle

parliamentary taxation levied at all after 1453 and the resentment can only have been caused by household purveyance, by the exploitation of the hereditary revenues by the household at Coventry and, possibly, by an attempt to levy the grant of archers made by the Reading parliament in 1453 in the changed circumstances of 1457. It is possible that when preparations were at last made to apportion the 1453 grant of archers among the counties and cities, in November and December 1457,[78] there was still nothing sinister about this. Dilatory routine alone may have been responsible, since the original grant had not envisaged their being made available before Easter 1456.[79] Defence of the realm in any case became an immediate, unavoidable issue when the French landed at Sandwich in late August 1457 and there were numerous commissions of array issued for defence of the coasts in August and September.[80] In November 1457 an approver charged one Robert Burnet of Stepney with uttering treasonable words about Queen Margaret herself raising men, but these were alleged to be for service overseas in default of action by Henry himself who had 'lost all his father had won', and was no longer himself capable of raising any army. Burnet also uttered the rash thought that it would have been better, in his opinion, if Henry's hurt at St Albans had been fatal.[81] The Yorkists later claimed that this attempt to levy the archers in 1457 was an example of Lancastrian tyranny, but this cannot be proved or disproved.

Henry's move to Kenilworth in August 1456 thus signified the collapse of normal political life. Signs are that in the autumn of 1456 Henry was still not entirely hostile to York, although the queen had already become notorious for this. York was able to attend a great council meeting, summoned to Coventry on 7 October 1456, when he was reported as standing well with Henry, but not with the queen, who would have had him 'distressed' if the duke of Buckingham had not prevented it. Buckingham appeared to be the most powerful peer then present at court, having likewise saved the young duke of Somerset from the wrath of the Coventry townspeople, after his men had killed several of them in an affray. The ministerial changes in which his two Bourchier half-brothers lost their offices were reported by the same informant to be much resented, and due to the queen's wishes.[82] A much longer great council, held there from 15 February to 14 March 1457, was specifically called to settle internal dissensions: 'for the restful rule of our land and subjects and the surety of the same'. The lists

---

[78] C.P.R., 1452–1461, 406–10; Coventry Leet Book, 304.
[79] R.P., V, 233.
[80] C.P.R., 1452–1461, 371, 400, 410, 405, 405.
[81] P.R.O., K.B.9/287/53.
[82] Paston Letters, I, 403, 407–9.

of writs of summons and the presence list given in the Coventry Leet
Book confirm that York was again summoned and attended, but not
Salisbury or Warwick. This second meeting of a great council at
Coventry in 1457 was most probably the assembly, as Stubbs surmised,
of which an undated, partisan account later appeared in the parliamentary attainder of the Yorkists in 1459. If so it indicates that consequent on York's initial bad example in the use of armed force to further
his objectives at Dartford in 1452 and at the first battle of St Albans,
he was still held primarily responsible for the disturbed state of the
kingdom. According to this later, partisan account in 1457 at Coventry
he was again made to take another solemn oath to eschew the 'wey
of fayt'. The duke of Buckingham, no longer his protector at court
this time, implored Henry on his knees to make this his last, final
offer of royal mercy for such an offence.[83]

In April 1457 the queen and Henry moved temporarily to Hereford
to support a commission of oyer and terminer headed by those peers
of the realm on whom the court could rely: Buckingham, Arundel,
Shrewsbury, Wiltshire, Beaumont, Audley and Chief Justice Fortescue,
sitting to punish Sir William Herbert and Sir Walter Devereux and
their associates in their home country. This was done excessively
harshly, according to the Paston Letters, rousing much local sympathy
for them.[84] Among others charged were Thomas Herbert, senior and
junior, of Little Troy, alleged to have raised men at Ross-on-Wye in
June 1456 to march against the king at Kenilworth, though, of course,
Henry had not, at that stage, yet moved to the Midlands, thus indicating
ex post facto rationalization in the spring of 1457 of events of the previous
year.[85] There was undoubtedly considerable unease at court about
the loyalty of the shires, for in July 1457 commissions were issued from
Kenilworth to fourteen magnates and knights in sixteen counties surrounding Kenilworth and Coventry, in a block stretching from Berkshire north to Derbyshire and Lincoln and including Hereford, Shropshire, Gloucester and Worcester to the west. Each of these fourteen
nominees was to be a kind of lord lieutenant to raise a posse of the
county to resist and suppress the king's rebels. Neither York nor
Warwick nor Salisbury was among those nominated.[86]

Why Henry decided to return to Westminster in early September
1457, after more than a year's withdrawal to the Midlands, is a matter
for conjecture. It was not news of an apparent French invasion and
sack of Sandwich on 28 August which brought him back, since this

[83] *P.P.C.*, VI, 333–4; *Coventry Leet Book*, 297; *R.P.*, V, 347.
[84] P.R.O., K.B.9/35/24, 44, 60, 70, 71, 72; *C.P.R.*, *1452–1461*, 353, 348; *Paston Letters*,
I, 416–17.
[85] P.R.O., K.B.9/35/32.
[86] *C.P.R.*, *1452–1461*, 370–1.

reached him on his way at Northampton, where he stayed from 2–7 September.[87] It appears that improving health had briefly roused him to his duty to govern the whole realm from its political and administrative centre once more. But even when he did return the first half of October was spent in Chertsey abbey and most of December, January and the first half of February 1458 in Reading, Abingdon and Chertsey abbeys again. His mere presence speeded up minor administrative processes. For example, during his long absence in the Midlands the abbot of St Albans had been trying in vain to establish the validity of his abbey's exemption from the 1456 resumption act. He describes how he had to wait month after weary month until the king's return to get his petition through the privy seal office, even though his agent was a king's councillor and a high exchequer official. This he finally achieved on 12 November.[88] But little or nothing was achieved in important matters of government. A great council meeting was summoned for some date after 12 October. It adjourned inconclusively on 29 November. Its declared purpose was 'to set apart such variances as be betwixt divers lords'. York was summoned, Salisbury brought from Doncaster, apparently under the escort of Viscount Beaumont. Probably because of poor attendance the council was perforce further adjourned to 27 January 1458, when, according to Abbot Wheathampstead, Henry in a brief appearance at Westminster personally addressed it on the evils of dissension among the lords.[89] York, Salisbury and the young Somerset were present, but absentees were still being summoned on 14 February. From 20 February until 14 March 1458 Henry was at Berkhamsted castle and this great council, which had originally been intended for October 1457, does not in fact appear to have done anything until the middle of March 1458.[90] What finally happened is described by the numerous London chroniclers. The great council, once assembled, turned out to be two separate armed camps. Henry himself was again absent.[91] Certain members summoned, who were considered to be impartial on the issues involved, held morning consultations in the city, at the Blackfriars, with York, Salisbury and Warwick and afternoon consultations, at the Whitefriars in Fleet Street, with Somerset, Northumberland, Egremont and Clifford, whose fathers had been slain at St Albans. They were billeted outside the city at the request of the civic authorities. All that was achieved was a formal accord on the limited issue of atonement and compensation for the

[87] *Coventry Leet Book*, 301; *London and the Kingdom*, ed. R. R. Sharpe, III, 382.
[88] *Registrum*, I, 265–8.
[89] *Ibid.*, 296–7.
[90] *P.P.C.*, VI, 290–4; *C.P.R., 1452–1461*, 428; *Paston Letters*, I, 426.
[91] Benet's Chronicle, 221: 'Rex tenuit magnum concilium apud Westmonasterium *rege absente* set consilio laborante circa pacem inter dominos.'

principals who had suffered death or injury at St Albans. Details appear
to have been left to the king, who decreed that York and his associates
should pay £45 *per annum* to St Albans abbey for masses for the dead.
Their dependants should be compensated from crown debts owed to
York, Salisbury and Warwick. A great 'love day' procession to St Paul's
followed, on Lady Day 25 March 1458, with Henry wearing his crown,
Salisbury and Somerset walking together before him, followed by York
and Queen Margaret behind, hand in hand. This grand, formal, empty
state occasion was aptly recorded for posterity in Lydgate's banal
verse.[92]

This formal healing of the rifts between sections of Henry's nobility,
first crystallized in the open armed conflict at St Albans on 22 May
1455, in fact settled nothing, because basic problems remained untouched by it. Who should control a feeble-minded monarch who was
yet not completely incapacited? How could those of his natural advisers
who felt themselves continuously at risk when not in his presence, obtain
security? Contending parties had been created in the state during
Henry's personal rule, even while he was in full possession of his senses.
His rule had always tended to promote faction, because it had never
been strong or wise enough to dominate opposing interests. The loss
of his wits had given unexpected but brief supremacy to Richard duke
of York, the party with whom he had never been able to work. This
brief authority had rested on the king's necessity, not his trust. As
soon as he recovered sufficiently to act he returned to his persistent,
partisan promotion of the rival Beaufort interest coupled now with
his slighting of the Nevills, which led to the first battle of St Albans.
But the political assassinations perpetrated there, and the hollow
atonement made for them three years later, provided no solution.
During these years a new interest had emerged to oppose the supremacy
of York, the mettlesome Angevin queen, who was creating a narrow
Lancastrian interest around the feeble king, centred on the rights of
her infant son. Since 1456 it had been impossible for any normal political
life to be maintained under such conditions.[93] 'And that same yere
[1458] alle thes lordys departyd from the Parlyment [sic], but they
come nevyr alle togedyr aftyr that tyme to noo Parlyment nor conselle,
byt yf hyt were in fylde with spere and schylde.'[94]

[92] *Registrum*, I, 298–308; Davies's Chronicle, 77; *Six Town Chronicles*, 145, 160;
Lydgate's verses printed in *Chronicle of London* (ed. Nicolas), 251–4.
[93] C. A. J. Armstrong, *op. cit.*, 43.
[94] Gregory's Chronicle, 203–4.

Chapter 16

THE LOSS OF THE THRONE

Foreign policy, the relations between monarchs, were matters for kings and princes alone in the fifteenth century and the renewal of diplomatic activity between England and France in 1458 after a lapse of nine years might be taken as good evidence that Henry was himself once more ruling, particularly as this represented a reopening of negotiations for peace. There had been indications, during a lucid period early in 1456, that this would represent his wishes. At that time the would-be French traitor Jean II duke of Alençon was trying to promote a new English invasion of Normandy. His overtures had been well received by Protector York, who said he looked forward to leading such a force himself before the autumn of 1456. But Alençon's envoy had had a different reception from Henry. He had expressed a most unchristian wish to fight Burgundy, not France, if he fought anyone before he died, to punish him for treacherously breaking faith with him in his youth. He said he desired only friendship with his uncle Charles, whom he hoped would aid him to discipline his own internal enemies, as he gladly would aid his uncle against his. He marvelled at the disloyalty of Charles's princes against such a noble king, but added that his own were no better.[1] Two English embassies were active in 1458. On 29 August Queen Margaret's former chamberlain, Sir John Wenlock, and Louis Gallet, called Henry's master of requests of his household, the father of Alençon's envoy Edmund Gallet, received Henry's authorization, under his sign manual, to open peace negotiations with France and Burgundy.[2] The proposals which Wenlock and Gallet put forward, oddly first to Burgundy and then to France, were for marriages with three Burgundian or three French princesses for the infant prince of Wales, for one of York's sons and for Henry duke of Somerset. At about the same time Richard Beauchamp, bishop of Salisbury, also appeared in Calais, discussing breaches of the truce with Burgundy and claiming to be Henry's personal envoy. He had ostensibly been sent to gather information about the life of his recently canonized predecessor St Osmund, but was really seeking, in conjunction with the Captain of Calais, the earl of Warwick, to open negotiations with

---

[1] Beaucourt, op. cit., VI, 52, 55, 137, citing MS fr. 18441 (depositions in the trial of the duke of Alençon).

[2] P.R.O., C.81/1469/26; Stevenson, Wars, I, 358–77.

Charles VII through Pierre de Brézé, seneschal of Normandy.[3]

In fact these diplomatic activities only serve to reinforce the picture gained from the scrappy evidence of domestic history at this time: doubts about the king's authority and confusion as to whom these envoys really represented. It has been suggested that, in reality, both these embassies in the autumn of 1458 were active merely on behalf of York, Warwick and their associates.[4] Both Wenlock and Gallet were to be found supporting York in 1459[5] and suffered forfeiture for it. The ambiguity of Sir John Wenlock's position is typical. Having fought for the king at St Albans, he was yet elected Speaker in the 1455 parliament and may have begun his successful career in the Yorkist interest at that point. Richard Beauchamp, bishop of Salisbury, was to be the envoy sent from Worcester in Henry's name to invite York and his associates to surrender in 1459, presumably as the person most likely to be acceptable to them. All that can be said with certainty is that both these embassies of 1458 were received with suspicion by Burgundy and France and serious doubts were entertained about their real allegiance. French historians, relying on a report made by the Count of Foix to Louis XI in 1461, on his recollections of Charles VII's relations with England at this time, accept that already in the spring of 1458 York made his own approaches to Charles VII to enlist some kind of aid against Henry, overtures which were contemptuously rejected by the high-minded Charles VII on the same grounds on which Henry had rejected Alençon's overtures: the dishonour of associating with a disloyal subject who was bound in allegiance to his own sovereign.[6] This cannot be disproved. The similar belief of the chroniclers Chastellain and d'Escouchy, however, that Queen Margaret had actually invited Brézé's sack of Sandwich in August 1457 to assist her against York's pretensions can, as Beaucourt realized, be firmly rejected.[7] When she did finally ask Brézé for naval help to prevent Warwick's return to England from Calais in 1460, after the encounters at Blore Heath and Ludford had made party divisions apparent, the novelty of the request, and the extreme danger to her person from her own supporters if it became known, were urgently conveyed to Charles VII by Brézé. This makes it clear that nothing

---

[3] Deposition of Jean Doncareau, Brézé's secretary, and his envoy to Henry's court, B.N. MS fr. 15537, printed by P. Bernus, 'Le rôle politique de Pierre de Brézé, 1451–1461'. *Bibliothèque de l'Ecole des Chartes* LXIX (1908), 303–47.

[4] Ramsay, *Lancaster and York*, II, 210–11; Storey, *op. cit.*, 185, although as Storey notes, nothing was said in York's parliamentary attainder about his having established private relations with foreign powers.

[5] *R.P.*, V, 349; *C.P.R., 1452–1461*, 585.

[6] *Mémoires de Philippe de Commines*, ed. D. Godefroy and Lenglet de Fresnoy (Paris 1747), II, 310–11; Beaucourt, *op. cit.*, VI, 144–5.

[7] *Loc. cit.*

similar had ever happened before.[8] The bishop of Salisbury's mission in 1458 was regarded with particular suspicion by the French, since the bishop claimed to have the especial backing not only of his fellow bishops but also of York, Norfolk, Salisbury and Warwick, for what he had to say.[9] As for Wenlock and Gallet, Charles VII insisted on sending the herald Maine back to England with them to assess the strength or weakness of Henry's own position there. Maine reported that Henry, early in 1459, was very poorly supported by his princes and nobles, a view confirmed by a conversation he had with an emissary from Constantinople who was there at the same time.[10] He also reported that it was then notorious in London that a 'great parliament', presumably a great council, had been planned to deprive Warwick of his captaincy of Calais. It had been broken off and Warwick was publicly declaring that he would insist on holding the office for the six remaining years of his original grant and, rather than surrender it, relinquish his English lands. This French report fits in with several rather obscure chronicle references to Warwick narrowly escaping assassination by members of the royal household when leaving Westminster palace, variously dated to November 1458 and early February 1459.[11] This incident was the first clear evidence of continuing dissensions at home after the loveday of 25 March 1458.

Doubts expressed abroad about Henry's own authority in his kingdom were certainly justified from the end of 1458. On 2 December 1458, 500 pikes and 500 leaden clubs were ordered to be made immediately available to the royal household for his protection, in view of the activities of 'certain misruled and seditious persons'. Three great serpentines were also ordered. The warrant for their purchase made Henry's master of ordnance, John Judde, assure him that with these he would be able to subdue any castle or place which rebels might try to use against him.[12] Since the Annunciation loveday Henry's itinerary had continued to suggest a minimal concern with affairs of state. He returned to the abbey of St Albans for Easter 1458, spending at least three weeks there; during May and early June he was with the queen at Greenwich and from late June to early August at the Woodstock royal hunting lodge. Most of September and early October were once more spent in the abbey of St Albans. At mid-May 1459 he began a second, prolonged withdrawal to Queen Margaret's

[8] Basin, op. cit., IV, 358–60.

[9] Stevenson, Wars, I, 367–9.

[10] C.C.R., 1454–1461, 318, 350. What he called a parliament, really the law courts in session in Westminster Hall, had just been interrupted by the duke of Exeter, which dates his visit to early 1459.

[11] Six Town Chronicles, 113; The Brut, 526; Davies's Chronicle, 78; Kingsford's London Chronicle, 169, cf. Registrum Johannis Whethamstede, I, 340.

[12] P.R.O., E.404/71/3/43.

Midland, Lancastrian domains, arriving in Coventry about the 23rd. It was from this midsummer of 1459 that the abbot of St Albans, in a typical conceit,[13] marked the final setting of the sun of Henry's royal dignity. From that point, he wrote, the dispensation of royal justice and mercy were entirely ignored. No details follow, but the clear implication is that he was referring to the harsh yet ineffective treatment he next described, which York, Salisbury, Warwick and their associates received in Henry's name.

Queen Margaret must be presumed to have continued principally to control Henry's movements and actions after, as before, the loveday. She was certainly with him at St Albans, where the abbot mentioned her receiving envoys in April 1458, at her palace of Greenwich when Henry was there, and had probably taken him to the Woodstock hunting lodge, since her love of hunting is specially well attested.[14] There are plenty of recorded examples of her backing up and reinforcing the royal will in matters which directly concerned her, although these in themselves do not constitute evidence of the new control which she exercised over him in his enfeebled state from 1456 because this had always been her habit, even before his illness.[15] York and his associates, who never directly criticized Henry, and were equally mindful that the law of treason also protected the queen, never presumed to criticize her in their public pronouncements. They now castigated the earls of Shrewsbury and Wiltshire and Viscount Beaumont as the evil, avaricious councillors who had assumed the role about the king previously occupied first by Suffolk and then by Somerset.[16] That Henry was always controlled by a never failing succession of bad men passes belief, but such an assumption was the only possible alternative to direct attacks on the king himself. The more outspoken chroniclers are unanimous in attributing responsibility for the events leading to the battle of Blore Heath, and its consequences, to Queen Margaret. They show that the queen and her council had taken over the realm through their control of the king. She decided all that was done about him.[17] With the assistance of some lords she even tried unsuccessfully to get him to abdicate in favour of the infant prince of Wales. Her own unpopularity was now reflecting on to the Lancastrian heir. Malicious rumour now had it that he was not her son, or Henry's.[18]

---

[13] Registrum, I, 336–7.

[14] Coventry Leet Book, I, 301; Letters of Queen Margaret of Anjou, ed. C. Munro (Camden Society, 1863), 100–1, 131, 137, 141.

[15] Ibid., 98–9, 119, 128, 132, 142, 147, 160, 164; A. R. Myers, English Historical Documents, IV, 280–1.

[16] Davies's Chronicle, 88.

[17] The Brut, 526, 527.

[18] Davies's Chronicle, 79–80, 92: 'fals heryres fostred as knowethe experyence'; Benet's Chronicle, 216.

At her command she had a menacing force of knights and squires of Cheshire and elsewhere, to whom she had given the prince's livery of the swan. These 'queen's gallants' were first prominent in the battle of Blore Heath.[19] Those in the know 'knewe welle that all the workyngys that were done growe by hyr, for she was more wyttyer then the kynge, and that apperythe by hys dedys, etc.'[20] From 1459, Henry had once again ceased to have any use for Richard duke of York, according to Abbot Wheathampstead. He was now thoroughly convinced that York was aiming at the throne.[21]

On 7 May 1459, 3,000 bowstaves, and sheaves of arrows sufficient for that number of yeomen archers, were ordered to be put in the keeping of Thomas Thorpe, keeper of the privy wardrobe, 'considering the enemies of everyside approaching us, as well upon the sea as on land'.[22] The return of the court to Kenilworth and Coventry a few days later was certainly a military move. Privy seal writs sent out, some signed by Henry himself, ordered selected subjects to meet him at Leicester on 10 May, equipped for two months' military service.[23] The recently published chronicle of John Benet supplies additional information that a great council was summoned to Coventry and met there after 24 June 1459 in the presence of Queen Margaret and the five-year-old prince. Those summoned who did not appear were Thomas Bourchier, archbishop of Canterbury, the duke of York and earls of Salisbury, Warwick and Arundel, William Grey, bishop of Ely, George Nevill, bishop of Exeter, and Viscount Bourchier. They were then indicted at the queen's instigation for their non-appearance.[24] It is understandable that they should have been reluctant to appear in the king's presence, to put themselves in his power, without the strongest guarantees for their safety. This mistrust lay at the heart of the problem now leading to hostilities. Henry VI did not command the trust of all his great subjects. York's later attainder confirms that his and his two principal allies' final fault was that they failed to respond to these repeated royal summonses and allegedly instead prepared to meet together to destroy Henry, the queen and the prince at Kenilworth.[25] They were alleged to have planned to make simultaneous, surprise armed marches on Henry at Kenilworth, with the same purpose in mind as at Dartford and St Albans. But the court at Kenilworth received rapid information of Salisbury's initial move from Middleham

[19] Davies's Chronicle, 79–80; Benet's Chronicle, 224; Gregory's Chronicle, 204.
[20] Ibid., 209.
[21] Registrum, I, 337–8.
[22] P.R.O., E.28/88/49.
[23] Paston Letters, I, 438.
[24] Benet's Chronicle, 223.
[25] R.P., V, 348.

and the king took to the field with a considerable force. By moving
to Nottingham castle and the river Trent crossing, he caused Salisbury
to divert west towards Richard duke of York at Ludlow, for greater
strength.[26] En route for Ludlow Salisbury was intercepted on 23
September by the queen's forces under Lord Audley, at Blore Heath,
on the road between Newcastle under Lyme and Market Drayton,
some ten miles north-east of Eccleshall, where she was residing. After
slaying Audley and routing the queen's Cheshire and Shropshire men
under his command, Salisbury went his way unhindered, to join up
with York. Warwick also, who had returned from Calais about 21
September as prearranged, was later noted at Coleshill in search of
the king, where he narrowly missed a chance encounter with a force
under Somerset's command. Finally York, Salisbury and Warwick met
together at Worcester and then withdrew on the approach of the king's
forces to Ludlow.

The conflicting story, as told by York and the earls, was that they
had been intending peacefully and loyally to come to Henry's presence,
but for this they required certain prior assurances for their safety. They
would not believe that the armed attack on Salisbury at Blore Heath,
and the subsequent advance of the royal host against them, had been
made at Henry's own will and pleasure. They were his loyal subjects,
prevented from their rightful access to his person by malicious persons,
bent on their destruction. This they had solemnly declared on oath
together, in the cathedral at Worcester, receiving the sacrament from
William Lynwode who, with the prior and others, had then taken
their sworn testaments of loyalty to the king. Garter king of arms had
also been sent with similar messages. A third and final communication
had been sent to Henry to the same purpose from Ludlow on 10
October.[27] No reply came. Thus from their point of view Henry had
been withdrawn from his people by an armed Lancastrian or Angevin
caucus. To them Henry was thus a puppet in the hands of evil men,
or the queen, who kept all York's communications from him even
when carried by Garter, the principal herald of the realm. That this
could actually be the case does not ring true. It was on record that
in the identical circumstances at St Albans in 1455, when Mowbray
herald, as York's personal emissary, gained access to the royal presence,
this had availed him nothing. Henry had declined to communicate
directly with York. If the king was manipulated before Ludlow as
before St Albans then he was willing to be so manipulated.

Henry's itinerary shows that he had left Kenilworth about 20

[26] From Nottingham he summoned his household chamberlain Thomas Lord Stanley
to his presence in vain (*R.P.*, V, 369). Stanley, whose brother William was with
Salisbury, sympathized with Salisbury and wished him well.

[27] Davies's Chronicle, 80–3.

September and was back in Coventry by 20 October. This was the period which the authors of York's attainder subsequently described as his marvellous, manly prowess for thirty days or so in the field, cheerfully enduring cold and rough lodgings in bare fields, in pursuit of his manifest traitors. On 12 October the royal host, advancing from Worcester to Ludlow, and plundering as it went, found York, Salisbury and Warwick entrenched at Ludford, to the immediate south of Ludlow town. Heralds had preceded them, proclaiming full pardon to all who would surrender within six days. Unscrupulous rumours that Henry was dead were allegedly being put about to strengthen his enemies' resolve, but these were confounded when he displayed his banner in the field and made a fighting speech to boot, demonstrating his determination to fulfil his 'courageous knightly desire'. This put great heart into all his host. Such an *ex parte* picture of a campaigning Henry at this time is not entirely incredible, at least as regards his capacity for physical endurance which was, after all, to be similarly demonstrated by his subsequent long years wandering as a fugitive. The accounts of the speech itself strain credibility since there appears in fact to have been no battle plan devised to give effect to his alleged bellicose intentions. No moves were made to overcome and secure the persons of the duke and earls once the royal army had run them to earth. That the king had been induced to sit a horse and appear in the field in armour, with his banner displayed, was in itself sufficient to cause considerable defections[28] and ruin morale among the duke's and earls' followers. This was particularly true of the professional Calais contingent under their captain, Andrew Trollope, whom Warwick had brought with him, but he had apparently not told them that they would have to oppose their lawful sovereign in the field. The royal host appears to have been greatly superior, in numbers, to their opponents, but no one was in effective command of it. Since there was no investment of the traitors' position they consequently went free. The following morning, St Edward's Day, the duke's and earls' camp was found abandoned. This can hardly have been what Queen Margaret had intended. There could be no resolution of the impasse except by a military verdict which led to the complete triumph of one sectional interest which would control the king. At Ludford the verdict was indecisive because Henry, by the mere fact of being king, and present on the field, determined the immediate course of events. York and his associates were not destroyed. York escaped safely to Ireland, Warwick, Salisbury and Edward earl of March to Calais, equally out of range of royal power as exercised by the queen.

[28] Including Lord Grey of Powys, Walter Devereux Esq., Sir Henry Radford (*R.P.*, V, 349); Walter Hopton, Roger Kynnarston, Fulk Stafford, William Hastings, William Bowes (*ibid.*, 368).

York's enforced visit to Ireland strengthened his position. The effort to replace him as lieutenant in Ireland by the earl of Wiltshire on 4 December, together with the nomination of his deputies there, was quite ineffective. The Irish parliament confirmed York's appointment, protected him with the law of treason, provided him with a force of archers to take to England if he wished, allowed him to issue his own coinage and refused to accept the authority of privy seal writs from England.[29] The appointment of the young duke of Somerset to replace Warwick as Captain of Calais from 9 October was equally futile. Refused admission by the garrison, he could only manage to secure the subsidiary fortress of Guînes; all efforts to reinforce him there were anticipated and frustrated and he was finally forced to surrender after defeat by Warwick at Pont de Neullay on 23 April 1460.[30] Warwick's naval control of the English and St George's Channels enabled York and the earls to communicate freely to concert plans to mount an effective expedition to secure possession of the king's person. They sent placards into Kent and elsewhere, expounding their aims as entirely loyal subjects of Henry, who himself could do no wrong. Their aims were to rid the kingdom of the traitors about the king, to end the prostitution of the crown by evil advisers, and to free the land from the intolerable burden of their incompetent, corrupt government.[31]

On 9 October, before the confrontation at Ludford, a parliamentary assembly was hastily summoned to meet at Coventry. The writs were sent out to sheriffs whose term of office had already expired on 29 September.[32] Although letters of loyalty were still being received from York, the queen had obviously determined upon the complete destruction of her enemies. She must have anticipated that when the parliament met they would have been completely defeated and at her mercy. In the actual circumstances she still proceeded with the new, extreme measure of a parliamentary attainder against York, Salisbury and his countess, Warwick, March, Rutland, their principal adherents and their families, but qualified the bill by a promise of pardon for humble submission.[33] A separate enactment deprived them of all their offices;[34] their lands were put in the hands of receivers; those who had opposed them were given immediate rewards from their lands, and the estates

---

[29] A. J. Otway-Ruthven, *A History of Medieval Ireland*, 386–8.

[30] Ramsay, *Lancaster and York*, II, 221–2, for references.

[31] Printed in Davies's English Chronicle, 86–94.

[32] *R.P.*, V. 367 (petition of the old sheriffs for pardon for illegally holding the elections as instructed by the writs).

[33] *Ibid.*, V, 349, 15 others: John, Lord Clinton, William Oldhall, Thomas Vaughan, Thomas and John Nevill, John Wenlock, James Pykering, John Conyers, Thomas Parre, John and Edward Bourchier, Thomas Colt, John Clay, Roger Eyton and Robert Bold.

[34] *Ibid.*, 366.

left over were mortgaged to defray the expenses of suppressing their rebellion. Numerous commissions of array were issued to try to ensure their being opposed if they attempted further resistance.[35] A propaganda defence of these measures which was compiled confirms that those responsible for them were not at all confident that public opinion would accept that York and the earls were guilty of treason and should thus be destroyed and their families utterly ruined.[36] This justification of the actions of the Coventry parliament claimed that Henry was a good and gracious king, ruling a loyal and contented people; that York and his associates had proved themselves incorrigible in their attacks upon him, at Dartford, St Albans and now Ludford; that they were but one rotten tooth in an otherwise healthy set, whose extraction had been twice postponed, but must now be carried out before the poison infected the whole mouth. By the civil law they had earned decapitation and the disinheriting of their heirs. Other men saw the act as 'a perilous writing' and 'mischievous indicting', likely to rebound on the heads of its authors, the culmination of a series of injustices which had begun with the destruction of Duke Humphrey at the Bury parliament of 1447, but never until this moment had been carried to these dangerous extremes.[37] It was the fear come true which York had expressed in 1450 and 1452 that his enemies at court were working to corrupt his blood. This new process of attainder was intended not only to eliminate the confederate duke and earls themselves, but to deprive their heirs and families of their entailed lands, in gross violation of the currently accepted practice of English common law that entails were sacrosanct, even against treason, a convention ominously last flouted by the tyrannous Richard II in 1398. The 'rout' of Ludford and the legislation of this Coventry parliament were thus typical examples of the dangerous mixture of weakness and forcefulness inherent in having Henry at the head of affairs.

When the earls finally mounted their inevitable expedition to capture control of Henry's person, apparently no question of deposing him in favour of York had yet been discussed. The emphasis of this enterprise, which was in preparation at Calais during the first half of 1460, was again on utter loyalty to King Henry; to rescue his person from control by evil advisers. This time the means was to be a 'competent fellowship', that is a limited force of professional soldiers, knowing what it had to do, whose loyalty could be entirely depended on, supported by a considerable artillery train[38] and a determination to assault even the city of London if necessary. Salisbury, Warwick and Edward earl

---

[35] *C.P.R.*, *1452–1461*, 526–614 *passim*; *Foedera*, XL, 446–8.
[36] The 'Somnium Vigilantis', ed. J. P. Gilson, *E.H.R.*, XXVI (1911), 512–25.
[37] *Paston Letters*, I, 535–6.
[38] *A Short English Chronicle*, ed. Gairdner, 74; *Bale's Chronicle*, 152.

of March finally crossed to Sandwich on 26 June 1460 where an advance party under William Nevill, Lord Fauconberg, had first secured them a bridgehead. The papal legate Francesco Coppini, recently accredited to Henry VI, accompanied them. Archbishop Bourchier received them at Sandwich and gave them episcopal protection and their numbers were swollen by many Kentish recruits as they made their way towards the capital. In the event, the threat of assault itself proved sufficient to gain them entry to the city on 2 July;[39] only the Tower resisted. Leaving Salisbury in charge of London and of the siege of the Tower, the rest set out to find the king. They encountered the royal army at Northampton on 10 July. The morning was spent in fruitless parleys; battle was joined in torrential rain early that afternoon.[40] Warwick gave orders not to spare the nobility, knights and esquires[41] and the capture of the king in his tent, in the meadows outside Northampton, between the river Nene and Delapré Abbey, was preceded by the deliberate slaughter of Buckingham, Shrewsbury, Beaumont and others about his person,[42] after the manner of St Albans in 1455. They were deemed to be the intimate secular advisers and councillors of the moment. Indeed, the preliminaries of the battle had also been a repetition of St Albans; a series of repeated, abortive parleys, designed to gain Warwick peaceful access to Henry's person. The complete victory of Warwick's forces in half an hour's encounter was, according to the abbot of St Albans and the chroniclers, due to the devastating treachery of Lord Grey of Ruthyn who led the king's vanguard over to the opposing side.[43]

From 10 July 1460, until he returned to the queen's custody at St Albans on 17 February 1461, Henry now performed acts of state at the will of the confederate earls.[44] The Tower of London was starved out by 18 July; Somerset, in Guînes, surrendered to Warwick in August. The great seal was taken by Warwick's younger brother George, bishop of Exeter, Viscount Bourchier was made treasurer and Margaret's chancellor, Laurence Booth, was replaced as keeper of the privy seal by Robert Stillington, archdeacon of Wells. A parliament summoned to Westminster for 7 October proceeded to repeal all the acts of the Coventry Parliament as the work of seditious and covetous persons, bent on the destruction of Henry's great, noble and faithful lords.[45]

---

[39] *Ibid.*, 150 and editor's note.

[40] Ramsay, *Lancaster and York*, 227–9 and reference given there.

[41] Davies's English Chronicle, 97.

[42] Gregory's Chronicle, 207.

[43] *Registrum*, I, 374; Davies's English Chronicle, 97; 'William Worcester' in Stevenson's *Wars*, II, pt. ii, 773, cf. Gregory's Chronicle, 207 who mentions treachery but is unspecific.

[44] 'Kept them in his majesty royal at pleasure of the lords' (Bale's Chronicle, 151).

[45] *R.P.*, V, 374.

So far the aftermath of St Albans in 1455 was exactly repeated.

Over ten weeks elapsed, after the earls' return to England, before York made his landing from Ireland, near Chester. Was this as originally planned, or did it represent the development of differences between them? York only appeared in London on the fourth day of the parliament, probably as the Commons were choosing their Speaker. He arrived with trumpets sounding and a naked sword borne before him. His surviving correspondence shows that, at least from 13 September, he had begun to date what he wrote by the year of grace, ignoring the regnal years of Henry VI.[46] He also now displayed 'the whole arms of England without any diversity',[47] whereas hitherto he had borne only the arms of his grandfather Edmund of Langley, late duke of York, fifth son of Edward III. In short, Richard 'Plantagenet'[48] had come to claim the throne. That this was no part of his original bargain with Warwick and Salisbury was soon evident. The abbot of St Albans described the consternation and dismay among the lords in the parliament chamber when he laid his hand upon the vacant throne to occupy it.[49] The Burgundian chronicler Waurin, although he undoubtedly presented the history of England since St Albans as a panegyric on Warwick, was nevertheless particularly well informed about events in England at this time. He maintained that the earls were very much aware that their oaths of loyalty to Henry had greatly aided them in their progress towards Northampton. Consequently Warwick, with the approval of Salisbury and of York's own heir, Edward earl of March, vainly remonstrated with York against his unexpected and unpopular move.[50] This must be accepted, because Pope Pius II in his Commentaries, writing a few years before Waurin, also makes the same point.[51] But York's mind, hitherto known only to himself and his own council, was at last firmly made up, declared and not to be changed. There are conflicting accounts in the chronicles of York's behaviour towards the king after his arrival. In Gregory's chronicle and the English chronicle there is an account of violence towards Henry and forcible possession of his apartments in the palace. In Abbot Wheathampstead's account, however, the only violence is

[46] K. B. McFarlane, 'The Wars of the Roses', *Proceedings of the British Academy*, L (1965), 93, n. 2.

[47] Gregory's Chronicle, 208.

[48] This was the ancient sobriquet of Geoffrey count of Anjou, father of Henry II, which it is assumed York took to mark his royal descent as superior to the Lancastrian line, although kings of England had never used it. He may have originally adopted it about 1448 in protest at Henry's renunciation of Anjou and Maine (see above, p. 35, n. 26). It must have been particularly offensive to Margaret of Anjou.

[49] *Registrum*, 376–80.

[50] *Chroniques*, ed. W. & E. L. C. P. Hardy (R.S. 1891), V, 312–18.

[51] Constance Head, 'Pius II and the Wars of the Roses', *Archivum Historiæ Pontificiae*, VIII (1970), 160.

the breaking of the seals to the king's apartments when York took up residence there. They were unoccupied as the king was using the queen's apartments. This seems the more credible account and is consistent with the rest of York's behaviour at the palace of Westminster and with the respect still shown later to Henry. York was claiming the throne as his by right of inheritance and his behaviour was that of one who believed himself already the rightful king. According to Wheathampstead he did not even visit Henry when Archbishop Bourchier suggested it because 'I know of no person in this realm whom it does not behove to come to me and see my person rather than that I should go and visit him'.

On 16 October York's legal counsel formally submitted his claim in the Upper House to the kingdoms of England and France and to the lordship of Ireland, by right of inheritance superior to Henry VI, as right heir of Edward III through his third son Lionel duke of Clarence. He demanded an immediate answer to it. Next day the assembled peers resolved to avoid the issue by laying the claim, through the chancellor, before the only authority superior to themselves, the hapless Henry himself, as a matter too high for any of his subjects. He requested them to find means to oppose it and they in turn countered by asking that he himself should use his own well-known bent for studying old writings to that end. For their part they then tried to pass the responsibility of providing an answer over to the king's judges. They, in turn, declared that they would not be drawn into a matter which was too high for them, since it properly concerned only the princes of the blood and the peerage. The king's sergeants and his attorney, subsequently summoned to give an opinion, naturally replied that what was too high for the judges was also too high for them. No initiative came from Henry.

Hence the lords spiritual and temporal, continually pressed by York for an answer, were finally forced, after free and secret debate among themselves, to set out all the objections they could think of to York's claim: all their previous oaths of loyalty, the parliamentary entail of the crown in the Lancastrian succession, the arms hitherto borne by York, those of Edmund of Langley, duke of York, who was only the fifth son of Edward III, the great number of legislative acts passed in the name of three successive Lancastrian kings, the assertion of Henry's grandfather that Edmund Crouchback of Lancaster, not Edward I, had been the elder son of King Henry III, whose rightful heir he, Henry IV, therefore was, through his mother, Blanche of Lancaster.

According to Abbot Wheathampstead York had previously been absolved from his oaths of fealty, homage and allegiance by the pope, so could brush such objections aside. This is unlikely, since the papacy had already denied earlier reports to this end,[52] and his actual answer to this objection of the lords was that oaths taken against right and truth required no absolution. They were *ipso facto* invalid against his Divine Right 'by title of inheritance ... as it accordeth with God's law'. Failure to act on his claim earlier could not prejudice this right: 'though right for a time rest and be put to silence yet it rotteth not nor shall not perish'.

Finally, on 25 October, in answer to York's continued importuning, the peers of the realm took it upon themselves to propose a compromise to Henry through the mouth of George Nevill, the chancellor. He first bound them all to stand by him, however the king might take it. This was that Henry should continue king until death or voluntary abdication, but disinherit his heir in favour of York and his heirs. In fact Henry took it passively. He was in an isolated position, with no queen or trusted adviser to give him the will to oppose it. Two near-contemporary explanations for his acceptance are extant: fear of death, 'for a man that hathe by lytylle wytte wylle sone be a feryd of dethe',[53] and intervention by the papal legate. Pope Pius II did later claim credit for Henry's acceptance of the compromise: 'by the wisdom of the legate [Coppini] the dispute was settled'. It is quite feasible that such papal pressure was put upon him by the legate who favoured the Yorkists and that tipped his weak mind towards accept-ance. Moreover, this solution did present a way round the thorny problem of York's oaths in the eyes of the church, since it involved his swearing allegiance yet again to Henry.[54] Important details of the settlement were that York and his sons all swore oaths to Henry, who bound himself, by indenture, to keep the agreement. York, as heir apparent, was given the protection of the law of treason and the titles and endowments of the heir to the throne (the principality of Wales, earldom of Chester and duchy of Cornwall, estimated to be worth 10,000 marks *per annum*) were all vested in him and his heirs. The statute of 1406 entailing the succession on Henry IV's issue was repealed.[55]

In spite of the face-saving all round there was in fact no royal dignity or power left to Henry at all. He had signed it all away. Follow-ing his acceptance of the lords' arbitration, the very next enactment on the parliament roll ordered all royal officers throughout the land to give the same obedience to the new heir to the throne as was due to the king himself, subject to the penalties of treason for non-compliance, whenever he should take it upon himself to raise troops

[52] *Papal Letters 1447–1455* (H.M.S.O., 1915), 152–3.
[53] Gregory's Chronicle, 208.
[54] Constance Head, *op. cit.*, 161, citing Pius II's *Commentaries*, III, 271.
[55] *R.P.*, V, 375–82.

and ride against rebels and disturbers of the peace.[56] The chroniclers now styled York protector and even regent of the kingdom[57] for Henry's lifetime, by authority of parliament. The analogy with Henry V's dominant ruling position in France over his father-in-law, the mad Charles VI, after the treaty of Troyes in 1420, was thus very close indeed.[58]

The problem of 'rebels' was immediate. The queen, the prince, the dukes of Exeter and Somerset, the earls of Northumberland, Pembroke, Devon and Wiltshire, Lords Clifford, Roos and other lords, were in no way party to the acts of this parliament. Early in December parliament was prorogued so that the validity of this settlement, made on the authority of only a section of the peerage, might, so to speak, be put to the test of trial by battle. From Jasper Tudor's castle of Denbigh, whither she had fled from Coventry after Northampton, Queen Margaret had gone by sea to Dumfries in Scotland. For ten or twelve days over the New Year she and the prince were closeted with the Queen Dowager of Scotland, Mary of Guelders, and the young King James III, in Lincluden abbey, arranging a treaty for Scottish military aid against York, probably involving a marriage of the prince with one of James III's sisters and the cession of Berwick to Scotland.[59] Twelve English lords assembled at York on 20 January 1461 before Queen Margaret and bound themselves to do all in their power to fulfil the terms of this humiliating treaty on behalf of King Henry.[60] By this date, the queen's party had already achieved a notable success. The forces of the dukes of Somerset and Exeter, the earl of Northumberland, Lords Roos, Nevill and Clifford, had overwhelmed York, Salisbury and York's son Edmund earl of Rutland at Wakefield Bridge, by York's castle of Sandal, on 30 December. It was alleged that they had been taken by surprise and treachery, against the law of arms, while their forces were dispersed in foraging parties, under protection of a truce. In any case the outcome had been that York and his son were slain in the mêlée and Salisbury was taken alive to Pontefract castle to be ransomed on the orders of Somerset, the official commander. This was

[56] *Ibid.*, 382–3.

[57] *The Brut*, 530; Davies's Chronicle, 106; 'William Worcester' in Stevenson, *Wars*, II, pt. ii, 774; *Chronicle of London*, ed. Kingsford, 172.

[58] S. B. Chrimes, *Lancastrians, Yorkists and Henry VII* (London 1964), 74.

[59] Treaty of Lincluden, 5 January 1461: *The Auchinlech Chronicle and Short Chronicle of the Reign of James the Second King of Scots*, ed. Thomas Thomson (Edinburgh 1819), 21; *Exchequer Rolls of Scotland*, ed. G. Burnett (H.M.S.O., 1884), VII, 8, 39, 157.

[60] Exeter, Somerset, William Percy, bishop of Carlisle, Northumberland, Westmorland, Devon, John Hales, bishop of Coventry, John Lord Nevill, Henry Lord FitzHugh, Thomas Lord Roos, Thomas Seymour and Ralph Lord Dacre of Gillesland: T. Basin, *Histoire des règnes de Charles VII et de Louis XI*, IV, 357–8, where the editor, J. Quicherat, prints the copy of their undertaking, sent to Charles VII of France.

duchy of Lancaster territory and 'the commune peple of the cuntre, whyche loued hym nat, took hym owte of the castelle by violence and smote of his hed'. Salisbury, his life spared on the battlefield, had yet died for his desertion of the Lancastrian House. York's head was fixed over the city gate of York, wearing a paper crown. He and his son lost their lives because of the now openly declared Plantagenet pretensions to the English throne.[61]

Henry had played no part in all this, after he had signed away his son's inheritance, but he was subsequently held to be legally responsible for these 'murders' as a dishonourable act, in violation of his solemn indenture with York and his family, which released them from the compact and gave legal justification for the usurpation of York's son, Edward of Rouen. Both sides in the conflict, the queen and the Yorkists, were acting in Henry's name. Edward of Rouen, now styled duke of York, was backed by an official royal commission to levy the king's lieges in the West Midland counties against Henry's 'rebels',[62] He had succeeded in checking the concentration of Lancastrian forces there by defeating the earls of Pembroke and Wiltshire on 2 February at Mortimer's Cross near Wigmore and driving them into the depths of Wales. Among those captured and quite needlessly executed on his orders was Henry's step-father, Owen Tudor.

Meanwhile the queen's forces, composed of the lords in Yorkshire who had routed York and Salisbury at Wakefield, her new, indisciplined Scottish allies and northern shire levies marched south. Their primary purpose was to recover Henry from the earls' captivity. Their progress south of Trent to St Albans can be plotted by the record of places plundered on the way: Grantham, Stamford, Peterborough, Huntingdon, Melbourn and Royston. The dread felt at the approach of this whirlwind from the north, and the desperate measures of protection organized, are graphically described in the chronicle of Crowland abbey whose demesnes escaped its ravages by a mere six-mile margin.[63] The bishop of Ely hastily strengthened the water defences of the isle of Ely and Wisbech castle and garrisoned them with Burgun-

---

[61] Bale's Chronicle, 152; *Three Fifteenth-Century Chronicles*, 154, 171–2; Davies's Chronicle, 106–7, from which the quotation is taken; 'William Worcester' in Stevenson, *Wars*, II, pt. ii, 775; *Registrum Johannis Whetehamstede*, I, 381–3; John Benet's Chronicle, 228, all tell substantially the same story. The alternative explanation that the outcome was due to York's military rashness comes from the First Crowland Continuation (Bohn translation), 421. The countess of Salisbury, who later named nine obscure men as her husband's murderers, claimed that Percy retainers under Sir Ralph Percy were accessories: Storey, *The End of the House of Lancaster*, 194, citing K.B.27/804, m.67.

[62] *C.P.R., 1452–1461*, 659 (commission under the great seal by authority of the council enrolled 12 February 1461).

[63] Crowland Chronicle (Bohn translation), 421–3.

dian cross bowmen against their advance.[64] The defence of the capital
was in the hands of Warwick with his forces acting nominally as the
army of the kingdom. He took the king with him and kept him with
him, even on the battlefield. This may have been desirable to show
that Warwick's was the legal army and the queen's the rebels, or it
may have been because the king was not an entirely docile puppet
at that time and Warwick did not dare to leave him in London.
Warwick chose to block the queen's army's approach by the eastern
route by constructing an extended and well-fortified encampment for
his army to the north-east of St Albans, with an outpost in Dunstable
to the north-west and a rear party in the centre of the town. But
strategic and tactical victory in the final encounter went to Margaret's
principal captain, Andrew Trollope, that professional Calais soldier
whose earlier defection with his men from Warwick to the king had
begun the disintegration of the forces opposed to Henry before Ludlow
in 1459. Warwick found himself outflanked. Dunstable was first taken
by surprise and from there an unforeseen night march made on St
Albans. Here on 17 February the queen's forces penetrated into the
town, when Warwick's scouts were reporting them as still nine miles
away. Finally, an uphill attack from the town on Warwick's left flank
made it break under pressure while he was trying to withdraw and
reorientate his whole encampment. The author of the most detailed
account of the battle[65] was scornful of Warwick's Burgundian hand-
gunners, mounted pikemen, elaborate cannon and defensive devices
which did not work. These may well have hampered them in the vital
hand-to-hand encounter which first broke Warwick's left flank and
then led to the collapse of his centre and right. Abbot Wheathampstead's explanation was that, compared with the hardy northern men,
too much sun had weakened the southerners' blood and softened their
resolution for confrontation with cold steel and lead hammers.
Treachery was inevitably another contemporary explanation: the
Kentish men in this vital position were commanded by one Lovelace,
a leader whose life had been spared at Wakefield on condition that
he should never again appear in arms. He chose to save his own skin
at the vital position and moment of the encounter. Whatever the details
of the final encounter, Andrew Trollope had won a resounding victory
for his new employer, Queen Margaret. Nevertheless, she was unable
to draw much advantage from it.

Trollope's former master, Warwick, successfully extricated himself
in the confusion of withdrawal and escaped to meet with the still

---

[64] *Three Fifteenth-Century Chronicles*, 76, 155, 172.
[65] Gregory's Chronicle, 211–15. See also 'William Worcester' in Stevenson, *Wars*,
II, pt. ii, 776–7; *Registrum Johannis Whetehamstede*, I, 388–401; Davies's Chronicle, 107–8;
Chronicle of London (ed. Kingsford), 173; *Three Fifteenth-Century Chronicles*, 76, 155, 172.

victorious earl of March in the Cotswolds, on his way towards London. Henry himself was left in the hands of his rescuers. He was subsequently accused of having acted dishonourably by his sudden desertion of Warwick and his supporters, or simply by his refusal to move with them on the battlefield. Instances of his proverbial ineffectiveness are immediately recorded. Bonville and Sir Thomas Kyriell, who had faithfully defended him and did not flee because they were promised their safety, were nevertheless summarily executed by command of Queen Margaret, who made the seven-year-old prince give the orders. When Henry took up his normal quarters in the abbey, the abbot requested him to issue a proclamation against plundering. This was done, but with no effect. Even the abbey suffered so badly that the abbot advised his brethren to disperse and himself retired to Wheathampstead.

Possession of Henry's person brought immediate military and political paralysis to the queen's hitherto successful forces. Presumably his presence inhibited action without his approval and his indecisiveness now infected the direction of affairs. Havering and uncertainty now followed decisive military success. Victory had been achieved under Trollope's command, in spite of the plundering hordes of worthless Scottish and northern levies, by the disciplined household and feed men of the queen's and the Lancastrian lords' retinues: footsoldiers, archers, clubmen and swordsmen, all marked by their own lords' badges and the badge of the prince. But no advantage was now taken of the open road to London, even though counsels there were known to be divided between submission and resistance. In similar circumstances threat of assault and bombardment by the confederate earls from Calais in the previous year had proved sufficient to gain them possession of the political, administrative and financial centre of the kingdom. Now, as 'William Worcester' put it: 'hoc fuit destructio regis Henrici et regine sue', for if they had gone on to London all would have been at their disposal. Advance seems to have halted at Barnet, where deputations for mercy were received from the city and their promised supplies of money and provision awaited. But a final agreement for the preliminary admission of divers lords with 400 men into the city, made when the northern levies on horseback were already plundering at Westminster and in the suburbs, was not fulfilled. Perhaps at bottom the queen was satisfied once more to have secured the king's person and content to repeat, yet again, the earlier, established pattern of Lancastrian withdrawal with the king from the south in time of crisis. In any case the earls of March and Warwick now forestalled any Lancastrian moves for possession of the capital. After experience of the earls' previous decisive action and their consequent collaboration with them in the previous summer, the city authorities were already predisposed, and financially committed, to their cause.

In theory Margaret and her allies had achieved as much in the capture of Henry at St Albans as the confederate earls had done in similar circumstances at Northampton. But the political circumstances of 17 February 1461 were no longer those of 10 July 1460. An alternative course of self-preservation and political mastery was available, much more likely to be a permanent solution than any attempt to recapture Henry's person. York's claim to the throne had been fatal to himself, but not to his heir. There was now a legally respectable case for Edward of Rouen to claim the throne *de jure*, in contrast to Henry's now admitted *de facto*, prescriptive title. This was a welcome salve for any uneasy consciences in that Henry could be deemed to have broken his oaths to the Plantagenets through Wakefield and St Albans, thus absolving them from their allegiance. These were to be the arguments enacted in the parliamentary legislation of 1461 to justify the ensuing Yorkist usurpation and must have fortified its perpetrators and justified their novel actions in their predicament after 17 February 1461. The exact date of Margaret's withdrawal to the north, at the end of her desultory negotiations for admission to London, is not known[66] so cannot be directly related to the peaceful entry of the future Edward IV there on Thursday 26 February.[67] Intentions to make Edward of Rouen king were tested out at an assembly of Yorkist supporters, reinforced by the London populace and numbering some three to four thousand persons, in St John's Fields on the Sunday afternoon. George Nevill, bishop of Exeter, was their orator and the acclaim of the assembly was secured. Next day Edward's title was proclaimed. The recorded personnel of a council meeting which approved it at the Yorkist town seat of Baynard's Castle on Tuesday 3 March reveals who were the authors of the move. They were the duke of Norfolk, the earl of Warwick, the archbishop of Canterbury, Thomas Bourchier, the Beauchamp bishop of Salisbury, the chancellor, George Nevill, bishop of Exeter, Lord Fitzwalter, Sir William Herbert, soon to be Lord Herbert and later earl of Pembroke, and Sir Walter Devereux, soon to be Lord Ferrers of Chartley. In spite of the unspecified addition *et multis aliis* to these names, their numbers were obviously small. Their action nevertheless turned out to be decisive. Edward was inside the capital with a disciplined, effective, armed force, and sufficient goodwill and popular support had been raised for their purpose. He was able to appear at St Paul's on the Wednesday morning and process to Westminster, where the populace could see him enter

[66] For details of the panic measures in London taken by great and small in fear of Margaret's advance see Cora L. Scofield, *The Life and Reign of Edward IV*, I, 147–8.

[67] The preferred date in a welter of conflicting dates: see C. A. J. Armstrong, 'The Inauguration ceremonies of the Yorkist Kings', *T.R.H.S.*, 4th ser, XXX (1948), for this and what follows.

into his 'right'. Received in chancery by the Yorkist lords, he donned
royal robes and a cap of estate and publicly took some form of oath
before them. Then, ceremonially seating himself on the marble chair
or King's Bench, in that part of Westminster hall occupied by the
Law Courts, he was acclaimed by those present. Next he proceeded
over the road to the Abbey to take formal possession of the vital
coronation regalia, which the monks had in their charge, including
the most important item of all, St Edward's sceptre. With this in his
hand he was then enthroned in the coronation chair, while a Te Deum
was sung and those peers present did him homage.

Such was the cleverly stage-managed process, in imitation of the
early stages of a coronation, by which a handful of Yorkist lords
inaugurated their new king. Had Margaret advanced on London the
opportunity for this charade would have been denied them. Her forces
had won the battle of St Albans, but her victory had proved of no
advantage to her. On the contrary, in the changed circumstances
following the compact of October 1460 between Henry and the Yorkists,
Henry was no longer the undoubted king and thus automatically able
to establish the right of the side holding him. There was, however,
still an undefeated Lancastrian army in the field and the new king
would have to survive a successful trial by battle against them before
he could proceed to his actual coronation. Some ten days were sufficient
to muster a field force in pursuit of the Lancastrians, who elected to
make no stand south of Trent. The city fathers, who had previously
committed their money, if not their hearts, to the confederate earls
in July 1460 now once again opened their purses in the Yorkist cause.
By 7 April they had loaned Edward £12,000.[68] The various sections
of Edward's army, his own, Norfolk's, Warwick's and Fauconberg's,
finally came together for joint action at Pontefract. In the ensuing
battle at Towton, some twelve miles south-west of York, three-quarters
of the surviving peerage of England were engaged, most of them on
the Lancastrian side. Historians now think there were possibly even
50,000 combatants in all.[69] The scale of the slaughter was in any case unprecedented. Edward IV required the permanent elimination not only
of his principal opponents, but of the substance of the Lancastrian
cause. This was to a large degree achieved at Towton on Palm Sunday
29 March, where the Yorkist footsoldiers, aided by a driving snowstorm
which blinded their opponents, finally won the day. The earl of

[68] P.R.O., Exchequer of Receipt, Receipt Rolls, E.401/877; Warrants for Issues,
E.404/72/1, m.22.
[69] J. R. Lander, *The Wars of the Roses* (London 1965), 21; Charles Ross, *Edward IV*
(London 1974), 36–7; but see Ramsay, *Lancaster and York*, II, 278, where he suggests
that from measurements of the most likely site of the battle only 5,000 combatants
could be accommodated in the Lancastrian lines.

Northumberland and Lords Clifford, Nevill, Welles, Mauley and Dacre, Andrew Trollope and Sir Henry Stafford, headed some 9,000 Lancastrian slain,[70] the earls of Devon and Wiltshire were taken at York and Newcastle and beheaded. Henry, Margaret and the prince, who awaited the result in York, fled the kingdom into Scotland, where Exeter and Somerset, Lords Roos and Moleyns, Chief Justice Fortescue and other faithful, subsequently joined their exile. On their way, on 25 April, to fulfil Margaret's compact and to crown Henry's shame, Berwick was handed over to the Scots.[71]

The Yorkist lords had rescued the kingdom from the consequences of Henry VI's 'inanity',[721]that most apt description of his predominant mental state, at least since 1455, if not of all his policies since his assumption of power in 1437. This alone had rendered the event of Edward IV's usurpation possible and desirable. The shortcomings and offences of Henry VI now at last had pride of place in all the pronouncements of the Yorkist lords, although their immediate aim had been self-preservation. The intermittent fighting commonly called the Wars of the Roses had originated from the gross misgovernment and mismanagement of the nation's affairs at home and abroad by Henry VI, in which the aristocratic enmities and struggles for power were generated and fostered. These had been quite absent in the reign of his predecessor Henry V. They appeared long before Henry VI went mad. He was both an incompetent and a partisan king. He generated faction. It says much for the conservatism and restraint of the fifteenth-century English aristocracy that it took ten years from 1450 before any of them ventured to propose the removal of the king himself. Kingship was the most fundamental bond of society in fifteenth-century England and ten years of sterile armed confrontations and battles were endured before the vital issue was finally faced up to. It was impossible to end any incompetent government because the king was the government. In 1461 Henry VI was at last deposed, primarily because of his own failings and not for the claims, ambitions or rights of his supplanter.

---

[70] 'William Worcester' in Stevenson, *Wars*, II, pt. ii, 778.
[71] *R.P.*, V, 478.
[72] K. B. McFarlane, *Proceedings of the British Academy*, L (1965), 97.

Chapter 17

THE LAST TEN YEARS

When Henry crossed the border to Scotland in April 1461, ten years of exile, concealment in his own realm, captivity and a final, brief, nominal restoration to the throne, in which he personally played no part, still lay ahead before his murder in the Tower on the night of 21–22 May 1471. Previously deposed kings of England, whose mere survival was dangerous to their supplanters, had not survived their depositions by as many months. By her treaty of Lincluden and her final stand near enough to the border to make flight to safety possible, Queen Margaret had secured for him several years of freedom to rally the still powerful Lancastrian cause. His grandfather had won the kingdom from exile; Henry's successor was to recover it from exile. Starting out from exile, with initial resources no greater than Henry's were at this time, his nephew, Henry Tudor, was likewise to secure a kingdom for himself in 1485. But no such efforts came from Henry during his four years of freedom in Scotland and northern England. From 1465 he was in the hands of his supplanters, safe only because the Lancastrian heir was still at large. Prince Edward's death at Tewkesbury sealed his father's fate. Henry was done to death immediately his survival ceased to be of use to his enemies.

On his arrival in Scotland, Henry was housed first in Linlithgow palace by command of the Queen Mother, Mary of Guelders, and later with the Dominican friars in Edinburgh.[1] The young prince was made welcome by the Queen Mother at Falkland. Action in the cause which was nominally Henry's was inevitably desultory and fragmented for lack of overall, effective leadership and direction. Henry was accused in a parliamentary attainder of rearing war at Ryton and Brancepeth on 26 June 1461,[2] but whether these were Scottish incursions into England, or risings of the Westmorland Nevills, there is no evidence that Henry himself was actually back in his own kingdom there at that time. The earl of Oxford, his eldest son Aubrey, Henry's former keeper of the wardrobe, Sir Thomas Tuddenham, and others were brought to the block for communication with Queen Margaret and planning a landing in Essex in February 1462. In Wales Harlech castle held out until 1468, but attempts were not made to relieve it until

[1] *The Exchequer Rolls of Scotland*, VII, xxxvi, xxxvii, 49, 60, 145, 211.
[2] *R.P.*, V, 478.

that year, when Jasper Tudor, earl of Pembroke, in three ships with fifty men, provided by Louis XI, set out from Honfleur. Although the place was too tightly invested by Lord Herbert's men to be relieved, the earl was still able to march inland, with his tiny force swelled by local support, and to take Denbigh before he was routed.[3] In Northumberland the three adjacent castles of Alnwick, Dunstan-borough and Bamborough were not finally subdued by the Yorkists until June 1464.

The strong fortresses of Northumberland, with their ready access by sea, were the obvious springboard for recovery of the kingdom. But something more than Scottish help was deemed necessary and in July 1461 Queen Margaret sent Somerset and Moleyns to the dying Charles VII to appeal for French aid. They returned with only empty promises from the new king, the wily Louis XI,[4] so the only indefatigable champion of the Lancastrian cause, Margaret herself, landed in Brittany on Good Friday 1462, bent on success in the same mission. She was armed with valuable plenary powers from Henry to mortgage Calais in return for effective assistance. At Touraine, on these terms, she won over her cousin to give limited but practical support against Edward, 'late earl of March'.[5] Her old advocate, Pierre de Brézé, ex-seneschal of Normandy and Poitou, was given command, with 43 ships and 800 soldiers, whose wages he had to pay himself. With this force Margaret returned to Scotland, picked up Henry, Somerset and a few Scottish reinforcements and landed near Bam-borough on 25 October. Alnwick, which had meantime been taken by the Yorkists, was recaptured, and all three garrisons then reinforced. But nothing more could be attempted. Setting out with Henry and de Brézé and some half of the original French force to return to Scotland, Margaret's fleet was wrecked in a storm. The French soldiers were captured on Holy Island and Margaret, Henry and de Brézé reached comparative safety in Berwick with little more than their lives.[6] In January 1463 an attempt by land to relieve the besieged castle of Alnwick, led by the earl of Angus and de Brézé, achieved nothing.[7] French help, for the price of Calais, had proved no more effective in restoring Henry to his throne than Scottish help for the price of Berwick.

    [3] *Ibid.*, 486; 'William Worcester' in Stevenson, *Wars*, II, pt. ii, 791; Scofield, *Edward IV*, I, 458–9.

    [4] Jacques Du Clercq, *Mémoires*, ed. M. Petitot (Paris 1820), 99–100.

    [5] Commines, *Mémoires*, ed. Lenglet-Du Fresnoy, II, 367–73; Jean de Waurin, *Anciennes Chroniques d'Engleterre*, ed. E. Dupont, III, 176–7.

    [6] Basin, *op. cit.*, II, 49–51; Commines, ed. Lenglet-Du Fresnoy, II, 373; G. Chastellain, *Oeuvres*, ed. Kervyn de Lettenhove (Brussels 1863–6), IV, 230–1.

    [7] 'William Worcester' in Stevenson, *Wars*, II, pt. ii, 780.

Henry, Margaret and de Brézé were back in Bamborough in June 1463 and it was from here that Margaret and de Brézé sailed for Sluys in late July, taking with them the young Edward prince of Wales, Exeter, John Fortescue, Edmund Mountfort, Robert Whitingham, Edmund Hampden, Henry Roos, Thomas Ormond, Doctors Morton and Mackerell and others, who were destined to become a permanent court in exile of some 200 persons in all.[8] Throwing herself upon the reluctant hospitality of the duke of Burgundy, the queen and her entourage were conveyed by him to the duchy of Bar where her father, René of Anjou, provided her and the prince with a permanent residence at St Michael in Barrois.[9] Here they existed in poverty until 1471.

The decision to remove to a remote and permanent place of safety with the Lancastrian heir must have been taken by Queen Margaret in view of the increasingly hopeless appearance of Henry's cause. Henry himself returned to Edinburgh into the care of the chancellor, James Kennedy, bishop of St Andrews, who claimed a special responsibility for Henry's welfare because he had once been personally instructed to look after him by King Charles VII of France. The rest of the year 1463 was a black one indeed. Edward IV succeeded in making a tripartite truce with France and Burgundy at Hesdin in the autumn, the first since 1449, one condition of which was that Louis XI should give no more help to his Lancastrian cousins. Early in December he also secured a truce for a year with Scotland, with a view to a lasting peace.[10] There was now a real danger of Henry's extradition from Scotland since, as Edward IV claimed, he had not become James III's liege man or subject and was therefore Edward's rebel and traitor.[11] Death also deprived Henry of two of his principal supporters in Scotland, Mary of Guelders and the earl of Angus. The Lancastrians' presence there was becoming precarious and Bishop Kennedy, who at Henry's plea first took him north to St Andrews for greater safety some time after 2 January 1464,[12] returned him to Bamborough before 22 February 1464. Here messages for Margaret were entrusted to Guillaume Cousinot returning to France. Cousinot also carried pleas for assistance to the Burgundian heir, the count of Charolais, to the duke of Brittany and to their Angevin relations. According to these,

---

[8] *Ibid.*, 781.

[9] Chastellain, *op. cit.*, IV, 278–314, 'ut ibi expectaret eventus mundi' ('William Worcester' in Stevenson, *Wars*, II, pt. ii, 781).

[10] Ramsay, *Lancaster and York*, II, 300–1 and references given there.

[11] MS Harley 545 f. 148, undated request for his extradition, printed by J. O. Halliwell, *Letters of the Kings of England* (London 1846), I, 125–6.

[12] Henry's trading charter to Edinburgh dated there on 2 January 1464 cited in *Exchequer Rolls of Scotland*, VII, xxxvii; Kennedy's despatch in Waurin-Dupont, III, 164–75.

expressions of goodwill and urgings for Henry to assert his rights were then reaching Bamborough from all over his kingdom and a little practical help from all his well-wishers abroad at this crucial time was all that was needed for success.[13] Two additional northern castles, Norham and Skipton in Craven, were indeed secured for Henry at this time,[14] indicating that Bamborough had become a centre for successful Lancastrian raiding parties. But in fact his overall position had worsened with the loss of his secure retreat in Scotland.

It was Lancastrian attempts from Bamborough to interfere with the conduct of Edward IV's peace negotiations with Scotland which now led to two engagements, at Hedgeley Moor and Hexham, which finally destroyed the remaining Lancastrian hold on the north of England. Warwick and his brothers George, the chancellor and John Nevill, warden of the East March, had been entrusted with the Scottish negotiations which were fixed to be held at York. John Nevill, travelling up to meet and conduct the Scottish envoys south to York, was intercepted on 25 April 1464 by Lancastrian forces under Somerset, Hungerford, Roos and Sir Ralph Percy, on Hedgeley Moor, some nine miles north-west of Alnwick. In the encounter Sir Ralph Percy was slain. Nevill was able to complete his mission, but the Lancastrian field force did not disperse and moved south into the Tyne valley. On 14 May Nevill, with Lords Greystock and Willoughby, moved north again from Newcastle to engage them afresh. On the 15th he attacked and trapped them in their encampment, in a meadow called the Linnels on the Devil's Water, south of the river Tyne, some two or three miles from Hexham. His victory was complete. Its melancholy significance was that all Henry's leading supporters still in England were either slain, captured in the field, or taken and executed soon afterwards. The fall of the Lancastrian-held castles swiftly followed.[15] Somerset and four others were executed immediately, Roos, Hungerford, Sir Thomas Findern and three more at Newcastle on 17 May, Sir Philip Wentworth, Sir William Pennington and five others at Middleham on the 18th, and fourteen more at York at the end of the month. A few weeks later Sir William Tailboys was captured hiding in a coalpit and beheaded at Newcastle. Alnwick and Dunstanborough capitulated on 23 and 24 June; Bamborough was battered into submission and its commander, Sir Ralph Grey, executed at Doncaster on 10 July. John

[13] Printed in Waurin-Dupont, III, 178–81, and re-dated by Scofield, *Edward IV*, I, 316.

[14] *Three Fifteenth-Century Chronicles*, 178.

[15] Charles Ross, *Edward IV*, 60–1; details in Gregory's Chronicle, 223–6; *Three Fifteenth-Century Chronicles*, 79, 179; 'William Worcester' in Stevenson, *Wars*, II, pt. ii, 781–2, and College of Arms MS L 9 printed by J. O. Halliwell in *Warkworth's Chronicle* (Camden Soc., 1839), 36–9.

Nevill was fittingly created earl of Northumberland by the grateful Edward IV. The Nevills had in fact wiped out all effective Lancastrian resistance in the north of England.

Indeed only Henry himself survived. Left in Bywell castle on the north bank of the Tyne at a safe distance from the field while the issue was decided, the last signs of him for over a year were his bycoket or crowned cap and other personal possessions found there by John Nevill when he took the castle. He presented these to Edward IV at Pontefract.[16] So complete was Henry's disappearance that Edward IV is alleged to have suspected he was once more being harboured in Scotland.[17] Gregory's chronicle, which quite wrongly describes his final capture as taking place on Furness Fells, the source of the belief that he had been sheltered in Furness abbey, also states that he had come from Scotland.[18] In fact he seems to have stayed in Lancashire, West Yorkshire and Westmorland all the time until his capture. He was several times housed by John Maychell of Crackenthorpe near Appleby, who was afterwards pardoned for it.[19] He was finally discovered one day in July 1465 among the gentry of Ribblesdale, at his dinner in Waddington Hall near Clitheroe, a seat of the Tempests of Bracewell, where Sir Richard Tempest had made him welcome. After a brief flight, his whereabouts were again betrayed, allegedly by William Cantelowe, a monk of Abingdon, but those rewarded for his capture were Sir Richard himself, his brother John Tempest, his relatives Thomas, John, Richard and Edmund Talbot, of nearby Bashall and Salesbury, and their associates together with the Yorkist knight Sir James Harington. His reward was Sir Richard Tunstall's various estates at Thurland, Lonsdale and Kendal in Lancashire, Yorkshire and Westmorland, granted by his grateful king on 29 July.[20] Tunstall, formerly Henry's carver, had probably been his main protector over the previous year and even warded off his would-be captors at Waddington Hall for a brief time. But Henry was soon afterwards taken in a wood called Clitherwood, near Brungerley stepping stones over the Ribble, accompanied only by two chaplains, Doctor Thomas Manning, former dean of Windsor, and Doctor Bedon, and a young squire named Ellerton. Brought to London on horseback, with his feet bound to his stirrups, he was met by the earl of Warwick at Islington

---

[16] *Chronicles of London*, ed. Kingsford, 178.

[17] Scofield, *Edward IV*, I, 380–1.

[18] *Ibid.*, 381; Gregory's Chronicle, 232; Thomas Basin, *Histoire de Charles VII et Louis XI*, II, 53, is the unreliable source of the story that he spent several years disguised as a monk, until betrayed by a monk.

[19] *Foedera*, XI, 575; *C.P.R., 1461–1467*, 536 (20 November 1466).

[20] *R.P.*, V, 586; *Foedera*, XI, 548; P.R.O., E.404/73/1/124B. Thomas Talbot received the largest cash reward.

on 24 June and paraded through the streets to the Tower.[21] Edward IV and his new queen had received the joyful news of his capture, brought in haste to them in Canterbury cathedral, on 18 July. They celebrated it with a Te Deum, a sermon and a procession to Becket's tomb.[22]

Henry was next confined in the Tower for over five years. Other notable fifteenth-century captives of English kings wrote poetry, political testaments, corresponded, plotted; with Henry there is no contemporary record of activity of any kind whatsoever. This was not due to the rigidity of his confinement for, we are told, any man might come and speak with him by licence of his keepers.[23] Equally there is no evidence of the hunger, thirst, mockings, derision, abuse and many other hardships which the hagiographic Blacman tract later alleged he now had to endure, in imitation of Christ.[24] Five members of Edward IV's own household, seconded with others to wait and attend on 'Henry of Windsor', are named in the issue rolls: William Griffiths, Edmund Clare, Nicholas Hatfield, Thomas Grey and Hugh Courtenay and, later, Robert Radclyff esquire and William Sayer. The highest number of his attendants at any time, some of whom were presumably guards, was twenty-two;[25] five marks a week were assigned for his maintenance and paid regularly to his attendants throughout his captivity. For example, Thomas Grey received £106 13s 4d advance payment for his diet and expenses, on 13 May 1469.[26] A priest, William Kymberley, who celebrated mass for him daily by personal command of Edward IV, received 7½d a day special reward, although he had to wait fifteen months for his first payment.[27] On occasion wine was sent to him from the royal cellars and velvet cloth supplied from the wardrobe for his gowns and doublets.[28] When he was led from captivity, by his old friend the bishop of Winchester, on 3 October 1470, he was alleged to have been not so worshipfully arrayed, nor so cleanly kept, as befitted such a prince,[29] but this may not have been his captors' fault. On the whole such scanty evidence as survives suggests a humane

[21] The fullest account with notes of the various relics of his stay still preserved in Ribblesdale houses in the eighteenth century is in Halliwell's edition of *Warkworth's Chronicle*, 5 and 40–3; Stow, *Annales*, 419; *Three Fifteenth-Century Chronicles*, 80; 'William Worcester' in Stevenson, *Wars*, II, pt. ii, 785; Waurin-Dupont, II, 284–6, although his interesting detailed account is wrongly dated.

[22] John Stone, *Chronicle*, ed. W. G. Searle (Cambridge Antiquarian Society, 1902), 93.

[23] *Warkworth's Chronicle*, 5.

[24] *Life of Henry VI*, 19.

[25] P.R.O., E.404/73/1/124B; Devon, *Issues*, 489; *Foedera*, XI, 712.

[26] P.R.O., E.404/73/2/1, 74/2/37, 74/2/79; Devon, *Issues*, 492; P.R.O., E.404/75/15 (his expenses and debts after his death).

[27] P.R.O., E.404/73/2/26.

[28] Scofield, *Edward IV*, I, 383, citing Household Accounts and Issue Rolls.

[29] *Warkworth's Chronicle*, 11.

and lenient captivity which Henry accepted with complete resignation. He could be a danger to Edward IV only as a puppet in the hands of his enemies and the careful preservation of his life in captivity was Edward's best safeguard against a resurgence of the Lancastrian cause.

Henry's brief restoration, from the end of September 1470 until 11 April 1471, or 'readeption' as it was then styled, was thus understandably ascribed by many of his astonished former subjects to a miracle, to the direct intervention of the hand of God. The shrewd Crowland chronicler heard many say as much, but, he added, so inscrutable are the ways of God that within six months, not one of those who professed to believe in the divine intervention dared acknowledge that he had wished Henry well.[30] Ten years had largely obliterated the memory of his ineffective rule, although a tradition of the chief evil consequences of it which had made most of his subjects welcome a change in 1461 survived: 'the murder of the good duke of Gloucester, the poisoning of John Holand duke of Exeter, the fostering of Suffolk and his mischievous and covetous clique, the loss of France, Normandy, Gascony and Guienne'.[31] The king himself was now remembered as an 'innocent man', which meant, in the words of the Tudor chronicler Hall, glossing the event, a nonentity, 'a man of no great wit ... neither a fool nor very wise',[32] but Edward's own rule since had been only fair promises of better times, unfulfilled: battle after battle, disturbances and insecurity, taxes, decline of trade and constant demands for military service. Things were at least as bad as they had been before, so why not have another king? In fact Henry's restoration owed nothing to the hand of God, or to the fickle wishes of Edward IV's subjects at large. The *deus ex machina* had been the French king Louis XI.

From 1464 Edward IV had resumed the normal, popular policy of all successful late-medieval English kings, the assertion of his 'rights' against the Valois and the recovery of the French inheritance. As the son and heir of Richard duke of York, who had constantly attacked Henry VI's ministers for their loss of the overseas possessions, this was especially to be expected. He made a personal declaration in 1467 to parliament that he would lead his armies across the Channel if they would give him the means to do so. The Commons responded with two tenths and fifteenths. Thus they revealed once again the basic popularity of this traditional policy. Alliances with Scotland, Denmark, Castile and Brittany were announced, and compacts with the duke of Burgundy were to be sealed by his marriage to Edward's sister Margaret. Edward was ready to challenge the 'ancient adversary of

[30] Crowland Chronicle (Bohn translation), 463.
[31] *Warkworth's Chronicle*, 11–12.
[32] Edward Hall, *Chronicle*, ed. H. Ellis, 285.

France'.[33] In fact, Louis XI broke up the intended coalition against
him. He invaded Brittany and compelled its duke to desert his allies.
He secured a treaty and truce with Burgundy. He dabbled in Lancastrian plots, raising counter fears of invasion in England and sending
Jasper Tudor's expeditionary force to Wales.[34]

It was a breach between Edward and his most powerful supporter,
Warwick, which finally presented Louis with a real bonus, the means
of removing this hostile English king from his usurped throne. How
and when that breach first arose and developed into armed rebellion
has been the subject of much debate by historians.[35] The best contemporary observers believed it grew out of conflict for the control
of high policy between them. Warwick, who was thought of abroad
as the real ruler of England under the king, favoured, and persisted
in fostering, a revival of Henry VI's discredited peace-marriage policy
towards France; peace and cooperation through a French marriage
for Edward's sister, not a Burgundian one.[36] Warwick's consequent
rebellion in concert with Edward's brother George duke of Clarence
may well have been intended to declare Edward a bastard and replace
him by Clarence.[37] It had nothing to do with Henry VI, Queen
Margaret, or the Lancastrian cause. It was launched from Warwick's
old base at Calais, whither the Nevills and Clarence had repaired to
celebrate Clarence's marriage to Warwick's daughter Isabel, a marriage
which had been expressly forbidden by Edward. In striking imitation
of that enterprise of 1460, which had triumphed with the capture of
Henry VI at Northampton, they landed in Kent in July 1469, preceded
by a manifesto of 'reform' which, *mutatis mutandis*, was identical with
the placards of that earlier occasion. The Wydevilles, Sir William
Herbert and Humphrey Stafford, the new Yorkist earls of Pembroke and
Devon, Lord Audley and Sir John Fogge now replaced the earls of
Shrewsbury and Wiltshire and Lord Beaumont of 1460 as the evil
advisers who had estranged the lords of the blood from the king's
council, appropriated his landed estate and revenues, caused his subjects
to be loaded down with taxes and purveyances, perverted the processes
of justice to serve their own ends, plundered the church, etc. The only
basic difference was that it was now Edward IV and not Henry VI
who was threatened with the fate of Edward II and Richard II.[38]
At no stage yet were Warwick and Clarence converted Lancastrians.

---

[33] *R.P.*, V, 622–3; 'William Worcester' in Stevenson, *Wars*, II, pt. ii, 789.

[34] See above, pp. 333–4.

[35] The evidence is re-surveyed by Charles Ross, *Edward IV*, 114ff.

[36] Crowland Chronicle (Bohn translation), 457–8.

[37] As stated in Edward IV's proclamations against them (*Warkworth's Chronicle*, 53
notes), cf. Ross, *op. cit.*, 133.

[38] *Warkworth's Chronicle*, 46–51 (notes).

23(a). Eight Henry of Windsor pilgrim badges.

23(b). Pilgrim's money box in St George's chapel, Windsor, by the tomb of Henry VI.

23(c). Statue of Henry VI on the lectern of King's College chapel, dating from the provostship of Robert Hacomblen (1509–28).

24. Henry VI invoked as a saint. Woodcut of *c.* 1490, pasted into a Lollard bible of *c.* 1440.

A possible restoration of Henry VI, as yet, never entered their minds.

In the event, although they were able to secure possession of Edward's person and destroy the so-called royal favourites, they were unable to establish any acceptable authority of their own. The lack of any effective government provided the opportunity for a Lancastrian rising in the northern borders, led by two members of the senior branch of the Nevills, Sir Humphrey Nevill of Brauncepeth and his brother Charles. Warwick found that his proclamation to raise the forces needed to suppress this rising was useless without the king's authority behind it. Men knew that, unlike Henry, Edward IV could only be forcibly restrained and could not be used as a puppet king, therefore he had to be released and seen to be evidently free before the necessary troops were forthcoming to suppress the Lancastrian rising. With peace restored, and his freedom regained, Edward now seized his opportunity to re-establish himself. He followed a policy of pacification, rather than punishment, for the uprisings, until new disturbances began in Lincolnshire early in 1470. Warwick and Clarence also became involved in this rising and after its suppression fled to the continent where the duke of Burgundy, and even Warwick's hitherto firm Calais base, refused to receive them.[39] Edward's 'great rebels' were thus driven into the arms of Louis XI who was able to insist on the impossible, their reconciliation with Queen Margaret of Anjou and with Edward prince of Wales. The restoration of the House of Lancaster was the unavoidable price they had to pay for the French king's invaluable assistance. With what reservations and reluctance Warwick and the queen sealed the compact has been variously estimated. It was inevitable that their agreement should frustrate the ambition of the treacherous Clarence. He could gain little from the success of a plan to restore the House of Lancaster, which was to be cemented by the marriage of the Lancastrian heir to Warwick's daughter Anne. He had to be satisfied with being designated residual heir, should the Lancastrian line utterly fail.

When Warwick landed in Devon on 13 September 1470 the king was still in Yorkshire, after quieting a minor rising in the north, possibly contrived by the Nevills to distract him. He began his march to London, but waited at Doncaster for the considerable force being assembled at Pontefract in his name by John Nevill, marquis of Montagu, Warwick's brother. The king still trusted Montagu's loyalty, even against his brother's enterprise, but Edward underestimated Montagu's resentment over his loss of the substantial earldom of Northumberland. The king had wished to conciliate the Percies and so had required him, earlier that year, to relinquish the earldom and the wardenship of the East March to the Percy earl of Northumberland, and accept in its place the superior, but empty title of marquis. When Edward heard

[39] For details see Ross, *op. cit.*, 126ff.

that Montagu had turned traitor and was bent on his capture, he fled across the Wash to Lynn and thence to Burgundy.

It was the report of Edward's precipitate flight which prompted the civic authorities in London to take possession of the Tower and caused Henry to be visited there on 3 October by Bishop Wainfleet and the mayor. They removed him from his captivity to the king's lodgings, which had been prepared for Queen Elizabeth's approaching confinement. She fled to sanctuary at Westminster. Loyalty could hardly be maintained to a king who had fled the country. Warwick and Clarence were duly proclaiming Henry's title on their advance towards London and already, on Sunday 30 September, a Dr William Goddard had been put up to preach to that effect at St Paul's Cross.[40] George Nevill, archbishop of York, entered the city with a considerable force on 5 October. Clarence and Warwick arrived with their army next day and removed Henry in state to the bishop of London's palace. On 8 October Warwick felt able to inform Louis XI that all was well. Henry was re-established in his kingdom.[41] On 13 October, the Translation of St Edward, they took him in procession for a crown-wearing to St Paul's, Warwick bearing his train and the earl of Oxford his sword. He was then returned to the bishop's palace and installed there with a new household. Sir Henry Lewes was appointed ruler and governor of it and over the next six weeks spent £1,001 22½d, largely out of his own pocket, establishing and maintaining it. Here Henry seems to have remained for five months of his nominal restoration, until Edward IV entered the palace on Maundy Thursday 11 April 1471 and returned him, together with the archbishop of York who then had custody of him, to the Tower.[42]

During these five months there is no evidence that Henry did anything at all. Authority was uneasily shared between Warwick, who assumed the title of his lieutenant, and Clarence. Warwick established himself in the bishop's palace with the king, taking the office of great chamberlain of England as well as his long-standing captaincy of Calais. Coroners, verderers, sheriffs, justices of the peace, judges, barons of the exchequer were now appointed or reappointed in Henry's name. Summonses for a parliament were issued in his name on 15 October. This duly met on 26 November at Westminster, to hear a sermon from the chancellor on the appropriate text 'Turn again to me O backsliding children',[43] and, after adjournment to St Paul's, it sat until Christmas and then again in the New Year. Who attended is not known and what little is known about its proceedings comes only from the

---

[40] Stow, *Annales*, 422; *London and the Kingdom*, ed. Sharpe, III, 385–6.
[41] Waurin-Dupont, III, 43–4.
[42] Stow, *Annales*, 423; P.R.O., E.404/71/6/36 (city of London 18 December).
[43] *Warkworth's Chronicle*, 12.

chroniclers, because the Yorkists later destroyed its records. Edward IV
and his younger brother Richard duke of Gloucester were attainted
and the attainders of his reign reversed. The making of a ten-year
truce and a peace treaty with Louis XI was authorized.[44] As seen from
abroad this extraordinary regime appeared to have been instantly and
well established, and Warwick, true to his compact with Louis, even
began raising an army to fight with him against the duke of Burgundy
in Flanders,[45] where Louis had already begun hostilities. But Queen
Margaret and the prince of Wales had still not sailed for England.
Warwick received £2,000 and more from 18 December 1470 to proceed
with an army of ships to France to fetch them.[46] Late in February he
went down to Dover to receive them, but still they did not come.[47]

There was one man at Margaret's court, Sir John Fortescue, formerly
Lord Chief Justice of England and in exile with her since 1463, acting
as tutor to Prince Edward, who tried to bend his mind squarely to the
problems of the Lancastrian restoration of Henry VI. He communicated
his advice, through the prince, to Warwick, in the belief that a
permanent government in Henry's name would now have to be provided for. How could a repetition of past disasters in this utterly unforeseen reversal of fortune be avoided? First Henry must reward no one,
however deserving, until his resources had been surveyed and his means
ascertained. Otherwise, from the start, he would again be living off
his subjects and he, and whoever he took to advise him, would once
again be the centre of intrigue and envy. Rewarding must be done
not by Henry but by a new council of uncontroversial membership:
twelve members, balanced by twelve ecclesiastics, together with a
further four temporal lords and four spiritual lords, elected for a year
at a time. The king should henceforth only act on advice given after
mature debate in this council, not only over patronage but on all affairs
of state. Thus a crucial mistake of the past, household and chamber
men giving the king advice and controlling affairs, might be avoided.
It was fundamentally for this reason, the alleged miscounselling of
Henry, he believed, that so many people had lost their lives. The new
council would be an adequately salaried body and would take no other
rewards; the money for this must be found. Looking at the past it was
obvious that under the old ways a single temporal lord had on occasion
managed to acquire as much of the king's livelihood as would have
paid adequate wages for the whole council. Actual alienation of the
king's livelihood would now be allowable only by act of parliament.

[44] Scofield, *Edward IV*, I, 563, citing *Foedera*, XI, 681–90.
[45] *Coventry Leet Book*, 362 (22 February); A. R. Myers, 'The Outbreak of War between
England and Burgundy in February 1471', *B.I.H.R.*, XXXIII (1960), 114–15.
[46] P.R.O., E.404/71/6/35.
[47] *Chronicle of London*, ed. Kingsford, 183.

The rest of the advice was concerned mainly with the details of how the new council would manage the finances, with an especial concern that a controversial great new household should not be established immediately. Henry himself should be kept for at least a year in a sure place or places best for his health and pleasance, with a few people and only the absolute minimum number of his old household men about him.[48]

All this was a sad admission, just short of spelling it out, that the fundamental problem would be the incapacity of Henry to rule, even if he could be roused from his comatose state after five years of captivity. It clearly demonstrates that a well-informed contemporary, who had participated in government during the 1440s, appreciated that the troubles of the 1450s, the first of the Wars of the Roses, had arisen from Henry's inadequacies as king. But Fortescue could only offer a superficial, administrative solution to the fundamental, political problem of a king who had to rule but who, long before his illness, had shown himself to be inherently incapable of ruling well or even adequately. Georges Chastellain expressed the immediate political situation of 1470–1 graphically and directly: Warwick, as mayor of the palace, was ruling for 'a stuffed wool sack lifted by its ears, a shadow on the wall, bandied about as in a game of blind-man's buff ... submissive and mute, like a crowned calf'.[49]

Clarence accepted the lieutenancy of Ireland on 18 February 1471.[50] His share in Warwick's government is obscure, but he was almost certainly already suborned by his brother in exile, through the good offices of their sisters, the duchesses of Burgundy and Exeter.[51] It was Louis XI's declaration of war against the duke of Burgundy which, during the first week of January, decided Burgundy to finance Edward's attempt to recover his kingdom.[52] Edward sailed from Flushing on 11 March with some 1,200 men, a mixed force of English and Burgundian mercenaries, in Dutch and Hansa ships. The threat hanging over the so-called Lancastrian regime seems to have become apparent towards the end of March when Clarence, Pembroke and Warwick appointed themselves commissioners to raise Henry's subjects against Edward. A similar commission was issued to the prince of Wales,[53] who was still on board ship with his mother at Honfleur. They had embarked on

[48] Identified and printed by Charles Plummer, *Fortescue on the Governance of England*, 348–53.

[49] Chastellain, *op. cit.*, V, 490, quoted by Ramsay, *Lancaster and York*, II, 363.

[50] *Foedera*, XI, 693, backdated to 29 September.

[51] Crowland Chronicle (Bohn translation), 464.

[52] *Foedera*, XI, 705–7 (25, 27 March).

[53] Ramsay, *Lancaster and York*, II, 363, citing Comines-Lenglet, I, 162, II, 197; Waurin-Dupont, III, 55; T. Basin, *op. cit.*, II, 252.

24 March, but contrary winds kept them in port until Easter Saturday 13 April.

It is possible that by her six-month delay, unwilling or unable to bring herself to the point of risking everything on the final throw, Margaret herself ruined the Lancastrian cause. Had the prince and heir apparent, now seventeen, been sent over with Clarence and Warwick; had Henry, willing in 1460 to renounce his inheritance to the Yorkists, been now persuaded to abdicate in favour of his son; had all their available forces been concentrated together, then the House of Lancaster might, even at that late stage, have acquired a new, effective centre of loyalty and purpose. But Edward IV seized back the initiative. His restoration with the aid of a very few of his peers – Gloucester, Rivers, Hastings, Say and Sele – owed little to anyone's efforts apart from his own. If his preliminary landing at Cromer had not been thwarted by the earl of Oxford, his final appearance at Ravenspur in Holderness might have been taken as a conscious imitation of Henry of Bolingbroke in 1399, especially as he kept up the pretence that he had come only to claim his duchy of York until he reached the Midlands, where William, Lord Hastings's men flocked to his support. The Percy earl of Northumberland now amply repaid his restoration of the year before merely by 'sitting still'.[54] Warwick was surprised and bypassed in Coventry, where he was awaiting Clarence's support. Clarence, as prearranged, brought his army, raised in Henry's name, to his brother's side.

In London George Nevill, archbishop of York, paraded Henry on horseback through the streets of the capital from the bishop's palace, in a vain attempt to inspire resistance and solidarity in the city, but he secretly sent to Edward to secure his grace and kept Henry out of sanctuary on Edward's instructions.[55] On Maundy Thursday, at dinner time, Edward entered the city in triumph, unopposed.[56] There was no will or desire to resist him. He went directly to St Paul's to offer and to secure the persons of King Henry and the archbishop from the bishop's palace. When he came face to face with his feeble supplanter, Edward held out his hand to him, but Henry, who actually appeared glad to see him, came forward to embrace him saying 'Cousin of York, you are very welcome. I hold my life to be in no danger in your hands.' Edward told him not to worry about anything; he would fare well.[57] We can only conclude that Henry was quite content to be Edward's

[54] *The Arrival of Edward IV*, ed. J. Bruce (Camden Soc., 1838), 6. This official account of his restoration, sent out after the event, gives the basic facts. A French version is printed in Waurin-Dupont, III, 96–145.

[55] *Warkworth's Chronicle*, 26.

[56] *Chronicles of London*, ed. Kingsford, 184; *Warkworth's Chronicle*, 15.

[57] As reported to Margaret of York, duchess of Burgundy, by an Englishman who left London on Easter Monday 1471; Waurin-Dupont, III, 210–14.

prisoner once more, perhaps looking forward to returning to his old quarters in the Tower. For the moment Edward kept him with him wherever he went, under close guard.[58]

On the vigil of Easter, 'paying more attention to urgent necessity than to absurd notions of propriety',[59] Edward set out to confront Warwick and Montagu at Chipping Barnet. Here, on Enfield Chase, to the north of the town, in the misty first light of Easter Sunday, with the good luck that favours all successful generals, he slaughtered the Nevills in time for a triumphant re-entry into London that same afternoon. Henry, who had been taken to Barnet by Edward, was once again, and for good, put back in the Tower, together with his keeper, the treacherous archbishop.

That day Margaret and the prince landed at Weymouth and moved north to Cerne Abbey, where on Easter Monday they had news of Barnet. Any plans to march on London were perforce abandoned. Feints were made to Shaftesbury and Salisbury, to convince the enemy that they were indeed moving east, but from Cerne they marched west, recruiting as they went, and mustered all the strength of the western counties they could gather at Exeter, under the earl of Devon and the self-styled duke of Somerset. The intention now was to proceed via the Severn valley to join with Jasper Tudor, and so on to Cheshire and to the duchy of Lancaster heart-lands. Edward, who had knowledge of their landing on Easter Tuesday, kept his nerve and patience, remustering his forces and holding the Feast of St George at Windsor. On the morning after, 24 April, he set out, furnished at last with reliable reports of their general movements. On 2 May, at Malmesbury, he heard that Bristol had received and refreshed them, but before they got to Gloucester, the town, castle and Severn crossing had been secured for Edward by his own servants under Sir Richard Beauchamp. Forced marches over the higher slopes of the Cotswolds brought Edward up with them at Tewkesbury on Saturday 4 May. His victory there, that day, was crowned by the death of Prince Edward, still on the field when struck down, but in flight towards the town according to the official Yorkist account, 'The Arrivall'; deserted and crying in vain for succour to his brother-in-law, Clarence, according to the independent account in John Warkworth's chronicle; deliberately assassinated by unnamed persons, along with the principal Lancastrian lords, according to the most reliable Crowland chronicler. This was truly the end of the House of Lancaster, though who can doubt that Henry, who had done so much to promote the Beauforts against York in his own days of power, would have rejoiced to see the ultimate triumph of his Tudor-

[58] *Ibid.*, III, 124.
[59] Crowland Chronicle (Bohn translation), 464.

Beaufort namesake when his Yorkist supplanters finally destroyed themselves by their internecine strife?

His son's murder at Tewkesbury undoubtedly sealed Henry's own fate. He was done to death in the Tower a few hours before Edward IV reached London on the vigil of the Ascension, during the night or early morning of 21–22 May. The Crowland Chronicler, writing in 1486, called his unnamed slayer a tyrant and the victim a glorious martyr. The only circumstantial account, in Warkworth, written soon after July 1482, suggests that Richard duke of Gloucester was responsible for it as the principal man in the Tower at the time. A chronicle in the Cotton collection, Vitellius A xvi, written before 1496, records that it was then said that Richard of Gloucester did it but that there could be no certainty of this.[60] His body was 'chested' and taken, heavily guarded, to lie with the face uncovered in St Paul's, where it bled on the pavement, and then to Blackfriars for the funeral service, where it bled again. From here it was carried by barge up-river to the Benedictine abbey at Chertsey, to be buried there in the Lady Chapel and, it was hoped, forgotten. Twenty-eight yards of Holland linen were used to wrap the body and money expended on wax, spices and torches. Calais soldiers were hired to guard it, barges, masters and oarsmen to convey the cortege to Chertsey and the Dominicans, Franciscans, Carmelites, Augustinians and Friars of the Holy Cross were all paid to celebrate obsequies and masses.[61] Neither the official 'Arrivall' account, that Henry died on Ascension day of pure displeasure and melancholy at the news of Tewkesbury, immediately after Edward IV's departure again from London into Kent, nor the statement in a latin chronicle that he expired 'feliciter' on the vigil of the Ascension, can be believed.[62] When his remains were exhumed in 1910 the best opinions then available confirmed the almost unanimous views of the contemporary chroniclers: the hair matted with blood on the skull showed that he had indeed died a violent death. That deed could only have been done on the orders of Edward IV himself. The Sforza ambassador in France reported as much to his master in Milan. Edward, he said, had decided to have the custody of King Henry no longer; with the prince of Wales, Warwick and all the powerful Lancastrian adherents dead he had had him secretly put to death and, rumour had it, Henry's queen as well. He had chosen 'to crush the seed'.[63]

In fact only the Angevin Queen Margaret remained, now utterly

[60] *Chronicles of London*, ed. Kingsford, 185; *English Historical Literature*, 101.
[61] Devon, *Issues*, 495–6.
[62] *Three Fifteenth-Century Chronicles*, 184.
[63] *Calendar of State Papers Milan*, I, 157, dispatch in cypher dated at la Fère, 17 June 1471.

bereft of her Lancastrian family and cause. Captured after the battle she was brought to London in a cart and took Henry's place in the Tower.[64] Later she was transferred to the more congenial wardship of her old friend, the dowager duchess of Suffolk, at Wallingford, until her cousin Louis XI pitied her and ransomed her from Edward after their treaty of Picquigny in 1475.[65] She died on 20 August 1482, near Saumur in Anjou, and was buried in her father's tomb in the cathedral of St Maurice in Angers.

---

[64] *Chronicles of London*, ed. Kingsford, 184; P.R.O., E.404/75/15 (2 June 1471), payments for the 'debts' of Henry and the current expenses of Margaret.

[65] B.L. MS Cotton, Vespatian, F. iii, f. 65, agreement between Louis XI and Edward IV for the delivery of Margaret of Anjou, 2 October 1475. J. J. Bagley, *Margaret of Anjou* (London 1948), 233ff., gives the details.

Part VI

APOTHEOSIS

APOTHEOSIS

The 'variable and divers fortune of king Henry the Sixt'[1] is not yet entirely told, for well within ten years of his death the 'sillie weake King'[2] had become the popular saint, embarked on by a burgeoning career of miracle working which, for the next fifty years, at least equalled, if it did not exceed, that of St Thomas of Canterbury. Long years of passive endurance and the violence done to the Lord's anointed at the end provided fertile ground for an image of innocent martyrdom. Although no Chaucer appeared to immortalize him, forbidden pilgrimages of gratitude for his ghostly interventions to the hitherto unremarked but easily accessible Thames-side abbey of Chertsey presaged a more than nationwide devotion.[3] Two further usurpations, within three years of his supplanter's death, each gave boosts to the popular cult and the ensuing official campaign for the canonization of the now saintly royal martyr should have been crowned with success, in due course, within a few years of what proved to be its final mention, in 1528.[4] But in the event Henry's heavenly kingdom, like his earthly inheritance, slipped through his fingers.

The earliest surviving evidence of the cult comes from York minster where his former secretary Dean Richard Andrew had erected a screen bearing images of all past kings of the realm, from the Conqueror to Henry. His statue on this screen was already being venerated there in 1473.[5] Archbishop Booth condemned this veneration as contempt of

[1] *Polydore Vergil's English History*, ed. Henry Ellis (Camden Soc., 1844), 112.

[2] This was King James I's description of him. He found comparisons made with himself particularly irritating: cited by R. Zaller, *The Parliament of 1621* (Berkeley 1971), 69.

[3] The cult has been exhaustively and authoritatively documented by the Jesuit Father Paul Grosjean in *Henrici VI Angliae Regis Miracula Postuma* (Société des Bollandistes, Bruxelles 1935), which contains the full latin text of B.L. MS Royal 13 C viii (the contemporary account of the miracles) and all relevant documents from English and papal archives. See also *The Miracles of King Henry VI*, ed. and trans. Ronald Knox and Shane Leslie (Cambridge 1923); Cardinal Gasquet, *The Religious Life of King Henry VI* and John W. McKenna, 'Piety and Propaganda: The Cult of King Henry VI', in *Chaucer and Middle English Studies in honour of Rossel Hope Robbins*, ed. Beryl Rowlands, 72–88.

[4] 'Yf my Lord of Canterbury and my Lord of Winchester ... do send the process hither ... the sentence of canonization shal shortly pass here', the king's proctors at Rome to Cardinal Wolsey, 13 April 1528 (*Letters and Papers Foreign and Domestic*, IV, pt. II, 1841, no. 4167).

[5] *The Fabric Rolls of York Minster*, ed. James Raine (Surtees Society XXXV, 1859), 83; Grosjean, 157. *

the church and disparagement of King Edward in 1479.[6] Edward himself enlisted the aid of the London livery companies to stop the 'great usage ... in going of Pilgrimage to King Henry' in the following year.[7] There is some evidence that the abbot of Chertsey himself, in the face of royal displeasure, quite understandably did his official best to discourage the pilgrims.[8]

By contrast Richard III took a different line. On 12 August 1484, no doubt from the same motives as had prompted Henry V to move the body of Richard II, whom his father had deposed and murdered, from Langley to Westminster, and to rescind the prohibitions of offerings at the shrine of Archbishop Scrope whom his father had executed, King Richard III gave Henry of Windsor's corpse an honourable 'translation' back to his birthplace. Here he was buried opposite his supplanter, in the second bay of the south choir aisle of St George's Chapel (the first perhaps being reserved for Richard himself). The charge made by Henry VII, in his supplication for papal approval of a further remove to Westminster abbey, that the Windsor burial carried out by Richard III was intended to be more obscure and inaccessible even than Chertsey, can hardly be sustained. An exhumation carried out at Windsor on 4 November 1910[9] revealed that in 1484 the remains of the earth burial at Chertsey had been reverently enclosed within a wooden casket, inside a small chest of sheet lead and then re-interred inside a full-sized, wooden, iron-bound coffin. This discovery thus confirmed, in part, John Rous's contemporary description of the event; not that the body was found in great part uncorrupted, but that the corpse was honourably treated and reburied with great solemnity to the south of the high altar at Windsor.[10] Nearby stood the chapel of Master John Shorn, another late-fifteenth-century cure worker, now the Lincoln chapel, as well as the canons of Windsor's greatest treasure, a piece of the True Cross. This point in the ambulatory was the culmination of pilgrimages which Henry's 'translation' now enormously enhanced. All that remains today of the contemporary scene is the elaborate wrought-iron money box with its four separate locks and Henry's initial, probably made in 1484 by John Tresilian, the king's smith, to receive the offerings of pilgrims at the tomb.

[6] *Ibid.*, 157–8 from Laurence Booth's register.

[7] *Acts of Court of the Mercers' Company 1453–1527*, with intro., by Laetitia Lyell (Cambridge 1936), 139 (4 November 1480).

[8] One of the Windsor pilgrims (Thomas Fullar, miracle no. 40) repeated his pilgrimage there because earlier he had not been made welcome at Chertsey (according to the Windsor scribe).

[9] W. H. St John Hope, 'The Discovery of the Remains of King Henry VI in St George's Chapel, Windsor', *Archaeologia*, LXII (1910), 533–42.

[10] John Rous, *Historia Regum Angliae*, ed. Thomas Hearne (Oxford 1745), 127.

Henry was a popular, invocatory saint to whom, usually joined with the Virgin, the faithful made their supplications, bending a coin or measuring the length of the body of the beneficiary and vowing a wax candle of equivalent length to be offered at the tomb on the subsequent pilgrimage in thanksgiving for the favour received. Further votive offerings, as portrayed in a woodcut of about 1490 which shows the royal saint in gigantic proportions, surrounded by his kneeling suppliants, were also left at the tomb; wax models symbolic of the cure or rescue, such as parts of the body, a whole naked boy, a horse or a ship, or real objects discarded, such as crutches, chains or garments.[11] Prayers, promptly answered at the site of the calamity, were the essence of his miracles. Subsequent cures at the tomb itself, or following the pilgrimage, were rare.

That the widespread devotion to Holy King Henry extended even beyond his kingdom of England is testified by the distribution of leaden pilgrim tokens purchased at the Windsor shrine.[12] Among his miracles appears the case of the infant Miles Freebridge, of Aldermanbury, London, who choked on a round silver token bearing the image of St Thomas of Canterbury, of the type which had been sold at Canterbury for the previous three centuries. Prayers to Henry, not Thomas, dislodged it from his gullet and revived him. The canons of Windsor were now producing their own Holy King Henry badges. Five distinct known types have been dug up: two depicting the king standing crowned in robes of state with orb and sceptre, either embossed on a round medallion or on a lozenge-shaped badge, one a standing cut-out of the king with his antelope, one of the king peering over a towered rampart and another of the king in a ship, a design based on the gold noble. Also within England, apart from his effigies in York, Durham and Ripon minsters, he came to be represented on screens or in stained glass in numerous parish churches. Prayers and hymns addressed to him abound in late-fifteenth and early-sixteenth-century manuscripts and printed Books of Hours.[13]

As Eton boys wrote in their grammatical exercises, 'King Henry

[11] MS Bodley 277, pasted in on fol. 376v., see Campbell Dodgson, 'English Devotional Woodcuts of the late fifteenth-century with special reference to those in the Bodleian Library', *The Walpole Society*, XVII (1928–9), 104–7.

[12] Brian Spencer, 'Pilgrim Badges of King Henry the Sixth', *Henry VI Society Newsletter* (December 1972), 10–13.

[13] Exhaustive list in Grosjean, 234–62. Modern survivals include paintings at Warfield (Berks.), Binham Abbey (Norfolk), St Michael's at St Albans, Eye (Suffolk), Ludham, Barton Turf, Litcham, Gateley and Witton (Norfolk), Alton (Hants.), Whimple (Devon); stained glass portraits in York Minster, All Soul's College, Oxford, St Mary's Hall, Coventry, Ashton-under-Lyme and King's College, Cambridge (details *ibid.*, 252–4).

doth many divers miracles. Divus Henricus non una miraculorum specie inclarescit.'[14] He was indeed no narrow specialist. His collected miracles have the appearance and range of a fifteenth-century coroner's roll as regards his exploits for his fellow men, except that the victims recovered: rescues from death by drowning, from crushings to death under cart-wheels, from hangings, woundings, fatal falls, lightning strikes, fires and assaults. Ruptures cured included one caused by a kick in a football match, an execrable, worthless and dangerous game, in the Tudor compiler's opinion. Madness, blindness, deafness, sweating sickness, plague, epilepsy, lameness, battle wounds, even heresies, were all cured or healed; shipwrecks were averted, childbirth made easy and deformed infants made normal by his intervention. But he was not above curing horses, cows or pigs and would find lost animals, or even a mislaid purse. He was pre-eminent in all he touched, for not only did he outshine St Thomas, but he stole the thunder of his successors. Prayers and vows alone to Henry were sufficient to cure scrofula, the king's evil, and the wise parents of a nine-year-old sufferer were recorded (after 1485, notably) as having rejected the ministrations of the live Richard III in favour of the more immediately accessible and effective offices of the dead Henry.

The canons of Windsor duly recorded the original, vernacular testimonies of the recipients of Henry's bounty themselves, and of their witnesses and supporters, who on occasion numbered as many as forty at a time, accompanying them on their pilgrimage. All that now survives is a latin edition of 172 miracles,[15] some given in detail, some only in epitome, but culled from what must have been at least 445 cases in the original vernacular accounts, as taken down at Windsor between 1484 and 1500. This latin edition seems to have been compiled for use by papal commissioners, since 77 of the case histories were subsequently marked as investigated and 23 of these declared proved to the satisfaction of investigators. Peak years of pilgrimage before 1500 were 1484, 1485 and 1486, with a resurgence in 1490 and 1491 and again in 1499, but there is evidence that devotion to 'Holy King Henry' continued long after. Henry VIII is recorded offering at his altar on 10 June 1529.[16] In 1543 a Windsor choirman, Robert Testwood, could not refrain from admonishing idolatrous Devon and Cornishmen, with their candles and wax images, who were offering to Good King Henry of Windsor, as they called him, vainly spending their goods on such a

[14] Roger Ascham, *The Schoolmaster*, ed. J. Upton (London 1711), 128.
[15] B.L. MSS Royal 13 C. viii and Harley 423, a partial copy; Grosjean, 1–307.
[16] *Ibid.*, 230, citing the Household Book, 21 Henry VIII from J. Payne Collier, *Trevelyan Papers prior to A.D. 1658* (Camden Soc., 1857).

long journey simply to revere his relics, to kiss a spur, and to have an old hat put on their heads.[17]

Henry VII promoted his uncle's canonization with three successive popes, Innocent VIII, at some date before 1492, Alexander VI, who appointed the archbishop of Canterbury and the bishop of Durham to inquire into Henry's life and miracles, before and after death, on 4 October 1494, and Julius II, who appointed a further commission, consisting of the archbishop of Canterbury and the bishops of Winchester, Durham and London, on 20 May 1504. In response to a request from this latter commission Julius gave them extra powers to appoint deputies, to travel about to take the testimonies of aged and infirm witnesses, on 3 May 1507.[18] But the matter was still *sub judice* in 1528 when a report from the archbishop of Canterbury and the bishop of Winchester, presumably under yet another commission of inquiry, was still awaited in Rome.[19] The break with Rome put an end to it.

The temptation is strong to see here a series of inquiries languishing over half a century and failing because of the weakness of the case. Francis Bacon, while partly blaming the length and inconclusiveness of the process on Henry VII's reluctance to pay for it, also says shortly, but without foundation, that the pope had to make a distinction between saints and fools if the honour was not to be cheapened.[20] Archbishop Morton's Register in fact provides contemporary evidence that there was no undue delay in Rome or elsewhere. The normal rate of progress towards canonization, allowing for unavoidable delays caused by deaths of popes and ecclesiastical commissioners, was certainly followed in this case. Current papal directives, entered in the Register about 1494 for the guidance of those involved in a process of canonization, stressed that the pope had to be petitioned not once but many times, and always in the most compelling terms; that he would never act precipitately; that the reputation of sanctity had to grow and grow until the pope felt compelled to issue a commission of local inquiry into the authenticity and extent of the belief. This, duly considered, and accepted at Rome, was followed by a further local commission to ascertain the facts of the candidate's life and miracles. All this had to precede further final, exhaustive inquiries at Rome into all the evidence submitted.[21] If, as seems to have been the case, the only

[17] John Foxe, *The Book of Martyrs*, ed. S. G. Potter (Newcastle-upon-Tyne and London 1873), 279.

[18] Wilkins, *Concilia*, III, 640 (1494); Grosjean, 207–9, from Arch. Vatic. Reg. Vat. 984, fols 49–50v. (1504), both of which contain references to an earlier bull of Innocent VIII; Grosjean, 215–16, from Arch. Vatic. Reg. Vat. 1204, fol. 228v. (1507).

[19] See above, p. 351, n. 4.

[20] *The Works of Francis Bacon*, ed. J. Spedding and others, 14 vols (London 1857–74), VI, 233–4.

[21] Grosjean, 169–76.

support for a saintly life which could then be produced was the jejune Blacman collection which attempted to describe an uninvolved, holy innocent, with its blatant manufacture of one solitary, incongruous, lifetime miracle (Henry, with his army in the field, feeding his whole host with a superfluity of bread from a small quantity of wheat, while his enemies went hungry), then this at least must certainly have presented serious difficulties to honest contemporary ecclesiastical opinion. Morton's instructions specified both a glorious life, with miracles performed while still on earth, as well as posthumous miracles. Neither the one nor the other was sufficient alone. Arguments that Henry was 'A Very Small King' and that a saint should achieve his sanctity in harmony, and not at variance, with his secular vocation, are valid ones.[22] They must have carried weight then as now.

The posthumous miracles also, while in a different category from the Blacman tract, are still at the mercy of the sceptic. A natural explanation can be offered for them all: the patient would have recovered anyway; the illness or injury looked much worse than it was; death was wrongly presumed; the therapeutic value simply of prayer alone, and of being prayed for, could be very high.[23] There is no record of the comparable occasions on which Henry's intervention must have been sought without success. But the fact remains that the great army of the faithful populace involved in these posthumous manifestations of Henry's sanctity believed that what they experienced, saw, heard and reported was true. Maintained over a sufficiently long period, and duly recorded by the legal processes of the church, this would in due course have been deemed sufficient, and may even yet be so. Thus divine judgement would be declared decisive over human reason.[24] But in a canonized Henry VI there could be no exemplar of kingship.[25] Decisions he took, and the courses of action he initiated and approved, on earth, had produced less good than evil.

From 1496, when Edward IV's new chapel of St George at Windsor was ready to become the chapel of the Order of the Garter, Henry VII was free to pursue plans for the eventual, official translation of his sainted uncle's relics. He pulled down almost entirely the old chapel of St Edward and St George, the home of Edward III's Order, on the site of the present Albert Memorial Chapel, and began to build there a new Lady Chapel to house seven chantry priests, his own tomb, and a shrine over the relics of Holy King Henry. Special indulgences

[22] 'Henry VI; A Very Small King', *The Times*, Saturday 19 August 1972.

[23] See Basil Clarke, *Mental Disorder in Earlier Britain*, 151–75, for a modern medical discussion of the healing miracles.

[24] As the papal bulls of 1494 and 1504 and the guide lines laid down in Morton's Register specified it should be.

[25] *The Times, loc. cit.*

for pilgrims to this new chapel of the Virgin at Windsor were obtained, with papal permission to transfer to it the endowments of Luffield priory in Buckinghamshire.[26] Among the miracles is a case of mariners carrying dressed stone from Caen for building Henry VII's new church at Windsor, who escaped the hot pursuit of pirates by continuously calling on the name of Good King Henry.

But contention arose to prevent these plans. The abbots and convents of Chertsey and Westminster now both asserted prior claims to the relics, Chertsey on the grounds that Richard III had removed them from Chertsey without authority and against their will, Westminster on the more compelling grounds that Henry VI himself, when he was their parishioner, had chosen his resting-place there and that it was the traditional burial place of the kings of England. The matter was heard out by the king's council both in the Star Chamber and, finally, at Greenwich on 5 March 1498. Eleven ancient eye-witnesses – John Ashby, former clerk to the signet, priests, servants, scriveners and crafts-men of the abbey, commissioned to make the tomb – all claimed that Henry had himself selected a spot in St Edward's chapel at Westminster as his burial place. The evidence is not entirely above suspicion. The date was very uncertain, generally given as forty years or more earlier. The most specific of the witnesses, a scrivener of seventy, who plumped for the autumn of 1458, claimed he then saw Henry take the cham-berlain's staff from the hands of Ralph, Lord Cromwell and with it mark out the length and breadth of the tomb.[27] Cromwell had in fact died on 4 January 1456. However, the sheer volume of their circum-stantial evidence convinced the king and council that the Westminster convent had indeed succeeded in revealing Henry's own intentions for his final resting place. Henry VII therefore ceased his building at Windsor and petitioned the pope for permission to move the relics to Westminster, which was finally granted in 1504.[28] On 24 January 1503 Abbot John Islip had laid the first stone of the magnificent new West-minster Lady Chapel which, it was hoped, would receive the relics of the new royal saint and, in due course, those of Henry VII himself.[29] Understandably, in the circumstances, the king bound the abbot and

[26] *Foedera*, XII, 563–6.

[27] Grosjean, 189.

[28] Pope Julius II (1503–1513) gave permission on 20 May 1504 (Grosjean, 212–14 from Arch. Vatic. Reg. Vat. 986, fol. 53v, 54v. and *Foedera*, XIII, 103–4). Henry VII's supplication, which from the great similarity of language between the two appears to have produced this bull (Grosjean, 176–8), is conjecturally dated 1496 solely from its position in Morton's register. It must, however, be dated *post* 5 March 1498 when the council gave its decision in the Chertsey-Windsor-Westminster contest. Morton died in 1500 so it is possible that the petition was addressed in the first instance to Alexander VI.

[29] Holinshed's *Chronicle* (1806 ed.), 529–50, cited by Grosjean, 203.

convent of Westminster to contribute £500 to the cost of it.[30] But at Henry VII's death in 1509 the process of canonization was still not concluded. Henry VIII, who himself intended to be buried in his father's Lady Chapel at Windsor, which Cardinal Wolsey had meantime appropriated and finished to contain his own mausoleum, clearly did not press sufficiently hard for the rapid completion of his great-uncle's cause. The relics of Holy King Henry still rest today to the right of the high altar in St George's Chapel at Windsor, where Richard III had reburied them. Henry VIII's will not only marked the end of the contest of Lancaster and York but also of all sixteenth-century hopes of canonization for Henry of Windsor. He left impartial instructions that the tombs and altars of both his great-uncle Henry VI and his grandfather Edward IV should be made more princely at his charge *where they were.*[31]

> Here, o'er the martyr-king the marble weeps,
> And, fast beside him once-fear'd Edward sleeps:
> The grave unites: where e'en the great find rest,
> And blended lie th'oppressor and th'opprest!
> (Alexander Pope, *Pastorals, Windsor Forest*).

[30] *Ibid.*, 201, citing the account of the abbey sacrist as printed by A. P. Stanley, *Memorial of Westminster Abbey* (London, 3rd ed., 1869), 521, for the payment.
[31] *Foedera*, XV, 111 (30 December 1546).

APPENDIX
GENEALOGIES
SELECT BIBLIOGRAPHY
INDEX

Appendix

ITINERARY OF HENRY VI, 1436–1461

Note: The sources correlated here are household accounts, instruments under the sign manual, signets and privy seal, other royal warrants to the chancellor or to the exchequer, records of council meetings at which the king's presence was recorded, the rolls of parliament, occasional town records, the very few chronicle references which fit and Winchester College records for his visits to Winchester. Dating under the great seal normally reveals the whereabouts of the chancellor, not the king. Failure to appreciate this largely invalidates the only previous itinerary of the king attempted (by Mabel E. Christie in her book *Henry VI*, 375–89).

1436   JULY 21[1]–30 Canterbury. AUGUST 4–5 Merton. SEPTEMBER 3 Westminster. OCTOBER 13 Kennington. 17–21 Westminster. NOVEMBER 1 Merton. 6 Kennington. 23 Westminster. DECEMBER 19–31 Eltham.

1437   JANUARY 1–8 Eltham. 18–MARCH 26 Lambeth. 27–APRIL 2 Merton. 5–8 Kennington. 9–17 Westminster. 18–20 Kennington. 21–22 Staines. 22–24 Windsor castle. 24–25 manor in Windsor park. 25–27 Easthampstead. 27–28 Merton. 28–29 Windsor castle. 29 Colnbrook. 30 Sheen. 30–MAY 2 Merton. 2–11 Kennington. 11–12 Staines. 12–16 Easthampstead. 16 Chertsey. 17–23 Merton. 23–JUNE 3 Sheen. 3–4 Kennington. 4 Tottenham. 5–8 Copped Hall. 9–14 Hertford. 16–JULY 12 Kennington. 12–15 Sheen. 15–16 Kennington. 16 Sheen. 16–17 Barnet. 18–19 St Albans. 19–20 Dunstable. 20 Dunstable, Brickhill, Stony Stratford. 21–26 Stony Stratford. 26–29 Northampton. 29–30 Market Harborough. 30–AUGUST 5 Leicester, 5–6 Loughborough. 6–8 Nottingham. 8–9 Newstead. 9–11 Nottingham. 12–13 Loughborough. 13–19 Leicester. 19–20 Nuneaton. 20–26 Kenilworth. 26–27 Stratford-on-Avon. 27–29 Winchcombe. 29–30 Chipping Norton. 30–SEPTEMBER 8 Woodstock. 9–12 Boarstall. 12–13 Aylesbury. 13–23 King's Langley. 23–24 Uxbridge. 24–NOVEMBER 5 Sheen. 6–14 Hospital of St John, Clerkenwell. 15–18 Sheen. 18–20 Staines. 20–28 Easthampstead. 29–DECEMBER 3 manor in Windsor park. 3–4 Colnbrook. 4–10 Sheen. 10–13 Hanworth. 14–18 Sheen. 18–20 Kennington. 20–31 Eltham.

1438   JANUARY 1–7 Eltham. 7–10 Kennington. 10–11 Staines. 11–15 Easthampstead. 15–18 manor in Windsor park. 18–21 Reading. 21–29 Sonning. 29–30 Maidenhead. 30–MARCH 4 Windsor castle. 4–5 Coln-

---

[1] Prior to this date the young Henry's movements, in so far as they can be ascertained, are recorded in the text.

brook. 5 Brentford. 6–10 Kennington. 10–14 Eltham. 14–15 Dartford. 15–17 Rochester. 17–26 Maidstone. 26–31 Leeds. 31–APRIL 1 Rochester. 1–2 Dartford. 2–3 Kennington. 3 Brentford. 3–4 Colnbrook. 4–25 Windsor castle. 25 Colnbrook. 25–MAY 21 Kennington. 21 Colnbrook. 21–26 Windsor castle. 26–30 Henley-on-the-Heath. 31–JUNE 9 Windsor castle. 9–10 Colnbrook. 10–14 Westminster. 14–25 Havering atte Bower. 25–27 Copped Hall. 28–30 Havering atte Bower. 30–JULY 1 Ingatestone. 1–2 Chelmsford. 2–3 Brentwood. 3–8 Havering atte Bower. 8–12 Westminster. 12–21 Windsor castle. 21–28 Easthampstead. 28–30 Odiham. 30–AUGUST 1 Kingsclere. 1–2 Andover. 2–5 King's Somborne. 5–8 Clarendon. 9–11 Salisbury. 11–12 Marlborough. 12 Faringdon. 14–26 Woodstock. 26–27 Banbury. 27–SEPTEMBER 13 Warwick. 15–19 Fulbrook Lodge. 24–OCTOBER 6 Woodstock. 7–11 Oxford. 13–24 Woodstock. NOVEMBER 1–14 Eltham. 14–19 Windsor castle. 21–24 Easthampstead. 24 Henley-on-Thames. 30–DECEMBER 1 Warwick. 1–3 Kenilworth castle. 4–11 Goodrest Lodge. 13 Kenilworth castle. 14–15 The Pleasance at Kenilworth. 19–31 Kenilworth castle.

1439 JANUARY 1–6 Kenilworth castle. 9–15 Goodrest Lodge. 26–29 Easthampstead. FEBRUARY 1–12 Windsor castle. 13–16 Easthampstead. 16–20 Windsor castle. 22–27 Eltham. MARCH 2–9 Fulham. 10–11 Westminster. 11 Dartford. 12 Rochester, Sittingbourne. 14 Canterbury cathedral. 15 Ospringe. 17 Rochester cathedral. 18–28 Hospital of St James by Westminster. 28–APRIL 17 Windsor castle. 18 Henley-on-the-Heath. 21–27 Windsor castle. MAY 1–8 Kennington. 8 Sheen. 10–16 Windsor castle. 17 Sheen. 18–27 Kennington. 29–JULY 8 Windsor castle. 9–20 Sheen. 23–27 Windsor castle. 28–29 Easthampstead. 30 Odiham. AUGUST 5–27 Windsor castle. 30 King's Langley. SEPTEMBER 2 Copped Hall. 3–12 Havering atte Bower. 12 Kennington. 14–19 Windsor castle. 25 Guildford. 30–OCTOBER 6 Windsor castle. 9–14 Kennington. 16–NOVEMBER 4 Windsor castle. 5–7 Eltham. 8–30 Kennington. DECEMBER 1–22 Westminster. 24–31 Windsor castle.

1440 JANUARY 1–12 Windsor castle. 15–FEBRUARY 24 Reading. 26 Windsor castle. 28 Eltham. MARCH 2 Rochester. 4 Sittingbourne. 5–6 Canterbury. 11 Kennington. 13–APRIL 29 Windsor castle. 30–MAY 5 Kennington. 10–14 Westminster. 14–21 Windsor castle. 24 Chertsey. 26–28 Windsor castle. 31 Sheen. JUNE 2–20 Kennington. 20–JULY 9 Windsor castle. 12–16 Easthampstead. 17–26 Windsor castle. 27 High Wycombe. AUGUST 1–3 Woodstock. 8–15 Windsor castle. 16–20 Sheen. 23–27 Windsor castle. 30–SEPTEMBER 3 manor in Windsor Park. 5–OCTOBER 7 Windsor castle. 8–11 Sheen. 13–14 Westminster. 14–17 Eltham. 18–29 Westminster. 29 Sheen. NOVEMBER 2–23 Windsor castle. 23–28 Westminster. DECEMBER 1–9 Windsor castle. 12–13 Easthampstead. 21–29 Windsor castle.

1441 JANUARY 8 manor in Windsor park. 15–26 Sheen. 27–30 Westminster. FEBRUARY 2–3 Windsor castle. 3–16 Westminster. 18–MARCH 4 Windsor castle. 5 Sheen. 7 Eltham. 10 Ospringe. 13 Canterbury and

Sittingbourne. 15 Rochester, Dartford. 15–16 Eltham. 17 Kennington.
18 Sheen. 23–26 Windsor castle. 27 Uxbridge, Kennington. 29
Royston. APRIL 1–3 Cambridge. 5 Hertford castle. 6–MAY 1 Windsor
castle. 3–JUNE 26 Sheen. JULY 1–14 Havering atte Bower. 14 Havering
atte Bower, Stratford, Kennington. 15 Kennington. 16–18 Sheen.
22–25 Westminster. 27–AUGUST 2 Sheen. 2 Sheen, Bagshot. 4 Basingstoke. 5–7 Winchester. 9 Hartfordbridge. 13–27 Sheen. 28–SEPTEMBER
8 Eltham. 9–11 Sheen. 14 Hanworth. 17 Copped Hall. 19–20
Waltham. 22 Hertford. OCTOBER 1 King's Langley, Hertford. 2–3
Hertford. 3 Hertford, Waltham, Tottenham, Westminster, Sheen.
4–12 Sheen. 12–27 Westminster. 27 Westminster, Uxbridge. Sheen,
27–NOVEMBER 10 Sheen. 11 Sheen, Westminster, Eltham. 12–27
Eltham with visits to Westminster. 28 Westminster. 29–DECEMBER 11
Sheen. 11 Sheen, Hillingdon. 11–14 Hillingdon. 14 Hillingdon, Sheen.
14–18 Sheen. 18 Sheen, Kennington, Eltham. 18–31 Eltham.

1442   JANUARY 1–8 Eltham. 8 Eltham, Dartford, Rochester. 9 Sittingbourne,
Ospringe. 10–11 Canterbury. 11 Canterbury, Ospringe. 12 Sitting-
bourne, Rochester. 13 Dartford, Eltham. 14–16 Eltham. 16 Eltham,
Kennington, Sheen, 17–19 Sheen. 19 Sheen, Staines. 20 Staines,
Easthampstead. 20–22 Easthampstead. 22 Easthampstead, Staines.
23 Staines, Sheen. 24 Sheen, Westminster. 24–28 Westminster. 29
The Wardrobe in London. 30 The Wardrobe, Westminster. 30–
FEBRUARY 2 Westminster. 2 Westminster, Eltham. 2–12 Eltham with
visits to Westminster. 12 Eltham, Westminster. 14 Westminster. 15
Westminster, Sheen. 16–MARCH 27 Sheen with visits to Westminster.
27 Westminster, Colnbrook, Windsor castle. 28–APRIL 9 Windsor
castle. 9 Windsor castle, Sheen. 9–20 Sheen. 20 Sheen, Colnbrook.
21 Colnbrook, Windsor castle. 21–26 Windsor castle. 26 Windsor
castle, Sheen. 26–MAY 5 Sheen. 5 Sheen, Colnbrook, Windsor castle.
5–11 Windsor castle. 11 Windsor castle, Colnbrook, Sheen. 11–17
Sheen. 17 Sheen, Colnbrook, Windsor castle. 18–JUNE 6 Windsor
castle, 6 Windsor castle, Sheen, Brentford, Langley. 6–12 Langley.
12 Langley, Clapham, Sheen. 12–18 Sheen. 18 Sheen, Colnbrook.
19 Colnbrook, Windsor castle. 19–JULY 10 Windsor castle, Brentford.
11–16 Fulham. 16 Fulham, Brentford, Colnbrook. 17 Colnbrook,
Windsor castle. 17–30 Windsor castle. 30 Windsor castle, manor in
Windsor park. 31–AUGUST 8 manor in Windsor park. 8 manor in
Windsor park and castle. 9 Windsor castle. 9–20 Windsor castle,
20 Windsor castle, Sheen. 20–24 Sheen. 25 Sheen, Kennington.
26–29 Kennington. 30–SEPTEMBER 3 Sheen. 3 Sheen, Colnbrook,
Windsor castle. 3–27 Windsor castle. 27 Windsor castle, manor in
the park. 27–30 manor in the park. OCTOBER 3–18 Eltham. 22–26
Easthampstead. 31–NOVEMBER 4 manor in Windsor park. 8–28 East-
hampstead. 29–DECEMBER 8 Windsor castle. 10–16 Sheen. 18–31.
Windsor castle.

1443   JANUARY 1–13 Windsor castle and manor in Windsor park. 16–30
Eltham. FEBRUARY 2–7 Westminster. 8 Brentford. 9–17 Windsor
castle. 18–19 Maidenhead. 21–22 Windsor castle. 24–MARCH 3 Sheen.

7–APRIL 11 Eltham. 11 Eltham, Kennington. 17–23 Windsor castle. MAY 5–18 Westminster. 19–23 Eltham. 24–26 Westminster. 26 Westminster, Sheen. 26–JUNE 20 Sheen. 23–JULY 1 Windsor castle. 2 Brentford. 3–8 Westminster. 8 Westminster, Sheen. 10–15 Windsor castle. 17–18 Easthampstead. 21–29 Windsor castle. AUGUST 3–6 Eltham. 15 Eton College. 16–26 Eltham. 27 Camberwell. 28 Brentford. SEPTEMBER 1 manor in Windsor park, Henley-on-the-Heath. 1–4 Henley-on-the-Heath. 9–10 manor in Windsor park. 15—OCTOBER 18 Windsor castle. 19 Colnbrook, Sheen. 19–29 Sheen. 30 Colnbrook, Windsor castle. 30–NOVEMBER 7 Windsor castle. 7 Windsor castle, Easthampstead. 7–10 Easthampstead, 10 Easthampstead, Sheen. 10–28 Sheen. 28 Sheen, Colnbrook, Windsor castle. 28–DECEMBER 10 Windsor castle, manor in park and Easthampstead. 10 Colnbrook, Sheen. 12–19 Sheen. 19 Sheen, Colnbrook, Windsor castle. 19–31 Windsor castle.

1444 JANUARY 1–7 Windsor castle. 7 Windsor castle, Colnbrook, Uxbridge, Rickmansworth. 8 King's Langley. 15 Sheen. 31–FEBRUARY 6 Westminster. 8–23 MARCH Sheen. 23 Sheen, Hillingdon. 23–26 Hillingdon. 26 Hillingdon, High Wycombe. 27–28 Watlington. 28 Watlington, Culham. 28–APRIL 4 Culham. 4 Culham, Abingdon. 4–16 Abingdon. 16 Abingdon, Culham. 16–19 Culham. 20–26 Woodstock. 27 Islip, Tetsworth. 28 Stokenchurch, High Wycombe. 29 Beaconsfield, Hillingdon. 29–MAY 7 Hillingdon. 8–25 Berkhamsted castle. 25 Berkhamsted, King's Langley, Chalfont. 26–29 Hillingdon. 29 Hillingdon, Chalfont. 29–JUNE 11 Berkhamsted castle. 12 Chalfont, Uxbridge. 13 Stanwell, Bagshot. 13–15 Bagshot. 15 Bagshot, Farnham, Alton. 16 Alton, Warnford. 17 Warnford, Southwick. 18 Southwick, Meonstoke. 19 Meonstoke, Tisted, Alton. 20 Alton, Farnham, Bagshot. 20–22 Bagshot. 22 Bagshot, Stanwell, Sheen. 22–JULY 20 Sheen. 20 Sheen, Staines, manor in Windsor park. 20–27 manor in Windsor park. 27 manor in Windsor park, Bagshot, Henley-on-Thames. 27–AUGUST 4 Henley. 4 Henley, Marlow, High Wycombe. 5 High Wycombe, Stokenchurch, Tetsworth. 6 Tetsworth, Islip, Woodstock. 6–12 Woodstock, 12 Woodstock, Langley in Wychwood. 12–20 Langley in Wychwood. 20 Langley in Wychwood, Woodstock. 20–25 Woodstock. 25 Woodstock, Islip, Tetsworth. 26 Stokenchurch, High Wycombe. 27 Marlow, manor in Windsor park. 27–SEPTEMBER 11 manor in Windsor park. 11 manor in Windsor park, Staines, Kingston. 12 Clapham, Eltham. 12–17 Eltham. 17 Eltham, Clapham, Kingston. 18 Staines, Windsor castle. 18–NOVEMBER 3 Windsor castle. 4–9 manor in Windsor park. 10 Sonning. 13–14 Wallingford. 17–19 Donnington (Berks.). 19 Donnington, Andover. 21–22 Winchester. 24 Dogmersfield. 25 Dogmersfield, Stratfield Mortimer. 28–DECEMBER 31 Windsor castle.

1445 JANUARY 1–20 Windsor castle, 23–29 Sheen. 31–APRIL 13 Westminster and Windsor castle. 16–18 Southwick. 22–27 Titchfield. MAY 1 Alresford. 2 Winchester. 5–8 Windsor castle. 11–14 Westminster. 15–21 Eltham. 26 Tower of London. 29–JUNE 6 Westminster. 7–9 Eltham. 12–14 Canterbury. 17 Dartford. 17–21 Eltham. 22–JULY

10 Windsor castle. 13–16 Westminster. 17 Windsor castle. 19 Sheen, Brentford, Westminster. 21–26 Windsor castle. 26 Windsor castle, Westminster. 27–AUGUST 2 Fulham. 4, 6, 7, 10 Westminster. 10–SEPTEMBER 7 castle and manor in park of Windsor. 10 High Wycombe. 13–22 Woodstock. 22–23 Osney. 23 Osney, Wallingford. 25 Marlow. 27–OCTOBER 5 Windsor castle. 12 Cambridge. 15 Royston. 18 Copped Hall. 24–29 Eltham. 31–NOVEMBER 16 Westminster. 18–19 Eltham. 21–DECEMBER 2 Westminster. 5–7 Windsor castle. 9–16 Westminster. 18 Eltham, Sheen. 19 Sheen. 21–31 Windsor castle.

1446   JANUARY 1–18 Windsor castle. 26–MARCH 21 Westminster. 22 Sheen. 25 Windsor castle. 27–APRIL 8 Westminster. 16–26 Windsor castle. 28 Henley-on-the-Heath. MAY 3–5 Guildford. 6, 9 Windsor castle. 14–17 Tower of London. 21, 25 Windsor castle. 31–JUNE 2 Tower of London. 3 Brentford. 10–17 Windsor castle. 19–20 Odiham castle. 20–21 Farnham castle. 22–JULY 23 Westminster. 25–26 Cambridge. 29 Brandon, Walsingham. 30 Walsingham. AUGUST 1 King's Lynn. 3–5 Bury St Edmunds. 6 Sudbury, Colchester. 7 Witham. 10–11 Stratford Langthorne. 13–29 Windsor castle. 31 Winchester. SEP-TEMBER 1–2 Alton. 4–13 Windsor castle. 21 Cookham. 25 Marlow. 30 Huntingdon. OCTOBER 4 Ramsey. 7 Leighton Buzzard. 9 Berk-hamstead castle. 10–NOVEMBER 3 Windsor castle. 4 Colnbrook. 6–7 Sheen. 8–15 Westminster. 16 Eltham, Dartford. 17 Gravesend, Rochester. 18 Rochester, Sittingbourne, Ospringe. 19 Ospringe, Canterbury. 20 Canterbury. 21 Canterbury, Ospringe. 22 Ospringe, Sittingbourne. 23 Sittingbourne, Gravesend, Dartford. 24 Dartford, Eltham, Westminster. 24–DECEMBER 1 Westminster, Sheen. 2 Sheen, Brentford. 3 Brentford, Colnbrook, Windsor castle. 4–12 Windsor castle, 13–19 Sheen. 19 Sheen, Colnbrook. 20 Colnbrook, Windsor castle. 20–31 Windsor castle.

1447   JANUARY 1–10 Windsor castle. 10 Windsor castle, Bagshot. 11 Bagshot, Guildford. 12 Guildford, Chiddingfold. 13 Chiddingfold, Midhurst, Arundel. 14 Arundel, Chichester. 15 Chichester. 16 Havant, Wick-ham, Botley. 17 Botley, Southampton. 18–23 Southampton. 24 Alres-ford, Alton. 25 Alton, Farnham. 26 Guildford. 27 Guildford, Newark priory (Surrey), Windsor castle. 28–FEBRUARY 3 Windsor castle. 3 Windsor castle, Uxbridge, Watford. 4 Hatfield, Hertford. 5 Hertford, Buntingford, Royston. 7 Royston, Cambridge. 8 Cambridge, New-market. 9–MARCH 6 Bury St Edmunds. 6 Bury St Edmunds, Thet-ford. 7 Pickenham, Litcham. 8 Walsingham. 9 Hilborough, Brandon Ferry. 10 Brandon Ferry, Mildenhall, Newmarket. 11 Newmarket, Cambridge. 11–14 Cambridge. 15 Royston. 16 Puckeridge, Ware. 17 Cheshunt, Tottenham. 18 Tottenham. 19–20 Westminster. 20 West-minster, Brentford, Colnbrook, Windsor castle. 20–MAY 4 Windsor castle. 4 Windsor castle, Bagshot, Farnham. 5 Farnham, Alton, Alres-ford. 6–8 Winchester. 9 Bishop's Waltham. 10 Alresford, Alton. 11 Alton, Farnham. 12 Farnham, Bagshot. 13–19 Windsor castle. 19 Windsor castle, Colnbrook, Brentford. 20–26 Westminster. 26 West-minster, Brentford, Colnbrook. 27–JUNE 12 Windsor castle. 12 Windsor castle, Colnbrook. 13 Westminster, Windsor castle. 13–16 Windsor castle. 16 Windsor castle, Brentford. 17–22 Westminster. 22 Westminster, Colnbrook. 23 Colnbrook, Windsor castle. 23–29 Windsor castle. 30 Colnbrook, Brentford, Greenwich. 30–JULY 15 Greenwich with visits to Westminster, Eltham. 16 Eltham, Greenwich. 17 Greenwich, Stratford. 18 Stratford, Havering atte Bower. 19 Barking, Westminster. 20–27 Westminster and Greenwich. 28 Westminster, Brentford. 29 Brentford, Colnbrook, Windsor castle. 29–AUGUST 1 Windsor castle. 1 Windsor castle, High Wycombe. 2 High Wycombe Stokenchurch, Tetsworth. 3 Tetsworth, Islip, Woodstock. 4 Woodstock. 5–7 Osney, Dorchester, Ewelme. 8 Ewelme, Reading. 9 Reading, Maidenhead, Windsor castle. 10–14 Windsor castle. 14–15 Eton College. 15–17 Windsor castle. 17 Windsor castle, Sonning. 18 Sonning, Theale, Newbury. 19 Newbury, Hungerford, Marlborough. 19–28 Marlborough. 28 Marlborough, Bishop's Cannings, Potterne. 29 Potterne, Trowbridge, Farleigh Hungerford. 30 Farleigh Hungerford, Bath. 31 Bath, Keynsham, Bristol. SEPTEMBER 1 Bristol, Sodbury. 2 Sodbury, Malmesbury. 3–4 Malmesbury. 4 Malmesbury, Lechlade. 5 Lechlade, Faringdon, Abingdon. 6 Abingdon, Dorchester, Wallingford, Sonning. 7 Sonning, Maidenhead. 8–13 Windsor castle. 13 Windsor castle, Colnbrook. 14 Colnbrook, Brentford. 15 Brentford, Westminster. 16 Westminster, Greenwich. 16–22 Greenwich. 22 Greenwich, Welling, Dartford. 23 Dartford, Gravesend. 24 Gravesend. 25 Gravesend, Rochester. 26 Rochester, Sittingbourne. 27 Sittingbourne, Ospringe, Canterbury. 28 Canterbury, Faversham. 29 Faversham, Maidstone. OCTOBER 2 Rochester. 3 Dartford. 4–5 manor in Windsor park. 8–17 Windsor castle. 18 Brentford. 23 Eltham. 26 Brentford. 27 Colnbrook. NOVEMBER 3 Windsor castle. 13 Westminster. 14 Waltham Abbey, Ware. 15 Buntingford, Royston. 20 Royston. 21 Buntingford. 22 Ware. 26 Westminster. 27–28 Brentford. 29–DECEMBER 9 Windsor castle. 9 Windsor castle, Brentford, Pleshey. 10 Pleshey. 11 Pleshey, Romford. 12 Romford, Greenwich, Dartford, Gravesend, Rochester. 13 Rochester, Sittingbourne, Ospringe, Canterbury. 14 Canterbury. 15 Ospringe. 16 Ospringe, Sittingbourne, Rochester. 17 Rochester. 18 Rochester, Gravesend, Dartford. 19 Westminster, Brentford, Windsor castle. 20–31 Windsor castle.

1448 JANUARY 1–22 Windsor castle. 22 Windsor castle, Brentford. 23–26 Westminster. 26 Westminster, Brentford, Windsor castle. 27–FEBRUARY 13 Windsor castle. 13 Windsor castle, Westminster. 14–18 Eltham. 19–25 Windsor castle. 26 Brentford, Eltham. 27 Eltham. 28 Eltham, Dartford, Greenwich. 29 Greenwich, Gravesend, Rochester. MARCH 1 Sittingbourne, Ospringe. 2 Ospringe, Canterbury. 3 Canterbury. 4 Canterbury, Ospringe, Sittingbourne. 5 Sittingbourne, Maidstone. 6 Maidstone, Cobham, Dartford. 7 Dartford, Eltham. 8–9 Westminster. 10 Greenwich. 11 Greenwich, Tower of London, Windsor castle. 12 Eton. 13–APRIL 11 Windsor castle, Brentford. 12 Brentford, Camberwell, Eltham. 13–17 Eltham. 17 Eltham, Clapham. 18 Brentford, Windsor castle. 19–28 Windsor castle. 28 Windsor castle, Merton. 29

Merton. 30 Merton, Greenwich. MAY 1 Greenwich. 2–27 Windsor castle. 27 Windsor castle, Brentford. 28 Clapham, Eltham. 29–JUNE 5 Eltham. 5 Eltham, Westminster. 6 Westminster, Waltham Abbey, Ware. 7 Buntingford, Royston. 8–9 Cambridge, Burwell, Mildenhall. 11 Brandon Ferry. 12 Brandon Ferry, Litcham. 13 Litcham, Walsing-ham. 14 Walsingham, East Dereham. 15 East Dereham, Norwich. 16 Norwich. 17 Attleborough. 18 Attleborough, Thetford. 19 Thetford, Bury St Edmunds. 20 Bury St Edmunds, Woolpit. 21 Bury St Ed-munds, Mildenhall. 22–JULY 1 Cambridge. 1 Cambridge, Royston. 2 Royston, Ware. 3 Ware, Waltham Abbey. 4 Edmonton, West-minster. 5 Westminster, Brentford, Windsor castle. 5–18 Windsor castle. 18 Windsor castle, Bagshot, Hartfordbridge. 19 Hartfordbridge, Basingstoke, Ashe. 20 Ashe, Wallop, Clarendon. 21–24 Clarendon, Shaftesbury. 25 Shaftesbury. 26 Shaftesbury, Todber, Sherborne. 27 Sherborne, Glastonbury. 28–29 Glastonbury. 30 Glastonbury, Wells. 31 Wells, Chew. AUGUST 1 Chew, Bristol. 2 Bristol, Bath. 3 Bath, Castle Combe, Malmesbury. 4 Malmesbury. 5 Malmesbury, Ciren-cester. 6 Cirencester, Lechlade, Faringdon. 7 Faringdon, Ewelme. 8. Henley, Marlow. 9 Windsor castle. 15–17? Eton. 17–SEPTEMBER 3 Windsor castle. 3 Windsor castle, Brentford. 4 Brentford, Westminster. 5 Sheen, Waltham Abbey. 6 Waltham Abbey, Ware, Puckeridge, Barkway. 7 Barkway, Cambridge. 8 Cambridge. 9 Cambridge, Hun-tingdon. 10 Huntingdon, Stilton. 11 Stilton, Wansford, Stamford. 12 Stamford, Easton, Grantham. 13 Grantham, Newark, Southwell. 14–15 Southwell. 16 Wellow, East Retford, Scrooby. 17 Scrooby, Doncaster. 18 Doncaster, Pontefract. 19 Sherburn in Elmet, Healaugh. 20–23 York. 23 York, Alne, Topcliffe. 24 Topcliffe, Northallerton. 25 Northaller-ton, Darlington. 26 Ferryhill, Durham. 27–29 Durham. 30 Ferryhill, Darlington, OCTOBER 9 Beverley. 13–15 York. 15 York, Sherburn in Elmet, Pontefract. 16 Pontefract, Blyth. 17 Blyth, Kettlethorpe, Lin-coln. 17–20 Lincoln. 21 Navenby, Grantham. 22 Easton, Stamford. 23 Milton. 24 Milton, Thorney. 25 Sawtry, Huntingdon. 26 Hunting-don, Cambridge. 27–28 Cambridge. 29 Cambridge, Royston. 30 Royston, Letchworth, Luton. 31 St Albans, Tittenhanger. NOVEMBER 1–2 Tittenhanger. 3 Tittenhanger, Eltham. 3–6 Eltham. 6 Eltham, Belsize, Edgware. 7 Edgware, Westminster. 7–9 Westminster. 9 West-minster, Eltham. 9–25 Eltham. 25 Eltham, Tower of London. 26 Tower of London. 29 Eltham. 29–DECEMBER 3 Eltham. 3 Eltham, Clapham, Brentford. 4–10 Windsor castle. 10 Windsor castle, Brent-ford, Eltham. 10–13 Eltham. 13 Eltham, Gravesend, Rochester. 14 Rochester, Canterbury. 15 Canterbury. 16 Canterbury, Ospringe. 17 Sittingbourne, Rochester. 18 Eltham. 19 Eltham, Brentford. 20 Windsor castle. 20–23 Windsor castle. 23 Brentford, Windsor castle. 24–31 Windsor castle.

1449   JANUARY 1–15 Windsor castle. 15 Windsor castle, Bagshot. 16 Bagshot, Farnham. 17 Alton, Alresford. 18–20 Winchester. 20 Winchester, Alresford. 21 Alresford, Alton. 22 Alton, Farnham. 23 Bagshot, Windsor castle. 24–FEBRUARY 10 Windsor castle. 10 Windsor castle,

Brentford. 11 Brentford, Westminster. 12 Westminster, Kingston. 13 Kingston, Greenwich. 14–22 Greenwich and Westminster. 23–27 Eltham. 27 Eltham, Greenwich, Westminster. 28–MARCH 1 Westminster. 2–22 Westminster and Greenwich. 22–24 Sheen. 24 Sheen, Windsor castle. 25 Windsor castle. 26 Windsor castle, Sheen. 27 Sheen, Westminster. 28–30 Westminster. 31–APRIL 6 Greenwich and Westminster. 7 Westminster, Brentford. 8–MAY 5 Windsor castle. 5 Windsor castle, Brentford. 6 Brentford, Westminster. 7–9 Westminster. 9 Westminster, Kingston. 10 Kingston, Westminster, Greenwich. 12–30 Westminster and Greenwich. 30 Colnbrook. 31 Windsor castle. JUNE 1 Windsor, Greenwich. 2–4 Greenwich. 5 Greenwich, Westminster, Brentford. 6 Brentford, Windsor castle. 7–?12 Windsor castle. 14–15 Alresford. 15–JULY 16 Winchester. 16 Winchester, Alresford, Holybourne. 17 Holybourne, Farnham. 18 Farnham, Bagshot. 19 Windsor castle. 20 Windsor castle, Staines. 21 Kingston, Merton, Sheen. 22 Sheen, Merton, Greenwich. 23–AUGUST 12 Eltham. 12 Eltham, Brentford. 13 Brentford, Windsor castle. 14–18 Windsor castle. 18 Windsor castle, Brentford. 19 Brentford, Hackney, Waltham Abbey. 20 Ware, Buntingford. 21 Royston, Cambridge. 22–25 Cambridge. 25 Cambridge, Ely. 26 Ely, Mildenhall, Brandon Ferry. 27 Brandon Ferry, Hilborough, Litcham. 28 Litcham, Walsingham. 29 Walsingham, East Dereham. 30 East Dereham, Norwich. 31 Norwich. SEPTEMBER 1 Wymondham, Thetford. 2 Thetford, Bury St Edmunds. 3 Woolpit, Newmarket. 4 Babraham, Barkway. 5 Ware, Waltham Abbey. 6 Hackney, Eltham. 7–9 Eltham. 10 Eltham, Sheen. 11–22 Sheen. 23–25 Westminster. 27 Sheen, Eltham. 29–OCTOBER 1 Eltham. 8 Westminster. 14 Worcester. 18 Gloucester. 25 Westminster. 25– NOVEMBER 5 Westminster. 5–DECEMBER 5 City of London and Westminster. 5–20 Westminster. 25 Windsor castle.

1450 JANUARY from about 16 to MARCH 30 Westminster. 30–APRIL 12 Windsor castle. 22–JUNE 7 Leicester. 13–18 Hospital of St John, Clerkenwell. 18 Blackheath, Greenwich, Westminster. 26–JULY 2 Berkhamsted castle. 7–15 Kenilworth castle. 17–19 Fulbrook Lodge. 23 Leighton Buzzard, Dunstable. 24 St Albans. 31–OCTOBER 8 Westminster. 9 Westminster, Brentford. 10 Brentford, Chertsey. 10–14 Chertsey. 14 Chertsey, Bagshot. 15 Bagshot, Farnham. 16 Farnham, Alton. 17 Meonstoke, Bishop's Waltham. 17–20 Bishop's Waltham. 20 Bishop's Waltham, West Meon, Alton. 21 Alton, Farnham, Guildford. 22 Farnham and Guildford. 23 Farnham, Guildford, Sheen. 23–NOVEMBER 5 Sheen. 5–DECEMBER 31 Westminster.

1451 JANUARY 1–28 Westminster, Dartford. 29 Gravesend, Rochester. 30 Sittingbourne, Ospringe. 31–FEBRUARY 1 Ospringe. 1 Ospringe, Canterbury. 2–8 Canterbury. 8 Canterbury, Dover. 9 Dover, Sandwich. 10 Sandwich, Canterbury. 11–12 Canterbury. 12 Canterbury, Ospringe. 13 Ospringe, Sittingbourne, Rochester. 14–17 Rochester. 17–18 Maidstone. 19–21 Rochester. 22 Dartford. 23 Blackheath, Westminster. 24–APRIL 3 Westminster. 3–16 Sheen and Westminster. 17–JUNE 10 Windsor castle or Westminster via Colnbrook and Brentford. 11 Westminster, Waltham Abbey. 12–21 Hertford. 22 Hertford, Westminster, Croydon. 24–25 Croydon. 25 Croydon, Sevenoaks. 26 Sevenoaks, Tonbridge. 27–JULY 1 Tonbridge. 1 Tonbridge, Mayfield. 2 Mayfield, Lewes. 3–6 Lewes. 6 Lewes, Bramber. 7 Bramber, Arundel. 8 Arundel, Chichester. 8–13 Chichester. 13 Chichester, Southwick. 14 Southwick, Winchester. 15 Winchester. 16 Winchester, Romsey. 17 Romsey, Salisbury. 18–21 Salisbury. 22 Salisbury, Andover. 23 Andover, Newbury. 24 Newbury, Reading. 25 Reading. 26 Maidenhead, Tottenham. 27 Sheen, Staines, Kingston. 28 Kingston, Eltham. 29 Eltham. 30 Eltham, Dartford. 31 Dartford, Gravesend, Rochester. AUGUST 1 Rochester. 2 Sittingbourne, Ospringe, Canterbury. 4–16 Canterbury. 17 Canterbury, Ospringe. 18 Ospringe, Sittingbourne, Rochester. 19 Rochester, Gravesend, Dartford. 20 Dartford, Eltham, Kingston. 21 Kingston, Sheen, Eltham. 22–26 Eltham. 27 Eltham, Kingston. 28 Kingston, Windsor castle. 29–SEPTEMBER 2 Windsor castle. 3 Windsor castle, Kingston. 4 Kingston. 5–8 Windsor castle. 9 Windsor castle, Uxbridge. 10 Uxbridge, St Albans. 11–13 St Albans. 14 St Albans, Dunstable. 15 Dunstable, Stony Stratford. 16 Stony Stratford, Northampton. 17 Northampton, Market Harborough. 18 Market Harborough, Leicester. 19–21 Leicester. 22 Leicester, Coventry. 23–26 Coventry. 27–OCTOBER 2 Coventry and Kenilworth. 3–4 Coventry. 5 Coventry, Fulbrook Lodge. 6 Fulbrook Lodge, Banbury. 7 Banbury, Woodstock. 8 Woodstock, Oxford. 9 Oxford, Wallingford. 10 Walingford. 11 Wallingford, Henley, 12 Henley, Windsor castle. 13–18 Windsor castle. 19 Windsor castle, Brentford. 20 Brentford, Westminster. 21 Westminster. 22 Westminster, Kingston. 23 Kingston, Westminster. 24–29 Westminster. 30 Westminster, Eltham. 31 Eltham, Westminster. NOVEMBER 1–DECEMBER 2 Westminster, 3 Westminster, Brentford. 4 Brentford, Windsor castle. 5–8 Windsor castle. 9 Windsor castle, Brentford. 10–13 Westminster. 14 Westminster, Eltham. 15–31 Eltham.

1452 JANUARY 1–11 Eltham. 12 Eltham, Westminster. 13–FEBRUARY 15 Westminster. 16 Westminster, Barnet. 17 Barnet, St Albans. 18 St Albans, Dunstable. 19–20 Dunstable. 21 Dunstable, Stony Stratford. 22 Stony Stratford, Northampton. 23 Northampton. 24 Northampton, Stony Stratford. 25 Stony Stratford, Dunstable. 26 Dunstable, St Albans. 27 Barnet, Tower of London. 28 Southwark 29 Southwark. MARCH 1 Welling. 2 Welling, Blackheath. 3 Blackheath, bishop's palace, London, Westminster. 4–21 Westminster. 22 Brentford, Colnbrook, Windsor castle. 23–28 Windsor castle. 29 Windsor castle, Bagshot, Farnham. 30 Farnham, Alton, Alresford. 31 Alresford, Southwick. APRIL 1 Southwick, Winchester. 2 Winchester. 3 Winchester, Alresford. 4 Alresford, Farnham. 5 Bagshot, Windsor castle. 6–27 Windsor castle. 28–MAY 26 Windsor castle and Sheen, with visit to Eton on Ascension Eve (17). 27 Sheen, Chertsey. 28–JUNE 3 Chertsey. 4 Chertsey, Sheen. 5 Sheen, Eltham. 6–21 Eltham. 22 Greenwich, Kingston. 23 Kingston, Chertsey. 24–29 Chertsey. 30 Chertsey, Guildford, Farnham. JULY 1–2 Farnham. 3 Farnham, Alton,

Alresford. 4 Alresford, Southampton. 5 Beaulieu, Christchurch. 6 Christchurch, Ringwood, Kingston Lacy. 7–9 Kingston Lacy. 10 Kingston Lacy, Canford, Poole. 11 Poole, Kingston Lacy. 12 Milton Abbas. 13 Sherborne. 14 Crewkerne, Forde Abbey. 15 Forde, Shute, Ottery St Mary. 16 Ottery St Mary. 17 Ottery St Mary, Exeter. 18 Exeter. 19 Exeter, Honiton. 20 Honiton, Donyatt. 21 Donyatt, Athelney, Bridgewater. 22 Bridgewater, Glastonbury. 23 Glastonbury. 24 Glastonbury, Wells. 25 Wells. 26 Wells, Bristol. 27 Bristol, Bath. 28 Castle Combe, Malmesbury. 29–31 Malmesbury. AUGUST 1 Malmesbury, Cirencester. 2 Cirencester, Gloucester. 3 Gloucester, Ross on Wye. 4 Ross on Wye, Monmouth. 5–7 Monmouth. 8 Monmouth, Hereford. 9–10 Hereford. 11 Hereford, Leominster. 12 Leominster, Ludlow. 13 Ludlow. 14–15 Much Wenlock. 16 Much Wenlock, Bridgnorth. 17 Bridgnorth. 18 Birmingham. 19 Birmingham, Coventry. 20 Coventry. 21 Coventry, Kenilworth. 22–27 Kenilworth. 28 Kenilworth, Fulbrook Lodge. 29 Fulbrook Lodge, Banbury. 30 Banbury, Woodstock. 21 Woodstock. SEPTEMBER 1 Woodstock, Tetsworth. 2 Tetsworth, High Wycombe. 3 High Wycombe. 4 High Wycombe, Colnbrook. 5 Colnbrook, Sheen. 6 Sheen, Eltham. 7–19 Eltham. 20 Eltham, Sheen. 21–27 Sheen. 28 Clapham, Eltham, Greenwich. 29–OCTOBER 7 Greenwich. 11 Colnbrook. 12 Watford. 13 St Albans. 15–16 Hitchin. 18 Huntingdon. 19 Peterborough. 24 Newark. 26 Stamford. 28–29 Peterborough. NOVEMBER 1–3 Cambridge. 4–5 Saffron Walden. 9 Barking. 11, 17 Eltham. 21 Maidenhead. 23–28 Reading. 29–DECEMBER 14 manor in Windsor park. 16, 17 Sheen. 21–31 Greenwich.

1453   JANUARY 1–16 Greenwich, with visit to Tower of London on 5. 19 Sheen. 23, 24 manor in Windsor park. 29 Eltham. FEBRUARY 1, 4, 5 Eltham. 7 Greenwich. 8 Barking. 18 Norwich. 23 Thetford. 28 Sudbury. MARCH 2–3 Berkhamsted. 5 High Wycombe. 6–APRIL 4 Reading. 5–JULY 3 Westminster. 6, 7, 14 Greenwich. 21 Sheen. 31 Kingston Lacy. AUGUST 5–OCTOBER 3 Clarendon. 13–DECEMBER 31 Windsor castle.

1454   JANUARY 1–DECEMBER Windsor castle, Christmas at Greenwich.

1455   JANUARY 1–APRIL 14 Greenwich with visits to Westminster. 19–MAY 9 Windsor castle. 10–21 Westminster. 21 Westminster, Watford. 22 Watford, St Albans. 23 St Albans, bishop's palace, London. 23–JUNE 4 bishop's palace, London. 5 Westminster, 6–8 bishop's palace, London. 12 Windsor castle. Later in June to Hertford. JULY 6 Westminster. 6–AUGUST 23 Westminster. 26 Hertford.

1456   FEBRUARY 25 Westminster. 25–APRIL 30 Westminster with possibly visits to Canterbury (17 March), Greenwich (26 March), Windsor castle (26 April). 30–MAY 5 City of London. 6–12 Westminster. 15 Sheen. 26 Sheen. JUNE 7, 16 Sheen. 22 Westminster. 29–JULY 6 Westminster. 7 Sheen. 8–15 Westminster. 16–AUGUST 14 Windsor castle. 18 High Wycombe. 20 Woodstock. 24 Kenilworth. 29–SEPTEMBER 8 Lichfield. 14–OCTOBER 14 Coventry. 14 Coventry, Coleshill. 19 Stafford. 20 Eccleshall. 24 Chester. 31–NOVEMBER 4 Shrewsbury. 6–DECEMBER 4 Kenilworth. 4 Kenilworth, Coventry. 4–15 Coventry. 18,

19 Kenilworth. 27–31 Leicester.

1457 JANUARY 1–7 Leicester. 10–FEBRUARY 11 Kenilworth. 11 Kenilworth, Coventry. 12–MARCH 14 Coventry. 14 Coventry, Kenilworth. 15–23 Kenilworth. 24 Coventry. APRIL 1–26 Hereford. 28 Worcester. MAY 10 Winchcombe. 13–JUNE 1 Kenilworth. 3–9 Coventry. 13–AUGUST 15 Kenilworth. 16 Coventry. 17–27 Kenilworth. 31–SEPTEMBER 2 Coventry. 2 Coventry, Rothwell, Northampton. 2–7 Northampton. 22, 25 Westminster. OCTOBER 8–12 Chertsey. 17–NOVEMBER 29 Westminster. DECEMBER 6, 7, 8 Reading. 30, 31 Abingdon.

1458 JANUARY 1–6 Abingdon. 17 Chertsey. 27–30 Westminster. FEBRUARY 3–13 Chertsey. 20–MARCH 14 Berkhamsted. 20 City of London. 21–28 Westminster with visit to London (25). 29–APRIL 20 St Albans. 29, MAY 2 Westminster. 6–JUNE 5 Greenwich. JULY 20–AUGUST 6 Woodstock. SEPTEMBER 10–OCTOBER 7 St Albans. 10–DECEMBER 3 Westminster. 16 manor in Windsor park. 18 Henley-on-Thames.

1459 JANUARY 3–12 Wallingford. 21–MARCH 12 Westminster with possibly visit to Sheen (about 4). 16–26 St Albans. APRIL 2–MAY 10 Westminster with possibly visit to Windsor (24–25). 14–19 Northampton. 23–JUNE 3 Coventry. 4 Nuneaton. 15 Burton-on-Trent. 19–about SEPTEMBER 20 Coventry and Kenilworth, from about 20 September to OCTOBER 12 in the field: Market Harborough, Nottingham, Walsall, Coleshill, Worcester. 12 Worcester, Ludlow. 12–14 Ludlow. 16 Worcester. 20 Warwick, Coventry. 20–DECEMBER 22 Coventry. Christmas at Leicester abbey.

1460 JANUARY 1–28 Leicester abbey. 30–FEBRUARY 10 Northampton. 22–23 Bedford. 23 Bedford, Dunstable. 24–25 Dunstable. 26–28 St Albans. MARCH 28 Royston. 28–31 Cambridge. APRIL 6–22 Peterborough abbey. MAY 4 Leicester. 6 Coventry. 12 Kenilworth. 20–JUNE 18 Coventry. JULY 7–13 Northampton. 16–25 bishop's palace London. AUGUST 2–18 Canterbury. 23–OCTOBER 6 Greenwich and Eltham. 7–30 Westminster. 31–DECEMBER 31 bishop's palace London.

1461 JANUARY 1–FEBRUARY 12 bishop's palace London. 17 St Albans. 19 Dunstable.[1]

---

[1] After this date Henry's movements, in so far as they can be ascertained, are recorded in the text.

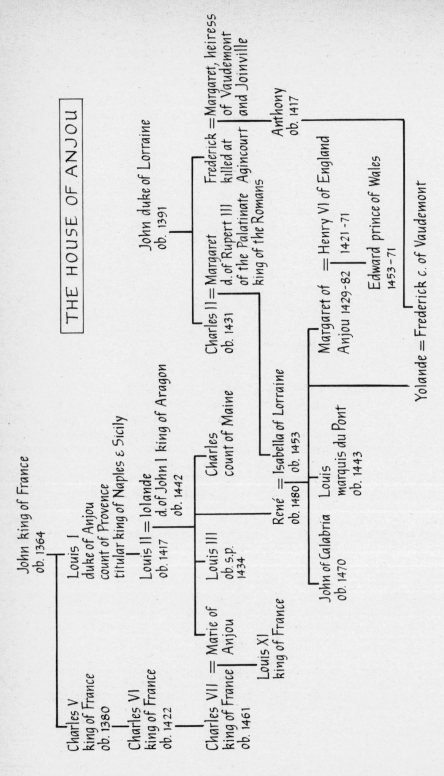

John king of France
ob. 1364

Charles V
king of France
ob. 1380

Charles VI
king of France
ob. 1422

Louis I
duke of Anjou
count of Provence
titular king of Naples & Sicily

Louis II = Iolande
ob. 1417   d. of John I king of Aragon
            ob. 1442

Charles VII = Marie of
king of France Anjou
ob. 1461

Louis XI
king of France

Louis III
ob. s.p.
1434

Charles
count of Maine

René = Isabella of Lorraine
ob. 1480 ob. 1453

John of Calabria
ob. 1470

Louis
marquis du Pont
ob. 1443

John duke of Lorraine
ob. 1391

Charles II = Margaret
ob. 1431   d. of Rupert III
            of the Palatinate
            king of the Romans

Frederick = Margaret, heiress
killed at   of Vaudemont
Agincourt   and Joinville

Anthony
ob. 1417

Margaret of = Henry VI of England
Anjou 1429-82 1421-71

Edward prince of Wales
1453-71

Yolande = Frederick c. of Vaudemont

1   The House of Anjou

LANCASTER AND YORK

Edward III = Philippa of Hainault

Lionel of Antwerp d. of Clarence = Elizabeth de Burgh

John of Gaunt =(1) Blanche of Lancaster (2) Constance of Castile (3) Catherine Swynford

Edmund of Langley d. of York

(1) Philippa = Edmund Mortimer e. of March ob. 1381

(1) Henry IV =(1) Mary Bohun ob. 1394 (2) Joan of Brittany ob. 1437

(1) Philippa = John I of Portugal

Peter d. of Coimbra

(1) Isabella = Philip d. of Burgundy

(1) Elizabeth = John Holand e. of Huntingdon d. of Exeter ob. 1400

(3) John Beaufort e. of Somerset ob. 1410

(3) Henry, cardinal bp. of Winchester ob. 1447

(3) Thomas d. of Exeter ob. s.p. 1426

(3) Joan = Ralph Nevill e. of Westmorland

Margaret = Thomas Courtenay e. of Devon (1414–1458)

Edward d. of York ob. s.p. 1415

Roger e. of March ob. 1398

(1) Thomas d. of Clarence ob. s.p. 1421

(1) John d. of Bedford ob. s.p. 1435

(1) Humphrey d. of Gloucester ob. s.p. 1447

John e. of Huntingdon d. of Exeter ob. 1447

Henry e. of Somerset ob. s.p. 1418

John d. of Somerset (1404–1444)

Joan = James I of Scotland

Edmund m. of Dorset d. of Somerset (c. 1406–1455)

Eleanor Beauchamp

Henry d. of Somerset (1436–1464)

Edmund ob. 1471

John ob. 1471

John ob. 1471

Henry V (1) = Catherine (2) = Owen Tudor d. of Charles VI ob. 1461 of France ob. 1437

Henry e. of Huntingdon d. of Exeter (1430–1475)

Edmund Tudor (1) = Margaret =(2) Henry Stafford e. of Richmond (3) Thomas ob. 1456 e. of Derby

Henry VII (1457–1509)

Edmund e. of March ob. 1425

Henry VI = Margaret of Anjou ob. 1422 (1429–1482)

Jasper Tudor e. of Pembroke

Edward p. of Wales (1453–1471)

Anne = Richard e. of Cambridge ob. 1415

Cicely Nevill = Richard ob. 1495 d. of York sister of Richard (1411–1460) e. of Salisbury (1400–1460)

Edward IV (1442–1483)

2 Lancaster and York

SELECT BIBLIOGRAPHY

Acts of Court of the Mercers' Company 1453–1527, ed. L. Lyell and F. D. Watney (Cambridge 1936).

ADAM OF USK, *Chronicon*, ed. M. Thompson (London 1904).

ALLMAND, C. T., 'The Anglo-French Negotiations of 1439', *B.I.H.R.*, XL (1967).

—— (ed.), 'Documents relating to the Anglo-French Negotiations of 1439', in *Camden Miscellany*, XXIV (Royal Historical Society, 1972).

Annales Monasterii Sancti Albani 1421–40, ed. H. T. Riley, 2 vols (R.S., 1870–1).

ARMSTRONG, C. A. J., 'The Inauguration Ceremonies of the Yorkist Kings', *T.R.H.S.*, 4th series, XXX (1948).

——, 'Some examples of the distribution and speed of news in England at the time of the Wars of the Roses', in *Studies in Medieval History Presented to F. M. Powicke*, ed. R. W. Hunt and others (Oxford 1948).

——, 'Politics and the Battle of St Albans, 1455', *B.I.H.R.*, XXXIII (1960).

ASTON, M., 'A Kent approver of 1440', *B.I.H.R.*, XXXVI (1963).

Auchinlech Chronicle and Short Chronicle of the Reign of James the Second King of Scots, ed. Thomas Thomson (Edinburgh 1819).

AVERY, M. E., 'The History of the Equitable Jurisdiction of Chancery before 1460', *B.I.H.R.*, XLII (1969).

BAGLEY, J. J., *Margaret of Anjou* (London 1948).

BALDWIN, J. F., *The King's Council in England during the Middle Ages* (Oxford 1913).

BALE's Chronicle, in *Six Town Chronicles of England*, ed. Ralph Flenley (Oxford 1911).

BASIN, T., *Histoire des règnes de Charles VII et de Louis XI*, ed. J. Quicherat, 4 vols (Société de l'histoire de France, Paris, 1855–9).

BEAUCOURT, GASTON DU FRESNE DE, *Histoire de Charles VII*, 6 vols (Paris 1881–91).

BEAUREPAIRE, C. DE, *Les Etats de Normandie sous la Domination Anglaise* (Evreux 1859).

BECKINGTON, T., *Correspondence of Thomas Bekynton Secretary to Henry VI and Bishop of Bath and Wells*, ed. G. Williams, 2 vols (R.S., 1872).

BELLAMY, J., *Crime and Public Order in England in the Later Middle Ages* (London 1973).

BENET, JOHN, 'Chronicle for the years 1400 to 1462', ed. G. L. and M. A. Harriss in *Camden Miscellany*, XXIV (Royal Historical Society, 1972).

BERNUS, P., 'Le rôle politique de Pierre de Brézé, 1451–1461', *Bibliothèque de l'Ecole des Chartes*, LXIX (1908).

BERRY herald, in *Histoire de Charles VII Roy de France par Jean Chartier, Sous-*

chantre de S. Denys, Jacques le Bouvier, dit Berry, Roy d'Armes, Mattieu de Coucy et autres auteurs due temps, ed. Denys Godefroy (Paris 1661), 369–480.

BETCHERMEN, LITA-ROSE, 'The making of bishops in the Lancastrian period', *Speculum*, XLI (1966).

Boke of Noblesse, ed. J. G. Nichols (Roxburghe Club, London, 1860).

BOSSUAT, A., *Perrinet Gressart et François de Surienne, agents de l'Angleterre* (Paris 1936).

BOURDEAUT, A., 'Gilles de Bretagne entre la France et l'Angleterre', *Mémoires de la société d'histoire et d'archéologie de Bretagne*, I (1920).

BROWN, A. L., 'The Authorization of Letters under the Great Seal', *B.I.H.R.*, XXXVII (1964).

——, *The Early History of the Clerkship of the Council* (University of Glasgow, 1969).

BURNE, A. H., *The Agincourt War* (London 1956).

BURNEY, E. M., 'The English Rule in Normandy, 1435–1450' (unpublished Oxford B.Litt. thesis, 1958).

Calendar of Charter Rolls, VI (*1427–1516*) (H.M.S.O., 1927).

Calendar of Close Rolls (H.M.S.O.): *Henry V*, 2 vols (1929–32); *Henry VI*, 6 vols (1933–47); *Edward IV*, 2 vols (1949–53).

Calendar of Fine Rolls (H.M.S.O.): *Henry V* (1934); *Henry VI*, 5 vols (1935–40); *Edward IV* (1949).

Calendar of Patent Rolls (H.M.S.O.): *Henry V*, 2 vols (1910–11); *Henry VI*, 6 vols (1910–11); *Edward IV* (1897); *Edward IV–Henry VI* (1900).

Calendar of State Papers and Manuscripts existing in the Archives and Collections of Milan, I, *1385–1618*, ed. A. B. Hinds (H.M.S.O., 1913).

CAPGRAVE, JOHN, *Liber de Illustribus Henricis*, ed. F. C. Hingeston (R.S., 1858).

CHANDLER, R., *The Life of William Waynflete* (London 1811).

CHASTELLAIN, G., *Oeuvres*, ed. Kervyn de Lettenhove, 8 vols (Académie royale de Belgique, Brussels, 1863–6).

CHRIMES, S. B., 'The Pretensions of the Duke of Gloucester in 1422', *E.H.R.*, XLV (1930).

——, *English Constitutional Ideas in the Fifteenth Century* (Cambridge 1936).

——, *Lancastrians, Yorkists and Henry VII* (London 1964).

——, *Henry VII* (London 1972).

——, and BROWN, A. L. (eds), *Select Documents of English Constitutional History, 1307–1485* (London 1961).

CHRISTIE, M. E., *Henry VI* (London 1922).

CLARKE, B., *Mental Disorder in Earlier Britain* (Cardiff 1975).

COMMYNES, P. DE., *Mémoires de Philippe de Commines*, ed. D. Godefroy and Lenglet de Fresnoy, 4 vols (Paris 1747); *Mémoires*, ed. J. Calmette and G. Durville, 3 vols (Classiques de l'Histoire de France au Moyen Age, Paris, 1924–5); *The Memoirs for the Reign of Louis XI, 1461–1483*, translated by Michael Jones (Penguin, Harmondsworth, 1972).

Complete Peerage of England, Scotland, Ireland and the United Kingdom, ed. G. E. Cokayne, in new edition by Vicary Gibbs, H. A. Doubleday and others, 13 vols (London 1910–59).

COMPTON REEVES, A., 'William Booth, Bishop of Coventry and Lichfield', *Journal of Midland History*, III (1975).

CONTAMINE, P., *Guerre état et société au fin du Moyen Age* (Paris 1972).

Coventry Leet Book, or Mayor's register 1420–1455, ed. M. D. Harris (E.E.T.S., 1907–13).

Crowland Chronicle: 'Historiae Crowlandensis Continuatio', in *Rerum Anglicorum Scriptores Veterum*, ed. W. Fulman (Oxford 1684); English translation by H. T. Riley in *Ingulph's Chronicle of the Abbey of Crowland with the Continuations* (Bohn, London, 1854).

CURTIS, E., 'Richard, Duke of York as Viceroy of Ireland, 1447–1460', *Journal of the Royal Society of Antiquaries of Ireland*, LXII (1932).

DAVIES, J. S. (ed.), *An English Chronicle of the Reigns of Richard II, Henry IV, Henry V and Henry VI* (Camden Society, 1856).

DELPIT, JULES (ed.), *Collection générale des documents français qui se trouvent en Angleterre* (Paris 1867).

DEVON, F. (ed.), *Issues of the Exchequer* (Record Commission, 1837).

DICKINSON, J. C., *The Congress of Arras, 1435* (Oxford 1955).

DICKS, S. E., 'Henry VI and the Daughters of Armagnac: A Problem in Medieval Diplomacy', *Emporia State Research Studies*, XV (Kansas 1967).

DODGSON, C., 'English Devotional Woodcuts of the late Fifteenth Century with special reference to those in the Bodleian Library', *The Walpole Society*, XVII (1928–9).

DU MONT, J., *Corps universel diplomatique du droit des gens*, 8 vols (Amsterdam and The Hague, 1726–31).

DUNHAM, W. H. JR., 'Notes from the parliament at Winchester, 1449', *Speculum*, XVII (1942).

——, '"The Books of the Parliament" and "The Old Record" 1396–1504', *Speculum*, LI (1976).

——, and WOOD, C. T., 'The Right to Rule in England: Depositions and the Kingdom's Authority, 1327–1485', *American Historical Review*, LXXXI (1976).

ELLIS, H. (ed.), *Original Letters Illustrative of English History*, three series in 11 vols (London 1824–46).

EMDEN, A. B., *A Biographical Register of the University of Oxford to A.D. 1500*, 3 vols (1957–9).

——, *A Biographical Register of the University of Cambridge to A.D. 1500* (1963).

ESCOUCHY, MATHIEU D', *Chronique*, ed. E. du Fresne de Beaucourt, 3 vols (Société de l'Histoire de France, Paris, 1863–4).

EVANS, H. T., *Wales and the Wars of the Roses* (Cambridge 1915).

Excerpta Historica, ed. Samuel Bentley (London 1833).

Exchequer Rolls of Scotland, VII, ed. G. Burnett (H.M.S.O., 1884).

FERGUSON, J., *English Diplomacy, 1442–1461* (Oxford 1972).

Foedera Conventiones Litterae ... et Acta Publica (etc.), ed. T. Rymer, 20 vols (London 1704–35).

FORTESCUE, SIR JOHN, *Fortescue on the Governance of England*, ed. Charles Plummer (Oxford 1885).

——, *De Laudibus Legum Anglie*, ed. and trans. S. B. Chrimes (Cambridge 1942).

GAIRDNER, J. (ed), *Three Fifteenth-Century Chronicles* (Camden Society, 1880).

GARILLOT, J., *Les Etats généraux de 1439* (Nancy 1947).

GASCOIGNE, T., *Loci e Libro Veritatis*, ed. J. E. Thorold Rogers (Oxford 1881).

GASQUET, F. A., *The Religious Life of Henry VI* (London 1923).

GILES, J. A. (ed.), *Chronicon Angliae de Regnis Henrici IV, Henrici V, et Henrici VI* (London 1848).

GILSON, J. P., 'A defence of the proscription of the Yorkists', *E.H.R.*, XXVI (1911).

GREGORY, WILLIAM, 'Gregory's Chronicle, 1189–1469', ed. James Gairdner in *Historical Collections of a Citizen of London* (Camden Society, 1876).

GRIFFITHS, R. A., 'Gruffyd Ap Nicholas and the Fall of the House of Lancaster', *The Welsh History Review*, II (1965).

——, 'Local rivalries and national politics: the Percies, the Nevilles and the duke of Exeter, 1452–55', *Speculum*, XLIII (1968).

——, 'The Trial of Eleanor Cobham: an episode in the fall of Duke Humphrey of Gloucester', *B.J.R.L.*, LI (1968–9).

——, 'Duke Richard of York's intentions in 1450 and the origins of the War of the Roses', *Journal of Medieval History*, I (1975).

——, 'Richard duke of York and the royal household in Wales 1449–50', *The Welsh History Review*, VIII (1976).

GROSJEAN, P., *Henrici VI Angliae Regis Miracula Postuma* (Société des Bollandistes, Brussels, 1935).

HALL, EDWARD, *Chronicle*, ed. Henry Ellis (London 1809).

Handbook of British Chronology, ed. M. Powicke and E. B. Fryde (2nd edn, Royal Historical Society, 1961).

HARDING, A., *The Law Courts of Medieval England* (London 1973).

HARDYNG, JOHN, *Chronicle*, ed. Henry Ellis (1812) and ed. C. L. Kingsford in *E.H.R.*, XXVII (1912), 462–82, 740–53.

HARRISS, G. L., 'The Struggle for Calais, An Aspect of the Rivalry between Lancaster and York', *E.H.R.*, LXXV (1960).

——, 'Cardinal Beaufort, patriot or usurer?', *T.R.H.S.*, 5th series XX (1970).

HASTINGS, MARGARET, *The Court of Common Pleas in Fifteenth-Century England* (Ithaca, New York, 1947).

HEAD, C., 'Pius II and the Wars of the Roses', *Archivum Historiae Pontificiae*, viii (1970).

Henry the Sixth: a reprint of John Blackman's Memoir, ed. M. R. James (Cambridge 1919).

HEYWOOD, J., and WRIGHT, T. (eds), *The Ancient Laws of the Fifteenth Century for King's College, Cambridge and for the Public School of Eton College* (London 1850).

Historical Manuscripts Commission, Third Report (muniments of the family of Neville of Holt, London, 1872).

——, *Eighth Report Part I* (muniments of Magdalen College Oxford, London, 1881).

Historie of the Arrivall of King Edward IV, ed. J. Bruce (Camden Society, 1838).

HOLMES, G. A., 'The Libel of English polity', *E.H.R.*, LXXVI (1961).

HOPE, W. H., ST J., 'The Discovery of the Remains of King Henry VI in St George's Chapel, Windsor', *Archaeologia*, LXII (1910).

HOUGHTON, K. N., 'Theory and Practice in Borough Elections to Parliament during the Later Fifteenth Century', *B.I.H.R.*, XXXIX (1966).

HUNNISETT, R. F., 'Treason by Words', *Sussex Notes and Queries*, XIV (Lewes 1954–7).

JACOB, E. F., *The Fifteenth Century* (Oxford 1961).

——, *Archbishop Henry Chichele* (London 1967).

JAMES, M. R., and TRISTRAM, E. W., 'The Wall Paintings in Eton College Chapel and in the Lady Chapel of Winchester Cathedral', *The Walpole Society*, XVII (1928–9).

JEFFS, R., 'The Later Medieval Sheriff and the Royal Household, 1437–1547' (unpublished Oxford D. Phil. thesis, 1960).

JEULIN, P., 'L'hommage de la Bretagne', *Annales de Bretagne*, XLI (1934).

JONES, T. A., 'Owen Tudor's Marriage', *Bulletin of the Board of Celtic Studies*, XI (1943).

Journal d'un Bourgeois de Paris 1405–1449, ed. A. Tuetey (Société de l'Histoire de Paris, 1881); trans. as *A Parisian Journal 1405–1449* by Janet Shirley (Oxford 1968).

JUDD, A. F., *The Life of Thomas Bekynton, secretary to King Henry VI and Bishop of Bath and Wells, 1443–65* (Chichester 1961).

KEEN, M. H., and DANIEL, M. J., 'English Diplomacy and the Sack of Fougères in 1449', *History*, LIX (1974).

KINGSFORD, C. L. (ed.), *Chronicles of London* (Oxford 1905).

——, *English Historical Literature in the Fifteenth Century* (Oxford 1913).

King's Works: The History of the King's Works, the Middle Ages, ed. H. Colvin and others, 2 vols (H.M.S.O., 1963).

KIRBY, J. L., 'The Financing of Calais under Henry V', *B.I.H.R.*, XXIII (1950).

KIRBY, T. F., *Annals of Winchester College* (London and Winchester 1892).

KNECHT, R. J., 'The episcopate and the Wars of the Roses', *University of Birmingham Historical Journal*, VI (1957–8).

KNOOP, D., and JONES, G. P., 'The Building of Eton College 1442–1460', *Transactions of the Quatuor Coronati Lodge*, XLVI (1933).

KNOX, R., and LESLIE, S. (eds), *The Miracles of King Henry VI* (Cambridge 1923).

KRIEHN, G., *The English Rising of 1450* (Strasbourg 1892).

LANDER, J. R., 'Henry VI and the Duke of York's second protectorate', *B.J.R.L.*, XLIII (1960).

——, *The Wars of the Roses* (London 1965).

——, *Crown and Nobility 1450–1509* (London 1976).

LEACH, A. F., 'Eton College' in *V.C.H. Buckinghamshire*, II (London 1908).

LECOY DE LA MARCHE, A., *Le Roi René*, 2 vols (Paris 1875).

LEONARD, F., *Recueil des Traitez* (Paris 1693).

LETTS, M. (ed.), *The Diary of Jörg von Ehingen* (Oxford 1929).

LEWIS, P. S., 'Sir John Fastolf's Lawsuit over Titchwell 1448–55', *The Historical Journal*, 1 (1958).

Liber Regie Capelle, a Manuscript in the Biblioteca Publica, Evora, ed. W. Ullmann (Henry Bradshaw Society, 1961).

LYLE, HELEN M., *The Rebellion of Jack Cade* (Historical Association, 1950).

LYTE, H. C. MAXWELL, *A History of Eton College* (4th edn, London, 1911).

——, *Historical Notes in the use of the Great Seal* (H.M.S.O., 1926).

MCFARLANE, K. B., 'England: The Lancastrian Kings', in *Cambridge Medieval History*, VIII (1936).

——, 'Bastard Feudalism', *B.I.H.R.*, XX (1943–5).

——, 'Parliament and "Bastard Feudalism"', *T.R.H.S.*, 4th series XXVI (1944).

——, 'Henry V, Bishop Beaufort and the Red Hat', *E.H.R.*, LX (1945).

——, 'At the deathbed of Cardinal Beaufort', in *Studies in Medieval History Presented to F. M. Powicke*, ed. R. W. Hunt and others (Oxford 1948).

——, 'The Investment of Sir John Fastolf's Profits of War', *T.R.H.S.*, 5th series, VII (1957).

——, 'William Worcester: A Preliminary Survey', in *Studies Presented to Sir Hilary Jenkinson*, ed. J. Conway Davies (Oxford 1957).

——, 'The Wars of the Roses', *Proceedings of the British Academy*, L (1965).

——, *Lancastrian Kings and Lollard Knights* (Oxford 1972).

——, *The Nobility of Later Medieval England* (Oxford 1973).

MCKENNA, J. W., 'Henry VI of England and the Dual Monarchy: Aspects of Royal Political Propaganda', *Journal of the Warburg and Courtauld Institutes*, XXVIII (1965).

——, 'Piety and Propaganda: the cult of Henry VI', in *Chaucer and Middle English Studies in honour of Rossel Hope Robbins*, ed. Beryl Rowlands (London 1974).

MARGARET OF ANJOU, *Letters of Margaret of Anjou*, ed. C. Munro (Camden Society, 1863).

MEEKINGS, C. A. F., 'Thomas Kerver's Case', *E.H.R.*, XC (1975).

MONSTRELET, ENGUERRAND DE, *La chronique de Monstrelet*, ed. L. Douët d'Arcq, 6 vols (Société de l'Histoire de France, Paris, 1857–62); trans. by Thomas Johnes, *The chronicles of Monstrelet* (with continuations), 2 vols (London 1840).

MORICE, P. H., *Mémoires pour servir de preuves a l'histoire de Bretagne*, 3 vols (Paris 1742–6).

MYERS, A. R., 'A parliamentary debate of the mid-fifteenth century', *B.J.R.L.*, XXII (1938).

——, 'The Captivity of a Royal Witch', *B.J.R.L.*, XXIV (1940); XXVI (1941–2).

——, 'The Household of Queen Margaret of Anjou', *B.J.R.L.*, XL (1957–8).

——, 'The Jewels of Queen Margaret of Anjou', *B.J.R.L.*, XLII (1959).

——, *The Household of Edward IV* (Manchester 1959).

——, 'The outbreak of war between England and Burgundy in February 1471', *B.I.H.R.*, XXIII (1960).

——, 'A Parliamentary Debate of 1449', *B.I.H.R.*, LI (1978).

—— (ed.), *English Historical Documents 1327–1485* (London 1969).

Narratives of the Expulsion of the English from Normandy 1449–50, ed. J. Stevenson (R.S., 1863).

NICHOLS, J. (ed.), *A Collection of all the Wills ... of the Kings and Queens of England ... from William the Conqueror to ... Henry VII exclusive* (London 1780).

NICOLAS, N. H. (ed.), *A chronicle of London* (London 1827).

—— (trans.), *A Journal by one of the suite of Thomas Beckington during an embassy to negotiate a marriage between Henry VI and a daughter of the count of Armagnac*, A.D. *1442* (London 1828).

Ordonnances des roys de France de la troisième race, 22 vols (Paris 1723–1846).

ORME, N., *English Schools in the Middle Ages* (London 1973).

OTWAY-RUTHVEN, A. J., *The King's Secretary and the Signet Office in the XV Century* (Cambridge 1939).

——, *A History of Medieval Ireland* (London 1968).

Papal Letters: Entries in the Papal Registers relating to Great Britain and Ireland, vols VII–XIII, ed. J. A. Twemlow (H.M.S.O., 1906–56).

Paston Letters, ed. J. Gairdner, 4 vols (Edinburgh 1910).

PAULI, R., *Geschichte von England*, V (Gotha 1858).

PERRY, G. G., 'Bishop Beckington and Henry VI', *E.H.R.*, IX (1894).

PLANCHENAULT, R., 'La délivrance du Mans en 1448', *Revue Historique et Archaeologique du Maine*, LXXIX (1923).

POWICKE, M. R., 'Lancastrian Captains', in *Essays in Medieval History presented to Bertie Wilkinson*, ed. T. A. Sandquist and M. R. Powicke (Toronto 1969).

Prétentions des Anglois à la couronne de France, ed. R. Anstruther, Roxburghe Club, vol. 64 (London 1847).

Proceedings and Ordinances of the Privy Council of England, ed. N. H. Nicolas, 6 vols (Record Commission, 1834–7).

PRONGER, W. A., 'Thomas Gascoigne', *E.H.R.*, LIII (1938); LIV (1939).

PUGH, T. B., 'The magnates, knights and gentry', in *Fifteenth-century England*, ed. S. B. Chrimes and others (Manchester 1972).

——, and ROSS, C. D., 'The English Baronage and the Income Tax of 1436', *B.I.H.R.*, XXXVI (1953).

RADFORD, L. B., *Henry Beaufort* (London 1908).

RAINE, J. (ed.), *The Fabric Rolls of York Minster* (Surtees Society, 1859).

RAMSAY, J. H., *Lancaster and York*, 2 vols (Oxford 1892).

RAWCLIFFE, C., *The Staffords, earls of Stafford and dukes of Buckingham 1394–1521* (Cambridge 1978).

Reports from the Lords' Committees ... touching the Dignity of a Peer of the Realm, 5 vols (London 1820–9).

ROSENTHALL, J. T., 'Richard duke of York: a fifteenth-century layman and the church', *Church History Review*, L (1964–5).

——, 'The training of an elite group: English bishops in the fifteenth century', *American Philosophical Society Transactions*, New Series, LX, pt. 5 (Philadelphia 1970).

ROSKELL, J. S., 'The office and dignity of Protector of England', *E.H.R.*, LXVIII (1953).

——, *The Commons in the Parliament of 1422* (Manchester 1954).

——, 'The Problem of the Attendance of the Lords in Medieval Parliaments', *B.I.H.R.*, XXIX (1956).

——, 'Sir William Oldhall, Speaker in the Parliament of 1450–1', *Nottingham Medieval Studies*, V (1961).

——, *The Commons and their Speakers in English Parliaments, 1376–1523* (Manchester 1965).

ROSS, CHARLES, *Edward IV* (London 1974).

Rotuli Parliamentorum, ed. J. Strachey and others, 6 vols (1767–77).

ROUS, JOHN, *Historia Regum Angliae*, ed. Thomas Hearne (Oxford 1745).

ROWE, B. H., 'King Henry VI's claim to France in picture and poem', *The Library*, 4th series, XIII (1933).

——, 'The Estates of Normandy under the duke of Bedford', *E.H.R.*, XLVI (1931).

SALTMARSH, S. J., 'King's College', in *V.C.H. Cambridge*, III (London 1959).

——, *King Henry VI and the Royal Foundations* (Cambridge 1972).

SANDQUIST, T. A., 'The Holy Oil of St Thomas of Canterbury', in *Essays in Mediaeval History Presented to Bertie Wilkinson*, ed. T. A. Sandquist and M. R. Powicke (Toronto 1969).

SCOFIELD, C. L., *The Life and Reign of Edward the Fourth*, 2 vols (London 1923).

Select Cases before the King's Council, ed. I. S. Leadam and J. F. Baldwin (Selden Society, London, 1918).

SHARPE, R. R. (ed.), *London and the Kingdom*, 3 vols (London 1894–5).

——, *Calendar of Letter-Books of the City of London*, 11 vols (London 1899–1912).

SHILLINGFORD, J., *Letters and Papers of John Shillingford, Mayor of Exeter 1447–50*, ed. S. A. Moore (Camden Society, 1871).

SOMERVILLE, R., *History of the Duchy of Lancaster*, I (London 1953).

SPENCER, B., 'Pilgrim Badges of King Henry the Sixth', *Henry VI Society Newsletter* (December 1972).

STANLEY, A.P., Memorials of Westminster Abbey (3rd edn, London, 1869).

Statutes of the Realm, ed. A. Luders and others, 11 vols (Record Commission, 1810–28).

STEEL, A. B., *The Receipt of the Exchequer, 1337–1485* (Cambridge 1954).

STONE, JOHN, *Chronicle*, ed. W. G. Searle (Cambridge Antiquarian Society, 1902).

STOREY, R. L., 'English Officers of State', *B.I.H.R.*, XXXI (1958).

——, *The End of the House of Lancaster* (London 1966).

——, 'Lincolnshire in the Wars of the Roses', *Nottingham Medieval Studies*, XIV (1970).

STOW, JOHN, *Annales or A Generall Chronicle of England* (London 1631).

STRONG, R., *Tudor and Jacobean Portraits* (H.M.S.O., 1969).

STUBBS, W., *The Constitutional History of England*, 5th edn, 3 vols (Oxford 1891–8).

Studies in English Trade in the Fifteenth Century, ed. Eileen Power and M. M. Postan (London 1933).

TAILLANDIER, C., *Histoire ecclésiastique et civile de Bretagne* (Paris 1756).

TAYLOR, F., 'Some manuscripts of the Libelle of Englysche Polycye', *B.J.R.L.*, XXIV (1940).

The Brut, or the Chronicles of England, ed. F. W. D. Brie, E.E.T.S., Original series, cxxxi-cxxxvi (London 1906–8).

THIELEMANS, MARIE-ROSE, *Bourgogne et l'Angleterre: relations politiques et économiques entre les Pays-Bas bourguignons et l'Angleterre, 1435–67* (Brussels 1966).

'Tractatus de regimine principum ad regem Henricum sextem', in *Four English Political Tracts of the Later Middle Ages*, ed. Jean-Philippe Genet (Camden Series, Royal Historical Society, 1977).

VALE, M. G. A., *English Gascony 1399–1453* (Oxford 1970).

VALLET DE VIRIVILLE, A., *Histoire de Charles VII et de son époque*, 3 vols (Paris 1862–5).

VAUGHAN, R., *Philip the Good* (London 1970).

VERGIL, POLYDORE, *Three Books of Polydore Vergil's English History*, ed. H. Ellis (Camden Society, 1844).

VICKERS, K. H., *Humphrey, duke of Gloucester* (London 1907).

VIRGOE, R., 'The Parliament of 1449–50' (unpublished London Ph.D. thesis, 1964).

——, 'Some Ancient Indictments in the King's Bench referring to Kent 1450–1452', in *Documents Illustrative of Medieval Kentish Society*, ed. F. R. H. Du Boulay (Records Publication Committee of the Kent Archaeological Society, XVII, Ashford, 1964).

——, 'The death of William de la Pole duke of Suffolk', *B.J.R.L.*, XLVII (1965).

——, 'The Composition of the King's Council, 1437–61', *B.I.H.R.*, XLIII (1970).

Vita et Gesta Henrici Quinti Anglorum Regis, ed Thomas Hearne (Oxford 1727).

WALCOTT, M. E. C., *William of Wykeham and his Colleges* (London 1852).

WALSINGHAM, THOMAS, *Historia Anglicana*, ed. H. T. Riley, II (R.S., 1864).

WARKWORTH, J., *A Chronicle of the First Thirteen Years of the Reign of King Edward the Fourth*, ed. J. O. Halliwell (Camden Society, 1839).

WARNER, G. (ed.), *The Libelle of Englyshe Polycye: A Poem on the Use of Sea-Power, 1436* (Oxford 1926).

Wars of the English in France during the reign of Henry VI, Letters and Papers, ed. J. Stevenson, 2 vols (R.S., 1861–4).

WAURIN, JEAN DE, *Anchiennes Cronicques d'Engleterre*, ed. E. Dupont, 3 vols (Société de l'Histoire de France, Paris, 1858–63); *Recueil des Chroniques*, ed. W. and E. L. C. P. Hardy, 5 vols (R.S., 1864–91).

WEDGWOOD, J. C., and HOLT, ANNE D. (eds), *History of Parliament, 1439–1509*, Biographies (H.M.S.O., 1936).

WEISS, R., 'Henry VI and the Library of All Souls College', *E.H.R.*, LVII (1942).

WHETHAMSTEDE, JOHN, 'Registrum', ed. H. T. Riley in *Registra Quorundam Abbatum Monasterii Sancti Albani*, 2 vols (R.S., 1872, 1873).

WICKHAM LEGG, L. G. (ed.), *English Coronation Records* (Westminster 1901).

WILKINS, D. (ed.), *Concilia Magnae Britanniae et Hiberniae*, 4 vols (London 1737).

WILLIAMS, ETHEL C., *My Lord of Bedford 1389–1435* (London 1963).

WILLIS, R., and CLARK, J. W., *The Architectural History of the University of Cambridge and of the Colleges of Cambridge and Eton*, 4 vols (Cambridge 1886).

WOLFFE, B. P., 'Acts of resumption in the Lancastrian parliaments, 1399–1456', *E.H.R.*, LXXIII (1958).

——, *The Crown Lands 1461–1536* (London 1970).

——, *The Royal Demesne in English History* (London 1971).

WRIGHT, T. (ed.), *Political Poems and Songs relating to English History*, II (R.S., 1861).

INDEX